T0113662

Ryōgen and Mount Hiei

Map of Mount Hiei

A. To Kyoto
B. To Ōtsu
C. Mudōjidani
D. Eastern Pagoda area
E. Western Pagoda area
F. Lake Biwa
G. Sakamoto
H. Yokawa area
I. Mount Hachiōji
1. Benten Hall
2. Myōō Hall
3. Peak of Mount Hiei
4. Sōjiin
5. Precepts Platform
6. Lecture Hall
7. Central Hall

比叡山概略図

Ⓔ
西塔地区

Ⓓ
東塔地区

大講堂
根本中堂
浄土院
常行堂
相輪橖
釈迦堂
椿堂
にない堂

文殊楼

Ⓗ
横川地区
横川中堂
根本如法塔
元三大師御廟

恵心院

元三大師堂

雄琴

Kuroda Institute
Studies in East Asian Buddhism

Studies in Ch'an and Hua-yen
Robert M. Gimello and Peter N. Gregory, editors

Dōgen Studies
William R. LaFleur, editor

The Northern School and the Formation of Early Ch'an Buddhism
John R. McRae

Traditions of Meditation in Chinese Buddhism
Peter N. Gregory, editor

Sudden and Gradual: Approaches to Enlightenment in Chinese Thought
Peter N. Gregory, editor

Buddhist Hermeneutics
Donald S. Lopez, Jr., editor

Paths to Liberation: The Marga and Its Transformations in Buddhist Thought
Robert E. Buswell, Jr., and Robert M. Gimello, editors

Sōtō Zen in Medieval Japan
William M. Bodiford

The Scripture on the Ten Kings and the Making of Purgatory
in Medieval Chinese Buddhism
Stephen F. Teiser

The Eminent Monk: Buddhist Ideals in Medieval Chinese Hagiography
John Kieschnick

Re-Visioning "Kamakura" Buddhism
Richard K. Payne, editor

Original Enlightenment and the Transformation of Medieval Japanese Buddhism
Jacqueline I. Stone

Buddhism in the Sung
Peter N. Gregory and Daniel A. Getz, Jr., editors

Coming to Terms with Chinese Buddhism:
A Reading of The Treasure Store Treatise
Robert H. Sharf

Studies in East Asian Buddhism 15

Ryōgen and Mount Hiei

Japanese Tendai in the Tenth Century

Paul Groner

A KURODA INSTITUTE BOOK
University of Hawai'i Press
Honolulu

Printed in the United States of America
24 23 22 21 20 19   6 5 4 3 2 1

Library of Congress Cataloging-in-Publication Data

Ryōgen and Mount Hiei :
Japanese Tendai in the tenth century / Paul Groner.
p.   cm.—(Studies in East Asian Buddhism ; 15)
"A Kuroda Institute book."
Includes bibliographical references and index.
ISBN 0-8248-2260-9 (alk. paper)
1. Ryōgen, 912–985.   2. Tendai (Sect)—History.
3. Priests, Tendai—Japan—Biography.   I. Series.
BQ982 .Y944 G76   2002
294.3'92—dc21   2002004637

ISBN 978-0-8248-8154-2 (pbk.)

Publication of this book was made possible
by a generous grant from the Tendai School's
Office of General Affairs

The Kuroda Institute for the Study of Buddhism
and Human Values is a nonprofit, educational corporation
founded in 1976. One of its primary objectives is to promote
scholarship on the historical, philosophical, and cultural ramifications
of Buddhism. In association with the University of Hawai'i Press, the Institute
also publishes Classics in East Asian Buddhism, a series devoted to the
translation of significant texts in the East Asian Buddhist tradition.

Frontis map: This map is based on a typical modern tourist map of Mount Hiei;
no maps survive that reflect Mount Hiei during Ryōgen's tenure.

Designed by Integrated Composition Systems

Contents

Tables and Figures

Tables

Figures

Preface

The idea for this book first came from Professor Sonoda Kōyū of Wakayama University who told me about Ryōgen when I went to visit him in Wakayama as I was finishing my doctoral dissertation on Saichō. Professor Sonoda kindly sent me copies of two documents from the *Heian ibun:* Ryōgen's will and a set of twenty-six rules, both of which are translated in the appendixes of this book. I did not begin working on Ryōgen until 1982–83, when I held a Japan Foundation Fellowship. Around the same time, a friend arranged an introduction to Hirabayashi Moritoku, the author of a biography of Ryōgen who was kind enough to discuss several issues with me. A good friend, Ichishima Masao of Taishō University, told me of a childhood illness that had been cured through prayers to Ganzan Daishi (Ryōgen). As a result, he named his son Gen, taking the character "gan" from Ryōgen's posthumous title Ganzan Daishi. Such stories helped me to understand the role of Ryōgen in contemporary Japan.

I had initially intended to write one or two short articles on Ryōgen to help with my tenure. The deeper I went into Ryōgen's biography, however, the more issues I found that interested me. My short project gradually evolved into a much longer work that lasted for many years. My studies of Ryōgen have been sporadic; I've worked intensively for short periods then put the manuscript away for considerable time as I worked on other projects. The result is a book that is somewhat idiosyncratic as it reflects my changing interests over the years.

Recently, several events helped me decide that it was time to publish this work. My own interests have taken me in other directions, and I came to feel that additional time spent on this study would not necessarily improve it. Thus I decided that the time had come to publish it so that others could use and build on it. In addition, the contingencies of the academic calendar and promotion to full professor necessitated distributing the text to readers. In the process of being considered for promotion, I became aware that Eishō Nasu of the Institute of Buddhist Studies in Berkeley had just finished a doctoral dissertation on Ryōgen: "Doctrine and Institution in Japanese Tendai Buddhism: A Study of Jie Daishi Ryōgen (912–985)." After meeting with Professor Nasu, we agreed that I would include three of his translations in my book: (1) the major source for the Ōwa debates, the *Ōwa shūronki;* (2) Ryōgen's will; and (3) Ryōgen's compilation of twenty-six rules. I am deeply indebted to Professor Nasu for agreeing to this arrangement and helping us to overcome what could have been an awkward situation. His fine translations enhance this study. Although I have edited his translations by eliminating notes that were already covered in the body of my book and adding a very few of my own, the translations are still substantially as I received them. I have been deeply impressed by his rendering of some of the more difficult passages.

An earlier version of chapter 12 is scheduled to be published in *Engendering Faith: Women and Buddhism in Premodern Japan,* volume 1: *New Directions in Western Research,* edited by Barbara Ruch (Ann Arbor: Center for Japanese Studies, University of Michigan, forthcoming). I thank Professor Ruch for permission to use a revised version in this volume.

The General Administration of the Tendai School (Tendai shūmucho) graciously provided a generous subvention that aided in the publication of the book. Needless to say, their generosity does not imply that they agree or disagree with the contents of this book. Saitō Enshin of Taishō University was invaluable in aiding me in the submission of the application for funds.

Finally, I owe debts of gratitude to several organizations and to many people who have supported me in this project over the years, either directly or indirectly. Besides the Japan Foundation mentioned above, a Sesquicentennial Fellowship and several summer grants from the University of Virginia provided me with the time to work on the book. The work of Hirabayashi Moritoku and Hori Daiji on Ryōgen should be acknowledged because of the many leads it provided as I pursued this study. In fact, without their pioneering work this work would have been much more difficult.

My brother-in-law, Fukasawa Shigeyuki, and his family have graciously provided hospitality during my many visits to Tokyo. Stanley Weinstein of Yale, my mentor and close friend, has freely offered his encouragement and advice. The many friends I have made in Japanese academic circles over the years have played a vital role in sustaining my enthusiasm. I have already mentioned several of them above. Although I cannot name them all, I would be remiss if I did not mention some of them. Ōkubo Ryōshun of Waseda, Sueki Fumihiko of Tokyo University, Yoshizu Yoshihide and Ikeda Rosan of Komazawa, Tonegawa Hiroyuki of Taishō University, and Nomoto Kakujō (editor of the *Zoku Tendaishū zensho* [Continuation of the collected works of the Tendai school]) have provided me with both material and spiritual sustenance (in several senses) over the years. In the West, Jackie Stone, Ruben Habito, Robert Rhodes, Neil McMullen and Jean-Noël Robert have helped through their research and interest in Japanese Tendai. The research of Daniel Stevenson, Daniel Getz, and Paul Swanson on Chinese T'ien-t'ai has helped me to look at Japanese Tendai in new ways. Two anonymous readers provided me with valuable advice. Patricia Crosby of University of Hawai'i Press has been enormously helpful with this project and others. Finally, I welcome the friendship of Professor Yoritomi Motohiro of the International Center for Japanese Studies, under whose auspices I have put the final touches on the book. I look forward to continuing these friendships and to developing new ones in the coming years as my work takes me in different directions.

I thank my wife and children for their understanding and support over the years. Finally, in the spirit in which Ryōgen honored his mother, I dedicate this book to my parents and thank them for their many years of support and understanding.

A Note on Dates and Ages

Dates are given in the format of month, day, and year. For example, Ryōgen died on 1-3-985, the third day of the first month of 985. Although the third day of the first month would actually fall near the end of 984, I have followed the convention found in many Japanese reference books of simply converting the Japanese year to the year that most closely corresponds to the Western calendar. Ages are given following Western conventions.

Abbreviations

BKD	Ono Genmyō, ed. *Bussho kaisetsu daijiten.*
BZ (Bussho kankōkai ed.)	Bussho kankōkai, ed. *Dainihon Bukkyō zensho.*
BZ (Suzuki ed.)	Suzuki gakujutsu zaidan, ed. *Dainihon Bukkyō zensho.*
DS	Tōkyō daigaku shiryō hensanjo, ed. *Dainihon shiryō.*
DZ	Hieizan senshuin fuzoku Eizan gakuin, ed. *Dengyō daishi zenshū.*
GR	Hanawa Hokinoichi, ed. *Gunsho ruijū.*
KT	Kuroita Katsumi, ed. *Shintei zōho Kokushi taikei.*
T	Takakusu Junjirō and Watanabe Kaigyoku, eds. *Taishō shinshū daizōkyō.*
TZ	Tendaishūten kankōkai, ed. *Tendaishū zensho.*
ZGR	Hanawa Hokinoichi, ed. *Zoku gunsho ruijū.*
ZTZ	Tendai shūten hensanjo, ed. *Zoku Tendaishū zensho.*

1

Ryōgen's Place
in the History of the Tendai School

The Japanese Tendai school is based on T'ien-t'ai teachings systematized by the Chinese meditation master and exegete Chih-i (538–597).[1] However, the institutional base of Chinese T'ien-t'ai was generally not very strong in the T'ang dynasty (618–907); as a result the T'ien-t'ai tradition is closer to a school of thought than a religious institution in Chinese history. In fact, much of Chinese T'ien-t'ai literature was lost during the T'ang dynasty as a result of the 845 persecution of Buddhism in China and later had to be brought back to China from Japan and Korea. However, T'ien-t'ai was revived during the Sung dynasty (960–1279).[2]

The situation in Japan was quite different. Tendai quickly came to dominate medieval Japanese religious life in both institutional and intellectual senses. A Japanese Tendai school with institutions and an unbroken lineage came to exist; such schools were generally not found in China. As Japanese Tendai developed, many interpretations, teachings, and practices unknown to Chih-i were introduced into the school. In fact, for much of its history, once the initial transmissions of texts had taken place, Japanese Tendai developed without much direct input from Chinese monks. The purpose of this study is to examine the development of the Tendai school during the tenth century and thereby elucidate some of the factors behind Tendai's rise to its preeminent position in Japan.

This study focuses on institutional history rather than doctrinal history. Ryōgen wrote few texts on doctrine that can be decisively attributed to him. Those that are extant are debate manuals or short commentaries and will be briefly mentioned in chapters 4 and 8. Among the texts on doctrine that survive are short texts on topics such as Pure Land and path structure.[3] However, Ryōgen's doctrinal positions can be best considered in the context of extended discussions in which his positions are contrasted with those of other medieval monks. A detailed consideration of their contents would require the investigation of similar works by other monks and would be tantamount to writing another study.

The dramatic rise of Tendai power during the tenth century can be highlighted by considering two images: the school at the time of the death of its founder Saichō (766/767–822) and Tendai late in Ryōgen's (912–985) life. When Saichō first established the Tendai school in the first two decades of the ninth century, it consisted of a small group of monks sequestered on the top of a mountain to the northeast of the capital at Kyoto. According to a register of the monks of the Tendai school compiled near the end of Saichō's life, more than half of the Tendai yearly ordinands (*nenbundosha*), monks ordained with official permission and support, had left Mount Hiei, leaving fewer than a dozen officially sanctioned monks. Because Saichō was also willing to accept monks from other schools, the total number of monks and novices on Hiei may have added up to several dozen at Saichō's death. The educational system that Saichō had set up for his monks was on the verge of collapse. Saichō had devoted substantial energy toward developing a training program in Esoteric Buddhism (*mikkyō*) that would be in agreement with and equal to training in T'ien-t'ai meditation. Saichō's early death at about the age of fifty-four before he could define his training program left his followers without a visionary teacher and a prestigious guide. Records dating from the decade after Saichō's death suggest that simply feeding the monks on Mount Hiei was a major problem. In addition, Saichō's successors argued among themselves over issues such as the leadership of the school and the balance between Esoteric Buddhism and traditional T'ien-t'ai doctrine, further weakening the school.

Within 150 years, the Tendai school had overcome almost all of these problems and emerged as one of the major monastic institutions in Japan. By the end of the tenth century, several thousand Tendai monks lived on Mount Hiei. Tendai monks were valued for their ability to perform rituals to ensure the prosperity and longevity of their patrons. Mastery of Tendai Esoteric rituals enabled practitioners to occupy important posts at court as guardian monks for court chaplains (*naigubu*) and guardian monks (*gojisō*) for emperors; in addition, Tendai monks dominated the Office of Monastic Affairs (Sōgō), an institution that Saichō had rejected. Tendai monasteries had begun to acquire important land holdings in the form of manors (*shōen*). Eventually nobles and the imperial family had to consider Tendai power when they made their political decisions. The Tendai educational program produced impressive scholars who were able to compete successfully with monks from other schools. In fact, Tendai educational institutions played major roles in the cultural life of Japan, eventually training most of the founders of the new Buddhist schools of the Kamakura period.

These shifts in Tendai fortunes coincide with major changes in Japanese political life. During much of Saichō's life, emperors such as Kanmu (737–806; r. 781–806) had been active in administering their domains. The Ritsuryō state, influenced by Chinese models, was still influential and administered much of the land. By Ryōgen's time, the emperor was gradually losing power to Fujiwara regents who would effectively control the throne. The centralized bureaucracy that had administered taxation was being replaced by a web of arrangements between officials and administrators of manors, with a resultant loss of at least some tax revenues for the court. Many of the families who had acquired wealth in the provinces had come to the capital; they were replaced by new administrators who represented those who had moved to the capital. The tenth century has been called a time of transition as the form of government was shifting.[4] Only a skilled leader would be able to guide the Tendai school through such perilous times.

Reasons for Choosing Ryōgen as the Focus of a Study of the Transformation of the Tendai School

Traditional Japanese scholarship on the history of Buddhism has tended to focus on the founders of schools. The educational system that produces the modern monk tends to revere the founder and directs young scholars to focus on the founders of their schools. Although historians such as Kuroda Toshio have called for efforts to place Buddhism within the broader context of Japanese history and society, simply perusing the entries in bibliographies of Japanese Buddhist scholarship reveals the preponderance of studies and books on the founders.[5] In contrast, later figures have often been neglected even though they sometimes played as important a role as the founder. In the case of Tendai, Ryōgen's biography reveals as much about later Tendai institutions as Saichō's biography discloses about the origins of the Tendai School.

A thorough study of the evolution of the Tendai school during the ninth and tenth centuries would include a discussion of such early Tendai thinkers and administrators as Ennin (794–864), Enchin (814–

891), Henjō (816–890), Annen (841?–915?), and others. In addition, it would consider parallel developments in other institutions such as Kō-fukuji and Tōdaiji in Nara and Kongōbuji on Mount Kōya. Discussions of the economic and institutional reasons for the decline of some of the major temples in Nara during this period would provide a useful contrast to the more successful institutions. Such a broad study is difficult at the present time because of the number of institutions that would be involved as well as the many lacunae in the primary sources. Consequently, I have chosen to focus on one figure, Ryōgen, the eigh-teenth head (*zasu*) of the Tendai school.

For several reasons, the biography of Ryōgen provides a useful frame-work for investigating many of the changes that occurred within the Tendai school. First, because many documents from the Tendai school were destroyed in fires and conflicts with other monastic institutions and governmental authorities, many of the developments in the school are difficult to trace in very much detail. However, two major biogra-phies of Ryōgen exist, providing a detailed and usually reliable account of his activities. Although the researcher might wish for more plentiful sources, when these biographies are supplemented with other sources, they provide a rich source for the investigation of Ryōgen's biography and the social forces that led to the transformation of the Tendai school. These biographies will be discussed in more detail below.

Second, Ryōgen lived during a period when the institutional char-acter of the Tendai school underwent many changes, and Ryōgen played an active role in the implementation of many of them. Under his lead-ership, alliances were forged with certain factions of the nobility. Sons from the ruling classes were ordained, granted special privileges, and given leading roles to play within school. As the Tendai school became involved in secular politics and factionalism, the rivalries between cliques in the school were exacerbated. In addition, the Tendai school acquired a number of large manors that were contributed by members of the ruling class. However, the families of the donors often maintained control over these manors and used them in ways that would benefit members of their clan. The strengthening of these alliances between families from the nobility and certain monastic factions provides the background for the vicious factionalism that emerged in the Tendai school during the late tenth century. Around this time, groups of armed monks dedicated to defending the interests of their cliques began to form. The study of Ryōgen's biography helps to elucidate all of these changes.

Third, late in his life Ryōgen attempted to control many of the changes within the Tendai school that had been set in motion by his activities. A set of twenty-six rules that he formulated provides an excellent source for investigating how some of the more serious religious practitioners within the Tendai school regarded many of the issues. Investigation of these and other issues within the context of Ryōgen's biography can elucidate the reasons for many of the changes within the school.

Fourth, Ryōgen's biography contains significant information about monastic biographies and careers during the middle of the Heian period. Ryōgen came from a poor family and lost his major teacher at an early age. Despite these disadvantages, he managed to rise to a prominent position within the school and become head of the Tendai school at the comparatively young age of fifty-three. Ryōgen's rise was made possible by luck and the shrewd use of the Tendai system of debates and examinations, as well as his mastery of Esoteric Buddhist ritual. Tracing how Ryōgen gradually acquired disciples and lay patrons through these means reveals much about the "ladder of success" of politically active monks. In addition, Ryōgen's biography provides a background against which the stories of other types of religious and secular practitioners can be placed. Among the figures considered in passing are Buddhist lay believers, reclusive and eccentric monks, and female lay and monastic practitioners.

Finally, Ryōgen's biography includes information about important developments in religious practice and doctrine during the middle of the Heian period. Ryōgen rose to prominence as a young monk through his skill in debate and later stressed debate as an educational tool when he was the leader of the Tendai school. The investigation of the debate topics yields information about which subjects were important to Tendai monks at this time and helps to elucidate the general shape of monastic education for scholarly monks. The debate system also influenced some texts concerning "original enlightenment" (*hongaku*) in subsequent centuries. In addition, Ryōgen's use of Esoteric ritual reveals the importance of Esoteric ritual to lay believers. Ryōgen's biography reveals details of how monks of different lineages competed with each other to win lay patronage. The appearance of Ryōgen's written work on Pure Land and the activities of his disciple Genshin (942–1017) indicate that the Pure Land tradition was emerging as a major component of Tendai thought during the latter part of Ryōgen's life.

Evaluation of Ryōgen's Place
in the History of the Tendai School

Even a brief discussion of Ryōgen's life calls to mind the work of the prominent Japanese historian Kuroda Toshio. Kuroda's description of *kenmitsu taisei*, sometimes translated as "exoteric-Esoteric system," refers to the institutional and ideological system that both Buddhist monks and court supported in their efforts to wield power in medieval Japan. Statements by Kuroda such as the following indicate the importance that he ascribed to the development of Tendai during the mid-Heian:

> From the tenth century, amidst the development of Pure Land Bud-
> dhism, the Tendai school took the lead in developing a system that, in
> the eleventh century, confirmed the exoteric and esoteric as coexistent
> entities—either as unified, as perfectly syncretized, or as mutually de-
> pendent. This system is referred to in this article as the *kenmitsu taisei*,
> with the word "system" signifying not a system of law or administrative
> control, but rather an ideological order.[6]

This study would have been very different without Kuroda's work in calling the attention of scholars to the role of Buddhism and its insti-
tutions in Japanese history and society. Kuroda also deserves credit for pointing out the importance of the history of Buddhist traditions after their founders' deaths. In fact, this study supports Kuroda's general conclusions by elucidating the burgeoning alliance between Tendai monks and the Japanese nobility as the *kenmitsu taisei* took form.

However, the study also differs with Kuroda at points. This study was written from the perspective of Buddhist Studies rather than secular and political history. The principal aim of the study was to elucidate developments within Tendai establishments rather than Japanese society at large. Thus, it focuses on the manner in which political and social events affected monasteries rather than on how those monasteries fit into Japa-
nese society at large. The shifting alliances between monks and patrons as well as among monks themselves are a major concern in Ryōgen's biography. The institutional doctrinal system of *kenmitsu taisei* was filled with sufficient dissension between the various doctrinal forms that it frequently is difficult to call it a system. Besides a focus that is narrower than that of Kuroda, this monograph has been written with the institutional and doctrinal backgrounds of Buddhism in India and China in mind, even though they do not play an overt role in the study. In fact, the study arose out of my desire to understand the forces that made me-
dieval Tendai different from other forms of Buddhism. The narrower,

and consequently more detailed, focus of the study calls several aspects of Kuroda's view of *kenmitsu taisei* into question. As Taira Masayuki has noted, Kuroda argued that medieval Japanese Buddhism was dominated by Esoteric Buddhism because the Japanese used Buddhism as a form of magic to advance their interests.[7] Esoteric Buddhism played a crucial role in Ryōgen's rise to prominence; however, he also used and emphasized exoteric Buddhist teachings throughout his life. The mastery of exoteric Buddhism played a key role both in his rise to power and in the educational system he instituted on Mount Hiei. However, monks were not the only ones interested in exoteric doctrine; the Ōwa debates, which focused on the teachings of the *Lotus Sūtra,* attracted considerable attention from lay Buddhists. A second area in which a more detailed focus reveals differences with Kuroda's view of *kenmitsu taisei* is found in the sectarian rivalries with the Hossō school that played a major role in Ryōgen's life. In many of Kuroda's writings, *kenmitsu taisei* is portrayed as a monolithic system that dominates and runs through Japanese Buddhism. However, this view at time obscures the serious doctrinal differences that ran through Japanese Buddhism during the Heian period. Such reservations about Kuroda's view of *kenmitsu taisei* do not indicate that Kuroda's arguments should be abandoned; rather, they point the way to a more nuanced view of Buddhist history.

My choice of Ryōgen as the central character in this study should not be interpreted as suggesting that Ryōgen can be held solely responsible for seemingly negative changes within the school, such as the seeming deterioration of monastic discipline, the appearance of warrior monks, and an apparent decline in serious scholarship by Tendai monks in the late Heian and Kamakura periods. These trends are found in many of the major monasteries during this period and affected almost every Buddhist school. The Hossō monastery, Kōfukuji, and the Shingon monastery on Mount Kōya, to mention several, eventually maintained warrior monks. The decline in monastic discipline affected virtually every tradition, including the Risshū (Vinaya school), the guardians of the ordination tradition.

In addition, Ryōgen cannot be given sole credit or blame for these developments even within the Tendai school. Many of the issues had emerged decades before Ryōgen appeared. For example, one of the key provisions of Saichō's educational plan had been to have Tendai monks remain sequestered (*rōzan*) on Mount Hiei for twelve years while they received special training. During this period, they were not to leave the confines of the mountain for any reason. However, Saichō's most promising student, Ennin, had to abandon his retreat after only six years. According to his biography, Ennin had announced that he would begin the twelve-year period in 823, the year after Saichō's death. After only six years, however, the other Tendai monks had asked him to abandon the twelve-year period, arguing that he should spread Tendai teachings beyond the confines on Mount Hiei. In the summer of 828, he traveled to Nara to lecture on the *Lotus Sūtra* at Hōryūji. The following summer, he lectured on the *Lotus* and the *Jen-wang ching* (Sūtra of the benevolent king) at Shitennōji.[8] Ennin did not abandon his plan to remain in seclusion on Hiei lightly; several years later, he went into seclusion in the Yokawa area of Mount Hiei. Although he made no vow to remain in Yokawa for twelve years, he clearly recognized the value of remaining sequestered on Hiei.

Ennin's decision to leave Hiei before the twelve-year period had been completed clearly made it easier for those who followed him to ignore Saichō's educational plan. Relatively little evidence exists that subsequent Tendai monks remained sequestered on Hiei for the full twelve years. One noteworthy exception was Enchin, who received a certificate (*iki*) attesting to the completion of the twelve-year period in 846.[9]

In 914, two years after Ryōgen's birth, the deterioration of Buddhist practice was described by Miyoshi no Kiyoyuki (847–918), a high official (*taifu*) in the Bureau of Ceremonies (Shikibu) in his *Twelve Opinions* (*Iken jūnikajō*), a memorial describing his views concerning proper government.

> The number of people initiated as yearly ordinands or in special (*rinji*) ceremonies permitted by the court has risen to two or three hundred per year. Of these more than half are evil and wild sorts of people. In addition, many people among the farmers privately [without government permission] shave off their hair and wantonly wear monastic robes in order to escape their tax and corvée labor obligations. As the years have passed, their numbers have increased until two-thirds of the population has shaven heads. They all keep a wife and children in their houses. Although they resemble monks outwardly, they eat meat and fish; their minds are like those of butchers. It is even worse when they assemble and behave like a band of robbers or secretly mint their own money. They do not fear punishments from heaven or concern themselves with the Buddhist precepts. If provincial governors try to make them behave according to law, they assemble and become violent. In previous years, when Fujiwara no Tokiyoshi, the governor (*kami*) of Aki, was surrounded and when Tachibana no Kimiyasu, governor of Kii, was threatened and robbed, it was precisely this type of evil monk who did so. . . . If the edict from the Chancellor's Office had been late, or the court's messenger had been

delayed, Tokiyoshi and Kimiyasu might have died terrible deaths. If such monks are not prohibited, then I fear that they may rebel [against the government]. Therefore I ask that when monks behave in such evil ways, they be arrested and forced to return their certificates of initiation and ordination. They shall then be required to [again] wear lay clothing and return to their former occupation. In addition, if privately initiated novices join together in evil groups, then they should be put in restraints and forced to do hard labor.[10]

Although allowances must be made for exaggerations in Kiyoyuki's description of the Buddhist order, his testimony describes an order that already was filled with men who had become monks to make an easy living. The gangs that some of the monks and novices had formed probably were the forerunners of the warrior monks who emerged at the end of Ryōgen's life. Although much of the *Twelve Opinions* is Confucian in tone, Kiyoyuki was in fact a devout Buddhist. In 902, Tendai monks gave him materials concerning the life of Enchin, one of the most eminent Tendai monks of his lifetime, and asked Kiyoyuki to write Enchin's official biography. Moreover, he had also had one of his sons ordained by Genshō (844–917), one of Ennin's students. In 907, Kiyoyuki wrote an account of the formation of a *nenbutsu* (repetition of the Buddha's name) organization for the Tendai monk Rinsei.[11] Thus, his statement should be read as an effort to reform the Buddhist order rather than discredit Buddhism.

Ryōgen is often criticized for the vicious factionalism that arose within the Tendai school at the end of his life and in the decades following it. Because this issue decisively affects any evaluation of his biography, two chapters are devoted to the topic. Chapter 2 sets the background for Ryōgen's biography by tracing factionalism from its inception shortly after Saichō's death to the the situation during Ryōgen's youth. Chapter 11 is a discussion of factionalism during Ryōgen's lifetime. By treating this issue in detail, I demonstrate that factionalism had its origins long before Ryōgen's administration of the Tendai school.

Just as Ryōgen cannot be assigned the sole responsibility for the problems that arose within the Tendai school, he also cannot be given sole credit for positive developments in Tendai practice. The academic quality of the educational institutions on Mount Hiei, an issue in which Ryōgen was vitally interested, had its origins in the activities of earlier monks such as Saichō and Ennin. In addition, Ennin pioneered the effective use of Esoteric Buddhist ritual to create alliances with patrons. Efforts to strengthen monastic discipline, another topic that concerned Ryōgen, are reflected in the sets of rules composed by earlier Tendai monks. Ryōgen was well aware of the efforts of his predecessors and frequently referred to them. To set Ryōgen's activities in their proper context, such precedents must be noted.

Sources for Ryōgen's Biography

One of the major reasons for focusing this investigation of Tendai during the middle of the Heian period on Ryōgen is the quality of the early biographies concerning him. Much of the biographical detail of many Tendai figures from the eleventh century onward is incomplete. False attributions of texts further complicate the situation. In Ryōgen's case, two early biographies give us material that is usually trustworthy.

Ryōgen's immediate disciples contributed to the compilation of each. The first, the *Jie daisōjōden* (Biography of the grand archbishop Jie), was composed from materials brought together by some of Ryōgen's disciples, especially Kakuun (953–1007). Because Kakuun died in 1007, twenty-four years before the final compilation of the biography, the materials presumably were ignored for a time before Tadanobu edited them into their final form. After several years, these primary source materials were then edited and polished by a layman, Fujiwara no Tadanobu (967–1035), who was probably chosen for his literary abilities and because he was Jinzen's nephew.[12] This procedure had been followed in the composition of earlier biographies. For example, the most authoritative biographies of Chien-chen (J. Ganjin) and Enchin had both been compiled first by the monk's disciples and then refined into a more literary style by laymen.

The *Jie daisōjōden* was edited into its final form in 1031, forty-six years after Ryōgen's death, probably because Ryōgen's surviving disciples wanted the details of their teacher's life to be compiled into a formal biography before they too had died. The comparatively late date of the biography is undoubtedly the reason for a number of questionable statements in the text, particularly the stories of Ryōgen's early years. The materials that Kakuun presented to Tadanobu probably fell into four categories: biographical episodes that Ryōgen told the disciples, events remembered by the disciples, episodes mentioned in Ryōgen's writings, and official documents concerning Ryōgen's biography.[13]

The *Jie daisōjōden* was probably a public document; it was edited by a high government official and was intended to be source material for the compilers of official biographies.[14] Because of the official bias of the compiler, the *Jie daisōjōden* includes much information about Ryō-gen's relations to emperors and regents, as well as about Ryōgen's appointments to the Office of Monastic Affairs. It does not include detailed information about such issues as Ryōgen's personality and his efforts to rebuild the Tendai monastic complex on Mount Hiei or about the rise of factionalism within the Tendai school.

These lapses were a source of dissatisfaction to Bonshō (964?–1032?), one of Ryōgen's disciples. To supplement the *Jie daisōjōden,* Bonshō wrote the *Jie daisōjō shūiden* (Gleanings for the biography of the grand archbishop Jie), a text that collected episodes and information that had been left out of the biography Tadanobu had edited. Bonshō included detailed information about internal Tendai affairs, such as the rebuilding of the monastic establishment on Mount Hiei and the factionalism that arose between the successors of Ennin and Enchin. In addition, Bonshō included a number of episodes that were based on the reminiscences of Ryōgen's disciples and that tended to be more hagiographic than the events recorded in the *Jie daisōjōden.* Although Bonshō was more interested in Ryōgen's religious aspirations than Tadanobu was, neither biography included very many entries from Ryōgen's writings. Consequently, Ryōgen's intentions and spiritual life are often unclear.[15]

Structure of This Study

Mid-Heian biographies of monks differ from what the modern reader expects from biographical writing. Medieval Japanese biography often focused on the external trappings of a career or on hagiographic stories rather than the inner struggle of the religious man. Many of the biographies consist of lists of the important people with whom a monk associated and the official honors he received, along with a few hagiographic details. While medieval biographies may seem disappointing at first to the Western reader, a careful investigation of their details sometimes reveals considerable information. In this study, I pay considerable attention to the people and places mentioned in Ryōgen's biographies, sometimes digressing for considerable portions of my narrative to explain the significance of an event or the people involved. In doing so, I have tried to reveal why Ryōgen's biographers felt that the mention of certain figures and places was important.

Because such digressions sometimes lead the reader away from the basic narrative, I have chosen to treat some of them as appendixes to certain chapters. The appendixes contain a number of primary sources for this study. They also contain descriptions of several figures that play important roles in Ryōgen's biography such as his major patron, Fujiwara no Morosuke, and the reclusive monk Zōga. These accounts have been included to provide the reader with biographies that contrast with that of Ryōgen. For example, although the modern reader may be more inspired by the biography of a reclusive monk such as Zōga, the biography of Zōga seems to have developed partly as a response to that of political monks such as Ryōgen.

A brief survey of the chapters may serve to give the reader an overview of the progression of topics. Although this biography generally proceeds along chronological lines, it is not intended to be a sequential survey of Ryōgen's life as much as a consideration of key themes in it. It begins with a survey of early Tendai factionalism in chapter 2. Because factionalism both within the Tendai school and with other schools played a major role in Ryōgen's life, the study begins with a consideration of early factionalism in the Tendai school.

Chapters 3 and 4 are concerned with the ladder of success in monasteries. How did a monk make a name for himself? Thus, the role of debates on exoteric Buddhism and Esoteric ritual are considered to elucidate how Ryōgen used them to build a network of supporters and how they furthered his career. In addition, the significance of Yokawa, an area of Mount Hiei opened by Ennin, is described. Ryōgen took over this underused area and made it the basis for his activities. Through the skillful use of such resources Ryōgen was able to gain the attention of a powerful patron, Fujiwara no Morosuke, the most powerful political figure in Japan during Ryōgen's life.

Chapter 5 considers the relationship between Ryōgen and Morosuke and what each obtained from it. Of particular importance was the ordination of two of Morosuke's sons and what each brought to the Tendai school. The differing circumstances of these ordinations reveals the political agendas of both Ryōgen and Morosuke. Morosuke's early death left Ryōgen without a patron and forced him to rely upon other figures to further his career and establish the Tendai school as the dominant force in Japanese religious life.

Chapter 6 is a study of the Ōwa debates, a dramatic set of discussions held between Tendai and Nara monks at the court. The debates are of interest not only because they reveal lay interest in exoteric doctrine and what topics were of particular interest, but also because they call the whole issue of "winners" and "losers" in such debates into question.

In fact, many of the "losers" in the debates went on to have successful careers. At the same time, some monks refused to participate; they represent a more reclusive and seemingly more spiritual group uninterested in Ryōgen's political use of ritual and debate. However, their biographies often exaggerate their spirituality, perhaps as a way of indirectly criticizing politically active monks such as Ryōgen.

The next five chapters all concern aspects of Ryōgen's tenure as head of the Tendai school. Chapter 7 examines his controversial appointment as head and the reactions of the Tendai monks who opposed him. In addition, the growing importance of Tendai appointments to the Office of Monastic Affairs is considered; although Saichō had fiercely criticized this institution, Tendai monks came to dominate it; their ascendancy would mark their mastery of the Japanese religious world at that time.

Chapter 8 is a study of the examinations used in the Tendai monastic education system. While this chapter begins with Ryōgen's reformation of the educational system, it considers developments both before and after Ryōgen. The Tendai monastic education system provides the institutional background for the innovations in Tendai doctrine that would later be characterized as *hongaku*. It also sheds light on how scholarly monks were trained in medieval Japan. The rigor found in the examinations suggests that claims that scholarship declined in medieval Buddhism should be questioned.

Chapters 9 and 10 examine the process of rebuilding the Tendai complex on Mount Hiei after a disastrous fire. The order in which buildings were reconstructed reveals their usages and the structure of the ritual year and leads to insights into which practices were popular among Tendai monks.

Such a major rebuilding project required major contributions, the focus of chapter 10. The need for such support was a major factor in strengthening Tendai ties with certain factions of the nobility. It also led to the acquisition of manors and the strengthening of ties with other temples and shrines. The acquisition of land required monks skilled in administration; in addition, monks who could defend Tendai holdings were needed to defend Tendai interests against competing claims. The concluding section of chapter 10 concerns the role of women in financing monasteries. Although little evidence for direct contributions by women exists, a number of rituals seem to have been directed toward them and probably resulted in contributions through male relatives.

Chapter 11 returns to the theme of factionalism and to traditional claims that Ryōgen bears the responsibility for the advent of warrior-monks (*sōhei*). The end of Ryōgen's career was marked by bitter factionalism between several groups of Tendai monks, a development that would haunt the Tendai school for centuries. It has led some some scholars to question his effectiveness late in life. However, the factionalism evident in the political life of the patrons of monasteries, the earlier history of factionalism within Tendai, the early experiences of Ryōgen's life, and the need for finances and patronage to rebuild a devastated monastic complex lead to a more charitable evaluation of Ryōgen. The death of Ryōgen is also considered in this chapter.

Chapter 12, a discussion of nuns, could be considered a digression from the main focus of this book. However, it arose while I considered a question as I wrote the study: the absence of nuns in Ryōgen's biography even though he paid extravagant attention to his mother. To investigate Ryōgen's treatment of his mother, the chapter provides a background for understanding the position of nuns during Ryōgen's lifetime. The chapter thus provides a view of a group of Buddhist practitioners that was very different from that of Ryōgen and his politically active allies.

The final chapter is a consideration of Ryōgen's posthumous career. A virtual cult arose around Ryōgen, making him the most commonly enshrined monk in Tendai circles. He was said to be responsible for the protection of the Mount Hiei complex, as well as for helping individual believers. The wide-open eyes of many images of Ryōgen reflect his role as a protector of those who believe in him and provide a marked contrast with images of other monks, in which downcast eyes reflect deep meditative states.

2

The Early History of Factionalism Within the Tendai School

From Saichō through the Mid-tenth Century

The problem of factionalism on Mount Hiei is a constant theme in this study. Ryōgen is constantly motivated by his desire to support monks in his own lineage, often at the expense of monks from other lineages. Any general assessment of his career must take the open fighting between his faction and other factions of the Tendai school into account. In this chapter, the history of factionalism within the Tendai school before Ryōgen's time is discussed to provide a context for the rest of the study. Considerable attention is paid to a bitter rivalry that arose among the immediate followers of Saichō and Gishin to trace the origins of the bad feelings between these groups. Although later Tendai leaders would often try to ameliorate the hard feelings between the groups, they were never completely successful.

Tendai was not the only religious institution with such troubles. The other major Buddhist schools, particularly Shingon and Hossō, had similar problems. In fact, at times monks might have warmer relationships with members of a seemingly opposing school than with the members of an opposing faction of their own school. In addition, an opposing school might well try to exploit the factionalism in an adversarial school. For example, Tendai monks probably learned about Buddhist logic from Hossō monks disaffected with the major Hossō institution, Kōfukuji.

This chapter is divided into three parts, corresponding to the two relationships that most affected Tendai sectarianism. The first concerns the relationship between two of Saichō's followers, Gishin and Enchō. The second focuses on Ennin and Enchin, the two figures around which the two major factions Sanmon and Jimon coalesced. The last part traces the lineages of the heads of the Tendai School who followed Enchin, demonstrating how Enchin's lineage controlled the school during Ryōgen's youth to the detriment of monks who traced their lineage from

Ennin. In a later chapter, I examine the bitter rivalry and fighting that arose between the two major factions of the Tendai school.

Saichō's Immediate Followers

The Rivalry between Gishin and Enchō

The rivalry between the factions that traced themselves back to Ennin and Enchin plays a major role in Ryōgen's biography, as well as in Tendai history in subsequent centuries. The conflict actually began before the time of Ennin and Enchin, shortly after Saichō's death. In fact, the two factions are called the Sanmon and Jimon, names that reflect the areas where each faction had its stronghold. The term "Sanmon" refers to Mount Hiei (Hieizan), where Ennin's faction was eventually based. The term "Jimon" refers to Onjōji, a monastery that Enchin made his head-quarters for a time.

Saichō had named two men as successors at different times during his lifetime. In 812, he appointed Enchō (771–836), one of his first disciples, as his successor, partly because Gishin (781–833) had returned to his home province of Sagami. Later, in 822, the year he died, he appointed Gishin, who had traveled with him to China as interpreter and later had come to Mount Hiei to serve as the first head of the Tendai School. Saichō probably appointed Gishin because of the authority he could bring to the position as a result of the initiations he had received in China. In a collection of lineages by Saichō, the *Naishō buppō kechimya-kufu* (Lineages of the realization of the Buddha Dharma), Gishin was often listed alongside Saichō rather than as Saichō's student. When Saichō was asked which of the two men should serve first, he replied that Gishin should do so because he was the senior monk.[1]

By the time Gishin was appointed as *zasu*, the court had recognized the Tendai school's autonomy by granting it permission to conduct ordinations without interference from the Nara schools. As *zasu*, Gishin pursued a policy of reconciliation with the Nara schools, perhaps believing that the reasons for the earlier antagonism between Tendai and Hossō had been ameliorated. Moreover, Tendai monks were poverty-stricken after Saichō's death. If the school were to survive and prosper, some form of accommodation had to be found. To help the monks on Mount Hiei, Gishin had to send some of them to live at Hōryūji and Shitennōji by securing them lectureships during rainy-season retreats.[2]

Ennin lectured on the *Lotus Sūtra* at Hōryūji in the summer of 828 and on the *Lotus* and *Jen-wang ching* at Shitennōji the following year. Finally, Gishin served as lecturer at the Yuima-e (Assembly on the sūtra of Vimalakīrti's teachings) in 832.[3] When Ninchū wrote the *Eizan daishiden*, Saichō's biography, several years after Saichō's death in 822, he did not mention the debates with Tokuitsu of the Hossō school or the break in relations with Kūkai (774–835), founder of the Shingon school, probably to minimize Tendai conflicts with the Shingon and Hossō schools.[4] These policies bore fruit with appointment of six Tendai monks to the official rank of *dentō man'i* (senior rank of the transmission of the flame) in 832, the same year Gishin went to the Yuima-e. Among the monks promoted were Ennin, Tokuen (b. 785), and Enshu (also read as Enshū, n.d.).[5] Because the senior rank of the transmission of the flame was conferred by the court and was the third highest monastic rank, it carried considerable prestige.[6] That same year, Archbishop Gomyō (750–834) of the Hossō school, who had so vehemently opposed Saichō's proposals to ordain monks with the *Fan-wang ching* (Brahmā's net sūtra, *T* 1484, J. *Bonmōkyō*) precepts, was invited to preside over the dedication of the Lecture Hall in the Tōdō area of Mount Hiei, a building that had been commissioned by the court.[7] The invitation to Gomyō must have been seen as an attempt by Tendai monks to ameliorate some of the bitterness that had arisen during the debates with Saichō. Gomyō's appearance at the dedication also might have been an indication that the dispute was over.

Enchō was probably dissatisfied with many of Gishin's actions. When Gishin suddenly died, Enchō and Kōjō (779–858), two of Saichō's most trusted disciples, had been away from Mount Hiei. Although their movements cannot be traced in any detail, such absences suggest that Gishin and Enchō were uncomfortable with each other. In addition, when Enchō wrote a letter to Kūkai in 831, asking if he and a number of other Tendai monks could study Esoteric Buddhism with Kūkai, Gishin did not sign it. Because Gishin was *zasu* at the time Enchō wrote, the absence of Gishin's signature on such an important document to the head of the rival Shingon school indicates that relations between Enchō and Gishin were probably strained.[8] Moreover, Enchō and other Tendai monks had probably been disappointed in Gishin's response to a request from the court during the Tenchō era (824–833) that the head of each school submit a summary of the school's doctrines to the court. Gishin compiled the shortest work submitted, the *Tendaishū gishū* (Collected doctrines of the Tendai school) in one fascicle. Although the text was an admirable summary of Chinese T'ien-t'ai doctrine, largely based on citations from Chih-i's *Fa-hua hsüan-i* (Profound meaning of the *Lotus Sūtra*) and *Mo-ho chih-kuan* (Great calming and contemplation), it did not mention the Japanese Tendai claim to a valid tradition of Esoteric Buddhism or Saichō's use of the *Fan-wang ching* for ordinations.[9]

Enshu

The antagonistic feelings between followers of Gishin and Enchō were exacerbated by one of Gishin's last acts. When Gishin was on his deathbed, instead of naming Enchō as his successor, he appointed his own disciple, a young monk named Enshu.[10] This appointment can only be seen as a direct snub to Enchō who outranked Enshu in seniority and had been promised the position by Saichō.

During Saichō's lifetime, yearly ordinands were appointed to one of two courses of study: Tendai and Esoteric. Enshu, the man chosen by Gishin to be the next *zasu,* had been a yearly ordinand in the Tendai school's Esoteric course for 814, the same year Ennin was initiated as a yearly ordinand in the Tendai course. In subsequent years, Enshu decided to go Mount Takao, an Esoteric center, to study with Kūkai or his disciples.[11] Consequently, Enshu's relations with the Tendai monks who had remained on Mount Hiei were probably not very strong. However, from Gishin's perspective, Enshu seemed a likely successor because he was trained in Esoteric Buddhism and thus could answer the Tendai need to develop an Esoteric tradition that might compare with Kūkai's Shingon school. In addition, Gishin might have felt that Enchō was too old to master Esoteric Buddhism or to travel to China to obtain additional training in Esoteric rituals. To Gishin, the future of Tendai must have seemed much more promising in the hands of a younger, more active monk such as Enshu who could travel to China for Esoteric initiations if necessary.[12]

Opinion among Tendai monks was bitterly divided when Gishin's decision was made public. Kōjō and Enchō were away from Mount Hiei when they heard of Gishin's sudden death and Enshu's appointment.[13] Enchō's supporters, led by Kōjō, bitterly opposed Enshu and were able to have Enchō appointed *zasu* by the court after eight months of protest. According to Nakao Shunpaku, Enchō probably enlisted the help of Gomyō and Kūkai in advancing his claim to be *zasu.* These two monks, both critical of Saichō, had become the highest ranking and most influential men in the Office of Monastic Affairs. Enchō must have seemed like an improvement because he had studied Esoteric Buddhism under Kūkai and had studied the precepts under Dōchū (735?–800), a disciple of Chien-chen. Barely two weeks after Enchō was named *zasu*, on 3-30-834, he conducted a dedication ceremony for the Chapel of the Western Pagoda (Saitōin) on Mount Hiei. The ceremony was conducted by Archbishop Gomyō as leader (*dōshi*) and Greater Bishop Kūkai as the invoker (*jugan*). Their prominent roles may have been a way for Enchō to acknowledge their help in the dispute with Enshu. In addition, Enchō's overtures to them represent a continuation of Gishin's efforts to heal the bitter antagonism that arose during Saichō's struggle to establish the school.[14]

Why would Gomyō, Saichō's bitter antagonist during the dispute over the establishment of the ordination platform on Mount Hiei, have been willing to aid Enchō and then officiate at a dedication on Mount Hiei? The direct evidence for Nakao's claim that Gomyō and Kūkai aided Enchō rests on brief and ambiguous entries in the *Tendai zasuki* (Records of the heads of the Tendai school) and *Eigaku yōki* (Essential records of Mount Hiei).[15] Nakao's argument is weakened by the lack of any mention of help from Gomyō and Kūkai in Kōjō's *Denjutsu isshinkaimon* (Concerning the essays on the One-mind precepts), a source that records Enchō's efforts to be appointed as *zasu* in detail; perhaps Kōjō was still sensitive about Saichō's strained relations with Kūkai and Gomyō or did not want to mention Kūkai because it might lead to comparisons between Shingon and the less-developed Tendai Esoteric tradition.

Indirect evidence for Nakao's assertion can be gleaned from Gomyō's biography. As a young man, Gomyō had studied under several of Chien-chen's (J. Ganjin, 688–763) disciples, Tao-hsing (n.d.) and Fa-chin (709–778). He had been a master of the precepts himself, called "a latter-day Upāli" by Fa-chin, a reference likening him to Śākyamuni's disciple renowned for his mastery of the precepts. Moreover, he had officiated at both *Ssu-fen lü* (Four-part *vinaya*, I 1428; Skt. *Dharmaguptaka Vinaya*; J. *Shibunritsu*) and *Fan-wang ching* ordinations. He thus was amply aware that Saichō's proposals were unprecedented in Buddhist history and opposed them as a member of the Office of Monastic Affairs. When Saichō's proposals were approved one week after Saichō's death, Gomyō attempted to resign from the Office of Monastic Affairs. However, the emperor refused to approve the request. Gomyō's stature had continued to rise until he was appointed archbishop (*sōjō*) in 827. He seems to have become acquainted with Kūkai at about that time;

both monks were members of the Office of Monastic Affairs and participated at several of the same monastic assemblies. Kūkai wrote several letters to Gomyō. Thus Gomyō might well have been open to cooperating with Enchō because of Enchō's overtures to Kūkai and because several years had passed since his opposition to the ordination platform on Mount Hiei. Moreover, he could be expected to preside at the dedication on Mount Hiei in his capacity as archbishop, the highest office in the Office of Monastic Affairs at that time.[16]

Enchō's interests matched those of Gomyō in certain ways. He had studied under Dōchū in Tōgoku before he had become Saichō's student. Dōchū was famous for his interest in the precepts and had studied under Chien-chen. Enchō had probably been interested in Esoteric Buddhism while he was in Tōgoku. With Saichō's permission, he had studied with Kūkai. After Saichō's death, he had attempted to renew those studies. Thus Enchō's interests and background gave him much in common with Gomyō.[17]

After Enshu lost his position on Mount Hiei to Enchō, Enshu and several others of the six recently appointed *dentō man'i* left Mount Hiei to go to the Hossō center at Murōji, (Nara prefecture), which was used as a retreat by Hossō monks. The departure of half of the monks named *dentō man'i* must have deeply shaken the Tendai school. Although the choice of a Hossō temple might have seemed unusual for a Tendai monk at that time, Gishin had established relations with Hossō monks, such as Gomyō, during his tenure as Tendai *zasu*. Shuen (also read as Shūen; 771–835), a Hossō monk who had been deeply interested in both Tendai and Shingon, resided at Murōji for various periods and had performed rainmaking ceremonies. In addition, Gishin had become a close friend of one of Kūkai's disciples, Shintai, who was living at Murōji. Enshu could thus study a variety of Esoteric traditions at Murōji under several masters who were favorably disposed toward his teacher Gishin.[18]

The competing Tendai factions at Murōji and Enryakuji, the monastic complex on Mount Hiei, attempted to bolster their claims by sending monks to China. Ennin from Enryakuji left for China in 838; although he was supposed to stay in China for only a short period, he was caught up in attempts to reach Mount T'ien-t'ai and the Hui-ch'ang persecution of Buddhism in China and did not return to Japan until 847. Ennin's experience of the severe persecution of Buddhism in China may have led him to carefully cultivate patrons at the Japanese court after he returned so that Buddhism might be protected in Japan. If this supposition is correct, Ennin's efforts to provide for the future of Buddhism also contributed to the factionalism that beset Tendai as different groups of monks appealed to various political factions.[19]

Ennin carried several sets of questions (*Tōketsu*) that Japanese Tendai monks had given him to ask their Chinese counterparts. These questions reflected early Japanese Tendai attempts to interpret the Chinese T'ien-t'ai tradition and to develop their own views. Some of the questions reflected Tendai efforts to establish an independent tradition of Esoteric Buddhism that did not rely on Kūkai's Shingon school.[20]

Enshu and his disciple Kenne (n.d.), representing Murōji, left for China between 842 and 844, approximately five years after Ennin.[21] Their decision to go to China was undoubtedly influenced by the knowledge that Ennin was in China and would bring back additional teachings. In 844, Enshu received a document testifying that T'ien-t'ai teachings had been transmitted to him by the eighth Chinese T'ien-t'ai patriarch, Kuang-hsiu (772–844), of the Ch'an-lin-ssu on Mount T'ien-t'ai. At the time, Kuang-hsiu was on his deathbed and knew he would not live long. T'ien-t'ai monks must have been well aware of the Chinese court's chilly attitude toward Buddhism that would result in the Hui-ch'ang persecution. As a result, they probably conferred the document attesting to Enshu's reception of T'ien-t'ai teachings with little thought about its implications in Japan.[22] The document itself lists eight patriarchs of Chinese T'ien-t'ai, culminating in Kuang-hsiu. The Chinese tradition was conferred upon four Japanese monks: Saichō, Gishin, Enshu, and Kenne. The lineage would thus have implied that Murōji Tendai was at least equal to that of Mount Hiei, and possibly that it superseded it.

While Ennin remained in China, Enshu returned to Japan with this document ready to press his case for an independent Tendai school at Murōji or perhaps to renew his claim as *zasu* on Mount Hiei. In 844, shortly after he returned, he was named head administrator (*bettō*) at a privately established temple, the Jion'in, a branch (*betsuin*) of Saiji.[23] Enshu eventually settled at Izumodera to the northeast of Kyoto (within the precincts of Shōkokuji).[24] Kenne returned to Murōji to pursue his claim to be the rightful inheritor of the leadership of Tendai in Japan. About this time, a Golden Hall (Kondō) was constructed at Murōji with Yakushi nyorai (Bhaiṣajyaguru) as the central figure on the altar; the arrangement was reminiscent of the Central Hall (Chūdō) at Enryakuji (established by Saichō when he carved an image of Yakushi shortly after arriving on Mount Hiei) and thus served as an architectural statement of Enshu's claims. Very little is known of Enshu's subsequent activities, except that he participated as the Tendai representative at lectures on the *Chin-kuang-ming ching* (*Suvarṇaprabhāsa-sūtra*) held at court in 850.[25]

Enshu's efforts to establish a viable Tendai tradition at Murōji failed for several reasons. First, Enshu's voyage was a private effort, probably supported by several of the major patrons of Butsuryūji in Yamato, the temple Kenne returned to after his voyage. They could not have provided him with the same degree of support that Ennin's participation in a court-sponsored voyage would have received.[26] Control of the officially recognized center of Tendai on Mount Hiei also gave Ennin and his allies a marked advantage.

Second, Enshu was exhausted from the struggle to become *zasu*. Both a passage in the document attesting to his lineage and his subsequent lack of activity reflect his weariness. Perhaps he took Kenne along with him hoping that Kenne could provide the energy to press their case later. However, Kenne seems to have had few accomplishments of his own. In the document certifying his lineage he is mentioned as being from the same province as Saichō and as a disciple of Enshu, but little other information about him has been found. The name of the temple Kenne settled in and perhaps founded, Butsuryūji, may reflect the hope that in the future when Maitreya appeared, their claims might be recognized.[27]

Third, Enshu and Kenne studied only exoteric T'ien-t'ai traditions in China at a time when the Japanese nobility had become fascinated with the Esoteric tradition. In part, the Buddhism transmitted by Enshu and Ennin reflects the contrast between the conservative Buddhism on Mount T'ien-t'ai, where Enshu studied, and the more progressive and syncretistic Buddhism in Ch'ang-an, where Ennin studied. Perhaps Enshu was overconfident of his understanding of the Esoteric tradition as a student of Shingon Buddhism on Mount Takao, or he may have misjudged the situation in Japan. He seems to have brought back very few texts and to have written only one;[28] in contrast, Ennin brought back 584 texts in 802 fascicles from China and wrote several major commentaries on Esoteric texts, successfully advancing a Tendai version of Esoteric Buddhism that could compete with that of the Shingon school. Ennin clearly outshone Enshu. However, if Ennin had not returned from China, Enshu might have been able to mount a significant challenge to Enryakuji.

Fourth, the difference in intellectual quality between Ennin and Enshu is striking. Enshu seems to have been content with receiving documentation to further his claims and returning to Japan after a short stay in China. In contrast, Ennin took the opportunity to observe as much about Chinese Buddhism as possible and record it in his diary. After his return, he was the author of major treatises and commentaries and established a number of practices on Mount Hiei that were based on his observations in China.

The movement to establish a separate Tendai tradition at Murōji came to an official end on 11-4-874 when Kenne gave Enchin the lineage document that he and Enshu had received in China.[29] Because Enchin, one of Gishin's disciples, had been *zasu* since 868, the future of Gishin's lineage on Mount Hiei must have seemed more secure than at any time since Gishin's death. Thus Kenne might have been willing to relinquish the failed effort to establish a separate Tendai lineage at Murōji.[30]

Ensai

Factionalism within Japanese Tendai even affected Japanese monks studying in China. Ensai traveled to China with Ennin in 838. While Ennin was authorized to stay for only a short time, Ensai (d. 877) was directed to remain for a longer time. Monks from several other schools were to go to China, including the Shingon monks Shinzei (800–860), Shinzen (d. 891), and Engyō (799–852); the Hossō monk Kaimyō (791–849); and the Sanron monk Jōgyō (d. 866).[31] The ship that was to carry Shinzei and Shinzen was destroyed, and they decided to abandon their plans to go to China. As a result, only Engyō (799–852) represented the Shingon school, while the Tendai school sent two monks. The dispatch of two Tendai monks may have reflected the dire situation of Tendai monks at this time; beset by internal dissension and external competition from the Shingon and Hossō schools, the Tendai school must have felt a serious need for the legitimation that study in China offered.

When Ensai and Ennin reached China, they applied for permission to go to Mount T'ien-t'ai, headquarters of the T'ien-t'ai school. However, only Ensai received permission to proceed to Mount T'ien-t'ai; Ennin was refused permission, probably because he was only a short-term student.[32] The two monks parted and Ensai proceeded to Mount T'ien-t'ai, carrying a copy of Prince Shōtoku's commentary on the *Lotus Sūtra* and a purple robe presented by the empress of Japan to be deposited at the monastery on Mount T'ien-t'ai. He also brought a series of questions from eminent Japanese Tendai monks for presentation to his Chinese counterparts. The questions, called the *Tōketsu*, reflected the major concerns of early Tendai monks. Ensai asked the T'ien-t'ai patriarch Kuang-hsiu for his teachings in 838.[33] Kuang-hsiu's response is not known, but Ensai did not receive the respect from Chinese monks or the documentation concerning a transmission that Enshu would receive five years later. While Ensai remained on Mount T'ien-t'ai, Ennin traveled to Ch'ang-an, where he engaged in the Esoteric studies that would make him famous.

During some of the time Ensai was in China, the Buddhist community was subject to criticisms from the court for being lax in discipline. These attacks culminated in the Hui-ch'ang persecution around 845. Ensai seems to have been influenced by some of the laxer elements among the clergy or perhaps by the court's efforts to laicize monks; according to Enchin, Ensai was involved in sexual relations with a nun, kept a wife and children, and engaged in farming and raising silkworms; in addition, he may have absconded with some of the money intended to support Ennin.[34] Because monks of Ensai's status were laicized during this time, Ensai may well have found that living with a woman and farming were the only way he could live. After all, he had no relatives and no connections that would have enabled him to continue as a monk during the persecution.

However, Ennin's mentions of Ensai are almost always respectful; he calls him "eminent priest" (*shōnin*), "meditation master" (*zenji*), and "master of Esoteric Buddhism" (*ajari*), and never mentions Ensai's lapses of discipline.[35] In 845, shortly before he returned to Japan, Ennin made unsuccessful inquiries concerning Ensai's whereabouts.[36] The court continued to be interested in Ensai. In 847, Ensai sent Ninkō back to Japan to obtain permission to extend his stay as a court-sponsored student; the court granted permission the following year and gave Ensai an additional 100 ryō of gold to finish his studies. In 850, they awarded him the title of *dentō daihosshi* (great Dharma-master who transmits the flame).[37]

In contrast to the respectful treatment of Ensai by the court and Ennin, Enchin clearly did not like Ensai. Even their first meeting in China was difficult. As Enchin wrote in his diary for 12-14-853,

> I saw that the person was the bodhisattva Ensai, a court-sponsored Japanese monk studying in China. I immediately went out of the gate to greet him at the north end of the bridge. I was so happy that I shed tears. Although I felt like that, Ensai did not seem very happy to see me and his

expression was dark. He seemed unable to feel at ease. I thought this very strange. Because we were from the same country, even if we had not known each other before, we should have felt closer than family when we met in a foreign country. How much more so should this have been the case since we had sat together at the same monastery [in Japan]. But now when we met here, Ensai seemed devoid of any true human feeling (*honjō*).[38]

Ensai explained that he had forgotten Japanese during his long stay in China. However, the next day, when Enchin gave Ensai a Japanese court document promoting him to *dentō daihosshi* and some money, Ensai was friendlier and spoke at length in Japanese. Enchin eventually became aware of some of the reasons for Ensai's reservations at their first meeting. Enchin wrote that he heard from Chinese monks that Ensai had became so jealous of Enshu's success in obtaining a transmission on Mount T'ien-t'ai that he had prepared a poison and employed a Korean monk to follow Enshu and kill him. However, Enshu returned to Japan before the plan could be carried out.[39] Ensai may have resorted to such drastic measures because he feared that Enshu would return to Japan and tell the court about his sexual transgressions, leading the court to deny a request Ensai had made for money.[40] However, Enchin's accounts of these events are so vitriolic that they cannot be taken at face value.[41] Moreover, Enchin continued to associate with Ensai even after he had heard these stories, and Chinese monks conferred high Esoteric initiations on Ensai even though they supposedly knew of Ensai's supposed violations of monastic discipline.

Enchin noted that Ensai had not striven to master Buddhist doctrine and clearly felt that the court's financial aid had been wasted. According to Enchin's diary,

> Another time, I asked Ensai about various topics of T'ien-t'ai doctrine, but he could not answer any of them. Two or three times he managed a simple answer, but after that time, I stopped [trying to speak of such matters] and we did not speak [of these issues] again. This saddened me greatly. How could a Tendai monk sent abroad to study have ended up this way!
>
> During the Chen-yüan period (785–804), the Japanese monk Enki who was studying in China falsely claimed that he had an eye ailment and hurriedly returned to Japan where he was made a temple administrator (*kōi*) in an outlying province. He was ashamed before the monks of his school. Now in the field of doctrine, Ensai must be regarded in this manner. . . . Ensai's understanding of doctrine does not even come up to the level of that of the novices and young boys of Mount Hiei. How much less so that of the monks? How pathetic.[42]

Despite Enchin's obvious dislike of Ensai, he agreed to travel with him to Ch'ang-an, where in 855 they both received the highest Esoteric initiations from Fa-ch'üan, one of the Esoteric masters Ennin had studied with earlier. During this time, Enchin recorded Fa-ch'üan's opinions about Ensai:

> The preceptor [Fa-ch'üan] said, "This thief [Ensai] lived in the province of Shan [in Chekiang] for a long time, caring for a wife, cultivating fields, raising silkworms, and rearing his children. He had no intention of coming to Ch'ang-an, but when he saw that you intended to come here, he became a demonic thief and accompanied you."[43]

Enchin continued, noting that Ensai had not been very assiduous about studying for the Esoteric initiations. However, Enchin's criticism of Ensai seems overstated. If Fa-ch'üan disliked Ensai so much, why would he have conferred Esoteric initiations on him? Does that action reflect the confused state of Chinese Buddhism soon after the Hui-ch'ang persecution? Fa-ch'üan's loose standards? Or was Ensai a more impressive monk than Enchin believed? Some of Enchin's criticisms may have been due to the resentment that had built up over the antagonism between the lineages of Gishin and Enchō. However, Enchin continued to respect Ennin. As Saeki Arikiyo has argued, Enchin's active dislike of Ensai may have been due to the hypercritical and uncompromising attitudes of both men.[44] In addition, the antagonism between the two men may have been intensified when one of Enchin's disciples, Hōchi, changed his name to Chisō and decided to accompany Ensai; Chisō remained with Ensai for the next several decades. He boarded the ship on which Ensai would try to return to Japan and survived the shipwreck that resulted in Ensai's death, returning in 877 to Japan, where he would become known as an expert in Chinese pronunciation.[45]

Ensai remained in China for a total of four decades. Other sources for his activities during this period describe him as a serious scholar. Ensai copied a number of texts and sent them back to Japan with Ninkō in 843. One of these texts, Chan-jan's *Wu-pai men-lun* (five hundred questions), survives; the text consisted of questions concerning the Fa-hsiang patriarch Tz'u-en's commentary on the *Lotus Sūtra*, the *Fa-hua hsüan-tsan*, and would have been a valuable source for Tendai monks debating Hossō monks. The copy was made in the New Japanese Hall (Shin Nihon-dō) at Kuo-ch'ing-ssu on Mount T'ien-t'ai, a structure that might have been built by Ensai for the use of Japanese monks studying on Mount T'ien-t'ai.[46] At some point, Ensai came to the attention of Emperor Hsüan-tsung

(r. 846–859), who ordered him to reside in the Hsi-ming Temple in Ch'ang-an. Later the emperor asked Ensai to come to court to lecture on scriptures and was so pleased that he conferred on him a purple robe (*hōi*), the highest honor the court bestowed on monks.[47]

Ensai is portrayed as a serious and helpful monk in documents concerning Shinnyo, an imperial prince who was ordained as a monk and traveled to China to study Esoteric Buddhism. Shinnyo, the third son of Emperor Heizei, was named crown prince in 809 but lost the position in the Kusuko disturbance the following year. After a demotion in rank in 821, Shinnyo was ordained a monk at Tōdaiji. He studied under a variety of teachers, but his Esoteric Buddhist studies under Kūkai were particularly important, and he eventually rose to *ajari*. He traveled to China in 864 to resolve certain doubts about the Esoteric tradition. Shinnyo met Ensai shortly after Shinnyo arrived in Ch'ang-an. For the next six months Ensai served as Shinnyo's translator and liaison to the Chinese court. Ensai also introduced Shinnyo to his own teacher, Fa-ch'üan. However, because even Fa-ch'üan could not resolve Shinnyo's doubts, Shinnyo decided to travel to India and had Ensai submit the proposal to the T'ang court. Shinnyo probably died after his departure from Canton on a ship in 865.[48]

Near the end of his life, Ensai became interested in Confucianism and collected several thousand fascicles of Buddhist and Confucian texts that he attempted to bring back to Japan; however, he died at sea in a storm in 877.[49] The Confucian texts may have been part of an attempt to bolster his own lineage of Tendai against that of Enchin, who had been named head of the Tendai school. Or perhaps he intended to establish his own tradition.

During Ensai's stay in China, he helped a number of Japanese monks. The remarks about him in contemporary sources were generally positive. As a result, some scholars have not accepted Enchin's negative comments about Ensai at face value. Although some of the reasons for Enchin's negative comments remain unclear, they do become harsher as time passes and surely reflect the distrust between members of the two factions.[50]

Ennin and Enchin

The major schism in the Tendai school is sometimes said to have originated in bad feelings between Ennin and Enchin, though evidence is often not given. In fact, as was noted above, the two factions are called the Sanmon and Jimon, names that reflect the areas where Ennin and Enchin had their bases of power. However, as the previous section demonstrated, bad feelings existed between the two factions from an earlier date. Thus, describing the tensions in the Tendai school in terms of factions descended from Ennin and Enchin is simplistic. Tendai monks from these factions could be both rivals and allies, much as Enchin and Ensai had been in China. A similar situation existed in the relationship between Ennin and Enchin. In this part of the chapter, the relationship between the two men is investigated by focusing on Enchin, who was twenty years younger than Ennin.

Enchin climbed Mount Hiei to join the Tendai order in 828; at approximately the same time, Ennin interrupted his twelve-year retreat to go to Hōryūji and Shitennōji to lecture; he then traveled north to proselytize. Enchin was ordained as a monk in 833, the same year that Ennin sickened and retreated to Yokawa. Enchin began his twelve-year retreat in 833, close to the time that Enshu was force to leave Mount Hiei. Although Enchin was a disciple of Gishin and could have left with Enshu, he decided to remain on Mount Hiei to complete the twelve-year retreat. Enchin's decision to complete the retreat despite the controversy indicates his seriousness, but it may also have been due to Kōjō's intervention to ensure that Enchin's stay on Mount Hiei went smoothly.[51] During much of the time Enchin was undergoing his twelve-year retreat on Mount Hiei, Ennin was in China (838–847). Thus Ennin and Enchin had few opportunities to meet; they were usually either on different parts of Mount Hiei, in different countries, or in different parts of Japan until 847. For example, for much of the time Enchin was completing his twelve-year retreat on Mount Hiei, Ennin was at his own retreat in Yokawa or in China.

Enchin was recognized as a very promising young monk near the end of his retreat. In 846, he was appointed head of Esoteric studies (*Shingon gakutō*) by the monastic assembly (*shugi*) on Mount Hiei.[52] His appointment even though he was young and from Gishin's lineage indicates that the Tendai school was still open to members of different factions.

The year after Enchin was appointed head of Esoteric studies, Ennin returned from China with new Esoteric transmissions. Because Esoteric transmissions were jealously guarded, one measure of factionalism is whether Ennin was willing to transmit some of his new teachings to Enchin. Sometime between Ennin's return from China and Enchin's departure for China, Ennin taught Enchin the ritual for Mahāvairocana of the Womb-realm (*Dainichi nyorai taizō son hō*).[53] The ritual was to be applied in accordance with the wishes of the practitioner. Enchin noted that when he studied it in China under Fa-ch'üan, one of Ennin's teachers, he found slight discrepancies in the ritual procedures he had learned from Ennin, but that the "flavor" of the transmissions was the same.[54] Perhaps because of these transmissions, in his conversations with his Chinese teacher Fa-ch'üan, Enchin referred to Ennin with terms such as "teacher and elder brother."[55]

Late in his life, Enchin's appreciation of Ennin grew deeper. Enchin completed a number of the plans that Ennin had begun but been unable to complete. In 888, Enchin constructed the shrine to Sekisan myojin, the deity that had protected Ennin on his journey to China.[56] When Enchin was on his deathbed, he is said to have written an eleven-article will (*yuisei*). The third article concerned his relation to Ennin:

> I followed Jikaku daishi [Ennin] and again penetrated the depths of the Esoteric tradition. On the fourteenth day of the first month, my followers should make offerings to the *maṇḍalas* (*mandara-ku*) and invite ten superior scholars to lecture on the profundities of the One-vehicle [in memory of] Ennin. . . . His disciples and my disciples should carefully follow the proper order and not be indolent in the performance of the ceremony.[57]

Because many of the other articles clearly reflect events after Enchin's death, modern scholars believe that the will was composed by later Sanmon monks because their position is advanced in a number of ways.[58] A set of three admonitions (*seikai*) from 888, however, reflects similar attitudes toward Ennin.[59] This document concerns Enchin's thankfulness toward Sannō myōjin (the protective deities for Mount Hiei), Kōjō and Ennin.

Not all of the relations between Ennin and Enchin were without friction, however. In 847, Enchin was named as one of ten monks (*jūzenji*) that were to constantly chant the *Greater Perfection of Wisdom Sūtra* to ensure the safety and longevity of Emperor Ninmyō (810–850; r. 833–850) at the Jōshin'in (Hall of the concentrated mind), a chapel commissioned in 846 on Mount Hiei.[60] On 2-15-850, several years after Ennin returned from China, he was commanded to lead the monks appointed to practice at the Jōshin'in in Esoteric services for the ailing Emperor Ninmyō at the *jijūden* (imperial living quarters) in the palace. The ceremony was the eight-character Mañjuśrī rite (*Monju hachiji hō*). This ritual, introduced to Japan by Ennin, was to be performed during eclipses and other astrological anomalies, illnesses, and political upheaval.[61] For Enchin, the head of Esoteric studies on Mount Hiei and one of the ten monks affiliated with the Jōshin'in, the appointment of Ennin to lead the ceremony might have been vexing, perhaps enough to lead to his decision to travel in China.[62]

Enchin's decision to travel to China only a few years after Ennin returned from a prolonged stay there has been cited by several scholars as evidence of Enchin's distrust and critical attitude toward Ennin.[63] A record of several of Enchin's dreams provides insight into Enchin's state of mind:

> In the spring of 850, Enchin dreamt of Sannō myōjin, who said to him, "You should quickly fulfill your intention of traveling to China to study the Dharma. Do not delay." Enchin replied, "The preceptor and *ācārya* Ennin traveled to China and mastered the threefold mystery. Now he has recently returned to Mount Hiei. Why should I be in a hurry to cross the ocean?" The deity encouraged Enchin again, saying, "If it is as you say, many people shave their heads and become monks. Long ago, why did you feel that it was so urgent that you have your head shaved and become a monk?"
>
> In the spring of the following year, the deity appeared again and spoke: "A mendicant should forget his health and life in the pursuit of the teaching. All superhuman forces will surely protect you as you cross the sea. Strive diligently and do not harbor any doubts." Enchin felt that his plan had received the deity's approval and submitted his request to the court.[64]

Enchin's dreams can be interpreted as revealing that he was dissatisfied with the Esoteric Buddhism taught by Ennin, perhaps because Ennin did not readily grant initiations to the members of Gishin's lineage. However, it can also be interpreted in a less sectarian manner as reflecting Enchin's fear of the dangers of the journey and his final decision to travel to China to study in order to advance his own practice. Moreover, close analysis of documents from Onjōji reveal that Enchin had been considering studying in China as early as 840, while Ennin was still in China.[65] Saeki Arikiyo suggests that Enchin might have been influenced by Ensai's travels to China at that early date because he had been a fellow student of Ensai on Mount Hiei.[66] Although Enchin's decision to study in China cannot be attributed solely to a rivalry with Ennin, Ennin's return might well have heightened his desire to go to China.

After Enchin had returned to Japan from China, virtually no sources place him together with Ennin. Ennin was busy with his duties as *zasu* on Mount Hiei while Enchin served as abbot of Onjōji. The two men would certainly have had much to talk about concerning their studies in China—both had studied with Fa-ch'üan—but no record of discussions between the men remains. Perhaps they felt uncomfortable with each other and had begun to see each other as rivals. They also may have differed in their attitudes toward Ensai.

Factionalism was expressed not only by access to Esoteric rituals, but by access to the texts upon which those rituals were based. One of the major reasons for the break in relations between Saichō and Kūkai had been Saichō's request for Esoteric texts.[67] Ennin brought back a massive collection of 584 works in 802 fascicles and fifty-nine *mandalas* and other ritual implements. Of the texts, 221 texts in 283 fascicles were Esoteric.[68] In his last will, dated 1-15-864, one day before his death, Ennin noted that the texts he had brought back had been kept in a repository (*hikyōzō*), probably at his residence, the Zentōin. However, Ennin now asked that the Esoteric texts be kept in the Sōjiin (Dhāraṇī hall), an institution that would be administered by his own disciples, and that circulation of them be restricted so that people not suitable for the Way would not be able to see them. In addition, the Esoteric texts in Saichō's collection were to be transferred to the Sōjiin. The exoteric texts that Ennin brought back were to be placed at the Central Hall, where the works Saichō had collected were kept. Thus two libraries were to exist on Mount Hiei, one for exoteric texts and the other for Esoteric works. The library at the Sōjiin was sometimes called the Shingonzō (Esoteric repository). The day after Ennin died, the major controller of the left (*sadaiben*) issued an order granting Ennin's request.[69]

Ennin's request could be viewed as an attempt to limit access of these texts to his disciples, but Ennin also was concerned with the dispersal of the texts he brought back and the possibility that "those not suited to the way might see the [Esoteric] texts."[70] This restriction seems to have referred to laymen more than to members of different factions on Mount Hiei. In fact, Ennin had specified that the monastic institution he had founded at Yokawa though administered by his disciples, was to be open to all monks. Thus the disposition of the Esoteric texts should not be considered as contributing to factionalism. This interpretation is supported by a note in Enchin's *Daibirushana jōdōkyō gishaku mokuroku* stating that he had access to a copy of a text brought to Japan by Ennin that had been deposited in the Sōjiin.[71] Moreover, a number of texts from the Sōjiin were copied and included in a library based on texts brought from China by Enchin.[72] In addition, Enchin honored Ennin's instructions concerning the texts during his long period as *zasu*. He ordered that when a master of Esoteric Buddhism died, if he did not have any disciples who had qualified as *ajari,* all of his Esoteric texts and implements were to be deposited in the Sōjiin, thus expanding the collection beyond the texts that Ennin had brought back.[73] However, even if Ennin's order had not been intended for sectarian applications, the potential for abuse existed.

The books brought back by Enchin were treated in a similar manner. At first the texts were deposited with the Nakatsukashō (Ministry of central affairs). In 859, Enchin renovated Onjōji and constructed a Chinese Hall (Tōbō) there for his books.[74] According to later sources, the deity Sannō myōjin appeared in a dream and told Enchin that a government office was not an appropriate place for the texts and that they should be placed in the Sannōin, Enchin's residence on Mount Hiei. However, another deity, Shiragi myōjin, then emerged and told him that because Mount Hiei would be the site of discord, the books should be placed at a site to the south, Onjōji. The library there was not built for several years, with the actual move occurring in 867. Presumably the books would have been stored at the Sannōin until they were moved later. However, because no early sources support the 867 date, the 859 date for the transfer of the books to Onjōji is more reasonable.[75] Because Onjōji was far from the monastic complex on Mount Hiei, many of the books were eventually brought to the Sannōin. By 925, thirty-five years after Enchin's death, well over one thousand texts were stored in the Sannōin.[76] Although Enchin's books were carefully protected against damage, little evidence exists that access was denied or granted in a sectarian manner during his lifetime.

Strains in relations between various groups of monks were certainly evident during the lifetimes of Ennin and Enchin. However, both monks strove to deemphasize partisanship among Tendai monks. The struggle between the disciples of Gishin and Enchō and the separatist movement led by Enshu had been resolved with the appointment of Enchin as *zasu*. At the same time, both Ennin and Enchin also supported their own followers for appointments to the institutions they founded. While such favoritism would play a key role in the open fighting between Tendai monks that eventually arose late in Ryōgen's lifetime, few signs of the vicious competition between the Sanmon and Jimon are found at this time. In the next part, factionalism during the fifty-year period after Enchin's death is examined, bringing the discussion of factionalism up to the time when Ryōgen was beginning to be a prominent young monk.

Factionalism during the Fifty Years after Enchin

Certain teachings and institutions contributed to the intensification of factionalism in Tendai during the tenth century. This discussion begins with a consideration of the ways in which Esoteric Buddhism contributed to the factionalism and sectarianism that characterized Japanese Buddhism during the mid-Heian period. It then proceeds to a consideration of the establishment of religious institutions that supported these trends.

Esoteric Buddhism and Factionalism

The increasing role of Esoteric Buddhism in the Tendai school contributed to the emergence of factionalism in the generations of Tendai monks beginning with Ennin and Enchin. When Ennin established a form of Tendai Esoteric Buddhism that could compete with the Shingon school, he also strengthened a form of Buddhism that was well suited to the factional tendencies that had emerged in his school. Through exoteric forms of Buddhism, any monk who was intelligent, learned, and eloquent might be able to attract disciples and patrons. Ryōgen himself was a prime example of the openness of the exoteric system in the early tenth century when, despite the death of his teacher, he attracted both disciples and patrons through his performances at debates. To become proficient in Esoteric Buddhism, however, the sponsorship of a qualified master of the tradition was necessary.[77] If a monk had not received a consecration into a particular Esoteric tradition from a master, then he could not practice the rituals or claim to be a master himself no matter how intelligent or able he was. The importance of lineages in medieval Buddhism is partly due to the importance of proving that one had access to certain teachings and rituals. Such a system could easily be used to convey the teaching to a master's chosen disciples and to ignore others who might have more seniority or be better qualified.

To some extent, the Japanese Esoteric tradition had displayed these tendencies from the beginning. Kūkai had specified that only Shingon monks could live at Tōji. Although Saichō had wanted to make

Enryakuji a Tendai temple, he also opened it to any monk who wished
to study Tendai. However, as Esoteric Buddhism came to dominate
Tendai, only monks of certain lineages were allowed to hold office at
certain Tendai institutions. For example, Ennin allowed only his own
monks to hold office at Yokawa. Enchin treated Onjōji in the same
manner.

The use of Esoteric Buddhism to control Tendai lineages can be illustrated by the appointment of masters of Esoteric Buddhism. When
Saichō conferred advanced consecration (*kanjō*) upon students, he had
done so with little government supervision. In a sense, conferral of the
status of master of Esoteric Buddhism qualified to transmit the teaching (*denbō ajari*) was roughly equivalent to an advanced degree. However, the court wished to control the new ritual technology that Esoteric Buddhism represented. As a result, the names of candidates for
ajari were to be proposed by the Tendai school to the court. After re-
viewing the selections, the government would grant its permission, and
an advanced Esoteric consecration would be held. In the Tendai school,
Ennin and his disciple Anne (794–868) put this system into place because it helped the *zasu* control the various temples under the Tendai
umbrella. Although originally no specific numbers for *ajari* had been
designated because it was a position awarded to whoever was qualified,
under this new system, specific numbers of *ajari* were allocated to various temples. For the Tendai school in the tenth century, the numbers
were twelve for Enryakuji, three for Gangyōji, four for Hōsshōji (the
temple founded by Tadahira), and one for Hōrinji.[78] Because appointment as *ajari* was often a prerequisite for being named to higher positions, such as *zasu*, the system easily led to increased factionalism. Thus
the status of *ajari* came to be treated as roughly similar to that of serving in the Office of Monastic Affairs, a step on the road to becoming
an eminent monk. The system would begin to fall apart near the end
of Ryōgen's life when his archrival Yokei assumed the right to appoint
ajari even though he was not *zasu*.

An emphasis on lineages is found early in Tendai. Saichō's *Kechimyakufu* (Lineages) for example, carefully demonstrates how he received teachings in T'ien-t'ai, Ch'an, *Fan-wang* precepts and Esoteric
Buddhism. Saichō compiled the text primarily to demonstrate the authenticity of his Chinese teachings, but such lineages could also be used
in sectarian manners to claim exclusive control over doctrines and ritual. Exoteric teaching lineages were more open than Esoteric lineages,
but eventually the emphasis on lineages that was so fundamental to Es-

oteric Buddhism would have counterparts in the exoteric Buddhist tradition as oral tradition (*kuden*) and in the arts.

As Esoteric Buddhism provided a ritual and doctrinal rationale for the increasing influence of factionalism, institutions controlled by one bloc of the school arose. The court had discouraged the use of ritual for private gain early in the Heian period, but as the system of regents governing in the place of young emperors was put into place, the court factions behind them commissioned religious institutions and supported certain monks. Thus religious factionalism came to reflect partisanship among the nobles.

Imperially Sponsored Temples

Sectarian tendencies among monks were directly related to patronage by different groups or individuals. In this section, some of the institutions established for the express purpose of performing rituals for individuals are described.[79] The *goganji,* literally "august prayer-offering temples," were one of the most important examples of this type of monastery. *Goganji* were established as religious centers where rites were conducted to further the longevity and fortunes of the emperor or a member of his family. Although the royal family had sponsored temples since the time of Empress Suiko (554–628; r. 592–628), the term "*goganji*" was not used until the middle of the ninth century, when it came to refer to temples with certain characteristics that typified the close relation between politics and religion during the Heian period.[80] A few temples established before the term was in use such as Enryakuji and Tōji were also referred to as *goganji* of Emperor Kanmu after the emperor's death. *Goganji* were established at the express wish of the emperor as well as when a monk applied to have a temple he had established designated as a *goganji.*

Few *goganji* were established during the first decades of the Heian period, but from the time of Emperor Ninmyō (r. 833–850), they proliferated until such temples as Gangyōji, Jōganji, Ten'anji, and Kajōji came to be mentioned prominently in documents in the middle and late ninth century.[81] Often the temples seemed to be a mixture of both official and private elements. Like many official temples, they had yearly ordinands assigned to them who were supported with court funds; but, like private temples, they were independent of the supervision of the Office of Monastic Affairs. Moreover, they often controlled land much like private temples. Although early *goganji* were supported through tax funds, as time passed their landholdings tended to come from imperial lands, making them more like private temples.[82] Some emperors established several such temples. By Ryōgen's time, the list of *goganji* established on Mount Hiei included the Jōshin'in for Emperor Ninmyō; the Shiōin (Chapel of the four kings), Sōjiin, and Saitōin for Emperor Montoku; the Hōdōin (Bejeweled banner hall) and Zuijii-in (Chapel for meditation that freely follows one's thoughts) for Emperor Seiwa; the Senkōin (Chapel of one thousand lights) for Emperor Uda; the Anrakuin (Chapel of ease and pleasure) for Emperor Yōzei; the Gonen'in (Chapel for guarding one's thoughts); and the Enmeiin (Hall of longevity) and Shin-enmeiin (New hall of longevity) for Emperor Suzaku.[83] With each hall or chapel entailing court or private support or both, the possibilities for factional tendencies were enhanced as noble patrons and monks congregated around the various institutions.

Most *goganji* flourished during the years when the emperor reigned and then declined as they came to be replaced by the temples of the next emperor and his supporters. The use of era names (*nengō*) in temple appelations such as Kajōji, Jōganji, and Gangyōji was unintentionally accurate because a temple's influence flourished during the years the emperor reigned. However, a few *goganji* managed to maintain their influence for a longer period by being named *goganji* by two or three patrons; among them was the Tendai Urin'in.

Most of these temples were established in and around Kyoto, though a few were in the provinces. Because most *goganji* were affiliated with either the Shingon school or Tendai school, the institution played a major role in the rise of these two schools to prominence in the early Heian period. By the end of the ninth century they had replaced most of the official temples in Nara as recipients of patronage of the court circles. In fact, the major temples of Nara that maintained their influence during the middle of the Heian period were Kōfukuji, Tōdaiji, and Yakushiji, all institutions that established an affiliation with powerful clans in a manner similar to the more successful *goganji*.[84]

Goganji played an important role in the development of the factionalism between schools and temples that came to typify Buddhism during the middle and late Heian period. An examination of the administrative details of these new temples reveals that they were much more suited to factionalism than their predecessors in Nara. *Goganji* were proposed by members of the imperial family, nobles, or monks. Sometimes a new temple was constructed, but in other cases a temple that already

existed might petition the court for the status of *goganji* because it wished
to have the prestige and financial support that accompanied this status.[85] Each of these groups usually had certain political goals, such as
the success of their branch of the family or their branch of a school, in
establishing a *goganji*. When a temple was designated a *goganji*, it was
often assigned to a specific monk. For example, Henjō was placed in
charge of Gangyōji, Ennin of the Jōshin'in at Enryakuji, and Kōjō of
the Shiōin at Enryakuji. These monks usually favored their own disciples as their successors and set up appointments so that only those in
their lineage could be named to major posts. A candidate for a high
post might be required to first be appointed as one of a limited number of officially authorized monks (*jōgakusō*) or a Master of Esoteric Buddhism.[86] Because in most cases only monks from the abbot's lineage
could attain such posts, the temple was controlled by that lineage.

During the Nara period and the first years of the Heian period, the
Office of Monastic Affairs had overseen appointments to the major positions at temples, but Saichō had replaced this system in the Tendai
school with lay supervisors (*zoku bettō*) because the Office of Monastic
Affairs had favored the Nara schools and monks. The monks who established the *goganji*, even though they were not always Tendai monks,
generally favored use of lay supervisors because such lay believers could
usually be depended upon to agree to their appointments.[87] As a result, the Sōgō declined in influence, and the effectiveness of the government's major institution for governing the order and controlling factionalism was seriously undermined.

Because *goganji* were established by or for the benefit of particular
patrons, the monks in charge were naturally interested in the welfare
of their sponsors. Although the performance of rituals for an emperor
did not seem to be an activity that led to factionalism during Saichō's
period, it later became closely connected with the support of the emperor's maternal relatives, as was the case with Ryōgen's support of Fujiwara no Morosuke against competing factions in the court and the
monks who served them.

Another institution that contributed to this situation was the "officially designated temple" (*jōgakuji*). The meaning of this term is not
completely clear; some scholars have argued that it referred to a designation awarded to only a limited number of temples, but others have
argued that it referred to limited governmental support, to a limited
number of monks given support, or to the official awarding of a temple's name.[88] The term dates back to the Nara period. These temples

were usually established by private individuals or groups, rather than the official temples established by the court. However, the court would recognize them by awarding them the status of *jōgakuji;* the term thus indicates a quasi-official status. The support and the privileges (such as the award of yearly ordinands or attendance at official assemblies of monks) varied with each temple. In addition, the laws concerning such temples changed over time. The court might attempt to control them by specifying that they focus on the protection of the state, but at other times the *jōgakuji* tended to support their patrons. In much the same way as *goganji,* the *jōgakuji* contributed to the increasing factionalism of the mid-Heian period.

Appointments as Zasu *and Factionalism*

Appointments as *zasu,* the head of the Tendai school, are the best demonstration of the factionalism that was developing in the Tendai school during the middle and late ninth century. However, they are not the only way in which factionalism was manifested. For example, Enchō was not only at odds with Gishin and Enshu; he also was involved in a dispute with Enshū over the location of the Shakadō (Śākyamuni hall) in the Saitō region of Mount Hiei that ended with Enchō's destroying a hut that Enshū had built. Enshū withdrew to a small building that he called the Isshinbō (Lodgings of the One-mind). Another dispute arose between Ensai (n.d.; not the monk who traveled to China) and Eryō (802–860) over the inscription on a bell. Ensai's group felt that they should determine the contents of the inscription because of the funds they had raised; but Eryō wished to honor his teacher Enchō in the inscription. The dispute continued over a number of years.[89] Although little is known about these events today, they are indicative of the tendency of younger monks to form factions around their teachers during this period.

　　After Enchō's death in 836, no *zasu* was appointed, perhaps because the court was undecided about which of the two factions would succeed in bringing back a vital tradition from China. During this time, Kōjō served as administrator (*bettō*) of Mount Hiei, a function that has led to the award of the honorific title *bettō daishi* (administrator-teacher) for him. Finally, Ennin was appointed *zasu* in 854; held the post for the next ten years. His disciple Anne who administered Mount Hiei from 864 to 868, succeeded him. Anne's administration marked a change in the responsibilities of the *zasu.* The office's original responsibilities focused on the propagation of teachings. Lay supervisors and other monastic officials were responsible for administrative tasks such as conducting ordinations. However, the *zasu* maintained control of the propagation of the teaching while gradually gaining administrative control of the Tendai school. As the *zasu* came to play a more important administrative role, the lay supervisor lost many of his administrative functions in the Tendai school and came to function as a major patron. For example, lay supervisors had overseen the ordination process and had arranged the appointment of Tendai monks to lectureships and positions in the provincial administration of the monastic order. These functions would be taken over by the *zasu*. The exact reasons for these shifts are not clear, but they might well have been connected with the increasing importance of Esoteric ritual during the administration of Ennin and Anne; the Tendai school had an important ally in Fujiwara no Yoshifusa during this time. The rituals performed to protect the court might well have entailed more control over the administration of the Tendai order.[90]

The court began preparing for a switch in lineages while Anne was in office. During Anne's administration, the court issued an edict noting that the *zasu* should be equally a master of Esoteric and exoteric Buddhism. It may well have referred to the future appointment of Enchin, who met such criteria.[91] Enchin was appointed the next *zasu* and served for twenty-three years (868–891), a period that gave him time to place his disciples in positions where they exerted considerable control on the Tendai school for the next half-century. The next *zasu*, Yuishu (826–893; r. 892–893) had studied under Henjō, the noble who had received instruction in Esoteric Buddhism from both Ennin and Enchin. Both Yuishu and Annen, the famous systematizer of Esoteric Buddhism, had been named masters of Esoteric Buddhism by Henjō. However, Yuishu had also studied under Tokuen (b. 786) and Enchin. As a result, he was named the second abbot of Onjōji in 891, the same year he was appointed *zasu*, but he died within a year. His association with Onjōji earned him a place in most Jimon lineages. However, Yuishu is much more associated with Henjō than with Enchin; in fact, most lineages trace Yuishu's connection with Enchin by tracing it through Henjō. Moreover, Yuishu is not mentioned in Enchin's biography as a disciple.[92] Thus the ties Yuishu had with both factions might have made him an excellent compromise candidate that would satisfy both lineages.

Yuishu was followed by Yūken (827–894; r. 893–894), a disciple of Tokuen. Tokuen was a disciple of Saichō who later became one of the

elder and more eminent monks in the Tendai school after Saichō's
death. Tokuen conferred the Esoteric initiations (*sanbu sanmaya*) Saichō received in China on Enchin. Yūken became prominent late in life,
receiving his Esoteric initiations from Enchin at age seventy and being
appointed the third abbot of Onjōji two years later, an event that places
him within Enchin's lineage. Within a matter of months, he was appointed *zasu* and court chaplain, but he died a year later.[93]

Kōsai (828–899; r. 894–899) studied under Kōjō, but he received his
full initiation into Esoteric Buddhism making him a master of Esoteric
Buddhism from Enchin at the same time as Yūken. He was appointed
the fourth abbot of Onjōji in 894, shortly before he became *zasu* and
court chaplain, making him the third consecutive abbot to have been
appointed abbot of Onjōji shortly before becoming *zasu*. In 897, he
served as lecturer at the Yuima-e.[94] The growing association between
appointments as abbot of Onjōji and Tendai *zasu* threatened to place
the Tendai school under the control of Enchin's Jimon lineage because
only monks in that lineage could be appointed abbot of Onjōji.

For the Sanmon monks, the equivalent of the appointment as abbot
of Onjōji was an appointment as abbot of the Hosshōji, a temple that
had been established by Fujiwara no Tadahira (880–949) and dominated by Sanmon monks. Thus the positions as abbot that a monk had
held were a crucial part of the road to appointment as head of the
Tendai school.

Three decades of Jimon administration were ended when Chōi
(836–906; r. 899–906), a disciple of Ennin and Anne, was appointed *zasu;*
he served in that position for seven years.[95] However, before Chōi was
appointed, an odd event seems to have occurred on Mount Hiei. Yūsen
(835–899), another disciple of Ennin, was appointed as administrator
rather than *zasu* of Mount Hiei for a short time, much as Kōjō had been
earlier during the dispute between Enchō and Enshu. He died suddenly,
one year after Chōi had been appointed *zasu*. Earlier Yūsen had served
as the first abbot of Ninnaji. Although very little is known of Yūsen's appointment as *bettō* rather than as *zasu*, perhaps the problem was his affiliation with Ennin.[96] Several documents include criticisms of Yūsen, either that his understanding of Buddhism was not profound even though
he was pious or that he had sexual relations with Empress Takaiko, Emperor Seiwa's consort; however, the veracity of these charges is unclear,
and they well may reflect sectarian dissatisfaction with Yūsen's appointment. Intimations were also made that Yūsen might not have had
the requisite Esoteric initiations to serve as *zasu*. At any rate, Yūsen's

appointment as *bettō* probably reflected the difficulty in switching the lineages from which the *zasu* came.

The rivalry between the two factions is not mentioned prominently in documents for several decades, but several indications that the hard feelings between the two groups had not vanished are found. In the edicts appointing *zasu* from Chōi onward, mention is made of the lineage of the appointee, suggesting that the court was aware of the factionalism. However, other rivalries probably were more pronounced than the Sanmon-Jimon competition at this time. For example, Kōjō strove to maintain the balance between the yearly ordinands appointed to Tendai (*shikan*) and Esoteric studies by suggesting that additional Tendai ordinands be added in 850. His efforts suggest that monks were also divided according to the type of studies and rituals they preferred.[97]

After Chōi's seven years as *zasu*, Enchin's lineage regained control of the *zasu* with the sixteen-year administration of Zōmyō (843–927; r. 906–922). Zōmyō had originally been ordained at Tōdaiji but then had gone to Mount Hiei for a Tendai ordination. There he studied Tendai exoteric teachings with Ennin, but his advanced Esoteric initiations were performed by Enchin. The examples of Zōmyō and other *zasu* indicate that the advanced Esoteric initiations were the key factors in determining eligibility for appointment as abbot of Onjōji and crucial in assigning Tendai monks to lineages. Zōmyō was appointed abbot of Onjōji in 899, and *zasu* in 906. He went to the palace periodically to conduct services for the well-being of the emperor, and obtained positive results. He also conferred the bodhisattva precepts and Esoteric initiations on the retired emperor Uda (867–931; r. 887–897). Zōmyō held various positions in the Office of Monastic Affairs and was the first Tendai monk to serve as an administrator (*hōmu*) of that institution. He was named archbishop in 925 and successfully petitioned the court for a posthumous title for Enchin.[98] When Zōmyō's administration ended, Enchin's lineage had controlled the leadership of the Tendai school for almost seventy years with the exception of Chōi's seven years as *zasu*. As a result, Ennin's faction had gradually lost its influence.

Because Ryōyū (855–923; r. 922–923) had studied with Enchin, Henjō, and Zōmyō and because Henjō had initiations from both Ennin and Enchin, Ryōyū's appointment might be interpreted as a lessening of factionalism.[99] However, Ryōyū is said to have accompanied Enchin during his later years. Enchin eventually conferred a text, the *Juketsushū*, which is said to contain much of what he learned in China on Ryōyū, with the stipulation that it should be shown only to advanced students; in fact, the name of the text was not to be used; it was simply to be called the "hidden scroll" (*kakuretaru maki*).[100] In later years, access to the *Juketsushū* helped to define the Jimon lineage.

Ryōyū was followed by Genkan (861–926; r. 923–926), who was ordained by Enchin at the age of nineteen when he followed Emperor Seiwa into the Buddhist order to continue serving his master. He studied both exoteric and Esoteric Buddhism with Ryōyū and Henjō. Later, he received advanced Esoteric initiations from Genshō[101] and in 903 was named abbot of Gangyōji, the temple founded by Henjō, at Genshō's suggestion. Genkan, in fact, was known by the title Kazan *zasu* (abbot of Gangyōji). He was renowned for his careful observance of the precepts. The appearance of Henjō in the lineages of the Ryōyū and Genkan is significant because Henjō had received Esoteric initiations from both Enchin and Ennin. Henjō's acceptance by the Jimon lineage also might have been based on his noble parentage. Genkan's teacher, Genshō, had been a student of Ennin's disciple, Chōi. Thus the appointment of Genkan represents the first appointment of a monk who had some of his training from members of Ennin's lineage in sixteen years. Genkan's ordination by Enchin, his noble background, and his close relations with the imperial family probably helped him break the dominance of Enchin's lineage on appointments as *zasu*.[102]

Ryōgen was ordained during the governance of the next *zasu*, Son'i (866–940; r. 926–940). Son'i was ordained as a monk by Enchin; however, Zōzen (837–906), who had studied Esoteric Buddhism under Ennin, conferred the dual (*ryōbu*) Esoteric initiations on Son'i. In addition, Genshō, also a member of Ennin's lineage, conferred the *soshitsuji* Esoteric initiation (one of the three major traditions of Tendai Esoteric Buddhism) on Son'i. However, Son'i dreamt about Enchin on the day of his initiation (*shukke*) and again two years later. Thus, Son'i may have had the approval of both lineages. Son'i spent twelve years on Mount Hiei after his ordination, following Saichō's rules for intensive study and practice. Son'i was famed for the efficacy of his Esoteric rituals and performed rites to pacify the nation, bring rain, and ensure safe births for the nobility. Five-altar rituals (*godanhō*) may have been performed during this time.[103] Son'i and subsequent *zasu* were called to the court to perform rituals when such natural catastrophes as earthquakes and droughts occurred, as well as when rebellions arose. Son'i counted Fujiwara no Tadahira among his patrons; Tadahira and his son Morosuke (908–960) would play key roles in Ryōgen's career. Son'i prayed for a safe birth for Fujiwara no Onshi (885–954) and then served as the guardian monk for her child, the future Emperor Suzaku. Such activities would typify Ryōgen's career. Son'i was so respected that he was posthumously awarded the rank of *sōjō* the same month of his death.[104]

Son'i was succeeded by Gikai (871–946; r. 940–946).[105] Genshō, Genkan, and Son'i are listed as his teachers, placing him in Ennin's lineage. During his service as *zasu*, the Sōjiin, the site of the ceremony of the Buddha of Abundant Light (*shijōkōhō*), burned down for the first time; several years later, Gikai performed the ceremony for a member of the nobility (rather than for the emperor) for the first time. The performance of such rituals comes to occupy an increasingly important place in the *Tendai zasuki* (Records of the heads of the Tendai school).

Enshō (880–964; r. 946–964) served as *zasu* for much of Ryōgen's career as a young monk.[106] His nineteen-year administration was one of the longer periods of service. Among the high points was the dedication of the Dainichiin, a *goganji*) for Emperor Murakami. He also maintained close ties with Fujiwara no Tadahira.

Conclusion

While the above description of the factional tendencies may seem tedious, they influenced much of what occurred during Ryōgen's lifetime and provide the background against which his career must be judged. Two opposing tendencies were often at work in the creation and maintenance of factions. The first was the recognition that Tendai monks belonged to the same school and needed to cooperate to further Tendai interests when other Buddhist schools threatened them. The internal conflicts were not to influence the behavior of Tendai monks when they were called upon to perform rituals to benefit lay patrons or protect the nation. The second tendency was the division of the Tendai school into an increasing number of lineages that strove to protect their interests against those of other groups of Tendai monks. Their conflicts become apparent when appointments to high monastic offices are considered.

By the time Ryōgen was a young man, Enchin's lineage clearly dominated much of Mount Hiei; they had built much of Mount Hiei and served as abbots of many of the major institutions on it. However, monks who came from Ennin's lineage through Genshō or Henjō were sometimes appointed to high positions; but even these monks sometimes had connections with Enchin's lineage. The most important aspect of determining a monk's lineage was often his Esoteric initiations because the ability to perform those ceremonies was a key aspect of winning patronage and power.

Several monks who were from Ennin's lineage would subsequently occupy important positions on Mount Hiei because of the patronage of the imperial family and members of the Fujiwara family. Their success set the stage for the increase in factionalism as both groups could offer suitable candidates to serve as head of the Tendai school. The importance of support from a faction became clear to Ryōgen early in his life. As is discussed in the next chapter, although the *zasu* Son'i would eventually preside over Ryōgen's initiation ceremony, the ceremony almost did not occur because Ryōgen had encountered various problems in obtaining his initiation. Such a background certainly must have led to Ryōgen's support for his own faction.

3

Ryōgen's Early Years

Family and Youth

Ryōgen's father was from the Kozu clan, descended from naturalized Chinese. His mother was from the Mononobe clan, a family that had been prominent earlier during the Asuka and Nara periods. Ryōgen was born in Azai county in the province of Ōmi, on the northeastern side of Lake Biwa approximately ninety kilometers from the Tendai monastery on Mount Hiei. Later sources contain a few more details about Ryōgen's parents, but these texts cannot be verified.[1] Ryōgen's family was probably poor, as is indicated by their inability to offer him any help after he climbed Mount Hiei and was struggling for recognition. The poverty of his mother late in life suggests that she was not from a wealthy family.

The biographies of many of Japan's most eminent monks begin with a story of the boy's miraculous conception, often accompanied with special signs from Kannon or other members of the Buddhist pantheon. Ryōgen's biography follows this pattern. His conception and birth are said to have been marked by various miraculous events. His mother had been saddened by her seeming inability to conceive a child. After praying to the Three Jewels, she dreamt that she was sitting in the middle of the sea and looking toward the sky when she saw the light of heaven come down and enter her bosom, a sign that marked the conception of Ryōgen.[2] He was born on the third day of the ninth month of 912.

The motif of light or a celestial body entering the mother at conception is common in Japanese Buddhist biographies. In some cases, the mother has a vision or dream of a Buddhist object, such as a pagoda, or of a Buddha or bodhisattva. She may also vow to ordain her son and encourage him to become a great monk. For example, this theme is found in the biography of the Tendai monk Senkan, mentioned later in this study. He is said to have been named Senkan because his mother had prayed to an image of a thousand-armed (*senju*) Kannon for his birth. She dreamt that she had received a lotus blossom and subsequently became pregnant.[3] Thus Senkan's name refers back to the image of the thousand-armed Kannon to which his mother prayed. The birth of Ryōgen's disciple Genshin is also preceded by his mother's prayers to the Buddha or to Kannon. As a result of her prayers, a monk appeared in a dream and offered her a jewel, which she accepted. She then became pregnant with Genshin.[4]

The accomplishments of the Japanese monks almost seem preordained with such stories. In contrast, in Chinese biographies of monks, the subject's accomplishments are often attributed to serious study or religious practice, not to events that occur at conception to foretell the monk's greatness. Moreover, the monks' mothers are not mentioned as frequently in Chinese monastic biographies. The Japanese emphasis on the importance of the monk's mother is found frequently around the late Heian and Kamakura periods for reasons that are not entirely clear. Ōsumi Kazuo has suggested that it may have been due in part to resistance to traditional Buddhist claims that women suffered from weighty karmic obstructions. By attributing a monk's accomplishments to his mother, the status of the mother was in fact raised. The pattern was similar to the manner in which female shrine attendants (*miko*) were said to give birth to the children of the deity (*kami*).[5]

Ryōgen's Introduction to Buddhism

The story of Ryōgen's introduction to Buddhism probably reflects the background of many of the young men who entered monasteries during the middle and late Heian period. Many of them were ordained more out of a desire to advance in the world than out of religious piety. Of course, such a statement does not suggest that all young men who entered monasteries had no serious religious aspirations. Rather, economic and social factors also played a significant role in the decision of many to enter a Buddhist order. Young men who entered monasteries for social and economic reasons might have later found that the religious vocation suited them, and some became pious practitioners.

According to the *Daisōjōden*, when Ryōgen was eight years old, he attended an agricultural festival with many of those from his clan. One of the elders of the province saw him playing in the field and was sufficiently impressed by the boy that he went to Ryōgen's father to tell him that his son was very bright, but that it would be difficult for him

TABLE 1

SOCIAL BACKGROUND OF TENDAI *ZASU*

	Nobles	Low-ranking nobles	Commoners	Average age at appointment
782–990	1	2	21	65
991–1069	1	8	2	71
1070–1190	18	9	0	61

TABLE 2

SOCIAL BACKGROUND OF ABBOTS OF KŌFUKUJI

	Nobles	Low-ranking nobles	Commoners	Average age at appointment
782–990	0	0	12	66.5
991–1069	0	5	3	62.0
1070–1190	9	7	0	59.5

to advance to a high position in the secular world. The elder instructed Ryōgen's father to have his son climb Mount Hiei, become a monk, and study with a Tendai teacher.[6] A similar story with slight variations is found in the *Shūiden*. Instead of an elder from the province, the man who spoke of Ryōgen's future greatness was an unidentified man of rank who was crossing a bridge when he saw Ryōgen fishing. He was sufficiently impressed that he asked a fisherman who was standing nearby to tell Ryōgen's father not to underestimate his son. Bonshō, the compiler of the *Shūiden*, complained that nobody had thought to ask the noble how Ryōgen had caught the noble's attention.[7] The assertion that commoners would find opportunities for advancement in the monastic world that they would not find in the secular realm is supported by studies of the backgrounds of high-ranking monks. The following figures compiled by Hirata Toshiharu reveal that during Ryōgen's youth, most high-ranking monks came from the families of commoners.[8] The tables divide Japanese history into three periods: 782–990, 991–1069, and 1070–1190. The first period reflects the situation at about the time of Ryōgen's lifetime. The dividing point between the first and second period is near Ryōgen's death in 984 and reflects changes in which Ryōgen participated. Three offices are con-

TABLE 3

SOCIAL BACKGROUND OF LECTURERS
AT THE THREE MAJOR ASSEMBLIES IN NARA

	Nobles	Low-ranking nobles	Commoners	Average age at appointment
782–990	0	0	78	70
991–1069	6	21	41	63
1070–1190	39	38	13	55

TABLE 4

SOCIAL BACKGROUND FOR APPOINTMENTS
TO HIGH MONASTIC OFFICES (PERCENTAGES)

	Nobles	Low-ranking nobles	Commoners	Average age at appointment
782–990	1	2	97	69
991–1069	8	40	52	64
1070–1190	50	40	10	56

sidered: heads (*zasu*) of the Tendai school, abbots (*bettō*) of Kōfukuji, and lecturers who served at all three of the major assemblies (*san'e kōji*) in Nara. In addition, the average age of appointment for each period was considered. In almost all cases, the average age drops as members of noble families are appointed to high posts. Table 4 expresses the overall changes in percentages. The figures clearly demonstrate that advancement to high offices by commoners was a possibility during Ryōgen's youth. Moreover, the situation had clearly begun to change four or five decades after Ryōgen's death when his two chief biographies were written.

Ryōgen subsequently went with his mother to the county of Shiga in Ōmi. The occasion of their journey may have been the death of Ryōgen's father. Although this event is not mentioned in any of Ryōgen's biographies, Hirabayashi has noted that Ryōgen's father is not mentioned after this time and suggested that he probably died about this time.[9] However, other scholars have noted that the mothers of monks were mentioned far more frequently than fathers in Japanese monastic biographies, suggesting that young boys may have been raised in the homes of their maternal relatives and that fathers may not have played a very important role in raising the child.[10]

Young Ryōgen and his mother later journeyed to the Bonshakuji monastery, one of the major temples of this period. Bonshakuji had been established in either 786 or 795 by Emperor Kanmu (737–806; r. 781–806) in memory of Emperor Tenji (626–671; r. 668–671) and as part of his attempt to strengthen state Buddhism. As a result, it had been given land and quickly developed into one of the major official temples of the early Heian. It was often the site of rituals to protect the state. In 915, several years before Ryōgen and his mother visited, the court had issued an edict noting that the monastery grounds should be freed of any ritual pollution.[11] Thus when Ryōgen went to visit the temple, it was still a major site for state Buddhism. Ryōgen went to play with a temple boy at the quarters of Kakue, a master of Esoteric Buddhism. When Kakue saw Ryōgen's features, he declared that Ryōgen was not an ordinary person and advised Ryōgen's mother that her son should be studying instead of playing. If he spent his time in the country, he would not be exposed to good teachers.[12]

During Ryōgen's childhood, young men from the families of commoners sometimes decided to become monks because it was possible to advance to high positions either in individual monasteries or within the governmental organizations that were supposed to supervise the Buddhist world. Ryōgen's father had been advised to have his son ordained because career opportunities still existed in monasteries for the sons of commoners at that time. Indicating that such considerations played a major role in a person's decision to become ordained or to have his son ordained does not preclude religious motivations. In many cases, a monk's piety developed later in his life. Ryōgen mentioned his own struggle to reconcile his desire for success with Buddhist ideals while he was in the midst of his rapid rise to leadership within the Tendai school.[13] Several centuries later, Jien (1155–1225), the head of the Tendai school, wrote about how his own piety developed later in life.[14]

Ordination

At the age of eleven, Ryōgen climbed Mount Hiei and was sent to the lodgings of Nittō Shōnin of the Hōdōin. There he was entrusted to the care of a teacher named Risen. Virtually nothing is known about Risen except that he seems to have been in Ennin's lineage. A document on

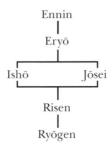

Figure 1. Ryōgen's Tendai Lineage

lineages, the *Tendai Hokkeshū sōjō kechimyakuzu,* includes the lineage shown in figure 1.[15]

The inclusion of a number of obscure monks in the lineage makes it more believable; if it were a forged document, Ryōgen might have been given a more illustrious lineage.

At the time Ryōgen began to study under Risen, Mount Hiei was divided into three major geographical blocks: Tōdō (Eastern pagoda), Saitō (Western pagoda), and Yokawa. The Tōdō area was the heart of the Tendai establishment. Saichō had been active primarily in this area, and the majority of Tendai monks had always lived there.[16]

The Hōdōin in Saitō, the hall with which Ryōgen was affiliated, had a tower that served as a symbol of the Dharma (*hōdō* or *sōrintō*).[17] A number of scriptures, including the *Lotus Sūtra, Fan-wang ching,* and Esoteric texts on *dhāraṇī* were placed in the tower, indicating that it functioned as a *stūpa* (reliquary). The tower eventually became the symbol of the entire Saitō area; as a result, the term "Hōdōin" was sometimes used to refer to the entire Saitō area.[18] The tower was about forty feet high and was traditionally said to have been built in 820 by Saichō, who consecrated it by placing fifty-eight fascicles of texts in it. Although this tradition has been questioned, the tower certainly had been constructed within a few years after his death.[19] The tower was later repaired and additional texts added in 861 and 919. A large hall called the Hōdōin, situated about ten meters away from the tower, was built in 850 by Eryō (approx. 802–860). In 859, Eryō was awarded two yearly ordinands for the Hōdōin, thereby establishing the economic base of the building.[20] In 876, the court ordered that eight monks be permanently installed in the Hōdōin.[21] The lodgings (*bō*) of Nittō Shōnin where Ryōgen stayed probably were one of a group of smaller buildings where monks lived.[22]

Ryōgen's loyalty to Ennin's lineage probably dated from his studies with Risen. The lineage in figure 1 lists Ennin as Eryō's teacher; in fact, Eryō was ordained by Gishin but studied primarily with Enchō.[23] Eryō's close relationship with Enchō and Ennin probably resulted in the Hōdōin's being the stronghold of the monks in Ennin's lineage during Ryōgen's youth. In contrast, the Tōdō area had fallen under the control of monks from Enchin's lineage during Enchin's twenty-three-year reign as *zasu*. Virtually all of Ryōgen's support in the early part of his career came from the monks of the Hōdōin.

When Ryōgen was sixteen years old, his teacher Risen died. This event was a major setback for Ryōgen for several reasons. First, Ryōgen seems to have been exceptionally close to Risen, perhaps because Ryōgen had lost his father at an early age. Indeed, later, he refused to acknowledge any other monk as his primary teacher (*honshi*). Second, at the time of Risen's death, Ryōgen had not yet received his full ordination. To be ordained, Ryōgen would have to fulfill several requirements. Passing the examination that qualified a person to be ordained would probably not have been very difficult for a youth with Ryōgen's talents. However, the sponsorship of an experienced and respected monk was necessary for the ordination to be carried out. Government regulations restricted the numbers of people who could act as sponsors and the numbers of people they could ordain.

Another monk to sponsor Ryōgen would have to be found. Because the monks of Mount Hiei were divided into factions, this was not an easy task. After Enchin served as head of the Tendai school for twenty-three years late in the ninth century, his disciples had controlled the school for another fifty years by monopolizing appointments as *zasu*. Ryōgen's teacher had belonged to a lineage that traced itself back to Ennin, the founder of lineages that were in competition with those spiritually descended from Enchin. Because the monks of Ennin's lineage probably controlled very few of the positions available for yearly ordinands, the death of Ryōgen's teacher meant that finding a place as yearly ordinand would be very difficult.[24] Even though Ryōgen must surely have been one of the most promising young men on Mount Hiei, his ordination was far from assured.

Nittō, the head of the lodgings in which Ryōgen lived, eventually resorted to his secular ties, rather than his monastic ones, to have Ryōgen ordained. Nittō had a lay patron who was the administrator of Asake county in Ise, a man named Funaki Yoshimi. Nittō took Ryōgen to meet Yoshimi and explained the situation. Yoshimi was an old retainer of the minister of the right, Fujiwara no Sadakata (872–932). Through Sadakata's help they were able to have Ryōgen added as one of the yearly ordinands allotted to Onkun (859–948), who had served as lecturer at the Yuima-e in 825, three years earlier.[25]

Onkun was a member of the Hossō school, a school that held doctrinal positions directly opposed to those of the Tendai school. However, he was from Yakushiji, a temple that had fewer Hossō monks than the Hossō center at Kōfukuji. Moreover, the Yakushiji monks were probably not on very good relations with the Hossō monks at Kōfukuji, partly because the Yakushiji Hossō monks belonged to the Nanji (Southern temple) tradition while those of the Kōfukuji belonged to the Hokuji (Northern temple) tradition.[26] In addition, Yakushiji was not exclusively Hossō; substantial numbers of Kegon and Sanron monks also lived there. Thus, Onkun was probably more amenable to allowing someone from another tradition to use his allotment for yearly ordinands than a monk from Kōfukuji might have been.

Ryōgen, in appreciation of Yoshimi's efforts to have him ordained, used the character with the Japanese reading "*yoshi*" and the Sino-Japanese reading "*ryō*" from Yoshimi's name in his monastic name, Ryōgen. In 928, at the age of sixteen, Ryōgen received his ordination on Mount Hiei from Son'i (866–940), the Tendai *zasu*. Onkun was Ryōgen's teacher in name only, since Ryōgen remained on Mount Hiei after his ordination instead of going to Yakushiji. According to the *vinaya*, a person should be twenty when he receives a full ordination so that he can make a mature judgment about this grave step.[27] Tendai monks were ordained with the *Fan-wang* precepts, however, which did not specify an age limit for ordination. In his efforts to tighten the ordination system, Enchin had specified that the candidate should be twenty[28] but this provision was clearly ignored by Ryōgen's time. A survey of biographies of monks at this time suggests that Ryōgen's ordination at sixteen was typical.[29] Monks would rarely have been ordained at an age much younger than sixteen at this time, however.

Monastic Education

During the middle of the tenth century, various monastic careers were possible. A monk might devote himself to the maintenance and practice of religious rituals at a particular hall in the monastery or to a particular set of religious exercises. However, if he were to have an illustrious monastic career, he generally had to engage in scholarly pursuits or be skilled in the performance of Esoteric rituals. Although a monk might receive impressive rewards for the skillful performance of Esoteric rituals, particularly if he obtained the desired result, such practices also entailed serious difficulties. Although rituals might be performed for influential lay patrons, people still died from illness or childbirth, and droughts sometimes did not immediately cease. Moreover, a monk had to gain the attention of the monastic and lay authorities before he would be allowed a chance to demonstrate his skill in ritual. Scholarship provided the monk with a more reliable way to demonstrate his abilities and capture the attention of potential patrons. The court had traditionally rewarded excellence in scholarship through appointments as lecturers for a series of monastic assemblies and then to government posts in the bureaus that were nominally responsible for the supervision of monks and nuns. These appointments included financial remuneration, the privilege of having a certain number of novices or monks serve the appointee, and collateral rights that were normally reserved for nobles of certain ranks. In fact, many of the appointments were considered to be equivalent to certain court ranks.

Because of the specialized training necessary for Buddhist scholarship, many of the monks who became scholars during the late Heian period entered monasteries when they were seven or eight years old.[30] Although Ryōgen probably entered the monastery later than many who pursued careers as scholarly monks, his brilliance helped him make up for the delay. Unfortunately, details of neither Ryōgen's studies as a child nor of the studies of other youngsters studying at Tendai monasteries at this time survive. However, records from Shingon and secular sources that are dated approximately two centuries later are suggestive of the type of training that Ryōgen might have received.

Records of the imperial prince Shukaku's (1150–1202) monastic education when he entered the Hokuin of Ninnaji survive and provide at least some indication of the type of education that an imperial prince received. Although Ryōgen and Shukaku lived almost two centuries apart and although Ryōgen did not have the same noble parentage as Shukaku, it is still useful to note the type of studies that were regarded as valuable for a young man embarking on a monastic career. Education focused on learning to read and memorize texts. An important element of the education was learning the thousands of Chinese characters necessary to study Chinese texts. Shukaku studied those works that were important to the Shingon school. In contrast, Ryōgen would have studied the *Lotus Sūtra* and other texts chanted to protect the state, the major works of Chih-i, who was the de facto founder of the Tendai tradition, and the sources of the Esoteric Buddhist tradition.

Monks from noble families were taught many of the same skills that most young men pursuing official careers learned. For example, Shukaku was taught calligraphy and the composition of poems and songs, as well as football (*kemari*), archery, and *go*. Shukaku was warned against becoming too involved in pursuits such as archery, football, and composition, however. Only a low level of competence was required. According to some texts, archery and football were prohibited.[31] In the Tendai school, Saichō had allowed his monks to study some secular subjects, but he died before he could specify the contents of these subjects. At least some Tendai monks were trained in construction skills so that they could supervise building projects both in temples and among the people. Saichō had urged Tendai monks to travel to the countryside and help people build bridges and dig wells, as well as spread Tendai teachings. Although it is not known what secular subjects Ryōgen studied, the vast amount of construction he supervised and his success in associating with the nobility during his later career suggests that he might have been well versed in some of these secular subjects.

Conclusion

The difficulties Ryōgen experienced in obtaining an ordination decisively influenced him in a variety of ways. Ryōgen came to understand the complexities of factionalism within Tendai and the importance of powerful lay patrons. Whereas other monks might wonder about the propriety of catering to a patron's needs, particularly when those needs were blatantly political, Ryōgen seems to have understood that such service to patrons was a necessary concomitant of a strong monastic institution.

The unusual circumstances of Ryōgen's ordination had another important effect on Ryōgen's career. Because his teacher had died, Ryōgen had no major teacher in the Tendai school who would make sure that Ryōgen was given the leadership of a particular hall on Mount Hiei. Although Ryōgen studied with a variety of teachers on Mount Hiei, he was never considered to be the intimate disciple (*nyūshitsu deshi*) of any of them. Ryōgen's decision a decade later to retire to Yokawa to practice and his need to ally himself with supporters from the nobility must be viewed in light of these facts.

Later on in his life, Ryōgen would be devoted to advancing the interests of his own faction of monks within Ennin's lineage to the detriment of those in Enchin's lineage. Ryōgen's basic attitudes about the importance of monastic factions may very well have been influenced by his experiences at this time. Throughout the rest of his life Ryōgen would loyally form and support his own faction of monks.

4

Ryōgen's Rise to Prominence

Lectures and Debates

Without an important monk to help him advance in the monastic hierarchy, Ryōgen had to depend on his own abilities. He quickly made his presence known on Mount Hiei by participating in debates and lectures. During the middle of the Heian period, lectures at monastic assemblies were important events at a number of the major temples in Japan. Lectures might be performed for a variety of reasons: as part of a prayer service to protect the nation or to help someone recover from illness, as a component of memorial services, or as a way to further scholarship. For example, the Yuima-e (Assembly for Vimalakīrti) served as a private assembly for Nakatomi no Kamatari (614–669), founder of the Fujiwara clan, later as a memorial service for him, and finally as an assembly that encouraged scholarship and produced merit for both the emperor and the Fujiwara clan.[1] According to Saichō, a major role of Tendai monks was the recitation of *sūtras* to protect the country; sometimes lectures on these texts were performed along with the recitations. In contrast to assemblies that functioned primarily as merit-making occasions, the lectures of the Ōwa debates, discussed later in this study, were held partly to further scholarship and partly to further Ryōgen's political agenda.

Lectures and debates took place in a variety of formats. They could be annual affairs, as the Yuima-e, or scheduled when a particular set of circumstances indicated that they were needed, such as the Ōwa debates or the first performance of the Yuima-e. Finally, lectures could be large public affairs, court ceremonies, or small events held within a particular monastery only for the monks of that institution.[2]

Sometimes debates or periods of questioning were held either as a part of the lecture or at its conclusion. These debates, sometimes conducted as formal examinations, provided both young and old monks with an opportunity to display their scholarship and eloquence and thereby gain recognition. Because Ryōgen did not have the political connections within the Tendai school that would have enabled him to receive appointments to monastic offices, he had to find means other than patronage from powerful lay believers or the sponsorship of eminent monks to advance his career at first. His early activities on Mount Hiei are intimately tied to his efforts to use debates to gain prominence. Later in life, when his ties with the nobility appeared to be threatened, he would again turn to debates as a vehicle to increase his visibility. Finally, as head of the Tendai school, Ryōgen was a forceful advocate of the role of debate in monastic education.

In 929, two years after his ordination, Ryōgen took part in a debate conducted on Mount Hiei for Tendai monks. His adversary was Jōe (907–984?), a young monk who was a disciple of Kiren (884–958) of the Eastern Pagoda section of Mount Hiei. Kiren was so impressed with Ryōgen's performance at the debate that he told Jōe to go and study under Ryōgen even though Ryōgen would have been several years younger than Jōe. It is unclear whether this account should be considered entirely true. Hirabayashi Moritoku has suggested that it may have been exaggerated to dramatize the admiration of one of the Tendai school's senior teachers for the young Ryōgen.[3]

Later that same year, services were held on Mount Hiei to celebrate the fiftieth birthday of Minister of the Right Fujiwara no Tadahira (880–949), who also served as the lay supervisor (*kengyō*) of Mount Hiei. A thousand monks assembled in the lecture hall (Kōdō) to chant fifty thousand fascicles of the *Sūtra for Longevity* (*Shou-ming ching*).[4] Although the assembly is not mentioned in Ryōgen's biographies, he was probably one of the thousand monks who participated in the ceremony. If this is so, then this occasion was Ryōgen's first glimpse of a man who later would serve as a powerful lay patron for Ryōgen.

Ryōgen's academic prowess brought him other disciples before long. A Tendai elder named Unnichi, who had studied with Ryōgen's teacher Risen, had two temple boys, Senga and Shōku.[5] Although he wished to ordain them, he had no way of doing so since he had no spaces for yearly ordinands at his disposal. When Kizō,[6] the administrator of the Hōdōin, heard about the situation, he offered to give them two spaces as yearly ordinands. The two boys were sent to practice under Ryōgen, who had been associated with the Hōdōin since he first climbed Mount Hiei. The older boy, Senga (914–998), was ordained in 931. Ryōgen was only twenty years old at the time, a mere three years older than his new disciple.

Ryōgen had never been to see Kizō at his quarters, yet Kizō had given him two disciples. To express his gratitude, Ryōgen decided to send the younger of the two brothers, Shōku (909–998), who was still too young to be ordained, to serve Kizō. Senga was appointed master of Esoteric Buddhism at Gangyōji in 968. Later, he would serve as the twenty-second head of the Tendai school (990–998) and hold positions in the Office of Monastic Affairs (969–998), eventually rising to supernumerary archbishop (*gon-sōjō*). Shōku too had a distinguished career in the Office of Monastic Affairs serving in it for twenty years (979–998) and eventually rising to greater bishop (*daisōzu*). Both men would play important roles in Ryōgen's later efforts to extend his control on Mount Hiei. Stories such as these indicate the manner in which Ryōgen was able to use his association with the institutions and individuals on Mount Hiei to gradually build a network of monks.

As Ryōgen's reputation spread on Mount Hiei, other monks wished to test him. According to the *Shūiden*, Ryōgen was asked to debate a monk named Senkan who belonged to the Sannōin in the Tōdō area of Mount Hiei. Because monks of Enchin's lineage controlled the Sannoin, this debate would be between monks of two rival lineages of the Tendai school.[7] Senkan's specialty was Buddhist logic, one of the most scholastic and complex topics of Buddhist scholarship. Although Buddhist logic was usually a Hossō topic, some Tendai monks studied it occasionally.[8] Ryōgen was invited to participate only two days before the debate was scheduled, hardly enough time to prepare adequately. Although he asked to be excused from the debate, he was not permitted to do so. As a result, he stayed up all night memorizing the text that he was to be tested on. On the day of the debate, he advanced a new interpretation of the problem under discussion and won the debate.[9]

Attempts to identify Senkan have led to doubts about certain elements of the story. A monk named Senkan is mentioned in Tendai sources; his voluminous writings later in life included a massive text comparing the positions of the Tendai, Hossō, and Sanron schools on the *Lotus Sūtra*, manuals on debate topics, and hymns to Amida. However, if he was the monk Ryōgen debated, he was six years younger than Ryōgen. Ryōgen's victory consequently does not seem very impressive.[10] However, Ryōgen may have impressed the audience because of his quick mastery of a topic such as Buddhist logic and the quality of his rhetoric rather than his victory over a monk who was his junior.

An alternative explanation involves the intense factionalism in the Tendai school that was prevalent at the time Ryōgen's biographies were compiled, some fifty years after Ryōgen's death. Because Senkan later became the most eminent scholar of his day in Enchin's lineage, his name could have been inserted in the story by Ryōgen's biographers to demonstrate the superiority of the Sanmon faction (represented by Ennin and Ryōgen) over the Jimon faction (represented by Enchin and Senkan). In addition, as is discussed later in this chapter, Enchin's lineage probably had a more developed tradition of studies in logic than Ennin's lineage; Ryōgen's victory might have served as proof of the development of studies of logic within Ennin's lineage. In addition, because Senkan clearly wrote more scholarly works than Ryōgen, Ryōgen's biographer might have fabricated the debate to salvage Ryōgen's scholarly reputation from criticisms made by members of Senkan's Jimon lineage. However, because no evidence disproving the historicity of the debate with Senkan exists, the general details of the account in Ryōgen's biography should probably be accepted. Certainly no mention of the debate is made in Senkan's biographies; these portray Senkan more like a reclusive scholarly monk than like one striving to advance his career through debates.

Ryōgen's Appearance at the Yuima-e

Little is known about Ryōgen's movements during his first years as a Tendai monk, but he probably spent most of his time on Mount Hiei. None of the sources on Ryōgen's biography mentions that his occasional appearance at assemblies or services in Nara or Kyoto would have required him to violate the twelve-year retreat (*rōzan*) that Saichō had made a centerpiece of his educational reforms.[11] However, by the time of his appearance, Tendai monks largely ignored the twelve-year retreat. Saichō had initially asked monks to observe it because he feared that they would defect to the rival Nara school, but the plan was not practical, and little evidence exists that many early Tendai monks observed it.

An episode from the biography of the monk Sōō (831–918), famed for his assiduous practice, suggests the rationale several Tendai monks used to justify ignoring the requirement. When Sōō was in the middle of his twelve-year retreat on Mount Hiei, he received a letter asking him to perform rituals for the daughter of Fujiwara no Yoshimi (813–867), who was then minister of the right. When he wondered whether he should break his period of seclusion, his teacher Ennin explained, "Of the eight fields of merit, nursing the sick is the most important. Of the ways in which karmic ties between people (*kechien*) are formed, those between teacher and parishioner are the most serious. . . . You say that you wish to comply with your original vow [to stay on Mount Hiei for twelve years]; but if you do not respond to his request, you will violate [the vow to] help sentient beings and turn your back on your obligations (*on*). You should go quickly."[12]

Ryōgen's accomplishments up to this time had gained him wide recognition on Mount Hiei, but he was still unknown outside the Tendai school. His chance for wider recognition came in 937, when at the age of twenty-five, Ryōgen accompanied the Tendai monk Kizō who had been appointed as lecturer at the Yuima-e (annual assembly on the *Vimalakīrti-sūtra* at Kōfukuji), at that time the most prestigious assembly in Japan.

Tendai monks rarely were appointed as lecturers for the Yuima-e because it was held at the Hossō stronghold, Kōfukuji. Prior to Kizō's appointment in 937, only five Tendai monks had held the position over the previous century; however, Tendai monks had received several of those appointments the previous decade, in 929 and 932.[13] Consequently, Ryōgen was fortunate in receiving a rare opportunity to attend the assembly. Kizō's appointment may have been due to his expertise in logic, a subject that was favored by the Hossō monks.[14] Kizō was the supervisor of the Hōdōin and the monk who had assigned Ryōgen to be the teacher of Senga and Shōku several years earlier. Because Kizō had been appointed lecturer for the Yuima-e that year, he was able to ask Ryōgen to accompany him, perhaps as a specialist in protocol (*igisō*), and thereby present Ryōgen to the rest of the Buddhist world.[15]

Vice Controller of the Left (*sachūben*) Fujiwara no Arihira (892–970) had been sent to the assembly as an imperial emissary.[16] To relieve the tedium of waiting at the Yuima-e, a private debate was held in the emissary's room. It had probably been arranged at the last minute to relieve the emissary's boredom. At Arihira's urging, four Tendai monks and four monks from the Nara schools were to be chosen to participate in the debate. The main lecturer was to be a Tendai monk. Arihira may have been particularly interested in the performance of Gishō (920–968), a Hossō monk from Gangōji and a member of the Fujiwara clan. Ryōgen and Gishō were to be the first pair of monks to debate. According to the *Daisōjōden*, Gishō was a senior monk and felt that it was beneath his dignity to debate with a monk as young as Ryōgen. The situation was saved only by intervention of Ninkō (874–949), the bishop (*sōzu*) from Kōfukuji.[17] Ninkō is said to have talked to Gishō privately and explained that Ryōgen was an exceptionally promising and gifted young monk. Only then did Gishō agree to debate Ryōgen.

The *Daisōjōden* account cannot be accepted as it stands, however, because Gishō was actually eight years younger than Ryōgen, not Ryōgen's senior.[18] In addition, according to the *Sanne jōitsuki*, the record of the Yuima-e debates, Ryōgen participated in the first *tsugai rongi*, a form of debate in which questioners were paired with those who were to answer them. This sort of one-on-one debate was more informal than the highly structured debates that were the focus of the Yuima-e. In the Tendai tradition, the term "*tsugai rongi*" refers to debates (*rongi*) in which young boys are the participants. In Ryōgen's time, it might have referred to the participation of men younger than the senior participants who normally participated in the Yuima-e.[19] As in the debate with Senkan, Ryōgen's victory was over a monk who was his junior. Ryōgen probably gained fame as the result of his eloquence, not because he defeated Gishō. The incorrect identification of Gishō as Ryōgen's senior in the *Daisōjōden* probably occurred because the text was compiled approximately ninety years after the debate and because the biographer wished to glorify Ryōgen's victory over an important Hossō monk. Finally, Ninkō's role in the debate may have been related to his studies under greater bishop Nyomu (867–938), the biological father of the imperial emissary Arihira and to his studies of Tendai Esoteric Buddhism, an unusual accomplishment for a Hossō monk, but one that might be explained by his Fujiwara parentage.[20]

According to the *Daisōjōden*, Ryōgen was threatened by some "bad monks" (*akusō*) from Nara at this time for daring to debate one of their senior monks. But if Gishō was seven years younger than Ryōgen, the monks may have been upset because the mismatch was to Ryōgen's advantage. The bad monks are described as covering their heads to hide their identities and brandishing their staffs to intimidate Ryōgen. Ryōgen remained calm throughout the encounter and with his forceful arguments made the bad monks lay down their staffs and repent their actions. If this account is historically accurate, it is significant as the earliest mention of monks from an identifiable temple covering their faces and wielding staffs, both actions typical of the warrior monks (*sōhei*) who were to become prominent during the next century.[21]

The meeting with Gishō was a propitious one; the two monks became close friends despite their doctrinal differences. Gishō is said to have

participated in lectures on Mount Hiei with Ryōgen and to have helped
at assemblies in honor of Ryōgen's mother. Like Ryōgen he eventually
prayed for Fujiwara no Morosuke. Although Gishō was from the Fujiwara clan, the exact identity of his parents is not known.[22]

Ryōgen's Studies 1: Logic

Relatively little is recorded about the contents of Ryōgen's studies. Because Ryōgen's first teacher Risen died before Ryōgen could even be
ordained, Ryōgen had to find his teachers wherever he was able. He
seems to have studied with a number of people.

According to a lineage from the Hossō temple Kōfukuji, Ryōgen studied Buddhist logic (*inmyō*) from the Tendai monk Kizō, who later took
him to the Yuima-e.[23] Ryōgen's teacher Kizō was part of a lineage that
included Kegon monks from Tōdaiji and Hossō monks from Yakushiji.
The presence of Kegon and Hossō monks in the lineage suggests that
the Nara schools did not form a cohesive block that opposed the Tendai
school. Kegon monks, in particular, held many doctrinal positions close
to those of the Tendai school. Earlier Ryōgen had been ordained as part
of the quota of yearly ordinands from Yakushiji. The presence of
Yakushiji Hossō monks as teachers of Tendai monks suggests that there
may have been a tradition of cooperation between some Tendai and
Hossō monks instead of unremitting opposition.

Hossō monks were taught logic and used it in their debates. Some
of the Hossō monks who later faced Ryōgen in debate wrote works on
logic, although it is not clear whether they had already written them by
the time they debated Ryōgen. It thus was crucial that Ryōgen be trained
in the logical tradition followed by Hossō monks if he were to successfully debate them.

Virtually nothing is known of the contents of Ryōgen's studies with
Kizō, and little is known about Kizō's background.[24] Although later
sources credit Ryōgen with the authorship of a work on logic that has
not survived, these sources are from the seventeenth century and probably too late to have much credibility, particularly since no mention
of such a work is made in the text on Buddhist logic written in 978
by Ryōgen's disciple Genshin, the *Inmyōsho shishū sōi ryakuchūshaku*
(*T* 2276, Brief commentary on four logical mistakes).[25] Ryōgen and
one of his opponents in the Ōwa debates, Chūzan, held similar positions on at least some if not many aspects of Buddhist logic, suggesting that logic was probably a technique in debate rather than a main

topic of debate in which Tendai and Hossō monks held clearly demarcated interpretations.[26]

Earlier Tendai monks had sometimes made efforts to develop a logical tradition within the Tendai school. Saichō brought back one work on logic from China and was later credited with the authorship of several works on logic.[27] However, he also stated in the *Shugo kokkaishō* (Essays on the protection of the state) that logic was useful primarily in refuting the wrong views of one's opponents, not in revealing the ultimate teachings of the One-vehicle.[28] Although this attitude adversely affected the study of logic among some early Tendai practitioners, others made efforts to master the subject. When Ennin traveled in China, he read commentaries on logic with two Japanese novices who accompanied him, indicating that he probably considered the study of logic an important element of monastic education. He also brought back a large number of works on the subject.[29] Enchin also brought back texts on logic from China; his bibliographic annotations indicate that he sometimes copied only one fascicle of a work on logic to complete a text that had been partially transmitted to Japan. The care with which he searched for these texts indicates a deep interest in the subject. In addition, the *Sannōin zōsho mokuroku*, the 925 bibliography of works in the library in Enchin's quarters on Mount Hiei, listed approximately a hundred works on logic, many of them by Japanese.[30] Enchin is also credited with the authorship of a text on logic.[31] Thus the monks of Enchin's lineage may have had a stronger tradition in logic than those in Ennin's lineage. If this is correct, Ryōgen's victory over Senkan in a debate on logic may have marked the resurgence of a tradition of studies of logic among those in Ennin's lineage.

Ryōgen's Studies 2: Esoteric Buddhism

While he was in his twenties, Ryōgen is said to have been trained in Esoteric Buddhism by Kakue (872–954). This period was particularly important for Ryōgen because it provided him with the instruction that would allow him to perform Esoteric rituals later in his life. According to the *Shūiden*, during the Tenkei era (938–947), Ryōgen received training in the three Esoteric traditions (*sanbu*) of Tendai, as well as in the *shoson yuga goma* (yogic fire ceremony for various deities) ceremony.[32] The *sanbu*, the three major traditions of Tendai Pure Esoteric Buddhism (*junmitsu*), all had the objective of the realization of Buddhahood: Taizōkai (womb-realm), Kongōkai (diamond-realm), and Soshitsuji. The *goma* ceremony consisted of an offering through fire to various deities (*shoson*), probably based on the *Chin-kang-ting yü-ch'ieh hu-mo i-kuei* (*T* 909, Manual for the diamond-peak yogic fire ceremony), translated by Amoghavajra.[33]

Little is known about Kakue, except that he was part of an Esoteric lineage that had been established by Henjō. Such lineages were usually based on the transmission of rituals. The development of Tendai Esoteric doctrine (*kyōsō*) can be traced through Saichō, Ennin, Enchin, Annen, and other Esoteric masters as they strove to interpret such issues as the relationship between Esoteric and exoteric Buddhism. In contrast, the development of Tendai Esoteric ritual (*jisō*) cannot be traced in a continuous line through the major early Tendai masters. Instead, ritual traditions were brought from China at separate times by Saichō, Ennin, and Enchin. These ritual traditions were transmitted only to certain disciples and retained their distinct identities to a large degree. For example, Ennin and his followers generally did not transmit rituals to Enchin and his followers. In fact, Enchin's fear that Ennin would not teach him because the two were from different lineages was probably one of the major factors that led him to go to China and bring back his own Esoteric tradition.[34] In addition, the transmission of ritual texts was subject to the production of apocryphal texts and spurious lineages as Tendai monks contended with the Shingon criticisms and claims.[35] During the first half of the tenth century, the rituals transmitted by Enchin assumed the preeminent role within Tendai ritual, primarily because of Enchin's twenty-three-year rule as head of the Tendai order and because his lineage dominated the major positions within the school during the next fifty years.

A fourth Esoteric ritual transmission has its origins in Henjō, one of the first nobles to become a Tendai monk. Because of his noble origins, Henjō was able to receive initiations from both Ennin and Enchin and thereby begin a new Esoteric lineage. Ryōgen's Esoteric teacher, Kakue, belonged to this lineage, which is shown in table 5.

Kakue eventually became head of the Gangyōji monastery, founded by Henjō, on the outskirts of Kyoto. Although little is known of the teachings of Kakue, more is known of Genshō. Genshō was known for his performance of the *goma* ceremony and was even called the "king of *goma*" by the Esoteric master Shōbō (832–909), founder of the Daigoji monastic complex outside Kyoto. In addition, he was famous for his mastery of debate and Buddhist logic.[36] The emphasis on the mastery of

TABLE 5

RYŌGEN'S ESOTERIC BUDDHIST LINEAGE

1. Henjō (817–890)
2. Saien (825–?)
3. Genshō (844–915)
4. Genkan (861–926)
5. Kakue (872–954)
6. Ryōgen (912–985)
7. Kyōu (n.d.)
8. Kakuchō (955–1037)[1]

1. Little is known about Saien except that he studied under Henjō and was a fellow student of Annen. He was named an *ajari* when he was sixty-three. Henjō and Genshō are discussed earlier in this chapter. Nothing is known of Kyōu. For Kakuchō, see Akamatsu Toshihide, "Fujiwara jidai Jōdokyō to Kakuchō."

both Esoteric ritual and exoteric learning was typical of Ryōgen and may have its origins in the teachings he received from Kakue, although similar leanings can also be seen in Saichō, Ennin, and Enchin. The Esoteric lineage that Ryōgen received from Kakue was known as the Kazan-ryū (Kazan lineage), because Gangyōji was at Kazan in Yamashina, Kyoto. It later came to be known as the Kawa no ryū (river lineage) because Ryōgen made Yokawa his headquarters. Although the Kawa no ryū tradition might at first appear to offer a compromise between the lineages of Ennin and Enchin, it never seems to have functioned in this way. Henjō obtained Enchin's sanction only because Ennin had died before Henjō's training in Esoteric ritual had been completed and because Enchin was *zasu*. Neither Henjō nor such followers as Annen saw themselves as representing a compromise between the two lineages. In fact, both Henjō and Annen viewed Ennin much more favorably than Enchin. The favoritism toward Ennin's lineage that Ryōgen displayed was thus consistent with being initiated into Henjō's lineage.

Ryōgen's later successes must have brought prestige to the lineage. However, it survived for only one or two generations after Ryōgen's death. As the antagonism between the lineages of Ennin (Sanmon) and Enchin (Jimon) intensified, monks found it impossible to maintain a tradition that included transmissions from both masters. Any elements that seemed to suggest Enchin's influence were probably eliminated as the lineage changed and was called by new names.

Ryōgen's Studies 3: Tendai and Bodhisattva Precepts

In addition, Ryōgen must have studied Tendai exoteric doctrine (*ken-gyō*) extensively; the contents of the debates in which he participated usually concerned Tendai teachings. The term "exoteric teaching" was used in contrast to Esoteric teachings (*mikkyō*), although the actual contents of what was referred to by these two terms might change depending on the context in which they were used. For example, the *Lotus Sūtra* could be interpreted in both exoteric and Esoteric terms. However, the term "Tendai exoteric teaching" often referred to those teachings expounded by Chih-i, for example, Saichō had divided the Tendai school's teachings into two courses, one based on the *Ta-jih ching* (*Mahāvairocana-sūtra*) and the other based on Chih-i's *Mo-ho chih-kuan* (Great calming and contemplation). According to later sources, Ryōgen's teachings were from a lineage consisting of Eryō and Manga.[37] Several ordination lineages exist; according to them, Ryōgen received his bodhisattva precepts ordination from Risen or Son'i.[38] Son'i, *zasu* at the time of Ryōgen's ordination, probably presided over the ordination ceremony.

Ryōgen's Ties with the Fujiwara Clan

When Fujiwara no Arihira returned to Kyoto from the Yuima-e, he praised Ryōgen's performance at the debates to the chancellor. As a result, Ryōgen's name became known to some of the Kyoto nobility. About 939, Kakue, the monk who had instructed Ryōgen in Esoteric Buddhism, was asked to go to Chancellor Fujiwara no Tadahira's office to perform religious services. Ryōgen accompanied his teacher. When the ceremonies had been completed, Tadahira asked Ryōgen to remain behind after all the other monks had departed. Tadahira was more than sixty years old at the time and was undoubtedly concerned about death. He thus asked Ryōgen to pray for an auspicious rebirth for him after his death.[39] Tadahira was probably interested in Ryōgen because he viewed him as a young monk of promise who could help Tadahira's family in the future. Ryōgen had established relations with the influential Fujiwara clan—but so had many other Tendai monks. In the coming years, Ryōgen would have to strengthen these ties and demonstrate his importance to the Fujiwaras if he were to realize the full potential of this important connection.

At the time Tadahira asked Ryōgen to conduct services for him, Tadahira was at the peak of his career, the most powerful man in Japan.

Tadahira had fashioned much of the apparatus that would enable the Fujiwara clan to dominate Japanese court life as regents for emperors. His innovations had led to a decline in the power of the imperial family; at the same time, he also strengthened the restraints on local leaders and improved the taxation system.

Tadahira was deeply interested in court ritual. His two sons, Saneyori (900–970), and Morosuke (908–960), are regarded as the founders of the two most important traditions of court ritual, the Kujō-ryū and the Ononomiya-ryū, but much of their writing was based on Tadahira's written and verbal instructions.[40] The establishment of these two traditions parallels the existence of the variety of separate traditions of Esoteric Buddhist ritual. In Tadahira's diary, the *Teishinkōki*, sixty religious services from 924 to 948 are mentioned; the name of the officiant is recorded fifty-one times. Forty-seven of those mentions were Tendai monks, demonstrating the importance of Tadahira's ties with Tendai monks. In twenty-three cases, the current *zasu* performed the ceremony. If those monks who either had been *zasu* previously or would hold the post later are included, then the number of services performed by the most eminent Tendai monks rises to thirty-seven. The Tendai *zasu* Son'i was particularly important to Tadahira and performed seventeen of the ceremonies and acted as Tadahira's teacher.[41] Tadahira obviously valued his relationship with the Tendai monks since he went to the trouble to record his relations in such detail. The close relations between Tadahira and Tendai were exemplified by the establishment of Hosshōji by Tadahira about 925, when he was minister of the left. Tadahira had rituals performed by Tendai monks for his fiftieth, sixtieth, and seventieth birthdays at the temple, and he had his gravesite put in the temple ground. Tadahira's descendants and members of the imperial household later patronized the temple. Within a decade, it had been named an imperial temple and awarded yearly ordinands; it continued to be used by the nobility throughout the Heian period. Yet Tadahira's interest in Buddhism lay primarily in claims that its rituals would protect him and his family from disaster. He does not seem to have had the depth of understanding of Buddhist teachings or rituals displayed by at least some other lay believers, including his son Morosuke.[42]

Tadahira's position as lay supervisor for Enryakuji had clearly played an important role in the establishment of his relations with the Tendai school. Although the post of lay supervisor had originally been established shortly after Saichō's death to oversee examinations of candidates for ordination and to facilitate relations with the government, by

Tadahira's time the *zasu* had assumed most of these administrative functions. The lay supervisor was primarily an influential patron who could call on Tendai services for his special needs.[43] Thus Ryōgen's meeting with Tadahira held the promise of future patronage and influence.

Tadahira died in 949, several years after meeting Ryōgen. Ryōgen, who was thirty-seven at the time, went to the bereaved family's home, possibly to participate in the services for the deceased. Tadahira's second son, Morosuke, in accordance with his deceased father's instructions, took Ryōgen as his teacher.[44]

About this time, Ryōgen seems to have had an inauspicious dream that foretold some disaster. He decided to ask the Fujiwara clan for permission to return to Mount Hiei to practice.[45] However, Tadahira's oldest son, Saneyori, objected. Only when Morosuke intervened and argued that Ryōgen could pray for their father's repose while he was on Mount Hiei did Saneyori relent and agree that Ryōgen could return to Mount Hiei. Ryōgen did not return to the central monastic complex on Hiei; rather he chose a deserted and seemingly unimportant area called Yokawa. By choosing to go on a retreat, Ryōgen would increase his reputation for serious practice and enhance his reputation as an effective performer of ritual. In addition, if his ritual performance was effective, he would further strengthen his ties with the lineage of monks descended from Ennin. Ennin and Yokawa are discussed in appendix 1.

The *Kuhon Ōjōgi*

The *Kuhon ōjōgi*, a text on the nine grades of rebirth specified in the *Kuan wu-liang-shou ching*, is attributed to Ryōgen.[46] The authenticity of the text has been questioned for several reasons. It is not cited in the *Ōjō yōshū*, the seminal text on Tendai Pure Land belief written by Ryōgen's student Genshin. In addition, it is not mentioned in a list of texts on the Pure Land that was sent to China along with Genshin's *Ōjō yōshū*. In fact, the text is not cited anywhere in extant materials until eighty-five years after Ryōgen's death, when it appears once in the *Annyōshū* (Collection concerning the [Pure Land of] peace and sustenance) compiled by Minamoto no Takakuni (1004–1077) about 1070. It subsequently begins to be cited more frequently.

The text has often been considered to have been a debate manual. However, several aspects of the text make this interpretation implausible. It is written more as a commentary on the *Kuan wu-liang-shou ching* than as a set of questions and answers that explores various aspects of a doctrine. In addition, no other evidence that the nine grades of rebirth had emerged as a debate topic by the late tenth century can be found.

To interpret the text, Kakehashi Nobuaki has suggested that its origins can be traced to the interactions between Ryōgen and the Fujiwara clan.[47] He notes that Tadahira had commissioned a set of paintings of the nine grades of rebirth in 946, several years before his death. His descendants continued to be interested in teachings concerning the nine grades. Pictures of the nine grades could be found at the Muryōjuin at Hōjōji and at the Byōdōin, both temples founded by Tadahira's descendants. In addition, Michinaga had declared his intention to be reborn in the highest of the nine grades.

Although the text contains a statement suggesting that it might have been ordered by Morosuke, the text's style indicates that it was not intended for the nobility; it contains references to doctrines that are too brief to have been of much use to anyone not well schooled in the tradition. In addition, some sentences take the form of commands, hardly the style for a text intended for powerful patrons. Thus Kakehashi suggests that the text originally took the form of notes for a lecture that Ryōgen asked one of his students to give to members of the Fujiwara clan. Moreover, Morosuke had recorded an occasion when Ryōgen asked one of his students to lecture on the *O-mi-t'o ching* (Smaller *Sukhāvatīvyūha*). Although the subject of the lecture was not the nine grades of rebirth, this scenario might well have been repeated at other times. Finally, the contents of the text include references to oral recitation of the *nenbutsu*, a practice that appealed to members of the nobility.

The lack of mentions of the text in contemporary literature might be explained by the hypothesis that it was held by people other than Genshin and the group surrounding him. The text might finally have been cited in the *Annyōshū* by Minamoto no Takakuni, a member of a family that had long been associated with Morosuke and his descendants. Unfortunately, no evidence concerning the date of the composition of the text by Ryōgen has surfaced. However, Kakehashi's interpretation of the work sheds light on another aspect of Ryōgen's relationship with his patrons.

Conclusion

Because Ryōgen's teacher died before Ryōgen could be ordained, Ryōgen's ordination and early education were probably more difficult than those of many other monks. His experiences during that time may well have taught him the importance of monastic alliances. In establishing himself on Mount Hiei, Ryōgen made excellent use of the debate system to demonstrate his abilities and attract both followers and patrons. He also began to demonstrate a flair for performing religious rituals in such a way that influential patrons would come to him. His retreat to Yokawa served as a period of austerities that enabled him to solidify his reputation as a performer of ritual, increasing his renown as a spiritually powerful person; because much of the Tōdō and Saitō areas were controlled by monks from Enchin's lineage, the move to Yokawa gave him a geographical base from which he could assemble and train his followers. In the next chapter, his relations with certain segments of the powerful Fujiwara clan develop further, and he emerges as one of the most influential young monks on Mount Hiei.

5

Ryōgen and the Fujiwaras
Patronage and Esoteric Ritual

With Ryōgen in seclusion at Yokawa, this chapter focuses on how he was chosen by Fujiwara no Tadahira's son Morosuke to perform rituals to help his branch of the Fujiwara clan prosper. In the first part of this chapter, the relationship between Morosuke and Ryōgen is discussed. Their alliance was not based solely on Ryōgen's ability as a performer of rituals, but also on similarities between the two men in terms of age, political ability, and deep interest in the ritual performances for their respective spheres of influence. The analysis of their relationship is carried further with an assessment of Morosuke's interests (included in appendix 2). The two men sealed their alliance with the ordination of Morosuke's son Jinzen. However, when another son, Takamitsu, also wished to be ordained after Morosuke's death, Takamitsu's religious aspirations threatened the very structure of the alliance between Ryōgen and Morosuke's descendants. Although Morosuke's interest in Ryōgen seems to have extended to Tendai practice, it was based primarily on his interest in the practical effects of Tendai ritual. To clarify the practical nature of their alliance, the ordination at Tōdaiji of still another of Morosuke's sons, Jinkaku, is examined.

The second part of this chapter analyzes how Ryōgen used Esoteric Buddhist ritual to carry out his plans and help his patrons. In doing so, he had to balance two aspects of Esoteric ritual. He had to argue that his rituals had their origins in practices imported from China by qualified monks and that the rituals remained true to their origins. At the same time, as other groups performed the same or competing rituals, he had to make innovations in how the rituals were conducted in order to compete.

Ryōgen's Alliance with Morosuke

The Goma *Ceremony at Yokawa*

Shortly after he had commenced his retreat at Yokawa, Ryōgen began a period of intense religious practice; for three hundred days he performed the *goma* ceremony for the repose of Fujiwara no Tadahira. The effort and the length of time involved in this practice must have impressed Tadahira's son Morosuke, who would become Ryōgen's most important patron. It also must have indicated that he shared in the spiritual powers that mountain ascetics were often believed to possess.

The *goma* ceremony is an Esoteric ritual patterned after the Vedic *homa* rite. In the *goma,* various offerings are burned in a fire, and the offerings are then conveyed to celestial deities through the smoke from the fire. The ceremony was used for a variety of worldly purposes, including the prevention of calamities, the encouragement of good fortune, and the defeat of enemies. In addition, the ceremony could also be interpreted in a more spiritual sense as helping with the religious austerities of a practitioner. For example, ritual actions that were said to encourage good fortune in a mundane sense could also be interpreted as the encouragement of merit and the wisdom (*fukuchi*) associated with the aspiration to enlightenment. Actions said to result in the defeat of enemies in the outside world could be interpreted as the practitioner's internal battle to eliminate ignorance and the defilements. Defilements were "burned" in the fires of the practitioner's wisdom, just as offerings were burned in the *goma* fire.

The exact format of the ceremony Ryōgen performed is not described in any sources. However, on the basis of ceremonies performed on Mount Hiei today, the late Tendai *zasu* Yamada Etai has suggested that it probably had at least two parts. The first was a preliminary part in which the practitioner purified himself, possibly through refraining from eating both grains and salt for one hundred days. During the second part, the *goma* ceremony itself, the practitioner fasted and did not lie down to sleep or rest. The *goma* might have consisted of the burning of a certain number of pieces of wood, perhaps as many as a hundred thousand, representing the defilements.[1]

The Reconciliation of the Seeming Conflict
between Religious and This-worldly Political Goals

According to the *Daisōjōden*, while Ryōgen was practicing, he had a dream that foretold his eventual appointment as head of the Tendai school. At first, Ryōgen was disturbed by the dream because he felt that he should be motivated by the desire to help others, not by the desire to advance his own career and become famous. Only when he found a passage in the *Tao-kan yu ching* that noted that assiduously striving for enlightenment resulted in worldly achievements (*shitsuji*) did he feel relieved.[2]

Ryōgen apparently did reconcile his religious aspirations and his desire for high office. After his death, a short set of vows that Ryōgen wrote when he was thirty-seven years old was discovered in the library, probably the one at Yokawa. In the essay, Ryōgen explained his views on what a monk's motivation ought to be when he participated in debates. His views presumably also applied to the performance of Esoteric rituals for powerful patrons.

> When I had just begun my studies and religious practice, I participated in debates in order to defeat my opponents, and thereby I did wrong. Now that I have performed my religious practices for a longer time, although outwardly I may appear to be acting in pursuit of fame, my actions are based on my intention to propagate the correct teaching.
> I ask (1) that the Buddhas of the ten directions protect this dull and foolish monk; (2) that all sentient beings empower (*kaji*) me; (3) that all who vie with me in debate not succumb to anger, lust, and ignorance; (4) that even if I fall into adversity, others not do so; (5) that those who hear my questions and answers develop the aspiration to enlightenment and that we plant the seeds for Buddhahood together; (6) that all those who neither hear nor see me still realize supreme enlightenment.[3]

The conflict between the aspiration for high religious goals and interests in holding high monastic offices either in one's own school or in the Office of Monastic Affairs is an old theme in Japanese Buddhism. Saichō, the founder of the Tendai school, had adamantly criticized Nara monks for seeking fame rather than pursuing enlightenment. He censured those Tendai monks who left Mount Hiei for not persevering in their religious quest, and he eventually replaced the *Ssu-fen lü* precepts with those of the *Fan-wang ching* to keep his disciples on Mount Hiei. Although Ryōgen seems to have resolved the conflict to his own satisfaction, some of his contemporaries, as well as some later Tendai monks, still felt ambivalent about the issue. Several of Ryōgen's disciples refused to participate in the Ōwa debates that Ryōgen organized between 961 and 963. In addition, others such as Genshin clearly decided that retiring to a quiet life in Yokawa was preferable to seeking the rewards of high monastic office.

A later story about Genshin and his mother clearly illustrates the conflicting feelings many had about participation in officially sponsored assemblies. When Genshin was young, he was invited to serve at a series of eight lectures on the *Lotus Sūtra* for Princess Shōshi (950–999). Genshin was given various presents to thank him for his participation in the services. He selected an appropriate present and sent it to his mother, writing her about how he had obtained it. She replied by scolding him, arguing that a monk should not be concerned with the fame and honor that came from participating in services for the nobility. Rather, he should be more like the Tendai monk Zōga, concerned with studying so that he could become a sage (*shōnin*). If he did so, then he could help save his mother. Genshin subsequently is said to have resolved to follow her instructions.[4]

Ryōgen's brief reflections and justifications of his ambition represent most of the introspection that exist in his biographies and few writings. In fact, such introspective statements were rarely found in mid-Heian biographies. Biographies often focused on information such as where a person was born, who ordained him, who taught him, what his accomplishments were, and what offices he attained. Other writings such as the *Ōjōden* (Biographies of those reborn in the Pure Land) were concerned with religious practices and experiences. These brief introspective passages may well have been intended as public justifications of Ryōgen's activities for critics within the Tendai school who felt that he was too openly political. For the most part, sources reveal little of the private thoughts of this man who dedicated his life to his own success and that of his allies.

A number of the monks associated with Ryōgen, such as Genshin and Zōga, chose to emphasize the private aspects of Buddhist life, withdrawing to isolated monasteries and refusing to participate in public functions. However, later authors sometimes exaggerated these aspects of their lives, perhaps as an indirect criticism of the political activities of monks such as Ryōgen. A more accurate view of many of these monks would lie between the extremes. Ryōgen undoubtedly had an introspective side even though sources reveal nothing about it; his ongoing relationship with such seemingly reclusive monks as Genshin suggests that the two men found common interests. As is discussed in the next chapter, even such seeming recluses as Zōga and Senkan engaged in many of the same activities as Ryōgen to raise funds for their monasteries.

Ryōgen and Fujiwara no Morosuke

Ryōgen's alliance with Tadahira's son Morosuke was not just a matter of chance or of Morosuke's desire to have someone perform memorial services for his father. Personal friendship undoubtedly played a role in the relationship; because Morosuke was but four years older than Ryōgen, the two were virtually contemporaries. Both men were deeply interested in ritual, with Morosuke playing a major role in compiling his father's instructions on court ritual.

In addition, political considerations played a major role in the alliance. Ryōgen lived during a period when the northern house of the Fujiwara clan had solidified its hold on the government by developing a system in which the Fujiwara leaders would serve as regents for emperors. Earlier, Tadahira had secured his power by arranging to have his older sister Onshi (885–954) introduced to the palace as a junior consort (*nyōgo*) for Emperor Daigo (885–930; r. 897–930). She gave birth to two sons who would later ascend the throne as emperors Suzaku (923–952; r. 930–946) and Murakami (926–967; r. 946–967). Tadahira's power as regent was based on his status as uncle of these young emperors. However, it was necessary to continue to produce a supply of daughters who would serve as consorts for emperors and give birth to sons who would be appointed as crown princes and later serve as emperors for this strategy to work for any length of time. Introducing a woman into the emperor's quarters, gaining his affection, ensuring her fertility, determining the sex of the offspring, making sure that the birth was safe, and guaranteeing the continued health of those children made the process fraught with difficulty and danger. Tadahira's eldest son, Saneyori, had introduced his daughter Fujiwara no Nobuko into Emperor Murakami's quarters, but she had died in 947. After her death, Saneyori had no further daughters and had to resort to other tactics to further his family's career.[5] Because of such problems, the nobility employed monks to pray for the birth and health of children.

At the time of Tadahira's death in 949, Emperor Murakami was on the throne, but he had not yet produced a male heir. Thus the first family to successfully introduce a woman to the emperor and have her bear a son would have a significant political advantage. Middle Counselor (*chūnagon*) Fujiwara no Motokata (888–953) from the southern house of the Fujiwaras had his daughter Yūhime (also pronounced Sukehime; n.d.) introduced into the court as imperial concubine (kōi).[6] When Yūhime gave birth to a son, Prince Hirohira (950–971), he posed a clear threat to the dominance of Tadahira and his family.[7] Motokata had asked a Tendai monk named Kansan to serve as a guardian monk (shugosō) for Hirohira.[8]

Morosuke had a daughter Anshi (also read as Yasuko; 927–964) who had been appointed junior consort for Emperor Murakami; she was pregnant with the emperor's child when Prince Hirohira was born. The future of Morosuke's lineage might depend on whether she gave birth to a son or daughter. If it were a son, then perhaps Morosuke would be able to have his grandson appointed crown prince over Hirohira. Thus when Ryōgen went to Yokawa to perform a goma ceremony for three hundred days, he did so not only to pray for Tadahira's repose, but also to pray that Morosuke's daughter would have a son. To realize this goal, Ryōgen was willing to devise new ceremonies or modify old ones. According to a legend recorded in the Asabashō, on the chance that Anshi was pregnant with a girl, Ryōgen performed a ceremony to Ususama (Skt. Ucchuṣma, the mystic king of the North according to some Taimitsu ceremonies) that was designed to change a fetus from female to male. According to the Asabashō, the ceremony was not performed for this purpose after this time.[9] However, the ceremony is mentioned as producing males in the Taiheiki and other sources.[10] Although it is not clear whether the story in the Asabashō concerning Ryōgen's ceremony is historically accurate, it is significant that such sources suggest that Ryōgen not only performed such ceremonies, but also was willing to devise new ceremonies or modify old ones to solidify his relations with his patrons in the nobility.[11]

When Anshi, in fact, did give birth to Prince Norihira, the future Emperor Reizei (950–1011; r. 967–969), Ryōgen's future possibilities were significantly enhanced. Morosuke arranged to have Norihira's birth treated as though his appointment as crown prince were assured. During the potentially dangerous period before Norihira was officially appointed crown prince, Ryōgen served as his guardian monk (gojisō). When Norihira was only three months old, he was formally named crown prince.[12] Morosuke had won his struggle with Fujiwara no Motokata over who eventually would have his grandson on the throne. For Ryōgen, this was a major victory.

Three years later, in 953, Motokata died at the age of sixty-five. According to the Eiga monogatari, he was so disappointed and frustrated over the birth of Norihira that he wished to die immediately and avoid seeing his grandson displaced as crown prince.[13] Yūhime was quite depressed by these events and became a nun in 964 with Senkan, a monk from Enchin's lineage, as her preceptor.[14]

New Appointments for Ryōgen

The next few years after Ryōgen's retreat to Yokawa were marked by appointments to a number of increasingly prestigious posts, many of them a result of his alliance with Morosuke. As noted above, in 950, Ryōgen was appointed to be a guardian monk[15] for the newborn crown prince Norihira. Because Ryōgen had earlier prayed for the birth of this child, the child's elevation to the post of crown prince as a replacement for Fujiwara no Motokata's grandson meant both future possibilities for Morosuke and impressive rewards for Ryōgen. This appointment would continue to yield benefits for Ryōgen because the crown prince was later beset by mental illness attributed to the vengeful ghosts of Motokata and Prince Hirohira, whom he had supplanted; as a result, ceremonies to protect him would be required throughout Reizei's life. Ryōgen's name, however, does not appear in the lists of officiating monks after Reizei assumed the throne. Perhaps Ryōgen believed that it was too dangerous to cater to a man with erratic behavior. When Ryōgen's disciple Jinzen went to perform ceremonies for Reizei, Reizei chased him out of the palace with a sword.[16]

The following year, 951, Ryōgen's teacher Kakue (872–954) left his post as master of Esoteric Buddhism at Gangyōji (Yamashina-ku, Kyoto), ceding his position to Ryōgen. Kakue had encouraged Ryōgen's mother to have her young son ordained and had later trained Ryōgen in Esoteric ritual. Ryōgen was only thirty-nine years old at the time, a very young age to be appointed to such a major post.[17] The position was important for several reasons. First, Gangyōji was the headquarters of one of the three major Tendai lineages, the one that traced itself back to Henjō. With Ryōgen holding key positions at both Yokawa and Gangyōji, it gave him influence in the lineages traced back to Ennin and to Henjō. By adding buildings to Gangyōji and increasing the number of *ajari* at the temple from three to four in 968, Ryōgen would eventually be recognized as the leader of Henjō's lineage, resulting in its absorption into Ennin's lineage.[18] Second, the Urin'in (also read Unrin'in, situated to the south of Daitokuji in Kyoto), which had formerly been the palace of an imperial prince, was a branch temple of Gangyōji. It continued to grow throughout the Heian period and to receive gifts from nobles. It also is mentioned in connection with monks who wrote

poems such as Henjō, and thus was a site where the type of religion that
appealed to nobles was cultivated.[19] Although Ryōgen's name is not associated with the Urin'in, he was probably associated with it through
Gangyōji. Third, because Gangyōji and Urin'in were much closer to the
capital than Yokawa, this appointment probably meant that Ryōgen
would have much more immediate access to Morosuke than before and
be able to solidify his relations with the Fujiwaras.

Three years later, on 10-16-954, Morosuke set out on a tour of Mount
Hiei with a retinue. When he arrived he was welcomed by large numbers of monks and the *zasu* at the Lecture Hall; Morosuke then proceeded to visit Ryōgen at Yokawa. While he was there, Morosuke toured
various buildings and witnessed a number of ceremonies, including the
uninterrupted recitation (*fudan nenbutsu*), the Lotus meditation (*Hokke
zanmai*), and lectures and questions on the *O-mi-t'o ching*. On the eighteenth, perhaps inspired by what he had seen, he surveyed the lay of
the land and vowed to build a Lotus Meditation Hall (Hokke zanmaidō)
at Yokawa. At the dedication ceremony for the hall, Morosuke stated
that the merit from the building was to be devoted to the future prosperity of his family. He specifically mentioned that he hoped it would
enable his family to continue to produce emperors, empresses, and
crown princes.[20] Moreover, Morosuke stated that if he could strike the
flint and light the fire for the permanent lamp (*jōtō*) in front of the main
image within three tries, his successful lighting of the lamp would indicate that the vow would be effective. When Morosuke lit the fire on
his first try, the assembled crowd was delighted. Later, much of the Fujiwara clan interpreted the success of Morosuke's lineage in politics to
the effectiveness of the vow. In addition, Jien, the author of the *Gukanshō*, and the authors of the *Daisōjōden* and *Genpei jōsuiki* mention the
event.[21] In return for the prayers and ceremonies performed by Ryōgen and his disciples, Morosuke promised to support Ryōgen's branch
of the Tendai school, the monks belonging to Ennin's lineage. Morosuke also made a similar vow at the Kitano Shrine dedicated to Tenjin,
the *kami* often identified with Sugawara no Michizane's ghost.[22] Morosuke's vows and the buildings he sponsored were symbolic of the spiritual and political alliance between the two men.

Angry Ghosts

The various rivalries between members of the same clan, such as that
between Motokata and Morosuke, or between members of the same

family, such as that between Morosuke and his older brother Saneyori, left lasting impressions on both the participants and their descendants. For example, Motokata's bitter and frustrated death was remembered by many at court. Later, when misfortune befell Morosuke's relatives and descendants, it was said to be due to the evil influence of Motokata's ghost. According to the *Eiga monogatari*, the mental illness of Morosuke's grandson Prince Norihira and the death of Morosuke's daughter An-shi were both caused by Motokata's vengeful ghost.[23] Kansan (also pronounced Ganzan), the Tendai monk who had prayed for Hirohira, emerged after his death as a vindictive ghost who sometimes aided the ghost of Motokata in afflicting Morosuke's descendants.[24]

The appearance of such vengeful ghosts was not a new phenomenon in the society of the Japanese nobility.[25] Those people who had died frustrated because they had not attained their goals, who had been cheated of their rightful position, or who had died prematurely in some unusual manner might become ghosts. Such ghosts afflicted the living and either had to be assuaged or defeated through religious ceremonies. Before the Heian period, the individual qualities of these ghosts were not emphasized very much. In other words, people generally did not conceive of the ghost as a particular individual carrying out vengeance directly specifically toward those individuals who had wronged him during his lifetime.[26] Rather, ghosts of particular people were thought to avenge themselves on society at large through epidemics or natural disasters. To assuage such ghosts and protect the populace, a *goryō-e* (spirit appeasing) cult had been established in Kyoto in the early Heian period.[27] If a ghost afflicted an individual, that person was usually chosen by chance rather than as part of a systematic plan conceived of by the ghost. In many cases, ghosts gradually were placated, lost their individual personalities and merged with the multitudes of ancestors.

The activities attributed to Motokata's ghost differed from many earlier cases in an important way. Motokata avenged himself by afflicting both those who had wronged him during his life and their descendants. Once ghosts had been endowed with individual personalities and the power to afflict individuals of their choosing, ghosts were increasingly used to explain the tragedies and successes that occurred at court. At the same time, the nobles needed new and more powerful ceremonies to protect them from this new threat.[28] Ryōgen and his contemporaries responded to this need by employing and modifying Esoteric rituals.

Morosuke's faction later not only worried about defending itself from the attacks of ghosts; it also had ghosts that sought to protect it. These ghosts, however, were thought to suffer because of their activities. Thus ceremonies were needed to help alleviate their pain. The following entry from the *Shōyūki*, the diary by Saneyori's adopted son Sanesuke (957–1046), dramatically reflects the fears and concerns that ghosts gave rise to during this period. It also reveals the tension and the psychological conflicts that arose when members of the same family competed for positions.

> Bishop Kanju visited (in 994) and said that recently when he had performed rituals because the crown prince's imperial concubine, Fujiwara no Jushi, had become pregnant, a dreadful spirit had appeared and said, "I am the spirit of the minister Fujiwara no Morosuke. While I was alive, I vowed to help my descendants prosper by using both Buddhist and non-Buddhist rituals. My wish to destroy the descendants of my elder brother Saneyori was especially fervent. The vow to cut off his descendants through yin-yang techniques was to be effective for the next sixty years and is still valid. Now because I vowed to cut off other lineages, I suffer unlimited torment without hope of escape. Whenever someone from Saneyori's lineage is about to give birth, I must appear and prevent it because of my vow. Only a few years and months remain of the sixty-year vow that I took during my lifetime. The [yin-yang] heterodox rituals have only two years of efficacy left; afterward it will be difficult to prevent pregnancies [that may harm my descendants]. This imperial concubine [Seishi, a granddaughter of my younger brother Morotada] already is possibly pregnant [with a crown prince]. Thus I have come to attack her and to cut off descendants other than my own."
>
> When I heard this, I remembered [similar] past events. Though we are flesh and bones, we should be prepared. The bishop said that we should immediately install an image of Daiitoku and pay homage to it.[29]

This passage illustrates a number of aspects typical of spirit possession during the middle of the Heian period. Although men were occasionally possessed by spirits, women, especially when pregnant, were particularly subject to possession.[30] The Buddhist monks or masters of yin-yang techniques who served as exorcists either made the possessing spirit speak while it was still in its victim or transferred it to a third person and forced it to speak. The third person was frequently a child that the exorcist brought with him. The spirit was made to identify itself and to state the reasons for its possession and what it required. The monks who performed these rituals of exorcism frequently lived in the mountains and employed techniques that were mixtures of Buddhism and shamanism with some Taoist elements such as the yin-yang techniques. The main motive of the possessing spirit was anger over unjust treatment. In the case of Morosuke, the anger initially may have been over his premature death before he could see his grandson installed as emperor or before Morosuke could serve as regent. Later Morosuke's ghost was seen as acting in revenge for his rival Motokata's possession of Morosuke's daughter Anshi and grandson Emperor Reizei.

The Ordination of Morosuke's Son Jinzen

The relationship between Morosuke and Ryōgen, already very close after the dedication of the Lotus Meditation Hall, became even tighter with the ordination of Morosuke's son Jinzen. Almost all of Morosuke's twelve sons followed courses that involved them in court politics. By 957, his eldest nine sons had all begun their careers. However, for his tenth son, Jinzen, Morosuke chose a different career, and had him ordained as a monk. In the eight month of 958, at the age of fifteen, Jinzen climbed Mount Hiei and was ordained by the Tendai *zasu* Enshō. Because of the friendship between Ryōgen and Morosuke, Jinzen became Ryōgen's disciple and probably went to live with Ryōgen. Special quarters for Jinzen, the Myōkōin (Hall of the excellent scents), were built shortly after he arrived on Mount Hiei. Jinzen probably underwent the traditional period of confinement (*rōzan*) on Mount Hiei in those quarters.[31] This treatment would certainly not have been given an ordinary monk.

The ties between Ryōgen and Jinzen are revealed in a will Ryōgen wrote in the fifth month of 972, found in appendix 3. Ryōgen left his seals of authority as abbot of Yokawa to Jinzen, effectively naming Jinzen as the next head of the section of Mount Hiei where Ryōgen's power was based. In the will, Ryōgen respectfully referred to Jinzen as "Zenji no kimi."[32] Jinzen was twenty-nine at the time, with only fourteen years of seniority as a monk. Ryōgen's special treatment of Jinzen was clearly based on his family ties rather than any extraordinary achievements Jinzen had as a monk.

What did Ryōgen receive from Morosuke in return? As is discussed later, Morosuke and his sons supported Ryōgen with the money and manors to build Mount Hiei into the preeminent religious institution in Japan.[33]

The Ordination of Jinzen's Older Brother Takamitsu

Shortly after Morosuke's death, an event occurred that underscored the political nature of Ryōgen's alliance with Morosuke's clan. Morosuke's eighth son, Takamitsu (b. 940), left his post at court and climbed Mount Hiei to ask to be ordained.[34]

Takamitsu's mother was Princess Gashi, a daughter of Emperor Daigo and the younger sister of Emperor Murakami. She died in 954, when Takamitsu was fifteen. As a youth, Takamitsu was known for his poetry, and several poems conveying his sense of the transiency of life at the time of his mother's death survive. Under Morosuke's sponsorship, he embarked upon a career as an official, as had Morosuke's other sons. He eventually rose to the junior fifth rank and simultaneously held positions as lesser captain of the palace guards of the right and supernumerary assistant governor of Bigo. However, Takamitsu seems to have been a sensitive youth and to have wished to retire to the life of a Buddhist monk even before Morosuke's death; however, he had not done so because of his father's opposition.[35] His religious feelings had intensified after Morosuke's death. In part, his interest in the religious life may have been motivated by the feeling that further advances as an official would be difficult because both of his parents were dead. Moreover, the center of political power was quickly moving to Saneyori, away from Morosuke's sons. Morosuke's other sons who were pursuing official careers were half-brothers. Their sister, Empress Anshi, and their nephews, the future emperors Reizei and En'yū, would probably aid them in their careers. However, Takamitsu may have believed that he could not hope for very much help from such sources. In fact, his younger full brother Tamemitsu (942–992) would go on to have an illustrious career, rising to chancellor, proving Takamitsu wrong. Or perhaps Takamitsu felt that Tamemitsu could carry on his family's political aspirations while Takamitsu pursued his religious vocation.

On 12-5-961, less than a year after Morosuke's death, Takamitsu went to Yokawa and asked to be ordained. His destination was no accident. His father had spent several days in Yokawa and had expressed an interest in being ordained there. Later, Takamitsu would dream of his father comforting him at Yokawa.[36] Takamitsu went to see Jinzen, his younger full brother, who had been ordained three years earlier. Jinzen was not happy to see him and tried to dissuade him from being ordained, as did Ryōgen. Takamitsu must have been disappointed; Jinzen was younger by only one year, and Takamitsu must have hoped for a more favorable response from a brother who was virtually his contemporary. In desperation, Takamitsu cut off his own topknot. Word of Takamitsu's intention was sent to Kyoto, but appeals from Takamitsu's wife and sister failed to bring him back.

When Jinzen had climbed Mount Hiei to be ordained, Ryōgen had welcomed him and built special quarters for him. As long as Ryōgen was alive, he continued to give Jinzen special treatment. Yet when Takamitsu climbed Mount Hiei, Ryōgen tried to dissuade him from being ordained and later acquiesced only when Takamitsu departed to Tōnomine. Even though Takamitsu climbed Mount Hiei for genuinely religious reasons and was free of the political motivations that led to Jinzen's ordination, Ryōgen seems to have been unsympathetic toward him. Ryōgen's seemingly unfeeling treatment of Takamitsu's sincere interest in religion was undoubtedly due to the threat that Takamitsu posed to the careful plans that Ryōgen and Morosuke had made for Takamitsu's brother Jinzen on Mount Hiei.[37] Morosuke had willed considerable landholdings to Jinzen and the Tendai school. Because Takamitsu was Jinzen's older brother, he could have thrown the plans for Jinzen's rise to prominence in the Tendai school into confusion. Takamitsu, though Jinzen's junior in monastic terms, was his senior in secular terms. Questions concerning Takamitsu's rights to the landholdings might have arisen. Finally, during this time, Ryōgen was establishing ties with Morosuke's son Koremasa (924–972); Takamitsu's rash decision could have led to bad feelings between the men if the situation had not been carefully managed.

Finally, in 4-1-962, four months after Takamitsu had climbed Mount Hiei, Morosuke's oldest son, Koremasa (924–972), who was head of the family, gave permission for the ordination. Takamitsu was ordained along with two attendants.[38] According to the *Tōnomine ryakki* (Brief record of Tōnomine), Takamitsu was ordained by Zōga (917–1003); but recent studies have suggested that although Takamitsu later studied under Zōga, Takamitsu was in fact ordained by Ryōgen.[39] Takamitsu was given the monastic name Nyokaku. Four months after his ordination, in the eighth month of 962, Takamitsu went to Tōnomine (to the south of Sakurai-shi in Nara-ken) to practice at the invitation of Kakuei, Jisshō's (892–956) disciple.[40] With Takamitsu in Tōnomine, the threat to Ryōgen's carefully orchestrated plans was at least temporarily resolved. The choice of Tōnomine was not random. To understand Takamitsu's choice, a review of the history of Tōnomine is included in appendix 4.

Morosuke's Son Jinkaku

Besides Jinzen and Takamitsu, one more of Morosuke's sons, Jinkaku (also read as Shingaku; 955–1043), was later ordained as a monk. Although Jinkaku was ordained after Morosuke's death, his biography is important because it demonstrates that the alliance between the northern house of the Fujiwaras and Ryōgen's Tendai lineage was not completely sectarian. Powerful lay patrons chose their monastic allies on the basis of personal relations and charisma more than on the basis of unwavering loyalty to a particular set of teachings, even though they sometimes were vitally interested in Buddhist doctrine.

Jinkaku was the son of Morosuke's beloved wife, Princess Kōshi; he was ordained as a Shingon monk at the age of nine, several years after Morosuke's death. He studied under Kanchū (906–977) and Kanchō (916–998) of Ninnaji at first, but went to Tōji in 979. His career suggests that the special treatment given to Jinzen in the Tendai school was accorded to the sons of the highest nobility in other schools. Jinkaku studied Shingon Esoteric Buddhism under Kanchō, whose mother was the daughter of Fujiwara no Tokihira (Morosuke's uncle). Jinkaku was appointed abbot of Tōdaiji several times, the first being in 992, when he was only thirty-seven and replaced Chōnen (938–1016); he was appointed again in 1016. He rose through the ranks of the Sōgō, beginning with an appointment as supernumerary master of discipline (*gon-risshi*) at the age of forty-three and culminating with the highest rank of grand archbishop (*daisōjō*) at sixty-seven. In 1002, he performed Esoteric services for Michinaga when he was ill, leading to his recovery; as a result, the following year, he was named abbot (*chōsha*) of the Shingon temple Tōji. He was again appointed to the post in 1023 and 1033. Jinkaku is credited with performing a number of Esoteric rituals that cured the illnesses of the imperial family, serving as the master of ceremonies at Michinaga's ordination in 1019, and conducting services to end droughts, but not with any scholarly works.[41] Jinkaku's career is typical of the successful monk from a noble family with its emphasis on the performance of rituals protecting the nobility and service in high administrative positions. In the next section of this chapter, some of these rituals are examined.

Ryōgen's Performance of Esoteric Rituals

The Private Performance of Esoteric Ritual

Mention has already been made of several of the Esoteric Buddhist ceremonies used by Ryōgen to ensure his relations with the Fujiwaras. This section begins with a consideration of state attempts to control Esoteric ritual and then focuses on the qualities that made Ryōgen a particularly able Esoteric practitioner.

The performance of an Esoteric ceremony for the benefit or prosperity of an individual or a particular group of people, often a family or clan, is typical of the Esoteric rituals performed during the tenth century. The private use of Esoteric rituals had flourished during the late Nara period, particularly during the turbulent period when the monk Dōkyō (d. 772) came close to usurping the throne and later during Emperor Kanmu's (737–806; r. 781–806) attempt to move the capital to Nagaoka. However, the court had strictly forbidden such private ceremonies as Emperor Kanmu had used to strengthen the Ritsuryō state during the early Heian period. Consequently, Saichō and Kūkai performed few such ceremonies. Saichō, for example, had performed ceremonies for the protection of the state and the emperor, but he had not performed them to ensure the prosperity of particular individuals other than members of the imperial family. Kūkai's Esoteric ceremonies were also primarily intended for the benefit of the state. When Esoteric rituals had been performed for private individuals, they had usually taken the form of memorial services for the deceased. This use of Esoteric Buddhism was consistent with the centralized Ritsuryō state under Emperor Kanmu and several of his successors.

As the more decentralized aristocratic state of the tenth century took shape, individuals began commissioning monks to perform Esoteric rituals for their own benefit. Esoteric rituals were no longer performed primarily for the emperor and the state. Signs of this change in the application of Esoteric rituals began appearing near the end of the ninth century. By 901, the court felt compelled to issue an edict reminding people about the prohibition on the private commissioning of ceremonies.

> According to an edict issued by the Ministry of Civil Administration on 10-5-785, "Monks, nuns, male and female lay believers all read *dhāraṇī* in order to attack those with whom they are angry; they perform Esoteric Buddhist ceremonies (*danpō*) and wantonly cast spells. From now on, unless an edict permitting it has been issued, no *dhāraṇī* are to be read or Esoteric ceremonies conducted in the mountains or at temples. If anyone violates this, he or she should be arrested and tried."
>
> The minister of the left [Tokihira] states that today people have forgotten the import of this edict and often perform such rituals. Because this could lead to the decline of Buddhism, the edict should again be proclaimed in government offices and the provinces. The various cere-

monies that focus on individual Buddhas, bodhisattvas, deities, and Ganesh [Shōden] are all prohibited. If a person is discovered performing such ceremonies, then he shall incur a serious crime. If a person knows of such activities, but does not inform the authorities, then he too should be severely punished. All such ceremonies should be prohibited except in the case of illnesses in which the names of both the patient and the presiding monk are recorded and submitted to the authorities and permission is obtained. Routine Esoteric ceremonies and prayers for the recovery of the ill are not the object of this prohibition.[42]

When Sugawara no Michizane (845–903) was demoted and sent to Dazai-fu in 901, the resulting political chaos once again opened the door to the use of Esoteric rituals by individuals. One of the first clear uses of an Esoteric ritual for an individual's benefit occurred in 903 when Morosuke's uncle, Tokihira (871–909), summoned the Tendai monk Sōō to perform a ceremony on behalf of his daughter Onshi, the junior consort, who was about to give birth. Sōō performed the ceremony of the Immovable King (Fudō myōō), and she delivered a child safely. A later investigation revealed that an old woman had been hired by Morosuke's father, Tadahira, to place a broken catalpa bow under Onshi's bed to curse her.[43] Thus Morosuke's father was one of the first to use religious rituals as a weapon in his private rivalries.

Much of Ryōgen's success was due to his use of Esoteric Buddhism to create and then strengthen his ties to particular factions of the nobility. Although the use of Esoteric rituals to protect major figures at court goes back to Saichō, Ennin, and Enchin, by Ryōgen's time the use of these had become inextricably entwined with the factions at court and eventually contributed to the growing factionalism within Buddhist schools.[44] Even Tendai monks reputed to be recluses saw the importance of these ties.

Ryōgen is not credited with the authorship of major works on Esoteric doctrine, as are Ennin, Enchin, and Annen. For the nobility with whom Ryōgen associated, Esoteric doctrine was abstruse and of little importance. They were primarily concerned with the performance of rituals that would benefit them in concrete ways. Ryōgen's interest in Esoteric Buddhism focused on such rituals. Although Ryōgen was said to have written several texts on Esoteric ritual, these must be considered of dubious authorship.[45]

Throughout his life Ryōgen performed Esoteric rituals and is credited with a number of major innovations in ritual. Below, Ryōgen's application and innovations in Esoteric ritual are considered in regard to three major Tendai ceremonies: (1) the ritual of the Seven Healing Buddhas (*shichi butsu yakushihō*), (2) the five-platform ceremony (*godanhō*), and (3) the ceremony of the Buddha of Abundant Light (*shijōkōhō*).

The Ritual of the Seven Healing Buddhas

When one of Morosuke's most important wives, Princess Kōshi (or Yasuko, d. 959), was about to give birth in 957, Ryōgen performed an Esoteric ceremony that focused on Bhaiṣajyaguru Tathāgata, the Healing Buddha and his six manifestations (*shichi butsu yakushi*).[46] Kōshi was the fourteenth daughter of Emperor Daigo and the younger sister of Emperors Suzaku and Murakami. She was a favorite of her father and later of her husband, Morosuke. In fact, Morosuke did not marry again after her death. Needless to say, Morosuke's close relation to an imperial princess was important in maintaining power. Kōshi died in childbirth two years later.[47] However, Ryōgen's performance of the ceremony in 957, followed by Kōshi's safe delivery, probably helped alleviate the anxiety Kōshi must have felt as well as won the gratitude of Morosuke and her imperial relatives.

Yakushi had long been popular in Japan as a Buddha closely connected with worldly gains. In Esoteric ceremonies, Yakushi was used primarily to prevent calamities and promote good fortune (*sokusai zōyaku*). The ceremony that Ryōgen performed was based on one that Ennin had performed for Emperor Ninmyō when Ninmyō was on his deathbed in 850. It had then fallen into disuse. Ryōgen revived its use and clarified the procedures to be followed in performing it. In fact, Ryōgen's efforts to clarify and organize the procedure to be followed in the ceremony resulted in his being credited by some sources as the person who originally devised it.[48] Ennin, in fact, had hung up pictures (*gazō*) of the seven Yakushi in front of a bamboo blind in the emperor's quarters (Seiryōden) at the palace to cure Emperor Ninmyō of an illness. However, Ryōgen used sculpted images, probably making the ceremony more impressive.

Ryōgen's efforts to revive the ceremony gave Tendai monks a clear claim to it as an exclusively Taimitsu ceremony. During the early and middle Heian period, Tendai monks had striven to develop rituals that would win them the support of the court and differentiate them from their rivals in the Shingon school. Many of the arguments they used to claim the right to sole performance of a ritual resembled the arguments put forth by Morosuke and Saneyori over court ritual: precedent, lineage, and procedure. Although Shingon monks performed rituals with a single Healing Buddha, they did not perform the ritual of the Seven Healing Buddhas until later, and even then most of their sources acknowledge that the ceremony was Taimitsu.[49] Thus Ryōgen played a major role in defining the ceremony as uniquely Tendai.

The ceremony itself was based on I-ching's translation of the *Ch'i-fo ching* and was used to cure illness, ensure safe birth, and deal with celestial anomalies such as eclipses.[50] After Ryōgen's time, it was performed frequently, but only by Tendai monks, and thus developed into one of the special ceremonies that the Tendai school used to accentuate their differences from the Shingon tradition. Ryōgen had revived a ceremony that was potentially more impressive than rituals common to both Tendai and Shingon that focused only on a single image of Yakushi. Using seven manifestations of Yakushi in the ritual meant that more altars and additional personnel could be used. Although only a single platform with seven images was used when the ceremony was performed for Morosuke's wife Princess Kōshi in 957, it subsequently developed into an elaborate ritual with several platforms and large numbers of officiating monks.[51] The ritual was eventually included as one in a list of four major Tendai Esoteric ceremonies (*sanmon shika daihō*).

The Five-Platform Ceremony

The five-platform ceremony was an elaboration on rituals focusing on the Immovable King (Fudō myōō). In the late tenth century, as the struggles between court factions increased, nobles came to increasingly believe in the powers of vengeful ghosts both to attack their enemies and protect their own faction. Monks responded to the situation by introducing Esoteric ceremonies that would enable a person to defeat (*gōbuku*) their enemies, both living and dead. The most commonly used ceremony for this purpose was the ritual for the Immovable King. Although this ceremony was also used to encourage good fortune and prevent calamities, it soon was primarily identified with the defeat of one's enemies. Ryōgen helped popularize these ceremonies among the nobility.[52]

In the second and eight months of 966, Ryōgen was summoned to the emperor's residence (Jijūden, literally, "hall of benevolence and longevity") to perform rituals to the Immovable King. He was accompanied by twenty monks (*bansō*).[53] In 967, when Emperor Reizei's insanity worsened, Ryōgen was summoned to the palace along with other eminent Tendai monks to perform the Five-platform ceremony, an elaborate variation of the Fudō ceremony. In 981, he officiated at the central platform (for the Immovable King) at a five-platform ceremony to help alleviate Emperor En'yū's (959–991; r. 969–984) illness. When the emperor recovered by the conclusion of the ceremony, everyone at court was very impressed, and Ryōgen was awarded the right to enter the palace in a hand-drawn carriage (*teguruma*), a privilege usually reserved for regents and aged grand ministers.[54]

The five-platform ceremony consisted of rituals performed on five altars to the five mystic kings (*godai myōō*): (1) Fudō (Acalanātha), (2) Gōzanze (Trailokyavijaya), (3) Gundari (Kuṇḍalī), (4) Daiitoku (Yamāntaka), and (5) Kongōyasha (Vajrayakṣa; or Ususama [Ucchuṣma] in Shingon and Jimon versions). Fudō myōō occupied the first altar, with the others arranged in a row (*rendan*). Eventually the altars were separated and arranged with Fudō myōō in the middle and the others in the four corners.[55] Although ceremonies on all five platforms were usually performed simultaneously, sometimes the ceremonies for each platform might be performed consecutively, each requiring ten days. Moreover, the ceremony performed at each altar was not always for the same goal, enabling the ceremony to be tailored to a variety of needs.

According to one source, the five-platform ritual was first performed in 940 at Hosshōji; but the same source also lists the first performance as occurring on Mount Hiei in 961.[56] Although Ryōgen did not participate in the performance in 961, he had been scheduled to do so. Thus he was certainly aware of it. The ceremony was not performed again until 967, when Ryōgen became the first person to conduct it at court. The five-platform ceremony typifies the trend that was developing during Ryōgen's lifetime toward the use of more elaborate ceremonies with more monks to defeat a patron's enemies. Prior to Ryōgen's time, a ceremony using a single platform with Fudō myōō would probably have been performed in similar situations. After Ryōgen's death, monks from the Sanmon (Ryōgen's) branch of the Tendai school continued to perform the five-platform ceremony, but it was also sometimes conducted by monks from both the Shingon school or the Jimon branch of the Tendai school.[57] As might be expected, the tendency of nobles to sponsor larger and more-elaborate ceremonies led to the decline of the single-altar Fudō myōō ceremony for subduing one's enemies. According to a comment dated 1046, "Ceremonies for subduing enemies usually consist of the ceremony of the five honored deities. Ceremonies for other Buddhas and bodhisattvas are not heard of very much."[58]

The Ritual of Abundant Light

The central figure in the ceremony of the Buddha of Abundant Light
is identified with several Buddhas, including the fierce aspect of Śākyamuni with light emanating from each of his hair follicles. Because Śākyamuni's light is brighter than that of any deity or heavenly body, all other
deities submit to him. In the main *maṇḍala* used for the ceremony at
the Sōjiin on Mount Hiei, the central figure was seated on the top of
Mount Sumeru with the world spread out below him; his position at the
center of the world was equivalent to that of the ruler.[59] In addition,
the central figure was identified with the polestar, around which all other
stars revolved, a Taoist and yin-yang (*onmyōdō*) association that contributed to the use of the ceremony for the ruler.[60] The ceremony was
appropriate whenever there were any unusual celestial phenomena,
such as a solar or lunar eclipse or an inauspicious alignment of the plan-
ets. Because such astrological phenomena were thought to adversely affect the star on which the emperor's life depended (*honmyōshō*), the *shijōkōhō* was performed to compensate for astrological anomalies. The
ceremony itself was based on the *goma* rite with offerings made in a fire.

The *shijōkōhō* was based on a ceremony performed in China at the
Ching-lung-ssu in Ch'ang-an to bring the emperor long life.[61] It was
first performed in Japan in 850, three years after Ennin had returned
from his studies in China. On 3-21-850, Emperor Ninmyō died; one
month later, on 4-17-850, the crown prince (Emperor Montoku, 827–
858; r. 850–858) was to be installed as the new emperor. Four days before the enthronement ceremonies, Ennin was asked by the future emperor in a letter conveyed by the middle captain of the left bodyguards
(*sakon'e no chūjō*), Fujiwara no Yoshimi, to chant the large *Prajñāpāra-
mitāsūtra* from the fifteenth through the eighteenth so that his reign
might be successful; but on 4-15, Ennin suggested that a new Esoteric
ceremony would be appropriate. When Yoshimi asked for clarification,
Ennin explained that the ceremony for the Buddha of Abundant Light
was used in China and was particularly efficacious as a ceremony to vanquish calamities and invite good fortune. In doing so, he described a
ritual that only he knew how to perform and that could not be carried
out by his Shingon or Tendai rivals.

Finally, on 9-4-850, the court authorized the performance of the ceremony by Ennin with twenty-seven monks. Ten days later, fourteen
monks were appointed as masters of Esoteric Buddhism who were to
perform the ceremony day and night in shifts.[62] They were to be in-

stalled in the Sōjiin, a structure that required ten years for construction (851–860).[63] This hall, supposedly built on land that Saichō had designated several decades earlier, was elaborate. It included one thousand copies of the *Lotus Sūtra;* eventually the Eastern Pagoda Hall (Tōdōin), one of the central institutions of Mount Hiei, was moved to the Sōjiin and performances of the Lotus meditation were held there.[64] The court lavishly supported the monks who served at it with grants of rice, cloth, and attendants. The financial and human resources of the hall, as well as the vital rituals performed to ensure the emperor's longevity, made it the centerpiece of Ennin's Esoteric Buddhist program. With the establishment of the Sōjiin, Ennin had created an institution that could rival the Shingon'in (Mantra chapel) established in the palace by Kūkai in 834.

The continual practice of the ceremony for the Buddha of Abundant Light was eventually abandoned as subsequent emperors and their patrons favored other temples, teachers, and ceremonies. When monks from Enchin's lineage were appointed *zasu*, they encouraged Esoteric rituals at their own temples and halls rather than at the Sōjiin.[65] However, when the *zasu* was from Ennin's lineage, the ceremony was still performed for the protection of the state and the emperor. The Sanmon branch of the Tendai school jealously guarded the ceremony, and it was not performed by either Shingon or Jimon monks. The ceremony itself was secret and used a *maṇḍala* that was laid out on a platform (*shiki-mandara*), rather than a painting to be hung in back of the platform (*kake-mandara*) that people could more easily see.[66]

Like several of the Tendai *zasu* before him, Ryōgen performed the *shijōkōhō* for emperors. He found that it fit in well with the attitudes of many of the nobility. For example, in his instructions to his descendants, Morosuke had suggested that the star controlling one's destiny should be called upon seven times upon awakening.[67] Tadahira, Morosuke, Saneyori, and their descendants were vitally interested in yin-yang techniques and applied them to various taboos concerning whether they should venture outside and which directions were safe. One of the most visible manifestations of their interest is found in the frequency with which era names were changed. During the fifteen-year reign of Emperor En'yū, the era name was changed five times because of such problems as earthquakes, fires, and unbalances among the five elements.[68] The prevailing beliefs in yin-yang and astrology resulted in an atmosphere conducive to the revival of the *shijōkōhō*.

In 975, Ryōgen performed the *shijōkōhō* at court along with twenty monks, including Morosuke's son Jinzen. As a reward, Ryōgen received one novice and was appointed supernumerary greater bishop (*gon-daisōzu*), and Jinzen was appointed supernumerary lesser bishop (*gon-shōsōzu*).[69]

In 977, Ryōgen departed from the precedent of reserving the ceremony for emperors when he performed it for the chancellor, Fujiwara no Kanemichi (925–977), who had a grave illness.[70] The chancellor is said to have recovered during the ceremony, though he died later that year. The performance of such an exalted ceremony in an unprecedented way for his patrons furthered his relations with the Fujiwaras. In fact, Ryōgen was appointed supernumerary archbishop as a result of his efforts, and several of the participating monks were appointed supernumerary masters of discipline. Prior to that time, the *shijōkōhō* had rarely been performed for nobles.[71] Ryōgen's use of the ritual to prevent calamity and bring good fortune for a patron from the nobility represent an important change in the use of the ceremony. It is also typical of Ryōgen's tendency to base his ritual performances on precedents set by Ennin as part of his program to revive and advance the fortunes of his lineage. Once again, Ryōgen was applying Esoteric ceremonies in new ways to serve his patrons.

Conclusion

Much of Ryōgen's popularity amongst the nobility was based on his accomplishments as a master of Esoteric Buddhism. Ryōgen was not alone in his use of Esoteric ritual; during the Heian period many monks attained high office through their mastery of Esoteric Buddhist ritual.[72] Although Ryōgen portrayed himself as firmly in Ennin's lineage, carefully adhering to precedent, in fact he was an innovator who revived a number of ceremonies that had been introduced by Ennin, using ceremonies for new purposes and adding new elements to older ceremonies to make them more impressive. Ryōgen constantly referred back to precedents set by Ennin in his use of Esoteric Buddhist ritual, an aspect of his activities that contributed to the factionalism that was developing in the Tendai school at that time.

After his death, Ryōgen became the subject of a large number of legends concerning his seemingly superhuman powers of discernment, qualities that presumably arose from his mastery of Esoteric ritual. According to the *Gishaku sōketsushō*, Ryōgen and Kanchō, one of the most eminent monks from the Shingon school, were commanded to participate in a five-platform ceremony at court in 981. When Emperor En'yū peeked through a curtain at the monks and looked toward Ryōgen, who was at the central platform dedicated to the Immovable King, he saw that Ryōgen looked exactly like the Immovable King with a fire in back of him, a sword in his right hand, and a rope in his left hand. When he looked toward Kanchō, he saw that he looked like Gōzanze myōō (Skt. Trailokyavijaya or Vajrahūṁkāra), the wisdom-king at whose altar he was practicing. However, Kanchō's appearance changed over time, probably because his concentration wavered, while Ryōgen's appearance remained constant.[73] Thus the legend compared the most eminent monks from the Tendai and Shingon schools, with the Tendai school emerging on top.

Ryōgen's skill at Esoteric ritual was certainly responsible for the strong alliance that he formed with Morosuke. However, personal friendship must also have played an important role. Both men were seeming underdogs early in their careers, struggling to make a name for themselves against men who were their superiors. Both were intensely loyal to their families or followers, vitally interested in ritual, and approximately the same age. Morosuke's decision to entrust his son Jinzen to Ryōgen and Ryōgen's careful treatment of Jinzen are evidence of the depth of their feelings for each other. However, Ryōgen's friendship with Morosuke would be cut short by Morosuke's death; as a result, Ryōgen faced new challenges.

6

The Ōwa Debates

The Death of Morosuke

Ryōgen's major patron, Morosuke, had begun to sicken by the beginning of 960. Because Morosuke was concerned about the future of his lineage, he had the ranks of five of his sons raised on 1-7-960. Before this time, nobles had raised the ranks of at most three sons at one time. The rank of another son, Takamitsu, was raised shortly afterward. When he had become ill, Morosuke had expressed a desire to be ordained as a monk and live in Yokawa. Work soon began on quarters for Morosuke at Yokawa, and Morosuke was ordained on 5-1-960, even though the emperor asked him to wait. In addition, fifteen men were initiated as novices so that the karmic merit from their ordinations might be made to aid in Morosuke's recovery. Despite these efforts, Morosuke died four days later, before he ever realized his desire to live at Yokawa.[1]

Ordinations were often administered to the nobility on their deathbed or in life-threatening situations, such as childbirth. In many cases, particularly near the end of the Heian period, such ordinations were often related to a belief that the ordination would result in enough karmic merit to heal an illness or help an individual through childbirth.[2] Even if the recipient died, many believed that the ordination would help him or her be reborn in the Pure Land. In many cases, the recipient had little intention of ever observing the precepts. For example, ordinations were administered to children who were too young to understand the vows. In some cases, if the patient's health did not improve, an additional ordination was conferred. In such cases, the ordination was clearly considered to be a merit-making ceremony or deathbed sacrament rather than an initiation into a religious life.[3] Morosuke's desire to be ordained was almost certainly based on genuine religious sentiment and interest in Buddhism, but the belief that the ordination might help him recover his health, or at least ensure a good rebirth, also must have influenced him.

On 5-4-960, Morosuke died at the height of his power, without seeing Norihira, the grandson he had striven to have named crown prince, crowned. His death at the relatively young age of fifty-two, the peak of his career, was mourned by many. In addition, his premature death played a role in the belief that he would become an angry ghost because he had died without realizing his ambitions. Emperor Murakami, who had taken Morosuke's daughter Anshi as wife and then made her empress, was said to have been so distraught at Morosuke's untimely death that he considered abdicating.[4]

Even though Morosuke had raised his sons' ranks, they were still too young to take leading roles in government. They eventually would prevail, and two of Morosuke's grandsons would become emperor. However, the next ten years would be a dangerous time: Morosuke's sons would have to preserve their positions at court and consolidate their power while waiting for a chance to advance themselves. Morosuke's death also affected Ryōgen because he had allied himself so closely to Morosuke and his sons.

During the years that Morosuke was the most powerful man in government, he had remained minister of the right. His older brother Saneyori, had, in fact, outranked him as minister of the left, but Saneyori had been content to play a passive role in government. With Morosuke dead, Saneyori became more active. By 967, he had become regent (*kanpaku*), and in 969 he became *sesshō,* an even higher degree of regent, ranks that Morosuke had never attained. In contrast, Morosuke's oldest son, Koremasa, only advanced to the post of adviser (*sangi*) during Saneyori's lifetime, certainly due in part to the understated rivalry between Morosuke and Saneyori.

The Ōwa Debates

In 961, shortly after Morosuke's death, Ryōgen was forty-nine and had just lost his most important patron. As a result, he began to take action to ensure that the northern house of the Fujiwara clan would remain aware of his contributions. At the same time, he must have hoped to consolidate his influence within the Tendai school. The result was the Ōwa debates, named after the era, Ōwa (961–964) in which they were held. The account below follows the *Ōwa shūronki* (Record of the Ōwa debates), supplementing it with other sources. A translation of this source is in appendix 5.

On 4-18-961, Ryōgen went to the court and suggested that the Hossō school's traditional domination of the six Nara schools was unfair to the other Nara schools. Emperor Murakami, a cousin of Morosuke, did not object. One month later (5-15), Ryōgen is said to have written to two Tōdaiji monks, Genkei (892–966) of the Kegon school and Ittei (884–947) of the Sanron school, about his dissatisfaction with Hossō dominance, thereby skillfully exploiting divisions within the Nara schools.[5] In Ryōgen's letter, he raised the question of whether the leader of the Hossō school should head the Nara schools. Because the abbot of Kōfukuji, the Fujiwara clan temple (*ujidera*), dominated the Hossō school, Ryōgen was questioning the whole system by which Kōfukuji monks had come to occupy the preeminent position in the Buddhist world.[6] In effect, Ryōgen was challenging the institution that had traditionally been patronized by much of the Fujiwara clan, a strategy that had become possible because the Fujiwara clan had divided into factions with each group requiring its own religious center.

During the next six months, the court received separate petitions concerning Hossō domination from the Kegon, Sanron, and Tendai schools. As a result, in the third month of 962, the court asked the various schools to submit evaluations of the relative merits of their teachings so that the court could judge them. However, before the schools could submit their reports, the format of the competition was changed. Because Emperor Murakami had copied the *Lotus Sūtra*,[7] the various schools were to present their views on this text at a series of lectures for the dedication of the imperial text. After three postponements, the debates were held for five days beginning on 8-21-963.

The debates attracted a considerable amount of interest from the court. Although debates and lectures were held in conjunction with a number of annual assemblies such as the Yuima-e at prominent monasteries, the Ōwa debates were to be held in the emperor's living quarters (Seiryōden). Monks from the Tendai and Nara schools (mostly Hossō monks) would directly oppose each other in every lecture. Because Ryōgen had directly challenged Hossō dominance of the six Nara schools, the stakes were high. The debates would focus on the *Lotus Sūtra*, a text about which the participating schools had rich commentarial traditions, suggesting that the arguments would be stimulating.

Finally, the intellectual content of the debates must have attracted attention of the court. The parables of the *Lotus Sūtra* made it one of the more understandable texts for lay believers. In addition, during the Nara and early Heian periods, the *Lotus* had been used for its magical efficacy to protect the nation, vanquish sins, or memorialize the dead. Saichō strongly recommended that the *Lotus* be chanted to protect the nation. With the establishment of the Tendai school, nobles gradually became interested in the content of the text. Saichō's lay patrons had been concerned with the Tendai interpretation of the *Lotus*. Saichō's famous defense of the *Lotus* had been conducted as a private exchange with the Hossō monk Tokuitsu and thus was probably not known widely by lay believers. However, by the early tenth century, the *Lotus* was frequently used as a subject of lectures, often for memorial services, at which members of the court were in attendance.[8] At the same time, chanting the *Lotus* as a magical text to eliminate disasters was declining, and perfection of wisdom *sūtras* had come to be mentioned more often than the *Lotus* in edicts asking that texts be chanted for protection.[9] However, Lotus meditations were still used to eliminate sins (*metsuzai*) or in hopes of having one's clan prosper. These uses of the *Lotus* did not preclude an intellectual interest by nobles in the teachings of the text. When the biographies of nobles such as Fujiwara no Michinaga (966–1037) and Fujiwara no Sanesuke (957–1046) are considered, the important place of lectures on the *Lotus Sūtra* becomes evident. Michinaga sponsored lectures on the *Lotus Sūtra* that were attended by nobles; the lectures of 1008 usually had between six and fourteen nobles in the audience. Sanesuke employed monks permanently at his mansion, built a hall dedicated to the *Lotus Sūtra,* and sponsored a series of thirty lectures on the text that lasted two and a half years.[10] Thus when the issues of its interpretation were explored in a direct confrontation in the palace, it must have attracted considerable attention. Some of this interest undoubtedly may have been superficial, an attempt to feign concern for issues only because powerful people were attracted to the subject, but more than a few nobles must have found the debates compelling. The *Shōyūki,* Fujiwara no Sanesuke's detailed diary, reveals that he frequently listened to lectures on Buddhist *sūtras.* Moreover, the interest of nobles was not limited to the intellectual side of Buddhism; some practiced the Lotus meditation.

The Ōwa debates were to consist of ten lectures on the eight-fascicle *Lotus Sūtra* and two associated one-fascicle *sūtras,* the *Wu-liang-i ching* (Sūtra of innumerable meanings) and *Kuan p'u-hsien ching* (Sūtra of the contemplation on Samantabhadra). These two texts were considered

TABLE 6

INITIAL LIST OF PARTICIPANTS
IN THE ŌWA DEBATES FROM THE NARA SCHOOLS

Name	School	Rank	Temple	Age in 963
Kanri[1]	Sanron	master of discipline	Tōdaiji	69
Genkei[2]	Kegon	master of discipline	Tōdaiji	68
Anshū[3]	Hossō	lecturer	Kōfukuji	71
Hōzō	Hossō	lecturer	Tōdaiji	56
Ninga	Hossō		Kōfukuji	
Tanshō[4]	Hossō		Tōdaiji	54
Hyōshū[5]	Hossō		Tōdaiji	
Senri	Hossō		unknown	
Shinki[6]	Hossō		Kōfukuji	33
Chūzan	Hossō		Kōfukuji	28

1. According to the *Honchō kōsōden* (*BZ* [Suzuki ed.], 63:69a–b), Kanri (894?–974) was from an impoverished family from Nara named Taira. His father died when he was young, and Kanri wished to help his mother through his prayers, eventually becoming a monk. Fujiwara no Tadahira is said to have taken an interest in the young monk and asked him to help remove a curse. If this account is correct, he may have known Ryōgen through Tadahira. Kanri first studied Hossō at Kōfukuji. Later he studied Sanron and Esoteric Buddhism at Daigoji with Enchin (862–929), a disciple of Shōbō who had combined Sanron with Esoteric Buddhist studies. Because of his connections with Enchin, Kanri was listed as a Tōdaiji monk (of the Tōnan'in) from the Sanron school in many documents, but his doctrinal interests seem to have focused on Hossō. He served as lecturer at the Yuima-e in 952; in 960 he was appointed supernumerary master of discipline and abbot of Daigoji. In 968, he was appointed greater bishop and the next year, abbot of Tōdaiji. Among his works is a fifteen-fascicle work on Yogācāra titled *Yuishikishō* (Essays on consciousness-only) and a text on logic, the *Inmyō shishu sōi shiki* (Private record concerning four logical errors). His interests in Esoteric Buddhism might have made him conciliatory toward Tendai; in 972, he presided over a ritual at Sōjiin on Mount Hiei as the monk reading the vows (*dōshi*). Moreover, earlier in his career he had participated in several rituals other than the Ōwa debates that focused on the *Lotus Sūtra* (*NS* 1.14:395–396). For an analysis of Kanri and his works, see Ueda Kōen, *Nihon jōdai ni okeru yuishiki no kenkyū*, pp. 7–13.
2. Genkei (892–966) was lecturer at the Yuima-e in 954, appointed supernumerary master of discipline in 961, master of discipline in 964, and supernumerary lesser bishop in 965.
3. Anshū (890?–971) studied Hossō under Hyōgen of Kōfukuji, served as lecturer at the Yuima-e in 958, as lesser bishop in the Office of Monastic Affairs in 971, and as abbot of Kōfukuji in 967 (*NS* 1.13:317–319).
4. Tanshō (909–987) served as lecturer at the Yuima-e in 966, was appointed master of discipline in 974, abbot of Tōdaiji in 978, and supernumerary lesser bishop in 981 (*NS* 1.17:66–67, 2.1:213).
5. Hyōshū served as a candidate at the Yuima-e in 955 (*Sanne jōitsuki*, BZ 123:298).
6. Shinki (932?–1000) was from the Taira clan; he was a candidate (*rissha*) at the Yuima-e in 964, lecturer in 975, supernumerary master of discipline in 982, and abbot of Kō

to the opening and capping *sūtras* for the *Lotus*. The three texts totaled ten fascicles. Thus each lecture concerned one fascicle. Two monks would participate in each lecture, one as the main lecturer (*dōshi*) and the second as a questioner (*monja*), who criticized the lecture. Twenty monks were to participate. The series was completed by an eleventh lecture that was to be given by the monk who did the first.

Ten of the participating monks were from the Nara schools, eight of them from the Hossō School, one from the Kegon school, and one from the Sanron school. Although representatives of the Kegon and Sanron schools had supported Ryōgen's petitions, they had traditionally been grouped with the Hossō school as the six Nara schools. The ten monks from the Nara schools included one master of discipline, one supernumerary master of discipline, two monks who had served as lecturers at the three major assemblies in Nara (*ikō*) but had not yet received appointments to the Sōgō, and Hōzō (905–969), a monk famed for his scholarship. Moreover, many of the lesser-known Hossō participants such as Shinki and Tanshō would later become major figures in their school. The monks initially invited to participate on the Nara side are listed in table 6.[11]

The Nara schools had assembled an impressive array of monks to represent them. In contrast, the ten monks on the Tendai side had few eminent monks on it. Ryōgen did not invite a number of Tendai monks who would have seemed like natural choices. For example, Ryōgen ignored Tendai monks such as Shunsen (900–964), who had been appointed supernumerary master of discipline in 963, and Zengei (903–980), who would serve as lecturer at the Yuima-e in the tenth month of 963, two months after the Ōwa debates.[12] Other eminent Tendai monks who were not asked were Archbishop Enshō, Greater Bishop Chinchō, Master of Discipline Kikyō, and Supernumerary Master of Discipline Bōsan.[13] Instead, Zen'yu[14] (912 or 913–990) was the only monk older than the fifty-one-year-old Ryōgen. In a society in which older monks were respected for their wisdom, this might put the Tendai school at a disadvantage. Zen'yu, Shōku, and Kakugyō were Ryōgen's disciples. Most of the rest were probably from Ennin's faction of the lineage, al-

---

fukuji in 983. In 996, he delivered the admonition to practice when retired emperor En'yū took the ten precepts and became a novice. By 994 he had risen to archbishop. He served as the teacher of Fujiwara no Michitaka (957–999), Kaneie's eldest son, and supervised the dedication of the Shakuzenji, founded by Michitaka (*NS* 2.3:709–713).

TABLE 7

LIST OF INITIAL INVITEES FROM
THE TENDAI SCHOOL AND THEIR MONASTIC AFFILIATIONS

Zen'yu	Enryakuji
Ryōgen	Enryakuji
Chikō[1]	Onjōji
Juchō[2]	
Shōku	Enryakuji
Senkan	
Zōga	Enryakuji
Yokei[3]	Onjōji
Nōe	
Gashū[4]	Tendai

1. Little is known of Chikō, but in the *Honchō kōsōden* biography of Shinki he is said to be from Onjōji (*BZ* [Suzuki ed.], 63: 71b).
2. The characters for Juchō are listed in small characters in the *Ōwa shūronki* (*BZ* [Bussho kankōkai ed.], 124: 87b), as though they were a note concerning a temple affiliation or activities at the debate, but they should clearly be in large characters indicating that he was one of the ten Tendai monks originally invited to participate. Nothing is known of his life.
3. Senkan is discussed in several other chapters in this study; Zōga is discussed below in this chapter. For a biography of Yokei, a monk from Enchin's lineage who would later rise to be one of Ryōgen's major competitors, see chapter 11 on Ryōgen and factionalism.
4. Nothing is known of Nōe. Little is known of Gashū, but he was posthumously appointed greater bishop in 1021 (Hirabayashi and Koike, *Sōryaku sōran*, p. 31).

though Yokei, Senkan, and Chikō were from Enchin's faction of the Tendai school. If a victory were won, it would belong primarily to Ryōgen and Ennin's lineage rather than to the Tendai school as a whole. The initial list of Tendai monks invited and their affiliations, when known, are listed in table 7.

Four of the participants originally chosen decided not to participate: Ninga and Senri of the Hossō school (see Table 6) and Senkan and Zōga of the Tendai school. They were replaced by Zōsō[15] and Sentō[16], both of the Hossō school, and Kakugyō and Suju of the Tendai school. Zōsō of the Hossō school also declined and was replace by Engei of the Sanron school, making a total of two Sanron participants.[17] The final schedule for the debates is shown in table 8.[18]

The debates began with Kanri lecturing on the *Wu-liang-i ching* and Yokei as the questioner. Although Yokei's questions were difficult,

TABLE 8

LECTURERS AND QUESTIONERS AT THE ŌWA DEBATES

	Time	Lecturer	Questioner
Day 1	Morning	Kanri (Sanron)	Yokei (Tendai)
	Evening	Genkei[1] (Kegon)	Nōe (Tendai)
Day 2	Morning	Anshū (Hossō)	Gashū (Tendai)
	Evening	Hōzō (Hossō)	Kakugyō (Tendai) (aided by Ryōgen)
Day 3	Morning	Ryōgen (Tendai)	Hyōshū (later replaced by Hōzō [Hossō] by imperial command)
	Evening	Zen'yu (Tendai)	Sentō (Hossō)
Day 4	Morning	Chikō (Tendai)	Shinki (Hossō)
	Evening	Tanshō (Hossō)	Suju (Tendai)
Day 5	Morning	Juchō (Tendai)	Ninga (Hossō); replaced by Chūzan (Hossō)
	Evening	Shōku (Tendai); replaced by Ryōgen?	Engei; replaced by Chūzan
Day 6	Concluding lecture		Kanri (Sanron)

1. Ankyō (897?–977), a Sanron monk from Yakushiji, is listed instead of Genkei in some later accounts (*Genkō shakusho, BZ* 62:198c; *Jinden ainōshō, BZ* 150:397).

Kanri is said to have replied with impressive eloquence.[19] The rest of the first day and the morning of the second day were completed without any problem. However, when the Hossō scholar Hōzō lectured during the afternoon of the second day, he advanced the Hossō tenet that some people lacked the seeds that would permit them to realize arhathood, *pratyekabuddhahood,* or Buddhahood. They could not acquire the seeds to realize these goals through practice, and thus were condemned forever to the realm of rebirth, never attaining any permanent spiritual goal. In addition, those who became arhats or *pratyekabuddhas* could never go on to realize Buddhahood. Hōzō's argument is said to have been based on a passage from the *Lotus Sūtra* that was read by Tendai monks as stating, "Of those who hear this teaching, there is not one who will not realize Buddhahood" (*hitori to shite jōbutsu sezaru nashi*).[20] This passage thus supported the Tendai position that everyone, without exception, could realize Buddhahood, a stance that was directly contrary to Hossō doctrine. Hōzō is said to have argued that this passage should be punctuated differently and read as meaning "Even if they hear this teaching, the one [group of those] without [the seeds for Buddhahood] will not realize Buddhahood" (*mu no ichi wa jōbutsu sezu*). The Tendai questioner Kakugyō argued for the Tendai position that all could realize Buddhahood, but he could not effectively refute Hōzō.

Kakugyō's role in the debate has been a subject of interest for modern scholars. Kakugyō took the place that had originally been assigned to Zōga, an able debater. At the time Kakugyō was a young Tendai monk;[21] his opponent, the experienced Hossō monk Hōzō (905?–969), clearly outmatched him. Although Hōzō soundly defeated Kakugyō, Hōzō's argument prepared the way for Ryōgen to intervene and defeat Hōzō the following day. Because Ryōgen played a central role in organizing the debates, he might very well have urged Kakugyō to draw Hōzō into the debate on the Buddha-nature so that Ryōgen could then directly challenge Hōzō. By defeating Hōzō, Ryōgen gained substantial prestige. If the above scenario is correct, then Zōga may have been unwilling to participate in Ryōgen's plan. Kakugyō eventually rose to the highest ranks in the monastic world, being appointed Tendai *zasu* in 998, archbishop in 1000, and grand archbishop in 1001. Hirabayashi has argued that Ryōgen may have promised Kakugyō his support in attaining high office in return for his participation in the Ōwa debates.[22] While Ryōgen's support certainly played a role in Kakugyō's rise, Kakugyō's grandfather was the major counselor (*dainagon*) Taira no Koremochi (881–939), a cousin of Fujiwara no Tadahira, indicating that family ties helped him advance.

According to the *Jie daishiden,* Ryōgen could not restrain himself from interrupting the discussion to defend the Tendai position, whereupon Hōzō asked that they continue the next day because it was already about 8:30 at night.[23] The next morning Ryōgen was scheduled to serve as questioner, but at the imperial command, the Hossō monk Hyōshū was appointed questioner and Ryōgen was allowed to continue his criticisms of Hōzō's arguments.[24] Because Hōzō was being criticized, it was decided that Hōzō should replace Hyōshū as questioner so that he could defend himself. Finally, Hōzō broke off the debate and asked, "Your rhetoric is like that of Pūrṇa (*maitrāyaṇīputra*). How can I match it?"[25] According to the Hossō history of the debates, the members of the court who had listened to the proceedings were moved by Ryōgen's elegant defense of the Tendai position.[26]

Who was Hōzō and why should Ryōgen have been so concerned with defeating him? Hōzō was born in Kyoto and was a member of the Fujiwara family, though his exact parentage is not known. According to the *Asabashō,* some sources claimed that he was a direct disciple of the Tendai monk Jōzō (891–964), a connection that might have given him access to Tendai teachings on a variety of subjects, including astrology.[27] He had studied Yogācāra, Sanron, and Esoteric Buddhism under many of the best minds of his day. He had been appointed lecturer at the Yuima-e in 960 and was recognized as one of the most scholarly monks of his day. Appointments as master of discipline in 964, abbot of Tōdaiji in 965, and lesser bishop in 968 followed. He was the author of several books including the *Hannya genmon* (Profound sentences concerning the perfection of wisdom; 10 fascicles), the *Hannya rishubun shiki* (3 fascicles), and a work on logic, the *Inmyō nisshōriron sho* (Commentary on Śāṅkarasvāmin's *Nyāyapravekśaka,* an introduction to Dignāga's views on logic that was popular in East Asia).[28] The *Hannya rishubun shiki* was probably a text on Esoteric Buddhism. In addition, Hōzō was a noted specialist in astrology (*sukuyō*), a topic that vitally concerned the court. In 961, he performed a weeklong astrological ceremony at the Jissōin at Tōdaiji that required nine other monks. That same year, he was also engaged in a debate with Kamo no Yasunori (917–977), the most noted astrologer of that time, over the proper way to determine the astral influences that influenced Emperor Murakami. The debate undoubtedly caught the attention of Morosuke's sons who, like their father, were vitally interested in astrology.[29] Thus, with his family connections to the nobility, his skill in exoteric Buddhism, and his abilities in astrology and Esoteric Buddhism, Hōzō was a serious rival to Ryōgen for influence with Morosuke's sons. In fact, along with Gishō and Ryōgen, Hōzō was considered to be one of the three most important monks for Morosuke's family. According to one person's dream, the three monks were manifestations of celestial bodies that appeared in this world to protect Morosuke and his family.[30]

Fujiwara no Fuminori's Efforts to Defeat Ryōgen

When it was evident that Ryōgen had been victorious over Hōzō, Fujiwara no Fuminori (909–996), head of the Ministry of Popular Affairs, traveled to the Kasuga Shrine in Nara to pray for help. According to the *Ōwa shūron nikki,* Fuminori was disturbed that the Fujiwara clan temple, Kōfukuji, was not only losing the debates, but also not even showing much fight. He chose Kasuga Shrine because of its close relationship with Kōfukuji and because Kasuga Myōjin was the Fujiwara clan deity (*ujigami*). He was met at the Kasuga Shrine by the Hossō monk Chūzan of Kōfukuji, scheduled to participate in the last lecture.[31] The two men must have traveled much of the night to return to Kyoto.

Although Fuminori might seem like a supporter of Hossō at first, his biography reveals that he was much more interested in Tendai. Fuminori, the great-grandson of the official and poet Nagayoshi (802–856) and son of the counselor Motona (885–965), served as head of the Ministry of Popular Affairs from 970 to 996 and middle counselor from 971 to 988, eventually rising to the junior grade of the second rank. His father had been an exemplary official, and Fuminori also became a powerful official. Because he was from a different branch of the northern house of the Fujiwara family, only distantly related to Morosuke, he felt no obligation to support Ryōgen. In fact, he probably felt that his family was competing with Morosuke's lineage. His interest in preventing the defeat of the Nara schools was probably not based on doctrinal considerations. In fact, he helped found the Fumonji, a Tendai temple on the western foot of Mount Hiei, sometime between 959 and 964, about the time of the Ōwa debates. One of Fuminori's youngest sons, Myōchō, (964–1014) was head of the Fumonji and was succeeded by his younger brother Mon'en (b. 986).[32] The two brothers devoted themselves to performing Esoteric Buddhist ceremonies for members of their family in much the same manner that Ryōgen had performed them for Morosuke and his lineage.

Myōchō was educated by Yokei and other monks of Enchin's lineage, and many of the Esoteric rituals performed by Myōchō were peculiar to Enchin's lineage of Tendai just as Ryōgen's were distinctive of Ennin's lineage. Fuminori helped establish another temple, the Daiunji, also in Iwakura at the western foot of Mount Hiei. Daiunji was presided over by Shinkaku (lay name Fujiwara no Sukemasa, d. 998), who had been married to Fuminori's daughter. In addition, the Shugakuin was founded and presided over by Kanshu (945–1008), the son of one of his retainers. These temples, on the outskirts of Kyoto (in modern Iwakura), provided the monks of Enchin's lineage with ready access to the capital and to the nobles they were serving. The roles that Fuminori's sons played in the temples and their appointments as abbots of them are reminiscent of the relationship between Ryōgen and Morosuke's son Jinzen. Later when Ryōgen opposed the appointment of

Yokei to a number of high posts, Fuminori supported Yokei, again demonstrating his antipathy for Ryōgen and his patrons. When the Tendai monks in Enchin's lineage fled Mount Hiei, temples such as Fumonji, Daiunji, and Shugakuin provided many of them with shelter.[33] Fuminori was thus one of Yokei's most important patrons. Thus Fuminori's support for the Hossō side at the Ōwa debates can be understood only in the context of the political factions at the capital, not as motivated by his approval of Hossō doctrine.

Returning to the Ōwa debates—Kasuga Myōjin is said to have helped Chūzan defeat Ryōgen in the next important event in the debates.

Ryōgen's Debate with Chūzan

According to the *Ōwa shūron nikki,* the debates continued following the preapproved schedule for the next few days. Finally, during the lecture by the Tendai monk Juchō that had been scheduled for the morning of the fifth day, the questioner, a young Hossō monk named Chūzan (also read as Chūsan; and sometimes known as Matsumuro, the name of his lodgings; 935–976) renewed the attack on the Tendai position concerning the universality of the Buddha-nature. The court was so impressed with Chūzan's arguments that he was commanded to continue his role as questioner in the next lecture. In addition, the court asked that a problem in logic be given in the last lecture. Because logic was a specialty of Hossō monks, this probably would have resulted in an impressive victory for Chūzan, who was known for his mastery of the subject. However, the Sanron monk Kanri objected, arguing that logic was not a suitable subject for a lay audience. Kanri was one of the most eminent monks at the debate. At that time, he had already lectured at the Yuima-e, had been appointed master of discipline in the Office of Monastic Affairs, and probably already had written his two works on logic, the *Inmyō nisshōriron shoki* (Subcommentary on Śāṅkarasvāmin's *Nyāyapraveśaka;* not extant) and the *Inmyō shishu sōi shiki* (Private record concerning four logical errors; *T* no. 2275). Because of Kanri's objections, the court agreed to continue the debates without a problem in logic. During the period for questions, Chūzan argued for the existence of *icchantikas,* those without Buddha-nature. He went on to attack Ryōgen's assertion that all had the Buddha-nature, attacking and belittling each point, arguing so eloquently that all in the audience were touched by his words. Instead of replying, Ryōgen sat silently and stared and made no reply to Chūzan's attacks.[34]

Because Ryōgen was not originally scheduled to speak on the fifth day, the description in the *Ōwa shūron nikki* of his silence may indicate that the court had asked him to participate on that day. Ryōgen's silence has been interpreted in a number of ways. Hirabayashi notes that Ryōgen had already skillfully presented his position and achieved his goal by attracting the support of the nobles in the audience. His silence was evidence of his tact and tolerance.[35] Neil McMullin suggests that Chūzan was an unknown monk of little political consequence, whereas Hōzō's Fujiwara relations had made him a worthy opponent.[36] Although these are both possible explanations for Ryōgen's silence, Chūzan's prowess as a scholar made him an imposing opponent, one whom Ryōgen may have been hesitant to face. Moreover, since Chūzan was barely thirty years old at the time of the Ōwa debates and had no official rank, Ryōgen had little to gain by defeating him and might have lost respect if he had been defeated.[37] Some biographical information about Chūzan helps to complete the background for this episode in the Ōwa debates.

Nothing is known of Chūzan's family.[38] He studied under the Hossō master Kūshō of Kōfukuji, entering the monastery at the age of twelve. A precocious child, he was skilled in debate, but is said to have been uninterested in a political career in monastic circles, several times refusing to serve as a lecturer at the Yuima-e.[39] He eventually was appointed the administrator of Saidaiji in Nara. His dislike of high office resulted in very sparse biographies; for example, most of the entries on Chūzan in both the *Genkō shakusho* and the *Honchō kōsōden* are devoted to the Ōwa debate.[40] However, a survey of his writings serves as evidence of the quality of his scholarship. He is credited with the authorship of several works on the *Lotus Sūtra:* the *Hokke shakumon* (Commentary on the *Lotus Sūtra*) and the *Hokke ryakuju* (Short verses on the *Lotus Sūtra*).[41] The *Inmyō shishū sōi shiki* (Private record of views on four logical errors), an unpublished five-fascicle text attributed to him on contradictions in Buddhist logic, is extant at Kōfukuji.[42] A number of texts on debate topics (*shiki*) are attributed to him, including works on the four aspects of consciousness (*Shibungi gokuryaku shiki;* T no. 2322), three objects of cognition (*sanruikyō*), and worthies and sages (*Hossōshū genjōgi mondō;* T no. 2320).[43] His discussion of the four aspects of consciousness, a central topic in Yogācāra doctrine is considered the most thorough treatment of the subject.[44]

Chūzan died at the age of forty-one in 976. His early death became the subject of several legends. For example, he is said to have predicted his own early demise. According to other sources, when he chanted the

Heart Sūtra beneath the Nachi waterfall at Kumano, the waters reversed their course, and a thousand-arm Kannon was manifested. Chūzan then climbed to the top and disappeared, giving rise to the theory that he had been a manifestation of Kannon. The same sources record a legend that he entered Jionjisan and never emerged, leaving behind a single straw sandal.[45] Such legends suggest that Chūzan was revered by later generations. Even during Ryōgen's time, Chūzan was recognized to be an exceptional scholar, well versed in the topics that might have made Ryōgen hesitate before challenging him.

A fourteenth-century work, the *Ainōshō*, includes a different story.[46] It is a dramatic but fictitious account that demonstrates the dimensions the Ōwa debates took in later literature. Although the story cannot be taken as literally true, it is related in some detail below because it suggests some of the ways in which monks might have argued at debates. The heart of the story concerns the evening lecture on the fifth day. According to it, Ryōgen and Chūzan were ordered by the court to oppose each other. The author of this version apparently combined the accounts of Ryōgen's victory with that of Chūzan to produce a dramatic but fictitious account. Because Ryōgen was angry over Kakugyō's defeat by Hōzō several days earlier (Ryōgen's defeat of Hōzō is not mentioned by the compiler of the *Ainōshō*), Ryōgen was asked to serve as lecturer. He explained the Tendai position that the one reality perfectly interpenetrated phenomena (*ichijitsu ennyū*) and that nonsentient objects such as trees and grasses realized Buddhahood (*sōmoku jōbutsu*). Chūzan replied with an explanation of Hossō's doctrine of the five types of nature (*goshō kakubetsu*). He continued, arguing, "Although nonsentient beings such as trees and grass possess the Buddha-nature in principle (*ribusshō*), they do not have the Buddha-nature of practice (*gyōbusshō*). Where then is the scriptural proof that they can realize Buddhahood?"[47] Chūzan thus claimed that Tendai monks had cited scriptural references to Buddha-nature in principle and misinterpreted them as referring to the aspect of Buddha-nature that provided the basis of religious practice.

To answer Chūzan's question about scriptural support, Ryōgen quoted a passage from the *Ta yüan-chüeh ching:* "The hells and heaven are all pure lands; both those with [Buddha]-nature and those without it realize Buddhahood (*Jigoku mo tengū mo minna jōdo to nari, ushō mo mushō mo hitoshiku butsudō wo jōsen*)."[48]

Chūzan was silent for a time and then was inspired by the deity Kasuga myōjin to change the Japanese punctuation of the scriptural passage and argue that it should be interpreted as meaning "If both the hells and the heavens are pure lands, then both those with the [Buddha]-nature and those without it can realize Buddhahood (*Jigoku mo tengū mo minna jōdo taramashikaba ushō mo mushō mo hitoshiku butsudō wo jōsen*)." The implication, of course, was that both of these options were absurd.

Ryōgen argued,

> "Chūzan's reading violates the spirit of the passage. Each tree and blade of grass has its own causes and effects. The mountains, rivers, and earth all possess the Buddha-nature. My critic has already agreed that they possess the Buddha-nature. If they possess the Buddha-nature, but cannot realize Buddhahood, then what is he calling Buddha-nature? If he says that they possess Buddha-nature but do not realize Buddhahood, then not even sentient beings can realize Buddhahood. The realization of Buddhahood by sentient beings is based on Buddha-nature in principle. The opening of flowers and bearing of fruit by grasses and trees is their practice!"[49]

He then closed his eyes and meditated for a while, whereupon the cherry tree at the left of the garden opened its flowers and the orange tree at the right bore three fruit.

Chūzan tapped his cypress fan[50] and said, "At this point, explanations will no longer suffice. My teaching is profound and difficult to understand." Thereupon the flowers dropped off, the fruit fell, and the trees appeared as they had before. The members of the Fujiwara clan withdrew, proud that their clan temple had won. However, as they left, they noticed that among the oxen tied up in front, the tongue of Ryōgen's ox was dribbling saliva that had a wondrous smell. Upon closer inspection, the pattern of the saliva was found to form a *waka* saying, "How satisfying for beings with feelings to hear that the grass and trees can realize Buddhahood." Sannō, the guardian *kami* of Mount Hiei, had composed the poem to prove that Ryōgen was correct.

Victors and Losers

How were the victors and losers determined in affairs such as the Ōwa debates? The issue is not easily resolved because sources disagree on who won and who lost. Tendai sources, such as Ryōgen's biographies, argue that the Tendai school won because Ryōgen defeated Hōzō.[51] However, Hossō sources, such as the *Ōwa shūron nikki*, consider the debates to have ended with a Hossō victory because of the strength of

Chūzan's arguments. According to the *Ōwa shūron nikki,* Chūzan refuted each of the points Ryōgen had made several days earlier. The emperor was so impressed that he sent an order to Fuminori's quarters summoning Chūzan the last night of the debates. Because Chūzan was honored by all in attendance, he received a wine cup for his performance. Another criterion for victory raised in the *Ōwa shūron nikki* is that Ryōgen's proposal that the Hossō school no longer be allowed to be the head of the Nara schools was not accepted. Because the Hossō school continued to dominate the Nara schools, it must have won the debate.[52] However, Ryōgen probably did not seriously hope to end Hossō's domination of the Nara schools; Kōfukuji was simply too strong. Moreover, the very structure of the debates would seem to indicate that Hossō domination was not the issue. The few Kegon and Sanron monks who participated were aligned with Hossō. If Hossō domination had been the issue, then at least some Kegon and Sanron monks might have been expected to participate on the side of Tendai. The *Honchō kōsōden* records a victory by Chūzan, as well as claiming that both Ryōgen and Chūzan were successful.[53]

Decisions in debates where monks were the audience probably rested on the monks' evaluation of the debaters' logical consistency, ability to cite sources, and skill in reconciling seemingly contradictory material.[54] However, when lay believers were the audience, different criteria might have been used. Thus even the monks recognized that questions on logic were not appropriate at the Ōwa debates. Of particular importance to a lay audience was the eloquence of the speaker. Descriptions of debates, such as the *Ainōshō* account of Ryōgen's debate with Chūzan, mention how moved the audience was by a speaker's oration. In addition, audiences probably enjoyed the differing readings for the same passage that were suggested. Finally, educated lay audiences probably knew many of the stories from the *Lotus Sūtra* and understood the rudiments of the doctrinal issues discussed. Thus they could probably judge the quality of the expositions as long as the discussion did not become too technical. Finally, the influence of a monk's patrons must have played a very important role at times.

Regardless of who emerged from the debates as victors, Ryōgen had accomplished his major goal: obtaining recognition for himself and his faction of the Tendai school from the court. The following year (964) Ryōgen was appointed court chaplain (*naigubu*), an official position that was the first of many to come. But Ryōgen was not the only monk who gained influence from the debates. Many of the monks who participated from both the Tendai and Nara schools went on to hold positions in the Office of Monastic Affairs or to become abbots of major temples.

The Tendai Monks
Who Refused to Participate in the Debates

Senkan

The four monks who chose not to participate were among the best-qualified people invited. Analyses of their biographies suggests that many of them must have been disturbed at Ryōgen's use of religious meetings to advance his own interests. In some cases, later authors exaggerated the monks' refusal to participate as a way of criticizing the political aspirations and agendas of monks such as Ryōgen.

Senkan (918–983), son of the governor of Sagami, Tachibana no Toshisada, began his monastic career in a manner similar to that of many other eminent monks. He was appointed court chaplain, one of the ten meditation teachers at court (*jūzenji*), and appeared in a number of officially sponsored assemblies.[55] He studied Buddhism with Unshō, probably at Onjōji. By 962, he had compiled a fifty-fascicle work titled *Hokke Sanshū sōtaishō* (Excerpts comparing [the interpretations of] the *Lotus Sūtra* by the three schools).[56] This text contrasted the positions of the de facto founders of the Hossō (Tz'u-en), Sanron (Chi-tsang), and Tendai (Chih-i) schools on the *Lotus Sūtra*. Although Senkan's work concerned the very text that would be discussed at the debates, he withdrew from the debates. Senkan's academic prowess is also revealed in medieval bibliographies. He and Genshin are each credited with the authorship of twelve position papers for debates (*gikasho*), more than any other monks of their time. According to the *Genkō shakusho*, Senkan's works were later used by Onjōji monks in debate.[57] He was also a master of Esoteric Buddhism, receiving the three advanced initiations in 970. But even before then, he was performing rain-making ceremonies; he is particularly famous for a successful ceremony in 962. Thus by the time the Ōwa debates were held, Senkan was a well-known monk.

About the time of the Ōwa debates, Senkan withdrew to Mount Minoo (Osaka-fu, Minoo-shi), perhaps because he wished to avoid participating. According to the biography of Senkan in the *Nihon ōjō gokuraku ki* (Accounts of Japanese births in paradise), compiled a year after Senkan's death, Senkan had "extensively studied both Esoteric and exoteric teachings; his learning was broad. He did not venture from his study except for mealtimes."[58] Senkan certainly could have traveled to Kyoto from Minoo for an important debate if he had wished to do so. Thus his refusal was probably due to dissatisfaction over Ryōgen's manipulation of the debates for his own political motives. Senkan's attitude toward the ostentatious display of learning is revealed in a short list of eight rules that he used to admonish laypeople. According to the fourth rule, "As for useless discussions, even if a person has the superior position, he should not engage in arguments."[59] This serious scholar clearly did not approve of the use of his learning for political motives or for the advancement of his career.

Senkan eventually turned toward Pure Land teachings. His practices included meditations on the setting sun.[60] According to later sources, Senkan was converted to Pure Land through a meeting with the *hijiri* Kōya (903–972), but early biographies include no mention of the meeting; these accounts must thus be viewed with suspicion.[61] However, he was noted for proselytizing among the common people. After his death, Senkan was identified as an incarnation of Kannon or Samantabhadra in some sources. He was said to have been so compassionate that people called him the "smiling Buddha" or the "Buddha saint" (*Butsuda shōnin*).[62]

Senkan was open to serving as an adviser and preceptor for nuns, and he had a number of noble women as his disciples. In 967, two months after Emperor Murakami's death, he served as the teacher (*kaishi*) in the ordination of the late emperor's imperial concubine, Princess Shōshi, and junior consort, Fujiwara no Yūhime. He was also the teacher of Middle Counselor Fujiwara no Atsutada's (d. 943) oldest daughter.[63] The connection with Yūhime may suggest that Senkan was patronized by people who were opposed to Morosuke and Ryōgen; however, he is said to have received word of a posthumous promotion in rank for Morosuke's wife Seishi, indicating that at least some of Morosuke's relatives must have felt comfortable with him.[64] Some of these women may have been drawn to seek teachings from reclusive monks because of their disillusionment with court politics. These patrons must have been valuable to monks such as Senkan who had decided to withdraw from mainstream political institutions, but who still needed patronage to manage their institutions.

Zoga

The other Tendai monk to withdraw from the debates, Zōga (917–1003), is said to have been the son of Counselor Tachibana no Tsunehira (922–983), but his dates make this impossible.[65] Zōga is said to have been a religious youth and to have gone to Yokawa to practice at the age of nine. Most biographies list Ryōgen as his teacher, but because Ryōgen was only five years older than Zōga, he probably was not Zōga's first teacher on Mount Hiei.[66] At some point, possibly in 949 when Ryōgen had received his advanced Esoteric initiations, Zōga became Ryōgen's student.[67] Zōga studied assiduously and mastered both exoteric and Esoteric teachings. He was so skilled in debate that he was called "a latter day Mahākaśyapa," after Śākyamuni's disciple who was so skilled in debate. Zōga was thus a natural choice for the debates at court.[68]

Zōga spent the thirty-seven years from 926 to 963 on Mount Hiei. His decision to leave Mount Hiei and his teacher Ryōgen in the seventh month of 963 must have been the result of considerable thought. A recently discovered diary of Zōga's dreams contains an entry from 8-2-948. In his dream, Zōga followed a river upstream into a deep valley where he saw a hut and an old man accompanied by a retinue of gods and goddesses. When he asked the old man his name, the old man replied that he was Vimalakīrti and that the land on which he lived would be propitious for Buddhist practice after he left.[69] Zōga's dream probably reflects his desires to retreat to a quiet place and pursue religious austerities; the mention of Vimalakīrti may be a reference to Kamatari, who is buried at Tōnomine and had established the Yuima-e. Ryōgen also left vows from 939 referring to a desire to retreat to the mountains.[70] Thus Ryōgen and Zōga may have talked together about the possibility of living quietly in the mountains. However, with time Ryōgen's plans changed, and he became active in the political and institutional side of Buddhism. Although no sources contain a clear statement of why Zōga chose to leave Mount Hiei, his departure only a month before the Ōwa debates at court suggests that he probably was trying to avoid participating.[71] Perhaps he objected to Ryōgen's overtly political agenda. Zōga also chose to go to Tōnomine because Takamitsu had gone there a year earlier and invited him; the two men had met during Takamitsu's nine-month stay at Yokawa. In addition, the monks at Tōnomine welcomed an accomplished Tendai monk such as Zōga; the abbot Senman (d. 981) and the master of the temple (*jishu*) Hyōsen personally supervised the construction of his quarters. After Zōga arrived at Tōnomine, he realized that it fit the description of the land he had dreamt about fifteen years earlier.[72]

Once he was at Tōnomine, Zōga devoted himself to training monks in the Tendai tradition. He was famed for his knowledge of Chih-i's *Mo-ho chih-kuan* (The great calming and contemplation), *Fa-hua wen-chü* (Words and phrases of the *Lotus Sūtra*), and *Fa-hua hsüan-i* (Discourse on the profound meaning of the *Lotus Sūtra*), which constituted the three major treatises of Chinese T'ien-t'ai. In 964, shortly after arriving at Tōnomine, he lectured on the *Mo-ho chih-kuan*; the following year he lectured on the *Fa-hua wen-chü*. From 964 to 973, he performed twenty-one-day Lotus meditations four times a year. In 974, he established an examination system similar to that on Hiei, in which a candidate would be examined over a broad range of issues (*kōgaku ryūgi*).[73] In 991, when Emperor Murakami's son Prince Tomohira (964–1009) wrote a four-fascicle subcommentary on the non-Buddhist works mentioned in the Chan-jan's commentary on the *Mo-ho chih-kuan*, he sent it to Zōga and asked him to check it.[74] Zōga is credited with the compilation of several texts, the *Hokke gengishō* (Excerpts from Chih-i's *Fa-hua hsüan-i*), the *Yugaron mondō* (Questions and answers on the *Yogācārabhūmi*), and the *Gika shiki* (Private compilation on debate topics).[75] Although the text on the *Yogācārabhūmi* was compiled in 981, long after the Ōwa debates, its contents suggest that Zōga would have been a valuable ally for Ryōgen if he had participated in the debates.

Additional evidence for Zōga's interest in the *Mo-ho chih-kuan* is found in the Shōkōkan version of the *Tōnomine ryakki*. When a Constant-walking Meditation Hall was established on Tōnomine with the help of Takamitsu's half-brother, Minister of the Right Koremasa, in 970, Takamitsu is said to have suggested that the monks recite the *O-mi-t'o ching* (Smaller *sūtra* on Amitāyus) and verses on Amida's thirty-two marks and perform the uninterrupted *nenbutsu* for a period of ninety days from the seventh through the ninth month of each year.[76] The ninety-day meditation period was in accordance with the *Mo-ho chih-kuan* and was substantially longer than the seven-day period for the Constant-walking Meditation that was employed on Hiei at that time. Because Takamitsu's teacher at this time was Zōga, who was noted for his mastery of Chih-i's works, Takamitsu may have studied the *Mo-ho chih-kuan* under Zōga, and the two monks may have decided to follow at least some of Chih-i's instructions on the performance of the Constant-walking Meditation rather than completely adopt the version followed on

Mount Hiei. The format of the Tōnomine Constant-walking Meditation would thus seem to be further evidence of Zōga's critical attitude toward Mount Hiei under Ryōgen. However, this interpretation of Zōga's view of the Constant-walking Meditation has been called into question recently through studies of an unpublished version of the *Tōnomine ryakki* called the Nishinomiya-zōhon. According to the description of the constant-walking meditation in the Nishinomiya version, Takamitsu (presumably with Zōga's agreement) practiced the constant-walking meditation used on Mount Hiei for the first seven days of each year and throughout the rest of the year from the fifteenth through the thirtieth days of each month. Even so, the frequency of this meditation would have made practice on Tōnomine more strenuous than Mount Hiei. When the two versions of the *Tōnomine ryakki* are compared, more evidence exists for the early composition of the Nishinomiya version than for the Shōkōkan version; however, no explanation about why the text was altered to suggest a ninety-day period has been suggested. The problem requires further investigation.[77]

Besides religious practice, Zōga was also concerned with the institutional aspects of Tōnomine. In 964, shortly after Zōga's arrival, Emperor Murakami had a Lotus Meditation Hall built at Tōnomine; the hall soon became the site for Zōga's practice of the Lotus meditation. Zōga may also have been behind Takamitsu's request to his elder brother Koremasa that resulted in a major building program at Tōnomine. In 969, Koremasa contributed some land (*sanmaiden*), the taxes of which were to be used for the ceremony. Six monks were appointed to perform the practice, and one attendant (*azukari*) was named to oversee the preparations. In 970, Koremasa had the Constant-walking Meditation Hall built; it served as the center for Takamitsu's practice. In 969, he and Fujiwara no Fuminori reestablished the boundaries of Tōnomine, thereby stopping farmers from encroaching upon land that had been owned by Tōnomine.[78] Fuminori had supported Chūzan in the Ōwa debates. His aid to Zōga probably reflects his appreciation of Zōga's refusal to participate in the debates. At the same time, his cooperation with Koremasa indicates that he would still cooperate with the members of Morosuke's lineage at times, such as in the reconstruction of the complex at Tōnomine as a mausoleum for Fujiwara no Kamatari, founder of the Fujiwara clan, even though he had opposed Ryōgen's faction on Mount Hiei. In 974, Zōga is said to have lectured on the *Vimalakīrti-nirdeśa,* an act reminiscent of the Yuima-e that had been established during Kamatari's lifetime and used to commemorate his death.[79]

The Hossō Monks
Who Refused to Participate in the Debates

Senri and Ninga

Of the Hossō monks who refused the invitation to the debates, virtually nothing is known of Senri, who was to replace Sentō. Because both men had the character *sen* in their names, they may have belonged to the same lineage at Kōfukuji.

Ninga from Kōfukuji had a reputation as a painstaking scholar. His interests extended beyond Yogācāra; he studied Esoteric Buddhism with Jōjo (888–957) of Daigoji.[80] The Daigoji tradition of Esoteric Buddhism had been founded by Shōbō (832–909), a monk who had combined Esoteric Buddhism with Sanron and Hossō. Later in life Ninga rejected all honors and withdrew to Tōnomine to practice the *nenbutsu* under Zōga. Ninga obviously disliked the political motivation behind the Ōwa debates. His decision to leave the Hossō school and go to study with a Tendai monk, Zōga, despite the long history of conflict between the Hossō and Tendai schools is probably due, in part, to their common distaste for the Ōwa debates. He is said to have refused appointment to the Office of Monastic Affairs by acting in an eccentric manner. According to the *Zoku honchō ōjōden, Honchō kōsōden,* and *Kojidan,* he lived with a widow to discourage people from treating him as a sage. The stories about eccentric behavior designed to make the devout leave him alone are reminiscent of stories about Zōga's eccentricities. After he died, although his body was placed in a coffin, it did not decay, a sign of his virtue.[81]

The Effects of the Ōwa Debates

The Ōwa debates are among the better-documented monastic disputes of the tenth century. They provided a sense of drama with the two sides clearly arrayed against each other, discussing issues on which each held explicitly defined positions that could be understood by an educated lay audience. Moreover, power and influence were at stake because Ryōgen had challenged the right of Hossō to be the head of the Nara schools. Although the Hossō school continued to dominate the Nara schools, Ryōgen used the debates to give new impetus to his career and within a few years was appointed head of the Tendai school and to the Office of Monastic Affairs. However, even the purported "losers" in the debate did not lose much. Hōzō, defeated by Ryōgen in the debates, continued to receive appointments and honors until his death. Kaku-gyō, defeated by Hōzō, went on to receive some of the highest positions in the Buddhist world. Other participants also garnered rewards. Iron-ically, Chūzan, who is said to have been recognized by the emperor as the victor, did not receive such promotions because of his personal choice, his obscure family origins, or his death at an early age.

The political nature of Ryōgen's challenge and his selection of Tendai participants bothered some of the participants, however. Some of the monks most skilled at debate and most knowledgeable about the doctrinal issues to be discussed refused to participate. Zōga's critical at-titude toward Ryōgen's quest for power and influence became the sub-ject of legends as time passed. However, Zōga's attitudes were not nearly as extreme as later legends make them seem. After he had retired to Tō-nomine, many of his activities to attract patronage and support were virtually identical to those of Ryōgen. Senkan, too, had to attract sup-port for his establishment. How, then, did they differ from Ryōgen? Neither monk sought high office or influence for himself. Both con-tinued to be interested in serious practice and scholarly activities. Later Japanese authors used them as foils to criticize the activities of Ryōgen and other political monks; later legends about Zōga are discussed in appendix 7.

Finally, mention must be made of an event that occurred at the same time as the Ōwa debates. On the third day of the debates, Kōya (903–972), who was nominally a Tendai monk,[82] was dedicating a copy of the 600-fascicle *Perfection of Wisdom Sūtra*. In 950, fourteen years ear-lier, Kōya had vowed to copy this work in gold letters with the help of anyone who wished to aid him. With the completion of the mammoth work, Kōya had decided to hold the dedication on the east bank of the Kamo River, in imitation of the Veṇuvana monastery founded on the banks of the Ganges shortly after Sākyamuni's enlightenment. The ded-ication, open to anyone, created great excitement. Six hundred monks and innumerable lay believers, both commoners and nobles, attended. Music (*gigaku*) was played; a boat with the head of a dragon plied the river. Sermons were delivered during the day, lamps lit at night, and the *nenbutsu* recited. Although both the Ōwa debates and Kōya's assembly were based on the dedication of texts, the contrast between them could hardly be more marked. The Ōwa debates were intended for a small number of the educated elite. Although Ryōgen and other Tendai monks argued for the universal salvation of all people, the Ōwa debates were directed toward the court elite. Moreover, opportunities for advancement in Ryōgen's Tendai school were available primarily for the sons of nobles. Women had little or no role as Tendai monastics. In contrast, Kōya's movement was primarily for the masses and for both men and women. Ryōgen carefully planned for his own fame and fortune; Kōya disdained personal advancement. Although no records survive about how Senkan or Zōga responded to Kōya's dedication, Hirabayashi has suggested that they might well have chosen to attend that event rather than the Ōwa debates.[83] Although little evidence exists of any connection between Zōga and Kōya other than their common disdain for the blatantly political use of Buddhist rituals, Senkan's activities sometimes resembled those of Kōya. For example, Senkan composed hymns and vows to help spread Pure Land beliefs among the people.[84] Kōya's dedication thus provided a model of Buddhist behavior that contrasted with Ryōgen's political usage.

In the next chapter, Ryōgen's appointment as head of the Tendai school and to the Office of Monastic Affairs, both due in part to the Ōwa debates, are investigated.

7

Ryōgen's Appointments
as Head of the Tendai School
and to the Office of Monastic Affairs

The Ōwa debates were a success for Ryōgen, as he drew the court's attention to both himself and his lineage. During the next few years, he received appointments as both head of the Tendai school and to the Office of Monastic Affairs. Appointments to the latter institution were particularly important because they were symbolic of the emerging Tendai dominance of the monastic world. This chapter concerns the significance of those appointments and the role that his alliance with Morosuke and his son Jinzen played in these appointments.

Ryōgen's success was not without difficulties, however, as a disastrous fire destroyed the heart of the monastic establishment on Mount Hiei shortly after his appointment as *zasu*. Chapter 9 concerns Ryōgen's efforts to rebuild Mount Hiei and focuses on the order in which the reconstruction took place and the roles of the various buildings.

Appointment as *Zasu*

On 8-27-966, Ryōgen was appointed the eighteenth head of the Tendai school, a post that he held until shortly before he died. For the two years before Ryōgen's appointment, the Tendai school had experienced considerable difficulty in choosing a *zasu*. The fifteenth *zasu*, Enshō, had served for eighteen years; however, the sixteenth, Chinchō (d. 964), had been appointed when he was seventy-eight years old and had served for only eight months before dying. The seventeenth, Kikyō (889–966), had been appointed at age seventy-six and lived for only a year afterward.[1] Thus by 966, the Tendai school was probably ready to appoint a younger man as head. Both Chinchō and Kikyō were probably well known to Ryōgen. Chinchō had served as supervisor of Yokawa, and Kikyō was from the same county as Ryōgen.

During the period before Ryōgen was appointed *zasu*, he was occasionally summoned to the palace to perform Esoteric ceremonies. In the sixth month of 964, he had been appointed court chaplain and meditation master (*naigubu jūzenji*), a post that enabled the court to call him for religious services.[2] On 10-16-964, he had led fifteen monks in the performance of the ceremony of the Buddha of Abundant Light at the palace to counteract a celestial anomaly. Although other Tendai monks performed Esoteric ceremonies at Tendai temples at this time for the state, Ryōgen had been asked to come to the palace, a sign of his growing influence.[3] In both the second (2–23) and eighth months (8–19) of 966, Ryōgen had led twenty monks in the Esoteric ceremonies of the Immovable King at the palace.[4] Ryōgen's popularity was growing at court, and his favored position led to his appointment by the court as head of the Tendai school on the twenty-seventh day of the eighth month, just eight days after he had performed ceremonies at court.

Many must have wondered about Ryōgen's qualifications. At the age of fifty-four, he was one of the youngest *zasu* ever appointed. Of the previous seventeen *zasu,* only the first, Gishin, had been appointed at a younger age. Like Ryōgen, Enchin had been appointed at fifty-four; but the rest had been at least sixty when they were named *zasu.* With thirty-nine years of seniority, Ryōgen had less seniority than all but five of the previous *zasu.* The Tendai *zasu* was expected to be a master of Esoteric Buddhism at Enryakuji, but Ryōgen held this position only at Gangyōji. In 1020, Michinaga remedied the situation by posthumously conferring upon Ryōgen the status of *yama no ajari* (Esoteric master of the mountain [temple], namely Enryakuji).[5]

Several of the Tendai monks passed over in favor of Ryōgen were very disappointed. Bōsan (899–967) of Onjōji, who was in Enchin's lineage, was Ryōgen's senior in both monastic rank and years of seniority. He had been appointed lecturer at the Yuima-e in 955 and supernumerary master of discipline in 961; he also served as the eleventh abbot of Onjōji. Although Ryōgen had participated in the Yuima-e in an unofficial capacity as a young man, he had not been appointed lecturer, and his appointment as supernumerary master of discipline in 965 came four years after that of Bōsan. When Ryōgen was appointed *zasu* in 966, Bōsan resigned his position in the Office of Monastic Affairs and went into a retreat on Nanzan. Bōsan is said to have died that same year in disappointment. Afterwards, he made an appearance as a vengeful spirit and later was posthumously awarded the rank of archbishop to assuage his anger.[6] Although historical records do not reveal the feelings of monks in Enchin's lineage when Ryōgen was appointed, many must have had misgivings. The previous two *zasu*, both from Ennin's lineage, had been appointed in their late seventies; their appointments might have been more acceptable to the monks of Enchin's lineage because the appointees were old and not very active. In contrast, Ryōgen was appointed at a comparatively young age and might prove to be a vigorous and long-lived leader.

Another disappointed Tendai monk was Gajō, who, like Ryōgen, was from Ennin's lineage but from a different branch. Gajō also held a post within the Office of Monastic Affairs, entering the same year as Ryōgen. Although Gajō had not advanced to higher posts in the Sōgō until 966, when he was appointed master of discipline, he had a more important qualification for *zasu:* he had been appointed abbot of the Hosshōji, a temple founded by Tadahira. Because the previous five Tendai *zasu* had all served as abbot of this temple before being appointed *zasu*, Gajō must have felt that he deserved to be head of the Tendai School. Gajō too died the next year. He occasionally made appearances as an angry ghost; finally, in the sixth month of 1010, after consideration for the posthumous award of *zasu*, he was given the rank of *hōin*.[7]

Appointments to the Office of Monastic Affairs

From 965 onward, Ryōgen received a series of appointments to the Office of Monastic Affairs. These along with several other posts, are listed in table 9.[8]

Ryōgen's first post as court chaplain and one of the ten meditation masters was not actually in the Office of Monastic Affairs, but it had been held by Tendai monks such as Saichō, Gishin, Ennin, and Enchin in the past. It had served as a stepping-stone on their path to prominence at a time when appointments to the Sōgō had not been readily available for Tendai monks. The posts of court chaplain and meditation master originally had been separate, but had been conflated by this time. The post of meditation master, established during the Nara period, actually had little to do with meditation; rather the appointee was supposed to be a monk of spiritual power gained through "pure practices" such as living in the mountains or perhaps meditation. This spiritual power was to be used to help him protect and cure people, particularly the emperor.[9] The origins of the court chaplain are more obscure; Hongō Masatsugu has suggested that Saichō may have brought the concept from the Chinese court and that it was then adopted by the Japa-

TABLE 9

RYŌGEN'S APPOINTMENTS
TO THE OFFICE OF MONASTIC AFFAIRS

6-964	court chaplain and meditation master	*naigubu jūzenji*
12-28-965	supernumerary master of discipline	*gon-risshi*
8-27-966	head of the Tendai school	*zasu*
12-26-966	master of discipline	*risshi*
3-11-968	supernumerary lesser bishop	*gon-shōsōzu*
5-11-971	chief administrator	*hōmu*
12-22-973	lesser bishop	*shōsōzu*
5-11-974	supernumerary greater bishop	*gon-daisōzu*
5-11-975	greater bishop	*daisōzu*
10-5-977	supernumerary archbishop	*gon-sōjō*
12-21-979	archbishop	*sōjō*
8-30-981	grand archbishop	*daisōjō*
8-30-981	permission to enter the palace in a *teguruma* (hand-drawn cart)	

nese, but Oyamada Kazuo views the origins as more Japanese.[10] The two positions were amalgamated sometime between 772 and 797.[11] For early Tendai monks, appointment as *naigubu jūzenji*, a position that lay outside the Sōgō, was one of the few ways that they could influence court circles because appointments to the Sōgō were closed to them for several decades after Saichō's death. Enchin commented on the importance of the post for the Tendai school. In fact, Tendai monks listed this position before positions in the Sōgō in official documents, even though posts in the Sōgō were usually regarded as higher. By the tenth century, monks from other schools usually resigned as *naigubu jūzenji* when they received appointments to the Sōgō, but Tendai monks held both concurrently, probably in memory of the important role that *naigubu jūzenji* held in Tendai history.

Several of the appointments corresponded with specific events in Ryōgen's life. For example, the appointment as master of discipline occurred the same day that an edict was issued commanding that formal debates be included for the assembly commemorating Saichō's death, the *rokugatsu-e* (also called the *minazuki-e*) or assembly of the sixth month. That same day, the Sōjiin received two additional masters of Esoteric Buddhism making a total of sixteen. The appointment to grand

TABLE 10

JINZEN'S APPOINTMENTS
TO THE OFFICE OF MONASTIC AFFAIRS

974	supernumerary master of discipline (965)
976	abbot of Hosshōji
977	resigned as abbot of Hosshōji
978	greater bishop (974)
981	supernumerary archbishop (977)
985	Tendai *zasu* (966)
1007	conferral of posthumous title of *daishi* (987)

archbishop was a reward for the successful performance of Esoteric ceremonies to enable Emperor En'yū recover from a grave illness. No specific reason is given in the *Sōgō bunin* for most of the rest of Ryōgen's appointments. However, some of them were undoubtedly given as a reward for the successful performance of Esoteric ceremonies. Moreover, his treatment must have been influenced by the presence of Morosuke's sons in the highest offices at court. After Saneyori's death in 970, Morosuke's sons dominated Japanese court life for the next seven years. Even when Saneyori's son Yoritada assumed the highest posts in 977, they were ceded to him by Morosuke's son Kanemichi. Ryōgen thus had high officials friendly to him during most of the time he was receiving appointments to the Sōgō.

In addition, Ryōgen's appointments can be correlated with those of Morosuke's son Jinzen. As Jinzen rapidly advanced in rank, often skipping ranks in the Sōgō, his teacher Ryōgen was also promoted so that he stayed ahead of Jinzen. Jinzen's ranks and the date of promotion are listed in table 10. The year in which Ryōgen was promoted to the same rank is given in parentheses.

Jinzen's appointment as supernumerary lesser bishop and as supernumerary archbishop trailed Ryōgen's by only four years each. In both cases, by the time Jinzen was advanced in rank, Ryōgen had already been promoted, preserving the proper difference between teacher and student. Moreover, on the same day that Ryōgen received his appointment as grand archbishop, Jinzen was appointed supernumerary archbishop. Jinzen's family connections must have been important in helping Ryōgen receive appointments to the highest levels of the Sōgō. He was only the second monk, after Gyōki, to be appointed grand archbishop and the third monk to receive permission to enter the palace in a *teguruma*.[12]

Ryōgen's appointments to the Sōgō were vital to the Tendai school. Saichō had striven to free the Tendai school from the Sōgō's control 150 years earlier. At first, Tendai monks had not wanted appointments in the Sōgō, nor had the monks of Nara been eager to have Tendai monks in the supervisory positions in the Sōgō. The first heads of the Tendai school had not held appointments in the Sōgō. However, by the middle of the Heian period, many of the administrative functions of the Sōgō had been taken over by the heads of individual temples or schools; in many cases, monasteries of other schools adopted the same administrative procedures as Enryakuji, bypassing the Sōgō by using a lay supervisor (*zoku-bettō*).[13]

Because appointments to the Sōgō carried financial rewards and prestige, Tendai monks eventually set aside their antipathy for the institution. Many of the functions to which Saichō had objected no longer seemed as important to Tendai monks, particularly because their independence from Nara control had been assured for many years. Consequently, in 890, a group of Tendai monks submitted a petition to the court asking that Enchin be appointed to the Sōgō. The court agreed and appointed him lesser bishop, skipping the previous stage of master of discipline. When Enchin received the appointment, there was so much rejoicing on Mount Hiei that the buildings were said to have shaken with the celebration. The appointment was also announced to the guardian deities on Hiei.[14] At the time of the appointment, Henjō, who was nominally Enchin's disciple but much closer to Ennin's lineage, was serving as archbishop, the highest position in the Sōgō, and probably helped smooth the way for Enchin's appointment. Henjō's appointments to the Sōgō were almost entirely due to the favoritism he received because he was the son of Yoshimine no Yasuyo (758–830), Emperor Kanmu's son. Consequently, Enchin's appointment to the Sōgō can be seen as a much more important breakthrough for the Tendai school than Henjō's appointments.[15]

Enchin's appointment occurred only after he had risen to the highest position within the Tendai school. After Enchin, the next seven *zasu* received appointments to the Sōgō only after they had been appointed *zasu*, the highest position in the Tendai school, a procedure that indicated how few Tendai monks actually were able to enter the Sōgō. Finally, from the time of Gikai (served as *zasu* 940–946) onward, appointments to the Sōgō preceded being named *zasu,* a procedure that indicates that a few eminent Tendai monks probably held positions in the Sōgō at most times.[16]

Although the Tendai school had a certain amount of success in obtaining appointments to the Sōgō during the late ninth and early tenth centuries, because of the opposition of the Nara schools, most Tendai monks appointed to the Sōgō advanced no further than the positions of master of discipline or lesser bishop, the lower ranks of the Sōgō. Tendai monks were rarely appointed to the higher ranks of the Sōgō. Even when they were successful, that success was largely due to the individual's political ties, as was the case with Yoshimine no Yasuyo's son Henjō. Takagi Yutaka has compared the success of the Tendai and Shingon schools in obtaining appointments to the Sōgō.[17] Because the Tendai and Shingon schools were founded at approximately the same time, the comparison effectively reveals the difficulty that Tendai monks had in rising to the top of the monastic hierarchy. The Tendai school generally received its first appointment to a particular position in the Sōgō, such as bishop, several decades later than the Shingon school. In addition, 80 percent of the Tendai appointees never advanced beyond lesser bishop whereas only 56 percent of the Shingon appointees never advanced beyond the lower positions. The situation finally changed with Ryōgen's appointments to the Sōgō. Ryōgen's career set precedents for Tendai monastic officials receiving appointments, and his administration opened the way for Tendai domination of the Sōgō.

Ryōgen's success in appointing his disciples to the Sōgō was due in part to his position from 971 to 983 as one of two chief administrators (*hōmu*) in the Sōgō, a post that gave him the authority to recommend Tendai monks for appointment and promotion in the Sōgō.[18] Ryōgen's appointment as chief administrator was clearly not the result of rising to the top of the Sōgō hierarchy; he was only supernumerary lesser bishop when he was appointed. Rather, the appointment was given because of his post as Tendai *zasu.* Other appointments as *hōmu* were given to the abbots of major institutions such as Tōji, Kōfukuji, and Onjōji. In fact, the Tendai *zasu* Zōmyō, Son'i, and Enshō had all held the position before Ryōgen, but none of them had used it to bring about Tendai domination of the Sōgō.

Originally, the highest-ranking official in the Sōgō had performed the administrative duties; however, this system seems to have deteriorated after Hossō monk Gomyō's (d. 834) administration.[19] The position of chief administrator was added to the Sōgō in 872, probably to free the other officials from the administrative burdens of Sōgō positions.[20] These duties had become particularly onerous when the Sōgō was moved from Yakushiji in Nara to Saiji in Kyoto. For the Kōfukuji monks who dominated the Sōgō early in the Heian period, the requirement that they travel between the two cities must have been a nuisance. As a result, many of the administrative duties were given to two monks, the chief administrators, while the other positions in the Sōgō were simply honorary without any administrative duties.[21] Although Hossō monks at Kōfukuji might have been uncomfortable with Ryōgen's appointment, no record of their opposition survives. Because the power of the Sōgō had declined significantly since the early Heian, control of the institution was not nearly as important as it had been in Saichō's time. In many cases, a monk well versed in Esoteric ritual, particularly one from the Shingon monastery Tōji, held one of the appointments; thus during Ryōgen's tenure, he usually shared the post with Shingon monks. The Sōgō was based at Saiji and later at Tōji, the official temples in Kyoto; by the twelfth century, abbots of Tōji were routinely appointed as *hōmu*. But in the tenth century, Ryōgen's position as chief administrator probably gave him occasions to go to Kyoto and further his ties with the Fujiwara nobility.[22]

Table 11, based on research by Ogami Kanchū, lists the numbers of monks from each school appointed to the Sōgō for representative years between 925 and 1030.[23] At first, Hossō monks clearly outnumbered Tendai monks. However, in 948, the numbers of Tendai monks in the Sōgō outnumbered those from the Hossō school for the first time. Even though Hossō monks regained numerical superiority around 960, by 968, shortly after Ryōgen was appointed *zasu*, the Tendai school had begun to dominate the Sōgō. By 985, the year of Ryōgen's death, Tendai monks in the Sōgō outnumbered those from the Hossō school by almost four to one.

The seeming contradiction of Tendai domination of the Sōgō with earlier Tendai antipathy for the institution led to a number of accommodations after Ryōgen's time. Because Saichō's criticism of the Sōgō had focused on the ordination system, the ordination platform on Mount Hiei continued to remain independent of Sōgō administration in most cases.[24] However, when the Jimon (Enchin's) faction attempted to establish its own ordination procedure, it was to be supervised by the Sōgō; meanwhile, Sanmon ordinations continued to be independent. Although the Sōgō played a limited role in Tendai ordinations, it performed an important function at Tendai ceremonies and rituals, espe-

TABLE 11

MEMBERSHIP OF THE SŌGŌ ACCORDING TO SCHOOL

Year	Hossō	Sanron	Kegon	Ritsu	Tendai	Shingon	Total
925	7	1	3	0	2	3	16
930	5	1	0	0	1	3	10
935	9	0	0	0	3	3	15
940	7	2	0	1	4	4	18
945	7	4	0	0	4	2	17
947	6	4	0	0	3	2	15
948	6	3	0	0	7	2	18
950	4	3	0	0	7	2	16
955	4	2	0	0	7	4	17
960	5	2	1	1	6	2	17
961	7	1	2	1	6	3	20
965	6	2	2	0	4	4	18
967	5	2	1	1	4	3	16
968	3	2	1	0	6	4	16
970	3	2	1	0	7	4	17
975	3	2	1	0	9	5	20
980	3	2	0	0	8	3	16
985	3	0	0	0	11	3	17
990	2	2	0	0	18	4	26
1000	4	1	0	0	15	5	25
1010	4	1	0	0	15	4	24
1020	4	0	1	0	16	5	26
1030	4	0	0	0	14	6	24

cially those that had an official function. By the twelfth century, Sōgō officials were present at many of the major assemblies on Mount Hiei, such as the *rokugatsu-e* held in memory of Saichō. In case any questions of procedure were raised, the Sōgō officials would consult precedents and advise the monks in charge of the ceremony. In addition, the Sōgō would invite the audience to the *rokugatsu-e*. By the twelfth century, those invited were from the Sanmon and Jimon factions of the Tendai school and the Hossō temple Kōfukuji.[25] Of course, the rights of the Sōgō to regulate temples were increasingly limited by the various abbots of temples who had gradually increased their power since the beginning of the Heian period.

Saichō had proposed that ordinations and other Tendai activities requiring government sanction be supervised by a lay supervisor. This system worked well for a time, often giving the Tendai school a direct liaison with the highest government officials. By the time Ryōgen became *zasu*, the lay supervisor does not seem to have directly supervised ordinations on Mount Hiei, giving the Tendai school much more autonomy than it had enjoyed in the ninth century. Although lay supervisors were still appointed into the twelfth century, they did not climb Mount Hiei and directly oversee ordinations, partly because this function was eventually taken over by the Sōgō.[26]

Conclusion

Within several years of the Ōwa debates, Saichō was appointed to a variety of posts, including court chaplain, head of the Tendai school, and various posts in the Sōgō. Service as court chaplain was a traditional way for Tendai monks to gain influence in the court. The appointment as *zasu* was controversial and left a number of Saichō's rivals unhappy, resulting in more tales of curses by angry ghosts. Because Ryōgen was young in comparison with previous *zasu*, his long tenure as *zasu* enabled him to transform many aspects of Tendai institutions. Finally, his appointments in the Sōgō led to appointments for other Tendai monks in the bureaucratic apparatus that was to oversee monasteries; the appointments in turn eventually resulted in Tendai domination of the Sōgō and domination of the monastic world.

In the next three chapters, several aspects of Ryōgen's administration of Mount Hiei are surveyed. Whereas this chapter has been concerned with the relations between the court and the Tendai school in regard to appointments, the next chapter focuses on internal developments in the Tendai school by considering the Tendai educational system. Chapter 9 is concerned with the rebuilding of the establishment on Mount Hiei after a disastrous fire. Chapter 10 is a discussion of how these developments were financed.

8

The Significance of Ryōgen's
Revival of the Examination System

When Saichō (767–822) established the Japanese Tendai school, one of his major concerns was the creation of an educational system on Mount Hiei for Tendai monks. Among the important elements of the system were a twelve-year confinement on Mount Hiei, the division of Tendai students into meditation and Esoteric courses, and the study of Tendai texts as well as those from other traditions. In addition, Saichō set up an examination and ordination system that bypassed the governmental Office of Monastic Affairs, which normally would have overseen such activities. Although certain elements of Saichō's plan, such as the twelve-year confinement on Mount Hiei, fell into general disuse within several decades of Saichō's death, many of the other elements, such as Tendai independence from the Office of Monastic Affairs, were maintained, though sometimes with significant changes.

Saichō's confrontational policies resulted in few appointments or rewards from the court for Tendai monks because such honors often depended upon favorable recommendations from the Office of Monastic Affairs, an institution dominated by Hossō monks. Although Tendai mastery and development of Esoteric ritual helped alleviate these difficulties, few Tendai monks received court appointments to major monastic posts until the time of Ryōgen. An important factor behind Tendai disappointments was the failure of Tendai monks to obtain appointments to the prestigious assembly of the Yuima-e that was held at Kōfukuji, the Fujiwara clan temple, which was affiliated with the Hossō school.

In this chapter, Ryōgen's revival and restructuring of the Tendai examination system so that it could compete with the Yuima-e is examined. The chapter is divided into four sections: (1) the Yuima-e, (2) the history and institutional significance of the examinations, (3) the format of those examinations, and (4) the contents and types of questions

asked at the examinations. Although the chapter is concerned primarily with the examinations during the tenth century, both earlier and
later developments are also considered to elucidate the development
of medieval monastic education. Monastic training and education has
not received the attention it deserves in modern scholarship in both
Japan and the West. However, a beginning to a remedy of the situation
has begun in Japan with formation of the study group focusing on debates (*rongi*); several of the essays from members of this group are cited
below. In the West, monastic education in Japan has been largely ignored as scholars have focused on the founders of the various schools.
This survey of the Tendai examination system does not touch on such
issues as training in meditation or Esoteric Buddhist ritual; rather, it focuses on how exoteric doctrine was studied and interpreted in medieval
Tendai.

The Yuima-e

The Yuima-e has already been mentioned in this study because it provided Ryōgen with the opportunity to first attract the attention of the
Fujiwaras. A more detailed examination of the Yuima-e is called for here
because the assembly served as model for the Tendai examination system and had a decisive influence on medieval monastic education.

Origins of the Yuima-e

The Yuima-e[1] can be traced back to when the founder of the Fujiwara
clan, Nakatomi no Kamatari (614–669), had been sick for a time in 656.
Hōmyō, a nun from Paekche on the Korean peninsula who had come
to Japan, had suggested that a special service that included the commissioning of an image of the layman Vimalakīrti and the chanting of
the *Vimalakīrti-nirdeśa* (C. *Wei-mo ching*; J. *Yuimagyō*) might help cure him.
When the services were conducted, Kamatari was miraculously cured
when he began chanting the chapter on asking about illness ("Wen-chi
p'in"). According to a variant tradition, the origins of the assembly can
be traced to the following year when the Chinese San-lun monk Fu-liang
(n.d.) of Gangōji served as lecturer at Kamatari's house in Suehara in
Yamashina.[2] Annual lectures on the *sūtra* seem to have been conducted
for the next twelve years, but the practice was discontinued after Kamatari's death in 669.

The *Vimalakīrti-nirdeśa* was probably chosen because Vimalakīrti had used an illness as an expedient means to teach others; thus the text probably seemed appropriate for curing illness. In particular, the text could be seen as using Buddhist teachings such as emptiness as the cure for illness. In addition, the *Vimalakīrti-nirdeśa* had been a popular text among the nobility in China and may have been an object of Prince Shōtoku's interest. Thus Kamatari's interest in the text was in keeping with East Asian Buddhism of that period.

The assembly was not held for approximately thirty years. Finally, in 705 Kamatari's second son, Fuhito (659–720), became ill. According to divination, Fuhito's illness had occurred because the assembly begun by his father had been abandoned. The next year, Chihō (n.d.), a Japanese monk who had studied Yogācāra in China, was asked to lecture on the *Vimalakīrti-nirdeśa*. For several years, either the translation by Kumārajīva (*Wei-mo ching; T* 475) or Hsüan-tsang (*Wu-kou-ch'eng ching; T* 476) was used. Fuhito was probably responsible for moving the Fujiwara clan temple to Nara, where it was called Kōfukuji, and establishing the Yuima-e at it.[3] In addition, from 706 onward, the Yuima-e was to begin on 10-10 and end on 10-16, the anniversary of Kamatari's death.

In 757, Fujiwara no Nakamaro, Kamatari's great-grandson, asked that 100 *chō* be given to Kōfukuji to pay for the annual performance of the assembly. Empress Kōmyō (701–760) also played a major role in carrying out the annual funding of the ceremony. Besides being a ceremony in honor of Nakamaro's great-grandfather, Kamatari, the assembly began to take on a new public significance. In the petition, Nakamaro specified that it was to support the imperial family, support Buddhism, comfort the souls of the clan, and encourage scholarship.[4] The tradition of examining monks following the lectures may have begun at about this time as part of the effort to encourage monastic scholarship. This aspect of the ceremony also was closely associated with the *Vimalakīrti-nirdeśa* because of the debates between Vimalakīrti and various monks and bodhisattvas. No exact date for the origins of the examinations is found in historical records.

As the Fujiwara clan rose to prominence, the Yuima-e came to be recognized as the preeminent monastic assembly because it was held at the Fujiwara clan temple. In 802, the lecturer at the Yuima-e was given the responsibility for lecturing at the Misai-e (held from the eighth through the fourteenth of the first month) in the palace. In 834, an edict specified that monks who had passed the test at the assembly were to receive appointments as rainy season lecturers at various temples.[5] From approximately 839 onward, serving as lecturer in the Yuima-e automatically entailed receiving appointments the following year as lecturer at two other major assemblies, the Misai-e and the Saishō-e. If a monk had served at these three assemblies, he received the title of *ikō* (literally, "past lecturer," indicating that he had served at the three major assemblies) and was eligible for certain other appointments, including positions in the Office of Monastic Affairs.[6] Although not all *ikō* were appointed to the Office of Monastic Affairs, approximately two-thirds did receive such appointments.[7] If the *ikō* was a Kōfukuji monk, he was eligible for appointment as abbot of that monastery. In 855, service as lecturer at the Yuima-e was considered to be one of the accomplishments that would qualify a monk as a lecturer or reader in the provinces. If the monk passed the test, then he had completed one of the five qualifications (*gokai*) for an appointment as lecturer in the provinces (*kōji*, not to be confused with the lecturers at the Yuima-e) or the three qualifications (*sankai*) for appointment as reader (*dokushi*) in the provinces.[8] Appointments as lecturers in the provinces were to go to monks at least forty-five years old. Because these appointments gave monks the opportunity to extend their influence into the provinces by serving a term (usually about six years) at the *kokubunji* (provincial monasteries), they played an important role in the expansion of Buddhism.[9] Although the provincial lecturers had originally been appointed both to oversee the monks and nuns in the provinces and to lecture, by the ninth century they primarily lectured.

Even when the Yuima-e had become an official assembly, it still retained much of its character as a merit-making service for the Fujiwara clan. According to the *Sanbō ekotoba* and other texts, the Yuima-e had brought the Fujiwaras prosperity: many emperors were born to Fujiwara women, and Fujiwara men were appointed to many high posts.[10]

The Format of the Yuima-e

The date of the beginning of examinations through debate of promising monks at the Yuima-e is not clear. Horiike Shunpō finds evidence of the presence of a candidate (*ryūgi* or *rissha*,[11] literally, "those who established the teaching") in examinations as early as 784; because the entry mentioning the candidate does not identify his presence as unusual, the beginning of the debates could have been earlier.[12] The addition of examinations would have been in keeping with the mission of the Yuima-e as a ceremony that promoted Buddhist learning. With time, the structure of the debates became more elaborate and officially sanctioned. Examiners (*shōgisha*, literally, "those whose mastery of doctrine was detailed") asked follow-up questions of the candidate. They would judge the candidate's answers and then publicly announce whether he had passed (*toku*), failed (*ryaku*), or performed indifferently (*mihan*). The examiners had to be learned monks, men who had already served as lecturers at the three major assemblies in Nara or who had been appointed masters of discipline in the Office of Monastic Affairs. In addition, efforts were made to match the examiners with the contents of the debates. In other words, if the subject was Sanron doctrine, an examiner from the Sanron school would be most appropriate. In 911, a judge (*tandai*) was added as the high official of the examinations; he was particularly responsible for questions concerning Buddhist logic. Early judges served for several years, giving the ceremonies continuity in personnel. From 961, the abbot of Kōfukuji generally served as judge, placing the Yuima-e firmly under the control of Kōfukuji. However, from 1025, two judges were appointed, one from another monastery.

The transition of the Yuima-e from a private into a public ceremony was reflected in the manner in which those monks eligible to be in the "audience" (*chōshu*) were chosen. According to the *Engishiki*, the Office of Monastic Affairs was to determine the thirty monks who served as the audience approximately one month before the assembly was held. But before the Office of Monastic Affairs could make its decision, the head of the Fujiwara clan was permitted to review the choices.[13] The Fujiwaras continued to influence the Yuima-e even after it had become a court-sponsored ceremony. For example, the court sent an official emissary to the ceremony, but usually chose a member of the Fujiwara clan. Fujiwara clan rules specified that certain members of the clan attend the ceremony; if they didn't, they would be suspended from their posts. Finally, the Fujiwara made gifts to the lecturers and other participants in the Yuima-e.[14] The Fujiwara attitude toward the Yuima-e reflected their belief that the karmic merit from the ceremony helped them maintain their domination of court life.

Because being chosen as part of the audience was an important step toward selection as lecturer at the assembly, the number in the audience was increased to forty in 900. Much of this increase was accounted for by an increase in the number of candidates for the examinations (since candidates were included in the enumeration of the audience). By this time, the Yuima-e had ten candidates.[15] In addition, various temples had claims on a certain number of positions in the audience. For example, edicts were issued giving one annual position in the audience to a Tendai monk from Gangyōji in 887 and one from Tōkōji in 905.[16] Other edicts specifying positions for monks from various temples are also found in the *Ruijū sandaikyaku*. Kōfukuji was guaranteed at least ten positions, and Yakushiji, the site of the Saishō-e, was to receive five.[17] The demand for positions in the Yuima-e reflects the ceremony's growing importance as a key step in the advance of monastic careers. Other monasteries had lectures and debates, but that of the Yuima-e was a necessary step toward high offices as provincial lecturers and positions in the Office of Monastic Affairs.

Efforts also were made to ensure that the assembly would not be completely dominated by the Hossō school. In 802, an edict had directed that monks from all six of the Nara schools be invited and had specifically criticized the rivalry between Hossō and Sanron monks.[18] In later edicts, the importance of including Tendai monks is specifically mentioned.[19] These edicts were effective to a certain extent; in the early Heian period (793–930), 31 percent of the lecturers were from the Kōfukuji, but by the middle of the period (930–1086), 62 percent came from that temple.[20]

The early Yuima-e were grueling examinations that took years for a monk to prepare for. Each of the temples that supplied monks had a series of preliminary steps that participants had to pass through. For example, the monks from Kōfukuji eventually had to go through the Hōkō-e (Vaipulya assembly, said to have been established between 707 and 715), Hokke-e (Assembly on the *Lotus Sūtra*, said to have been established in 817), and Jion-e (Assembly in honor of Tz'u-en, the founder of the Hossō school, established in 951). These assemblies all took approximately a week to complete and were structured in a manner similar to the Yuima-e, with lecturers and examinations.[21] Because completing the various requirements could take years, most candidates at the Yuima-e were in their forties.[22] Another decade might pass before one was appointed lecturer at the Yuima-e. Thus a monk appointed as lecturer at the age of fifty was considered to be young. Many were in their seventies when they were appointed.[23]

A monk who was named as lecturer or candidate usually had approximately six months to prepare. Some of them wrote texts that give an idea of the issues on which they were tested. For example, Shōhan (962–999) of the Kōfukuji was tested at the Yuima-e in 984, one year before Ryōgen's death, on problems in the first fascicle of Tz'u-en's *Fa-yüan i-lin ch'ang* (*T* 1861).[24] Other years, topics such as the eight levels of consciousness were chosen. Because the topics generally seem to have focused on topics vital to Hossō, Kōfukuji monks were obviously at an advantage. Other favorite topics were the *Hua-yen ching* (*Avataṁsaka*) and problems in Buddhist logic.[25]

Later Developments in the Yuima-e

The nature of the Yuima-e examinations eventually changed from a testing ground for the brightest and most able monks to a more formalistic ritual that enabled the sons of the nobles and the rich to advance in the monastic world. This shift can be traced in the appointments of the sons of nobles to positions in the Yuima-e.

Even in the Heian period, the Fujiwara clan probably played some role in determining which monks received invitations to serve as lecturers. However, few monks from the Fujiwara clan served as lecturers at the assembly during Ryōgen's youth in the tenth century, indicating that monks from the lower classes could advance to high monastic ranks. However, by the twelfth or thirteenth century, candidates from the nobility or rich families were given the general topic and sometimes answers beforehand to prepare. Table 12 shows the distribution of temples that had monks appointed lecturers and indicates the number of lecturers from the Fujiwara clan.[26] These figures indicate that members of the Fujiwara clan did not dominate appointments to the Yuima-e until the eleventh century. They also suggest that the monastic world was relatively open during Ryōgen's youth. Despite the competition that existed between the Tendai and Hossō schools, six monks from the Tendai temple Enryakuji served as lecturers at the Yuima-e between 900 and 950. However, from the eleventh century onward, Kōfukuji (along with Tōdaiji) completely dominated the lectures. Small numbers of the monks from Yakushiji, Daianji, and Tōdaiji were from the Sanron school; and, between 859 and 940, about half of the Tōdaiji lecturers were from the Kegon school. All of the lecturers from Kōfukuji, however, were Hossō. In addition, all of the temples listed but Enryakuji also sent Hossō monks as lecturers. Thus, the Hossō school increasingly dominated the Yuima-e. In the last half of the eleventh century, the Tendai school managed to establish its own system of officially recognized assemblies to qualify its members for official appointments.

The increasing numbers of nobles entering monasteries received special treatment at the Yuima-e. They were given appointments while they were still young and often without much regard to their academic

TABLE 12

LECTURERS AT THE YUIMA-E
ACCORDING TO TEMPLE AFFILIATION AND DATE

	859–900	901–950	951–999	1000–1050	1051–1099	1100–1150	1151–1180
Fujiwaras	1	3	3	16	25	24	19
Kōfukuji	10	21	24	36	41	38	23
Yakushiji	6	4	4	2	0	1	0
Gangōji	5	7	2	0	0	0	0
Tōdaiji	8	11	12	11	7	10	6
Saidaiji	1	1	1	0	0	0	0
Enryakuji	1	6	4	1	0	0	0
Daianji	3	1	2	1	0	0	0

achievements. In contrast, monks from the commoners still had to maintain the same high standards as before. The result was that by 1169 one candidate was supposed to be from the noble classes (*kishu*), one from "good" families (*ryōke*), and one from monks who had trained and studied (*shugaku*) assiduously.[27] The differences were reflected in the ages of the appointees. In the twelfth century, when monks from the common classes were appointed to the Yuima-e, they were often in their forties as candidates and in their fifties and older as lecturers. However, monks from the noble or rich classes were appointed at a much younger age, frequently in their teens; they often served as lecturers in their twenties.[28] In addition, they did not have to wait a decade or more to be appointed as a lecturer at the Yuima-e. They advanced to prominence much more quickly than did monks from the common classes. Soon monks from common families found appointments extremely difficult to obtain. From 1185 to 1292, 16 percent of the lecturers were from noble families, 63 percent from "good" families, and 21 percent from common families.[29] The figures for appointments as abbot of such major temples as Kōfukuji and Tōdaiji were even more slanted against commoners. The result was a decline in the learning of the candidates for the examinations; they were too young to have mastered doctrinal material. In addition, they frequently were given the questions (and sometimes the answers) before the examinations.[30]

In the following sections, the Tendai examination system is described. The similarities in format and in the general historical developments between the Yuima-e and the Tendai examinations are indicated.

The History and Institutional
Significance of the Examinations

The Tendai Examination System before Ryōgen

The origins of the examination system in the Tendai school are said to date from 798, when Saichō invited Nara monks, primarily from the Hossō school, to Mount Hiei for the Shimotsuki-e (Assembly in memory of Chih-i, de facto founder of the Chinese T'ien-t'ai school) to discuss the *Lotus Sūtra*. Although disputes concerning the differences between the Hossō and Tendai positions probably took place, the contents or format of these meetings are not known. Apparently, no young Tendai monk was tested as a candidate at the discussions, and they thus cannot be considered to be examinations in the strict sense of the word. However, when Saichō returned from China, he is said to have held the Shimotsuki-e again in 801 and on the fifth day to have added an examination to test his disciple. Three Hossō monks served as examiners: Enjaku (d. 822) of Daianji, Ryōun of Yakushiji, and Jikō of Tōdaiji.[31]

The Shimotsuki-e consisted of a series of ten lectures on the eight-fascicle *Lotus Sūtra* and its opening (*Wu-liang i ching*) and capping (*Kuan P'u-hsien ching*) *sūtras*, each of which was one fascicle; examinations were probably held sometime after the day's lectures had been completed. As a result, Tendai examinations have traditionally been held at night, often concluding at a very late hour in an atmosphere that must add to the solemnity of the proceedings. In the early ninth century, because Tendai monks had not yet participated at the major assemblies in Nara, they were not yet qualified to serve as judges in an examination system; consequently, monks from Nara presided over the first examination as judges. The examination was probably not held for the next few years, but was revived in 809, when Gishin served as judge (*hakushi*) and tested his disciple Enshu; this was probably the first occasion when a Tendai monk served as the judge for an examination.

From 846, an examination system was also instituted at the Minazuki-e (or Rokugatsu-e, Assembly for Saichō). Both Tendai and Nara monks were candidates for the examinations in this assembly, but the judges were almost always from the Nara schools. Because this examination also followed lectures on the *Lotus Sūtra,* the Minazuki-e assemblies were sometimes known as Hokke-daie (great *Lotus* assemblies).

The sources that maintain that *shimotsuki-e* examinations began during the lifetimes of Saichō and Gishin are all very late and include little information other than the brief account summarized above.[32] Moreover, examinations are not mentioned prominently in the biographies of early Tendai monks such as Ennin and Enchin, suggesting that they were probably not a vital step on the ladder to prominence during that time. Inoue Mitsusada has suggested that Tendai scholarship declined after Annen's time.[33] However, because a debate or examination system of some sort was in place during Ryōgen's youth, accounts of the early history of the examinations probably should be accepted, but with caution because they may have been embellished as part of a later attempt to legitimate the Tendai examination system.

Ryōgen's Reform of the Examination System

On 9-10-966, two weeks after his appointment as *zasu*, Ryōgen submitted ten items for approval to the court. Little is known about the contents of his proposals, but among them were details of a change in the examination system and a request that the court increase the number of masters of Esoteric Buddhism at the Sōjiin by three, to sixteen.[34] These proposals are important for several reasons. First, they indicate that Ryōgen intended to take an active role in shaping and reforming the Tendai school from the very beginning of his administration. Ryōgen's decision to use examinations in administering the order is not surprising because debates at Enryakuji, at Kōfukuji, and at court had played major roles in Ryōgen's career. Second, they reflect his interest in reviving the study of Tendai exoteric teachings and promoting the Esoteric Buddhist tradition followed by Ennin's lineage.[35] Ryōgen may have been responding to the interests of the nobility to whom he was increasingly catering with his proposal to revive examinations.[36] The sons of nobles were better educated than commoners and might have been interested in a more academic approach to Buddhism than commoners were. However, within two months, a huge fire would destroy the center of the Tendai establishment on Mount Hiei; as a result, Ryōgen's energies for the next few years would be devoted to fund-raising and rebuilding the Tendai monasteries and chapels.

Three days after he submitted his proposals, Ryōgen was called to the palace to lead twenty monks in the performance of the ceremony of the Buddha of Abundant Light for seven days because of some natural anomaly; the major participants were rewarded with permission and funds for an additional student each. While he was there, Emperor Murakami personally questioned him about his ten proposals.[37] In the twelfth month of 966, just three months after he had been appointed *zasu,* Ryōgen was promoted from supernumerary master of discipline to master of discipline, granted three additional *ajari* for the Sōjiin, and given permission to institute a new examination system on Mount Hiei as part of the Minazuki-e.[38] Ryōgen's initial petition had been to hold the examinations in conjunction with the Shimotsuki-e, but circumstances led to their performance as part of the Minazuki-e. Examinations were not included as part of the Shimotsuki-e until 1044; after that time, they were held twice every year at the Minazuki-e and Shimotsuki-e.[39]

The first performance of the examinations proposed by Ryōgen was planned for 967, with Kaikō as candidate (*rissha*) and Bōsan as judge (*tandai*). Because Bōsan had been passed over when Ryōgen was appointed *zasu,* he was not inclined to accept the appointment. When Kaikō resigned as candidate for reasons that are no longer clear, the examination had to be postponed. Perhaps Kaikō resigned because he sympathized with Bōsan's frustration over being passed over for Ryōgen as *zasu.*[40] Instead of waiting for the next performance of the Shimotsuki-e, about six months later in the sixth month of 968, the examinations were held for the first time during the Minazuki-e. Zengei (899 or 903–980) served as *tandai,* replacing Bōsan, who had died the previous year. Shun'ei (b. 924) was the candidate. In addition, Kakuen (b. 931), who had probably replaced Kaikō as *rissha* at the canceled examinations in 967, was tested.[41] The two candidates were examined on the Tendai interpretation of the three views (*sangan*) and on Buddhist logic.[42]

In 967, semiannual examinations to be held in the spring and fall were established at Ryōgen's quarters, the Jōshinbō (also known as the Lecture Hall for the Four Seasonal Assemblies [Shiki-kōdō]) in Yokawa on Mount Hiei. The spring and fall assemblies were part of a series of four annual gatherings, one for each season. Each of the four assemblies was to focus on a particular text. In the spring, they lectured on the *Nirvāṇa-sūtra.* Summer was devoted to the *Avataṁsaka-sūtra* (either the sixty- or eighty-fascicle text). The *Lotus Sūtra* was the topic in the fall. The winter assembly topic was based on the *Mahāsaṃnipāta, Vimalakīrti-nirdeśa,* or the large *Prajñāpāramitā-sūtra.* The assemblies usually were for a period of five days, though sometimes they were longer. Ryōgen had begun the four seasonal assemblies in 967 shortly after the Ōwa debates to encourage the monks under his direct control to debate and apply themselves to the study of exoteric doctrine. The participants would take turns serving as lecturers or being in the audience. To qualify as a candidate at the Minazuki-e, a monk was expected to have served in the Jōshinbō assembly for six or seven years.[43] Funds for the assembly were to come from twenty *chō* of the Kioka manor, which had been given to Ryōgen by Fujiwara no Morosuke, and the merits from the lectures were to ensure Morosuke's salvation; if anyone dared to misappropriate these funds, Ryōgen asked his followers to exhume his remains and leave them at the culprit's gate.[44] The stress placed by Ryōgen on debates is seen in his will:

> For the eight lectures on the anniversary of my death, debates certainly should be performed. The people of the world may feel that a taboo should exist against such debates on the anniversary of a death, but my main practice was debate. My disciples understand this. If they feel that they should repay their obligations to me, then they should lecture and debate rather than perform other ceremonies. Through such lectures and debates, good is spread to all sentient beings; they cause the defilements to be cut off and wisdom to arise so that one will quickly realize Buddhahood.[45]

Why Ryōgen Reformed the Tendai Examination System

Ryōgen's proposal served several purposes in helping him govern the Tendai school. First, Ryōgen obtained court sanction for the examinations and defined them as extending beyond Tendai doctrine; he called the system "*kōgaku ryūgi*," meaning "examination on 'broad learning'" (that is, doctrinal positions beyond those of the Tendai school).[46] In doing so, Ryōgen set up the examinations as an alternative to the Yuima-e, which was dominated by Hossō monks. Ryōgen's petition in 967 states that only Tendai monks serve as judge at the *kōgaku ryūgi*, further reinforcing Tendai claims to an independent examination tradition.[47]

The appointment of the Tendai monk Zen'yu as lecturer at the Yuima-e in 967 suggests that Hossō monks might have been trying to counter Ryōgen's proposal by opening the Yuima-e to more Tendai monks.[48] If this was Hossō policy, it apparently met with failure: the Tendai examinations flourished, and only a few Tendai monks were appointed as lecturers to the Yuima-e after Ryōgen proposed holding *kōgaku ryūgi* in 966. Although Tendai monks were named lecturers in 967, 977, 988, 990, 999, 1010 and 1020, the monks appointed in 988, 999, and 1010 declined invitations to lecture at the Yuima-e and were replaced by Hossō monks. The appointment of Tendai monks as Yuima-e lecturers in 988 and 990 coincides with the increasing factionalism between Sanmon and Jimon blocs and may represent Hossō attempts to exploit Tendai divisions. However, the Yuima-e had ceased to be important for the advancement of Tendai fortunes. After 1020, Tendai monks were not asked to serve as lecturers at the Yuima-e.

A second reason for the proposal was to place monks from the various factions within the Tendai school under Ryōgen's control by establishing objective standards for examining monks. The status of Tendai monks in the middle of the tenth century depended to a large degree on their ties to a particular teacher and their expertise in Esoteric ritual. This situation gave rise to factionalism because the allegiance of a monk to his particular Esoteric teacher was emphasized. Each faction maintained certain differences in the way rituals were performed or interpreted; as a result, advancement was not necessarily due to any objective public standard. Because so much of the Esoteric tradition was kept secret, senior monks exercised considerable latitude in supporting their favorite monks. In addition, monks often belonged to various halls dedicated to the performance of Esoteric rituals; these buildings had been established and financed by various emperors as august prayer-offering temples (*goganji;* see chapter 2). In establishing the examination and debate system, Ryōgen awarded status and promotions primarily on the basis of a public display of knowledge of Buddhism that he oversaw. Monks received the training needed to be chosen as candidates by participating for a number of years in the seasonal assemblies at the Jōshinbō, Ryōgen's quarters in Yokawa. In addition, Ryōgen expected to be the final arbiter in the Minazuki-e examinations by occasionally serving as examiner and determining the appropriateness of a monk's answer.[49] The manner in which the examination system served to balance the Esoteric Buddhism is made clear by the Shingon school's request in 1113 that it be allowed to substitute Esoteric consecrations for participation in the examination and lecture system.[50] In addition, the modern scholar Uejima Susumu has pointed out that the claim that Esoteric Buddhism came to dominate Buddhism during the Heian period fails to give the examination system the credit it deserves for keeping exoteric Buddhist doctrine vital.[51]

Third, Ryōgen's appointments of Bōsan and then Zengei, both members of the Jimon faction, as the first *tandai* at the Minazuki-e examinations suggest that Ryōgen was attempting to draw upon their experience at the Yuima-e and to appeal to monks from outside his own bloc of the Tendai school. Esoteric Buddhism was more difficult to use to appeal to and control other factions of the Tendai school because it depended on personal relations between master and disciple and a strict adherence to lineages, but exoteric teachings could serve as a public forum to allow Jimon monks to participate in Tendai life.

Finally, the examinations and debates focused on exoteric subjects (especially the *Lotus Sūtra*), thereby helping to reestablish the balance between Esoteric and exoteric learning.[52] The renewed consideration being given to exoteric studies probably contributed to the growing emphasis on Tendai teachings on such subjects as quicker paths to enlightenment through adherence to the *Lotus Sūtra;* such teachings would have helped supporters of exoteric Buddhism compete with Esoteric masters.[53] Ryōgen's interest in exoteric doctrine should not be interpreted as a rejection of Esoteric ritual but rather as a return to the Japanese Tendai position expounded by Saichō that Perfect teachings and Esoteric Buddhism had the same purport. In many cases, Tendai monks performed both exoteric and Esoteric practices as did Saichō and Ryōgen. However, more than a few monks favored one tradition over the other.

The Establishment of an Independent Tendai Lecture System

Part of Ryōgen's goal in setting up an examination system was to free Tendai monks from the need to rely on appointments to the Yuima-e as candidates and lecturers for advancement. Tendai monks came to occupy the majority of positions in the Office of Monastic Affairs within a decade after Ryōgen instituted the Tendai examinations. Although his success was partly due to his patrons, whose support helped him and his disciples advance rapidly through the ranks of the Office of Monastic Affairs, the examination system certainly played an important role in legitimizing his disciples and helping them qualify for court appointments.[54]

The process of setting up a system of court-sanctioned Tendai assemblies and examinations was finally completed in the late eleventh century when the Tendai school set up an officially authorized series of three assemblies that paralleled those of the Nara temples. Political considerations lay behind this new system of examinations. The temples at which they were held were set up as a religious base by cloistered emperors to rival the Fujiwara-dominated system of temples in Nara.[55] This system began in 1072 with the Hokke-e at Enshūji and was followed by the Daijō-e (Mahāyāna assembly) at Hosshōji in 1078. The two assemblies were immediately linked together and were referred to as the "two assemblies" (*ryō-e* or *ni-e*). Even after the third assembly, the Saishō-e at Enshūji, was added in 1082, the term "two assemblies" was still used at times.[56] As their names indicate, the Hokke-e was primarily a lecture series on the *Lotus Sūtra* and the Saishō-e was a lecture series based on the *Suvarṇaprabhāsa*. The choice of the *Suvarṇaprabhāsa* was based on the use of this text in the Misai-e, an assembly that was held at the beginning of the year at the palace and that was one of the three major assemblies of Nara. The Daijō-e consisted of lectures on the following five (groups of) *sūtras: Avataṁsaka, Vaipulya, Prajñā-pāramitā, Lotus,* and *Nirvāṇa*. The choice and order of the lectures was based largely on the Tendai exegetical system of five periods or five flavors, but without the period of the *āgamas*.

An examination was held only at the Hokke-e. Passing the examinations qualified a person to serve as lecturer at the three Tendai assemblies, a procedure clearly based on the precedents of the Yuima-e and the two assemblies associated with it. Moreover, after having served as lecturer, a monk could be appointed to various offices, including those in the Office of Monastic Affairs. Monks from the Jimon and Sanmon factions of the Tendai school were supposed to serve as judge at the examination in alternate years.[57] The system was discontinued around the end of the Nanboku period, when the Enshūji and Hosshōji burned.

Later Developments in the Examination System

Tracing the later development of the examination system is a difficult task because many of the texts vital to such a study are still unpublished and have not been adequately studied. In addition, the burning of Mount Hiei by Oda Nobunaga in the sixteenth century resulted in the loss of many sources. As a result, scholars are far from understanding the changes in the Tendai educational system. In this section, several of the significant later developments in the system are described.

During the Kamakura period, the number of candidates increased, indicating that the examinations may have begun to evolve from a grueling test to a formalistic ritual service at about this time. In 1214, at about the same time the numbers of candidates were increasing, an imperial emissary was dispatched to witness the examinations at the Minazuki-e.[58] Much pageantry surrounding his arrival and subsequent activities was introduced. Similar shifts occurred in the Yuima-e; in both cases, the special treatment accorded the sons of the nobility played a major role in the changes in the assemblies.

New topics were introduced; discussions of Esoteric doctrine, the precepts, and Pure Land came to play important roles in the tradition. Exoteric topics developed in new ways; efforts to determine the essential message of the *Lotus Sūtra* and express it in the concise form used in the presentation of examination questions probably contributed to the emergence and development of secret oral traditions (*kuden*). An investigation of the debate literature from the Muromachi period might reveal some of the ways in which Tendai scholars answered the challenge posed by the new Kamakura schools.

Finally, the examination itself was interpreted in the light of original enlightenment (*hongaku*) teachings. The candidate was said to manifest the realization of Buddhahood in this very existence (*sokushin jōbutsu*), and the Lecture Hall was considered the Buddha Land of Eternal Tranquil Light (Jōjakkōdo). Dainichi nyorai (Mahāvaircocana) was enshrined as the main image, symbolizing the agreement of Esoteric and exoteric doctrine.[59] The performance of the ceremony at night was said to reflect the purported fact that all Buddhas had realized Buddhahood during the night. The *tandai* was representative of the eternal Śākyamuni portrayed in the *Lotus Sūtra*, the Buddha who had attained supreme enlightenment in the distant past; through his efforts the candidate was led to supreme enlightenment. The imperial emissary symbolized the agreement of Buddhism and the state.[60] Such changes reflected the shift of emphasis as the examination evolved into more of a ritualistic formality than an actual test of the candidate's abilities. The format of the literature for the examinations also changed. Instead of *shiki,* the extensive question-and-answer formats that explored the details of individual topics, debate or examination manuals were written that were composed of short discussions of each of the topics on which a monk might be examined.[61]

Major changes also occurred after Oda Nobunaga burned the Tendai establishment on Mount Hiei in 1571. The examinations were revived through the efforts of Tenkai (1536?–1643) and others in 1589. To revive the examination system, Tenkai had to enlist the support of Tokugawa Ieyasu (1542–1616), who, in fact, attended many examinations. Ieyasu's interest in the examinations has been described by Tsuji Zennosuke as being motivated by political agendas such as bringing the monasteries under his control and providing a place where he might consult in private with his advisers. However, Sonehara Satoshi has pointed out other goals that might be typified as more religious. When the examinations were held in front of Ieyasu, he was emulating previous rulers who had presided over debates. His position could be likened to that of the world-ruling king who protected Buddhism. But, more important, Ieyasu seems to have taken an active interest in the debates, perhaps even influencing the choice of topics. A common theme was how a person who had committed evil might still find salvation, a topic that must have seemed germane to a man such as Ieyasu, who had risen to power through military force and political intrigue. Finally, Tenkai may have used Ieyasu's presence at the examinations to further his efforts to install Ieyasu as a *kami*. Just as *kami* might be said to gain additional power after being exposed to the teachings of Buddhism, so might Ieyasu, deified after his death, be said to have gained power by having presided over the examinations during his lifetime.[62]

The Tendai examinations eventually were held every four years and were open to virtually an unlimited number of monks, many of them from temples in the provinces. The timing of the ceremony was occasionally altered to correspond with key anniversaries of the Tendai school or because of disasters such as the Kantō earthquake or World War II. The numbers of candidates for most of the examinations from 1599 until the present day are recorded; the highest number to participate was 533 in 1941 and the lowest was 77 in 1874, during the Meiji persecution of Buddhism. With the increase in numbers of candidates, the ceremony came to play a role as a ritual that brought together monks from the various parts of Japan.

Today approximately three hundred candidates appear when the ceremony is held every four years.[63] Because such large numbers could not be expected to pass the stringent tests used earlier, they were given the examination questions beforehand and memorized or read the answers. The examination of the first candidate is still stringent and may take three hours, but subsequent candidates are examined in an increasingly cursory fashion. In addition, the examination extends over several days, with a lecture on the *Lotus Sūtra* being held from nine at night and the examinations beginning at 11:30. Special readings of technical terms and the melodies used in chanting the answers have been set. In addition, various elements to make the night ceremonies more impressive have been instituted.

The role of imperial messengers sent to witness the ceremonies was also expanded until the processions surrounding his arrival, his inspection of various treasures of the monastery, and his entertainment through debates by young boys (*tsugai rongi*) became as important as the testing of candidates.[64] The debates by young boys, usually of elementary school age, imitate Ryōgen's debate at the Yuima-e. Although the rigor with which the examinations were conducted declined in most cases, Tendai scholars have argued that many monks took the examinations seriously until this century; evidence of their importance is found in the voluminous but still unpublished material on Tendai debates. In addition, the Tendai school has rigorously kept many of the old traditions associated with the examinations.[65]

The Format of the Early Tendai Examination

Few sources survive that contain many details about the examinations used during Ryōgen's time. The following discussion is based on episodes in the biographies of Ryōgen's disciples Kakuun (953–1007) and Genshin (942–1017) and supplemented with an early record from Onjōji.

According to Kakuun's biography, Ryōgen and other Tendai monks are said to have urged the young monk to be a candidate in the examination. He appeared wearing a plain robe (*hōi*), causing everyone to sigh with admiration.[66] His topic (*gi*) was the four types of Tendai meditation. Kakuun answered the various questions. When he discussed the meditation on Amida's Pure Land, he was in tears without realizing it, and the audience too began to weep. After he had answered nine of the ten questions correctly, the judge, Zengei, felt that his knowledge on the subject had been exhausted. Ryōgen was concerned because no candidate had ever received a perfect score (*zentoku*) in the examination and insisted on taking over the questioning. Ryōgen asked Kakuun to discuss the seed syllables of the six manifestations of Kannon. Kakuun replied that he had not studied Esoteric Buddhism and could not answer. Ryōgen said that since the examination was based on broad learning, he had no excuse not to know about Esoteric Buddhism. Kakuun consequently received a score of nine passes and one indeterminate. Kakuun went on to study Esoteric Buddhism and was also known as a master of logic and Yogācāra Buddhism.[67]

The story of Kakuun demonstrates a number of features of the early examination system. According to Ryōgen's rules, the candidate could be chosen either through a seniority system or because he was particularly promising.[68] Only one monk was chosen as a candidate each year. This practice seems to have changed during the first half of the eleventh century: the number of candidates at Onjōji was increased to two in 1034, three in 1037, and four in 1041. Each of the candidates in a given

year had a different set of questions.[69] At Enryakuji, only one candidate
was tested at first. However, after the Kōgaku ryūgi was instituted as part
of the Shimotsuki-e in 1044, two candidates were tested annually at Enryakuji, one at each of the two examinations on broad learning on
Mount Hiei. By the beginning of the Kamakura period, the *zasu* had
acquired the right to appoint the candidates at each of the two meetings. According to the *Tendai zasuki*, Jien first did this in 1193; four years
later, when Prince Shōnin (1169–1197) was serving as *zasu*, six candidates were appointed.[70] The number seems to have stayed at about five
or six. The distribution of candidates between the various areas on
Mount Hiei also was specified as factionalism on Mount Hiei became
more pronounced: three candidates were to come from the Eastern
Pagoda region, two from the Western Pagoda area, and one from
Yokawa. This apportionment of candidates may not have been typical,
however: citations in the *Tendai zasuki* show a fluctuating number of
candidates and do not mention any set numbers of men from each
area.[71] In 1214, when Jien was reappointed as *zasu*, ten candidates were
appointed.

The examination had a format of ten questions on one or two major subjects; the configuration of ten questions had been introduced in
798 in the test for yearly ordinands (*nenbundosha*). A candidate had to
answer at least five questions satisfactorily to pass.[72] As the story of
Kakuun makes clear, virtually no one was allowed to answer all ten correctly. In fact, later sources list the scores of some of the most eminent
members of the Tendai school to demonstrate that even scholars such
as Genshin did not receive perfect scores. The receipt of a perfect score
would have indicated that the candidate was virtually a Buddha.[73]

The term "*san*," wooden sticks that had various questions written on
them, is used in Kakuun's story to refer to the problems to be discussed.
The judge prepared the candidate's questions by writing them on pieces
of wood that were then sealed in a box. The candidate would take a *san*
from a box and read it aloud; the *san* would then be given to the *tandai*
or passed to the questioners who examined the candidate. This procedure ensured that the candidate would not know the question he was
to answer until the time of the examination. The term "*san*" originally
came from "*sangi*" (divination sticks) because they resembled the sticks
in shape.[74] The questions on the *san* were short, consisting of as few as
six to eight characters;[75] and the candidate would have to expound on
the subject or question and clarify it in the course of his examination.

Although no questioners (*monja* or *nanja*) are mentioned in Kakuun's story, in later Tendai examinations a number of monks (usually five) would be responsible for asking follow-up questions to probe the degree of the candidate's knowledge about each of the ten questions he was to answer.[76] During the examination, the candidate was seated on an elevated seat, facing an image of the Buddha with the questioners seated behind him. His answers were thus directed more toward the Buddha than to the scholars who interrogated him.

The follow-up inquiries posed by the questioners sometimes assumed a set format. A typical pattern would be (1) the basic idea of the issue, (2) the *sūtra* and *śāstra* citations relevant to the issue, (3) an analysis of the central passage, (4) calling other passages into question, (5) returning to the main idea (as in the first inquiry).[77] A variety of criteria were used by different factions of the Tendai school to judge the candidate's performance. For example, if the candidate could explain the question but not cite the relevant passages (or vice versa), then he was graded "indeterminate." If he could neither explain the passage nor cite the relevant passages, he failed the question.[78]

Only one major topic, the four types of meditation, is mentioned in the story of Kakuun's examination. However, almost all candidates had to be concerned with two major topics: a primary (*gōgi*) and a secondary (*soegi*) topic. Examples of major topics would be such subjects as the four types of meditation (*shishu zanmai*) or the three views. Five questions would then be asked about each major topic, with each of these questions being investigated through five follow-up questions. The questioners might make further inquiries after the follow-up questions to clarify points. Thus a candidate had to reply to at least fifty questions during the grueling examination. The *Tandai kojitsuki* (Record of precedents for judges) describes the difference between the primary and secondary topics as follows: "The primary subject plants the seeds that lead to Buddhahood; the secondary subject assists in the planting, [just as] the classification of the eight teachings assists the *Lotus Sūtra* in the actual planting of the seeds." Later in the same text, the following opinion is recorded: "The primary topic elucidates the essential teaching, the cardinal message. When one has passed the examination, he has mastered the teachings of the school. The secondary topic furthers [the study of] the essential teachings. The secondary topic includes problems from *Abhidharmakośa*, *Mahāvibhāṣa*, and logic."[79]

One of the few cases when two topics were not used occurred in the case of special candidates who had been advanced over those who had more seniority (*chōotsu rissha*) at the Onjōji in 1027–1028; such candidates were required to discuss only one topic.[80] However, this special dispensation seems to have been abandoned quickly.

Most of the students tested seem to have passed. They probably would not have been allowed to appear if they were not capable of doing well in the examination. However, evidence does exist that occasionally students were not passed. Some sources indicate that unsuccessful candidates had to leave Mount Hiei.[81] But as the following story suggests, in other cases they may have been given a second chance. According to the *Mii zokutōki,* Hyōban was a candidate at the Onjōji examination in 1026. No score is recorded for him in that examination, but five years later he appeared again as a successful candidate with a score of eight passes, one indeterminate, and one fail.[82] Scores for a number of other candidates are missing from the *Mii zokutōki;* information does not exist to verify whether the candidates failed in these cases or whether the records have lacunae. Successful candidates usually had scores of seven or eight passes; no one in the *Mii zokutōki* received a perfect score.

The severity of the examinations can be determined from the score of Genshin, one of Ryōgen's best students and probably the outstanding Tendai scholar of the late tenth century: seven passes and three indeterminates.[83] The judge, Zengei, considered Genshin's answers overnight before passing him, an indication of the seriousness with which early examinations were treated. According to another interpretation, Genshin may have advanced a new interpretation of the subject that confused the judge.[84]

The examinations were sufficiently difficult even several centuries after they had begun that candidates must have felt themselves under considerable pressure. In 1232, the candidate was a monk from Yokawa named Kōshin. After the first question had been asked and he was being questioned on it, Kōshin suddenly left his seat, ran barefoot to the dining hall, where he disrobed, and disappeared. Although the other monks searched, no trace of him was found.[85]

The questioners did much of the work of examining the candidate, but the final decision about the score of the candidate belonged to the judge, who reserved the right to further examine the candidate; the *tandai* was the man ultimately responsible for correcting errors and praising accurate and meticulous answers. The *tandai* in Genshin's examination was Zengei, the same man who presided over the first Minazuki-e *kōgaku* examination and over Kakuun's examination. Miidera sources also suggest that a *tandai* held his position from year to year.

TABLE 13

EARLY *TANDAI* FOR TENDAI DEBATES

Name	Dates served	Dates of birth and death	Rank at appointment
Zengei	968–976	903?–980?	Supernumerary master of discipline (*gon-risshi*)
Zen'yu	977–979	913–990	Supernumerary master of discipline
Shōku	980–997	909–998	Supernumerary master of discipline
Jitsuin	998	945–1000	Greater bishop (*daisōzu*)
Myōgō	999–1001	954–1002	Supernumerary master of discipline
Kakuun	1002–1003	953–1007	Dharma-bridge (*hōkyō*)
Genshin	1004–1007	942–1017	Supernumerary lesser bishop (*gon-shōsōzu*)

The *Tandai shidai* records the names of judges for the debates at En-ryakuji. The first seven are shown in table 13.[86]

When the numbers of *tandai* at Onjōji increased to five in later years to coincide with the increasing numbers of candidates, only one of the *tandai* was to be new in any given year.[87]

A monk called a *chūki* (secretary) was appointed in later examinations to record the questions, answers, and scores, but he is not mentioned in early records. By the twelfth century, one or two secretaries were appointed at each examination.[88] Few, if any, records of early debates recorded by *chūki* would seem to exist, and none have been published.

Nobles and the Examinations

Although this discussion of examinations in the Tendai school has not been concerned with laymen, evidence does exist that some lay believers were interested in the examinations. Before the actual examinations began, candidates usually read a statement (*hyōbyaku* or *keibyaku*) about the purpose of the examination as they stood before the *tandai*. Early examples of these statements discuss in florid language the subjects upon which the candidates would be tested. The preparation of such statements would seem to indicate that the candidates had prior knowledge of at least the general subject area upon which they would be examined. A number of candidates had laymen compose their statements, incorporating various references to non-Buddhist Chinese literature as a demonstration of broad knowledge. Thirty-one statements are collected in the *Honchō bunshū* and two in the *Chōya gunsai.*[89] A number of nobles from prominent families of the eleventh century are among the authors, including Fujiwara no Akihira (989–1066) and his two sons, Fujiwara no Atsumoto (1046–1106; one statement each) and Fujiwara no Atsumitsu (1063–1144; twenty-one statements). Nine statements by Ōe Masafusa (1041–1111) survive. The most popular topics were the two truths (twelve statements), the three bodies of the Buddha (nine statements,) the three sermons for *śrāvakas* (eight statements), the Buddha lands (four statements), and the ten such-likes (three statements). Participation by these nobles demonstrates the interest that they maintained in the examination system and Buddhist teachings and indirectly suggests that some nobles would have been intensely interested in such meetings as the Ōwa debates. Very few statements by monks of the Heian period survive. In more recent statements of purpose, the *tandai* and other officials of the examination are praised, and the candidate makes disparaging remarks about his own abilities.

Examination Topics

Examination Topics in Logic and Hossō Doctrine

Ryōgen's proposal did not limit the examination system on Mount Hiei to Tendai doctrine. The term *"kōgaku"* (broad learning) that Ryōgen used to describe the examinations suggested that doctrinal issues from a variety of schools would be used. In practice, when Tendai monks went outside their own school, they usually focused on issues in Hossō and logic, topics that reflected Tendai competition with the Hossō-dominated Yuima-e. Although only a few early records of examinations at Enryakuji survive, a list of topics used from 1017 to 1045 at Onjōji is extant. Onjōji monks were usually tested on Tendai topics, but the examinations occasionally included Yogācāra issues, such as the four types of *nirvāṇa*, four types of conditions, three types of perfuming, and seeds.[90] In addition, topics such as the three bodies of the Buddha, bodhisattvas, or Buddha lands might have included Hossō interpretations, but not enough is known of the contents of the examinations to ascertain this. Tendai interest in Hossō doctrine can be traced back to Saichō, who cited a variety of Yogācāra texts in his debates with Tokuitsu. Saichō was particularly adept at exploiting some of the differences between interpretations advanced in translations by Hsüan-tsang and Paramārtha. After Saichō's death, Tendai monks concentrated on Esoteric Buddhism and the study of Yogācāra declined. However, both Ennin and Enchin were sufficiently interested in Hossō that they brought back a number of Yogācāra texts, and Enchin is even said to have written two works on Yogācāra topics.[91]

Topics in the *Abhidharmakośa* are also mentioned in records from Onjōji and several other temples where Tendai and Nara monks occasionally debated. The *Abhidharmakośa*, although a Hīnayāna text, was traditionally studied as part of the Hossō curriculum. Thus training in *Abhidharmakośa* would have prepared Tendai monks for debates with Hossō monks.[92] Onjōji interest in the *Abhidharmakośa* can be traced back to Enchin, who studied it under Ts'un-shih in China; Enchin brought commentaries on the text by Yüan-hui, T'un-lin, and Hui-hui back to Japan and then wrote a short commentary (*ryakuchū*) on the verses of the *Abhidharmakośa* in 870, after his return to Japan.[93]

Many Tendai monks studied Buddhist logic, a discipline traditionally included in the Hossō curriculum, as a secondary subject. In fact, logic was included in the first examination on broad learning held in 968. Such studies helped Tendai monks compete with Hossō monks in public debates and probably contributed to the eventual Tendai domination of institutions such as the Office of Monastic Affairs.

The influence of the inclusion of *Abhidharmakośa* and Hossō doctrine as well as Buddhist logic in the Tendai curriculum is apparent when the works of one of Ryōgen's most able students, Genshin, are surveyed. One of Genshin's earliest works was a text on Buddhist logic, the *Inmyō ronsho shisōi ryakuchūshaku* (Short commentary on four logical errors from the *Inmyō ronsho*), written in 978 when he was thirty-six years old. The text is a discussion of a complex section from the Fa-hsiang patriarch Tz'u-en's (632–682) *Yin-ming ju-cheng-li lun-shu* (*T* no. 1840) that concerns four types of logical errors in arguments. Genshin did not limit himself to Tz'u-en's text, but also quoted from works by other Hossō monks and cited the opinion of his own teacher, Ryōgen. At the beginning of the work, Genshin described the events behind his decision to compile it. In 978, the Tendai monk Gonkō was selected to be tested at the Hokke-e. Although he was to be examined on Buddhist logic, he had difficulty understanding the subject and asked Genshin for help. Genshin consequently wrote this three-fascicle text on the subject, cit-

ing the opinions of Tendai monks such as Genshō and his teacher Ryōgen when possible, but also relying on Hossō sources.[94] Buddhist logic
continued to occupy Genshin's attention for many more years. Fourteen years later, in 992, he sent a copy of the work to China with the
Chinese merchant Yang Jen-lu. Genshin asked the monk Hsing-ch'an
of Mount Yün-huang to ask Fa-hsiang monks for their opinion of the
text. When he received no answer, he again sent a copy to China for an
opinion five years later, entrusting it to Ch'i-yin. These incidents suggest both the seriousness of Genshin's scholarship and his fascination
with logic throughout his life.[95] Genshin's interest in this subject was
stimulated in part by the format of the Tendai examinations on broad
learning.

Genshin also wrote many works concerning the *Abhidharmakośa* and
the *Ch'eng wei-shih lun*, two major sources in the Hossō curriculum.[96]
The fourteen-fascicle text *Daijō tai Kushashō* (Mahāyāna compared with
Abhidharmakośa), completed in 1005 while Genshin was a judge at the
examinations on broad learning, was a painstaking comparison of passages from the *Abhidharmakośa* with selections from Mahāyāna works,
such as the *Yogācārabhūmi* (*T* 1579) and *Abhidharmasamuccayavyākhya*
(*T* 1606) on similar subjects. More than three thousand quotations
from 158 texts have been identified in the text; but the *Ch'eng wei-shih
lun* was treated as the most authoritative source for Yogācāra, reflecting the role of the Genshin's work in preparing Tendai monks for debates with Hossō monks. In the preface to the *Daijō tai Kushashō*, Genshin praised the manner in which Hīnayāna doctrine was systematically
explained in the *Abhidharmakośa* and lamented the lack of a similar text
for Mahāyāna doctrine.[97] In his discussions of Yogācāra in the *Daijō tai
Kushashō*, Genshin generally adopted Dharmapāla's doctrinal stance,
the orthodox position for Hossō scholars, instead of becoming involved
with the variant theories advanced by other Yogācāra scholars.[98] However, Genshin's studies of these subjects was obviously motivated by more
than the desire to compete with Hossō monks. He was reputed to have
always said, "*Abhidharmakośa* and logic are superior teachings for this
defiled world (*edo*); (through) consciousness-only, we expect the Pure
Land. But the essential teachings (*shūgi*) of our school rely on Buddhahood."[99] Genshin was not the only Tendai monk of his generation
to be well versed in these subjects; his fellow student, Kakuun, was
praised for his astute questioning of Henku on Yogācāra and logic.[100]
The *Abhidharmakośa* was studied by some members of the Kurodani lineage of the Tendai school such as Enkan (1281–1356).

Tendai monks continued to study Yogācāra doctrine and Buddhist logic for approximately a century, but eventually discontinued such studies. In the list of topics used at the Onjōji examinations between 1017 and 1045, logic appeared only once and Yogācāra doctrines four times.[101] An event in 1072 reveals the Tendai rationale for rejecting logic. During the *Lotus Sūtra* lectures at the Enshūji, Raishin (1011–1078) of the Kōfukuji suggested that a problem in logic be included. The Tendai monk Raizō (1009?–1076) of Miidera argued that logic was not part of the Tendai curriculum and therefore he could not answer. Raishin, however, noted that logic was a powerful tool for determining the validity of statements and that it had been a subject at the *minazuki-e* examinations on Hiei. Raizō replied that he had not studied logic as a youth, but instead had put his energy into Tendai meditative exercises such as the three views in an instant (*sangan isshin*). When he was older, he had spent his time in Esoteric practices. Logic was useful for refuting heterodox teachings, but not for revealing absolute truth. Although India had many heterodox teachings, China had only Confucianism and Taoism, neither of which could be classified as completely heterodox. In Japan, because even Hīnayāna Buddhism was not present, the study of logic was of little value. As a result of this argument, an edict was issued stopping the use of logic at the assembly. However, some Tendai monks began to study logic during the Tokugawa period, a practice that resulted in disputes over topics in logic with Hossō monks.[102]

Kōen (d. 1169), the Tendai editor of the *Fusō ryakki*, commented that Tendai monks began rejecting logic when Saichō's disciple Gishin was appointed as the first Tendai lecturer at the Yuima-e; however, his claims about Gishin are probably a sectarian attempt to defend Tendai interests.[103]

Some Reflections on the Uses of Buddhist Logic in East Asia

Buddhist logic has been mentioned thoughout this study in connection with the debate and examination systems. A few comments on how the topic came to be so closely linked to Hossō sectarian interests in China and Japan may help explain why Tendai monks were interested in it only at certain times. Buddhist logic was not inherently a Yogācāra topic in India, though scholars with Yogācāra leanings often studied it; rather it developed gradually as Buddhists debated members of other philosophical and religious groups in India.

The way in which teachings on logic were transmitted to China led to a close association with the Fa-hsiang (J. Hossō) tradition. Logic is mentioned occasionally in some early Chinese Buddhist writings, particularly those of Ching-ying ssu Hui-yüan (523–592). In fact, most Chinese Buddhist scholars did not choose to make logic an independent field of study. The first independent texts on logic did not appear until Hsüan-tsang returned from India to translate the *Yogācārabhūmi*, an encyclopedic work that serves as one of the seminal texts in the Yogācāra tradition. The fifteenth and thirty-eighth fascicles of Hsüan-tsang's translation of that massive work concern logical issues, particularly those that arise in determining the validity of arguments. According to these passages, logic was particularly useful in refuting the wrong views of non-Buddhists.[104] At the same time Hsüan-tsang was translating the *Yogācārabhūmi* (646–648), he also translated two independent texts on logic to help his students understand logical issues: the *Yin-ming ju-cheng-li lun* (Skt. *Nyāyapraveśaka*) by Śaṅkarasvāmin (*T* 32:11–13) and the *Yin-ming cheng-li-men lun* (Skt. *Nyāyamukha*). These texts were translated in 647 and 650, about the same time that Hsüan-tsang was translating the *Yogācārabhūmi*. Hsüan-tsang seems to have initially translated the first of these works to supplement the *Yogācārabhūmi*, not out of a desire to establish Buddhist logic in China. As he translated the text, Hsüan-tsang seems to have discussed it; as a result, monks who had been in his translation workshop produced a number of commentaries on it. In the process of discussing logic, he may also have talked about a major debate in Kanyakubja in India in which he participated when he was thirty-nine. The debate, performed before the king, left a lasting impression on both Hsüan-tsang and his listeners. As a result, logic was seen as a topic to be used in disputations. Earlier Chinese developments of logic, such as the famous dispute over whether a white horse is a horse, may also have predisposed the Chinese to use logic primarily as a tool in debate.

The author of the *Yin-ming ju-cheng-li lun,* Śaṅkarasvāmin, is said to have been a disciple of Dignāga, but recent scholarship has suggested that he was a Nyāya scholar. His work is an introduction to aspects of the new logical traditions developed by Dignāga in the *Pramāṇasamuccaya*. Because Dignāga's *Pramāṇasamuccaya* was not translated into Chinese, East Asian logic developed in different directions than that found in India and Tibet, where logic was intricately bound up with questions of epistemology.[105] The second independent work on logic translated by Hsüan-tsang three years later, Dignāga's *Nyāyamukha*, did not call forth as much interest from the Chinese as the *Yin-ming ju-cheng-li lun*.

Although commentaries were written on it by some of the monks at Hsüan-tsang's translation center, they were mostly composed with the intention of supporting and deepening insights into the *Yin-ming ju-cheng-li lun.*

As had been the case with Hsüan-tsang's Yogācāra translations, variant interpretations soon arose, but eventually, the Fa-hsiang commentarial tradition as explained by Tz'u-en and Hui-chao came to be recognized as orthodox. The major commentary on the *Yin-ming ju-cheng-li lun* was Tz'u-en's *Shu* (Commentary) in three fascicles. The beginnings of sectarian arguments over logic can already be seen in this text, with Tz'u-en's criticisms of Wen-kuei, a proofreader at Hsüan-tsang's translation center.[106] The friction was more evident in two texts written by Tz'u-en's successor as head of the Fa-hsiang tradition, Hui-chao (650–714): the *Yin-ming ju-cheng-li lun tsuan-yao* and the *Yin-ming ju-cheng-li lun i-tuan.*[107] The first of these texts collects the positions of Tz'u-en's school considered by Hui-chao to be authentic; the second text refutes those teachings on logic he considered heterodox. Thus with Hui-chao's works, logic was inextricably tied to Hossō sectarian teachings. This tendency was further stressed in the writings on logic of the next patriarch of the Fa-hsiang School, Chih-chou (668–723). Monks from other schools also studied logic. For example, Ch'ing-kan, a T'ien-t'ai monk who was on Mount T'ien-t'ai when Saichō visited, was the author of a text on logic. His work has not survived, but it is cited in Japanese texts. The events surrounding its transmission to Japan, however, are unclear.[108]

In China and Japan, logic developed mainly around the issues concerning the construction of valid arguments, a set of topics that had played an important role in the *Yogācārabhūmi.* Reliance on the word of Buddha took precedence over logical argument. Thus logic was to be used when other means failed to convince an opponent. In addition, logic may have played an important role in Hossō discussions about the status of external objects.

When logic was transmitted to Japan, the sectarian aspects of its study increased. Whereas the Fa-hsiang school ceased to exist as an independent school in China after several generations, its Japanese counterpart, the Hossō school, existed for centuries because of Fujiwara support for its clan temple at Kōfukuji. In addition, Japanese sectarian tendencies were particularly pronounced as the Hossō and Tendai schools debated a variety of doctrinal topics. Even within the Hossō school, factions developed. Thus two major traditions of logic existed within Japanese Hossō, a tradition based at Gangōji that began with

Dōshō (629–700), who studied with Hsüan-tsang. It included such luminaries as Gomyō (750–834), the monk who had opposed Saichō's proposals to ordain monks with the *Fan-wang* precepts.

A second lineage began with Genbō (d. 746) who studied with Chih-chou. It was based at Kōfukuji. This tradition used texts by Hsüan-tsang's disciples, and thus was more sectarian than the Gangōji lineage. The first few monks in its lineage did not write works, perhaps indicating the existence of an oral tradition. Finally, Zenju (723–797) wrote a twelve-fascicle commentary on Tz'u-en's *Yin-ming lun shu*, the *Inmyō ronsho myōtōshō*. In it, he defended Tz'u-en's position against that of Wen-kuei and others whom he considered to be heterodox.[109] The stronger sectarian qualities of the Kōfukuji lineage were manifested in its tendency to keep its tradition secret by limiting the spread of texts on logic.[110] In contrast, Kyōshun (688–778), a monk from Daianji who belonged to the Gangōji lineage of logic, wrote a commentary on Wen-kuei's work on logic. This would have been difficult if he had been influenced by the more sectarian writings of Hui-chao and Chih-chou.

For the first hundred years, the study of logic in Japan focused on commentaries written on Tz'u-en's works on logic. However, beginning with the ninth century, Japanese monks began to write independent works on specific logical problems. The reasons for this change are not entirely clear but are probably related to the inclusion of problems in logic in the examinations at the Yuima-e and other assemblies in Nara. Many of the texts on logic written by monks during Ryōgen's lifetime reflect this trend. The emergence of this new genre of writing on logic gave Japanese monks more latitude to develop their own positions.[111]

Tendai monks studied logic, but most wrote very little on the subject, reflecting their attitude that it was merely a tool to defeat their opponents rather than a means to reveal the truths of the One-vehicle or an integral part of Tendai studies. Their interest in logic paralleled their need for logic in debates with members of the Hossō school. As a result, interest in logic was notable from the time of Ennin through that of Genshin, but declined until Tendai monks finally abandoned its study in 1072.[112] However, the study of logic and the *Abhidharmakośa* seem to have been popularized at Onjōji and the Anrakuritsuin on Mount Hiei.[113]

The Questions Used in the Early Examinations

No complete records of the Tendai topics used in examinations around Ryōgen's period survive; however, several early sources of information do survive. The first is the record of general topics used at Onjōji from 1017 to 1045. The second is the accounts of examinations found in some of the biographies of Ryōgen's disciples such as Genshin and Kakuun. The third is the bibliographical entries concerning works written by Ryōgen's predecessors and successors on examination topics. Finally, several early texts attributed to Ryōgen and his contemporaries are extant.

The topics mentioned in the records of examinations at Onjōji and in the biographies of Ryōgen's disciples generally focus on those subjects that Tendai and Hossō monks had debated since the time of Saichō, includings such issues as whether arhats and *pratyekabuddhas* could realize the supreme enlightenment of a Buddha and the classification of doctrines (*kyōhan*). The Ōwa debates on the *Lotus Sūtra* were a particularly important influence on the topics chosen by Tendai monks.[114] At Onjōji, examination topics were based on the major headings in Gishin's *Tendai Hokkeshū gishū* (Collected doctrines of the Tendai Lotus school), a handbook on Tendai written shortly after Saichō's death. This source was chosen because of Gishin's position as Enchin's teacher.[115] In this system, examination topics were divided into the two major areas of doctrine and meditation. Among the doctrinal topics were the four teachings, five flavors, One-vehicle, ten such-likes, and two truths. The topics associated with meditation were the four types of meditation and the three types of delusion.

Another major theme in early examination topics was the realization of Buddhahood with one's current body. Ever since Saichō had introduced this topic, Tendai monks had striven to define it and defend it against Hossō criticisms. *Sokushin jōbutsu* is one of the most popular topics among those listed in early Onjōji records. Moreover, the court emissary who attended the examinations was supposed to arrive in time for the lecture on the chapter on Devadatta, the scriptural foundation for *sokushin jōbutsu*, indicating that it was one of the high points of the lectures on the *Lotus Sūtra*.[116] In fact, examination texts probably played an important role in the development of an indigenous form of Tendai Buddhism by giving monks the opportunity to focus on issues that may have been of secondary importance in China. Several other topics that were frequently debated were closely connected with the rapid realization of Buddhahood. For example, the six levels of identity (*rokusoku*) were a description of the path to Buddhahood in terms of *tathāgatagarbha* (Buddha-nature) teachings that played a major role in many Tendai discussions of *sokushin jōbutsu*. Discussions of whether the three major types of delusion (*sanwaku*) could be eliminated with one practice or would require a variety of practices also played an important role in describing the shortened Tendai path. A number of topics such as the ten such-likes (*jū nyoze*) and the three views concerned the Tendai definition of enlightenment.[117]

A striking characteristic of these topics was the absence of many of the aspects of Japanese Tendai that had distinguished it from Chinese T'ien-t'ai. For example, Esoteric Buddhism and the interpretation of the *Fan-wang* precepts played virtually no role in the early examination system. The question on Esoteric Buddhism that Ryōgen asked Kakuun was atypical. Discussions of *sokushin jōbutsu* usually focused on the interpretation of the *Lotus Sūtra* passage on the Nāga girl's realization of Buddhahood and excluded Esoteric Buddhism. This bias toward the exoteric tradition in discussions of *sokushin jōbutsu* may have been due to the manner in which exoteric and Esoteric topics generally had been discussed separately since Saichō's time and to Saichō's insistence that the Perfect Tendai teaching was in agreement with Esoteric teachings, perhaps suggesting that some monks might be satisfied with the study and practice of only one of these traditions. In addition, the secretive nature of Esoteric Buddhist transmission would have made it inappropriate for the "public testing" that occurred in the examinations.

A more extensive list of Tendai topics can be collected from entries in Muromachi- and Tokugawa-period bibliographies; these texts list works compiled on examination topics by monks who lived around Ryōgen's time. Many texts on specific examination topics were called *shiki* (literally, "personal records" or "personally compiled records" [*shishūki*]) because they included a particular monk's own views on an examination topic.[118] These texts were usually compiled in a question-and-answer format that focused on issues concerning a particular passage from a major work of the school. For example, Tendai *shiki* were usually based on sections from the *Fa-hua hsüan-i*, *Fa-hua wen-chü*, and *Mo-ho chih-kuan*, the three most important T'ien-t'ai works by Chih-i. These passages might be discussed in terms of seemingly contradictory passages from other works in the Tendai tradition, argued in terms of doctrines from competing schools, or debated as to their value for practice. The various positions held by members of the school would then be discussed through questions and answers. The format of *shiki* gave Tendai monks the freedom to choose key passages from the major Tendai texts by Chih-i and develop interpretations that would fit Japanese needs. Among the important trends evident in *shiki* were deep interests in the rapid realization of enlightenment and in this world as a pure land. The freedom to advance variant interpretations is explicitly mentioned in a note appended to Genshin's text on the six degrees of identity, a topic associated with realization of Buddhahood in this very life. In the note, Genshin's student Kakuchō notes that Genshin had encouraged others to develop their own views and that he had stated that his work should be discarded if this was not the case.[119] Genshin's reflections on his text were due in part to the criticisms of a more mature scholar contemplating one of his early works, but they are also an indication that monks involved in the debate system had a degree of freedom in advancing their interpretations of the material.

A small number of early Tendai *shiki* have survived and been published; a few unpublished *shiki* may exist in temple collections. For example, Ennin's disciple Rinshō wrote *Sokushin jōbutsugi shiki* (Personal compilation concerning the realization of Buddhahood in this very existence), a text that contains important information about early Tendai views on this central teaching, but until recently it existed only in a woodblock edition that was difficult to obtain; Sueki Fumihiko has recently published and annotated this and several other early texts connected with examinations.[120] A thorough bibliography and study of extant examples of this genre might add to our knowledge of the development of Japanese Tendai doctrine. Although in recent years Ōkubo Ryōshun has done extensive research on *sokushin jōbutsu*, Misaki Gisen on the realization of Buddhahood by trees and grasses, and Sueki Fumihiko on both of these topics, many of the sources and debate topics have not yet been studied adequately.[121]

The scope of the problem can be demonstrated by considering one of the best-known *shiki*, the *Sokushin jōbutsugi shiki* attributed to Annen. To begin with, the title is uncertain; bibliographies list texts on this topic attributed to Annen under four different titles. Although these are probably simply alternate titles for the text, different manuscripts with this title have been reported, indicating that the published text requires additional study. In addition, bibliographic references to the text appear only in works compiled after the early eighteenth century. One of the most distinctive aspects of the text is that it discusses the issue of realization of Buddhahood in this very existence only in terms of the *Lotus Sūtra* and exoteric doctrine. Although Saichō introduced the topic in these terms, by Annen's time the Shingon school was a major rival of Tendai. How could Annen, the systematizer of Tendai Esoteric Buddhism, not have considered Esoteric Buddhism in a discussion of *sokushin jōbutsu*? These and similar problems led Nara Hiromoto to suggest that *Sokushin jōbutsugi shiki* may be one of approximately fifty *shiki* on the topic that were compiled by Tendai monks between the Heian and Kamakura periods. Nara has argued that one of these texts might have been attributed to Annen at a later date.[122] Although Nara's position can and should be challenged on the basis of the contents of the text, the bibliographical problems that he raises are an indication of some of the issues that remain to be investigated in this genre of literature. Ōkubo Ryōshun has suggested that the *Sokushin jōbutsugi* traditionally attributed to Kūkai may have been compiled at a later date, a position that may help explain why Annen was not concerned with Esoteric doctrine in his *Sokushin jōbutsugi shiki*.[123]

The Tendai school was not alone in producing *shiki;* Hossō monks also compiled a number of *shiki*. These were similar in structure to Tendai *shiki* and like their Tendai counterparts were intended to aid in the debates and examinations. Yūki Reimon, one of the leading Japanese scholars of Yogācāra, has argued that these works are much higher in quality than most researchers usually realize; they are particularly important in tracing Japanese developments in the interpretation of Yogācāra doctrine and deserve more attention than they have been given.[124] The same comments could be made about Tendai *shiki*.

A list of topics treated in early Tendai texts and the purported authors of *shiki* on them is given in table 14.[125] Those Japanese texts that are extant are marked with an asterisk.[126] Further research is needed to refine the list.

The authors of the *shiki* have been listed in approximate chronological order. Because Saichō, Ennin, Anne, and Annen were predecessors of Ryōgen, the number of *shiki* that they wrote, even allowing for a number of apocryphal texts, indicates that Tendai examination topics must have undergone considerable development before Ryōgen's time, probably because these topics were often discussed in debates on Mount Hiei and in encounters with Hossō monks.[127] The inclusion of texts by the Chinese T'ien-t'ai patriarchs Hui-ssu and Chih-i in these bibliographies may indicate that their texts (or excerpts of their texts) sometimes might not have been used only as the locus classicus for an examination topic, but may have served as debate texts similar to *shiki*.

Among Ryōgen's disciples, Genshin, Kakuun, and Kakuchō all contributed to the examination tradition by writing a number of *shiki*, with Genshin being the most prolific with at least twelve such texts being attributed to him. Five of Genshin's examination manuals are included in the third volume of his collected works.

TABLE 14

TOPICS IN TENDAI DEBATE

Three views (*sangan*): Saichō, Ennin, Annen, Senkan, Ryōgen, Kakuchō, Sange

Three bodies of the Buddha (*sanshin*): Anne, Ennin,* Annen, Enshō, Genshin,* Sange

Six levels of identity (*rokusoku*): Hui-ssu, Chih-i, Hsing-man, Annen, Ryōgen, Senkan, Genshin, Kakuun, Kakuchō, Sange

Two truths (*nitai*): Saichō,* Annen, Senkan, Genshin, Kakuun, Sange

Ten such-likes (*jūnyoze*): Ennin, Senkan,* Genshin,* Kakuchō, Sange

The divisions of the sermons in the *Lotus Sūtra* for *śrāvakas* with higher, middling, and lower faculties that enable them to enter the higher teachings (*sanshū*): Anne, Annen, Senkan, Genshin,* Kakuun

The seven stages of the sage in the Hīnayāna path (*shichishō*): Annen, Senkan, Ryōgen

Three types of delusion (*sannaku*): Annen

Twelve links of dependent origination (*jūni innen*): Saichō, Annen, Senkan,* Genshin, Kakuun

Buddha lands (*Butsudo*): Enchō, Ninchū,* Kōjō, Eryō,* Ryōgen

How able practitioners are drawn to higher teachings (*hishō*): Ennin, Annen, Senkan, Ryōgen,* Genshin

The teaching that although the terminology of some teachings may seem to belong to the distinct teaching, their meaning is that of the common teaching (*myōbetsu gitsū*): Ryōgen*

Bodhisattvas (*bosatsu*): Annen, Senkan, Genshin, Kakuchō

Realization of Buddhahood with this very body (*sokushin jōbutsu*): Anne, Rinshō,* Ennin, Annen,* Senkan,* Zōga, Genshin,* Kakuun, Sange, Ankai

Entrusting the *sūtra* (*shokurui*): Annen, Senkan, Kakuchō, Kakuun, Kurodani (Zen'yu?)

Five flavors (*gomi*): Ennin, Senkan, Ryōgen, Genshin

Nine categories of rebirth into the Pure Land (*kubon ōjō*): Ryōgen*

Ten meanings of the character "*myō*" (wonderful) in the title of the *Lotus Sūtra* (*jūmyō*): Senkan*

Senkan (919–984), a contemporary of Ryōgen, was one of the most prolific writers of *shiki*. As Ryōgen's opponent in a debate on logic and later as the recipient of an invitation to the Ōwa debates, he must have been one of the most respected figures in Tendai debate, and he undoubtedly contributed much to the Tendai examination and debate tradition; his works must have been particularly valued at the examinations at Onjōji because he was one of the most accomplished scholars from Enchin's lineage.

The actual questions used in the examinations were called *sandai* or *san no dai* (topics of the divination sticks) because they were presented to the candidate written on boards that resembled divination sticks. A collection of ninety *sandai* attributed to Ryōgen is extant.[128] Ryōgen supposedly lectured on these at the rate of one per day during the ninety-day summer rainy season retreat. As he expounded on the issues, he is said to have used boards to write down the topics. Other sources suggest that Ryōgen initially defined two hundred or three hundred questions. As the examination system developed, additional questions were devised until some texts included more than six hundred questions.[129] The various questions were eventually classified into three major categories: (1) major doctrines of the Tendai school (*shūyō*), (2) comparisons of Tendai doctrine with those of other schools (*gika*), and (3) supplementary questions (*mon'yō*) that do not fit into either of the first two categories, including general questions about Buddhism.[130]

The relatively stable configuration of the topics included in *gika* indicate that they may have developed earlier than the other two categories. *Shūyō* probably developed soon after, or in parallel with, *gika,* but *gika* played a more important role in the early history of the examination system, primarily because one of the main goals of the system around Ryōgen's time was to enable Tendai monks to debate Hossō monks. Competition between the two schools in debates eventually waned, however, as each school maintained its own examination and debate system. As a result, the emphasis of the examination topics within the Tendai school seems to have shifted to determining the essence of Tendai thought. Instead of vying with Hossō monks, competition occurred between the Jimon and Sanmon factions of the Tendai school or between the Eshin and Danna lineages within the Sanmon. Although the efforts of these groups to determine their own interpretations of essential teachings has not been adequately studied, they clearly contributed to many of the phenomena that characterize Tendai from the late Heian period onward, especially the emphasis on oral transmission and lineage. In addition, the debate structure gave Japanese monks the opportunity to take Chinese T'ien-t'ai writings out of their original context and develop their own interpretations. Thus Japanese thinkers sometimes stressed passages of texts by Chih-i and Chan-jan that might have received much less attention in China.

TABLE 15

THE SIXTEEN *GIKA*

Classification of doctrines (*kyōsō*), *Fa-hua hsüan-i* 1

Ten such-likes (*jū nyoze*), *Fa-hua hsüan-i* 2

Twelve links of cause and effect (*jūni innen*), *Fa-hua hsüan-i* 2

Two truths (*nitai*), *Fa-hua hsüan-i* 3

Retinues (*kenzoku myōgi*), *Fa-hua hsüan-i* 6

Five flavors (*gomi*), *Fa-hua hsüan-i* 10

Three sermons in the *Lotus Sūtra* designed to appeal to *śrāvakas*
    of varying capacities so as to lead them to enlightenment (*sanshū*),
    Fa-hua wen-chü 4

Realization of Buddhahood with this very body (*sokushin jōbutsu*), *Fa-hua*
    wen-chü 8

Three bodies (*sanshin*), *Fa-hua wen-chü* 9

Entrusting (*shokurui*), *Fa-hua wen-chü* 10

Six types of identity (*rokusoku*), *Mo-ho chih-kuan* 1

Four types of meditation (*shishu zanmai*), *Mo-ho chih-kuan* 2

Three views (*sangan*), *Mo-ho chih-kuan* 3

How able practitioners are drawn to higher teachings (*hishō*), *Mo-ho*
    chih-kuan 3

The teaching that although the terminology of some teachings may seem
    to belong to the distinct teaching, its meaning is that of the common
    teaching (*myōbetsu gitsū*), *Mo-ho chih-kuan* 6

Buddha lands (*Butsudo*), *Wei-mo shu* 1

"*Gika*" has been interpreted as meaning "the determination of errors" (*toga wo kotowaru*).[131] In debate, it generally referred to topics in which Tendai was contrasted with other teachings. The topics were usually organized into sixteen or seventeen major categories, each based on a passage from one of Chih-i's works. Although the lists of categories vary according to source, the above list is typical. The work and fascicle number for the central passage for each category are given in table 15.[132]

The compiler of the sixteen categories is not known, but some traditional works attribute it to Senkan and others to Ryōgen.[133] Because the list of *shiki* and their authors given earlier in this chapter indicates that almost all of the *gika* had been the subjects of treatises by Tendai monks by the late tenth century, lists of *gika* might have been formulated during Ryōgen's lifetime. Although the contents of lists of *gika* found in various Tendai examination manuals vary, the core elements

TABLE 16

SIX ADDITIONAL *GIKA*

Ten meanings of wonderful (*myō*), *Fa-hua hsüan-i* 7

One-vehicle, *Fa-hua wen-chü* 10

Buddha-nature, *Nieh-p'an shu*

Seven goals of Hīnayāna practice, *T'ien-t'ai ssu-chiao i* 6

Bodhisattva, *T'ien-t'ai ssu-chiao i* 7

Nine categories of rebirth into the Pure Land, *Kuan-ching shu*

---

seem consistent. Scholars vary on the relationship between *gika* and *shūyō*. Some have argued that the tabulation of *gika* probably began later than the compilation of *shūyō* and may not have been formalized into a catalogue of sixteen for one or two centuries.[134] However, other scholars have argued that *shūyō* developed later, as certain problems within *gika* came to be emphasized.[135] The latter position seems to be more in agreement with the materials I have surveyed.

As the examination system developed, six more *gika* were included (table 16). *Gika* were added and dropped to fit the needs of lineages. Among those added were several from the *Lotus Sūtra*. The classification of doctrines was not used by some lineages after a monk died suddenly while he was being questioned on it.

The basic list of *shūyō* is said to have been derived from a list of one hundred primary questions and one hundred secondary questions on which Ryōgen lectured over a period of one hundred days. His disciples Genshin and Kakuun are then said to have respectively chosen eighty-two and eighty-four of these questions. Within a few decades, Kan'in (n.d.) added ten more questions that were accepted by the lineages of both Genshin and Kakuun.[136] *Shūyō* were eventually organized into six major categories (table 17).

The distinction between *shūyō* and *gika* was not always clearly defined. Even a topic seemingly central to Tendai, such as the ten such-likes, could be treated in both fashions. Candidates could explain it in terms of Tendai teachings without referring to outside views or they could contrast it with interpretations of the *Lotus Sūtra* advanced by monks such as Fa-yün (467–529), an earlier commentator on the *Lotus Sūtra*. Categories of *shūyō* such as the two vehicles or five periods were as suited to use as *gika* as they were to *shūyō*.[137] In a system probably instituted after topics from logic and Hossō doctrine were no longer used in exami-

TABLE 17

THE SIX *SHŪYŌ*

Classification of doctrines (*kyōsō*)
Five periods (*goji*)
Buddha (*Butsubu*)
Bodhisattva (*bosatsu*)
Two vehicles (*nijōbu*)
Miscellaneous (*zōbu*)

nation, *shūyō* are used as primary questions and *gika* are secondary.[138] In later Tendai examination manuals, the categories are often muddled to the point where they cease to have much meaning.[139]

The role of the third major category of miscellaneous questions in the examinations remains unclear. *Mon'yō* seem to have been the last category to develop and to have consisted of issues that arose later and that had not been included in earlier categories. An example would be whether meditations on Amida were focused on a Buddha to the west or on one's own mind.[140] However, questions were sometimes switched from *mon'yō* to *shūyō* in different texts. Unlike *shūyō* and *gika*, no subdivisions or set numbers of questions were established for *mon'yō*. In addition, the term "*sandai*," which designated the questions given to candidates in examinations, was not used for *mon'yō*, indicating that these questions might have been used in some other fashion than as examination topics.

Conclusion

The examinations on broad learning played a major role in Ryōgen's efforts to gain appointments in the Office of Monastic Affairs for Tendai monks. In addition, although Ryōgen is not remembered as the author of doctrinal treatises, his interest in the examination system helps elucidate how he was able to train students with the academic talents of Genshin. With the establishment of the three Tendai assemblies in the late eleventh century, the Tendai school established a system of assemblies that was patterned after the assemblies dominated by the Hossō monks of the Kōfukuji. In subsequent centuries, the role of the examinations on broad learning evolved in new ways. Most of its history has still not been examined in a critical manner, but the examination and debate system clearly underwent a number of changes, at times declining in rigor and at other times being revived. The examinations on broad learning also served as the model for examinations conducted at a number of the chapels and halls on Mount Hiei, as well as at some of the Tendai temples in other parts of Japan.[141]

Examinations on broad learning provide a means to explore some of the doctrinal changes that occurred in Japanese Tendai. During the century after Ryōgen, the examinations stimulated Tendai interest in exoteric Tendai doctrine, logic, Hossō, and *abhidharma* doctrine. When competition with Hossō monks no longer concerned Tendai monks, the format of the examinations allowed Japanese monks to freely examine the classical texts of Tendai, selecting those issues that seemed to them to be most important. As the examinations were repeatedly held, topics were examined, often orally, in different ways, giving rise to the new interpretations for which medieval Tendai is known today. If the numerous texts on examinations and debates, many of them still unpublished, were surveyed they might well reveal much about the evolution of monastic education and the development of Tendai doctrine from the mid-Heian period onward, as well as the ways in which Tendai monks responded to the challenge posed by the emerging Kamakura schools.

9

Rebuilding the Tendai
Establishment on Mount Hiei

Ryōgen used his position as *zasu* to help his lineage dominate the Tendai school. A major fire shortly after his appointment provided him with both a major challenge and a major opportunity. If Ryōgen had not been able to rebuild the Tendai establishment on Mount Hiei, the Tendai school might have declined and lost much of its influence. No major thinkers had emerged from the school for several decades, and it seemed to have lost much of its vigor. Ryōgen spent much of the rest of his life in rebuilding the Tendai monastery on Mount Hiei, often restoring buildings to greater splendor than before. In the process, he extended and strengthened his control over much of the mountain. This chapter traces the process of rebuilding, focusing on the order in which buildings were restored and their functions in the life of Tendai monks. Many aspects of religious practice can be elucidated through an investigation of the reconstruction process.

The Fire on Mount Hiei

Only a few months after his appointment as *zasu*, Ryōgen and Mount Hiei suffered serious setbacks that threatened the very existence of the Tendai establishment. On 10-28-966, a fire started in the quarters of Zōkai in the Tōdō area and spread to many of the surrounding buildings. Because Saichō had made the Tōdō area the center of his activities on Mount Hiei, it had become the most developed part of the Tendai monastic institution.[1] Consequently, the fire destroyed many of the most important structures at the Tendai monastery. Thirty-one buildings were reduced to ashes. The extent of the devastation can be understood by considering the halls that were destroyed. Among them were the Lecture Hall (Kōdō), Mañjuśrī's Tower (Monjurō), the Hall of the Four Kings (Shiōin), the Hall of Longevity (Enmeiin), the

167

Constant-walking Meditation Hall (Jōgyōin), the Lotus Meditation Hall (Hokkedō), the Dhāraṇī Hall (Sōjiin), and the quarters of the former *zasu* Kikyō.[2] The Lotus Meditation Hall, Constant-walking Meditation Hall, and Mañjuśrī's Tower were used for three of the four meditations described in Chih-i's *Mo-ho chih-kuan* and were consequently vital to the Tendai exoteric practice. The Dhāraṇī and Longevity halls were the centers of Esoteric practice and ceremonies to protect the state. In addition, many of the halls had been built by eminent Tendai masters and were representative of their major achievements. The Dhāraṇī and Constant-walking Meditation halls had been built by Ennin and were the centers of practices that he had brought back from China. Finally, the death of Ryōgen's beloved mother the previous month added to the new *zasu*'s distress. The rebuilding of the monastery would have to be undertaken while Ryōgen was in mourning.[3]

The difficulty of rebuilding the establishment on Mount Hiei can be better understood if an earlier fire is considered. On 3-6-936, while Son'i was *zasu* and Ryōgen was a young monk of twenty-four, a fire broke out and destroyed the Central Hall (Chūdō) and forty other buildings on Mount Hiei.[4] The Central Hall had been the one of the first buildings constructed by Saichō when he climbed Mount Hiei.[5] Soon after, a library (*kyōzō*) was built to its south and a hall dedicated to Mañjuśrī to its north; both were about the same size as the original structure. Because the first building was between the two other buildings, it was called the Central Hall. The library contained many of the books brought back from China by Saichō; and the Mañjuśrī Hall contained an image of Tobatsu Bishamon (Skt. Vaiśravaṇa), a fierce deity that protected the state, carved by Saichō. As a result, the Monjudō was sometimes called the Bishamondō. Finally, the Central Hall itself contained the image of the Healing Buddha (J. Yakushi nyorai; Skt. Bhaiṣajyaguru) carved by Saichō shortly after he climbed Mount Hiei. Thus the Central Hall had deep associations with Saichō and the founding of Mount Hiei. The complex eventually deteriorated and was rebuilt by Enchin from 882 to 888 into one large building, nine bays long and four bays deep,[6] with additional eaves (or rooms) off the eaves (*magobisashi*).[7] The library and Monjudō each occupied two of the nine-bay length at either end of the building; the Yakushidō (Hall for the Healing Buddha) occupied the central five bays. The front half of the building was an area for worshipers (*gejin*). Enchin, criticized for changing the architecture of one of the original buildings on Hiei, responded, "The original three buildings were like the three truths; the building now is like the one truth. Since the three truths are identical to the one truth, how could I have gone against our founder's intentions?"[8]

The loss of the Central Hall in the fire of 936 was deeply felt, even though the monks did manage to save the image of the Healing Buddha that Saichō had carved. Although the building was rebuilt within three years, it was smaller than the former building. The new building did not have covered walkways (kairō) surrounding it and connecting it with other halls, a necessity during the winter. In addition, its eaves were too narrow to accommodate the large numbers of monks and laymen who would congregate at it for religious ceremonies. Finally, the new hall had never even been formally dedicated. Son'i had planned a dedication ceremony but had died before it could be held. Subsequent zasu had been too busy with administrative tasks to hold a dedication.[9]

Ryōgen is said to have begun planning for the reconstruction of the Tōdō complex the same day as the fire.[10] During the next few years, he had to raise the funds to rebuild the destroyed buildings. Because the halls had been built over a period of decades, the restoration of the monastery on Mount Hiei was not to be an easy task. Ryōgen had to strengthen existing alliances and form new ones with the nobles to succeed at this task. It is to Ryōgen's credit that he succeeded brilliantly. The buildings in Tōdō were completed in six years. In the process, Ryōgen made a number of improvements and changes. When Ryōgen's success is compared to the failure of earlier efforts to reconstruct the Central Hall on the same scale as it had been before the fire of 936, the importance of his accomplishment is evident.

Ryōgen's accomplishments in constructing buildings throughout his tenure as zasu are listed in chronological order in table 18; these have been taken from Ryōgen's early biographies and historical sources about Mount Hiei such as the Tendai zasuki (Records of the heads of the Tendai school) and Kuin Bukkakushō (Records of the nine halls and Buddhist pavillions).[11] The list reveals that even as the Tōdō area was rebuilt, Ryōgen continued building in other areas such as Yokawa. Serious building continued even after Tōdō's reconstruction. The list also includes a number of mentions of services constructed at the new buildings to convey the interest and support for the buildings by the nobility.

TABLE 18

CHRONOLOGY OF RYŌGEN'S REBUILDING OF MOUNT HIEI

10/28/966	Fire burns Mount Hiei.
4/967	The Lotus Meditation Hall (Hokkedō) in Tōdō is rebuilt (*Tendai zasuki, Shūiden*).
967	The Constant-walking Meditation Hall (Jōgyōdō) in Tōdō rebuilt in time for annual observances (*Tendai zasuki, Shūiden*)
968	The Constant-walking Meditation Hall (Jōgyōdō) in Yokawa is built and fourteen monks installed in it (*Mon'yōki*).
969	The Tower for Mañjuśrī in Tōdō is rebuilt (*Jie daisōjōden, Shūiden*).
970	The Dhāraṇī Hall (Sōjiin) in Tōdō burns during reconstruction; construction on the lecture hall (*kōdō*) ceases and efforts are concentrated on the Jeweled Pagoda (Hōtō), which served as the center of the Sōjiin, as well as its gates and towers (*Shūiden*).
4/971	The Sōjiin is rebuilt and the assembly for the Buddha's relic held there; in addition, an Esoteric consecration hall (*kanjōdō*) and mantra hall (*shingondō*) with eaves and covered corridors on four sides (*shimen*) are constructed (*Shūiden*).
971	Kakue's quarters, the Myōgōbō at Kazan chūin, are rebuilt.
971	The lecture hall at Tōdō is rebuilt and new images installed (*Shūiden*).
1/15/972	Yokawa is recognized as administrative equal of Tōdō and Saitō.
972	The Hall for Longevity (Enmeiin) and Hall for the Four Guardian Kings (Shiōin) are built and dedicated, marking the completion of the five major halls in Tōdō (*Shūiden*).
4/3/972	The dedication for the completion of the rebuilding project is attended by imperial emissary, nobles, and members of the Bureau of Monastic Affairs (Sōgō).
5/972	Ryōgen composes his will, specifying the disposition of many buildings.
11/973	Ryōgen stops an ordination ceremony, predicting the imminent collapse of the ordination hall (*kaidan'in*) in Tōdō (*Jie daisōjōden*).
1/14/975	Ennin's quarters (Hokkaibō) are rebuilt and the practice of offerings to him begun (*Shūiden*).
975	Yokawa is reorganized; quarters for masters of Esoteric Buddhism (*ajaribō*), miscellaneous buildings (*zōsha*),[1] treasure house (hōzō), and temporary quarters for ordinary monks (*daishu kariya*) are built (*Shūiden*).
975	The central hall at Yokawa, originally constructed by Ennin in 829, is rebuilt; a life-size image of Fudō myōō is carved and dedicated.

TABLE 18 *(continued)*

3/28/975	The regent (*kanpaku*) Fujiwara no Kanemichi is invited to the central hall at Yokawa for the assembly for the Buddha's relic (*Shūiden*).
976	Kanemichi has services for the seventeenth anniversary of his father Morosuke's death held at Yokawa (*Nihon kiryaku*).
977	One hundred copies of the *Lotus Sūtra* are deposited at the shrine on Chikubu Island in Lake Biwa.
11/1/978	Services for the first anniversary of Fujiwara no Kanemichi's death are held; Kanemichi's heir, Fujiwara no Asateru, builds a four-bay by five-bay building with a large (*jōroku*) golden Kannon; a golden Dainichi (Mahāvairocana) also is commissioned. The cloistered emperor En'yū has a golden Śākyamuni and six multicolored Jizō installed in a Shakadō (Hall for Śākyamuni). Kanemichi's wife has a hall built so that these images can be brought together and be presented to the Jōshinbō (Hall of the concentrated mind) (*Shūiden*).
4/1/979	A hall for *kami* (*shinden*) is built for the deities protecting Mount Hiei, as well as *torii* (gates), covered walkways, and miscellaneous buildings (*zōsha*) at Karasaki on the shores of Lake Biwa (*Shūiden, Tendai zasuki*).
8/18/979	A Nyoirin Kannon ritual is conducted for seven days at the Dannain in Tōdō for the birth of Emperor En'yū's son (*San'inki*).
8/28/979	Residents of Mitsuhama and Nōka are exempted from taxes (*Tendai zasuki, Eigaku yōki*). Ryōgen successfully appeals to the court for a suspension of taxes on Sakamoto, that had been levied by Muneaki, an appointee of the governor of Ōmi, Tachibana no Tsunehira.[2] Muneaki is relieved of his post (*Shūiden*).
979	Saitō is reorganized with the reconstruction of the Constant-walking Meditation Hall and the construction of the Jeweled Pagoda, Hōdōin, library (*kyōzō*), bell tower, Hall for Śākyamuni (Shakadō), worship hall (*raidō*), and bridges (*Shūiden, Tendai zasuki*).
979	Three-story grass-thatched building and several tens of other buildings are constructed at Hosoehama in Azai-gun. A three-day assembly is held, including a festival for the Buddha's relics. Many monks and various local officials attend; Prime Minister (*taishōkoku*) Fujiwara no Yoritada and the major captains of the left and right, Asamitsu and Naritoki, send offerings (*Shūiden*).
980	Three-day uninterrupted *nenbutsu* services are held at Hosoehama (*Shūiden*).
980	The Zentōin (Ennin's quarters) are rebuilt (*Tendai zasuki*).
980	Reconstruction of the central hall (*Chūdō*), surrounding walkways, worship hall, and central gate in Tōdō are planned, but the site is too small, so a different site is chosen (*Shūiden, Tendai zasuki*).

Continued on next page

TABLE 18 *(continued)*

9/30/980	The central hall is dedicated with many monks from Nara attending (*Shūiden, Tendai zasuki*). Emperor En'yū said to have attended (*Dō kuyō*). Services are held the next day at the Mañjuśrī Hall (*Shūiden; Tendai zasuki*).
980	A *kami* hall (*shinden*) is constructed near the Mañjuśrī Hall in Tōdō (*Kuin Bukkakushō*).
980	A refectory (*jikidō*) and miscellaneous buildings (*zōsha*) are constructed to the east of the central hall in Tōdō (*Shūiden, Tendai zasuki*).
980	The En'yūin is ordered constructed by Emperor En'yū (*Shūiden;* but the *Nihon kiryaku* lists this as 983).
981	Fujiwara no Kaneie orders the construction of the Eshin'in at Yokawa to carry out his deceased father Morosuke's wishes and to express respect for Ryōgen; it is named an imperial temple (*goganji*) (*Jie daisōjōden*).
981	The Constant-walking Meditation Hall at Tōdō is moved to the site of the Hachibudō (Hall for the eight types of supernatural beings); quarters for the imperial emissary (*chokushibō*), administrative offices (*mandokoroya*), and a bathhouse (*yuya*) are built (*Shūiden, Kuin Bukkakushō*).
10/25/983	The Medicine Buddha Hall (Yakushidō) at Yokawa is dedicated (*Nihon kiryaku, Shūiden*).
11/27/983	The Eshin'in at Yokawa is dedicated (*Nihon kiryaku, Shūiden*).
984	The Hōdōin in Saitō is refurbished (*Jie daisōjōden*).

1. The term "miscellaneous buildings" (*zōsha*) refers to a variety of buildings situated in the northern part of the monastery, it includes such edifices as kitchens, storage areas, and lodgings for servants, Nihon daijiten kankōkai, ed., *Nihon kokugo daijiten*, 12:272d.
2. Tachibana no Tsunehira is reported to have been the father of Zōga, but his dates would make this virtually impossible (Inagaki Taiichi, s.v. "Zōga," in Tsunoda, ed., *Heian jidaishi jiten*, 1:1397d).

Rebuilding the Tendai Establishment

Ryōgen began to rebuild the halls on Mount Hiei as soon as possible. His activities during this period are recorded in great detail in the *Shūiden*, revealing that his successors viewed this accomplishment as one of Ryōgen's most important achievements. Ryōgen may have been helped in his efforts to rebuild by the experience he had gained in other projects. He had been a young monk during the fire on Mount Hiei in 936 and may have helped with rebuilding Gangyōji after a fire in 957; he surely participated in construction at Yokawa.[12]

One of Ryōgen's first concerns was to rebuild the key structures most important for Tendai practice. In terms of exoteric practice, this consisted of the halls for at least some of the four types of meditation. The four types of meditation (*shishu zanmai*) were formulated by Chih-i on the basis of Indian *sūtras* and described in his meditation manual, the *Mo-ho chih-kuan*.[13] Saichō had noted that the *Mo-ho chih-kuan* was to be the basic text for the monks in his Tendai meditation course (*shikangō*). Elsewhere he had stated that halls for the four types of meditation were to be built on Mount Hiei.[14] In 812, Saichō built a hall for one of the meditations, the Lotus meditation (*Hokke zanmai*), a confession ceremony that was one form of the half-sitting–half-walking meditation.[15] To Saichō, the Lotus meditation was probably the most important of the four types. In addition, a tower for Mañjuśrī may have been the site of constant-sitting meditations.[16] However, Saichō died before most of the other forms of meditation could be practiced or the halls for them built.[17]

The Lotus-Meditation and Repentance Hall

By the fourth month of 967, six months after the fire, one of the most important halls for Tendai exoteric practice, the Hokke zanmaidō (Lotus Meditation Hall) had been completed so that the Lotus confession (*Hokke senbō*) services could be held that same spring. To understand the importance of this structure and why it was one of the first rebuilt, we must survey earlier Japanese uses of the Lotus meditation.

As noted, in 812 Saichō constructed a Lotus Meditation Hall and had five or six monks chant the *Lotus Sūtra* without ceasing.[18] Consequently, sources such as the *Sanbō ekotoba* (Words and pictures concerning the Three Jewels) credit him with transmitting the ceremony to Japan.[19] However, a number of other sources suggest that the ceremony was not performed completely correctly during Saichō's lifetime. Thus, Ennin, not Saichō, is credited with the most important transmission of the ceremony. Ennin first taught his students about it soon after he returned from China.[20] According to Ennin's biography, "Saichō transmitted the basic elements of the meditation, but Ennin propagated the details."[21]

The Lotus Meditation Hall built by Saichō was in the Eastern Pagoda area of Mount Hiei. During the Tenchō era, Saichō's disciple Enchō built a Lotus hall in the Western Pagoda area.[22] Genkan performed the ceremony in Tōnomine in 900; and in 950, by order of Emperor Murakami, six monks were installed to perform the ceremony. A Lotus Meditation Hall was finally built at Tōnomine in 964; several months later Zōga went to the hall to practice.[23] Although the practice of the ceremony by monks might seem consistent with Chih-i's original intent of seeing the "true characteristics of phenomena," the commissioning of Lotus meditation halls by nobility had other reasons behind it: using the merit from the ceremony to pray for the repose of the dead, ensuring good fortune in this life and the future, and protecting the nation. The following examples demonstrate such usages. When Fujiwara no Tadahira's wife, Minamoto no Junshi, died in 925, the Lotus meditation was performed at Gangyōji on the twenty-eighth day after her death to pray for her repose. In 946, Prince Shigeakira (906–954) had it performed on the anniversary of the death of his wife, Fujiwara no Kanshi (906–945). The ceremony was also performed to help cure sickness as when it was used in 939 to help heal a grave illness of Fujiwara no Onshi, the empress (*chūgū*) of Emperor Daigo. Finally, it was occasionally used to protect the state.[24]

Morosuke's use of the meditation in 954 to help ensure the prosperity of his branch of the Fujiwara clan in the present and future was similar to earlier applications of the ceremony to this-worldly needs. However, the use of the ceremony to ensure the prosperity of one particular group of people who were competing with other groups for power meant that the ceremony probably was being employed for more private and more selfish goals than had been the case when the ceremony was performed before Morosuke's time for the repose of the dead or for the protection of the nation. The ceremony's confessional aspects, which destroyed bad karma and created merits, undoubtedly made it appropriate for such applications. In 1005, several decades after Morosuke commissioned a Lotus Meditation Hall at Yokawa, Fujiwara no Michinaga commissioned a hall at Jōmyōji in Uji and used the ceremony in the same way as Morosuke, for the benefit of his lineage.[25]

The ceremony is described in the *Sanbō ekotoba* as follows:

> This confession ceremony is based on the *Kuan P'u-hsien ching*. It is one of the four types of Tendai meditations, namely the half-sitting–half-walking meditation. When Chih-i performed this meditation, he quickly realized the Lotus concentration, attained enlightenment, and clarified his mind. He saw the bodhisattva Samantabhadra; and then Samantabhadra, mounted on an elephant, touched Chih-i's head. Chih-i explained all of the difficult passages in the *sūtra* and composed a one-fascicle text on the Lotus meditation that was propagated throughout the world. If the meditation is performed in accordance with this text, then all of the wrongdoing that a person has committed with the six faculties

will be eliminated through the power of the One-vehicle. Although Hī-nayāna confessions can vanquish minor wrongdoing, Mahāyāna confessions can save a person from major sins.

According to the manual, [This ceremony may be practiced if one wishes to] see the Buddhas that have emanated from Prabhūtaratna, purify the six faculties, enter the realm of the Buddhas, be saved from various obstacles [to the path], or enter the ranks of the bodhisattvas. If you have violated the four *pārājika* offenses or committed the five heinous crimes and thereby lost your status as a monk, then [through this confession] you can become pure once again.[26] If you wish to attain these merits, then you should practice this ceremony in a quiet place for twenty-one days.[27]

The ceremony was performed four times each year, at the beginning of each season, with each performance requiring twenty-one days.[28] Although the ceremony as formulated by Chih-i had confessional aspects, its ultimate goal was to lead to the realization of emptiness, an aspect that has virtually vanished in the *Sanbō ekotoba* passage. In part, this was due to the increasing popularity of the ceremony among the nobility, for whom such abstract issues were much less important than repentance for past wrongdoing and the creation of merit. The growing popularity of Esoteric Buddhism, in which mastery of the nonsubstantiality of phenomena might be used to control phenomena, might have indirectly affected the interpretation of the ritual.

The Constant-walking Meditation Hall

Several months later in 967, the Constant-walking Meditation Hall was completed in time for the annual performance of the uninterrupted recitation (*fudan nenbutsu*) during the eighth month.[29] Along with the Lotus Meditation Hall, this building was a center of Tendai exoteric practice. In addition, the two types of meditation were considered to produce significant merit for those who sponsored them. Because the two meditations were performed at certain times each year, Ryōgen was anxious to complete them so that the meditations could be held on schedule.

Fourteen years later, in 981, Ryōgen changed the arrangement of the two halls, moving the Constant-walking Meditation Hall to a spot adjacent to the Lotus Meditation Hall. Both halls were built in the same architectural style with a corridor connecting them; they were subsequently known as the *narabi-dō* (adjacent halls) or *ninai-dō* (because the two halls connected by a corridor resembled the arrangement of two packages carried by balancing them on the ends of a stick).[30] During this period, these two meditation practices overshadowed the other two practices in Chih-i's fourfold classification. The close connection of the two also was typical of Tendai practice; the Kamakura tendency to choose only one practice and reject others had not yet become popular. Thus, the biographies of some monks and lay believers from this period mention that the *Lotus Sūtra* was chanted in the daytime and the *nenbutsu* chanted in the evening. The biographies of the *Hokke genki,* a collection of stories of *Lotus Sūtra* devotees, include many examples of practitioners reborn in the Pure Land. In a similar fashion, the biographies of Pure Land devotees found in early collections such as the *Ōjō gokurakuki* (Records of birth in the land of utmost bliss), *Zoku honchō ōjōden* (Continuation of biographies of those reborn in Pure Land), and *Shūi ōjōden* (Gleanings of biographies of those reborn in Pure Land) include many stories of practitioners who recited the *Lotus Sūtra.* Finally, Ryōgen's instructions about the services to be performed at his death reflect this tendency. For the forty-nine-day period following his death, twelve monks were to chant the *Lotus Sūtra* in the Hokkedō and fourteen monks were to recite the *nenbutsu* in the Jōgyōdō. The services were to be performed three times (*sanji*) each day.[31]

By the time Ryōgen rebuilt the Constant-walking Meditation Hall, the practices performed in such halls were significantly different from the meditation specified in Chih-i's *Mo-ho chih-kuan.* Pure Land devotion had played little part in the religious austerities described by Chih-i. Rather the meditation was based on the *Pan-chou san-mei ching* (*T* nos. 417–419, *Bhadrapālāsūtra*), a text concerned with visualizations of a number of Buddhas. According to Chih-i, the constant-walking meditation consisted of a ninety-day period during which the practitioner constantly circumambulated an image of Amitābha, recited his name, and meditated on his special physical characteristics. The ultimate goal of the meditation, however, was to realize the nonsubstantiality of the mind and the Buddha. The recitation of Amitābha's name was thus used as an expedient object of meditation to enable the practitioner to remain alert and focus his attention, not to further his wish to be reborn in Amitābha's Pure Land. In fact, Chih-i had assigned Amitābha's Pure Land, Sukhāvatī, a low rank among Buddha Lands because both ordinary people and sages could be born in it.

Saichō probably intended to have his disciples practice this strenuous meditation, but he died before he could put his plans into effect.[32] A constant-walking meditation was first performed in Japan under the instruction of Ennin in 851, when Ennin instructed his disciples to perform the ceremony.[33] In the seventh month of 856, Saichō's remains were moved to the Jōdoin (Pure Land chapel), where a similar *nenbutsu* ritual was performed, using the ceremony for memorial purposes.[34]

According to the *Jikaku daishiden,* the constant-walking meditation transmitted by Ennin was based on a practice performed at the Chulin-ssu (Bamboo forest monastery) on Mount Wu-t'ai in China.[35] Ennin reports in his diary of travels in China that he saw the sites where Fachao had performed the five modes of the *nenbutsu* in 840; however, Ennin did not record anything about actually witnessing the ceremony even though long entries concerning other ceremonies are found in the diary. In 841, while he was in Ch'ang-an, Ennin noted that a disciple of Fa-chao named Ching-shuang had been commanded to lead three-day *nenbutsu* services at various monasteries. Ennin probably witnessed this ceremony at the Tzu-sheng-ssu; about this time, he may have obtained Fa-chao's *Ching-t'u wu-hui nien-fo lüeh-fa-shih-i-tsan* (Brief procedures and hymns for the five modes of the *nenbutsu* of the Pure Land; *T* no. 1983) in one fascicle (or two), a text that he brought back to Japan with him. Although Ennin did not write in any detail about the ceremony in his diary, the constant-walking meditation he taught his disciples was probably based on his experiences in the Tzu-sheng-ssu.[36]

The entries in Ennin's biography and travel diary have led modern scholars to suggest that the constant-walking meditation on Mount Hiei was based on a ceremony devised by Fa-chao that became popular on Mount Wu-t'ai several decades before Ennin traveled to China. Little was known about Fa-chao and his teachings until the caves at Tun-huang were opened. On the basis of documents found at Tun-huang, considerable information about Fa-chao and his teachings has emerged.[37]

Fa-chao (d.c. 800) was a monk who had a series of visions while he was performing his religious austerities. During a ninety-day retreat, Amitābha appeared before him and taught him a way of reciting the *nenbutsu* in five modes (*wu-hui nien-fo*), which were said to have been based upon the way in which the leaves on trees in the Pure Land produced the sounds of preaching when the wind blew through them.[38] Fa-chao was successful in gaining court patronage and spread his practice through many parts of China. At the time Ennin traveled to China, it would have been one of the most popular forms of Buddhist practice. Among the key influences on Fa-chao was Shan-tao, the Pure Land thinker who would later influence Genshin and Shinran. Thus Ennin's Pure Land practices served as a means of introducing this important thinker to later generations of Japanese devotees. Fa-chao was also influenced by the T'ien-t'ai tradition; his teacher had spent time at Yü-ch'üan-ssu, the site where Chih-i had delivered a number of his most important lectures. Fa-chao's T'ien-t'ai connections made it easier for Ennin to adopt his practices and introduce them to Japan.

The earliest description of the practice of constant-walking meditation in Japanese Tendai is found in the the *Sanbō ekotoba,* a work compiled in 984 by Minamoto no Tamenori (d. 1011). The description thus reflects the ceremony as it was performed during Ryōgen's time. According to the text,

> the *nenbutsu* was brought from China by Jikaku daishi [Ennin] and first performed in 868. Within the four types of meditation, it is called the constant-walking meditation. It is performed without cease from the dawn of the eleventh day [of the eighth month] until the night of the seventeenth when the cool autumn wind is blowing and the full moon is shining. The practitioners constantly circumambulate the Buddha and thus their physical sins are all eliminated. They chant the *sūtra* without interruption and thus their verbal transgressions are all vanquished. They steadily think of the Buddha and thus all mental offenses vanish. . . . Those who wish to reach that Pure Land must despise this world and desire the Pure land. As for despising this world, whether you are standing or sitting, you must loathe the sufferings of this body. As for desiring the Pure Land, whether you are awake or asleep, you must aspire to the pleasures of that land. If you see spring flowers in the morning, you should think of the seven rows of [blossoming] trees [in the Pure Land]. When you hear the autumn wind in the evening, you should think of the rippling of the water of the Pure Land and its eight good qualities. You should focus your mind on the setting sun as it sinks in the west. If each day you intend to do at least a little good, then you shall surely be reborn there. Even if you have committed the five heinous sins, you shall surely be reborn there.[39]

Similar passages that were probably influenced by the *Sanbō ekotoba* are found in the *Konjaku monogatari* and the *Eiga monogatari.*[40]

Although the above passage identifies the meditation as the constant-walking meditation from Chih-i's *Mo-ho chih-kuan,* it is clearly different from the meditation described by Chih-i. First, the Japanese form of the meditation is performed for seven days whereas the meditation described by Chih-i was to be performed for ninety days. Second, the Japanese meditation was performed at a particular time of the year as an annual ceremony whereas Chih-i's meditation could be performed at any appropriate time. Third, in the Japanese meditation, the practitioner recites a *sūtra,* the *O-mi-t'o ching,* but in Chih-i's meditation the

name of the Buddha is recited. Fourth, the object of the Japanese meditation is to vanquish sins and be reborn in the Pure Land, whereas
Chih-i's meditation is designed to lead to the realization of the three
views in an instant.[41] In fact, Ennin may not have called the meditation a constant-walking practice, indicating that he clearly recognized
the difference between the traditions.[42] The differences between the two
meditative practices probably existed from the time Ennin first transmitted the constant-walking meditation to Japan. Although most of these
differences can be traced to Fa-chao's ritual practices, the practice on
Mount Hiei differed in several ways from that of Fa-chao. For example,
Fa-chao had recommended twenty-one days of practice. By Ryōgen's
time, it was practiced for seven days each at the halls in Tōdō, Saitō, and
Yokawa, making a total of twenty-one days, but at three different sites.[43]

After Ennin's time the constant-walking meditation was transmitted
by his disciples, especially Sōō and Henjō. However, the Lotus meditation seems to have been more popular at the end of the ninth century
because of Enchin's efforts to promote it. During Ryōgen's lifetime, the
constant-walking meditation gained in popularity until it became virtually the only one of the four meditations practiced. As Ryōgen complained, "During the twelve years monks are confined on Mount Hiei,
they should practice the four types of [Tendai] meditation. However,
now only the constant-walking meditation is performed. The other meditations have virtually ceased to be practiced.[44]

Halls for the constant-walking meditation were built in various places
throughout Japan. The first was built in Tōdō on Mount Hiei sometime
between the first performance of the constant-walking meditation in 851
and Ennin's death in 865.[45] Halls were subsequently built at many other
sites, including Saitō on Mount Hiei in 893, Yokawa on Mount Hiei in
968, and such Tendai monasteries as Miidera in 875, Gangyōji in 886,
and Tōnomine in 969. Eventually most of the major Tendai centers had
a Constant-walking Meditation Hall. Images of Amida were usually installed, and the walls or pillars were sometimes painted with scenes de-
picting the Pure Land. Today on Mount Hiei, Constant-walking and Lotus Meditation Halls exist only in Saitō and are said to date from 1599.[46]

Mañjuśrī's Tower

Work continued on the other halls that had been destroyed in the 966
fire. In 969, Mañjuśrī's Tower was finished. Because Chih-i had used texts
in which Mañjuśrī was the protagonist as the authority for his treatment

of the constant-sitting meditation, this building originally may have been
the site of that practice; however, the building was referred to as both
a Single-practice Hall (Ichigyō zanmaiin) and a Constant-sitting Hall
(Jōza zanmaiin).[47] Although the constant-sitting meditation was not as
popular as the constant-walking or Lotus meditations on Mount Hiei,
it still was one of the basic Tendai practices.

Mañjuśrī's Tower was closely associated with Ennin, and Ryōgen
chose to first rebuild those structures that were associated with Ennin
and his lineage. Ennin had constructed it in 861 with help from the nobility. Unfortunately, little is known of the reasons behind its construction. However, from Saichō's time, Mañjuśrī had played a major role in
the Japanese Tendai tradition.[48] Ennin too was a devotee of Mañjuśrī,
traveling to Mount Wu-t'ai, where Mañjuśrī is said to reside, and dream-
ing that he was under Mañjuśrī's protection. In 850, shortly after returning from China, he performed the eight-character ritual dedicated
to Mañjuśrī (Monju hachiji hō) in the palace. This ceremony, based on
the Wen-shu-shih-li p'u-sa pa-tzu san-mei fa (Ritual for the eight-character
[mantra] of the bodhisattva Mañjuśrī; T no. 1185A), translated by Bod-
hiruci, was a mixed Esoteric ceremony used to vanquish disasters and
promote good fortune.[49] When Mañjuśrī's Tower was constructed,
stones from Mount Wu-t'ai were placed under its platform, and its central image was carved from a fragrant log from Mount Wu-t'ai.[50]

According to the Jie daisōjōden, at the dedication in 969, people remembered that Ennin had brought back earth from Mount Wu-t'ai, the
sacred mountain in China where Mañjuśrī was said to reside. However,
the soil had been contaminated and lost in the fire. Ryōgen then produced a container with the inscription that it too contained earth from
Mount Wu-t'ai that had been brought to Japan by Ennin. The dedication of the new hall to Mañjuśrī was carried out properly, using items
from Mount Wu-t'ai just as Ennin had done a century earlier.[51] Although no way exists of determining the authenticity of the story, the
dramatic way in which Ryōgen produced the items needed to make
the ceremony fit in well with his other uses of ritual. The story still cap-
tures the imagination of Tendai monks. The current Monjurō was built
in 1642 to replace the earlier Monjurō burned in Oda Nobunaga's raz-
ing of Mount Hiei. In 1984, the Tendai zasu Yamada Etai went to Mount
Wu-t'ai and brought back earth to bury at the base of the current image of Mañjuśrī.[52]

Ryōgen moved the location of the Mañjuśrī Tower from near the Lecture Hall to the Kokūzō peak, which was to the east of the Central Hall,

probably so that it would be safer from fires. Similar measures were taken with other buildings as Ryōgen sought a better arrangement for the buildings in the Tendai establishment. In a number of cases, his biographers recorded predictions or wondrous events that confirmed the new location chosen by Ryōgen and probably served to defuse criticisms of his changes. In the case of the Mañjuśrī Tower, a bodhisattva is said to have appeared several generations before Ryōgen. When Tendai monks went to build him a hall at Kokūzō, he said that the land was a good place, but already belonged to another bodhisattva; as a result, the building was not completed. When Ryōgen had the Monjurō moved to Kokūzō, the monks discovered the foundation of that earlier building, thereby confirming the earlier bodhisattva's prediction.[53] The Monjurō was dedicated on 10-1-980, the day after the dedication of the Central Hall. Two hundred monks participated in the ceremonies, and nobles attended it.[54]

Rebuilding the Sōjiin

Ryōgen's interest in the Sōjiin was obvious immediately after his appointment as *zasu*. On 9-10-966, two weeks after his appointment, he submitted a ten-point proposal to the court. Although little is known about its contents, Ryōgen is known to have asked that the number of masters of Esoteric Buddhism at the Sōjiin be increased by three to sixteen, a provision approved on 12-26.[55] The early date of Ryōgen's proposals, before the devastating fire on Mount Hiei, is important as indicating the central role the Sōjiin played in his plans. When the Sōjiin burned, it was one of the first buildings that Ryōgen rebuilt. But shortly after it had been completed, it burned down again, on 4-21-970.[56] Ryōgen was enraged by the carelessness that had led to the fire and three months after the fire issued twenty-six rules in an attempt to tighten discipline among the monks.[57] In addition, Ryōgen halted construction on the Lecture Hall long enough to build those parts of the Sōjiin that were necessary for the celebration of the traditional annual ceremony for the Buddha's relic (*shari-e*) on 4-25-971.[58] As in the hurried rebuilding of the Lotus Meditation Hall and Constant-walking Meditation Hall, Ryōgen's building schedule reveals a sensitivity to the needs of having certain structures finished so that annual performances of major rituals could be conducted. However, the performance of the ceremony of the Buddha's relic at the Sōjiin was only a part of his plan to restore the practices begun by Ennin to a prominent place in Tendai. Ryōgen's interest in the Sōjiin also arose from his desire to restore it to its previous status as the chief center of Esoteric practice on Mount Hiei, a move that would also indicate that his lineage was assuming the paramount position on Mount Hiei, surpassing the monks in Enchin's lineage.

To appreciate the role that the Sōjiin played for Ryōgen, we must understand the history of the structure. The full title of the Sōjiin was the Hokke sōjiin (Lotus Dhāraṇī hall), a name that reflects the structure's origins as the repository of a thousand copies of the *Lotus Sūtra*. The Sōjiin was thus said to be one of six pagodas planned by Saichō, each with a thousand copies of the *Lotus Sūtra,* to protect the nation. As a result the hall was also known as the Tōdōin (Hall of the eastern pagoda), the central building in the Tōdō area.[59] Apparently the thousand copies of the *Lotus Sūtra* had still not been completed at the time of Ennin's death, since he asked his disciples to finish them before the year ended.[60]

The actual building of the Sōjiin and its role as a center of Esoteric practice began after Ennin returned from China. At that time, the Tendai school desperately needed to import Esoteric teachings and rituals from China if it hoped to compete with Kūkai's Shingon school. One of Ennin's major reasons for traveling to China had been to bring back the dual (*ryōbu*) Esoteric tradition on which Shingon was based. In fact, Ennin brought back a system based on three texts (*sanbu*) that would give the Tendai Esoteric tradition a character different from that of the Shingon tradition. Establishing the doctrinal basis for Tendai Esoteric Buddhism would not be sufficient for Tendai, however, because Kūkai's successors had begun to import new rituals that could be used for specific purposes such as the protection of the state. These rituals often focused on a single deity or bodhisattva (*besson*), sometimes one not even included in the dual *maṇḍala* system.

An example of such a ritual is provided by the story of Jōgyō (d. 865), a monk with affiliations to both the Sanron and Shingon schools. In 838 Jōgyō had traveled to China, where Amoghavajra's disciple Wents'an had told him about a new ceremony to protect the emperor, the ritual for the demon (*yakṣa*) general Taigen (Skt. Aṭavaka). The central figure, Taigen, was portrayed as a multiarmed, multiheaded figure with three blood-red eyes, wrapped in snakes, treading on a demon. Jōgyō explained to the court that the ceremony was practiced in China where it protected the nation and the emperor against bandits and epidemics and ensured that the weather would be appropriate for the season. In 840, the year after he returned, Jōgyō began to perform the ritual at the Hōrinji in Ogurusu, Uji. He asked that it also be performed in the

TABLE 19

FUNDING FOR THE MONKS OF THE SŌJIIN (DAILY AMOUNTS)

Offerings to the Buddha	6 *masu* of rice
Offerings to the twelve gods	3 *masu* of rice
Oil for lamps	4 *gō* of oil
Incense	1 *masu*
Servants (*zōshi*) (5)	6 *masu*, 4 *gō* of rice
novices (2)	1 *masu* each of rice
hall boy (*dōdōji*) (1)	2 *masu* of rice
errand boys (*kushi*) (2)	1 *masu*, 2 *gō* each of rice

palace in a manner similar to the rituals performed in the Shingon Chapel (Shingon'in) established by Kūkai. His request was granted in 851, and the ceremony was performed annually from the eighth to the fourteenth of the first month by fifteen monks. About this time, various reports of the efficacy of the ritual, particularly in regard to protection from Korean attacks, came to the attention of the court.[61]

Just as Ennin had provided a doctrinal basis for Taimitsu, he also imported rituals that could compete with the ceremony for Taigen. At the same time that Jōgyō was urging the court to adopt the ceremonies propitiating Taigen, Ennin was advocating the adoption of the ceremony for the Buddha of Abundant Light to protect the emperor.[62] Ennin's arguments are virtually identical to those used by Jōgyō. Both noted that the ritual was used to great effect by the Chinese court and urged that a specific chapel be established for the performance of the ceremony. For the Tendai school, that institution was the Sōjiin.

Ennin's proposals came right as Emperor Ninmyō died and as Emperor Montoku was being installed. With the help of Fujiwara no Yoshifusa, Ennin's arguments were accepted. In 850, just a few months after Emperor Montoku had assumed the throne, the court ordered fourteen monks to constantly perform the ceremony.[63] The number of monks authorized suggests that the court was attempting to be evenhanded in its patronage of Shingon and Tendai. According to an order from the chancellor's office (*dajōkanpu*) issued on 9-16-850, the court supported the Tendai monks with a daily allotment of white rice, lamp oil, and incense (table 19).[64] The amounts of rice supplied to the fourteen monks was to be the same as that supplied to the monks of the Jōshin'in (Hall of the Concentrated Mind), the *goganji* (august prayer-offering temple) of the previous emperor (Ninmyō). According to a document dated 853 included in the *Kuin Bukkakushō* (Records of the nine halls and Buddhist pavilions), each monk at the Sōjiin was to receive 4 *masu*, 6 *gō* of rice. The amounts of rice supplied to the Sōjiin thus would probably have supported more than the specified number of people and given it a financial base sufficient for supporting a major religious institution.[65]

Work on expanding the Sōjiin was begun several years later at the command of Emperor Montoku and finally completed in 862 after ten years of work.[66] The structure was far more than a site for rituals; it included a library, quarters for monks, a hall for Esoteric consecrations (*kanjōdō*), a separate building where the major *maṇḍala* for Esoteric rituals were displayed, and walkways around and between the buildings. Ennin invested more of his efforts in this complex than any other, producing one of the most impressive Tendai sets of buildings on Mount Hiei. In addition, the Sōjiin was the site for the performance of advanced Esoteric consecrations (*denbō kanjō*) that qualified the recipient to become a master of Esoteric Buddhism. When the complex was dedicated in 866, even Jōgyō and several other monks from the Shingon and Hossō schools participated.[67]

The Sōjiin, however, was not for all Tendai monks; along with the Shuryōgon'in in Yokawa, it served as the headquarters for Ennin's lineage, and thus played a sectarian role in internal Tendai politics. The Esoteric texts that Saichō had brought from China were placed in it. Shortly after Ennin's death, the Esoteric works that Ennin brought from China were also placed in it so that access could be limited only to those monks qualified to read the texts. Exoteric texts, however, remained in the Konpon kyōzō, the library founded by Saichō, which was in the Central Hall.[68] The Sōjiin thus played a central role for monks in Ennin's lineage, giving them access to vital texts and perhaps limiting access to others. Finally, Ennin had stipulated that only members of his lineage should be appointed abbot of the Sōjiin.[69]

The treatment of Ennin's books undoubtedly alienated members of other lineages. In fact, the Sōjiin began to lose some of its prestige when Enchin was named Tendai *zasu* and stipulated that advanced consecrations were permitted at the Onjōji, a temple he had refurbished as the headquarters for his disciples. Just as the abbot of the Sōjiin was to be from Ennin's lineage, the abbot of Onjōji was to be from Enchin's lineage.[70] The texts that Enchin had brought back from China had been deposited with the Ministry of Central Affairs (Nakatsukashō); later they had been placed at Enchin's quarters at the Sannōin in Tōdō, the building where Enchin resided during his tenure as *zasu,* when the deity Shiragi myōjin had told him in a dream that the government offices were not an appropriate site for them. Eventually they were moved again to the Tōin at Onjōji.[71]

As Enchin's lineage came to dominate the Tendai school, the Sōjiin slipped into decline. By 872, the court felt it necessary to admonish the monks at three halls built at imperial request—the Sōjiin, Jōshin'in, and Shiōin—for not performing their assigned rituals regularly. Monks were making excuses for not attending the rituals, going to other temples, and loaning out texts without permission.[72] Neither the Sōjiin nor the ceremony for the Buddha of Abundant Light are mentioned much in the *Tendai zasuki* from Enchin's time until 941, when the Sōjiin burned down for the first time.[73] In the twelfth month of that same year, the *zasu* Gikai had the *shijōkōhō* performed for an unspecified member of the nobility, the first time it had been performed for someone other than the emperor.[74] This new usage of the ceremony suggests that it was not being performed with the same regularity; if it had been performed regularly for the emperor, it might have been more difficult to use it to benefit someone else.

After the Sōjiin burned down for the first time in 941, it was partially rebuilt with a pagoda and walkways, but not on its original scale with quarters, library, and separate buildings for the various advanced Esoteric ceremonies.[75] The reconstruction must have been finished within three years inasmuch as Myōtatsu is said to have led a performance of the *shijōkōhō* there in 944.[76] The regular performance of the ceremony was revived by Enshō (*zasu* from 946 to 964), a member of Ennin's lineage. At first, Enshō performed the ceremony in the Dainichiin (Hall for Mahāvairocana), perhaps because the Sōjiin was not in suitable condition, but after several performances he moved it back to the Sōjiin.[77] The pattern of decline and revival of the Sōjiin and the *shijōkōhō* continued during the centuries after it had been revived by Ryōgen.[78]

Ryōgen's indefatigable efforts to rebuild the Sōjiin, not once but twice, were the result of his determination to give the Esoteric tradition established by Ennin new life and to make it the centerpiece of the rituals he used to attract his patrons.

The Central Hall

Ryōgen made improvements to many of the halls he rebuilt. The Central Hall in Tōdō, for example, was enlarged to hold the large number of people who came to Tendai ceremonies.[79] The eaves were made wider than before, and walkways were constructed around it. In addition, Ryō-gen felt that the building should have a large dedication ceremony to mark its completion. He had criticized the lack of such a ceremony when the hall had been rebuilt after the 936 fire. Consequently, Ryōgen or-ganized an impressive celebration that was held on 9-3-980 and is de-scribed in detail in the *Shūiden*. More than 200 monks were especially invited to attend, and 150 musicians played for the services. Young boys performed various dances. The celebration for the dedication was con-ducted on such a large scale that various contemporary sources men-tion it.[80] The detail with which the services are described suggests that the compiler of the *Shūiden*, Bonshō, attended them and may have been disappointed in the failure of the author of the *Jie daisōjōden* to include them in his biography. However, this view is difficult to reconcile with Bonshō's age.[81] Various members of the nobility attended and read po-ems or composed music for the occasion. The massive celebrations Ryō-gen planned for the dedication of the Central Hall and other buildings were part of his efforts to attract lay interest in Buddhism. As he re-marked in the dedication for the Central Hall, "We have established as-semblies in various places; but very few people will come from nearby places to hear the Dharma. However, many people will travel from far off to hear music. . . . Thus through music, karmic ties to Buddhism are formed."[82]

The composition of the guests and participants at the dedication cer-emonies for the Central Hall reveal a number of significant aspects of the Tendai institution. A number of high officials, such as Morosuke's son Fujiwara no Tamemitsu[83] (942–992), are mentioned in various doc-uments, suggesting that the nobility was represented at the dedication. By the time of the dedication, more monks were coming from aristo-cratic families, and Ryōgen had been repeatedly honored by the court; thus the attendance of members of the nobility is not surprising. Ac-cording to the *Dō kuyō* (Record of offerings at [dedication of] the hall), Emperor En'yū, Chancellor Fujiwara no Yoritada, and other high court officials attended; but this account has been rejected as spurious because the ranks of the officials are inaccurate.[84] These documents exaggerate the amount of contact between the Tendai school and the court.

In addition, a significant amount of factionalism is evident in Ryō-gen's attitude by 980. Ryōgen invited a number of monks from the Nara schools to participate in the ceremony. In addition, Tendai monks from his own lineage who had previously been critical of Ryōgen took part in the procession; among them were such monks as Zōga. One group was not represented: monks from Enchin's lineage. After Enchin's lineage appealed to the court, Ryōgen was directed to include several representatives in the dedication, including Yokei, the current leader of the faction.[85] This account suggests that when Ryōgen rebuilt many of these structures, he might have claimed certain rights of appointing their officials. After all, the Central Hall was the first building on Mount Hiei; by failing to invite the representatives of a major group on the mountain Ryōgen excluded them from one of the most important and oldest centers on the mountain. The origins of the Central Hall lay in Saichō's establishment of a temple when he first climbed Mount Hiei. Another indication of Ryōgen's factionalism was his appointment of members of his faction to serve as abbots of the various reconstructed buildings.

Other Buildings

When Ryōgen began the construction of the New Lecture hall, he planned to make it considerably larger than the one that had burned down. Instead of five bays square, the new building was seven bays square. The Lecture Hall was completed in 971; the Hall of Longevity and the Hall of the Four Guardian Kings were completed in the second and third months of 972, thereby restoring most of the Tōdō buildings that had burned. To celebrate, Ryōgen planned a large dedication ceremony. It was held on 4-3-972, with more than 200 monks invited and 150 musicians performing.[86] When the dedication was over, music and dance were performed. Pageantry on a large scale was often a part of Ryōgen's activities for the next decade (as we have seen in connection with the dedication of the Central Hall).

Ryōgen is also credited with the construction of many other structures in the Tōdō area including the Hall for Consecrations and the Mantra Hall (Shingondō) in 970, both for Esoteric practice, as well as covered walkways between the two buildings. In 980, the dining hall (*jikidō*) with nine bays on each side was built; the following year, the lodgings for imperial messengers, administrative center, and bathhouse were completed. The restoration of the *jikidō*, was accompanied by the performance of religious services dedicated to the memory of Chih-i, de facto founder of the Tendai school, and debates.[87] Such ceremonies had originally been performed at the T'ien-t'ai monastery, Kuoch'ing-ssu, and had been introduced to Japan by Ennin.[88] Thus, even in rebuilding an edifice with a seemingly practical function such as taking meals, Ryōgen was able to stress the ceremonial connections with Ennin.

Ryōgen also built new halls in other areas on Mount Hiei and some of the major Tendai monasteries. In the Saitō area, Ryōgen built a library and bell tower for the Hōdōin, the hall where he had stayed as a young monk, and in 984 had the Hōdōin itself rebuilt. In 975 in Yokawa, the third major area on Hiei and the complex with which Ryōgen most closely identified, the Central Hall, was rebuilt and a new life-size image of Fudō myōō was dedicated. In 983, Fujiwara no Kaneie, minister of the right, traveled to Yokawa to participate in the dedication of the Eshin'in.[89] The construction of the building fulfilled a vow that had been made by his father, Morosuke. Later, Morosuke's son Jinzen would succeed Ryōgen as abbot of the hall and as *zasu;* on 10-20-986, the Eshin'in was recognized as an official temple (*kanji*) and awarded three yearly ordinands (*nenbundosha*), treatment that was based on that accorded the Hosshōji founded by Fujiwara no Tadahira. The merit from the temple and the rituals performed at it were to help Kaneie's lineage prosper.[90] Genshin was the third abbot of the temple and was so identified with the building that he would be known as Eshin sōzu (the bishop of Eshin'in) and his lineage as the Eshin-ryū. The building was five bays square and situated to the south of the Shuryōgon'in (Hall for the practice of the meditation of heroic valor). The Eshin'in thus played a major role in Yokawa's increasing importance.

Besides Mount Hiei, several halls were completed at the Gangyōji monastery outside Kyoto, including the Myōgōbō in the Central Hall (Chūin) and the monks' quarters dedicated to Ryōgen's early teacher, Kakue; Kakue had taught Ryōgen Esoteric Buddhism and had later resigned his position as master of Esoteric Buddhism at Gangyōji in favor of Ryōgen. The rebuilding was necessary because of serious fires in 949 and 957.[91] The newly constructed monastery must have been impressive: Emperor Kazan chose it when he secretly decided to take his vows as a monk in 986, the year after Ryōgen's death. Kazan remained there for two years.[92]

In Tōdō, the Lotus Meditation Hall and Constant-walking Meditation Hall could be completed rapidly because the main images in them had been saved from the fires. In other cases, new images had to be carved. For example, in the Lecture Hall new images of Dainichi (Vairocana), flanked by Kannon (Avalokiteśvara) and Miroku (Maitreya) were installed. Other images of Mañjuśrī and six deities were also placed in the hall.

Conclusion

The impressive scope of Ryōgen's construction activities is evident simply by looking at the list of structures he either renovated or built anew. Ryōgen's activities display his abilities as an administrator and supervisor of massive building projects; he was also frequently involved in the selection of sites and may have participated in architectural decisions. Ryōgen was not simply interested in construction, however; construction was driven by such concerns as the ritual calendar. In many cases, careful study of the buildings reveals significant changes in both the performance and objectives of rituals from the guidelines specified in Chih-i's *Mo-ho chih-kuan*. The growing influence of lay patronage is also evident when the performance of the rituals at the Lotus Meditation Hall and the Sōjiin is considered. As the competition between factions of the Fujiwara clan became more intense, the nobility demanded and paid for increasingly elaborate ceremonies and buildings to protect themselves. The competition between lineages within the Fujiwara clan was reflected in the lineages within the Tendai school. In his efforts to rebuild Mount Hiei, Ryōgen constantly referred to rituals that Ennin had instituted. Rarely, if ever, was Enchin, the leader of the Tendai school, looked up to as a model during these years, a bias that would create serious problems by the end of Ryōgen's tenure. In the next chapter, some of the sources for financing these projects are investigated.

Ryōgen as *Zasu*

Financing the Spread of Tendai Influence

Financing for the Tendai school has been a constant underlying theme in much of this study. Ryōgen's decision to become a monk was based in part on the difficulty commoners had in advancing in the secular realm. When he finally was named a yearly ordinand (*nenbundosha*), the appointment as an officially recognized monk undoubtedly brought some financial reward. His success in performing Esoteric rituals for the nobility was rewarded with buildings and appointments to the Office of Monastic Affairs, resulting in further support for Ryōgen and his faction. Even his plans for reforming the education system on Mount Hiei involved assigning funds for that process. In this chapter, a more systematic review of the sources of funding for Ryōgen's plans is undertaken. Because early sources for the Tendai finances are limited and scholarship on this subject has not progressed very far, the discussion is not detailed. The chapter is divided into three parts: finances on Mount Hiei, Tendai influence beyond Mount Hiei, and the role of women in financing Tendai expansion.

Finances on Mount Hiei

Financing the Rebuilding of Mount Hiei

Until Ryōgen's time most of the finances for Mount Hiei had come from taxes, particularly those of the province of Ōmi where Mount Hiei was situated. For example, in 831, official offerings (*kuryō*) for the official provincial temple (*kokubunji*) were ordered divided with Mount Hiei so that twenty-four Tendai yearly ordinands could be supported.[1] In the *Shijōshiki* (Rules in four articles), Saichō had asked that the two yearly ordinands given to the Tendai school each year be required to practice on Mount Hiei for twelve years before they descended the mountain. The revenues that the court provided in 831 were to be used to support these monks.

During the subsequent years additional funds from tax revenues were given to Mount Hiei. According to the *Engishiki,* fifteen thousand sheaves (*soku*) of rice from the taxes (*shōzei*) of Ōmi were to be given to the Saitōin (Western pagoda hall) and thirty thousand to the Jōshin'in (Hall of the concentrated mind). Forty thousand *soku* from the taxes of Mino were given to the Sōjiin (Dhāraṇī hall) and another forty thousand to the Shiōin (Hall of the four kings).[2] In addition, smaller amounts of white rice, brown rice (*kokumai*), and sesame oil were routinely given to the monastery for Esoteric rituals, oil for its lamps, offerings for monks, or funds for the repair and maintenance of its buildings.[3] Taxes continued to be a source of income in Ryōgen's time, though not enough to fund all of Mount Hiei's needs. For example, the Lotus Meditation Hall established with Morosuke's help and the Shuryōgon'in were supported with taxes from Ōmi and Mino. However, provision also was made that private sources might be used if taxes proved insufficient.[4]

Emperors had supported particular chapels and halls on Mount Hiei as centers dedicated to the performance of ceremonies to ensure their health and longevity. For example, Emperor Ninmyō supported the Jōshin'in, Emperor Montoku the Sōjiin and the Shiōin, and Emperor Suzaku (923–952; r. 930–946) the Enmeiin.[5] Sometimes specific amounts from taxes were designated for the support of various buildings. For example, in 878, ten *koku* each of white and brown rice were to be given annually to the Shiōin (Hall of the four kings) from Mino. In 886, fifteen thousand sheaves of rice from the taxes of Ōmi were given to the Shakadō (Śākyamuni hall) in Saitō; much of it was to be loaned as seed rice so that the interest would support the Shakadō over the years. However, because the practice of endowing specific halls was largely confined to emperors, it could not provide Mount Hiei with all of its support. Interest in specific halls might decline once the emperor died, and the funds assigned to a specific hall might have other claims put on them by subsequent officials. Thus, the Tendai school had to constantly seek new sources and defend its existing claims.

At first, contributions from private donors played a relatively small role in Mount Hiei's finances in comparison with the large amounts allocated by the state. The first instance of a private gift occurred in 863 when Prince Hitoyasu (d. 872) gave Enryakuji ninety-four *chō* of land

for the spread of Buddhism (*denbō kuryō*) and Prince Tsuneyasu gave it
120 *chō* to help the poor and distressed (*kyūkyūryō*).[6] These gifts, however, were exceptional. Until Ryōgen's time most of Mount Hiei's
finances came from official sources such as taxes, the interest on com-
pulsory loans of seed grain to farmers (*suikotō*), and grants when temples were established by emperors or their associates.

Donations for the support of a particular building must have contributed to the factionalism that was growing on Mount Hiei, but economic factors may not have been a major source of rivalry at first because the amounts of money involved were probably adequate for the
small number of monks on Mount Hiei and because government taxes
rather than private funds were involved. Once the powerful lay believers who were the power behind the throne began funding particular
halls, the monks were inevitably drawn into secular factional disputes.
Moreover, because powerful lay patrons began to build halls for the conduct of rituals that would benefit them and their descendants in their
struggles against other nobles, the monks were drawn into these conflicts. In addition, as particular halls came to have resources of their
own, the central authority of the *zasu* was weakened, especially late in
the Heian period.

Private gifts began to play a major role at Mount Hiei early in Ryōgen's career. For example, when Morosuke dedicated the Lotus Meditation Hall, he had stated that the merits from it were to help his lineage prosper. Donations accompanied the dedication to pay for the
services conducted there. For example, Morosuke had arranged that
revenues from the Tomoyui manor (with more than sixty *chō* and also
in Ōmi) be given to the Lotus Meditation Hall.[7]

Morosuke's death in 960 was the occasion for a substantial transfer
of lands to the Tendai school. Eleven manors in a variety of provinces
were left to Morosuke's son Jinzen; this large gift to a son who had just
begun his training at a monastery was unprecedented.[8] Jinzen was
eighteen years old at the time, with three years of seniority. The actual
transfer of the land took place approximately a year after Morosuke's
death and was carried out by Morosuke's oldest son, Koremasa, at a
time when Morosuke's sons were out of power. Their eventual success
in regaining power was attributed in no small part to Ryōgen's prayers.
In addition, Jinzen would not forget Koremasa's help and provided for
his descendants later. However, because Jinzen was young, the actual
management of these lands was left to Ryōgen.[9] In addition, several
manors were given directly to Ryōgen. Among them was the Okaya

manor in Ōmi with more than 160 *chō* of land.[10] On 5-4-962, Morosuke's son Koremasa donated eight thousand sheaves of rice from his private lands in Ōmi and Mino to the Shuryōgon'in at Yokawa.[11]

Appointments for Morosuke's Son Jinzen

The donors of estates needed to make sure that their contributions would be used as they intended. Morosuke had his own son ordained partly to perform rituals to ensure the clan's prosperity, but also to oversee the donations. In return, Ryōgen seems to have promised to educate Morosuke's son Jinzen, to help him advance through the monastic ranks, and to allow him and his relatives to administer at least part of Mount Hiei. In fact, Jinzen's rapid advance through the ranks of the Office of Monastic Affairs also helped Ryōgen gain higher appointments because the teacher was expected to maintain a higher rank than the student. Ryōgen's position as head of the Tendai school and an administrator in the Office of Monastic Affairs gave him the authority to influence appointments in both organizations. In sponsoring Jinzen, Ryōgen was also able to help the Tendai school, gaining authorization for new positions for it from the court and new sources of income from the Fujiwara clan.

In 971, Ryōgen conferred a number of Esoteric initiations upon Jinzen. He then petitioned the court for permission to grant the status of master of Esoteric Buddhism upon Jinzen. Because the number of *ajari* at each temple was limited by the court, monks usually were at least in their forties before they were given this status. Ryōgen had been thirty-nine when Kakue had given his position at Gangyōji to Ryōgen; Jinzen, however, was only thirty-one. Ryōgen realized that because of Jinzen's connections with the Fujiwara family, Jinzen could probably receive special permission to receive the position of *ajari* without waiting for one of the positions on Mount Hiei to fall vacant or for his turn. Ryōgen petitioned the court for permission to confer the status of *ajari* upon Jinzen in a special manner. Jinzen would not be counted as one of the *ajari* that the Tendai establishment was officially allotted, but in a special category because of his family connections. The Tendai school would thus gain, at least temporarily, an additional *ajari*, and Jinzen's special status would be recognized. The position was called *isshin ajari* (literally, "a special position as master of Esoteric Buddhism that is limited to that particular person"), and Jinzen was the first person to receive such an appointment.[12] Later, this position would be conferred upon many sons from imperial and noble families by decree even though the recipients often had not received training in Esoteric Buddhism.

Shortly after he had submitted his petition, Ryōgen celebrated his sixtieth birthday. Many of the most illustrious nobles from Kyoto attended the services in his honor. Because the guests undoubtedly included members of Jinzen's family, it is not surprising that the court granted permission for Jinzen to be made an *ajari* under the conditions specified by Ryōgen.

In 972, Ryōgen became ill and wrote a will specifying how the various properties under his control should be treated. Most of the buildings that Morosuke had built and the manors that had belonged to Morosuke were to go to Jinzen. Moreover, Ryōgen specified that his seals of authority over Yokawa were to go be given to Jinzen on the day of Ryōgen's death, indicating that Jinzen was to be appointed the head of Yokawa despite his young age of twenty-nine.[13] The Yokawa area was expected to become a religious area dedicated to the repose of Morosuke and the prosperity of his descendants.

Jinzen also received special consideration in appointments to the Office of Monastic Affairs (Sōgō) as the first son of a minister of state (*daijin*) to receive an appointment to the Sōgō.[14] He was given special treatment, obtaining his commissions at a young age and skipping many of the intermediate ranks on his way to archbishop (*sōjō*).[15] While he was still in his early thirties, Jinzen held such positions as abbot of Yokawa and Hosshōji, the temple dedicated to the repose of the Fujiwaras. At the same time, he accompanied Ryōgen when he performed rituals at the palace, an honor normally reserved for more-senior monks. Finally, he succeeded Ryōgen as *zasu* at the very young age of forty-two. The special treatment Jinzen received from Ryōgen and the preferred arrangements that Jinzen made for his relatives and disciples opened the way for increasing numbers of sons of nobles to become monks and bring their wealth with them to benefit both their families and the Tendai school.

Jinzen's Tenure as Zasu

Jinzen served as *zasu* for only four years. During that time, however, he strengthened his family's grip on the Tendai school, particularly on the Yokawa complex that his father had helped Ryōgen to build. For convenience, his accomplishments have been listed in chronological order in table 20.[16] The prominent places that Emperor Kazan and Emperor

TABLE 20

JINZEN'S TENURE AS *ZASU*

10/20/985	Jinzen has the Eshin'in, previously built by Kaneie and Ryōgen, designated an imperial temple (*goganji*) for Ichijō, soon to be emperor; three yearly ordinands (*nenbundosha*) are authorized for it. Jinzen asks for an order prohibiting fishing and hunting from north of Ōtsu and south of Koromogawa.[1]
10/985	The Shingondō (Mantra hall) at Yokawa, previously designated Emperor Kazan's imperial temple, is given twenty *chō* of land.
2/27/986	Jinzen is named *zasu*.
3/987	The Myōgōbō (Lodgings of wondrous actions; Henjō's former lodgings) at Gangyōji is designated an imperial temple for Emperor Ichijō; the Jitokuji is constructed there, and five masters of Esoteric Buddhism (*ajari*) authorized. Ryōgen's disciple Kakugyō plays a major role in establishing Jitokuji.
8/988	At Emperor Ichijō's request, Jinzen has the ceremony of the Buddha of Abundant Light (*shijōkōhō*) performed at the Sōjiin (Dhāraṇī hall). An offering of 84,000 clay *stūpas* is performed at Jitokuji to cure Emperor Ichijō's illness.
9/16/988	Jinzen serves as the preceptor at the ordination of retired emperor Kazan, who remains sequestered at Yokawa for a time, accompanied for much of his stay by Gonku, a disciple of Jinzen.[2]
10/29/988	Jinzen serves as the preceptor at the Mahāyāna ordination of retired emperor En'yū, who had received the Hīnayāna precepts at Tōdaiji earlier that year; Esoteric consecrations also performed.
1/989	At the request of the regent, Fujiwara no Kaneie, the ceremony of the Buddha of Abundant Light is performed in the palace.
2/989	Retired Emperor En'yū asks that a *sonshōhō* ceremony be performed for Emperor Ichijō.
6/989	A seven-day Medicine Buddha (*yakushi*) ceremony is performed at the Central Hall on Mount Hiei for the ailing Kaneie. Other ceremonies are performed about this time for retired emperor En'yū's empress, Fujiwara no Senshi,[3] who had fallen ill.
9/8/989	Jinzen resigns his position in the Office of Monastic Affairs and as *zasu*, even though the court asks him three times to remain. Jinzen ignores the court's requests, turns his emblems of authority over to the temple officials, and goes into retreat.[4]
1/26/990	Jinzen petitions the court to designate his quarters, the Myōkōin, as an imperial temple (*goganji*) for Emperor Ichijō. In his petition, Jinzen mentions the hardships he had endured living on Mount Hiei and how his health had deteriorated.[5]
2/14/990	A grant is given to Jinzen of income from one hundred households, which Jinzen in turn gives to the Myōkōin. The Myōkōin is designated

Continued on next page

TABLE 20 *(continued)*

	an imperial temple for Emperor Ichijō with two yearly ordinands. At the same time, Jinzen finalizes the arrangements for the future of Myōkōin.[6]
2/17/990	Jinzen dies.

1. *NS* 1:22:66–69; however, according to some sources the Eshin'in was designate a *kanji* in 985 (Shibuya, ed., *Tendai zasuki, p. 47*).

2. Several different dates are found in historical sources for this event; according to the *Tendai zasuki* (p. 47), he was ordained in 987. The *Nihon kiryaku* (*KT* 11:158) has a date of the tenth month of 988. I have followed the *Hyakurenshō, KT* (*fukyūban*), p. 5. Gonku (944–1008) would later be one of the first masters of Esoteric Buddhism at Jitokuji; he eventually served as its abbot. He was appointed to the Office of Monastic Affairs and served from 995 to 1008. He was later known as Kazan sōzu (bishop for [Emperor] Kazan).

3. Senshi (962–1002) was Fujiwara no Kaneie's daughter and the mother of Emperor Ichijō.

4. Shibuya, ed., *Tendai zasuki,* p. 47.

5. *Sanmon dōshaki, GR* 24:494a.

6. Ibid., 493–495, 498–499; *Nihon kiryaku, KT* 11:167–168. Jinzen's detailed will is found in *NS* 2.1:531–541.

Ichijō played in these movements are significant. Morosuke's son Kaneie rose to be regent when Kazan retired and Ichijō was named emperor. The personal services that Jinzen provided in serving as a teacher for Kazan and praying for Ichijō must have been viewed as a vital contribution to Kaneie's efforts.

Jinzen spent much of his four years as *zasu* building a temple complex at Myōkōin. By the time of his death, the central building was five bays square. In addition, two corridors each fifteen bays long, an eleven-bay by two-bay administrative building, a five-bay bath house, and an eleven-bay by two-bay living quarters had been built. He ensured the financial stability of Myōkōin by bequeathing to it ten of the eleven manors that his father had given him. The manors that Morosuke had given to Ryōgen were also bestowed on Myōkōin. These manors were not to be disposed of by the abbot of the monastic complex unless the appropriate members of Jinzen's lineage had first been consulted. Thus the manors did not completely belong to the Tendai school, but rather to one segment of it dominated by a particular family. In addition, Jinzen specified that the stipends to be given the various officials of Myōkōin.[17]

Three days before his death, Jinzen specified that Jinkō (971–1038) be appointed abbot (*kengyō*) of the complex even though he was only twenty-eight years old and had a mere fifteen years of seniority.[18] Jinkō was the grandson of Morosuke and the sixth son of Fujiwara no Tamemitsu (942–992), who would later be appointed chancellor. The monks who were to assist him were all older, and most had more seniority. The appointment of Jinkō clearly illustrates the intention of Jinzen to keep the Myōkōin complex under the control of Morosuke's lineage.

Although Jinkō was appointed the first abbot, ultimate control of Myōkōin was to go to Jin'en (977–1031) as soon as he was of age; after Jin'en's death, Myōkōin was to be administered by his descendants. Jinzen's favoring of Jin'en was probably based on the roles that Jin'en's grandfather and father, Fujiwara no Koremasa and Yoshichika, had played in seizing power from Morosuke's brother and nephew, Saneyori and Yoritada.[19] Koremasa had faithfully carried out Morosuke's intentions in making sure that Jinzen received the manors allocated to him. He had later given Jinzen additional property. Later, when Emperor Kazan had become a monk after reigning for only two years, Yoshichika had followed him into religious life; Jinzen served as their teacher. As a consolation prize, his son Jinkō and his descendants were to receive Myōkōin and continue to pray for the success of the descendants of Morosuke and Kaneie. Thus, Jinzen was rewarding those who had made the largest contributions to Yokawa and the success of his lineage.

In addition, Jinzen named seven men, most of whom were very young, as meditation masters (*zenji*). The oldest, Jakuen, was thirty-five, with fifteen years of seniority. Nyogen was only seventeen, with two years seniority; Dōmyō was seventeen, with three years seniority.[20] Like Jinkō, all of these young men appointed belonged to the Fujiwara clan, particularly to Morosuke's lineage. Jin'en was the fifth son of Fujiwara no Yoshichika and was thus Morosuke's great-grandson through Koremasa's lineage. Nyogen was Morosuke's grandson and Kinsue's (956–1029) fourth son. Dōmyō was the great-grandson of Kaneie and the fourth son of the major counselor Fujiwara no Michitsuna (955–1020).

A directive from Jinzen's time includes the amounts of rice devoted to supporting the positions at the Myōkōin, indicating the scale of the institution (table 21). Additional amounts for oil lamps, offerings, and cloth to supply personnel were specified. Supplies from manors were to be used for the upkeep of the Myōkōin. The positions at the Myōkōin are listed in hierarchical order with stipends corresponding to ranks with the exception of the meditation masters. Because of their noble

TABLE 21

SUPPORT FOR THE MYŌKŌIN

Position	Numbers holding the position	Masu *of rice* per day
Abbot (*kengyō bettō*)	1	7
Assistant abbot (*kōtō*)	1	5
Master of the hall (*chiin*)	1	4
Administrator (*azukari*)	2	3
Meditation master (*zenji*)	7	5
Lecturer (*jōgō*)	3	2
Ordained servant (*shōji*)	6	1.5
Servant (*shimobe*)	6	1[1]

1. *Sanmon dōshaki, GR* 24: 498b.

birth, these men received an amount surpassed only by the abbot. These provisions reinforce the impression that Myōkōin was intended as a sinecure for the sons of Morosuke's lineage.

Besides the property associated with Morosuke and Ryōgen, Myōkōin continued to receive donations from other Fujiwaras including temples given to it as affiliated temples (*betsuin*). Later registers of Myōkōin's holdings show significant changes from Jinzen's register. The manner in which Myōkōin maintained control over these lands (or whether it maintained control) deserves further study.[21]

Other monks connected with the Fujiwara clan found shelter at Myōgōbō, in Gangyōji. When Emperor Kazan suddenly decided to renounce the throne and be ordained, Fujiwara Yoshichika (951–1008), Koremasa's son and Kazan's half-brother, lost his political power and went to Myōgōbō to be ordained. Yoshichika was called the Iimuro *nyūdō* (the high official from Iimuro who has entered the way), and his son, Narifusa, the Iimuro *chūshō* (middle captain of Iimuro).[22] Emperor Kazan, ordained by Jinzen, was a great-grandson of Morosuke and son of Emperor Reizei; his mother was Fujiwara no Koremasa's daughter Kaishi. Thus both of his parents were descended from Morosuke. In fact, many of the people associated with Myōkōin were associated with Morosuke's lineage, with more than a few being the fourth, fifth, or sixth son of their particular family. Thus becoming a monk was a career path for some of the men who might not be the family's prime representative at court. As representatives of victorious segments of their lineage, they prayed for the continued good fortune of their close relatives. Others, such as Fujiwara no Yoshichika and his sons, who had been vanquished in political intrigues, might perform rituals to ensure the success of their victorious cousins.

When Jinzen died at the young age of forty-seven, he left most of his disciples without sufficient training. They went to a number of Tendai monks, most of them with noble pedigrees, to study: Jinkō to Kakugyō (also read Kakukei, 927–1014), Jin'en to Kakuun, Nyogen to Myōku,[23] and Dōmyō to Myōgō (955–1003).[24] What did these Tendai monks gain by agreeing to serve as teachers for these young noblemen? In many cases, their careers received a significant boost. Kakugyō had been appointed to the Office of Monastic Affairs in 987, at the late age of sixty-five. However, several years later, when he became Jinkō's teacher, his opportunities to meet with nobility increased. He performed various ceremonies for Fujiwara no Michinaga, and in 1008, along with his student Jinkō, was appointed guardian monk for the future emperor Go-Ichijō (1008–1036; r. 1016–1036). Two of Kakugyō's quarters, the Shōrengein and Daijōin, were designated imperial temples. Kakugyō's career subsequently advanced rapidly as he was appointed *zasu* of the Tendai school in 998 and rose to grand archbishop in the Office of Monastic Affairs by 1001. He died in 1014. Thus although he advanced to high position late in life, his affiliation with the Fujiwara clan made the last twenty years of his life illustrious. Nyogen's teacher Myōku (946–1020) was the grandson of Emperor Daigo and son of Prince Ariaki. He was a disciple of Enshō and Ryōgen; Jinzen petitioned the court so that Myōku could be named master of Esoteric Buddhism in 988. In 1004, he resigned a post in the Office of Monastic Affairs in favor of his student Nyogen. He subsequently performed a variety of services for Michinaga; as a reward, Michinaga had him reinstated to the Office of Monastic Affairs as a supernumerary greater bishop. In 1013, he was appointed supernumerary archbishop as a reward for his successful performance of Esoteric services to cure Emperor Sanjō. When Kakugyō died, Michinaga tried to have Myōku named Tendai *zasu,* but the court objected because Kyōen (944–1019) was older. Myōku finally was named *zasu* in 1019, but he died a year later.

The young men from the Fujiwara clan appointed to leadership roles in the Myōkōin went on to have successful careers and extend their clan's influence to other sections of Mount Hiei. For example, in 1004 when Nyogen was only thirty-one years old, his teacher Myōku resigned from the Office of Monastic Affairs so that Nyogen could be appointed supernumerary master of discipline. In 1011, he was appointed super-numerary lesser bishop, and in 1018, lesser bishop. When Myōku was appointed *zasu*, he gave Nyogen the position of abbot of the Hōdōin, the central institution in the Western Pagoda area of Mount Hiei. At the time, Nyogen was forty-six; he died that same year.[25]

Dōmyō's career was similar. He studied with Myōgō, who was even-tually appointed archbishop (*sōjō hōin*). Myōgō used his influence to have Dōmyō appointed abbot of the Sōjiin, the chief Esoteric center in the Eastern Pagoda area. Dōmyō was later appointed a master of Eso-teric Buddhism at the Sōjiin and played an important role in extend-ing Fujiwara influence into the Tōdō area. In 1015, he was also ap-pointed administrator of the Tennōji in modern Ōsaka.[26]

The careers of several other young monks from the Fujiwara clan and their Tendai teachers could be described with much the same pattern. As the sons of the Fujiwara clan entered the Tendai school, they brought wealth and influence to the school. Because they began their adminis-trative careers at a younger age than other monks, they had ample op-portunities to extend Fujiwara influence to various halls on Mount Hiei as well as temples in the Kyoto area. When the diaries of nobles are con-sulted, these same men often appear as guardian monks, masters of Es-oteric Buddhism performing rituals to ensure the health and prosper-ity of those in their clan, and as officiants at funerals and memorial services for their relatives among the nobility. Although the sources do not often record the monetary rewards they received for these activi-ties, they must have been substantial and contributed substantially to the changes in the Tendai school initiated by Ryōgen.

Tendai Expansion Beyond Mount Hiei

The Expansion of Tendai Power to the Provinces

In the proposals submitted shortly before his death, Saichō had asked that Tendai monks be appointed as lecturers and readers after they had served twelve years on Mount Hiei. Lecturers and readers served in the provincial temples, where they were responsible for overseeing the con-duct of monks in the province. By asking that his monks receive such appointments, Saichō was laying the foundation for Tendai expansion into the provinces. However, the system of lecturers and readers had a major weakness as a base for Tendai expansion; because the terms were limited to six years, the *kokubunji* could not serve as a permanent base for Tendai power. In addition, the lecturers were to be at least forty-five years old.[27]

The institution of the *betsuin* served as a more permanent base for Tendai expansion. Many aspects of this institution remain unclear, but *betsuin* may have been religious institutions established on monastic land holdings. The term *in*, translated as "chapel" or "temple," originally indicated an area within a monastery enclosed by a wall or fence. Thus, many of the major Nara monasteries had a number of *betsuin* within their boundaries, often with separate provisions for funding.

The term *betsuin*, here translated as "affiliated temples," seems to have referred to their location in a place other than the main temple. Although the term is mentioned in documents relating to Saichō, most of these usages have been questioned. The first clear mentions of *betsuin* must be dated one or two decades after his death. The earliest Tendai *betsuin* is the Tado jingūji in Ise, mentioned in a document dated 839. During the ninth and tenth centuries, *betsuin* had their status approved by the government. In most cases, the *betsuin* was given to the home temple and the relationship recognized by the court. At times, the relationship between temples could be so complex that some *betsuin* had their own *betsuin*. Although the exact social and economic relationship between the home temple and the *betsuin* is not clear, the home temple had the right to appoint monastic officials to the *betsuin*.[28] For example, numerous *betsuin* belonged to Jinzen's Myōkōin, giving Jinzen and his successors the right to appoint monastic officials to those sites. The term "*betsuin*" appears most frequently in regard to temples of the Tendai and Shingon schools; however, more *betsuin* were given to the Tendai school than to the Shingon school, indicating the emphasis Tendai placed on moving into the provinces. During the eleventh century, the term "branch temple" (*matsuji*) became more common and was used in the same way as "*betsuin*" for a time.[29]

Provincial Temples

Saichō had intended to use the *kokubunji* as bases for Tendai expansion into the provinces with appointments of Tendai monks as lecturers and readers at the temples.[30] The monks appointed to these positions not only supervised the monks in their province and performed rituals in support of the nation, but were also responsible for the supervision of construction projects that benefited the people. Some training in construction techniques might well have been given at Mount Hiei and might have aided Ryōgen in the rebuilding of Mount Hiei. Determining the extent to which Saichō's plans were put into effect is difficult because of the paucity of remaining sources. Moreover, the *kokubunji* system had begun a slow decline several decades after Saichō's death.[31] One striking example of the success of Saichō's strategy, however, is found in the biography of Anne, one of Ennin's foremost disciples. Anne was sent to Dewa as a lecturer. During his tenure, he converted many of the people there to Tendai. Previously the area had been a stronghold of the Hossō school because of the Hossō monk Tokuitsu. Because Tokuitsu had been a very able advocate of Hossō and had later opposed Saichō in a famous series of written exchanges, Anne's success was very much appreciated in Tendai circles and probably was a major reason for his eventual appointment as *zasu*.[32]

One incident from Ryōgen's biography suggests that the Tendai school, in fact, influenced at least some of the remaining *kokubunji*. In 984, Ryōgen was completing the rebuilding of the Stūpa Hall in the Western Pagoda area of Mount Hiei; however, he did not have enough gold to finish the base of the tower (*roban*) that topped the hall and the bells (*hōtaku*) that hung under the corners of the eaves. Because Mount Hiei did not have the resources to supply the needed gold, Ryōgen could only pray that somehow it would be supplied. Later Ryōgen received a letter from the governor of Mutsu, Fujiwara no Tamenaga,[33] along with the needed gold. According to the letter, some thieves had broken into the provincial temple and stolen a copy of the *Ta pan-jo ching* (*Mahā-prajñāpāramitā-sūtra*) that had been written in gold (*kindei*). The text was very large, 600 fascicles, and often used for magical purposes. While the thieves were in the act of burning the *sūtra* to obtain the gold, the abbot (*jishu*) of the temple discovered and seized them. Although the *sūtra* was destroyed, the gold was recovered. Because the abbot wished to use the gold for a Buddhist project of some sort, he sent it to Mount Hiei. The gold was the exact amount needed to complete the required implements for the Stūpa Hall.[34] The story can be interpreted several ways. It suggests that Tendai monks controlled or influenced the *kokubunji* in Mutsu and used its resources for Tendai purposes. However, the gold might have been sent to Ryōgen at Tamenaga's suggestion because of the strong relationship between his father, Koremasa, and Ryōgen. Unfortunately, not enough is known about the expansion of the Tendai school in such provinces to determine whether this pattern occurred frequently or not.

Taking Over Other Institutions

The rivalry between Kōfukuji, the Fujiwara clan temple, and Mount Hiei lies behind much of the rivalry between Hossō and Tendai; it is particularly evident in the Ōwa debates. However, as the Fujiwara clan developed, certain branches of it needed their own religious centers. Thus, Ryōgen's ties with one branch of the Fujiwaras were solidified through the vows of Morosuke to support Yokawa and the ordination of Morosuke's son Jinzen. Ryōgen also strove to extend Tendai influence by creating ties to other Fujiwara religious institutions. For example, Tōnomine was the cite of the Fujiwara mausoleum. When Takamitsu and Zōga went there, they strengthened the Tendai ties with the complex that had been established by Jisshō.[35]

The rivalry between Kōfukuji and Mount Hiei was exemplified by their struggle over the Gion Shrine in Kyoto, an institution traditionally affiliated with Kōfukuji, the Fujiwara clan monastery. According to the *Konjaku monogatari*, Rengeji, a branch temple of the Tendai complex on Mount Hiei, was to the east of Gion; a tree with splendid fall leaves grew on the premises of Rengeji.[36] Rōzan, the respected Hossō abbot of the Gion, sent a man to cut a branch of the tree. However, the Tendai abbot of Rengeji was angry that Rōzan would do so without even acknowledging him and expelled the man. Rōzan then ordered the man to return with others and cut down the tree and bring it back. However, the abbot of Rengeji knew that Rōzan would try to take the tree, so Rengeji cut it down himself. Rōzan became even angrier when he was told of this.

At that time Ryōgen was visiting Hosshōji, a nearby Tendai temple, to perform rituals for the regent. The abbot of Rengeji went to tell Ryōgen of the events. Ryōgen was angered by the story and sent a messenger to summon Rōzan, but Rōzan refused to come, claiming that the Tendai *zasu* had no authority to summon a monk who had been appointed by Kōfukuji. Ryōgen was angered by Rōzan's refusal and sent men to have the shrine officials at Gion write documents making it a branch temple of Enryakuji. Ryōgen then argued that because Gion was a branch temple of Enryakuji, Rōzan should be expelled. Rōzan responded by immediately calling on warriors Taira Kimimasa (n.d.), Taira Muneyori (d. 1011), and others to defend him. Ryōgen responded with armed force of his own, a monk skilled in martial arts named Eika and another monk named Nyūzen, who was Muneyori's brother. When the two sides faced each other, Muneyori's forces saw Nyūzen and left. The Tendai forces subsequently expelled Rōzan.

Kōfukuji then appealed to the court for a decision against the Tendai school's seizure of Gion. In the meantime, Ryōgen died. As part of its strategy, Kōfukuji asked Chūzan, one of their most skilled debaters, to argue for them. However, the night before the case was to be held, Chūzan sent all of his disciples away. From the outside, they heard Chūzan talking to someone, but they were sure that he was alone. Afterward, Chūzan told them that he had been speaking with Ryōgen's spirit. The next day he suddenly developed a cold and could not appear in the court. As a result, Gion became a branch temple of Enryakuji.

Among the elements that call the historicity of the story in question, other than the supernatural elements, is the absence of any corroborating contemporary historical records. However, Gion did pass from the control of Kōfukuji to Enryakuji in 974, perhaps suggesting that an element of truth might be found in the outcome of the story. However, because Chūzan died before Ryōgen, he could not have played a role. Rather, his role in the story may well be due to his victory over Ryōgen in the Ōwa debates: his defeat by Ryōgen in this story redresses the balance between the two monks. In addition, Ryōgen's posthumous appearance is typical of beliefs about his supernatural power that were circulating during the century after his death. The argument in the story is not so much over an aesthetic issue such as a branch of fall foliage as over the boundaries of the two temples. It was settled through the threat of force, a detail that is reminiscent of Ryōgen's implied threat to use force against the Tendai monks of the Jimon lineage, discussed in the next chapter.

The story reveals an important aspect about the general status of temple and shrine lands. The ownership of these lands was often in dispute. The temple or shrine ideally had documents that proved that the government had recognized that the manor (*kanshōfushō*) belonged to the temple or shrine. In fact, only two of the manors given to the Tendai school by Morosuke during Ryōgen's lifetime belonged to this class: Okaya and Tomoyui. In the case of Tomoyui, surviving documents reveal that Ryōgen had Morosuke intercede to have its status certified.[37] In many other cases, arrangements for the manor were made privately, and the title could be called into question when one of the principals in an agreement died or suffered a reverse in his fortunes at court. In addition, new lands opened by the tenants of tax-exempt lands were not necessarily exempt from taxes. Finally, supporting documentation might be forged, much as it seems to have been in the *Konjaku mono-*

gatari story. For example, a number of temples, including Onjōji, possessed documents of questionable authenticity defining the limits of the temple in such a way that they included areas important for farming or trade.[38]

The people who administered the land and those who lived on it were not above playing temples against each other to gain financial advantages. Thus, the story of the shrine attendants writing a document that enabled Enryakuji to gain control of Gion was probably not unusual; they may well have had reasons to prefer Tendai control over that of Kōfukuji, especially because they seem to have been in conflict with the monks of Kiyomizudera, a temple affiliated with Kōfukuji.[39]

The role of the shrine attendants (*jinin* or *jinnin*) is important in another way. These were lower-level shrine employees who performed a variety of duties for the shrine including disposing of the dead, cleaning the premises, and overseeing the shrine's lands and collecting rents; however, as time passed, they also engaged in various occupations including making weapons and engaging in trade. An area might be controlled either by laying claim to the land on which people lived or by organizing the people who lived on the land so that they functioned in a manner to the temple's advantage. Onjōji sometimes seems to have preferred land claims while Enryakuji preferred to focus on organizing the inhabitants.[40]

Finally, one other aspect of the transfer of the site deserves mention. Gion was famous as a site for rituals to calm angry ghosts (*goryō-e*) and to alleviate the plagues that sometimes struck Kyoto. Frequently, the *goryō-e* might focus on the losers in political battles and maneuvering, serving as a way to placate both the deceased who had lost power and their supporters who might still be alive. Both the winning Fujiwara factions and their Tendai supporters might well have wanted to control the site and employ the rituals in ways that placated people and supported their rule.[41]

Tax Exemptions

Besides extending Tendai control to additional holdings, Ryōgen worked to strengthen Tendai rights in areas under its control. An example of this can be seen in an incident concerning the Hie Shrine for the deities protecting Mount Hiei (located in Shiga-gun in Ōmi). According to Bonshō in the *Shūiden*, the area around the shrine had always been exempted from taxes; however, the area probably would not have been exempted from taxes even when Saichō had just founded the Tendai establishment.[42] In 975, the governor of Ōmi, Tachibana no Tsunehira, sent the lieutenant of the left palace guards, Taira no Muneaki, to collect taxes from the people of the Mitsuhama and Ōtsu areas. Ryōgen protested and submitted a petition to the court. As a result, Muneaki was removed from his post, and the court reaffirmed the special status of these areas. The special status was important for Enryakuji. These areas played an important role in the commerce of Japan; moreover, the area served as the gateway to Mount Hiei and as a town where Tendai monks could escape the cold and isolation associated with Mount Hiei.

Additional information about this incident is found in other documents. According to the *San'inki*, from the tenth day of the eighth month of 979, a seventy-day service for Nyoirin (Wish-fulfilling) Kannon was held at the Dannain in the Eastern Pagoda area of Mount Hiei to pray for the birth of a crown prince for Emperor En'yū.[43] A boy, Yasuhito (the future Emperor Ichijō), was born the next year in the sixth month. Four weeks later the court rewarded Mount Hiei by ordering that the people in the area from Mitsuhama to the village of Nōka would be exempted from taxes paid to the state. This area included East Sakamoto, the gateway to Mount Hiei, as well as Mitsuhama and Nōka, and thus probably included the shrine to the deity Hie and the surrounding land.[44]

Other Shrines and Temples

As scholars such as Kuroda Toshio and Allan Grapard have noted, the tradition called "Shintō" today was not a separate entity during the Heian period; shrines dedicated to the *kami* were frequently integrated with temples in complex arrangements. Mentions of *kami* in Ryōgen's biographies support this view. In fact, Ryōgen's biographies contain relatively few entries concerning the *kami;* however, several entries concerning Ryōgen's efforts to spread his lineage's influence do include passages concerning shrines and *kami*. The context in which they occur supports the contention that Buddhism and "Shintō" existed in a virtually seamless network.

In 977, at the age of sixty-five, Ryōgen went to the island of Chikubu at the north end of Lake Biwa, near his birthplace in Azai county in the province of Ōmi. The shrine there had long had unofficial relations with the Tendai school, various monks from Mount Hiei had traveled there to practice. In addition, various officials, including retired emperor Uda, had traveled to the island and made contributions to the shrine. Traditions associating the island with Kannon and Benzaiten also began around this time.[45] Ryōgen journeyed there partly to perform services to repay the deity of his birthplace for the favors he had received while young, but also to strengthen his lineage's ties with the shrine. While he was at the shrine he commissioned one hundred copies of the *Lotus Sūtra* and performed various ceremonies. Afterward, the monks who had participated boarded a boat with the head of a dragon and went around the island scattering flowers as offerings, chanting, and listening to music. Perhaps as a result of these ceremonies, Ryōgen was named administrator of the Chikubu Shrine, thus bringing it under the control of his faction.[46]

The refurbishing of monasteries that had fallen into disrepair also gave Ryōgen an opportunity to extend his influence. Sūfukuji, in Shigasato, Ōtsu, was founded at the request of Emperor Tenji (r. 668–671). By the early Heian period it was included in lists of the ten major temples. The temple had suffered from a disastrous fire in 921. Ryōgen had performed elaborate rituals there for his mother's sixtieth birthday in 945, indicating that he had close connections with the temple. It would burn again in 965 and be reconstructed. About 981, Ryōgen received an order from the court ordering the temple repaired; he had his disciple Anshin refurbish the temple and then "privately" (*shi*) appointed him abbot.[47] Because both the Chikubu Shrine and Sūfukuji were close to Mount Hiei, geographic proximity would seem to have played a major role in extending Tendai influence. By the late Heian period Sūfukuji had declined and was rarely mentioned.

Financial Aspects of Ryōgen's Attitudes toward Women

For the most part, the role of women as supporters of Tendai remains obscure. In fact, the prohibition forbidding women from entering the confines of Mount Hiei would seem to suggest that they could not have played an important role in the life of the Tendai school. Rules concerning property rights probably made it difficult for women to directly support Tendai. When property was given with the expectation that it would pay for rites so that a clan could prosper, that clan was defined in patrilineal terms.[48] All of these factors indicate that women played only a peripheral role in the rise of the Tendai school.

However, women may well have supported Tendai monks; Ryōgen

had performed Esoteric rituals to help Morosuke's daughter Anshi as well as Morosuke's wives during childbirth. Women must have indirectly supported Tendai institutions by encouraging their fathers, husbands, and sons to commission rituals from Tendai monks. This section has been placed in this chapter to acknowledge their role, often unrecorded in Tendai fortunes. Additional information is included in the chapter on nuns. Several women supported Tendai monks in their travels to China. Genshin's mother and sisters were known for their outstanding scholarship. Thus although women are rarely mentioned directly as contributing to Tendai fortunes, their contributions should be mentioned. In this section, two ways of exploring their contribution are explored. The first is Ryōgen's use of the ritual for the Buddha's relics to attract women. The second, Ryōgen's filial piety toward his mother, is less directly concerned with women's support of Mount Hiei, but it does indicate that Tendai and other schools sometimes supported laywomen, particularly the mothers of monks. Such support must have made the Tendai school seem more open to women.

Women and the Ritual of the Buddha's Relics

Ryōgen's use of the ritual for the Buddha's relics to appeal to women may be considered an acknowledgment of the role of women in the rise of the Tendai school. Rites in honor of the Buddha's relic (*shari-e*) in Japan date back to shortly after the introduction of Buddhism.[49] Offerings to the Buddha's relic were said to be equivalent to offerings made to the Buddha while he was alive; the merit from such offerings could eliminate bad karma and ensure a person's rebirth as a human being or god.[50] The Chinese *vinaya*-master Chien-chen brought relics with him from China and installed them at the Tōshōdaiji in Nara. The Tōshōdaiji celebration was held annually on the fifth and sixth days of the fifth month in memory of Chien-chen, with music and dance an integral part of the ceremonies.[51] Because Chien-chen brought the T'ien-t'ai texts that Saichō first read to Japan, his introduction of relics to Japan might well have interested later Tendai monks.

The Tendai celebration for the Buddha's relic had been started by Ennin after he had seen a similar ceremony in China and decided to bring back several relics.[52] A *shari-e* was first performed by Tendai monks in Japan on the fourth day of the fourth month in 860, when Ennin installed a relic that he had brought from China in a pagoda in the Sōjiin on Mount Hiei. The ceremony was repeated annually. Although no day was set for it, the performance usually was held in late spring or early summer according to Ennin's biography; however, according to the *Sanbō ekotoba*, it was held when the cherry blossoms bloomed. Hundreds of laymen as well as monks usually attended the event.[53] Because the merit from the *shari-e* was also used to protect the nation, it was a major Tendai ritual. In 866, rules were issued requiring all monks on Mount Hiei to attend it.[54] The ritual received major support when the retired and ordained emperor Uda climbed Mount Hiei to witness it and gave seven *chō* of land to support the ritual.[55]

In 977, Ryōgen made a major change in the ceremony by moving it from Mount Hiei to the capital. According to entries in both the *Eiga monogatari* and *Konjaku monogatarishū*, Ryōgen wished to perform the celebration at a place where his beloved mother could see it.[56] Because women were prohibited on Mount Hiei, she never had. However, this explanation for Ryōgen's decision cannot be accepted because Ryōgen's mother had died more than a decade earlier, in 966. Even so, the association by later sources of Ryōgen's filial piety toward his mother with the performance of the *shari-e* in Kyoto is significant because it suggests that Ryōgen's loving treatment of his mother made a major impression on people.

The *Shūiden* presents a more trustworthy account of Ryōgen and the *shari-e*. According to it, Ryōgen wished to allow women and other people who could not climb Mount Hiei to witness the ceremony and thereby to gain the merit that would naturally arise from their appreciation of the celebration (*zuiki*).[57] Ryōgen might have been responding to the interest that women displayed in *shari-e* held at Tōshōdaiji and Kazanji (Gangyōji). Although little is known of the Gangyōji *shari-e*, Ryōgen probably witnessed it in person while he held monastic offices at the temple earlier in his life.[58]

In 977, Ryōgen held the ceremony for the Buddha's relic twice. The first time was on Mount Hiei on the twenty-first day of the third month.[59] Exactly one month later, the ceremony was held on the eastern outskirts of Kyoto in Yoshidadera in Kaguraoka. For the ceremony on Hiei, two seven-jeweled pagodas and the palanquins for them were constructed. The robes for the eight groups (*hachibushu*) and the implements for performing the ceremony were remade.[60] The entire procession included 350 monks. In appreciation of these efforts, the court awarded a number of ordinands to the Tendai school.

After successfully performing the ceremony on Mount Hiei, Ryōgen next made preparations for holding the ceremony in the capital. Yoshi-

dadera was to the east of the modern campus of Kyoto University.[61] Ryōgen had several buildings constructed as the location of the ceremony
including a multistoried lecture hall. In preparation for the ceremony,
the three deities of Hiei were honored in front of the Hie Sannō Shrine,
and practice sessions for the ceremony were held. Emperor En'yū asked
that the relics be brought to the palace so that he could pay reverence
to them.[62] In later years, the ceremony for the Buddha's relic was a major event in the capital, with specific mentions of how it was held so
women could participate. Detailed descriptions of it are found in both
Eiga monogatari and *Konjaku monogatarishū*.[63] During the Kamakura period, women connected with Risshū (Vinaya school) were especially en-
thusiastic in their worship of other sets of relics.[64]

The ceremony for the Buddha's relic was not the only Tendai ritual
that appealed to women. On the fifth day of the Great Lotus Assembly
(Hokke dai-e), a set of lectures on the *Lotus Sūtra* held on Mount Hiei,
monks carrying firewood held a procession in the capital. The lectures
on that day concerned the Devadatta chapter of the *Lotus Sūtra*, a chapter that particularly appealed to women because it contained the story
of how the young Nāga girl realized Buddhahood. The practice of carrying firewood was based on a passage in the Devadatta chapter of the
Lotus Sūtra in which Śākyamuni tells how he had served Devadatta in a
past life to obtain the *Lotus Sūtra*. As a part of his service, Śākyamuni
had "drawn water and gathered firewood," practices that Japanese lay
believers emulated in the procession. This procession probably was held
during Ryōgen's lifetime.[65]

Ryōgen and His Mother

Ever since Buddhism was founded, it has been criticized for taking sons
away from their parents. In India, such criticisms were partially refuted
by formulating a rule that required prospective monks or nuns to have
the consent of their parents or spouses before they could be ordained.
In East Asia, similar charges were leveled against Buddhist monks. In
China, where filial piety was said to be the basis of morality, more elaborate ways of harmonizing Buddhism with filial piety were devised.[66]

In Japan, the question of a monk's responsibilities to his parents, particularly his mother, was an important issue. Saichō's rule that monks
spend twelve years on Mount Hiei without leaving made it difficult if
not impossible for monks to help support their aged parents. In his register of Tendai yearly ordinands, Saichō noted that two of the twenty-

four Tendai yearly ordinands he had received from the court had left Mount Hiei and presumably returned to lay life to support their mothers, indicating that the support of aged parents, especially mothers, was a serious concern for monks.[67] The departure of the monks suggests that Saichō had not formulated any special way of dealing with the problem.

The story of the Sanron monks Eikō and Gonzō (also read Gonsō or Kinsō 753–827) and Eikō's mother illustrates that some monks supported mothers while retaining their status as monks. Eikō supported his mother by having a servant bring a portion of what he begged. When Eikō died suddenly, his friend Gonzō hid Eikō's death from the mother by having the servant bring food. However, one night Gonzō and the servant drank alcohol and the servant blurted out that Eikō was dead. The mother died soon afterward. Gonzō began an annual series of eight lectures on the *Lotus Sūtra* to commemorate her death.[68]

A century later, Tendai monks were still troubled by the situation, as is illustrated by the biography of Son'i, who served as *zasu* of the Tendai school from 926 to 940. His conception is said to have occurred after his mother meditated on Kannon in a manner reminiscent of Ryōgen's own conception almost forty-five years later. As a young boy, Son'i underwent a period of seclusion in a temple from the age of ten to thirteen, an impressive accomplishment for so young a boy. When he climbed Mount Hiei at the age of thirteen, he probably was expected to undergo the twelve years of seclusion specified in Saichō's rules. However, after he received the tonsure at sixteen and was appointed a yearly ordinand, he took leave of his teacher and went to Kyoto and Nara to serve his mother.[69] Later, Son'i returned to Mount Hiei, completed the twelve-year confinement, and became one of the most eminent Tendai monks of his day. When Ryōgen was ordained as a Tendai monk, Son'i presided over the ceremony. Thus Ryōgen had probably heard of Son'i's difficulty in simultaneously serving his mother and performing his religious austerities.

Whereas Tendai monks such as Son'i seem to have interrupted their monastic careers to help their mothers, other monks were forced to give up their status as monks entirely. In 800, Kōshō of Daianji was granted permission to return to lay status because he could not bear the religious practice and he wished to support his old mother.[70] Temporary and permanent interruptions of religious practice to support an aged mother were probably not unusual.[71]

Ryōgen's treatment of his mother and his concern about the moth-

ers of some of his disciples suggest a change in the Tendai school's indifference to the problem of a monk's relationship with his parents.
Ryōgen was devoted to his mother, perhaps because his father had died
when he was very young. When he was a young monk in his early twenties, Ryōgen decided not to retreat to the mountains because his
mother needed his support. In a set of vows that he wrote when he was
thirty-seven, he described his decision:

> Twelve or thirteen years ago, when I had just begun my quest for en-
> lightenment, I had no wish for fame and fortune and only desired to re-
> tire to a deep valley to the south of the southern mountain [Mudōji]. But
> my old mother was still alive and without even coarse foods. And so I went
> to live near her.[72]

Ryōgen soon returned to being an active participant in Tendai affairs, but did not forget his mother. During the last twenty-three years
of his mother's life, beginning with her sixtieth birthday, Ryōgen conducted a number of major religious services in her honor. In the East
Asian tradition, the sixtieth birthday is considered to be especially important because one sixty-year calendrical cycle has been completed during a person's life. Ryōgen celebrated his mother's sixtieth birthday at
Sūfukuji in 945, where he performed religious ceremonies for three days
and copied six Mahāyāna *sūtras*.[73] The observances concluded with a
debate format that included lectures by six monks and questions by six
monks. The merits from these rituals were presumably dedicated, at least
in part, to his mother's well-being. Ryōgen's former debate adversary
at the Kōfukuji Yuima-e debates, Gishō, participated.[74] Gishō's appearance demonstrates that Hossō and Tendai monks did maintain cordial
ties at times even though they often competed. The mobilization of so
many monks and the use of a temple with imperial ties for a private ritual is an impressive indication of both Ryōgen's growing power and his
devotion to his mother.

In 955, when Ryōgen's mother was seventy, he had a house built for
her in Nōka, near the bank of Lake Biwa and to the northeast of Mount
Hiei.[75] From there, his mother could look up at the mountain on which
her son was practicing. A few impoverished mothers of monks had lived
near temples since the Nara period. However, the practice had become
more popular during the middle Heian period.[76] Because women were
prohibited on Mount Hiei, Ryōgen could not ask his mother to live on
the mountain, but he could have a house built in a village near the
mountain.

In 965, Ryōgen continued his tradition of celebrating his mother's birthday every ten years with elaborate religious services. For her eightieth birthday, *sūtras* were copied and lectures held with eighty monks invited. In addition, a number of buildings were constructed, as well as special boats with the head of a dragon or a seabird (*ryūtō gekishu*), ensuring that the boat would travel like the dragon and use the winds as well as the bird.[77]

After his mother's death in 966, Ryōgen may have been too busy to conduct memorial services in a suitable way because the disastrous fire on Mount Hiei occurred just one month after her death. However, in 979, thirteen years after her death, to fulfill his mother's wish at her death, he performed the time-consuming and expensive one-hundredday *goma* service at the Daikichisanji in Azai-gun, his birthplace.[78] On the concluding day of the *goma* ceremony, he made offerings to the accompaniment of music. When he visited her grave, he surprised the populace with the depth of his filial piety.

Ryōgen did not stop with honoring his own mother; he was also concerned with the welfare of his disciples' aged mothers. In his will of 972, Ryōgen mentioned several buildings in Nōka, the same village where he had built a house for his mother. The buildings were to be used by the mothers of two of Ryōgen's disciples, Genzen and Myōgō. Ryōgen wrote of his concern over the fate of these old women, who had no means of support, and encouraged his disciples to care for them. By providing support for these women, he hoped that his disciples would be able to practice and study without worrying about their mothers.[79] Ryōgen lived for another twelve years after writing his will and probably was able to provide for the welfare of a number of the aged mothers of his disciples.

Ryōgen's elaborate services in honor of his mother were much more significant than one individual monk's filial attitude toward his mother. They were symbolic of the Tendai school's growing interest in responding to the religious needs of women. When the compilers of the *Eiga monogatari* and *Konjaku monogatari* incorrectly stated that Ryōgen had moved the *shari-e* from Mount Hiei to the outskirts of Kyoto so that his mother could see it, they probably were influenced by stories of the elaborate way in which Ryōgen had served his mother.

Ryōgen's attitude toward his mother is similar to those of other monks during the middle and late Heian period. For example, Japanese monks who were about to travel to China to study were aware that they might not ever see their aged mothers again and held elaborate lecture series in honor of their mothers. For example, Chōnen (938–1016), a Sanron monk from Tōdaiji, hesitated to go to China because he worried about his mother, but she encouraged him to go. Before he left, he drew pictures of Mañjuśrī and Maitreya for her and copied scriptures. In case she died before he returned, he held a five-day lecture series in her honor, focusing on the *Lotus Sūtra* and the *Jen-wang ching*. The ceremony was to serve as her memorial service if she died before he could return, a practice called *gyakushu*. While he was in China, he made a copy of an image of Śākyamuni. The original image was believed to have been done to comfort King Udayana while Śākyamuni was in heaven preaching to his mother. The story of Śākyamuni's filial piety might have been a deep comfort to Chōnen while he was in China.

Mothers also missed their monastic sons while they were in China. A diary that includes poems by the mother of the Tendai monk Jōjin (1011–1081), who had traveled to China, is famous for its exposition of a mother's love for her son the monk. In addition, mothers increasingly appear in monastic biographies around this period and are credited with the achievements of their sons.[80]

Mothers were mentioned in Japanese monastic biographies from late in the Nara period; however, they began to play a particularly important role in biographies from the middle of the Heian period onward. The reasons for the sudden importance of the mothers of monks are still not completely understood, but several possible causes have been suggested. The role of women in society, particularly among the nobility, seems to have begun to change around Ryōgen's time. Women began to move to their husband's homes after marriage, whereas before they might have remained in their own homes. Instead of being praised for hard work or leadership, attributes that might have been prized in a matriarchal system, women were praised for their excellence as mothers, a role that contributed to the stability of the patriarchal system that was being established. The mother was praised not just for her fecundity, but also for her role in child rearing and ensuring that her husband's family line continued. The mother's efforts to raise and educate her children, even when her husband had died, were the subject of a number of entries in official compilations. The ideal mother was portrayed in Buddhist terms as the embodiment of compassion and caring, in contrast to the images of the woman as impure or a temptress that might be used to justify the prohibition of women from the precincts of Mount Hiei. In the case of the Fujiwara clan, the role of women as wives and mothers of emperors was perhaps their most important function in ensuring the clan's continued prosperity.[81] As George Sansom commented, "The true basis of Fujiwara power was not the rank of the ability of Fujiwara men, but the matrimonial success of Fujiwara women."[82] He might have added that their fertility was of equal importance.

The chronology of these social changes and when they occurred in various places and among different social classes is difficult to ascertain. Even among courtiers and nobles, scholars are in disagreement about the time when marriage patterns shifted from uxorilocal (residence at the wife's parents' house) and duolocal (each spouse residing at his or her parents' home) to a virilocal (the couple living at the husband's parents' home) pattern. The shift to a virilocal pattern among the Fujiwaras may have occurred several centuries after Ryōgen's time.[83] Although the surnames of clans (*uji*) such as the Fujiwaras were passed down in a patrilineal fashion, the households (*ie*) of the nobility were usually organized on matrilineal lines. William McCullough has assembled an impressive amount of data demonstrating the financial independence that many upper-class women enjoyed during the Heian period because they often inherited substantial amounts of property. In addition, the mother or the maternal grandparents were primarily responsible for raising the children. If we carry this explanation further, Ryōgen's respect for his mother would have been well received among the nobility because it reflected the ongoing importance of the position of the mother as the head of the household as well as her vital role in maintaining Fujiwara power by bearing emperors and ministers. Because source materials for marriage and the role of the mother among the lower classes are not plentiful, speculation on the societal effects of Ryōgen's emphasis of the role of his mother is substantially limited to its relationship to the upper classes; its effect on the lower classes is more difficult to understand.

The emphasis placed on motherhood eventually resulted in the construction of special halls for women (*nyonindō*) within the borders of the sacred precincts of Mount Hiei and Mount Kōya. There the mothers of monks could meet their sons and pay homage to the sacred sites. Although the Women's Hall on Mount Hiei is said to have been built by Enchin, such halls seem to have been constructed well after Ryōgen's time; the mothers of both Ryōgen and Saichō were eventually enshrined at the Hanatsumidō (Hall for picking flowers), which was in Higashidani (East valley) on the path from Sakamoto to Tōdō at a point where Saichō is said to have met his mother.[84] Once a year on the eighth day of the fourth month (the Buddha's birthday known as the flower festival), women were permitted to go as far as the Hanatsumidō to offer flowers to the Buddha. This practice may have been part of an attempt to replace offerings to a *kami* with a more Buddhist practice.[85] Ryōgen's mother was also enshrined as Myōken bosatsu (bodhisattva) at the Annyōin at the foot of Mount Hiei; however, this tradition seems late, possibly dating from the Edo period.[86] Mount Kōya had women's halls at most of its seven major entrances to the mountain. It also seems to have allowed women access further up the mountain than Mount Hiei did and to have recorded more instances of women sneaking into the sacred precincts. Ryōgen's mother was not the only mother of an eminent monk enshrined; Kūkai's mother was enshrined in the Jison'in at the foot of Mount Kōya and En no gyōja's mother at the Boshidō near Ōmine in Yoshino

Eison (1201–1290), the founder of the Shingon Ritsu tradition, whose mother died when he was seven, may have paid one of the ultimate compliments made by a Japanese monk to mothers. Eison spent much of the rest of his life proselytizing among women, conferring various sets of precepts, and establishing an order of nuns. Eison argued that although women were burdened by heavy karma from the past, their compassion as mothers could certainly overcome those obstacles to salvation.[87]

The relationship of monks and their mothers may well have given women a means to participate and empathize with the world of Buddhism. The result may well have been contributions to Buddhist establishments by either the women themselves or by male members of their families. Of course, another way for women to participate in Buddhism was open: they could become nuns. But this is a subject for a later chapter.

Conclusion

The fire on Mount Hiei at the beginning of Ryōgen's stewardship as *zasu* on Mount Hiei was a disaster. Ryōgen's place in history, as well as that of the Tendai school, depended on whether he could rebuild the complex. To do so, he needed substantial financial help. However, he served at a time when the traditional sources of revenue such as taxes would not have provided sufficient help to rebuild. A new source of help came in the form of Ryōgen's alliance with Fujiwara no Morosuke and his son Jinzen. As a result, Ryōgen was able to rebuild and expand the monastic complex on Mount Hiei to a degree that ensured his place in the history of Japanese Buddhism.

Other contributions came from temples and shrines that were brought into the Tendai fold. Finally, women probably played a role in supporting the Tendai establishment, either by directly contributing or by encouraging the men in their lives to contribute to it. Although their contribution to the order may seem odd (inasmuch as they were barred from climbing Mount Hiei), Tendai monks often performed rituals to ensure safe childbirth and to help their male relatives succeed.

At the same time that Ryōgen's alliance with Morosuke and the members of his clan enabled him to rebuild the Tendai establishment on Mount Hiei, the alliance resulted in major changes to the structure of Mount Hiei. The sons of nobles held key positions even though they had little experience; moreover, they made sure that their positions were handed down to members of their family. When Ryōgen had become a monk, he had done so with the understanding that although advancement in the secular world was closed to him, the monastic world was still open. By the time he died, advancement in the monastic world of Mount Hiei was much more restricted and available primarily to the sons of the nobility. Such changes in the structure of Mount Hiei led to resentment and bitterness among those monks who found the positions they coveted closed to them. As a result, factionalism became an increasingly intractable problem for Ryōgen during the last years of his life. In the next chapter, the history of factionalism on Mount Hiei during and after Ryōgen's time is surveyed.

Factionalism and Ryōgen's Efforts to Control the Order

In earlier chapters, the history of factionalism in the Tendai school from the time of Saichō onward has been described. Although relations between Tendai factions of monks were sometimes bitter, many of these problems had been ameliorated by the need to present a united front at court and to oppose monastic adversaries such as the Hossō school at Kōfukuji. In the last half of the ninth century, Enchin's appointment as *zasu* had demonstrated that a member of Gishin's lineage could rise to the highest office. As a result, the breakaway movement centered on Murōji ended. In the ensuing years, however, the antagonism between the two lineages once again became evident, particularly in appointments to key posts in the Tendai school. Finally, during Ryōgen's time, an open schism occurred.

Any assessment of Ryōgen's tenure as *zasu* depends on an evaluation of his role in the vicious factionalism that became evident late in his career. This chapter is divided into three parts. In the first, factionalism during Ryōgen's tenure as *zasu* is examined. The second part concerns the events after Ryōgen's death that culminated in the expulsion of Jimon monks from Mount Hiei. These events cannot be ascribed solely to Ryōgen's failings as a leader, but rather are the culmination of a long series of events. To help readers further evaluate Ryōgen's role, the third part focuses on his efforts to control the Tendai order.

Factionalism on Mount Hiei during Ryōgen's Tenure as *Zasu*

Ryōgen's Efforts to Support His Faction

Factionalism is a constant theme through Ryōgen's life. Ryōgen had to go outside of the Tendai school to find a monk who would sponsor his ordination. One of his early debates was against Senkan, who would become a leading Jimon scholar. In the Ōwa debates, he primarily chose monks from Ennin's lineage to represent the Tendai side, ignoring those monks from Enchin's lineage. The few he did choose refused to participate. Monks from Enchin's lineage opposed his appointment as *zasu*. After he became *zasu*, some monks from Enchin's faction did not support the new examination system. The rebuilding of Mount Hiei after a disastrous fire was accomplished by the creation of deep ties with Morosuke and his lineage, an alliance that drew Tendai monks further into court politics. In his will of 972, Ryōgen named monks from his own lineage to supervise the many halls he either constructed or had rebuilt, again ignoring the many qualified monks who were from Enchin's lineage. The increase in numbers of monks during Ryōgen's tenure as *zasu* also benefited his group and enabled it to increase its domination of Mount Hiei. Because Ryōgen had a long tenure as *zasu* and rebuilt so much of the monastic establishment on Mount Hiei, his favoritism must have been a major irritant to Tendai monks in other groups.

The competition between the two factions developed into a bitter rivalry during a series of events late in Ryōgen's life. In 980, Ryōgen conducted a lavish dedication for the Central Hall, inviting monks from the Nara temples. Because Saichō had founded this hall, a dedication should have included monks from all of the groups on Mount Hiei; however, monks from Ryōgen's own lineage held most of the important ceremonial posts in the dedication, and those from the Jimon were conspicuously absent. After a protest from the Jimon monks, the court directed Ryōgen to include Yokei in the dedication. The conscious omission of Jimon monks from the original plans was probably part of a plan to claim the administrative posts of this important building for Sanmon monks. Enchin had significantly expanded the Central Hall during his administration, but later it had burned down twice and been rebuilt by Son'i and Ryōgen.[1] The composition of the dedication ceremony was a symbolic gesture establishing Sanmon control over the building.

On 11-29-981, the court appointed the supernumerary lesser bishop Yokei (919–991) to the post of abbot of the Hosshōji (in modern Higashiyama-ku, Kyoto), the temple that had been established by Fujiwara no Tadahira and the *zasu* Son'i in 925, on the occasion of Tadahira's promotion to minister of the left. The temple took its name from Son'i's quarters, the Hosshōbō. Hosshōji had quickly become a vital temple for Tendai interests. In 934, the temple was named an official temple (*jogakuji*) and an imperial temple dedicated to Emperor Suzaku. It received yearly ordinands; soon Esoteric rituals including advanced initiations were performed there. Rituals in honor of Tadahira's fiftieth, sixtieth, and seventieth birthdays were also held at Hosshōji. In 949, with Tadahira's death, it became a *bodaiji*, a temple to pray for the repose of the Fujiwara dead. The temple was also important because it served as a Fujiwara clan temple and thus could serve to counter Kōfukuji, also a Fujiwara clan temple. In other words, Hosshōji was devoted to those Fujiwaras in Tadahira's lineage while Kōfukuji was often used by members of other factions of the Fujiwara clan. Hosshōji was in Kyoto, giving Tendai monks a valuable base in the capital. Thus, if Yokei were named abbot of Hosshōji, a Jimon monk would control one of the most important Tendai temples. In addition, the abbacy of Hosshōji was a traditional step in the advancement of a monk to appointment as *zasu*. The appointment was also connected with court politics because Yoritada supported Yokei while factions aligned with Morosuke's descendants supported Ennin's descendants.[2]

Because Yokei had been appointed abbot of Onjōji in 979, he was the leader of the faction of monks associated with Enchin. Within two weeks of the appointment, monks from Ennin's faction objected, arguing that the post of *zasu* of Hosshōji had always been awarded to a monk from Ennin's faction in the past. This tradition had included four generations of leaders of the Fujiwara clan and nine abbots of the Hosshōji; after three generations of appointments, Ennin's faction argued, a precedent had been set, and it should be maintained. The problem was not with Yokei's qualifications or behavior; they simply did not want the post to fall from the control of Ennin's faction. They argued,

> When Chancellor Tadahira established the Hosshōji, he appointed a member of Ennin's faction as abbot. Since that time, four generations of Fujiwara clan heads have appointed nine abbots [of Hosshōji] without naming anyone from another lineage. Yet now the current chancellor [Yoritada], the fifth head of the clan, has misunderstood precedent and appointed Yokei from Enchin's lineage as the tenth abbot.[3]

The court did not accept this argument and noted that the position originally had not been guaranteed to monks from Ennin's lineage. The monks from Ennin's lineage had been appointed in the past simply because more qualified monks were in that lineage and because a suitable monk from Enchin's lineage had not been available. The appointment of Yokei had been based on his wisdom and behavior, factors that were the main qualities necessary for the appointment.[4]

When the court failed to respond to their claims, more than 160 Sanmon monks led by 22 monks who held posts either as master of Esoteric Buddhism or in the Office of Monastic Affairs went to Kyoto to Chancellor Yoritada's mansion to ask him to rescind the appointment. When violence was threatened, the court bowed to the pressure and withdrew the appointment.[5] This was the first recorded occasion of Tendai monks marching on Kyoto to press their demands; it was a performance that would be repeated many times in the coming centuries. Although the immediate issue was resolved, the bad feelings between monks from the two lineages had been brought into the open and could not easily be suppressed again.

Why had the Sanmon monks objected so vehemently to Yokei's appointment as abbot of Hosshōji? They had accepted Yokei's other honors such as appointments in the Office of Monastic Affairs and the designation of the monastery he oversaw, the Daiunji, as a *goganji*. Although Ryōgen's name is not mentioned in connection with the protests, he had presumably played a role in the decision to march to Yoritada's house to protest; at least he had done nothing as *zasu* to stop the monks under his control from demonstrating their displeasure. Hirabayashi Moritoku has suggested that Yokei's appointment threatened the carefully laid plans that Ryōgen had made for Jinzen's succession. Yokei's other appointments had not been a threat to the dominance of Ryōgen on Mount Hiei, but if Yokei became abbot of Hosshōji, he might use that position as a step to appointment as *zasu* on Mount Hiei. Moreover, Yokei's appointment as abbot to a temple founded by Morosuke's father might throw the alliance between Morosuke's lineage and Ennin's lineage into question. Ryōgen could not allow the appointment to go unchallenged.[6]

After the incidents surrounding Yokei's appointment as abbot of Hosshōji, rumors began on Mount Hiei that Ennin's faction was planning to burn some of the major buildings controlled by the monks of Enchin's faction, including the library that contained the texts that Enchin brought to Japan at the Senjuin on Mount Hiei, as well as the Kannon'in and the Ichijōji at the foot of Mount Hiei. It was also said that they were plotting to kill five leading monks who belonged to Enchin's faction, including Yokei and his leading disciple Mokuzan (934–998). Yokei and many of his followers felt compelled to leave Mount Hiei for their own safety. During 982, Yokei and several hundred followers went to the Kannon'in[7] in Iwakura, Bishop Shōsan (939–1011) and several tens of followers to the Shugakuin in Kita-shirakawa, Supernumerary Master of Discipline Kanshu (945–1008) and thirty followers to the Gedatsuji (in Iwakura, Yamashiro), and Master of Discipline Mokuzan to the Ichijōji. Yokei had been preparing these monks, his disciples, for leadership position since 980. Shōsan and Mokuzan had already been named masters of Esoteric Buddhism. These temples were at the western foot of Mount Hiei, close to the capital and to the nobles who were major patrons of Yokei and his followers. Among those patrons was Fujiwara no Fuminori, who had tried to arrange for Ryōgen's defeat at the Ōwa debates and who became a major patron of the Jimon monks. Approximately three hundred monks from Enchin's lineage still remained on Mount Hiei to guard sites associated with Enchin.[8]

In the first month of 982, an imperial emissary, Assistant Director of the Housekeeping Bureau (*kamon no suke*) Taira Tsunemasa, climbed Mount Hiei and stayed at Yokei's former quarters, the Senjuin. He found that nobody was living there and that, consequently, the texts brought to Japan by Enchin were in danger of being destroyed. To prevent this, he organized six groups of twenty-one monks who lived nearby to protect the building. Each group was responsible for guarding the library for a five-day shift.

In the first month of 982, Ryōgen was summoned to court and asked about the veracity of the rumors. He is said to have replied,

> When we inspect both Buddhist and non-Buddhist writings, we find that arson and murder are heinous crimes. Buddhism warns that [those who commit them] will fall into hell at death and undergo many eons of suffering. Even if one were forced to perpetrate them upon pain of death, they are still foul crimes that ought never be committed. Now when we consider the events [surrounding the controversy over the appointment] of the Hosshōji abbot, the anxious words of our group were not motivated by the desire for individual benefits or fame, but out of our wish that the sites important to our lineage not decline.[9]

Once again violence had been temporarily avoided.

Yokei and the Imperial Family

The reasons for Ryōgen's opposition to Yokei becomes clearer if events at court around this time are briefly surveyed. Because the familial relations at court that must be considered are complex, the lineages of the major figures involved are shown graphically in figure 2.

When Morosuke's older brother Saneyori died in 970, Morosuke's

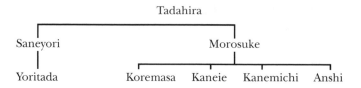

Figure 2. Lineage of Tadahira's Major Descendants

eldest son, Koremasa (also known as Koretada, 924–972) became regent, and control of the court passed to the lineage that had been Ryōgen's closest allies. About this time, however, a bitter feud between Koremasa's two full younger brothers was developing. The elder of the two, Kanemichi (925–977) had not had a very auspicious beginning to his career and was surpassed in rank by his younger brother Kaneie (929–990) in 968.[10] Kanemichi was so incensed that he refused to appear at court rather than be seated in a place inferior to that of his younger brother. Four years later, when Koremasa was about to die at the age of forty-eight, everyone felt that Kaneie would succeed him as regent. However, Kanemichi had foreseen this possibility and had obtained a written statement from his sister Anshi, who was Emperor En'yū's mother and Morosuke's daughter, declaring the importance of passing the succession to the regency and other offices in order of birth. Emperor En'yū is said to have agreed that the calligraphy was that of his mother. As a result, Kanemichi was promoted ahead of Kaneie to minister and was named named regent.

Relations between the two brothers continued to worsen over the next few years as both strove to introduce their daughters as a possible consort for Emperor En'yū. Kanemichi's daughter Fujiwara no Kōshi (also read as Teruko, 947–979) became an empress with Kanemichi's sponsorship but never did produce an heir. In the meantime, Kanemichi did whatever he could to prevent Kaneie's promotion and eventually succeeded in having him demoted. In the meantime, Kanemichi promoted his cousin Yoritada (924–989), Saneyori's son, ahead of Kaneie. When Kanemichi was on his deathbed in 977, he asked that his cousin Yoritada be named regent. Yoritada, of course, represented a threat to the dominance of Morosuke's lineage and consequently to Ryōgen's dominance on Mount Hiei. Since Emperor En'yū still had not produced an heir, Kaneie and Yoritada both tried to solidify their position by introducing their daughters to him as consorts, each hoping that his daughter might become a favorite of the young emperor, be raised to the status of empress, and produce a crown prince. The situation had been further complicated by Koremasa's daughter Kaishi's introduction as Reizei's consort; she eventually would give birth to a son who would become Emperor Kazan.[11] In addition, Kaneie's daughter Chōshi (d. 982) served as consort for Reizei, the former emperor.

For a time, it appeared as though Kaneie had lost when Yoritada's daughter Fujiwara no Junshi (957–1017) was named empress, but she proved to be barren. In 980, Kaneie's daughter Fujiwara no Senshi produced a son who would later be enthroned as Ichijō. Several years later, Emperor En'yū abdicated and Kazan (968–1008; r. 984–986) was enthroned; En'yū's problems were attributed to the angry ghost of Motokata, the loser in a succession dispute with Morosuke. After En'yū left the throne, he was ordained on both Mount Hiei (under Yokei) and at Tōdaiji.[12] En'yū's dual ordination indicates that a person with sufficient social status could ignore some of the rivalry between the various schools. Within two years, Kazan left the palace in the night to become a monk, tricked by Kaneie and his sons according to some accounts, and Kaneie's very young grandson was enthroned as Emperor Ichijō (980–1011; r. 986–1011). Because Kaneie had a clear claim to the position of regent as Ichijō's grandfather, Yoritada was forced to step down. The court was once again under the control of Morosuke's lineage. In addition, Chōshi, another of Kaneie's daughters, gave birth to a son who would become Emperor Sanjō (976–1017; r. 1011–1016) and succeed Ichijō. Moreover, the illustrious Michinaga was Kaneie's son. Thus, Kaneie's lineage came to dominate court life. (The lineages that led to the dominance of Kaneie's lineage are shown in figure 3.)

The above description of the intrigues of the various players in this game is only a sketch of the intrigues involved. The participants were subject to such uncontrollable factors as the fecundity of their daughters, the sex of the children they bore, the affections of emperors (who were sometimes mentally unbalanced), epidemics, health, and luck. The protagonists believed that one of the few ways they could exercise any control over such factors was to sponsor religious rituals. Just as Morosuke had once commissioned Ryōgen to perform rituals to promote Morosuke's career and ensure the fertility of his daughters, so did the various figures in these rivalries. Although extant sources do not give a full record of the activities of Yokei, diaries by court nobles do suggest that he was patronized by Yoritada and to some extent by Emperor En'yū, who was often under Yoritada's influence.[13] Because

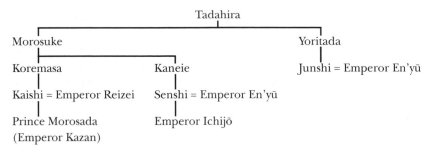

Figure 3. Lineage for Kaneie

En'yū was the grandson of Morosuke, he would have been expected to pursue a policy in favor of Kaneie; however, the young emperor was probably both influenced by Yoritada and also wished to use Yoritada to blunt Kaneie's control. As he grew older he seems to have favored a more independent course. After he retired he spent much of his time at the En'yūji, his *goganji,* which was administered by the Shingon monk Kanchō.[14]

The split between the factions controlled by Yokei and Ryōgen thus was exacerbated by the support the two men received from competing factions at court. Yokei's career is briefly surveyed against this background. Yokei was ordained by Myōsen in 935 at the age of sixteen and received advanced initiations in Esoteric Buddhism by Gyōyo in 967 at the age of forty-eight; he was appointed a master of Esoteric Buddhism at Enryakuji shortly thereafter, probably to fill one of the additional positions for the Sōjiin that Ryōgen had petitioned for shortly after becoming *zasu.*[15] Yokei was appointed a supernumerary master of discipline in 969 and remained at that level for a number of years. However, his career accelerated about 977, the same year when Yoritada was named regent, when he was made a full master of discipline. By 979, he was lesser bishop and abbot of Onjōji, a step that had led to appointment of *zasu* in the past. With his appointment as Hosshōji abbot in 981, he had a good claim to be *zasu.*

In 980, Yokei asked that the Daiunji monastery (in modern Agura-chō, Iwakura, Sakyō-ku, Kyoto) be designated the *goganji* temple for the reigning emperor, En'yū, and that it be granted five masters of Esoteric Buddhism.[16] Shortly thereafter, En'yū had the Rendaibō, a cloister within the Daiunji, also named a *goganji* and given four masters of Esoteric Buddhism. The result was a major establishment for the practice of Esoteric Buddhism, an institution that performed the same types of role as the Sōjiin on Mount Hiei. The conferral of the right to select advanced masters of Esoteric Buddhism had previously been held by the *zasu*. When Yokei began submitting his own petitions for appointment as *ajari* even though he was not *zasu*, two centers of power in the Tendai school were established. The Sanmon matched the Jimon's petitions by submitting their own requests for additional *ajari*. By the late Heian period, approximately three hundred positions for *ajari* had been created. Being named *ajari* was no longer the culmination of a long period of practice but simply a higher rank at temples.[17]

En'yū's close relations with the Jimon monks are also indicated by a brief stay at the Ichijōji temple on 10-27-988 when he was a retired emperor. He subsequently proceeded to climb Mount Hiei to receive the precepts and Esoteric initiations.[18] The former emperor's stop at the Ichijōji indicated that he recognized the complaints of the Jimon faction. However, Mount Hiei continued to maintain its monopoly on ordinations within the Tendai school at that time, forcing En'yū to go there for his ordination.

The location of the monastic complex at Daiunji in the northern suburbs of Kyoto must have been more appealing to the court than Mount Hiei, which required an arduous climb. In addition, Onjōji had not adopted the practice of confining their monks for a set number of years; even though this system was not actively in place at this time, the difference in the training between the two monastic complexes might have enabled monks in Enchin's lineage to move about more freely than those from Mount Hiei. With the establishment of these temples, tensions between the monks in Enchin's faction and those in Ennin's faction had worsened. Daiunji at the western foot of Mount Hiei complemented Onjōji at eastern foot of Mount Hiei, giving Enchin's faction strongholds in several locations. In a very short time, Yokei had assembled an impressive array of monks and established a monastery close to the capital for the performance of rituals for the reigning emperor. He revived the Esoteric tradition of Enchin, conferring advanced initiations on at least eighteen monks in his lineage.[19] The four most eminent—Shōsan, Mokuzan, Myōchō, and Kanshu—were called the "four kings of Enchin's lineage," perhaps a reference to the four heavenly kings installed to protect Buddhist monasteries; the same monks, with Kyōso (955–1019) replacing Myōchō, were referred to as Yokei's divine feet (*shinsoku*), suggesting that they carried out Yokei's plans. In 981, in preparation for his appointment as abbot of Hosshōji, he was named supernumerary greater bishop. Other awards followed, perhaps to demonstrate the court's support after the Sanmon faction had forced him to leave Mount Hiei. On 2-15-982, he was presented with special robes. On 3-21-982, he performed a ceremony of the immovable king at the Hall of Benevolence and Longevity in the palace.[20] Yokei's temple Daiunji continued to grow; in the third month of 985, Princess Shōshi (950–999), who by this time had been named grand empress, had a Lecture Hall, a Godaidō (hall dedicated to the five mystic kings), a Kanjōdō (Esoteric consecration hall), a Lotus Meditation Hall, an Amida Hall, and a Mantra Hall (*shingondō* with both *maṇḍalas*) built and renamed it the Kannon'in.[21]

While a survey of the activities of Yokei's disciples lies beyond this study, reference might be made to several highlights to demonstrate the continued importance of the pattern of patronage by nobles in return for the performance of rituals. Yokei's major disciples received appointments in the Office of Monastic Affairs, often awarded for the successful performance of rituals. Shōsan was called upon to perform rituals to heal the ailments of Fujiwara no Michinaga, Grand Empress Shōshi, Fujiwara no Senshi, and others. In fact, Michinaga served as Onjōji's lay administrator.[22] In 999, Kyōso conducted Shōshi's funeral and in 1015 conducted Esoteric rituals for an eye ailment of Emperor Sanjō. In 997, he was selected to be the author of a response to criticisms by Chinese T'ien-t'ai monks of the Japanese Tendai teaching of realization of Buddhism in this very life. The efforts of these monks were rewarded with additional support for temples under their control. For example, in 1001, the court granted Mokuzan four masters of Esoteric Buddhism for Ichijōji, increasing his temple's ritual power. In short, the Jimon monks were a very real threat to Ryōgen and his descendants.

Fujiwara no Kaneie responded to the commissioning of rituals by Yoritada with additional support for Ryōgen. In self-conscious imitation of his father Morosuke's establishment of the Lotus Meditation Hall at Yokawa and at Ryōgen's suggestion, in 979 Kaneie commissioned the construction of a temple building to be dedicated for the success of his lineage. The result was the Eshin'in, built to the south of the Shuryōgon'in in Yokawa; Kaneie happily contributed building supplies and one hundred *koku* of rice. On 11-27-983, Kaneie sponsored an elaborate dedication of the Eshin'in, complete with music, and gave the temple to Ryōgen as a symbol of the ongoing alliance of Ennin's faction and Morosuke's lineage. Yokei, Ryōgen's rival from the Jimon faction, participated as the chief priest in the ceremony, indicating that the two factions might still work together at court-sponsored functions, much as competing nobles still might appear together at court.[23]

In ceremonies reminiscent of those performed before to ensure the birth of an heir to the throne, ceremonies for Nyoirin Kannon were performed in 980 for the birth of a crown prince for Emperor En'yū—successfully, it appears, for a son was born who would become Emperor Ichijō.[24] In 984, Kaneie's daughter Senshi and her young son went to Gangyōji monastery outside Kyoto for a performance of rituals to the Nyoirin Kannon; they stayed in Ryōgen's quarters at the monastery. When Senshi's son was in fact named crown prince that year and two years later ascended the throne, his election was attributed in part to the efficacy of this ritual. By holding the ceremony at Ganyōji, Ryōgen made it accessible to a woman, Senshi, who would have been barred from a ritual on Mount Hiei. He also responded to the increasing activity of Yokei's faction in temples near Kyoto. Ryōgen demonstrated his seemingly superhuman powers of perception during the preparations for the ceremony. When the main image for the ritual was missing, Ryōgen suggested that it might be found in the repository where the founder of the monastery, Henjō, had kept scriptures. Jōan (925–998), the monk in charge of lodgings, checked there, but could not find it. Later, when he went to search for it again at night, he found the image on top of a small shrine in the repository. The monks who lived at Gangyōji had never seen the image before and were amazed by Ryōgen's prescience.[25]

Three years later, on 10-20-986, shortly after Kaneie had become regent, the Eshin'in was designated an official temple and awarded three yearly ordinands.[26] Later it became the headquarters for Genshin and his Eshin-lineage (ryū), one of the major subgroups within the Sanmon.

The building of the Eshin'in represents part of a solution to a problem that seemed to recur almost every generation. As lineages became broader, adherence to Morosuke's lineage was no longer an adequate criterion for Ryōgen because several members of the lineage could complete for leadership. Most of the major figures of each generation would require at least one temple to further their interests; in fact, when Kaneie dedicated the Eshin'in, he mentioned the Hosshōji founded by Tadahira and the Lotus Meditation Hall established by Morosuke as precedents.

Although it is tempting to explain many of the political and religious events of this period by referring to the factionalism at court and on Mount Hiei, a number of other events reveal that Ryōgen served and maintained relations with Yoritada and Emperor En'yū. On 10-5-977, Ryōgen performed the ceremony of the Buddha of Abundant Light for Yoritada, who had a serious illness; the regent is said to have been cured by the ritual.[27] In 977, he also brought Buddha's relic to the palace so that Emperor En'yū could pay homage to it.[28] Ryōgen received his appointment as grand archbishop in 981 when Emperor En'yū recovered from what was probably malaria while Ryōgen played a central role in a five-platform ceremony of the immovable king. However, the participation of Yokei and the Shingon monk Kanchō demonstrate that Emperor En'yū was also a patron of these monks. Like Ryōgen, they were awarded significant promotions in the Office of Monastic Affairs for their participation.[29] On 3-23-983, Ryōgen and Jinzen were to conduct services at the En'yūji, the emperor's recently constructed *goganji*. The assembly was to be patterned after the Misai-e, the assembly held at the palace around the new year, and had a number of high court officials participating. The actual ceremony was based on one performed at the pagoda at the Urin'in, a branch temple controlled by the Gangyōji that was under Ryōgen's control. The ritual might well have been based on performances developed by Ryōgen and his disciples. However, the services were suspended because of confinements (*monoimi;* taboos preventing certain actions for a specific period of time).[30] Such examples suggest that much as competing members of the nobility continued to associate at court, so did monks when circumstances demanded it. Such structures as family ties and belonging to the same Buddhist school or tradition must have ameliorated conflicts. Thus, the rivalry between Yoritada and Kaneie never escalated into open violence, perhaps because the two men were cousins; in fact, Yoritada had maintained much more cordial relations with Kaneie than had Kanemichi, Kaneie's own brother. However, these checks on competition would eventually fail for the Tendai school, just as they occasionally did within the noble classes, leading to violent confrontations between the followers of Ryōgen and of Yokei.

Ryōgen's Death and the Ensuing Factional Disputes

Shortly before Ryōgen died, he gave the temple seals and keys to Jinzen and retired to a temple, Guhōji, in Sakamoto at the foot of Mount Hiei, where he would die.[31] Sakamoto was favored by the monks when they became ill because the climate and amenities were better than on Mount Hiei. By conferring the seals and keys on Jinzen, he helped ensure the smooth succession of Morosuke's son Jinzen as the next *zasu*. In fact, less than two months after Ryōgen's death, Jinzen was named *zasu*.[32] Yokei and others were certainly better qualified in terms of seniority and their accomplishments; however, Jinzen did hold a higher rank in the Office of Monastic Affairs because he had been promoted so rapidly. Jinzen was not known as a scholar, but he did perform many Esoteric rituals and was known to be quite effective. As the *Ōkagami* stated of Jinzen and his brother Jinkaku,

> Those [of Morosuke's sons] who became monks were the Iimuro Provisional Archbishop and the present Zenrinji Archbishop. Although simply called monks, the last two have been the greatest wonder workers of our day. There is nobody inside or outside of the Court who does not trust or revere them as though they were buddhas.[33]

Although Jinzen may have been a noted thaumaturge of his day, he was only forty-two years old when he was appointed *zasu*. Compared to Ryōgen, who had been fifty-four, Jinzen was exceptionally young for such a high monastic post; he had few, if any, remarkable achievements to his name other than those that derived from his parentage. In this sense, he was similar to Fujiwara sons who received high court ranks because of their connections. Certainly, ambitious monks in Enchin's lineage must have questioned his appointment, and even some ambitious monks in Ennin's lineage must have felt qualms.

Jinzen would repay Ryōgen's support by securing the posthumous appellation of Jie from the court for his teacher two years after Ryōgen's death. The title Jie daishi by which Ryōgen was often called was never officially bestowed on him and does not appear until several decades after his death.

According to Jinzen's biography, after unsuccessfully attempting to perform services to cure Emperor Reizei of his mental illness, Jinzen "came to hate the way [of performing such services] and only sought Buddhahood."[34] Jinzen sickened and tried to resign from being both *zasu* and provisional archbishop after only four years; however, when the court refused to accept his resignation from the position of both Tendai *zasu* and provisional archbishop, he handed over his seal and keys, the symbols of his office, to the three chief administrators of the monastery and retreated to live a quiet life.[35] Jinzen would live for five more months, dying at the young age of forty-seven. Before he died, he made arrangements for the tidy succession of the lands under his control as head of Myōkōin.[36]

When a new *zasu* was to be appointed, Yokei from the Jimon was chosen and appointed *zasu* on 9-29-89. The monks in the Sanmon were furious; they blocked the road so that the imperial emissary, Lesser Counselor Minamoto no Yoshitō, could not pass and seized the edict.[37] The court was furious and decided to press its case. On 10-4, Lesser Counselor Fujiwara no Tokikata was dispatched to Mount Hiei as an imperial emissary with an escort of the imperial police; this time the edict appointing Yokei was read. Finally, on 10-29, another imperial emissary, Greater Controller of the Right Fujiwara no Arikuni, read an edict in front of the Zentōin, Ennin's quarters, that pardoned the monks for blocking an imperial messenger, but also lambasted the Sanmon monks for their interference with court appointments. Arikuni chose the Zentōin, the hall where the artifacts from Ennin's studies in China were stored, to deliver the edict, effectively accusing the monks of departing from the tradition of scholarship and practice begun by Ennin. The edict that he read, translated in part below, reflects the frustration that the court must have felt in trying to decide how to deal with the Tendai monks.

> Since the time of Ennin and Enchin, Tendai monks have split into two factions. Although the majority of *zasu* have been from Ennin's lineage, three or four have been appointed from Enchin's line.[38] They were venerable elders who were appointed by the court with the protection of the Sannō deity because they exhibited superior wisdom and were assiduous in their religious practice. Recently, Jinzen has resigned as *zasu*, and administrative affairs have piled up. Consequently, we appointed the top-ranking Tendai monk in the Office of Monastic Affairs, Greater Bishop Yokei, as *zasu* and sent Lesser Counselor Minamoto no Yoshitō as imperial messenger to read the edict of appointment to the chief temple administrator (*jike*). However, several hundred monks assembled on the mountain and blocked his way so that he was unable to complete his mission and had to return to the capital.
>
> Now, refusing an order and being rude to an imperial emissary are extremely grave violations of law. The four bishops Raga [Senga?], Shōku, Shōsan, Kakugyō, and the monk Tōen seem to have been the ringleaders of the wrongdoing. Senga and the others said they knew nothing of this even when they swore an oath before the *kami*. When we asked the three main administrators to summon Tōen for questioning, they said that they did not know where he was. However, the events are clearly known to us through the letter of complaint [concerning Yokei's appointment] that the three administrators submitted several days earlier.
>
> Because Buddhism (*shōbō*) is protected by imperial law (*ōbō*), these monks should be punished in accordance with our [secular] law. However, because we have been aided by the spirit of Ennin in many ways, we

hold Ennin's disciples in high regard and especially excuse them from wrongdoing. But the monks of your lineage should clearly understand the imperial will and not falter in your practice or study so that your lineage will prosper. You should understand that it is men who are responsible for promulgating the [Buddhist] way and thus carry out your duties with a loyal and chaste attitude. Those who perform such evil deeds will surely be admonished and chastened by the spirit of Ennin.

Buddhism and imperial law should stand side by side. From now on, those people who use Buddhism to harm imperial law will be punished in accordance with imperial law. These fellows are like worms in the body of a lion that eat it from within;[39] you should be aware that it is your own lineage that will destroy you.[40]

Yokei made serious efforts to govern Mount Hiei. On 10-29, the same day the court had its edict read, Yokei conducted Esoteric consecrations on Mount Hiei with aid of soldiers (*seihei*), but even then arrows flew, disrupting the service.[41] Despite the court's strong admonitions to the Tendai monks, Yokei was unable to govern Mount Hiei effectively; when he tried to conduct ordinations or Esoteric consecration ceremonies, the participants were chased away. He resigned on 12-27, three months after his appointment. The court appointed him supernumerary archbishop that same day. Until that time, *zasu* had always served until they died or became too ill to perform their duties. Now, because of growing factionalism on Mount Hiei, Yokei had been forced to resign. Less than two years later he would die.

Yōshō (904–990?) was appointed the new *zasu*, but would resign within a year.[42] His appointment may have been a final effort by the court to reach a compromise between the two factions. Yōshō was a student of Enshō rather than Ryōgen. Although Enshō had also been a member of Ennin's lineage, he had not been nearly as sectarian as Ryōgen. Moreover, Yōshō may have had ties to some Jimon monks. As a young man he was sickly; finally he went to get advice from an unnamed practitioner in Minoo who cured him. Minoo was the site that Ryōgen's contemporary Senkan had chosen for his retreat. Thus, Yōshō might well have known Senkan, the most illustrious scholar of his day in the Jimon lineage. Moreover, Yōshō was a recluse, interested in practice in secluded places rather than in scholarship or building institutions, and consequently was unhappy as *zasu* and soon resigned. A number of dates for his death are found in sources, including 990 and 993.[43] The court continued to make occasional efforts to treat the two factions equally even as factions of court tended to support certain monastic lineages. For example, the court granted Jinzen the posthumous title of Jinin (compassionate forbearance) and Yokei the title Chiben (words of wisdom) on the same day, 4-15-1007.[44]

The Expulsion of Jimon Monks from Mount Hiei

With Yōshō's resignation as *zasu*, the court stopped trying to impose its will on the selection of *zasu* and appointed Ryōgen's students. Senga served as *zasu* for eight years and Kakugyō (also read Kakukei) for sixteen. A major fight between the Sanmon and Jimon factions occurred in the eighth month of 993, when some Jimon followers of Jōsan, a disciple of Shōsan of the Kannon'in, destroyed a number of items at the Sekisan zen'in. This shrine was dedicated to the deity of Mount Ch'ih in Shantung who had protected Ennin during his journey to China. Ennin had vowed to establish a shrine for the deity, but died before he could build it. His disciple Anne, the next *zasu*, was able to obtain an official's villa as a site for the shrine; it was in Shugakuin, in the western foothills of Kyoto, probably not far from the Jimon stronghold at Kannon'in. The deity Sannō was enshrined in the eastern foothills to protect Mount Hiei.[45]

The monks from the Kannon'in are said to have destroyed an umbrella and staff that had belonged to Ennin and several items sacred to the deity.[46] The Jimon attack was thus directed against the central figure, Ennin, in the Sanmon lineage and against the shrine for the deity that supposedly had protected him on his return from China; the deity could thus be said to be central to the Sanmon lineage. During the meetings held on Mount Hiei by the Sanmon monks to decide their course of action, Hyōdai, a monk who lived at the Sekisan zen'in, became enraged and falsely charged Jimon monks with seizing items intended for Sanmon monks. In the ensuing conflict incited by Hyōdai, approximately forty of the Jimon buildings on Mount Hiei were burned, including the Senjuin and the Rengein (a *goganji* of retired emperor Reizei). The lodgings of a number of prominent monks, including the former *zasu* Ryōyū, Ryōgen's rival Bōsan, and Mokuzan, were also destroyed. Approximately a thousand monks led by Kyōso and four others left Mount Hiei. Kyōso's group of monks, carrying an image of Enchin, first went to Daiunji (Kannon'in) in Iwakura.[47] Later many moved to Onjōji.[48] As the *Fusō ryakki* account notes, "After this event, monks of Enchin's lineage lived in different places, not on Mount Hiei."[49]

The schism between the two lineages was complete. However, the Jimon lineage did not decline. In a society as rife with factionalism as

Japan, many accepted an alternative to the Sanmon faction. Records of the following decades show numerous occasions when the court supported Jimon temples. Jimon monks developed a scholarly tradition that rivaled the Sanmon, as well as their own versions of a number of Esoteric rituals. The leading monks of the faction, such as Kanshu and Shōsan (939–1011), who had left Mount Hiei in 981, eventually became abbots of Onjōji and de facto leaders of the Jimon. Kanshu, for example, had Fujiwara no Michinaga as a patron.

Differences in teachings played virtually no role in the schism,[50] but in subsequent decades both factions attempted to gain the advantage in the controversy by advancing arguments based on doctrinal positions. The Sanmon argued that the Jimon was in fact a part of the Tendai school and should be under the control of Enryakuji but then advocated the seemingly contradictory position that Jimon monks were to have no role in the administration of Mount Hiei. Jimon arguments either advocated the independent status of their faction or maintained that the Jimon tradition represented a purer form of Tendai. Several of these arguments are briefly described below.

Sanmon arguments that the Jimon should be under their control took several forms. Because the headquarters of the Jimon, Onjōji, had been a branch temple of Enryakuji, it should still be under the jurisdiction of Mount Hiei. However, Jimon monks could counter that if Enryakuji monks had been serious in their claims that the Jimon was an integral part of Tendai, then Onjōji monks should have been permitted to hold positions in the administration of Mount Hiei. In reply to such objections, Sanmon monks argued that a monk from a branch temple such as Onjōji should not be allowed to hold a position such as *zasu*. After Yokei, the court occasionally attempted to appoint a Jimon monk as *zasu*. However, Sanmon protests were so vigorous that this soon became a formalistic way of honoring eminent Jimon monks with no one expecting the candidate to exercise power. In all, beginning with Yokei, nine Jimon monks were appointed as *zasu*, but each served only a short time. The last was Kōken in 1190.

Jimon monks countered arguments that a monk from a branch temple should not hold power by noting that Onjōji was older than Enryakuji because it had been established as a clan temple for the Ōtomo clan. According to their claims the temple had been established at the request of Ōtomo no Ōji (648–672), the son of Emperor Tenji and an unsuccessful aspirant to the throne in the Jinshin disturbance. However, from the Heian period onward, some sources listed Ōji as an emperor.

Jimon monks claimed that the temple was actually established by his son Ōtomo no Yotamaro in 686. By arguing that the temple was established at the wish of three emperors—Tenji (626–671; r. 668–671), Kōbun (Ōtomo no Ōji, 648–672; r. 671–672), and Tenmu (d. 686; r. 673–686)—they could claim that it was an older imperial temple than Enryakuji. Moreover, the well on its premises was said to have provided the water for the first bath immediately after the birth (*ubuyu*) of three future emperors: Tenmu, Tenji, and Jitō (645–702). With this fabricated history, Jimon monks could argue that because Onjōji was older, it should not be a branch temple of the newer Enryakuji. Archeological finds place the temple in the Hakuhō period (645–710) with Ōtomo Sukuri as its founder, but it apparently had fallen into disrepair by the time Enchin gave it his support. Thus Jimon monks manufactured a history for the temple that associated it with royalty long before Enryakuji had been founded.[51]

Another attempt by Onjōji to establish its independence can be seen in its petitions to the court for permission to establish its own ordination platform. Much as Saichō used the ordination platform to establish the independence of the Tendai school from the officials of the Office of Monastic Affairs, Jimon monks wanted to establish a platform to declare themselves independent of Sanmon control. Court permission was required to establish an ordination platform, indicating official recognition of Onjōji's independent status. Jimon monks first applied to the court in the fifth month of 1039, after the Jimon monk Myōson (971–1063) had resigned as *zasu* after holding office for just a few days. They argued that Onjōji had an ordination tradition that could be traced back through Enchin to Gishin and was entitled to its own platform. Gishin had received the bodhisattva ordination at the same time as Saichō in China. Sanmon monks countered that a single school could not have two platforms. The precepts were supposed to serve as the basis of harmony (*wagō*) in the order; two platforms would create discord. Jimon monks countered this argument by noting that if the temples were already separate, then they should have separate platforms. Furthermore, they noted that the Jetavana monastery (J. Gion shōja) had two platforms. Because Myōson was supported by the regent (*kanpaku*) Fujiwara no Yorimichi (992–1074), Michinaga's eldest son, the petition might have succeeded, but the court kept postponing its decision. As a result, Myōson's many supporters asked that he be reappointed as *zasu* in 1048; but he served for only a few days, and the issue of the ordination platform was not resolved.

The issue of the ordination platform emerged again in 1074 when Emperor Shirakawa (1053–1129; r. 1072–1086) asked the Jimon monk Raigō (1004–1084) to pray for a son. Raigō did so and the empress bore a son. As his reward, Raigō asked that Onjōji be granted an ordination platform. When the court refused, he withdrew to the temple and fasted until he died, returning as an angry spirit. The child died at the age of four. Sanmon monks subsequently prayed for a son for the emperor; one was born who became Emperor Horikawa.

In 1163, Sanmon monks brought up the issue of the ordination platform, arguing that Onjōji candidates for ordination who had been going to Tōdaiji should be required to go to Enryakuji instead. The court agreed with the Sanmon position but could not enforce its decision.[52]

The issues between Sanmon and Jimon monks revolved around lineages and appointments rather than doctrinal issues. However, as might be expected, the factions did develop separate stances on some issues. For example, in the examinations, Jimon monks would have regarded Gishin's *Tendai hokkeshū gishū* and the essays by Senkan on doctrinal issues as basic sources while Sanmon monks would have ignored them.

Ryōgen's Attempts to Control the Order

Ryōgen can be criticized for not keeping factionalism under control. Certainly many court nobles were disturbed by the events on Mount Hiei. However, factionalism was also a part of court life, so much so that monastic factionalism can be viewed as an almost inevitable outcome of Ryōgen's efforts to gain support from Morosuke and his descendants. But even as Ryōgen accepted, and sometimes actively contributed to, factionalism, he also tried to control some of the abuses on Mount Hiei. In this section, several of his efforts are considered. The discussion begins with a consideration of a set of rules written by Ryōgen and then concludes with two pieces of evidence that Ryōgen made attempts to tighten monastic discipline.

The Composition of the Twenty-six Rules

On 7-6-970, Ryōgen issued a set of twenty-six rules for the order.[53] The set of rules was composed to tighten monastic discipline shortly after the Sōjiin had burned down for the second time. After the fire, Ryōgen redirected all his efforts from rebuilding other structures to the Sōjiin so that it would be ready for the annual performance of the *shari-e*, traditionally held in that building, the fourth month of the next year. In fact, the first of the twenty-six rules concerns the *shari-e*. Besides the immediate issue of the Sōjiin and *shari-e*, the composition of the rules was influenced by the need to bring together the disparate lineages that existed on Mount Hiei under Ryōgen. Each of the various imperial temples had been established under the guidance of a particular monk. In most cases, the founding monk left instructions that successive abbots were to be from his lineage. Thus, Mount Hiei was inhabited by various lineages that could conceivably compete with each other. The rules served as guides for all the monks on Mount Hiei, establishing Ryōgen as the clear source of authority for all of the various factions on Mount Hiei.

The code reflected Ryōgen's detailed knowledge of previous sets of rules compiled for the Tendai order. These began with Saichō's petitions to the court concerning Tendai administration.[54] Among the topics found in the codes by both Saichō and Ryōgen are the ordination and education system and the twelve-year sequestration on Mount Hiei. Other sets of rules cited include the *Enryakuji kinseishiki* issued by Saichō's immediate disciples led by Ninchū in 824, a chancellor's order issued in 6-21-866 supporting a number of Ennin's initiatives, Ennin's *Shuryōgon'in shiki* of 4-2-836, and several other sets of rules that do not survive.[55] Ryōgen's rules also refer to the *Fan-wang ching*, indicating that his rules were designed to supplant rather than supersede the *Fan-wang* precepts.

Hori Daiji divides Ryōgen's rules into four major categories.[56] The first concerns the system of lectures and examinations that Ryōgen revived on Mount Hiei (rules 2–5, 11). Monks who attend examinations are admonished for paying more attention to the food served by lecturers and candidates to the audience than to the actual lectures; in addition, they are criticized for being more interested in how the lecturers advanced in monastic circles than in the actual teachings presented in the lectures. Such attitudes are criticized for being more in keeping with secular than with monastic attitudes and as violating the spirit of Buddhism.

The second category of rules concerns ceremonies on Mount Hiei, particularly ordinations, commemorative offerings for the founders of the Tendai school, and Esoteric consecrations (rules 1, 8–10, 15, 23–25). Monks are criticized for appearing at these ceremonies without practicing the chanting of scripture, the verses in praise of the Buddha (*bonbai*), or the ritual actions of the monastic officials. As is discussed below, when Ryōgen recited the *Fan-wang* precepts for the fortnightly assembly, he prepared by practicing the recitation every day. Ryōgen expected the same of his students and was critical of them when they did not treat ceremonies seriously. In particular, Ryōgen was interested in Buddhist chanting (*shōmyō*) and is listed in a number of *shōmyō* lineages.[57] Ryōgen cautioned his monks, noting that if a monk assiduously strives to realize enlightenment, he must watch his activities whether walking, standing, sitting, or lying down. In addition, the rules criticize monks for not attending fortnightly assemblies, rituals that served as the basis for monastic discipline. In rule twenty-three, he threatened to expel those who did not attend the fall and spring assemblies in which scriptures were chanted for the Sannō *kami* that protected Mount Hiei, a threat that he carried out a decade later. For a monk such as Ryōgen who had based his career on the skillful conduct of religious ceremonies, a casual attitude on the part of Tendai monks must have been particularly galling.

The third category concerned deportment (rules 6–7, 12–14, 16, 22, 26). Monks were cautioned to wear straw sandals rather than wooden shoes in the halls. Fancy and colorful robes were prohibited for young monks. The boundaries for the sequestration on Mount Hiei were laid out. Impure items (such as meat and pungent onions [*kunsei*]) were not to be kept in the pure confines of the mountain in baskets (*warigo*). Monks were to be prompt in paying for the items used in the performance of rituals. Moreover, they were to take pains to follow the traditions of Mount Hiei as they were laid out in the rules issued by Saichō and others. In particular, they were to practice all of the four Tendai meditations (not just the Pure Land constant-walking meditation) during their twelve-year confinement on Mount Hiei. Only suitable monks were to be chosen to be candidates for the examinations. Monastic officials were warned about criticizing each other and urged to preserve the dignified behavior that should accompany their offices. Finally, the timely submission of registers of monks every spring and fall was required.

The fourth category concerned activities prohibited to monks (rules 17–21). Monks were criticized for letting horses and cattle loose in the sacred precincts of Mount Hiei. Some monks wore head coverings (*katō*) that concealed their identity at ceremonies and even carried weapons with which they fought, actions lambasted as being no better than those of butchers. Monks were not to be allowed to willfully administer punishments to attendants (*dōji*); after all, such servants might become monks in the future.[58]

The rules supplement, rather than replace, the *Fan-wang* precepts.

If the rules had been followed carefully, many of the disciplinary problems that arose later in Tendai history might have been avoided. However, the pressures that led to factionalism were so intense that they probably could not have been avoided except by refusing to perform services for the lay patrons who financed the order. In the next two sections, two indications that Ryōgen did make an attempt to control the order are examined.

Ryōgen and the Fan-wang Precepts

Ryōgen's interest in the *Fan-wang* precepts is noteworthy as one aspect of his attempt to regulate monastic behavior. Saichō had petitioned the court, arguing that the *Fan-wang* precepts should be substituted for the *Ssu-fen lü* (*Dharmaguptaka vinaya*) precepts in Tendai ordinations. One week after his death, the court had approved his petition. However, Saichō had never specified how the *Fan-wang* precepts were to be interpreted so that they could serve as a guide to monastic discipline. Although some Tendai leaders such as Ennin and Enchin had attempted to supplement the *Fan-wang* precepts either with monastery rules or by referring to other texts, their efforts do not seem to have had any long-term effect on monastic discipline on Mount Hiei. Moreover, other Tendai scholars, such as Annen, had argued that the *Fan-wang* precepts could be interpreted as expedient practices for monks and did not have to be taken literally.[59]

Ryōgen has been credited with both weakening and attempting to strengthen adherence to the *Fan-wang* precepts. The argument that he weakened it is primarily based on a statement by the Tendai scholar Fukuda Gyōei (1867–1954) that Ryōgen had proposed that all Tendai monks be ordained with the five lay precepts giving novices the same status as monks and making all eligible for monastic office.[60]

Fukuda gave no source for his claim that Ryōgen allowed monks to be ordained with the five lay precepts, nor have subsequent scholars who have discussed the claim.[61] Fukuda's claim does not seem to be supported by any documentation from sources dating from Ryōgen's time or several decades afterward. In recent years, Tendai scholars have simply ignored Fukuda's argument, and the basis for Fukuda's argument still remains obscure.[62]

Other evidence suggests that Ryōgen attempted to control the abuses of monastic discipline by reviving the use of the *Fan-wang* precepts. For example, Ryōgen revived the fortnightly *fusatsu* (*poṣadha*) ceremony.

The Buddhist precepts traditionally have been observed by requiring attendance at a fortnightly meeting at which all the precepts are recited. If a monk has violated any of the precepts, he is expected either to have confessed his wrongdoing before the meeting or to do so at the meeting. The fortnightly recitation of the precepts was thus a vital element in monastic discipline. Although Saichō mentioned it in the *Sange gakushō shiki,* he apparently did not put it into practice before he died.[63] According to the *Tendai zasuki,* Ennin first performed the fortnightly assembly on 5-15-860.[64] Ryōgen's revival of the ritual is in keeping with his restoration of various rituals introduced by Ennin. Although the fortnightly assembly seems to have been continued after Ennin, in 888 Enchin complained that many monks did not bother to attend it.[65] The practice apparently died out sometime later. The sporadic performance of the ceremony indicates that it was not regarded as necessary for the governance of the order.

On 4-15-971, at the Shuryōgon'in at Yokawa, Ryōgen began the fortnightly recitation of the *Fan-wang* precepts. To prepare for the occasion, Ryōgen had practiced reciting them every day for several weeks. When the day for the first public recitation arrived and Ryōgen began to chant, the characters chanted are said to have appeared in light that issued from his mouth.[66] This motif is probably based on a passage from the *Fan-wang ching* in which the "light of the precepts" is said to issue from a practitioner's mouth when he chants the precepts at the fortnightly assembly.[67] In the *sūtra,* the light is said to be beyond any color or cause and effect, serving as a symbol for the unconditioned essence of the precepts. In Ryōgen's biography, the light assumes a more physical shape and is included in the story to illustrate the spiritual power that he brought to the ritual rather than his rigid adherence to the precepts. In a similar manner, ordinations include a section in which the candidate is asked if he will adhere to certain basic rules. Although the candidate must answer that he will do so, in most cases candidates did not adhere to the precepts. Although Ryōgen probably did not plan to adhere to all fifty-eight of the *Fan-wang ching* precepts, he did use some of them in the set of temple rules he composed, indicating that he regarded them as important sources.

Purging the Order

The background for this event lies in rituals performed to the guardian deities of Mount Hiei. In 979, Ryōgen performed a ceremony in honor of the three territorial deities *(jishu sanshō)* of Mount Hiei. The first of these, Ōyamagui no mikoto (Ninomiya no gongen), had been installed since Saichō's time. The other two had been brought from other places and installed as guardian deities; they were Miwa myōjin of Yamato (Ōmiya no gongen), and Usa hachiman of Buzen (Shōshinshi gongen). For the festival, Ryōgen had a divinity hall built at Karasaki on the shores of Lake Biwa; four miscellaneous buildings and two corridors connecting them were also constructed. A palanquin, new costumes for the twenty men who were to carry it, and adornments for horses were also commissioned. More than twenty musicians boarded a dragon-headed boat and were rowed from Totsu-hama to Karasaki on Lake Biwa. Young boys from the best families were chosen to dance the Azuma-asobi, a *gagaku* piece adapted from the songs of the eastern provinces that had become popular at shrines by the mid-Heian period. They performed music and dances on the boat all day.[68]

The next year, in 980, Ryōgen eliminated about one-fourth of the monks on Mount Hiei from the monastic roles. According to the *Daisō-jōden,* on 4-1-980, he had the *Diamond Sūtra* read for the three deities who guarded Mount Hiei. Although all Tendai monks were supposed to attend the assembly, only two thousand of the twenty-seven hundred on the registers appeared. As a result, Ryōgen purged the monks who did not show up from the registers. Although the action seems precipitous and drastic, the rules compiled by Ryōgen in 970 often referred to monks who did not attend monastic rituals with sufficient gravity.[69] Moreover, control of the monastic registers had been one of the earliest areas in which *zasu* had exerted their administrative control. Gishin had included this prerogative in a set of rules he had compiled.[70] For a monk such as Ryōgen who had built his career on the basis of the performance of ritual, such laxity must have eventually been too much to bear. Moreover, Buddhist orders have often been strongest when monastic discipline was enforced by their leaders. On the other hand, if the monks eliminated from the roles were primarily from factions that were angered over Ryōgen's increasing factionalism, the event can be interpreted as a sign of the deepening split among Tendai monks.

The *Daisōjōden* refers to an event that occurred ten days later. A man came and told the story of an old woman from the Ishitsukuri clan who had become ill the previous year and was lying on her deathbed. After praying to the Three Jewels one night she had a dream in which a monk appeared before her. When she asked who he was, the monk replied that he was Sannō, the guardian deity of Mount Hiei, and that if she made an offering to all the monks on Mount Hiei, she would recover from her illness. When the old woman complained that she could not afford to feed the three thousand monks on Mount Hiei, the deity replied that there were only two thousand monks on the mountain. She recovered and prepared to feed the monks. Sannō appeared to her once again and designated a day. When the old woman went to make her offering, it occurred on the day that Ryōgen reduced the number of monks on Mount Hiei to two thousand.[71]

The story as it is presented in the *Daisōjōden* and other sources is unconvincing as it stands. Ryōgen probably would not have eliminated one-fourth of the monks on Mount Hiei from the roles simply as an expedient so that an old woman could make an offering to the order. Hirabayashi has suggested that it may have been fabricated to demonstrate that Ryōgen had supernatural approval for his actions when he purged the order of one-fourth of its monks, an action that might well have contributed to the factionalism that beset the Tendai school in his later years if these monks had belonged to the Jimon.[72]

Although the sources unfortunately do not provide the evidence for a definitive interpretation, one possible explanation may lie in Ryōgen's efforts to define the administrative role of the *zasu*. Appointments as *zasu* usually involved the approval of the various temples and administrative divisions that the Tendai *zasu* oversaw. References to such approval several months following the appointment frequently appear in several sources.[73] Ryōgen's efforts to rebuild Mount Hiei and to support his own faction undoubtedly left many monks dissatisfied, particularly those of the Jimon faction. They might well have been hesitant to participate in certain monastic assemblies. Ryōgen's action can thus be seen as part of the efforts to control the various temples on Mount Hiei that had been endowed by a variety of sources and that were semiautonomous. His choice of rituals for the territorial deities of Mount Hiei would have been an appropriate venue to reassert his authority. In so doing, Ryōgen was continuing the efforts of many *zasu* to assert administrative control over a disparate collection of monks and institutions.

Conclusion

The rise of factionalism within the Tendai school must be contrasted with developments in other temples to place it into a context. During the Nara and early Heian periods, official temples such as the *kokubunji* were not as divided by factionalism as the Tendai school in the mid-

Heian period. Appointments as abbots were often awarded to monks of various schools, and terms of appointments were usually limited to a specific term, often four years. However, such systems also had negative effects. Appointments as abbots were given to older monks who were sometimes not as vigorous as younger monks might have been. During his limited terms, an abbot might spend his first year or two becoming accustomed to the job and its demands. By the time he had learned the job, he was preparing to leave it. *Kokubunji* also might change their doctrinal affiliation depending on the temple's leaders. For example, when Ennin's disciple Anne was appointed lecturer at the *kokubunji* in Dewa, the laymen and monks of the area all converted from Hossō to Tendai.[74] Finally, patrons were less likely to give substantial property to institutions they could not control. As a result, the *kokubunji* declined while other monasteries grew.[75]

At least three factors can be singled out to explain the growing factionalism of the tenth century. First, the patterns of appointments of abbots to temples began to change during the late ninth century. The rise of *goganji* dedicated to the protection of emperors and the nobles who benefited by their reign led to factionalism. The monks who founded such temples might specify that successive abbots come from their lineage. As factionalism intensified in the court, so did it become more pronounced among Buddhist monks. Second, the rise in popularity of Esoteric Buddhism meant that monks jealously guarded the right to perform certain rituals, teaching the secrets associated with the ritual only to certain followers. Third, the use of manors to finance temples necessarily entailed the rise of monks who specialized in either directly administering and protecting property or in arranging for these functions. Rights to manors had to be defended against intrusions from other temples, government authorities, and the failure of farmers to pay rents.

Ryōgen is sometimes blamed for the origins of monastic warriors.[76] In fact, fights between groups of monks from Kōfukuji and Tōdaiji occurred decades before the clashes between Jimon and Sanmon monks late in Ryōgen's life.[77] The battles between Sanmon and Jimon monks might have seemed particularly deplorable to many, however, because they occurred between members of the same school. Although Ryōgen certainly might have done more to ameliorate the factionalism in the Tendai school, factional tendencies probably were an inevitable result of the alliances that monks made to help finance Buddhist activities. The presence of similar tendencies in Hossō and Shingon monasteries indicates that such developments often accompanied the rise of powerful monasteries at this time.[78]

The stories of seemingly reclusive monks such as Zōga and Genshin indicate that some Buddhists were critical of the political nature of Ryōgen's activities. However, Buddhism had been an integral part of Japanese politics from its introduction to Japan, and the rise of warrior monks can be seen as another manifestation of the relationship between monks and politics.

12

Ryōgen and the Role of Nuns in Ninth- and Tenth-century Japan

Nuns figure in Ryōgen's biography primarily by their conspicuous absence. However, Ryōgen was interested in the salvation of women; he moved the location of the *shari-e* from Mount Hiei to Kyoto so that women could witness it. In addition, he periodically conducted elaborate performances in honor of his mother's birthday. Despite his mother's interest in Buddhism, Ryōgen never attempted to ordain her as a nun, nor did he recommend that the mothers of his disciples be ordained. In fact, he is mentioned only once or twice in connection with nuns, the most notable being the case of Princess Sonshi, who is discussed below. In this chapter, the relation between Ryōgen's interest in the welfare of women and his reluctance to ordain woman as nuns is investigated.

To understand Ryōgen's views, one needs to investigate the position of nuns during his time. Consequently, this chapter also is intended as a general description of nuns in the early and mid-Heian period, focusing on the complex ways in which the rules in the *Vinaya* affected women. If the manner of ordinations of women can be clarified, much about their status and practices can be elucidated. The discussion also covers a broad array of topics, including the role of women in society and why women were barred from Mount Hiei, but finally returns to Ryōgen in the conclusion. The chapter is divided into five parts. First, a typology of ordinations for nuns during this period is suggested to clarify what was meant by the term "nun." If the procedures and precepts conferred in ordinations are clearly understood, then the patterns of monastic discipline and the status of women in terms of traditional *Vinaya* hierarchies can be illuminated. Second, the decline of officially recognized nuns during the early and mid-Heian period is investigated. In the third part, some of the explanations for this decline are suggested. Fourth, a number of examples of the nuns from the Heian period are

examined to further refine the description of nuns during the early
Heian. Fifth, the motivations of women for becoming nuns, their
lifestyles, and their religious practices during the early and mid-Heian
period are examined.

Patterns of Ordination

The Vinaya *and Nuns*

The rules of the *Vinaya,* the primary source for Buddhist monastic discipline and procedures to be followed in governing Buddhist orders,
have traditionally served as a model for the behavior of Buddhist practitioners. Even when monastics did not follow many of its rules, the
Vinaya was often regarded as an ideal to which monastics might return.
The *Vinaya* also has provided the basic categories for a hierarchy of religious practitioners. However, when the role of the *Vinaya* in the lives
of Buddhist practitioners has been considered, it has usually been examined in terms of male practitioners. When nuns have been discussed
in terms of the *Vinaya,* they have sometimes been viewed as the female
equivalent of monks, performing many of the same religious practices
for the same goals as monks. Among the differences between monks
and nuns are the eight weighty rules (*gurudharma*) that subordinate
nuns to monks in certain ways, but even these rules left nuns with considerable autonomy.[1]

Historically, the relationship between women and the *Vinaya* has been
more problematic than has been recognized. While the *Vinaya* provided
hierarchies of practitioners and specified many of the basic patterns of
behavior for religious women, it also severely limited their options in
some cases. This was particularly true of areas where the ordination lineages of nuns had been cut off and could not be reestablished. In Sri
Lanka, Southeast Asia, and Tibet, women lost status and opportunities
to practice as a result of the *Vinaya* rules concerning ordination. This
situation occurred because valid ordinations for nuns were said to require two separate ceremonies, first in the order of nuns and then in
the order of monks. Each order was to have ten correctly ordained members attend the ceremony. Thus if no correctly ordained nuns existed,
additional nuns could not be ordained, and the ordination lineage
ended. Few countries were willing to invest the resources required to
bring ten nuns from a foreign country to reestablish an order of nuns.

In most of these locales, women worked out their own ways of being devout Buddhists that differed from the patterns specified in the *Vinaya*.

The situation in Japan was more complicated than most for several reasons. First, two texts served as primary sources for sets of rules and procedures for ordination: the *Ssu-fen lü* and the *Fan-wang ching*. These two texts provided women with several options in forming religious orders, determining the requirements for ordination, and deciding upon appropriate behavior and religious practice. Second, although the ordination lineages for nuns were cut off in Japan, they were eventually reestablished. During this process a variety of ordination procedures and styles of religious practice for women developed. In many cases, ordinations were only as significant as the recipients and their teachers wished them to be. Third, the intimate involvement of the court in Buddhist affairs had a major influence on the status of nuns and their practices. When the court valued adherence to the *Vinaya* as a model for monastic behavior and supported female monastics, an order of nuns flourished. When state interest in nuns waned, women were left to improvise their own modes of religious behavior and had difficulty defining their relation to the *Vinaya*.

Types of Ordinations

Ordinations can be classified in several different ways. The differences between initiations for male and female novices, initiations for probationary nuns, and full ordinations (*upasampadā*, J. *gusokukai*) for monks and nuns are specified in *Vinaya* texts. Although these distinctions were recognized and important in Japan, particularly for men, they were not always as relevant for women.

Ordinations can also be classified according to the text upon which they are based. In the Japanese case, Tendai ordinations relying on the *Fan-wang ching* and Nara ordinations based on the *Ssu-fen-lü* would exemplify this division. The use of the *Fan-wang ching* to ordain monks led to a variety of ambiguities. For example, as Saichō, the founder of the Tendai school, indicated, both laymen and women, as well as monks and nuns, could receive the same set of precepts. In addition, the lack of clear detail in the precepts led to a variety of interpretations and sometimes to the complete disregard of the precepts. Many of these issues became important in Tendai history.[2]

Any consideration of the ordinations of nuns must take the above distinctions seriously, but another set of criteria is particularly important in the Japanese case, the relationship of ordinations to the state. Three patterns of ordination can be identified when the authority for ordination is considered. In discussing these categories, I use examples from the Nara period (710–784) because the patterns were clearly delineated at that time.

The first type is officially sanctioned ordinations. Typically, monks or nuns ordained in this way were the inhabitants of the state-sponsored temples in Nara such as Tōdaiji and the official monasteries (*kokubunji*) and nunneries (*kokubun niji*, also known as Hokkeji or *Lotus* [*Sūtra*] nunneries) in the provinces. Officially ordained monks and nuns (*kansōni*) were recognized in terms of both court and *Vinaya*. Their ordinations were sanctioned and supervised by the state. Full ordinations could be performed only on a limited number of government-sanctioned ordination platforms (*kaidan*).[3] Government officials judged applications for ordination, supervised the examination of candidates, verified the identities of those ordained, and issued official documents (*dochō, kaichō*) attesting to the candidate's status as a novice or monk. Terms such as "novice" (*shami, shamini*), "monk" (*sō*), and "nun" (*ni*) were probably used with precision in such documents. The ritual procedures and the status conferred on those ordained during the Nara period closely followed the requirements set forth in the *Ssu-fen lü*.[4] The court-sponsored mission to China that invited Chien-chen to Japan is indicative of the close connection between the government and *Vinaya* in Japan.

A second type of ordination consists of those that were privately performed (*shido* or *jido*) by a group or individual without any government sanction. The use of the term "*do*" (initiation) in "*shido*" (private initiation) suggests that the government did not consider such monks or nuns to be fully ordained (*jugusokukai*).[5] In fact, such practitioners were often referred to as *shami* or *shamini* (male or female novice), even though they had not met the exact *Ssu-fen-lü* requirements for this status. In addition, because even candidates for official ordination often had been practicing several years before they were granted permission to become monks or nuns, private ordinations at times might be considered to be analogous to government-sanctioned initiations as novices. As a result, privately ordained male and female practitioners were sometimes called *shami* or *shamini*.[6]

Typical of this pattern were the many ordinations performed by Gyōki (670–749) using a set of bodhisattva precepts, probably those from the *Yü-chieh lun* (*T* 1579, Skt. *Yogācārabhūmi;* J. *Yugaron*).[7] The court discouraged this type of ordination, partly because the state lost tax revenue, but also because such groups were deemed to be potentially seditious. Privately initiated novices might explain karmic laws in ways that could be interpreted as critical of the government.[8] Although Gyōki and his followers were persecuted at times, they eventually won recognition from the state in 731. At least some of Gyōki's followers, both men and women, welcomed government recognition and became fully ordained officially sanctioned monks and nuns.[9]

A third pattern of ordination, similar to the second in that it too was not officially sanctioned, was the self-ordination (*jisei jukai*). It differed from the second type insofar as no organization or teacher was necessarily involved in the actual initiation or ordination. Rather, an individual might decide to simply shave his or her head and put on Buddhist robes. This decision might be taken out of genuine religious fervor, to secure a better living, or both. Not all self-ordinations were performed by simply shaving the head and putting on robes. Self-ordinations could also involve a stringent set of austerities before an image of the Buddha for a long time.[10] In such cases, the ordination was only completed when the practitioner received a supernatural sign from the Buddha. The government had little control over the privately ordained and self-ordained and did not even consider them monks or nuns. The established Buddhist orders usually discouraged such ordinations because they exercised little control over such practitioners.

The self-ordination tradition may have appealed to some Japanese because it could be easily combined with shamanistic traditions. The practitioner might claim that he could go on meditative journeys to Maitreya's Tuṣita heaven in a manner reminiscent of shamanistic journeys to the realm of the gods. Members of some groups during the Nara period used the term "*ji*" (compassion) in their names to indicate their relation to the bodhisattva Jishi (Maitreya).[11] After a self-ordination, a person might practice alone or become a part of a larger group.

Private Ordinations of "Nuns"

Women called nuns (*ni, ama*) appear in both secular and religious literature composed during the Heian period. Such references contributed to the view that an order of nuns had continued to exist without any serious disruption throughout the Heian period. In addition, ambiguities in language and documentation played an important part in contributing to the view that the order of nuns continued to exist. In recent times, to the best of my knowledge, the modern Japanese

scholar Ishida Mizumaro was the first person to suggest that the order
of nuns had ceased to exist during the Heian period in a seminal article in 1978.[12]

Ishida suggested that the women who are referred to as nuns (*ni* or
ama) in Heian-period texts were probably novices (*shamini*) when
viewed from the traditional categories of the *Vinaya*. Because the Japanese terms for female novice (*shamini;* Skt. *śrāmaṇerikā*), probationary
nun (*shikishamani;* Skt. *śikṣamāṇā*) and fully ordained nun (*bikuni;* Skt.
bhikṣuṇī) all contain the element "*ni*," the term "*ni*" could be and was
used in an ambiguous manner.[13] Equivocal usages of words for "nun"
are not limited to Japan. Similar ambiguities for the Tibetan terms for
"nun" (*ani, jomo,* and *gema*) have been reported from Tibetan areas.[14]
In Sri Lanka, the term "*upāsika*" (pious laywomen) embodies similar
ambiguities, being used to refer to a range of women from married
householders to celibate practitioners who stay in hermitages.[15]

How were "nuns" initiated or ordained during the early Heian period? Biographies of nuns often described them as "leaving home"
(*shukke*), an ambiguous term that could refer to their initiation as
novices, status as probationary nuns, or full ordination as nuns.[16] In contrast, fully ordained monks were often said to "ascend the ordination
platform and receive the precepts" (*tōdan jukai*), a description that
clearly indicated that they received full ordinations on an officially sanctioned ordination platform. In the case of nuns, when precepts were
mentioned, they were often referred to with ambiguous phrases such
as "she received the precepts (*jukai*)." The set of precepts or the contents of the precepts are rarely mentioned. Thus many of the categories
that applied to male practitioners such as the distinction between
novice or monk or knowledge of whether a person received a set of precepts from the *Vinaya* or the *Fan-wang ching* are very difficult to apply
when nuns are mentioned. In many cases, the precepts conferred were
probably bodhisattva precepts from the *Fan-wang ching* (or the *Yogācārabhūmi*, in a few cases) since these had more liberal provisions for
conferral than those from the *Ssu-fen-lü;* but in other cases, they could
also have been the five lay precepts or the ten precepts conferred on
novices.[17]

The two elements that are never mentioned in entries on nuns that
would have suggested that official ordinations continued are (1) ascending the ordination platform and (2) ordination within an established order of nuns. The names of preceptor or instructor nuns, years
of seniority in an order, or government documents concerning nuns

would have indicated court recognition or an established institutional structure. The absence of ordination platforms is made particularly evident by occasional efforts to establish such an institution for women. In the next section, the significance of these categorizations of ordinations is developed further in a discussion of the decline of officially recognized nuns.

The Ordination of Nuns
during the Late Nara and Early Heian Periods

Until recently few scholars commented on the decline of nuns. Instead, the order was assumed to have continued without interruption from the Nara through the Heian period until nuns once again became more visible during the Kamakura and Muromachi periods.[18] Several factors led scholars to make this assumption.

The history of early Japanese Buddhism indicates that nuns played an important role. The first Japanese to be ordained was a woman named Shima, who was the daughter of Shiba Tattō. From the age of eleven she was instructed by a Korean layman who had formerly been a monk. Several years later, in 588, she traveled to the Korean kingdom of Paekche with two female attendants to obtain a proper ordination, where she was given the religious name Zenshinni.[19] She returned in 590 at the age of seventeen or eighteen with her two disciples. The account in the *Nihon shoki* may indicate that the women initially became nuns because the Japanese felt that a woman should serve the Buddha, who was regarded as a foreign *kami*. She thus would have been expected to fulfill a role similar to that of the *miko* (female shrine attendant) at Shinto shrines.[20]

When the three women returned as nuns, they ordained other women. However, these ordinations were not valid according to a strict interpretation of the *Vinaya* because a nun had to be ordained twice, first in the order of nuns with at least ten nuns participating, and then in the order of nuns in front of at least ten monks. Moreover, when the three women were in Korea, they would not have been of sufficient age to be fully ordained according to the *Vinaya*. However, early Japanese Buddhists ignored such ritual niceties, and the order of nuns flourished. A survey of Buddhism ordered by the court in 624, when a governmental supervisory system for Buddhism was first established in Japan, indicated that there were forty-six Buddhist institutions, with 816 monks and 569 nuns.[21] Thus nuns made up a significant proportion of the clergy. One of the reasons for the large number of nuns might be that early Japanese monks probably had many occasions to meet women. Because many monks were installed in clan temples to perform ceremonies for the clan, they must have come into contact with women as they performed their ritual duties and thus influenced a number of their female followers. In addition, women had traditionally played important roles in religious ceremonies at shrines, a pattern that might have influenced Buddhism.

Nuns also played an important role in the movements around Gyōki (also known as Gyōgi), a monk who actively spread Buddhism among the masses, especially townspeople and low-level government officials. Even when such proselytization was prohibited, many people continued to support Gyōki. During the latter period of his preaching, women seemed to join the movement in large numbers, making up the majority of the movement in some locales.[22] Of the approximately forty-nine places of practice established by Gyōki, thirteen were for nuns (*niin*), indicating that women as well as men helped do the physical labor to construct many of Gyōki's projects. Twelve of these centers for nuns were near centers for male practitioners.[23] When restrictions on Gyōki's followers were lifted and men over sixty were permitted to be officially ordained, the same right was extended to women over fifty-five.

Gyōki is often associated with women in the legendary stories included in the *Nihon ryōiki*, a text compiled about seventy years after Gyōki's death. Unfortunately, details about the ordination procedures and practices of the women are not known. Perhaps they were attracted to Gyōki's groups because he directed his preaching specifically toward women. Women may also have been attracted to Gyōki's movement as a reaction against the rise in this period of Confucian attitudes that deprecated women.[24]

The seemingly high status of nuns in early Japan is also indicated by the existence of officially sponsored convents. When the *kokubunji* with twenty monks each were set up throughout Japan to protect the nation in 741, nunneries where the *Lotus Sūtra* would be chanted to vanquish wrongdoing were also established, probably because Empress Kōmyō had been so impressed by the manner in which Gyōki established institutions for nuns alongside those for monks. The *Lotus Sūtra* was probably chosen for the nunneries because of the famous passage from the Devadatta chapter in which the Nāga girl is transformed into a man and realizes Buddhahood.[25] Passages in historical texts indicate that the nunneries were not supported as lavishly as the monasteries. For example, provincial monasteries were to have twenty monks, but the nunneries, ten nuns. Monasteries were given ninety *chō* of land each, but the nunneries received only forty. Provincial monasteries were supposed to have seven-story pagodas, but no such provision was made for nunneries.[26] The Hokkeji nunneries seem to have had monks as administrators, a practice that continued at least into the ninth century.[27] Although historical records indicate that the nunneries were not treated very well, archeological investigations reveal that in a few locations—Shimotsuke, Mikawa, and Mino—the nunneries had large buildings and probably flourished for a time.[28]

Because the decline of official ordinations of nuns was not marked by any government proclamation or protest by nuns, many scholars assumed that the order simply continued to exist throughout Japanese history. Government edicts in works such as the *Engishiki* continued to be written as though officially ordained nuns were present. In most cases, however, such laws seem to have been citations or paraphrases of earlier edicts and do not necessarily imply that the people or institutions to which they referred actually existed. In other cases, the term "*sōni*" (monks and nuns) is replaced by the term "*sō*" (monks or monastics); however, because the term "*sō*" could be read as including both monks and nuns, the shift in emphasis was not immediately noticeable.[29] In other words, although official documents from the early Heian period, such as the *Engishiki,* often discuss the administrative procedures for monks and nuns in equal terms, actual examples of such equal treatment are virtually nonexistent. For example, early-Heian-period documents or records of nuns being promoted to the various monastic ranks do not exist; moreover, no documents (*iki*) commending them for their religious achievements have survived. Nuns were not named as the main participants in lectures such as the Yuima-e.

The most important development for Buddhist women during the late Nara and early Heian periods was the decline and virtual disappearance of official full ordinations as an option. This decline had at least three aspects: (1) the exclusion of nuns from court-sponsored rituals, (2) limits on court-sponsored initiations and ordinations for women, and (3) placing monks in charge of nunneries.

First, nuns were no longer included in the assemblies sponsored by the state. Ushiyama Yoshiyuki indicates that the last court assembly where monks and nuns sat together occurred in 727 when six hundred monks and three hundred nuns were ordered to chant the *Diamond Sūtra.*[30] Although nuns were sometimes allowed to participate in assemblies in the provinces at *kokubunji* after that time, limitations on their participation in assemblies at court had taken away one of the main reasons for government support of nuns. Occasionally nuns would participate in assemblies without monks, the most conspicuous case being in 773 when a total of 269 nuns and court attendants (*nyoju*) assembled in honor of the deceased female emperor Shōtoku (718–770; r. 749–758, 764–770).[31] Another noteworthy occasion when nuns served as lecturers in a monastic assembly occurred in 902 when lectures on the *Lotus Sūtra* and *Tsui-sheng-wang ching* (*Suvarṇaprabhāsa-sūtra*) were held for more than 150 nuns at the Danrinji, the nunnery established by Tachibana no Kachiko.[32]

Second, with one of the most important rationales for court support of nuns gone, the court began to limit its sponsorship of nuns' ordinations. Officially sanctioned ordinations had been performed in several ways during the Nara period. Large numbers of men and women were sometimes initiated when a noble was ill or on special occasions (*rinji dosha*) so that the karmic merit from the ceremony might be dedicated to the recovery of the ailing person or the good fortune of the emperor. Because these initiations were conducted under official sanction, the participants had no problems receiving full ordinations. A thousand women were initiated between 730 and 750, and almost twelve hundred between 790 and 810. But the number declined precipitously after that, with only twenty-five being initiated from 810 to 830. The last special initiation of women occurred in 828.[33]

Another procedure involved the naming of yearly ordinands, those people initiated in special services at the beginning of the new year in the palace or other designated place. The merit from the performance of the ceremony was dedicated to the emperor and the state. To be chosen a yearly ordinand, the candidate had to be able to pass certain tests, such as chanting scriptures, to ensure that the candidate could perform the rituals to protect the state at official temples such as the *kokubunji*. However, in 798, as part of the court's efforts to reform the Buddhist order, the test requirements changed and became more academic in nature. Candidates had to pass tests on doctrine. These new rules did not mention women.[34] The year before, perhaps in anticipation of the coming restrictions, so many women interested in Buddhism flocked to the Hokkeji in Yamato seeking ordination that the court warned them to desist.[35]

Subsequent regulations concerning yearly ordinands assigned them to specific schools or temples. Both the Tendai and Shingon schools

had barred women from their main temple complexes and consequently were not concerned with female yearly ordinands. Other yearly
ordinands were assigned to the imperially sponsored temples that
copied Mount Hiei's regulations sequestering monks.[36]

The third and last indication that officially sanctioned nuns were declining concerns the officials in charge of nunneries. Although the evidence concerning the sex of the heads of nunneries is fragmentary,
nunneries seem to have been led by nuns before 750. However, from
the middle of the eighth century onward, monks seem to have occupied the key administrative positions of *chin* (superintendent) and *bettō*
in nunneries. Once monks held these positions, central to the financial health of the nunneries and their relationship to the court, nuns
obviously lost an important component of their autonomy.[37]

The cessation of official ordinations of women seems to have been
a gradual process that occurred from the middle of the eighth century
to the ninth century. Rather than being marked by any noteworthy event
that was recorded in historical records, the decline of official ordinations of nuns is demonstrated by their almost complete absence in historical records and biographies. Moreover, when biographies of nuns
appear, they do not include the basic information that is characteristic
of biographies of officially ordained monks. Such data as the nun's temple, the name of a preceptor nun, the number of years of seniority she
had accumulated at key points of her career, and sectarian affiliation
are conspicuously absent.[38]

Factors in the Decline of Officially Ordained Nuns

In recent years, a number of explanations for changes in the status of
women during the Heian period have been advanced. Although none
of these conclusively clarifies the changes in status of nuns during this
period, many of them undoubtedly contributed to the situation. Below
several of these explanations are considered.

Societal Changes

Tracing and dating shifts in societal patterns that occurred centuries
in the past are difficult. In the case of Japan, interpretations are decisively affected by the limitations inherent in sources arising from such
factors as the social class, sex, and location of the people being discussed.
Social changes must often be inferred from chance remarks made in

official records or diaries. As a result, the chronology of changes affecting the status of women in Heian-period Japan is uncertain, making conclusions about how general changes in society affected the status of nuns difficult. Despite these problems, a general decline in the status of women and their loss of autonomy must be noted during this time. Among the changes were shifts from matrilocal to virilocal marriage, from clans in which women had rights comparable to men to clans controlled by a patriarch, and from rights of inheritance for women to limits on those rights. Japanese scholars have arrived at dates for these changes that range from the eighth century to the eleventh and twelfth centuries. For the purpose of this study, it is sufficient, without exploring the arguments for these dates in detail, to note that the earlier date would correspond to the decline in the status of nuns.[39] About the same time, the status of female shamans at certain court-sponsored shrines was also declining.[40]

Buddhist, Confucian, and Imported Views on Blood Pollution

During recent years, Japanese scholars have discussed whether concerns with blood pollution, Confucian doctrine, or Buddhist attitudes toward women might have played significant roles in the decline of the status of women during the Heian period. Because the order of nuns was autonomous and was roughly equal to the order of monks during much of the Nara period, its decline during the early Heian has been said to parallel the loss of autonomy of women in general.[41] Attempts to explain the decline of nuns in terms of religious ideologies must focus on which traditions became prominent or changed at the same time that the status of nuns declined. Simply listing statements advanced by a tradition that seems misogynist to the twentieth-century reader does not adequately explain the shifts. Because the evidence for Buddhist misogynist views has been documented elsewhere, this section focusses on Confucianism and blood pollution.

From the Kamakura period on, Buddhist and secular works mention the pollution of women from menstruation and childbirth in connection with their inferior status. Such "disabilities" were said to be evidence of the heavy karmic burden they bore. Women's pollution does not seem to have been an original part of Japanese culture. Menstruation was treated as a necessary aspect of women's ability to produce new life. Taboos connected to childbirth have little to do with blood pollution at first; rather, they reflect the dangers of bringing new life into being, and are closer to taboos connected with death. In both cases, a being is in transition from the realm of spirits to the world of humans.[42] Relating menstruation and childbirth to blood pollution seems to have been transmitted through a variety of traditions from China and Korea. Taoism and yin-yang thought were probably influential, as were Korean folk customs.[43] By the early Heian period, such claims of blood pollution had become widespread enough to have been quantified and incorporated in codes such as the *Engishiki*. However, any ritual pollution from menstruation or childbirth was only temporary and would be removed after a time. Although temporary pollution would not have been a sufficient reason for barring nuns from rituals, combined with ideological influences and social factors, such beliefs undoubtedly contributed to the decline of official nuns. By the late Heian period, ideas about pollution had been so ingrained in Japanese thought that they became a prime reason why women were said to be permanently inferior.

Much speculation by modern scholars has focused on whether Confucianism influenced the status of women in Heian-period Japan. Confucian teachings were known and studied in Japan from an early period and influenced the literate classes, including those interested in Buddhism. The Confucian classics were an important part of the university educational system that prepared men to serve in the court bureaucracy. Thus if a man could read Chinese texts, he presumably must have had some knowledge of Confucian traditions. For example, Kibi no Makibi (695–775), an influential scholar and politician of the late Nara period, equated the Confucian five constants with the Buddhist five lay precepts.[44] Similar statements equating the usefulness of Confucian and Buddhist teachings for governing the nation are found in the *Man'yōshū* and *Shoku Nihongi*.[45]

During the late Nara and early Heian periods, reports surfaced of a number of cases of sexual misbehavior between men and women at Buddhist institutions. Moreover, women were reported leaving their families to join Gyōki's groups of "nuns." As a result, several edicts placed restrictions on the free association between men and women at all monasteries, stating their objections in Confucian terms. As a result, Gyōki may have decided to establish nunneries and associate them with monasteries so that any criticisms of mixing of the sexes could be defused.[46]

Confucian views on women also contributed to the abandonment of appointments of women as emperors after the Buddhist monk Dōkyō came close to usurping power by winning the female emperor Shō-toku's favor. With the death of Emperor Shōtoku and the resulting hesitation to install a woman as emperor, nuns no longer received the financial and ideological backing they had enjoyed earlier under such influential women as Empress Kōmyō. However, such evidence does not prove conclusively that Confucianism played a major role in the decline of nuns. During the time when these events occurred, nuns still were treated reasonably well in Japan, suggesting that Confucian statements that women were inferior might not have decisively influenced Japanese attitudes toward nuns. In addition, Confucian influence declined around the midninth century, when the court no longer sponsored missions to China and the university system and civil service examinations no longer offered access to those not of the highest noble classes.[47] Thus, although the coincidence of these events and the decline of nuns is suggestive, the evidence is still not sufficient to charge Confucianism with the main responsibility for the decline of nuns.

Another approach to identifying Confucian influences on nuns has been to trace certain Confucian terms and concepts through Japanese history. Confucian teachings concerning women have been summarized as "the three subordinations" (*sanjū*), a term found in such early texts as the *I-li*, one of the thirteen Confucian classics: namely, women were subordinate to their fathers when children, to their husbands when married, and to their sons when old. The Confucian tradition also stressed the importance of chastity and fidelity on the part of women. Even after a women's husband had died, she was expected to remain faithful to him and not remarry.[48]

During the Kamakura period, the Confucian "three subordinations" were often coupled with the Buddhist term "five obstacles" (*goshō*). The five obstacles for women stipulate that they cannot reincarnate as Brahmā, Indra, Māra, a world-ruling king, or a Buddha. The association of these two terms has sometimes been used as evidence that Confucianism played an important role in the decline of women in Japanese Buddhism. However, the three subordinations and five obstacles are not found in close association during the Nara and early Heian period. Indeed, the phrase "three subordinations" was rarely found in Japanese literature during the Nara and early Heian periods whereas the phrase "five obstacles" was more common.[49] Such evidence suggests that misogynist statements in Buddhist literature may have been important in the weakening influence of officially recognized nuns.

A more convincing attempt to link Confucianism with the decline of nuns has been the examination of Confucian attitudes against the remarriage of widows. Forty-six examples of chaste widows are found the *Ruijū kokushi;* approximately half of these were taken from the *Sandai jitsuroku* (Actual records of three reigns). In four cases, with dates ranging from 865 to 873, widows found consolation through Buddhist devotions, providing evidence that a combination of Confucian and Buddhist attitudes influenced some women.[50] Widows "unflinchingly guarded their chastity, made images, copied scriptures, and worshipped day and night." One woman, "after her husband's death, built a hut at his graveside, and placed her faith in the Buddha's teachings." Another "built a hut at the side of her husband's grave, became a nun, observed the precepts, and practiced austerities." Thus, becoming a nun proved to be a way for a widow to remain chaste and faithful to the memory of her husband. Pure Land teachings enabled women to practice with the goal of ensuring their own salvation as well as that of their deceased husbands. With time, the emphasis on Confucian virtues within Buddhism became stronger. In the *Ōjōden,* Confucian virtues such as chastity are typical of those women reborn into the Pure Land, but are not required of men.[51] Thus Confucianism probably influenced a shift in the role of nuns from an autonomous order that performed rituals for the state to a possible vocation for widows.

Confucian views on the proper role of women, chastity, and widow remarriage certainly influenced changes in the roles of both women and nuns, but the role of Confucian teachings should not be overemphasized. Because Confucianism did not become widespread in Japan until the eleventh and twelfth centuries, it alone does not provide a satisfactory explanation for changes throughout society in the relationship between women and Buddhism.[52]

Buddhism had its own misogynist attitudes, some adopted from Indian and Chinese society, as well as those that emerged from attempts to persuade monks of the value of celibacy. Although Confucian attitudes would eventually combine with Buddhism to produce a potent argument for the inferiority of women, the evidence for assigning the major responsibility for the decline of nuns during the late Nara to Confucianism or to imported ideas of pollution is fragmentary. Although some sources are suggestive, how well they actually reflected the social situation is problematic. At times, arguments that suggest that Confucianism played a major role in the decline of nuns appear to absolve Buddhism of responsibility, even though Buddhism had a misogynist tradition strong enough to play a major role when combined with other sources.[53] The decline of nuns is better assigned to a complex of traditions.

Chien-chen and Ordination Lineages

During the first half of the eighth century, Japanese monks became concerned about the authenticity of their ordinations. The court, viewing their concerns as a possible means of exerting its control over monks and nuns by supervising their ordinations, dispatched two Japanese monks, Eiei and Fushō, to China to persuade qualified Chinese monks to come to Japan to perform ordinations. When Chien-chen and his followers arrived in Japan in 754, ordinations that strictly followed the *Vinaya* could be performed at last in Japan. After a series of discussions, it was decided that Japanese monks should all be reordained.[54]

However, Chien-chen's arrival posed a serious problem for nuns in Japan. Even if the order of nuns in Japan had been recognized as performing valid ordinations at one time, discrediting the authority of the order of monks would have led to the conclusion that ordinations for nuns also would have to be reestablished. Moreover, the attention Chien-chen and his ordinations received from the court inevitably would have led to questions about ordinations for nuns. Because only three nuns accompanied Chien-chen, orthodox ordinations of nuns that had to be presided over by ten qualified nuns could not be performed.[55] An ordination manual by Chien-chen's disciple Fa-chin (709–778) listed chapters on ordinations and precepts for nuns, but these chapters are not extant; they either were never composed or were lost.[56] Even if they were composed, Fa-chin undoubtedly followed the *Ssu-fen-lü*, which required at least ten nuns for the ordination. Although the nuns could presumably have continued to use the ordination system they followed before Chien-chen's arrival, the attention lavished on Chien-chen when he first arrived and the importance placed on his ordinations by the court would have continued to call the validity of the nuns' ordinations into doubt.

Little evidence exists that directly supports the negative implications for nuns of Chien-chen's arrival in Japan. In fact, only fragmentary records of the activities of nuns of this period survive, but some of those records suggest that a few of the nuns were scholarly, borrowing and copying works. Among the texts mentioned in these documents are the *Ssu-fen lü* and the *Hua-yen ching*, indicating that the nuns were interested in problems of monastic discipline and participated in the rise of the Kegon tradition in Japan about the time of the dedication of the Daibutsu in Nara.[57] In addition, no private or official statements lamenting the interruption of the nuns' ordination lineage have surfaced. This lack may not be so surprising, however, because even the argument concerning whether all monks should be reordained on the ordination platform at Tōdaiji is found only in one or two sources. Once the monks had been reordained, the issue ceased to be important and was not included in histories. However, the differences between the validity of ordination lineages for monks and for nuns must have been apparent to anyone who thought seriously about such subjects.

A mission could have been mounted to either send Japanese nuns to China or Korea for a full ordination or bring foreign nuns to Japan. However, even bringing ten Chinese monks such as Chien-chen and his followers had been a major enterprise requiring many years.[58] The possibilities of such a mission's success would have been small indeed. However, hopes for such a mission may have been behind the lavish support, discussed below, that Tachibana no Kachiko gave to monks who traveled to China about 840.

Empress Kōmyō and the Patronage of Nuns

If Chien-chen's arrival in Japan suggested why a full-fledged order of nuns could not be readily established in Japan, the death of Empress Kōmyō hastened the decline. Kōmyō had been exposed to Buddhist teachings as a young girl in the Fujiwara family. Once she became the empress (*kōgō*) as the chief consort of Emperor Shōmu, she used her position to carry out a variety of Buddhist activities. Among them was the establishment of medical facilities, a hall to benefit the impoverished, the copying of the Buddhist canon, and the establishment of the *kokubunji* system. A major influence on her was the Buddhist monk Genbō, a scholar-monk who had traveled to China. Through Genbō, Kōmyō and others at court learned about the national system of temples established during the Sui dynasty in China. She may also have heard about Empress Wu of the T'ang and the system of temples established to support her claim to the throne.

According to the *Shoku Nihongi* and *Nihon kiryaku*, Kōmyō was a moving force behind the construction of the *kokubunji*. The very idea of *kokubunji* nunneries that were to be paired with monasteries might well have come from Kōmyō. She gave freely of her wealth to establish the *kokubunji* system, and the Hokkeji nunnery in Yamato was established at the palace she had inherited from her father, Fujiwara no Fuhitō. The monk Kyōshun was appointed as abbot of the Hokkeji at her suggestion. In addition, the decision to tie the nunneries to the *Lotus Sūtra* also may have reflected her views.[59]

Kōmyō's death must have affected a number of the institutions established at her insistence. The medical facilities, for example, declined after her death. Although *kokubunji* nunneries continued to exist in many locales, by the early Heian period they had begun to disappear, either falling into ruin or being converted to monasteries. Thus Kōmyō played a key role in the establishment and maintenance of an order of officially ordained nuns. With her death, the *kokubunji* nunneries lost their most influential patron.

Because sources are insufficient, the details of Kōmyō's involvement with the order of nuns is unclear. In particular, if Chien-chen had an adverse affect on the order of nuns, then we must wonder how Empress Kōmyō reacted. Although she seems to have been a supporter of Chien-chen, her support of the Hokkeji may have temporarily ameliorated the effects of questions raised about the ordinations of nuns.

If the above scenario is correct, then the relationship between officially ordained and privately ordained nuns may well be questioned. Because the *Vinaya* is the normative source for monastic ordinations, it is the source for our standard image of nuns. However, officially ordained nuns may not have been very common in early Japan; they may have been a phenomenon that occurred primarily when a powerful patron like Kōmyō was present.[60] The privately ordained nuns discussed below may have been much closer to the norm during both the Nara and Heian periods. If this is the case, then the decline of officially recognized nuns during the Nara period might not have led to very many protests because nuns' ordinations were merely returning to a much more common format.

The Exclusion of Women from Buddhist Sites

A major factor in the decline of nuns was the increasing incidence of enforced seclusion for men beginning their monastic careers. Saichō had begun this practice with his proposal that young Tendai monks spend at least twelve years on Mount Hiei without leaving its confines. To help protect the men from sexual temptation, women were barred from Mount Hiei.[61] The system spread rapidly during the early Heian period and was adopted at a number of imperially sponsored temples.[62] Moreover, the major temples within the Shingon tradition such as Kongōbuji also adopted the practice. Eventually, even some of the temples that did not require their monks to remain in seclusion adopted the practice of barring women from their confines. Among them was Tōdaiji, where women were barred from the hall with the giant image of the Buddha.[63] It is not clear whether women were also barred from the ordination platform at Tōdaiji and the two ordination platforms associated with it. However, no evidence exists that women were ordained on these ordination platforms during the Heian period.[64]

According to traditional accounts, barring women from Buddhist sites began in the early Heian period.[65] However, these restrictions may not have been particularly misogynist measures in the context of religious culture of that period. According to the *Sōniryō* (Regulations for monks and nuns), men were not to spend the night at nunneries and women were not to spend the night at monasteries. This pattern was adopted at a number of monasteries during the early Heian period, including some of those that required monks to be sequestered. For example, Zenrinji, founded by Kūkai's disciple Shinshō (797–873), required its monks to be sequestered for six years, but permitted women to visit as long as they did not stay overnight.[66] Other temples had boundaries that most monks were not allowed to cross. At some, even the ruler of the country could not enter. Thus the restrictions on women at Mount Hiei and Mount Kōya were only one type of attempt to ensure the purity of monks.[67] In fact, the exclusion of women from certain areas was so unremarkable that no rationale or story supporting the exclusion of women from such sites was even formulated for several centuries.[68] Thus, at first, women were excluded from sites such as Mount Hiei and Mount Kōya that were devoted to rituals protecting the state; if monks remained celibate and therefore pure when performing these rituals, the rituals might be more effective. Although the original intent of these restrictions might not have been to exclude women from Buddhist learning, this practice severely limited women's ability to study and practice with monks at the temples. The restrictions would have profoundly affected women who wished to become officially recognized nuns when the requirements for appointment as yearly ordinands were made more academic and would have contributed to the decline of officially ordained nuns.

The prohibitions on women were eventually justified with traditional Buddhist arguments warning that women were temptations, that they were impure, unable to attain the five higher statuses as gods or buddhas, and subject to heavy karmic burdens. Some of these rationales were similar to those used to limit attendance at palace rituals during the Nara and early-Heian periods. However, from the mid- to late-Heian, such statements increased. They cannot all be read merely as misogynist arguments, however; they usually were accompanied by promises of salvation that applied even to those who suffered from adverse circumstances—such as being born as women. For example, sometimes such statements were found in the context of extolling a teaching's power to save even those with heavy karmic burdens.[69]

By the eleventh century, concepts of pollution and purity came to play a key role in the maintenance of such prohibitions. Mountain *kami* were said to be female and jealous of any other females in their domains. Medieval legends about women who tried to climb the mountain and were physically stopped by the mountain itself suggest that women may have been prohibited from climbing the mountains as ritually polluting because of their menstrual cycles.[70] However, much more than blood pollution was involved in prohibiting women from these sites; even young girls, women past menopause, and women not currently menstruating were also prohibited from the mountain. Taboos on blood had been combined with Buddhist statements about women's inferior nature to strengthen the ban on women; as a result, by the late Heian period women were banned from an increasing number of major monasteries in Japan.

These bans did not completely exclude women from all major Buddhist activities. Ryōgen moved certain ceremonies, such as the *shari-e*, from Mount Hiei to Yoshida in Kyoto so that women could participate.[71] Women were allowed to have graves in the sacred precincts of certain monasteries that they had been unable to enter during their lifetimes. But the overall effect of these limitations was to force women and nuns to practice Buddhism in ways that differed from those practiced by men at the major monasteries.

Ryōgen had been concerned about the welfare of his mother and other women, but he nevertheless had not allowed them on Mount Hiei. His biography takes the prohibition for granted, never offering any rationale for it. A hundred fifty years after Ryōgen's time, the prohibition still was in force on Mount Hiei. In 1150, "a nun secretly climbed to the Tendai peaks [on Mount Hiei] to stay at Mudōji temple. The monks of that temple were greatly surprised and chased her away. The monks thought that this was bizarre."[72] The statement that the monks thought she was bizarre may reflect the establishment of a more coherent ideology concerning purity and pollution that justified the prohibition. By the sixteenth century, however, many women, usually the mistresses of monks, were on Mount Hiei, but the date and the extent to which the prohibition on women was ignored is not clear.[73] Mount Hiei was finally officially opened to women in 1872, when Westerners came to Japan.

In conclusion, social and ideological factors combined to deprive nuns of much their status as autonomous court-recognized agents during the eighth and ninth centuries. If officially recognized nuns no longer existed, what sort of women were called "nuns"? In the next section, several cases of individual nuns and their ordinations are considered to further refine the analysis.

Examples of Nuns

Several examples of ordinations of nuns found in secular literature reveal the ambiguity of terms such as "*ama*" and "*ni*" during the mid-Heian period. According to the *Eiga monogatari*, Fujiwara no Teishi (976 or 977–1001), junior consort of Emperor Ichijō, became despondent when her brothers were exiled over an attempted assassination of the abdicated emperor Kazan. In 996, "as the carriages [with her brothers] moved away, the Empress (*chūgū*) cut off her hair with a pair of scissors and became a nun (*ama*)."[74] Teishi continued to frequent the palace, probably dressed as a nun. Eventually she resumed relations with Emperor Ichijō, who still loved her, and gave birth to a son. Her rank was raised to *kōgō* (a higher rank of empress) in 1000. She died the following year giving birth to a daughter.[75] Most nuns, however, seem to have remained chaste although they often resided in the same homes they had stayed in as laywomen.[76]

The pattern of cutting one's own hair (or a lock of it) and becoming a "nun" is common in the literature of this period.[77] However, the actual conferral of the precepts is rarely mentioned. In terms of the typology of ordinations mentioned earlier, Teishi's action was a self-ordination. Such ordinations could sometimes by completed by a special arrangement with a particular Buddhist teacher as the following story of Princess Sonshi demonstrates. In all cases that I have found, the teacher was a monk, never a nun, suggesting the absence of independent orders of nuns during this period.

Ryōgen and Sonshi

Only two nuns are mentioned in connection with Ryōgen. The first is the mother of his disciple Myōgō, a woman Ryōgen refers to as an "old nun" in his will when he gives her a house in Nōka. Nothing is known of this woman; however, she apparently was not part of any order inasmuch as she was dependent on the Tendai order for her dwelling.[78]

The second nun is Sonshi, the second daughter of Emperor Reizei. Because Ryōgen had been the guardian monk of Emperor Reizei and had performed ceremonies to protect Reizei from his bouts of mental instability, Ryōgen may have felt protective toward Reizei's offspring. Sonshi's mother was Fujiwara no Kaishi (945–975), the daughter of Koremasa (924–972). When Reizei was named emperor, Sonshi was installed as priestess (*saiin*) of the Kamo Shrine even though she was only two years old. She continued to serve until 975, when she was ten. In 980, when Sonshi was about fifteen, she was installed as a wife of an uncle, Emperor En'yū, who had succeeded her father on the throne. With such illustrious relatives, she might have had a fulfilling life at court, but she seems to have been ill fated. Many called her "the fire princess" because a fire broke out soon after she arrived at court. Moreover, she did not win the emperor's favor. Two years later, in the ninth month of 982, she cut the hair on her brow and became a nun. Several explanations were offered for her decision to become a nun. According to some her decision resulted from a long-held desire, perhaps due in part to religious aspirations she developed during her service at the Kamo Shrine. But other sources attribute the decision to an illness (*jake*), which might have been either physical or mental. Because her father, Emperor Reizei, suffered from mental illness, Sonshi might well have been plagued by some inherited form of derangement.[79]

Sonshi's story is interesting for several reasons. It illustrates how a woman who was disturbed by various events might ordain herself by either cutting her own hair or having it cut. Sonshi did not stop at that stage, a step that was roughly equivalent to becoming a novice, however; two years later, she was ordained by Ryōgen. Sonshi's story thus shows a hierarchy of initiations. However, the difference between the two steps is not completely clear: they may represent initiations as a female novice and then as a full-fledged nun or perhaps as a self-ordained novice and then as a novice recognized by an eminent monk.

Ryōgen's role in the full ordination is suggestive of the same concern for the salvation of women that he displayed in the elaborate Buddhist services he had performed for his mother and by moving the *shari-e* so women could witness it. Despite Ryōgen's obvious concern for women, Sonshi is one of only two nuns ever mentioned in connection with this eminent monk. Perhaps he felt compelled to ordain her because of connections with some of his most powerful patrons. The modern scholar may even wonder whether Ryōgen might have broken precedents for a head of the Tendai order by ordaining Sonshi. Unfortunately, the story is not so clear-cut. The source for Ryōgen's ordination of Sonshi is a prayer titled Vows (Ganmon) written by Yoshishige no Yasutane (931–1002), which places the date of the ordination on "the nineteenth of the last month."[80] If the passage is interpreted as referring to the month before Sonshi's death on 5-2-985, then Yoshishige would be placing the ordination two months after Ryōgen's death. No definitive explanation has been proposed for this discrepancy. Perhaps it is merely the result of a copyist's error.

Ryōgen's deep concern for his own mother and the mothers of his disciples even as he remained uninterested in ordaining nuns became increasingly typical of many high-ranking monks during the Heian period. Indian Buddhist texts had extolled the nurturing qualities of mothers as well as cited the suffering of childbirth as evidence of the inferiority of women.[81] From the mid- and late-Heian periods, Japanese monks had extolled motherhood. Their attitude fit in well with changes in Japanese society as women were praised for producing heirs for lineages, but not for acting as autonomous individuals.[82]

Another Tendai monk, Senkan, may have taken a different approach to nuns and been more open to serving as an adviser and preceptor for nuns. Senkan is known to have had a number of noble women as his disciples. In 967, two months after Emperor Murakami's death, he served as the teacher in the ordination of the late emperor's imperial consort, Princess (*nyōō*) Shōshi, and junior consort (*kōi*), Fujiwara no Yūhime. He was also the teacher of Middle Counselor Fujiwara no Atsutada's (d. 943) oldest daughter.[83] Some of these women may have been drawn to seek teachings from reclusive monks because of their disillusionment with court politics. These patrons must have been valuable to monks such as Senkan who had decided to withdraw from mainstream political institutions but still needed to support their own monasteries.

The descriptions of these ordinations do not specify what precepts were conferred. Because Ryōgen and Senkan were Tendai monks, they might have been expected to confer some or all of the precepts from the *Fan-wang ching;* however, they might have conferred the ten good precepts, the ten precepts for novices, or even the five lay precepts. If the precepts conferred were from the *Fan-wang ching,* it is not clear how ordinations for a pious laywoman, a novice, and a full nun would have been differentiated. In the case of monks, such differentiations depended on whether the candidate had ascended the ordination platform. Because such a possibility was not open to women, most "nuns" would probably have been considered novices by contemporary monks. In *Genji monogatari,* in two of the few passages where the set of precepts conferred on a woman becoming a nun is mentioned, the five precepts (*gokai*) are conferred upon lay believers.[84] Although in the latter passage, the woman receiving the five precepts wishes for a more impressive set, the ordination seems sufficient to allow her to lead some type of quasi-monastic status. In both of these ordinations, the woman receiving the precepts is ill, again demonstrating the common pattern of receiving ordinations at times of adversity.

Tachibana no Kachiko and Princess Seishi

The two most prominent female Buddhist devotees during the early Heian are several empresses associated with the Tachibana clan. Perhaps because they were not from the politically dominant Fujiwara clan, they exhibited different forms of religious behavior than many other noble women of their era.[85] They are particularly important in this study because they made the only recorded attempts to establish nunneries during the early- and mid-Heian periods. As members of the imperial family, they were supported in ways that ordinary Buddhist laywomen would not have been, and thus they cannot be considered typical of female devotees. If women of this stature were not full-fledged nuns, it would suggest that women without imperial support certainly were not considered fully ordained "nuns" in the strict sense of the word.

The first of these women was Tachibana no Kachiko (786–850), Emperor Saga's empress. According to her obituary (*hōden*), Kachiko's devotion to Buddhism was evident in both her private and public activities.[86] When she was young, a nun named Zen'un undergoing austerities at the Hokkeji nunnery predicted that Kachiko would be the mother of both an emperor and an empress. Later, when the prediction proved to be true, Kachiko went to find the nun, but discovered that Zen'un had already died.[87] Kachiko's records of her dreams include Buddhist elements. For example, five or six days before she was named empress, Kachiko had dreamed of herself wearing Buddhist necklace and ornaments (*butsu yōraku*).

Kachiko sent a Japanese monk, Egaku, to China with pennants and monastic robes she personally had made.[88] There Egaku was to present them to several meditating sages (*jōshōsha*) and Mañjuśrī, the bodhisattva who embodied wisdom, on Mount Wu-t'ai. In fact, Egaku presented the robes to Chi-an, a prominent exponent of Southern school Ch'an Buddhism, and invited him to propagate Ch'an in Japan. Chi-an suggested that his disciple I-k'ung would be appropriate for the mission.[89] As a result, I-k'ung (n.d.) traveled back to Japan in 847 with Egaku and Ensai's disciple Ninkō. I-k'ung resided at the Western Chapel at Tōji Temple after his arrival in Japan. He is considered the first representative of Southern school Ch'an in Japan. He subsequently returned to China; nothing is known of his later life.

Kachiko ordered the construction of the Danrinji for I-k'ung. This temple, near Emperor Saga's country palace Saganoin just to the west of Kyoto, was a large monastic complex with twelve chapels (*in*). With the help of her son Emperor Ninmyō, the tax revenues of five hundred households were assigned to the Danrinji. The Danrinji was also to be used for nuns who observed the precepts (*bikuni jiritsusha*).[90]

When Kachiko's son, Emperor Ninmyō, sickened, she "cut her hair and became a nun," but Ninmyō died anyway, and Kachiko followed him within two months. Near the end of her life, Kachiko lived in one of the buildings at Danrinji where she practiced meditation under I-k'ung. Kachiko's ordination was typical of that of many men and women during the early-Heian period. In many cases, women were ordained upon the death of a male (rarely a female) loved one such as father, husband, or son. For such women, the economic and political repercussions of the death of important male figures may have contributed to their decision to withdraw from secular society. In contrast, for men, the death of a beloved woman rarely served as the immediate cause for ordination. The other common pattern is an ordination near the end of one's life, often when one was on one's deathbed. Because the object of such ordinations was to obtain a better rebirth rather than to enter a religious order as a nun, such ordinations should probably be considered lay sacraments.[91]

Kachiko's death only two months after her ordination suggests that she might fit both of these patterns. However, because the entry concerning her ordination states that she became a *bhikṣuṇī* (fully ordained nun) and because she lived at Danrinji for a time, she does seem to have intended to live a cloistered life.[92]

The Danrinji continued to function until it was destroyed by fire in 928. Several centuries later, in 1321, a Zen nunnery named Danrinji was established on the site.[93]

Kachiko's daughter, Seishi (also known as Empress Junna, 809–879), was the wife of Emperor Junna (786–840; r. 823–833) and the eldest daughter of Emperor Saga. When Emperor Junna abdicated in 833, he retired to his town palace, the Junnain (near Saiin, Junnain-chō, Ukyō-ku, Kyoto), where he died in 840. Two dates are found in sources for Seishi's decision to become a nun, 840 and 842. Although the reason behind her decision to become a nun is not explicitly stated in either source, both correspond to major events in her life. If the date 840 found in the *Sandai jitsuroku* is accepted, she probably became a nun (*ama*) because of the death of her husband.[94] However, if the date 842 found in the *Shoku Nihon kōki* (Later records of Japan continued) is accepted, "cutting her hair and entering the path" (*nyūdō*) can be associated with the loss of the position of crown prince by her son, Tsunesada (825–884), who had been designated crown prince in 833.[95] In fact, Seishi may have been heavily involved in the losing side of a plot known as the Jōwa disturbance (*Jōwa no hen*) to maintain her son's position. When her side lost, both she and her son were forced to withdraw from court life; a conventional response to such disgrace was embarking upon a religious life.[96] Although no decisive argument for either date has been advanced, the 840 date may well have been a fabrication by imperial historians to comply with Buddhist and Confucian views that a woman might guard her chastity on the death of her husband by becoming a nun. Such a view would have been more acceptable to court historians than portraying her as a politically active woman.[97]

Seishi continued to live in the Junnain for the next several decades. When her son Tsunesada lost his position as crown prince in 842, he went to live with his mother at the Junnain. He received the precepts as a novice in 848, and his full ordination in 860. During this time he followed the precepts and was chaste. The clear descriptions of Tsunesada's precepts contrast with the vaguer descriptions for the precepts received by most women. Another crown prince who had lost his position and became a monk was Shinnyo (799–865?), who was ordered to train and confer the two advanced Esoteric initiations (*ryōbu daihō*) on Tsunesada.[98]

Tsunesada's presence at the Junnain "nunnery" suggests that it was not a nunnery in the sense of the word used in discussing the *kokubun niji*, that is, an institution where monks could not live that was dedicated to the religious practices of nuns. Rather, the Junnain was used by members of its chief patron's retinue for their religious practices. Hence, it was a private institution rather than a public one like the *kokubun niji*. For unknown reasons, the Junnain does not seem to have been officially recognized as a religious institution until 864.[99]

Among Seishi's religious activities was the care of abandoned children and orphans found in the capital. Infants were supplied with wet nurses when necessary. Because Seishi devoted two-fifths of the income from her landholdings to this project, the care of the children probably was continued after they were weaned. Child care and the nursing of sick religious figures might well have occupied much of the time of the nuns who followed Seishi.[100] Seishi also sponsored large religious meetings. Among the most noteworthy were five days of lectures on the *Lotus Sūtra* held behind the Junnain in 863. The lectures were accompanied by meals for almost thirty thousand people. Emperor Seiwa (850–880; r. 858–876) and his mother supplied a large amount of food and money to make the observance possible.[101]

The Junnain burned in 874, and Seishi and her retinue were forced to leave it.[102] Although it was rebuilt, it apparently was not suitable for the empress. As a result, in 876, Seishi asked that the Saganoin, the country palace of her father Emperor Saga, be designated a temple to be called Daikakuji. The temple was to be dedicated to the repose of Emperors Saga and Junna, her father and husband. Because the Saganoin had fallen into disrepair, she wished to have it repaired and publicly recognized as a temple so that woodsmen and herd boys would not mistakenly violate its precincts.

Seishi probably hoped to spend the rest of her life at Daikakuji, turning it into another nunnery.[103] However, when her son Tsunesada became active in supporting it, granting it jurisdiction over a large number of manors and having fourteen officially recognized monks (*jōgakusō*) installed at it, the former palace clearly was destined to become a monastery. Tsunesada also had scriptures copied and six images of Amida carved for the temple. The temple's monks were to have many of the special privileges given to monks of other favored temples such as the right to attend the Yuima-e and other major monastic assemblies.[104] Finally, in 881, two years after Seishi's death, Tsunesada asked that the Danrinji and Junnain, the nunneries established by his grand-mother and mother, as well as the tumuli for Saga, Kachiko, and Seishi be placed under the jurisdiction of the Daikakuji monastery adminis-trator, a man from the high nobility (*kugyō bettō*). In his petition, Tsune-sada noted that Seishi had willed that the Junnain was to serve as a nunnery for the nuns who had served her during her lifetime and for nuns in the capital who could not support themselves.[105] Although Tsunesada probably intended to carry out his mother's will, placing the Junnain under the Daikakuji's administrator indicated the virtual impossibility of establishing an autonomous nunnery during the early Heian period. Seishi was also responsible for the establishment of a hospital near Daikakuji that was dedicated to the care of sick monks and nuns.

Another View of Ordinations and Institutions

At the beginning of this chapter, a typology of ordinations based on examples from the Nara period was suggested. Now, on the basis of examples such as Seishi, that typology can be refined further, partic-ularly in relation to the development of a Tendai ordination tradition. Much remains unclear about the ordinations and status of women such as Seishi and her nuns. Seishi's decision to become a nun in 840 is recorded as "cutting her hair and becoming a nun" (*ama*) and as "cut-ting her hair and entering the path" (that is, becoming a householder nun or *nyūdō*), without any mention of a formal ordination or of a preceptor.[106]

Tendai attitudes toward the precepts might have led to a new version of nuns' ordinations because the requirements for bodhisattva ordina-tions were much less strict than for *Ssu-fen-lü* ordinations. Sections of the *Fan-wang ching* and *Ying-lo ching*,[107] the two most authoritative scrip-tures for the Tendai bodhisattva precepts, might have allowed an order of nuns to be established by using self-ordinations or by having monks ordain the first nuns. After that, nuns could either have ordained other nuns or continued to be ordained by monks. Although Saichō had cited some of these provisions in his writings, successors such as Ennin and Enchin found it necessary to tighten the rules for ordination so that the order could be strictly managed, often adopting many of the stip-ulations found in the *Ssu-fen-lü*.[108] In addition, the court continued to require that all ordinations be performed on officially recognized plat-forms. As a result, if ordinations conferred upon women were not held on such platforms, the recipients of the ordination would not be officially recognized as full-fledged nuns.[109] They might have qualified as novices, however, because initiation ceremonies historically had been held at a variety of locations, including within the court itself as when yearly ordinands were initiated.

Seishi was concerned with ordinations, but no record exists of an ordination conferring the status of a full-fledged nun on her or her followers. Twenty years after she first became a "nun," Ennin conferred the full bodhisattva precepts (*bosatsu daikai*) on the empress in 860, giving her the religious name Ryōso; but Ennin's biography mentions that more than 150 people received the bodhisattva precepts at the same time. The ordination was followed by the conferral of the Esoteric *sanmaya* precepts and consecrations on more than 270 people and the performance of the first bodhisattva fortnightly assembly.[110] All of the precepts that a person had been ordained with were to be recited each fortnight by the members of the order to ensure that the precepts had been properly followed. Thus performance of the fortnightly assembly was an important ritual in assuring that the precepts conferred in an ordination actually were intended as guides for conduct. Without such fortnightly assemblies, the precepts easily could be forgotten. However, in the case of Seishi, the fortnightly assembly seems to have been used as a merit-making ceremony; no provisions seem to have been made to continue the practice with an order of the 150 people who had received the precepts.

Because of the large number of people involved, Seishi's bodhisattva ordination cannot be considered a ceremony conferring the status of a nun on her; instead, it was probably part of a ceremony designed to create karmic ties with Buddhism for the recipients. The ceremony could be performed repeatedly without necessarily conferring any lasting change in the recipient's social or religious status. Fifteen months later, Seishi received the bodhisattva precepts from Ennin again together with more than 170 people.[111]

Another episode concerning Ennin and Seishi provides important information into the ordination system for nuns. According to Ennin's will, "Empress (*taikōgō*) Junna [the title by which Seishi was known] wished to establish an ordination platform for bodhisattva nuns so that the Way would flourish. However, [I realized that] I would pass away before the platform could be established. The *Ken'yō daikairon* [Treatise clarifying and extolling the Mahāyāna precepts] was composed to further this goal. I ask that you aid in accomplishing [her] vow."[112] Since these events occurred at the end of Ennin's life, the empress' request was probably made at least twenty years after she had first become a "nun." Ennin's interest in nuns and their ordinations may have dated back more than twenty years; in 840, while he was in China, he met a number of nuns and went to see the ordination platform for nuns at Shan-kuang-ssu.[113] Seishi's request to Ennin is not surprising since he was one of the chief architects of Tendai attitudes toward the precepts following Saichō's death and the head of the Tendai school for ten years. The empress' request may indicate some misgivings with her status as a "nun." If she had been ordained with the full 348 precepts of the *Ssu-fen lü*, she might not have been so interested in a Tendai ordination. Her request to Ennin suggests that she desired to establish an official order of nuns that was ordained on an officially recognized platform and was fully equivalent to the order of monks.

Ennin died before he could build an ordination platform for nuns or complete the compilation of the *Ken'yō daikairon*. The ordination platform for nuns was not built. Tendai indifference to Seishi's request may imply that the Nara schools were not actively ordaining full-fledged nuns at this time. If they had been, then the competition between the Tendai and Nara traditions might have led the Tendai monks to establish an ordination platform for nuns. Nara monks might have pointed out that even though Tendai doctrine insisted on universal salvation, the Tendai school did not even ordain nuns. Although no such argument is recorded, because the ongoing debates between Tendai and Hossō focused on the issue of universal salvation, Nara monks could certainly have made such an argument. However, the lack of such arguments indicates that the ordination of nuns was not a major issue for either monks or their most influential lay supporters. The *Ken'yō daikairon* was completed by Ennin's disciple Anne after Ennin's death, but it contains no reference to an ordination platform for nuns. Perhaps Ennin never explained his views to Anne.

Although the details of the later history of the Junnain and the nuns who lived in it is not known, it still functioned as a center for nuns late in the tenth century. According to the *Sanbō ekotoba*, a guide to Buddhist ceremonies and important figures in Japanese Buddhist history that had been prepared for Princess Sonshi, who became a "nun" in 984, the Junnain was the site of semiannual confession services (*keka*) for nuns dedicated to Sākyamuni Buddha's disciple Ānanda. These ceremonies, performed on the eighth day of the second and eighth months, enabled nuns to repay the debt they owed Ānanda for helping them establish the order of nuns. When the Buddha's stepmother asked the Buddha for permission to become the first nun, the Buddha at first denied her request; only after Ānanda interceded did the Buddha grant her permission to establish an order of nuns.[114]

The Junnain is one of the few examples of an institution devoted to "nuns" that can be found in the ninth and tenth centuries. It was so closely tied to the careers of Seishi and her descendants that it probably had serious financial problems after their deaths; although Minamoto no Tamenori's description of the Ānanda rite of penance in the *Sanbō ekotoba* indicates the continued performance of that ritual by nuns, it does not explicitly describe the Junnain as an active nunnery.[115] The Junnain and the Hokkeji in Yamato[116] are the only institutions for nuns mentioned in the *Sanbō ekotoba,* and Seishi is the only example of an identifiable Heian-period Japanese nun mentioned in the text, suggesting that the author of the text probably did not have many examples of nuns or convents that he thought worth mentioning even though he was writing for Princess Sonshi, a woman who had become a nun.

The activities of Kachiko and Seishi set a pattern for several other women during this time, sometimes influencing their adversaries. Fujiwara no Junshi (809–871), Emperor Ninmyō's junior consort and mother of Emperor Montoku, was an integral part of the victorious faction in the Jōwa disturbance. Like Kachiko, Junshi supported Japanese monks who traveled to China. After the Shingon monk Eun (798–869 or 871) returned from China, he was installed at the Anjōji, a temple that Junshi commissioned and to which she donated land. The temple followed Enryakuji's example and maintained yearly ordinands and a system of sequestering its monks for set periods. In a request for the three yearly ordinands in 859, Junshi noted that the monks were to practice in place of her (*mi ni kawarite*). Although she had the religious aspiration of a man, Junshi felt that her female body was an obstacle to serious practice.[117] Junshi was politically active on behalf of her grandson Emperor Seiwa for several years, but then, lamenting the death of her son Montoku, Junshi took the tonsure (literally, "shed her ornaments [*rakusai*] and became a nun [*ama*])" on 2-19-861.[118] Although traditional histories suggest that she became a nun out of sorrow over her son's death, several years elapsed between the two events. Such views may reflect the Confucian bias of the compiler; in fact, she may well have been carrying out a long-held desire to pursue a religious life.[119]

In the sixth month of 861, she invited several monks from the Tō-daiji ordination platform to her dwelling at Higashi Gojō no miya and had them confer the bodhisattva precepts on her. Later that month, she invited Ennin to her residence. He stayed for four days, lectured on the *Lotus Sūtra,* and conferred the bodhisattva precepts on more than a hundred people, including Junshi; he also conferred the Esoteric *sanmaya* precepts and an Esoteric initiation on her.[120]

Several aspects of Junshi's religious life are noteworthy. The conferral of precepts from both Tōdaiji and Tendai monks in the same month suggests that the sectarian rivalries motivating many monks often did not move their lay disciples. Instead, the loyalties of lay believers and nuns often focused on individual teachers. The practice also indicates that both Nara and Tendai monks were willing to overlook ordinations of lay believers and nuns performed in their adversary's temples, a practice that would not have been allowed for monks in most cases. Anjōji, the monastery established by Junshi, was typical of many patronized by the women of noble families during the early Heian period; even though the monasteries followed the yearly ordinand system and kept monks sequestered, both practices that either excluded women or severely limited their access to monasteries, noblewomen actively supported these institutions. Anjōji had been established so that ceremonies could be performed that would help the imperial family. Junshi and other women like her who made lavish donations to monasteries and monks probably believed that monks kept in seclusion could perform these ceremonies more effectively than nuns. Junshi's establishment of the monastery Anjōji is particularly noteworthy when contrasted with Nara-period activities of Buddhist women such as Empress Kōmyō, who strove to provide nunneries for religious women.

Evidence for a clearly delineated Tendai full ordination for nuns finally appears in the twelfth century in a manuscript discovered at Manshuin, a Tendai chapel formerly on Mount Hiei but which eventually moved to the outskirts of Kyoto in the seventeenth century. This manual was probably compiled during the Eikyū era (1113–1118) by a Tendai monk, possibly Ryōyū (fl. 1087–1094) or Chūjin (1065–1138), at the Manshuin for a noble woman.[121] It clearly divides the ceremony into two parts: an initiation ritual (*shukke sahō*) and a full ordination (*jukai*), thereby ensuring that no confusion would arise about the status of the recipient. The ceremony combines a number of Esoteric Buddhist ritual elements and cited several stories such as the anecdote concerning Utpalavarṇa mentioned below.

Patterns of Practice for Nuns

The ordinations in the above examples indicate that by the mid-Heian period, women who were called "nuns" (*ama*) took a variety of precepts or sometimes may have taken no precepts at all. The above discussion focused on women of the noble class because source material is more detailed for them. If similar sources existed for nuns from lower classes, an even greater variety of ordinations and practices undoubtedly would be apparent. For example, more than seven hundred nuns were ordained in 986 at the Rokuharamitsuji in Kyoto, but little is known of them.[122]

The broad variety of ordinations and practitioners does not necessarily indicate that their practice was lax. Cutting the hair or giving up fashionable clothing for religious garb to become a nun was a public statement that a person was abandoning most if not all of his or her worldly ambitions. In many cases during the mid-Heian period, such a drastic step was not taken until a person was seriously ill or perhaps near death. If the person happened to recover from illness, restoration of the previous style of life was not easy, especially if he or she was not from a family of considerable means.[123] However, notable exceptions to this rule, such as Fujiwara no Michinaga (966–1027), did exist.

Deathbed ordinations further complicate attempts to determine whether a woman was becoming a nun or undergoing a religious ceremony to ensure a better rebirth at the end of her life with little hope or intention of living as a monastic in this world. As a result, one of the criteria for clarifying vague statements of religious intent such as "leaving home" must be a woman's subsequent behavior. Thus, in the following section, the lifestyles of nuns and the institutions where they lived are considered.

Institutions

By the mid-Heian period, few institutions existed that could be called nunneries. Most of the nunneries that had been established during the Asuka period or the *kokubun niji* of the Nara period had ceased functioning, been turned into monasteries for monks or into branch temples of monasteries, or fallen into disrepair. In a few cases, early nunneries such as some of the *kokubun niji* and the Hokkeji in Nara survived in some form, but such cases were rare and are poorly documented.[124] Several of these are surveyed below.

The nunneries established as an integral part of the *kokubunji* system are an obvious place where nuns might have lived during the Heian period. However, the *kokubunji* system lost much of its vitality during the first part of the Heian period. In particular, the number of mentions of nunneries decreases. In those sources that do mention "*kokubunji*," the term usually should be interpreted as referring to monasteries only.[125] When nunneries were referred to in official documents they were mentioned specifically as *kokubun niji* or Hokkeji.[126] Although entries in the official documents of the first half of the ninth century occasionally do mention the nunneries, they never include enough detail to indicate that the institutions were prosperous. In almost all cases, they are mentioned in connection with the nunnery's being destroyed and the need to either construct a new edifice or requisition another temple to take its place. For example, the nunnery in Izu burned down in 836. A temple, the Daikōji, was requisitioned to replace it, but the date of this exchange is not known. The *kokushi* (provincial teacher) petitioned the court for funds to rebuild the original nunnery in 884; however, the Daikōji does not appear in lists of designated temples until 855.[127] The time lag involved in replacing the nunnery certainly does not suggest a vital order of nuns. Finally, in the chapter on taxes in the *Engishiki,* although allocations of rice and salt are mentioned for monks at provincial temples, none are mentioned for nuns.

In the provinces where officially designated temples had gradually come to assume the place occupied by *kokubunji,* only one mention of a nunnery has survived. In 887, the designated nunnery (*jōgaku niji*) in Mushiroda-gun (in modern Gifu) was chosen to replace the *kokubunji* in Mino because the halls of the Mushiroda-gun nunnery were imposing. Because nuns would probably not have lived there after it was converted to a monastery, the nuns, if any still lived there, must not have been very influential.[128]

The fate of one Nara nunnery, Sairyūji, is particularly instructive. Sairyūji was established along with the Saidaiji monastery by the female emperor Shōtoku. The two temples were probably commissioned in imitation of the Tōdaiji monastery and Hokkeji nunnery established by Shōtoku's parents, Emperor Shōmu and Empress Kōmyō. Shōtoku may have wished to demonstrate that her own power to grant patronage was equal to that of her illustrious parents. The nunnery was given various grants of land and taxes, including 10,000 *soku*[129] of grain from Echigo province, indicating that a large nunnery was planned. However, it probably was allowed to decline soon after Shōtoku's death as part of the reaction against Shōtoku and her politically ambitious adviser, the monk Dōkyō. A century later, in 880, an edict states, "We order Saidaiji to incorporate (*setsuryō*) the Sairyūji. Both temples were founded by the Takano (Shōtoku) emperor. Sairyūji shall be used as a place where the robes of the Saidaiji monks are to be washed."[130] Matching nunneries with monasteries was common, as can be seen from both the *kokubunji* system and Gyōki's chapels. As the status of nuns declined, some of them may have taken on the task of washing the robes of monks, a duty mentioned in several other documents.[131] In fact, washing robes was one of the few ways nuns could support themselves. Others were by consorting with monks, guiding pilgrims, telling fortunes, or begging.[132] If a nunnery was not available, many such nuns probably lived in private dwellings near the monastery.[133]

Few new nunneries were established during the Heian period. Besides the Danrinji and Junnain mentioned above, only three other nunneries are mentioned; one of them was the Jōjuin in the Iwakura district of Kyoto, established by Fujiwara no Yoshiko (1021–1102), an empress who was the consort of Emperor Goreizei (1025–1068; r. 1045–1068). Yoshiko moved into the Jōjuin about 1074. Although her presence in the Jōjuin might have given it a character like a convent, it seems to have become a monastery after her death. The origins of another, the Kannōji in Settsu, are not completely clear, but it is associated with a dream of Princess Seishi (later known as Empress Junna); it was later rebuilt by Minamoto no Yoritomo during the Juei era (1182–1185). Very little is known of the third, the Myōshinji in Kumano.[134] In most cases, nuns seem to have remained in their homes to practice as "householder nuns." Only women with imperial connections could muster the resources to set up a nunnery. The fate of most of these nunneries remains obscure, but they probably did not last long. Nunneries undoubtedly had financial difficulties because they rarely received significant contributions of land. Nuns were excluded from most, if not all, of the various ceremonies used to protect the state or powerful leaders; as a result, few incentives existed for patrons to support them in return for special services that would prevent bad fortune or cure illness.

Hierarchies of Female Practitioners

The ambiguous ways in which terms such as "*ama*" were used led some monks to argue that such women were at best novices, a conclusion that might have been suggested by the use of terms such as *"shami"* and *"shamini"* to refer to privately ordained men and women. One of the clearest expressions of this view is put forth by the Sanron scholar Chinkai (1091–1152) who wrote in his *Bodaishin shū,*

> Male and female novices receive the ten precepts, and probationary nuns (*sakiama*) [Skt. *śikṣamāṇā*] observe six precepts. *Bhikṣu* [fully ordained monks] observe two hundred fifty and *bhikṣuṇī* [fully ordained nuns] follow five hundred. But the nuns (*ama*) of this realm are novices, not *bhikṣuṇī*. They can only be called *bhikṣuṇī* after they have climbed the ordination platform. Thus they are only novice nuns (*shamini no ama*) who have taken the ten precepts.[135]

Ishida Mizumaro, in a seminal article on ordination platforms for nuns (*bikuni kaidan*), makes a similar argument.[136]

Although monks may not have recognized religious women as full-fledged nuns, the women themselves sometimes structured their institutions and ordinations in a hierarchical manner reminiscent of the levels specified in the *Vinaya*. For example, a document discussing the status of the Junnain after Seishi's death contains the phrase "greater and lesser nuns" (*daishōni*), suggesting that some sort of hierarchy existed at the nunnery during her lifetime.[137] Women often were ordained more than once, as was the case with both Seishi and Princess Sonshi mentioned above. In most cases, so little is known of the structure and contents of the ordinations that definite conclusions cannot be drawn. However, Katsuura Noriko has used a different approach to suggest that nuns did have a hierarchy that roughly paralleled the *Vinaya* distinctions of novice (or probationary nun) and nun. By focusing on the hairstyles of ordained women as well as the number of times they were ordained, Katsuura suggested that some women followed a two-part pattern of ordinations.[138]

The first ordination often involved cutting the hair shoulder-length. Such women were referred to by such terms as *"ama," "ama-nyūdō,"* or *"ama-sogi."* This ordination was followed at a later date by another ordination that involved completely shaving the head (*teihatsu*). Often, but not always, the latter ordination was performed only when the recipient was near death. Women with such ordinations were designated by terms that normally were used for men to distinguish them from the more ambiguous ranks of the *ama*. Among the terms used were *"sō"* (monk or monastic) and *"hosshi"* (teacher of the Dharma).[139] The awkwardness of the terms indicates the difficulties some had in finding appropriate terminology to refer to these women.

One of the best examples demonstrating a clear hierarchical structure in orders of nuns and their desire to have full ordinations recognized is found in the story of the ordination of Fujiwara no Michinaga's daughter Empress Shōshi (also known as Jōtōmon'in, 988–1074). The first ordination recorded for Shōshi is found in a vivid passage in Murasaki Shikibu's diary. In 1008, Shōshi was undergoing a difficult childbirth; at stake was not just the mother's health, but also the political fortunes of Michinaga and others. Murasaki described the ordination as follows. "When the [monks] started to shave Her Majesty's head and made her take vows, we were all thrown into utter despair and wondered what on earth was happening; but then she safely delivered."[140] The ordination, accompanied by a slight shaving of the head (or more likely cutting her locks), was performed as part of various religious rituals to protect Shōshi from evil spirits, probably her rivals and their ancestors. Those watching were "thrown into utter despair" because such an ordination might be performed as a last resort. However, when Shōshi recovered she was not expected to lead a cloistered life.

Shōshi underwent other ordinations later in life with different expectations. According to the *Eiga monogatari*, in 1026, when Shōshi "received the commandments" (*kai ukesase*), her hair was only trimmed so that she looked "like a little girl with a nun's cut" (*amasogitaru chigo*).[141] After this ordination, she began to devote her considerable talents and resources to a religious life. Shōshi was apparently dissatisfied with her ordination—work began on an ordination platform for nuns at the Muryōjuin (also known as the Amida Hall) at Hōjōji. Shōshi hoped to receive a full ordination on the platform the following year. With Shōshi's support, the work "was being pushed forward day and night, and there was great happiness among nuns everywhere," probably because this would enable them to receive a full ordination along with Shōshi.[142] The ordination platform was completed in 1027. Comments were made that an ordination platform for monks also should be built at Hōjōji. About this time, however, the rivalry between the Tendai monks of Mount Hiei and Miidera (Onjōji) was intensifying to the extent that Miidera would attempt to obtain recognition for its own ordination platform independent of Mount Hiei. Allowing the Hōjōji platform for nuns to proceed thus would have undermined Mount Hiei's position that it should control all Tendai ordinations. As a result, the Tendai monks of Mount Hiei opposed the nuns' platform, and it was abandoned.[143] Shōshi eventually completed her ordination and had her "remaining hair" shaved in 1039 at the Hōjōji in a ceremony conducted by Archbishop Myōson, though probably not on the ordination plat-form.[144] After Hōjōji burned down in 1058, the ordination platform was not mentioned again.[145]

What did the different levels of ordination and hair style represent to the recipients? Partial cutting of the hair may have signified that they had the status of probationary nuns. Such a practice is found in Sung China. According to the *Shih-shih yao-lan* (Essential reading for Bud-dhists), an introductory text on Buddhism compiled by Tao-ch'eng in 1019, probationary nuns resembled nuns, but had long hair.[146] Cutting the hair also signified that they had renounced lay concerns. Re-nouncing all family ties, however, was much more difficult. Like Seishi, many continued to be concerned with their children for the rest of their lives. Only when such a nun was at the point of dying and completely ready to cut off all secular ties did she have her head shaved. Finally, women might have had their heads shaved completely because they be-lieved that they would be transformed into men and realize Buddha-hood (*tennyo jōbutsu*) after death.[147]

The issue of hierarchies also arises when women were permitted to be ordained as full-fledged nuns using the *Ssu-fen lü* precepts. This move-ment was begun by Eison (1201–1290) and the monks around him in the Kamakura period revival of the Risshū. Among the women men-tioned in rosters of his followers are two groups, "novices in accord with the Dharma" (*hōdō shamini*) and "novices in appearance" (*gyōdō shamini*). The former were women, usually in their late teens or early twenties, who took the ten precepts of a traditional initiation for novices. The latter group consisted of women, usually older, who took the five lay precepts but shaved their heads. The numbers of the latter group were significantly larger than the former group. No provision for a group of novices in appearance is made in the *Vinaya* in which Eison was so in-terested; thus the group probably represented the earlier tradition of women who received lay ordinations but dressed as nuns as described in this chapter.[148]

Ordinations and Life Cycles

Nuns' lives followed different patterns from monks'. Many monks en-tered monasteries while they were still young and sometimes were ex-pected to become scholar-monks. In contrast, women usually became nuns later in life because they were expected to marry and bear chil-dren first. Because Buddhism was associated with impermanence, death, and rebirth, women often were ordained because of illness, disappointment in love, or at the death of a child, husband, or relative. In the early Heian, the death of a child was a common reason for a woman, especially one from the imperial classes, to become a nun; however, by the late eleventh century, the death of a husband had become a more common reason for ordination. The growing influence of Confucian views on the chastity of widows played a major role in this shift.[149]

When young women attempted to become nuns before marriage, they were often discouraged by their parents or relatives. Typical was a woman known simply as "the daughter of Ono no Takaki," who asked her brother, the monk Enkyō, to instruct her in Buddhism. He gave her the *Kuan wu-liang-shou ching* (The *sūtra* of the visualization of the Buddha of Immeasurable Life) and extracts from various scriptures, which she studied constantly. On the fifteenth of each month she prostrated herself on the ground facing west and chanted, "Adoration to the Pure Land of Peace and Sustenance, [land of] the sun-meditation in the West." However, her parents admonished her, saying, "Such activities are not for young people; you will exhaust yourself and damage your looks." Shortly after giving birth to a daughter, fathered by the major controller of the right (*udaiben*) Fujiwara no Sukeyo (847–897), she died at age twenty-five. At her death, music was heard in the air, a classic indication of rebirth in the Pure Land, indicating that Amitābha's entourage had escorted her back to the Pure Land.[150]

Arguing that the decision to become a nun was often precipitated by disappointments in life does not mean that these women were insincere; indeed, they often were admirably sincere in their religious devotions. Moreover, being ordained as a nun late in life seems to have been a widely recognized and respected practice and did not carry the disapproval that it may have entailed at times in other Buddhist societies such as Sri Lanka and Tibet.[151]

From the mid-Heian period on, many emperors and nobles renounced the activities and responsibilities of lay life late in life or on their deathbeds. The term "*shukke*" (literally, "leaving home") applied so often to such male practitioners who remained in their homes to practice Buddhism as *nyūdō* (literally, "those who have entered the path") is the same used in many cases to refer to the ordination of nuns.[152] Such practitioners usually did not have the luxury of long years of study necessary to master abstruse doctrine or to perform complicated meditations or rituals. Women who followed this pattern were called by such terms as "*ama-nyūdō*" (literally, "a nun who has entered the path," but here with the sense of householder nun), "*ama-nyōbō*" (nun-wife), or "*ie no ama*" (house-nun), all expressions that suggested that the women had cut their hair to varying degrees, but had remained householders.[153]

Religious Practices

Monks had a choice of a variety of religious practices such as Esoteric Buddhist rites, Lotus confessional meditations, the scholarly study of exoteric texts such as the *Lotus Sūtra* and its commentaries, or the performance of devotional practices such as the *nenbutsu*. Most, but not all of the nuns from this period, however, performed devotional practices.[154] When a nun chanted a *sūtra* or the name of a Buddha, those practices usually were devotional in nature rather than practices designed to aid in visualizations or other complex meditative exercises. For example, Princess Sonshi is said to have been devoted to the recitation of the Devadatta chapter of the Lotus, a text that recorded the sudden realization of Buddhahood by an eight-year-old Nāga girl.[155] This text also served as the basis for Tendai interpretation of the realization of Buddhahood in this lifetime, but its significance for Sonshi was undoubtedly its portrayal of a young female realizing Buddhahood despite having the various physical obstacles that were attributed to women.[156] Sonshi was also said to have steadfastly focused her mind on rebirth in the Pure Land at the time of her death.[157]

Nuns tended to focus on devotional practices for several reasons. Their educational opportunities were limited. Unless they were aristocratic women they had many fewer opportunities to learn the Chinese characters necessary to read Buddhist scriptures that would have given them insights into Buddhist meditational practices or introduced them to Esoteric rituals. With so many of the major temples and monasteries closed to them, nuns could not cultivate the close relationships with their teachers that would have led to a broader variety of practices. Finally, because many women were ordained late in life, they were naturally concerned with preparing for their own deaths or with practices that would aid deceased (primarily male) members of their family. As a result, Pure Land practices and the caretaking of graves are often mentioned in connection with nuns. Although some women from the elite certainly achieved high levels of education, they wrote diaries, novels, and poetry rather than abstruse doctrinal treatises on Buddhism.

Scholarly Nuns

Some women from the families of nobles were conversant with Buddhist scripture.[158] Few, however, were famed for their mastery of the intricacies of Buddhist doctrine. When women who had mastered doctrine were mentioned, comments were often made on how unusual the phenomenon was. For example, the remark is made of Princess Shūshi (997–1050) that "perhaps because she was descended from a line of distinguished scholars, she has been reading the Tripitaka and consulting the sacred texts in a manner scarcely to have been expected of a woman." When she became a nun in the third month of 1024, Michinaga compared her with Queen Śrīmālā.[159] Similar attitudes about women and the academic study of Buddhism are expressed in biographical entries concerning Genshin's (942–1017) older sisters. Their scholarly achievements were so unusual that biographers felt compelled to comment on them. The following two passages from biographies indicate both that Genshin's sisters were very learned and that such attainments were unusual among nuns. "After [Gansai] had entered the Buddhist path, she chanted the *Lotus Sūtra*. Moreover, she understood its most profound principles. She was quiet and calm, honest without any deception, completely observed the precepts, and deeply concerned about any wrongdoing. Although she was physically a woman, she was more like a pious layman (*shinnan*)"[160]

Gansai, probably the first- or second-oldest of Genshin's sisters, died between 1004 and 1011. The term "*shinnan*" is usually used as the translation for *upāsaka* (pious layman). The compiler of the text could not bring himself to compare Gansai to a monk, but he had to acknowledge that Gansai was more scholarly than the usual pious laywoman. His hesitation in calling Gansai a *bikuni*, despite her observance of the precepts, contributes to the impression that such women did not belong to an established nunnery. Similar attitudes are expressed concerning another of Genshin's sisters, Ganshō: [Ganshō] had set her mind on Buddhism since she was young. She did not marry. Although she had a body with the five obstacles, she clearly understood the two truths. Her scholarship and piety excelled that of her brother."[161]

In each case, the woman's scholarly achievements are seen as being unusual and like those of men. In both cases, the biography continues on to discuss their devotional activities without any remark about the recitation of the *nenbutsu* or the chanting of *sūtras* being unusual. Nothing about the women's teachers, ordination, or institutional affiliation is mentioned, indicating that they probably did not belong to any well-established order or nunnery. When their biographies are compared to those of monks, the lack of this data is especially striking. Genshin's sisters had names that are clearly religious; thus they can be considered "nuns" in the loose sense of the word that was commonly used during the Heian period. The two nuns, along with their mother, who also became a nun, probably lived together, possibly at home.

A Rationale for Ordination

How did nuns feel about their lower status in the Buddhist world? Because nuns wrote little, speculation is difficult. However, a rationale that excused the various limitations placed on the ordinations of nuns and their ability to follow precepts was found in a number of texts that are important for the history of nuns during the Heian period. The prevalence of the following story may indicate that nuns were aware of the limitations placed upon them, but determined to do the best they could to live a religious life. The story, an apocryphal tale concerning the nun Utpalavarṇā (J. Rengeshiki or Uharake) who lived during Śākyamuni's lifetime is repeated in texts such as Ennin's *Ken'yō daikairon*, the *Sanbō ekotoba,* and a Tendai ordination manual for nuns from late in the Heian.

Utpalavarṇā urged young noblewomen to be ordained as nuns. When they replied that they could not follow the precepts because they were young, she encouraged them to be ordained anyway even if they later broke their vows. When the young women replied that they would surely fall into hell and suffer for breaking their vows, the nun encouraged them to be ordained even if they did go to hell for breaking their vows. Utpalavarṇā finally told them a story about her past lives. Many eons ago, she had played by dressing up in various clothes and changing her voice, finally putting on the robes of a nun. Later, during the time of the Buddha Kāśyapa, she was reborn as a human being and became a nun because of the merit she had accrued by wearing those robes. However, she eventually grew arrogant, broke her vows, and was reborn in hell where she suffered for a long time. But because of the merit from having been a nun, she was reborn as a woman during the time of Śākyamuni, became a nun, realized arhathood, and mastered the six superhuman abilities. Thus she urged women to become nuns even if they broke the precepts because they would be creating the merit that might help them realize the path in a later life.[162]

The story justifies the type of behavior that may well have been followed by many of the nuns who were ordained and continued to live in the same homes they had occupied as lay believers, observing some of the precepts, but not suffering from public criticism if they violated minor or even some of the major rules. Nuns were not the only people who followed this pattern, of course; many monks and "lay-renunciants" (*nyūdō*) did not completely observe the precepts.[163]

Conclusion

This chapter began as an attempt to elucidate the lifestyles of nuns by determining what sets of precepts and procedures nuns followed in their ordinations so that the paucity of "nuns" in Ryōgen's biography might be explained. When source materials quickly indicated the difficulty of this task, the role of the court or government in ordinations of nuns became the focus of the investigation. When the court supported an order of nuns that conformed for the most part to the structures found in the *Ssu-fen-lü,* the order of officially sanctioned nuns flourished. When the court adopted the position that nuns were not needed for the performance of rituals to support the state, the order of officially recognized nuns withered.

Although the contents of ordinations often seemed ambiguous, the freedom pious women found in privately conducted ordinations gave them a variety of opportunities to improvise and develop lifestyles that suited their needs. Even so, certain aspects of practice and hierarchy specified in the *Vinaya* continued to capture the imagination of nuns. Nuns were more often celibate than their male counterparts. Completely shaving the head remained a powerful symbol of commitment to Buddhism for women, even though it was often performed close to death, rather than earlier in their lifetimes. The hierarchical structure of types of practitioners specified in the *Vinaya* was still an attractive model even though many aspects of its rules were ignored.

Nuns were clearly not just a female analogue of monks. They were ordained at different points in their life cycle and had fewer educational opportunities than monks. They often were unable or unwilling to cut off relations with their families and lived in ways that were part monastic and part lay. Often, their religious practices focused on devotional practices and were connected with the salvation of deceased relatives. Although sometimes nuns were not held in as high regard by their contemporaries as monks, other writers praised their sincerity and struggle to overcome the social obstacles to living a religious life.

The paucity of nuns in Ryōgen's biography becomes more understandable through this study. Ryōgen focused his efforts on supporting official Buddhism, the very type of Buddhism that paid little attention to nuns because nuns did not participate in the rituals to protect the state. For Ryōgen and his supporters, nuns probably had little social status. As a result, Ryōgen does not seem to have ordained either his own mother or the mothers of his disciples. Ryōgen was not unconcerned with the spiritual lives of women, however. He honored women as mothers and lay believers, even moving the *shari-e* so that they could appreciate it. The attention paid to mothers fit in well with the views of his patrons, the Fujiwaras, who were interested in the political role that women could play as the mothers of emperors. Neither Ryōgen nor the nobles that were his patrons seem to have displayed much interest in or support for the autonomous lives that women might live as nuns.

13

Epilogue

Ryōgen's Posthumous Career

Saichō, Ennin, and Enchin had all been honored by the court with the posthumous title of *daishi* 'great teacher.' The tradition of honoring eminent monks with this title had begun in 866 with the award of the title to Saichō and Ennin. In all, only eight monks would receive the court-bestowed title during the Heian period. In Ryōgen's case, a posthumous title was conferred on him slightly more than two years after his death. The court ordered that he be given the posthumous title Jie (compassionate and wise).[1] However, the court probably never conferred the title of *daishi* on him during the Heian period. The use of the title in such expressions as Ganzan daishi or Jie daishi arose in the Kamakura period or later and was never authorized by the court.[2]

After their deaths, Tendai figures such as Saichō and Ennin became the subject of brief stories (*setsuwa*) that extolled their powers or virtues. While there are a few such stories, about Ryōgen, which have been mentioned in earlier stories, the *setsuwa* literature concerning him is less developed than that for such contemporaries and disciples as Zōga and Genshin. Stories concerning Ryōgen generally focus on his relationships with the precepts and relate such episodes as how he revived the fortnightly assembly or how he postponed an ordination ceremony shortly before the ordination platform collapsed, thereby saving people from injury. Stories about his devotion to the *Lotus Sūtra* or his mastery of Esoteric Buddhist ritual are few.[3] In fact, Ryōgen's biography does not become the subject of many later legends; most of these stories have already been mentioned in earlier chapters. However, legends about Ryōgen's posthumous career as a spirit protecting his lineage of the Tendai school abound.

Even in early biographies such as the *Jie daisōjōden*, Ryōgen is virtually deified. His death is said to have been similar to that of Saichō, with purple clouds hovering above, a sign that he was reborn in the

Pure Land.[4] In addition, he was one of three major monks who served Fujiwara no Morosuke and who all died on the third day of the first month. According to the dream of an unidentified person, all three monks were, in fact, celestial bodies (*sankō tenshi*).[5] Ryōgen's title of Ganzan, literally, "the first (month) and third (day)," is derived from the date of his death. In the *Genkō shakusho*, Ryōgen was considered to be like the sun, the brightest of these three bodies, because he had defeated both Gishō and Hōzō in debate.[6] Another story in the *Jie daisō-jōden* describes how Ryōgen's disciple Myōfu died and was then revived in 980. Upon awakening he told how he had asked the officials in the land of the dead what practice would guarantee his rebirth in the Pure Land. They told him that Ryōgen was a temporary transformation (*gonge*) of a deity and that by serving Ryōgen, Myōfu would surely be reborn in the Pure Land.[7] In the *Jie daisōjō shūiden*, Ryōgen is said to have been the reappearance of Śākyamuni or the rebirth of Ennin.[8] The identification with Ennin was based on Ryōgen's prodigious efforts to establish and protect Ennin's lineage. Thus, Ryōgen had been idealized within fifty years of his death, when these biographies were compiled. In addition, as the monk who had restored the Tendai establishment after a disastrous fire, Ryōgen was sometimes said to be the rebirth of Saichō.[9] In later texts, Ryōgen is identified with Kannon, Kokūzō (Akaśagarbha), Fudō myōō, Shōgun Jizō (an armored figure of Kṣitigarbha), dragons, and *kami*.[10] During droughts, Ryōgen was believed to control rainfall.[11]

Ryōgen is also part of a group of five key figures in Tendai history called the "three sages and two teachers" (*sanshō nishi*). The three sages were Saichō, Ennin, and Enchin. These three men had all traveled to China and brought back Tendai teachings and practices; in addition, they had also contributed to Tendai institutional life by establishing and developing various temples. The two teachers were Annen and Ryōgen. Annen is famous for his various works on Esoteric Buddhism; he was also the author of important texts on exoteric themes such as the realization of Buddhahood with this very body, the realization of Buddhahood by grasses and trees, and the Sudden-Perfect precepts. However, he played little role in the development of Tendai institutions, and very little is known about his life. In contrast to all of these figures, Ryōgen wrote relatively little. However, he played a major role in the history of the Tendai establishment, both building Tendai institutions and defending them against internal and external threats. Of the five, Ryōgen is enshrined in more temples than any of the others.[12]

Assemblies Honoring Ryōgen

As Ryōgen's will, translated in appendix 3, demonstrates, Ryōgen was vitally concerned with the rituals surrounding his own death. These instructions might well have served as the basis for his mausoleum. For example, in keeping with Ryōgen's love of debate, debates on the five teachings were held four times each year at Ryōgen's quarters, a practice so well known that his lodgings were often called Shiki-kōdō (Lecture hall for the four seasonal assemblies). Ryōgen's mausoleum is to the north of the Jōshinbō. In fact, Ryōgen's posthumous career is so closely identified with his mausoleum that the monks of Yokawa began calling him "the great teacher of the mausoleum" (Mimyō daishi) shortly after his death, partly because his spirit was said to intervene whenever Mount Hiei's fortunes were threatened and partly out of fear of his posthumous powers.[13]

A story of the origins of the painting of Ryōgen that serves as the central image helps elucidate the power that his mausoleum held. Once when Ryōgen was meditating at his lodgings in the Jōshinbō, his disciple Jinzen noted that Ryōgen's shadow remained even after the meditation had ended and Ryōgen had stood up. Jinzen copied the shadowy image. When he had finished copying one part of the image, that part of the image disappeared until Ryōgen died. The story suggests that Ryōgen's spirit had moved into the painting itself, which would continue to have the powers that Ryōgen had displayed during his lifetime.[14]

Assemblies (kō) honoring Ryōgen were performed on the monthly or annual anniversaries of his death. Traditional Tendai sources trace the origins of the Ganzan-e back to the lectures and debates that Ryōgen held at his quarters in Yokawa; these were continued after his death to honor his memory.[15] By the late Heian or early Kamakura period, an assembly called the Ganzan-e was performed at Ryōgen's quarters on Mount Hiei. The name of the assembly was based on Ryōgen's death on the third day of the first month, and the assembly was held annually on that day. Every fifth year, Tendai monks conducted a more elaborate assembly, which an imperial emissary attended. An image or picture of Ryōgen was probably installed, and lectures on the Lotus Sūtra were conducted. The format of the assembly reflected Ryōgen's interest in lectures and was probably associated with the debates he had held at his quarters.[16] At various other sites, monthly assemblies were conducted on the third day of each month, usually to ask for Ryōgen's protection.[17]

A number of ritual texts devoted to the commemoration of Ryōgen's deeds were compiled. Lectures (*kōshiki*) on Ryōgen's life and merits, as well as hymns (*wasan*) honoring Ryōgen are said to have been produced by two of his disciples, Genshin and Kakuchō. However, the dates and authenticity of these texts have not been firmly established. One of the texts attributed to Genshin was written in a style called *tōkanshiki* so that if the top and bottom character of each line is taken they will reveal the lines "Homage to the Great Archbishop Jie, protector of Tendai Buddhism, who has manifested himself as the greatest general, the being who benefits even those sentient beings with bad karma."[18] The text, attributed to Genshin, reveals that Ryōgen was thought of as a manifestation of Nyoirin (Wishfulfilling) Kannon. Although the text seems to be accepted as authentic by Yagi Kōe, Murayama Shūichi places it much later because the sentiments expressed in it reflect views of Ryōgen during a later period.[19] A similar statement identifying Ryogen with Kannon is found in the *Gukanshō,* compiled by Jien (1155–1225).[20] Although Kannon is often thought of as a gentle embodiment of compassion, one of the thirty-three manifestations of Kannon specified in the *Lotus Sūtra* is as a great general.[21] Thus, the commemorative lecture emphasized Ryōgen's role as a martial defender of Tendai, someone so powerful that he could help even those with bad karma. In addition, two of the more popular ritual texts are attributed to the Tendai exegete Hōchibō Shōshin (1136–1220 or 1131–1215), who valued Ryōgen's institutional contributions to Tendai even though Shōshin himself refrained from playing major administrative roles.[22] Eventually, at least seven of these ritual texts were chosen for recitation in daily services at the Daishidō, the hall dedicated to Ryōgen at Yokawa; the texts were read in rotation, with a different being used each day. Besides the two texts attributed to Genshin, one to Kakuchō, and two to Hōchibō Shōshin, one text is said to be by Emperor Go-uda and one by an unknown author.[23] Ryōgen's major accomplishments were often described in these texts. Some of them may have been accompanied by illustrations. A text from the fourteenth century includes pictures of Ryōgen at the Ōwa debates and being granted permission to enter the palace in a palanquin. The picture of the Ōwa debates shows the two monks debating in front of an altar surrounded by monks listening to the discussion. Several lay officials also appear in the picture, but most of them seem uninterested in the proceedings.[24]

Rituals honoring Ryōgen were used not only to repay the debt that all Tendai monks owed Ryōgen for protecting their community. Often

monks and lay devotees prayed to Ryōgen for help with personal problems or for help with threats toward the Tendai establishment. Sometimes a man would vow to perform rituals for Ryōgen for a certain number of days. A favorite activity was the recitation of the Fumon chapter
of the *Lotus Sūtra,* which concerned Kannon.[25] Belief in Ryōgen might
lead to this-worldly goals such as wealth or health.[26]

Ryōgen as the Founder of Monastic Traditions

Ryōgen's popularity as an object of devotion is due to his status as a protector of Tendai temples. One aspect of that status is reflected in his portrayal in a threatening manner as a protector of Ennin's lineage or of the
Tendai school as a whole. At other times, he was described as someone
who introduced certain abuses into the Tendai school. For example, according to the *Sange yōki senryaku* (Abbreviated records of the Mountain
School), a text compiled from earlier records by Shunzen about 1399,
the rise of warrior monks is attributed to Ryōgen. According to the text,
"During Ryōgen's period of tenure [as *zasu*], he explained, 'Without literary talents, we do not have the etiquette to become familiar with those
above; without military strength, we do not have the power to threaten
those below. Thus both the literary and military [arts] are needed to govern the world.'" Elsewhere the text states, "Those monks who are dumb,
without talent and unable to study should make up the martial ranks."
The text continues, noting that during the Period of the Semblance of
the Dharma (Zōhō), faith was sufficient to lead people to respect Buddhism, but in the Period of the End of the Dharma (Mappō), faith is weak;
thus military power is needed to quell disturbances in the school's
manors and to protect its landholdings.[27] In a biography of Ryōgen, the
Jie daishiden by Ranpa Keishin written in 1469, Ryōgen is said to have established a group of warrior monks in 975, arguing that just as Mañjuśrī
carried both a book and a sword, so must monks. The claim that Ryōgen
established warrior monks was repeated in the massive Tokugawa compilation concerning Japanese history, the *Dainihonshi.* However, as has
been discussed in the chapter on factionalism during Ryōgen's tenure
as *zasu,* the actual use of warrior monks developed after Ryōgen's death.

The use of alcohol on Mount Hiei was also said to have originated
during Ryōgen's tenure as *zasu.* According to the *Sange yōryakki senryaku,*

As for the prohibition on liquor on our mountain, our great teachers formulated this rule. However, gradually people's will [to follow it] weakened and the monks frequently broke it. Thus some wished to secretly

hold drinking parties and wantonly cause the rule to be abrogated. During the time of Ryōgen, [alcohol] was prohibited in accordance with the rules, but later the regulations were revised.

When it was time to dedicate the Eshin'in, the minister of the right from Kujō [Kaneie] was the lay patron and was asked to climb Mount Hiei. After the dedications were read, when all were at the reception, the minister of the right said to the *zasu* and archbishop [Ryōgen], "When I consider the situation on the mountain, cold winds are here that cause us difficulties. Autumn mists and cold give rise to illness and give it a basis. And yet you say that you do not need the nourishment of the [king of the] hundred medicines. Wouldn't [alcohol] aid the basic energies of the four elements?"

Ryōgen replied saying, "As for the instructions left to us by eminent predecessors, we can reject them only with difficulty because it would be similar to confusing the teaching."

Again [Kaneie] stated, "The ritual offerings are at an imperially ordered assembly (*chokue*). Any difference of opinion would go against the imperial command." Then he ordered the imperial emissary to take out the bottle that he kept with him. The minister of the right took a cup and had it offered to the archbishop.

After that time, alcohol was brought out at lectures or offered to those who came to the equinox services (*higan*). And so today people speak of this as, "The great teacher Jie saw into the future. He was awarded seats in assemblies, praised the five pungent herbs (*goshin*) and permitted drinking parties."

[Such words] are the height of groundless suspicion. They are slanderous songs filled with biased rumors. Within the sevenfold boundaries [of Mount Hiei] how could one take the five pungent herbs? In the beginning, in the hospitals of the multitudes of valleys, such items were taken to aid in the practice and study of those who were ill. This is for the world outside [of the monastery] and was not explained for the three thousand monks [on Mount Hiei]. [Drinking alcohol and eating the five pungent herbs] is a means of conversion in the latter period of the Dharma. It is not the case that it is only for the most vulgar who do not understand.[28]

Ryōgen, in fact, had forbidden the consumption of alcohol in the sixteenth of his twenty-six rules. The story is treated with ambivalence, being related in detail but then followed by a qualified denial. The contents reveal that at least some monks on Mount Hiei believed that Ryōgen had first permitted drinking. However, the story does not appear in many sources. The use of alcohol is justified in two ways in the passage. The medicinal use is, in fact, in keeping with the traditional interpretations of the rule against alcohol in the *Fan-wang ching*.[29] The mention of expedient means of conversion to be used in the latter days of the law (*matsudai*) provides a rationale for the changes in practice that came to be prevalent on Mount Hiei. Finally, the mention of the prohibition of the five pungent herbs reflects the prohibition of these in the *Fan-wang ching;* many of the markers at the boundaries of monasteries mentioned that alcohol and pungent herbs were prohibited.

Ryōgen's reputed association with armed monks and his support of Ennin's lineage over that of Enchin led to the development of legends concerning monks who denounced him. A monk from Onjōji named Gaen is said to have borne a grudge against Ryōgen and to have spread false stories accusing Ryōgen of reckless conduct and eating meat. Ryōgen became angry and posted a vow denying the charges at the three major centers on Mount Hiei. The story probably was based on his authorship of the twenty-six rules.[30]

Ryōgen is associated with certain objects used in the daily lives of monks. A type of pickled radish is called *jōshinbō* after Ryōgen's quarters.[31] The silken robes (*soken*) used in daily practice as opposed to those used in official functions were also said to have originated with Ryōgen when Emperor Murakami bestowed such a robe on Ryōgen in 981 for performing a ritual that cured an illness; however, Emperor Murakami was not on the throne at that time, clearly indicating that the story is a fabrication. Moreover, this type of robe was not used until the thirteenth century. The *soken* robe itself was also associated with warrior monks and may have been part of the complex of legends that associated Ryōgen with the advent of armed monks. The name of the robe indicates that it originally was white, but eventually a variety of colors was used to indicate ranks. Although these robes were particularly associated with the Tendai school, both Shingon and Nara monks eventually adopted them.[32]

Folk Religion

Ryōgen's posthumous reputation as a protector at times conflicted with Buddhist teachings. For example, his biography is included in the *Goshūi ōjōden* (Continuation of the gleanings of the biographies of those reborn in the Pure Land). The compiler, Miyoshi no Tameyasu (d. 1139), noted that Ryōgen was said to have remained on Mount Hiei to protect it and thus had not been born in the Pure Land. However, because such a belief would have invalidated Ryōgen's inclusion in a collection of those reborn in the Pure Land, Tameyasu added that he believed that Ryōgen would eventually be reborn in the "western mountains when he ceased guarding Mount Hiei."[33]

As was mentioned above, some images of Ryōgen seemed to embody his spirit and to have special powers. In fact, images of Ryōgen begin to appear during the Kamakura period. According to Murayama Shūichi, the earliest record of an image is dated to 1203, when lower-ranking monks serving in the halls (*dōshu*) of Mount Hiei threatened the scholar-monks (*gakusō*). An image of Ryōgen was placed in the Shuryō-gon'in at Yokawa to protect it. Later images were placed at all three of the major centers on Mount Hiei during the Genkyū era (1204–1206). The earliest extant image is at Genkōji in Kobe.[34] During the Bun'ei era (1264–1275), the Tendai monk Eijō (1234–?) vowed to make thirty-three images of Ryōgen that would reflect Ryōgen's identification with the thirty-three manifestations of Nyoirin Kannon. He later doubled his vow to sixty-six with the intention of placing one in each of Japan's provinces; these images were to help protect Japan from the Mongol invasions. Eventually, his vows raised the number to ninety-nine images. Eijō beseeched the buddhas that anyone who made an offering to the image obtain the karmic connection that would enable him or her to be reborn in the Pure Land.[35]

Certain images eventually came to be associated with legends and known by special names. The icon at the Zōrindō at Higashidani in Tōdō on Mount Hiei was called the Konoha daishi (Tree-leaves great teacher). When one of the monks had been assigned the job of raking the leaves in the courtyard for a major assembly, he became sick and could not perform his duty. The icon is said to have slipped out of the hall and raked the leaves for the monk. If all the monks in Higashidani sleep with their feet toward the image, when they wake up they are said to find their positions reversed with their heads toward the image.

The image at the Fujimotobō in the Kaishindani in Yokawa is called the Reifuri daishi (Bell-ringing great teacher). An image of Fudō myōō was installed at the Fujimotobō. The abbot of the Fujimotobō was devout and practiced every day without fail. One day the abbot heard that his mother was ill and went to visit. He asked the abbot of the neighboring hall to perform the practices for Fudō myōō while he was gone. The next morning the neighbor went to perform the services; although he saw no sign that the Fujimotobō abbot had returned, he did hear a bell ringing and so assumed that the Fujimotobō abbot was performing the services. The next day when the Fujimotobō abbot returned he went to greet his neighbor before going home. The neighbor told the Fujimotobō abbot what had happened, and the Fujimotobō abbot returned home. Just as he was about to enter, he heard a bell ringing. When he went in, he saw no sign that a human had been there, but he did see that the image of Ryōgen next to the Fudō myōō seemed virtually alive.[36]

The date of the earliest portrait of Ryōgen is not clear; one of the early examples is found in Fujiwara no Kanezane's (1149–1207) diary; he reports that he had the Mahāyāna Hall (Daijōin) at Mudōji constructed in 1194 and a portrait of Ryōgen drawn for it in honor of Fujiwara no Kiyoko (1122–1181).[37] In addition to portraits, pictures of Ryōgen were printed. An early reference to this practice can be found in the *Genkō shakuhso*, compiled in 1322: "Ryōgen's visage was virtuous and valiant. He held up a mirror and copied his reflection, saying, 'Wherever you place my image it will repel evil spirits.' From that time on, printed images [of him] spread everywhere. People today paste them on the doors of their houses everywhere."[38] Both icons and portraits of Ryōgen probably became widespread around the late-Heian or early-Kamakura periods. Portraits can be divided into four types: (1) Ryōgen alone; (2) Ryōgen flanked by two attendants (*dōji*); (3) Ryōgen flanked by his two top disciples, Genshin and Kakuun; and (4) a set of portraits intended for Esoteric rituals that include Sanskrit characters, Nyoirin Kannon, and Fudō myōō.[39] Certain images or paintings were said to be particularly powerful and might bring their monasteries wealth and renown. This was the case with a portrait said to have been drawn by Ryōgen himself that escaped the flames when Mount Hiei was set ablaze by Oda Nobunaga's troops. The portrait eventually became the focus of a dispute between Seiraiji in the city of Tsu in Mie Province and Kan'eiji in Tokyo.[40]

The spread of printed images, in particular, enabled Ryōgen's stature as a protector to spread to the population at large. The beliefs underlying these images and portrayed in them associated Ryōgen with Fudō myōō or with Kannon. For example, woodblocks were used to print thirty-three copies of a small image of a robed monk with an elongated left eyebrow. The thirty-three repetitions of the monk clearly identify it with Kannon's thirty-three manifestations. The image was called the Mame daishi (Demon-vanquishing great teacher); a play on the word "demon-vanquishing," pronounced *mame* (a homonym for bean) led to the image's also being called the Bean Great Teacher. Another explanation attributes the title Bean Great Teacher to the small size of the images. These woodblock prints were used as amulets to protect against illness and bad fortune.[41] A variation of this is attaching the amulet to the ends of bamboo grass and placing it at the four corners of a field; insect pests are then thought to be repelled.

In a similar manner, another folk belief relates how Ryōgen came to be called Tsuno daishi (The horned great teacher). The elongated eyebrow mentioned above may be a reference to the horns. One story behind this representation notes that when a plague god attacked Ryōgen, it was only able to reside in the tip of his little finger. Nevertheless, Ryōgen's body was wracked with pain and he developed high fevers. To expel the plague god, Ryōgen sat before a mirror and meditated on the perfect fusion of the three truths (*ennyū santai*) until he manifested himself in a demon-quelling mode, naked with horns. This form was later copied and given to people as an amulet. Woodblocks of Ryōgen in this form were pasted on the gates of homes to protect them from pestilence and from robbers, a practice that probably dates back to the Kamakura period. It was even used by Tendai scholar-monks (*gakusō*) to protect themselves against the disturbances of the monks who performed the more menial jobs around the various halls (*dōsō*). In the Aomori region, temples, regardless of sectarian affiliation, distribute new amulets of Tsuno daishi around the time of the New Year; if a household has not received a new amulet, the New Year has not been properly welcomed. The connection with the New Year is probably based on Ryōgen's death shortly after the New Year. When this practice became prevalent in Aomori is not known.[42] The image is also installed in Buddhist altars in the Kyoto region to pray for a husband for a woman who has not been able to meet a suitable man.

A related image, in which Ryōgen wears the mask of a demon, is found at Rozanji. The story behind it is that Ryōgen was said to have a kind and handsome face. When he was summoned to the palace, rumors of his good looks spread among the women. To end such talk, Ryōgen went to the palace wearing the demon's mask. The image itself is probably based on Ryōgen's association with Fudō myōō.[43]

By the Tokugawa period, a pilgrimage route devoted to Ryōgen with eighteen temples had been established in the Kantō area.[44] In other areas, worshipers chanted the phrase "Namu Jie daishi."

Ryōgen and Divination

Finally, Ryōgen is said to have been the founder of the fortunetelling systems found at Japanese temples and shrines; this is reflected in references to him as the "founder of divination" (*omikuji no ganso*) on maps for pilgrims from the Edo period until the present.[45] The claim may be related to the manner in which the topics for debate were drawn from a box, similar to the manner in which numbers corresponding to fortunes were drawn from a box for divination. The Tendai monk Tenkai, who restored Mount Hiei after it had been burned in 1571, was said to have been a fervent believer in Ryōgen and to have received his posthumous advice. Tenkai prayed to Ryōgen for some means so that others might benefit from his advice. In a dream, Ryōgen revealed that he had deposited one hundred verses that he had composed in a particular place. Each verse had been numbered. When a person had a wish, he or she could draw a stick or piece of paper from a box with a number. The number would correspond to the verse that would advise the believer about whether the wish would meet with success. One set of procedures used in this divination required the recipient to purify body, mouth, and mind and recite the chapter on Kannon from the *Lotus Sūtra*. In addition, various *dhāraṇī* dedicated to Kannon were recited 333 times each, before the believer selected a fortune; as a result, the system was sometimes called the Kannon-divination system (*Kannon-sen*). At Ryōgen's quarters in Yokawa, the recipient of the divination is questioned by a monk who then recites the scriptures and shakes a box until a fortune falls out. The vigor with which the box is shaken reflects the level of the monk's concentration. The monk then interprets the verse for the divination. The requirements of recitation and faith in the system made the *Kannon-sen* more rigorous than most divination at temples. This form of divination seems to have continued to the present day.[46]

The actual fortunes consisted of four verses of five characters each. The recipient (or the monk representing him or her) would choose the appropriate line to read depending on the person's age, the season or month, or the event the person wished to know about. For example, if the issue was related to a person's age, the first line was read if the subject was fifteen years or less, the second if the subject was between sixteen and thirty, and so forth. If the subject was between sixty-one and seventy-five, the first line was read. The fortunes are said to be effective for such issues as illness, lost items, desires, marriages, and journeys. In some versions of the verses, separate sections of the text were established to enable a person to apply the verse to such issues as birth, death, travel, and fortune.

Perhaps to counteract charges that fortunetelling did not belong at temples, precedents in China were cited and the claim made that

Kannon in the form of Ryōgen brought them to Japan.[47] In fact, the text attributed to Ryōgen can be traced to a text used at the Upper T'ien-chu-ssu (Indian temple) in Hang-chou that was in use during the Southern Sung dynasty. The divination system may have been formulated to give Buddhist temples a means to compete with the divination practices found at Taoist temples; however, the actual text has little Buddhist content.[48]

When the text first appeared in Japan is not clear. However, one of the oldest artifacts used in ordinations at a temple, a box holding the sticks with the numbers of fortunes on them, has been found at Tendaiji in Iwate Prefecture. The inscription on the container for the divination sticks has a date of 1408. When the time for the practice to spread from Mount Hiei to Tendaiji is considered, the text's introduction to Japan can probably be dated to the late-Heian or Kamakura periods.[49] Although the beginnings of the *Kannon-sen*'s use in Japan may be placed in the twelfth century, the text did not become popular until the Tokugawa period. In addition, early mentions of the text do not necessarily indicate any relation with Ryōgen; the identification of the text with Ryōgen does not appear until the early Tokugawa period. By the late seventeenth century, Ryōgen's divinations had spread to Kan'eiji in Tokyo.[50] Although the reasons for identifying it with Ryōgen are not clear, Tenkai's devotion to Ryōgen and interest in divination may have played a role in the transformation. Ryōgen and Tenkai were sometimes grouped together at the "two great teachers" because both had played key roles in the revival and establishment of Tendai institutions. In subsequent years, the text was printed and expanded numerous times with sections concerning certain problems. The pictures found in many of the editions undoubtedly appealed to those who could not read.

Ryōgen as Demon

Because Ryōgen was viewed as a force that could control evil both by preventing it from affecting his allies and by punishing his enemies, he eventually came to be seen as a demon of sorts. For example, he is portrayed as the chief of the *tengu* (goblin) in the *Tengu zōshi*, an illustrated scroll that depicts eminent monks as *tengu* that was compiled in 1296. In other documents compiled about this time he is called the "king of demons" (*maō*).[51] Such depictions probably arose from legends that he would resort to violence to defend his supporters. In addition, unlike the ideal monk, who was expected to be free of all attachments, Ryōgen was vitally concerned with power and could be portrayed as being attached to this world rather than as having gone on to an existence where he was freed of such defilements. The sense of questionable virtue is also suggested in the *Heike monogatari* where the lines from a text attributed to Genshin for the Ganzan-e were used to suggest that Taira no Kiyomori (1118–1181) was a rebirth of Ryōgen.[52] A number of legends arose that recognized his portrayal as such seemingly evil figures but explained them away as expedient means. As was noted above, when Ryōgen copied his image by looking in a mirror, he drew himself as a horned demon. The description of this image as an expedient so that the women of the palace would not be attached to the handsome Ryōgen also belongs to this category. In this mode, naked with horns, he is known as the Oni daishi (Demon great teacher).[53]

By the Kamakura period, the Tendai school sometimes used Ryōgen's reputation as a vengeful person to their advantage. Several documents mention punishment by Ryōgen's spirit for violations of Tendai property. Thus Ryōgen was one of several divinities that helped the monastery control its manors through threats of supernatural retribution. The Shingon school used Kūkai in a similar manner.[54]

Ryōgen's Influence on Subsequent Tendai Developments

Tendai after Ryōgen's death was dramatically different from what it had been early in his life. In terms of social composition, the school would come to be dominated by the sons of nobles who would guard the domains that had been nominally given to the Tendai school and pass control down to members of their clan who became monks. Eventually, lineages of monastic fathers and sons emerged. The nobles often dominated the ranks of the scholar-monks, in a manner similar to the way in which they dominated court cultural life. Although monks from the lower classes could sometimes gain recognition for their scholarly attainments in the Tendai school, the increasing numbers of nobles who appeared in the examinations at young ages effectively limited most of the upper positions in the Tendai hierarchy to the nobles.

The financial structure of monasteries had also been decisively changed. Funding from official tax sources had been replaced by grants of manors. The need to defend and administer these landholdings led to new classes of monks who could carry out these duties. At times the friction between scholar-monks and administrative monks would lead to conflict and bitterness within a school as deep as that between rival schools. The importance of strategic alliances with nobles and warriors would become increasingly evident.

Many aspects of Tendai practice changed during Ryōgen's lifetime. Esoteric ritual already had assumed a key place in Tendai life before Ryōgen's ordination. But under Ryōgen it developed further and was used in new and innovative ways. The use of rituals to both curse one's enemies and protect one's interests became a common theme in Tendai Esoteric ceremonies. Their performance for powerful patrons was vital to alliances with lay supporters. Tendai monks eventually needed to develop more-powerful and more-elaborate rituals and to defend them from those who would copy them. The result was an increased emphasis on lineage, sectarianism, and secret transmissions.

Newer forms of practice also emerged, most notably Pure Land. Ryōgen's interest in Pure Land is evident from his authorship of a commentary on the nine grades of rebirth. At the same time, Ryōgen complained that Pure Land practices such as the uninterrupted *nenbutsu* had come to dominate Tendai practice and tried to establish a more traditional balance of Tendai meditative practices. About the time of Ryōgen's death, groups of Tendai monks devoted to Pure Land practices such as the *kangaku-e* (assembly to encourage learning) and *nijūgo zanmai-e* (assembly of the twenty-five concentrations) emerged. Lay practitioners also participated in these groups. The authorship of the *Ōjō yōshū* by Genshin played a major role in the development of Pure Land.

Although texts concerning *hongaku* (original or innate enlightenment) thought did not appear during Ryōgen's lifetime, they began to appear during the next century. Some of these, such as the *Hongaku-san* (Hymn to original enlightenment), were attributed to Ryōgen. A commentary on the hymn was attributed to Genshin. Although Ryōgen was not the author of texts on original enlightenment, some of the developments in the Tendai school that dated from Ryōgen's time would contribute to *hongaku* exegesis. In particular, the tendency to take scriptural passages out of context and elucidate them in debates may have developed into the unregulated explanations that characterize some *hongaku* literature. The growing numbers of nobles and their concern with lineage contributed to the secrecy typical of some *hongaku* transmissions.

I have refrained from a more extensive discussion of Tendai history after Ryōgen's death for two reasons. First, our views of later developments frequently are called into question with the careful reading of documents. Japanese scholars have focused on a relatively small number of sources by the founder of the Tendai school and some of his major successors. As a result, we do not yet understand many aspects of Tendai history. Major texts that may well call our current understanding of Tendai history into question have been appearing frequently in series such as the Zoku Tendaishū zensho (Continuation of the collected works of the Tendai school). Frequently, scholars have been too quick to suggest overarching models to describe social and doctrinal developments. My concern has focused more on the description of events around Ryōgen's time than on how they fit into Tendai history as a whole. Second, Jacqueline Stone's recent book on original enlightenment and Mikael Adolphson's book on monastic warriors admirably describe some of the subsequent developments in Tendai history.[55] As we digest and build on their work, the history of Tendai institutions and doctrine and their relation with other facets of Japanese culture and history should become clearer.

Appendix 1
Ennin and Yokawa

The Tendai establishment on Mount Hiei is divided into three major geographical areas (*santō* or the three pagodas): Saitō (Western pagoda), Tōdō (Eastern pagoda), and Yokawa. Saitō and Tōdō received their names because they were the sites of two of the six pagodas that Saichō had planned to construct throughout the country to protect it.[1] Each of these pagodas was to contain a thousand copies of the *Lotus Sūtra*. Tōdō and Saitō are only one or two kilometers apart, and the walk is easy.

Yokawa is to the north of Saitō and Tōdō. It is five kilometers from Saitō and even farther from Tōdō. Because the path between from Yokawa and Saitō goes down a substantial hill and then back up another slope, walking between Yokawa and other parts of Mount Hiei involved a strenuous walk.[2] Saichō considered Saitō and Tōdō to be the center of the monastic complex on Mount Hiei. Yokawa was mentioned in Saichō's writings only as the northernmost boundary of the Mount Hiei complex and as the site of the Shuryōgon'in (Hall for the practice of the meditation of heroic valor; Skt. *Śuraṅgama-samādhi*).[3] Saichō did not treat it as the site of a pagoda, such as those that served as the focal points of the Saitō and Tōdō areas, and did nothing to develop it.

Yokawa was opened up by Saichō's disciple Ennin (794–864), probably about 831, nine years after Saichō's death.[4] According to the *Jikaku daishiden*, Ennin's main reason for retreating to Yokawa was illness. However, he also undoubtedly wished to escape from the bitter factionalism that had arisen between the followers of Saichō's two foremost disciples, Gishin and Enchō, in the Tōdō and Saitō areas on Mount Hiei during the decade after Saichō's death. This factionalism came to a climax when Gishin, shortly before his death in 833, appointed his disciple Enshu to be the next *zasu* of Enryakuji. The appointment was not popular among the followers of Enchō, Saichō's senior disciple, and

Enshu and his followers were eventually forced to leave Mount Hiei, virtually splitting the school in half. In addition, a clique led by Ninchū, the presiding officer (*jōza*), opposed many of the administrative measures that Kōjō advocated.[5] Finally, the development of the Western Pagoda center would be the occasion of considerable strife as factions led by Eryō and his disciples strove to gain preeminence in that area.[6] During the years before he went to Mount Hiei, Ennin had spent some time in the north, probably in the Tōgoku area with a community of monks sympathetic to the Tendai tradition that had been established by Dōchū (735?–800?) and Kōchi (fl. 794–835). Ennin hoped to create a community in Yokawa that would embody the strict training and discipline he had experienced under Kōchi.[7]

Ennin's teacher Kōchi had studied under Dōchū, a disciple of Chien-chen (J. Ganjin, 688–763), the Chinese master of *Vinaya* who had both performed the first orthodox ordinations in Japan and brought the first T'ien-t'ai texts to Japan. Dōchū was famous for his strict observance of the precepts, and Kōchi seems to have followed his teacher's lead in advocating strict observance of the precepts. He was also known to the local populace as a bodhisattva (*bosatsu*).[8] After several years with Kōchi, Ennin traveled to Mount Hiei to study under Saichō, probably because Dōchū had helped Saichō earlier.[9] In 817, Ennin accompanied Saichō on a journey back to Tōgoku to proselytize. There he saw Saichō supervise the construction of two pagodas that would each hold a thousand copies of the *Lotus Sūtra* and that would be part of his plan to build a network of six pagodas to protect the nation. In 817, when Ennin returned to Tōgoku with Saichō, Ennin must have visited the monastic order in which he had spent time when he was a young man and remembered the strict practices of his youth.

After Ennin returned to Mount Hiei, he continued his austerities until he was exhausted. According to the *Jikaku daishiden*, "When Ennin was about forty, his body was weak and his eyesight was failing. Since he felt that he did not have long to live, he sought out a quiet dark place along a river in the north of the mountain and built a hut out of grass. There he cut himself off from people and waited for the end."[10] After three years of practice, he dreamt that he was given some medicine from heaven. When he drank it, it tasted like honey. When he asked where it had come from, the man who had appeared beside his bed with the medicine told him that it was the medicine that gave longevity to the deities of the Heaven of the Thirty-three (Vedic) Gods. When Ennin awoke, the taste of the medicine still remained in his mouth. He began to recover his strength, and his eyes regained their sight.

After he had recovered, Ennin copied the *Lotus Sūtra* in a special manner. This copy became the spiritual center of the *stūpa* or pagoda that Ennin built, the eventual focal point of the monastic center at Yokawa. Instead of relying on a large number of copies of the *Lotus Sūtra* to give his *stūpa* the spiritual authority and power it needed to be the center of a new area on Mount Hiei, Ennin relied on a special way of making a single copy of the *Lotus Sūtra*. According to later sources, Ennin made the brush out of the soft inner portions of grass and his ink out of stone. As he wrote each character, he made offerings and meditated on the Buddha.[11] In addition, Ennin performed the four types of Tendai meditation during this period. When he had finished copying the *sūtra*, he built a small container for it and later installed this container in a hall. The hall was called the Konpon nyohōdō (Basic hall in accord with the Dharma) and became the basis of the Shuryō-gon'in, the center of the monastic complex at Yokawa.[12] In building a pagoda, Ennin gave notice that Yokawa might eventually have the same status as Saitō and Tōdō, the two major monastic centers on Mount Hiei. Shortly after his retreat at Yokawa had ended, Ennin left Japan to study in China.

Immediately before he left for China, Ennin wrote two documents concerning Yokawa: (1) Rules for the Shuryōgon'in (*Shuryōgon'in shiki*) and (2) a list of disciples in charge of the various buildings in Yokawa. Because the *Shuryōgon'in shiki* reveals Ennin's commitment to the type of serious religious practice that Saichō had originally proposed for Mount Hiei, it is translated here.

1. In accordance with Saichō's will, women may not enter the confines of our mountain monastery.
2. All those within the Shuryōgon'in, including the servants, may not drink alcoholic beverages. Anyone who does so may not associate with monks.
3. Those within the Shuryōgon'in shall take horse chestnuts (*tochi*) as their food. During the three months of fall [the seventh, eighth, and ninth months of the lunar calendar], they shall beg for their food and continue in this spirit.
4. All those in the Shuryōgon'in, no matter what their rank, shall regard each other as they might their parents, teachers, or siblings. They shall not constantly point out each other's faults.

5. All those in the Shuryōgon'in shall regard those under them in rank with compassion and shall respect those above them. If they do not do so, although they are still different from those of heterodox religions, how can they be called Buddhists?

6. If a lay believer and donor wishes to have religious services performed in the Shuryōgon'in, then he must have the service performed by monks in accordance with the rotation based on their seniority. If there are any monks from outside areas (*kyakusō*), then they may be appointed to perform the ceremony. If the donor does not agree to issue his requests or invitations in accordance with seniority, then no services will be performed for him within the Shuryōgon'in.

7. When those of the Shuryōgon'in are walking, standing, lying, or sitting, their minds should be in accord with the Dharma. They should contemplate the true nature of phenomena (*jissō*) and not discriminate. No other thoughts should enter their minds.

8. Those within the Shuryōgon'in should not look at objects in a covetous manner (*kōjiki*).[13]

9. Those who are engaged in studying within the Shuryōgon'in should not be motivated by the prospect of fame or profit from the secular world, but should do so to help sentient beings, to benefit the nation, to encourage Buddhism, and to realize enlightenment.[14]

Several elements of the *Shuryōgon'in shiki* are noteworthy. When Ennin prohibits women from entering the monastery on Mount Hiei and bans drinking alcohol, he reiterates the ideals about Buddhist practice that Saichō had expressed in his last instructions to his disciples.[15] The admonition against being motivated by the desire for fame and the admonition to keep Buddhist ideals in mind at all times whether one is walking, standing, sitting, or lying down are similar to Saichō's admonitions to his students, as is his endorsement of rituals to protect the nation.[16] Ennin's prohibition on special relationships between lay patrons and particular monks was an attempt to limit the favoritism and factionalism that had adversely affected much of the rest of Mount Hiei. Yokawa was to be a religious site devoted to serious practice.

The same day, Ennin also specified how Yokawa was to be administered while he was studying in China. Overall control of Yokawa was given to his chief disciple, Anne, who would later succeed Ennin as Tendai *zasu*. The names of thirteen buildings in Yokawa are listed along with the names of thirteen other disciples who were to oversee them during Ennin's absence. Ennin thus carefully made sure that the ideals upon which the founding of Yokawa was based would be maintained during his absence.[17]

After he returned from China, Ennin was unable to spend much time in Yokawa. However, shortly before his death in 864, Ennin set forth additional instructions about the future of Yokawa. Although any monk was welcome to come and stay at Yokawa, the administration of Yokawa was to be entrusted only to those of his lineage. Although Ennin was probably partially motivated by his desire to provide for his own disciples, his main motive was to insure that the ideals that lay behind the founding of Yokawa would continue to be observed.[18]

After Ennin's death, Yokawa seems to have gone into a steep decline as a Tendai center. It was probably too far away from the Saitō and Tōdō areas to attract many monks. But even more important, Ennin's rules prohibited the monks of Yokawa from establishing the type of close ties to individual patrons that played such important roles in the lives of Ryōgen and other eminent Tendai monks. During the century between Ennin's death and Ryōgen's entry to Yokawa, the *Shuryōgon'in kengyō shidai* records the names of only three supervisors (*kengyō*) of Yokawa: Anne, Jiei, and Chinchō.[19] In contrast, fourteen monks served as *zasu* of the Tendai school and eleven monks as supervisors of the Hōdōin of Saitō during this same period.[20] Of the three monks who served as supervisors of Yokawa, the first two were Ennin's disciples, suggesting that the post was filled for at most a few decades after Ennin's death. Although the third supervisor, Chinchō (884–964), is said to have been a disciple of Ennin's student Chōi (d. 906), this claim is questionable because Chinchō was still supervisor during Ryōgen's lifetime. Chinchō's activities in Yokawa suggest that Tendai interest in the area may have revived somewhat during the early years of Ryōgen's life.

Chinchō refused to let any monks build lodgings in Yokawa unless they were willing to live there permanently, apparently because he was waiting for some monk to come and revive the area. He is said to have been delighted when he heard that Ryōgen wished to live in the area.[21]

Appendix 2
A Note on Morosuke's Interests

The depth of the relationship between Ryōgen and Morosuke can be better understood by considering Morosuke's personality and interests. In both the *Ōkagami* and *Eiga monogatari*, Morosuke is portrayed as a model of rectitude, etiquette, and good sense. His instructions to his descendants, the *Kujōdono yuikai*, also reflect such qualities. Thus even while Morosuke was the effective head of government, he always held a rank lower than that of his elder brother Saneyori to preserve the proper Confucian relationship between elder and younger brothers. But at the same time, Morosuke seems to have resented his elder brother's precedence. When Saneyori was given as wife a woman who was from a higher-ranking family than Morosuke's first wife, Fujiwara no Seishi, Morosuke conducted an affair with and eventually married Emperor Daigo's fourth daughter, Princess (*naishinnō*) Isoko (904–938), even though men of his rank had not been allowed to marry women of that rank in the past.[1] When she eventually died childless, he married her younger sister, Princess Gashi (also known as Masako), who bore him several children. After her death, he married Princess Kōshi, also a daughter of Emperor Daigo, who bore him two children. Although the marriages seem to have been based on genuine affection, Morosuke also used them to further his own career. Morosuke's multiple marriages resulted in twelve sons and seven daughters; many of them served in important court posts or married strategically.[2] In contrast, Saneyori never took another woman as his primary wife after his first wife's death. While Morosuke outwardly acknowledged his brother's superior status, he worked hard to ensure his own nuclear family's success. Morosuke's own efforts to balance the demands of propriety with his desires for advancement parallel Ryōgen's efforts. Ryōgen had to operate within the parameters set for Buddhist monks. Yet at the same time, he was a master of manipulating those parameters to further his ambitions.

311

The rivalry between the two brothers became more evident after Morosuke's death as their descendants competed for supremacy in both the political and ritual spheres. Their rivalry in court etiquette and ritual is similar to that found among Buddhist lineages, and merits mention. An understanding of the deep concern that the nobility had for court ritual helps explain their lavish support for masters of Buddhist ritual such as Ryōgen. Morosuke wrote a diary, the *Kyūreki*, in which he discussed teachings on ritual handed down by his father.[3] He later collected the sections on ritual and classified them in a text called the *Kujōdono ki* (Record of Morosuke; however, the extant text was edited after his death). Finally, late in life Morosuke compiled the *Kujō nenchūgyōji* (Morosuke's record of annual ritual observances), a detailed description of the etiquette and order of court activities. Although Morosuke was vitally concerned with correct behavior, he was not above ignoring precedent as he had in his marriages to three princesses. Besides yearly observances, the text included discussions of such disparate topics as mourning and the reclamation of land. Morosuke's prescriptions were handed down and served as the basis of his lineage's views on ritual, a lineage named the Kujō-ryū after Morosuke's residence.

Morosuke's elder brother Saneyori was the founder of a tradition of ritual behavior called the Ononomiya-ryū, named after Saneyori's mansion at Onomiya. Many of Saneyori's views were included in his diary, the *Seishinkōki* (also known as the *Suishinki*),[4] which unfortunately has not survived, although parts of a work on ritual, the *Ononomiya kojitsu kyūrei* (Ancient practices and old examples of the Ononomiya lineage), do exist. Saneyori's adopted son Fujiwara no Sanesuke (957–1046), actually the child of Saneyori's son Tadatoshi (928–973), continued Saneyori's tradition of ritual exegesis in his diary, the *Shōyūki*, and a separate work on ritual, the *Ononomiya nenchūgyōji* (Annual rituals according to Saneyori). Sanesuke devoted considerable energy to discussions of precedent. Often he criticized Morosuke's procedures and praised those suggested by Saneyori. Although the criticisms may seem picayune by today's standards, consisting of arguments about such issues as where a person should enter and exit a room, these issues helped define the various factions at court in a ritual sense. Besides ritual, Sanesuke also discussed such topics as *kami*, ritual pollution, mourning, and respect for superiors.[5]

Appendix 3
Dying Instructions of the Great Archbishop Jie

On the third day of the fifth month of the third year of Tenroku [972], I begin writing these instructions [to be carried out] after my death.[1]

Yokawa Jōshinbō (Concentrated mind quarters),[2] a cypress bark–roofed house (*hiwadabuki-ya*)

A main house (*omoya*) five bays (*ken*)[3] long with four eaves (*hisashi*), three outer eaves (*magobisashi*), and one extended outer eave (*mago-magobisashi*).
A shingle-roofed house (*itaya*) in the west.
A main house thirteen *ken* long with four eaves.
Two shingle-roofed houses to the east.

The above-mentioned buildings will be permanently entrusted to Myōkōbō[4] [Jinzen]. He should keep these buildings in repair in order to provide for other disciples. This should give the disciples a special advantage so that they can fulfill their wish to complete their residence on Mount Hiei. All resident monks are to serve him [Jinzen] faithfully and should not defy his wishes. Any monk who does not follow this order will be permanently expelled from our lineage (*ichimon*).

Shingondō (Mantra hall), five *ken* long with four eaves and two outer eaves

The above-mentioned hall was built by the order of the late lord Kujō[5] [Fujiwara no Morosuke]. His lordship, however, passed away while lumber was being prepared for construction. Therefore, the project was entrusted to the former empress[6] (*saki no chūgū*) [Fujiwara no Anshi] who continued to support the construction project. Half of the lumber and other material for the construction had been prepared while the lord was alive.

The princess also sent one hundred *koku*[7] of rice for the construction (*sakuryōmai*). In addition, I personally made arrangements to obtain the rest of the lumber and other materials needed. I made every effort to complete the construction in time for the annual memorial service (*goshūki*) [for lord Kujō]. Therefore, I used my personal funds to obtain more than half of the materials needed to build the hall. Because of the damage caused by wind and rain over many years, the roof now suffers serious leaks. Although I would like to repair the roof, my days are numbered. The administration of this hall is entirely entrusted to Zenji no kimi[8] [Jinzen] and so the named Myōkōbō is entrusted with the residence hall in the east. If he does not have enough resources for its repair, he should consult the prime minister (*dajōdono*) [Fujiwara no Koremasa] and other sons [of Morosuke] to help complete the repair. The dual *maṇḍala* (*ryōbu mandara*),[9] the main statue (*honzon*), and other objects offered by the late lord [Fujiwara no Morosuke], and [a picture scroll of] the Pure Land [of Amida] offered by the [former] empress [Fujiwara no Anshi] are all to be enshrined in this hall. They should not be handled carelessly. Strive to carry this out.

Original residential quarters (*konpon bōchi*) in the south ravine (*minamidani*)[10]

My cremation (*enju no hi*) is to be held at my original residence. The estate of the residential quarter will be entrusted to Myōkōbō.

Hongakubō (Original enlightenment quarters) at Saitō[11]

This residence was originally made up of three shingle-roofed houses. For the convenience of the reconstruction of the residents, it was traded for the south residence of Byōdōbō [Enshō].[12] I have a written document of the exchange (*kaebumi*). The transaction was confirmed by the head monk (*inju*) and the senior administrator (*jōkō*)[13] [at Saitō], as well as Kōen [n.d.] *ajari*. But according to the agreement on the day of the trade, of the three houses, the one to the south, the permanent residence of the late master, was excluded from the trade. The estate [of Enshō] was, therefore, exchanged for the two shingle-roofed houses [of Hongakubō] to the north. The reconstruction project on the east ridge should be completed soon after the trade.

The estate on the east ridge belonged to the late Byōjuin. His disciples signed a document collectively to transfer the estate to me. (At that time, the head administrative officer (*bettō*) of Hōdō [in] also signed the document.)

But the late Ennichi *hosshi*[14] [n.d.] forged a document [of ownership to the estate] and deposited it at the residence of Byōdōbō [Enshō] before he left for his assigned province. The head priest and the senior administrators [of Saitō] ruled that [the document] was invalid and agreed that the ownership [of the estate] should belong to me per the original contract.

Although the official document has not yet been issued, the ruling states,

> "The ownership of the three houses at Hongakubō all belong to you. But three priests are currently living in the Hall for *Samādhi* of Freely Following One's thoughts (Zuijiidō).[15] Therefore, you should be careful not to create disputes with members of the same lineage (*dōmon*)."

I would like them to find other places to live and to evacuate the residence soon. My days are numbered. At this time, I entrust the residential land for the lodgings to the Master of Esoteric Buddhism Senga.[16] The master of Esoteric Buddhism Shōku[17] should also understand the conditions [of Hongakubō at Saitō]. I would like them to appeal the case [concerning the estates at Saitō] to the head priest and chief administrators [at Saitō] as well as the Master of Esoteric Buddhism Kōen and completely reconfirm the ownership of these two estates to the south and north [of Saitō]. These estates have already become part of the heritage of our lineage. I have already enshrined Yakushi [the Medicine] Buddha as the primary image, as well as a thousand-armed Kannon,[18] an image of Shōden (Gaṇeśa),[19] and other statues at the site. I have deeply committed myself to developing the site. In addition, I have already brought in lumber to build a fifteen-*ken*-long gallery house (*rōya*). I [temporarily used a part of the lumber] to build a music pavilion (*gakuya*) for the opening service of the lecture hall (*kōdō*). The music house is only thirteen *ken* long because the site was not large enough. The rest of the lumber for two *ken* is stored at Nōka.

I definitely want to build a cypress bark–roofed house of three *ken* with four eaves and one outer eave, for use as a residence (*shukubō*) along with a [Buddha] hall. I have explained the details of my plan to the Master of Esoteric Buddhism Senga and our fellow practitioner Jōan.[20] If I die before I complete the construction, I would like to ask both masters of Esoteric Buddhism (*ajari*) to work together to build the house in order to maintain our legacy.

An estate for a residence in Tōdō

Located to the north of the administration office (*mandokoro*) of the Jōshin'in (Hall of the concentrated mind).[21] The land for housing belonged to the *tani no zasu* (head of the valley), Master[22] [Ryōyū]. His disciple Enken *daihosshi*[23] inherited the estate [from Ryōyū] and resided there. On the day he passed away, the estate was entrusted to his disciple Kōmyō. I bought the estate from Kōmyō [n.d.]. The price was 180 *kan*. A [sale] transference document for the estate, a document of contract, a document requesting payment, and other documents are all available. The temple stipend (*jiryō*) inherited from the master at Byōdōbō, Abbot [Enshō], is henceforth given to Myōkōbō. If he is given a chance to take the position [of *zasu*] on Mount [Hiei], he should establish a temple there with an abbacy. Originally a storage house was built on the land. I dismantled the storage house and built a house last year, since I urgently needed extra housing (*zōsha*) while I hurriedly built a reliquary for the Sōjiin (Dhāraṇī Hall). I would like to expand the original plan of the site about a few *shaku*[24] and build two cypress bark–roofed houses of three *ken* long with four eaves and with one outer eave in the east and west from the center, and three galleries in the south, west, and north. I have not finished my project. My days are numbered. I would like [my disciples] to complete this project.

Kazan chūin Myōgōbō (Myōgō lodgings of the central chapel of Gangyōji)[25]

This residence was where the great master and senior administrator (*daishi jōkō*) [of Mount Hiei, Kakue] died. After the great master passed away, a fire broke out. The residence was completely consumed by the fire. Although he had many disciples, no one was qualified to inherit the site. Therefore, I privately built an eleven-*ken*-long shingle-roofed house with two eaves. Last year, I also built a palace-style house (*shinden*)[26] of three *ken* long with four eaves and one outer eave. The honorarium for the lecturer of Musashi province, Ryakukyū [n.d.], should be used to cover the cost of cypress bark roofing and interior modeling. The articles, such as some silk fabric presented last year, have already been put into the account. (This amounts to approximately fifty *kan;* Genzen[27] knows about the official documents [of the account].) The funds were loaned for the preparation of the opening ceremony of an assembly hall.

The building still needs some work. Many due articles have not been received. With the help of the senior (*hōnō*) and assistant administrators (*kōtō*), please collect the dues quickly and complete the construction by the end of this year. Our fellow practitioner Jōan has known [the plans for the construction of this site] from the beginning. I would like him to be in charge of [the rest of] the construction. I would like him to commute or stay there once in a while and carefully supervise the maintenance [of the site]. The legacy of the great master should not be left in disrepair. But [the practitioner] Heiyu no kimi already has another lodging place there. He is allowed to commute and stay there, too. Among other fellow practitioners, those who wish to reside there should also be given proper assistance to do so. I also want to build a cart shed (*kuruma yado*) in the southeast corner (*tatsumi no sumi*), a seven-*ken*-long house, a priestly residence house in the east, a gallery in the west, and other buildings. But I do not have enough funds. After this old priest [Ryōgen] passes away, I hope someone will build [these buildings]. The remainder of the honorarium for Ryakukyū, if there is any, should also be used to build necessary buildings according to the funds available.

The hall (*in*) at Nōka[28]

A cypress bark–roofed house, five *ken* long with three eaves. There is a breezeway (*gonrō*) in the east.

A shingle-roofed large kitchen (*ōtakiya*), four *ken* long with two eaves.

Genzen's mother has lived in the above-mentioned house for years. After this little priest [Ryōgen] passes away, I fear that both mother and son will not have anyone to rely on. While I lie in my sickbed and think of their situation, I can not help but cry [for them]. I would like my fellow monks to visit and offer her help. After the old nun passes away, Genzen should manage the place. If his residence on Mount Hiei is not suitable, he may dismantle the house [at Nōka] and rebuild it on Mount Hiei.

An administration office building (*mandokoroya*), an eleven-*ken*-long shingle-roofed building with two eaves. This building is affiliated with the prayer-offering site (*goganjo betsuin*). The manager of the temple (*inshi*), as well as Myōkōbō, should know of this arrangement.

A cabin (*kiya*) on the northern border, seven *ken* long with two eaves. This house was once destroyed by a fire. Anshin,[29] as a director (*gyōji*), worked hard to rebuild the house. Therefore, Anshin should manage it. The manager (*inge*) of [Nōka] in should allocate a budget [for its remodeling] if necessary.

Two storage houses. They should be built west of the administration office. Funds [for the construction of the buildings] were entrusted to Senga. Purchase lumber for the construction and build them as soon as possible; use them as special storage houses (*betsunōsho*) for [Nōka]in.

Lumber for a nine-*ken*-long house with two [eaves]. The lumber was delivered from the Tomoyui manor.[30] All of the lumber has been delivered. The house should be built in a suitable place between the mountain and [Nōka]in.

I have also ordered Tomoyui manor to prepare and deliver lumber for a *shinden*-style house. [I fear that] if I die of this illness, [the people of Tomoyui manor] might not complete my order. Three senior administrators of the temple (*sangō*) and Senga should remember the order and demand its delivery.

I have also ordered Okaya manor[31] to prepare and deliver lumber for a seven-*ken*-long house. [Administrators] should have the lumber readied as soon as possible. The lumber ordered for these two houses is needed to establish [Nōka]in. [The administrators] should take proper measures to [complete the project].

A shingle-roofed house, three *ken* long with four [eaves], at Koyama. Heiyu no kimi knows about this house.

The above-mentioned house was built to take care of Myōgō's mother, who does not have anyone to rely on. The construction was completed last year, and she has already moved into the house. Since my schedule is very tight, I have yet to visit her. My days are numbered. After I leave this world, she will become more and more dependent. Lying in my sickbed, I lament her situation. My fellow practitioners should remember this, and occasionally visit her and inquire about her comfort. Myōgō is a student with a keen intellectual appetite. He also wishes to fulfill his filial duties once he has successfully established his career, but he is not yet able to do so. I sympathize with his situation.

Okaya manor

Farmland, more than 160 *chō*. There is a certificate of title [for the estate]. The above-mentioned manor was originally owned by the late lord Kujō. When he passed away, the land was donated to Lotus Hall (Hokkedō) according to his will. The original area of the farmland [of the manor] was approximately 120 *chō*. The expected annual farm income (*jishi nenryō*) is twenty to thirty *koku* [of rice]. After the temple gained title of the land, I made a careful inspection of the area of farmland [of the manor and discovered it] to be 160 *chō*. An official document from the chancellor's office (*kanpu*) was issued exempting it from farmland tax (*sozei*)[32] and tax in kind (*kanmotsu*). Fifty people of the manor, including a manager (*shōji*) and tenant farmers (*shōko*), are exempted from miscellaneous labor services (*zōyaku*).

Revenue from the annual farm income [of the manor] has increased every year. Last year, the income reached 160 *koku*. The administrative policy of this old priest [compels the supervisor of the manor] to continue land reclamation by effectively utilizing the resources of the manor and trying to increase the revenues from farm income. The manager of the temple should understand this very well.

Annual farm income [of the manor] should be divided into three parts. One-third [of the revenue] should be appropriated to cover the expenses to maintain the perpetual lamp (*jōtōryō*) of the Lotus Hall. [This amount should be] three *gō*[33] per day. If there is a surplus, it should be applied to the clothing expenses of the monks who serve in that hall (*dōsō*). The temple should not be overstocked with the silk goods annually supplied by the imperial storehouse bureau (Kuraryō). The manager of the temple should be careful to maintain other necessary supplies.

One-third [of the revenue] should be appropriated to cover the maintenance expenses of the temple. If the Lotus Hall does not need repairs, the budget may be applied to maintain other halls, reliquaries, and miscellaneous buildings.

One-third [of the revenue] should be appropriated to cover the expenses for the eight lectures (*hakkō*) [on the *Lotus Sūtra*]. The eight lectures, at which I have officiated for years, are held for the sake of both others and ourselves throughout the Dharma-realm. Since the lord [Fujiwara no Morosuke] passed away, I have officiated at the lectures during his memorial [service] days (*kijitsu*) to transfer merit for his enlightenment (*bodai*). The prime minister, the lord [Fujiwara no Koremasa], however, currently takes care of [the memorial services for Morosuke]. The services need not be held twice. Therefore, after I pass away, the lectures should be conducted during the memorial days, either at the beginning or the ending.

The eight lectures that are held during the annual memorial service (*isshūki*) should include doctrinal debates (*rongi*). Some people place a taboo on this. This [seems] ridiculous to me. [Doctrinal debate] is the main practice (*hongō*) of this ailing priest. To attain Buddhahood, one should practice [debate]. [All] my disciples should understand this. If they appreciate my advice, they must practice both lecture (*kōzetsu*) and debate. Other virtuous [practices] are not necessary. The merit created by sponsoring the eight lectures is transferred to all sentient beings and eliminates their defilements (*bonnō*), generates wisdom, and helps in the swift realization of Buddhahood. [The merit of the lectures] is also transferred to the late lord and will help him escape the cycle of birth and death in the three realms and attain the wondrous state of the true [thusness] (*isshin*). [Merit] will also be transferred to the spirit of this old priest.

The twenty-*chō* rice field was purchased from Kiyohara Naohira [n.d.]. Income from the farm is available to us from this year. The rent should be appropriated to cover the maintenance expenses of the private residences.

Tomoyui manor

This includes farmland of more than sixty *chō*. This manor was originally owned by Tsuno Yoshiko's [n.d.] ancestors. [The transfer of ownership of the estate] was mediated by the late judge (*hanji*) and senior clerk (*daisakan*), Taketsure [n.d.]. With an official certificate of ownership (*kugen*) attached, [the estate] was permanently incorporated [into the temple]. I consulted the late lord of Bōjō[34] about [the acquisition of] the estate. The lord issued his official notice to the province to register [the manor]. During the period when the [currently] abdicated emperor [Reizei] was on the throne, I consulted his highness about [the acquisition of] the estate. [His highness] ordered the Council of State and Ministry of Popular Affairs to issue an official document to the province. The province executed the order. The documents are kept in the county office. [The manor] has been exempted from farmland tax. Sixty people of the manor, including a manager and tenant farmers, are exempted from miscellaneous corvée labor. Farm income collected from the above-mentioned manor should be appropriated to cover the expenses to maintain the Hokkedō lamp during seasonal repentance services (*shiki senbō*) to the extent of one lamp per night. The remainder [of the farm rent] is entrusted to the manager of the residence (*bōshi*). [The remainder] should be appropriated to cover the expenses of the perpetual lamp for the main figure [of the Lotus Hall] and the repair of residential houses after consultation with Zenji no kimi.

Tate[iri] manor[35]

The size of the farmland is recorded on the certificate of title (*kenmon*). [The manor] is in Yasu county. This manor was owned by the late Hata

Chikanari, a former provincial secretary (*jō*). According to his will, the estate was donated to cover the expenses of the perpetual lamps for services for the dual *maṇḍala* and the *Ta pan-jo ching* (*Mahāprajñā-pāramitā-sūtra*). Therefore, [the revenue of the manor] should be appropriated only for these expenses. It should not be diverted to other purposes.

Kurodae-nishi manor[36]

The size of the farmland is recorded on the certificate of title. [The manor] is in Takashima county. This manor was donated by Tsuno Takeyasu [n.d.], Tsuno Shigekata [n.d.], and others for the salvation [enlightenment] of their ancestors. Farm income [from the manor] should be appropriated to cover the expenses of the perpetual lamp. The remainder is entrusted to the manager of the residence. [The remainder] should be appropriated to cover the maintenance expenses of the residential houses and other miscellaneous expenses after consulting with Zenji no kimi.

Takaya manor

The size of the farmland is recorded on the certificate of title. [The manor] is in Kanzaki county.[37] This manor was donated by Kuwana Tadamura [n.d.] and others to help their ancestors attain Buddhahood. The management rules of the farm income [of the manor] are to follow the example of Kurodae manor.

Mitsu-no-mikuri [manor]

[The manor] is in Shimane county in Izumo province. This island was donated by the late commander of the large sling corps (*ōyumi no shi*) Tsurakuni [n.d.]. Annual revenue [from the manor], made in kind, such as seaweed, is appropriated first to cover the expenses of monks of Hokkedō. [The remainder] is then used for offerings given to monks participating in services, such as the uninterrupted (*fudan*) [Pure Land] practices or the eight lectures [on the *Lotus Sūtra*].

Shitsumi-no-ho [manor]

[The manor] is in Wakasa province. The size of the estate is recorded on the certificate of title. The estate was purchased for thirty *kanmon*. [The purchase] was mediated by Teimyō [n.d.].

This inlet was originally owned by the former emperor Yōzei [868–949; r. 876–884]. Ownership was transferred to the late supernumerary governor (*gonnokami*) of Mikawa province, Tōkata [n.d.]. After he passed away, [the estate] was purchased from his widow. Henceforth, the estate is permanently entrusted to Myōkōbō.

Item: Collections of scriptures on exoteric and esoteric teachings

I lost the catalogue of scriptures while moving from one place to another on Mount Hiei. Therefore, I am not able to identify them immediately. A [new] catalogue should be made as soon as possible. This [scripture collection] is entrusted to Zenji no kimi. [The collection] should be kept in the scripture repository (*kyōzō*) as it always has been. [The scriptures] may, however, be perused [by Jinzen] whenever necessary. If any disciple or monk needs to borrow [scriptures] from the repository, he must obtain written loan permission. Loaned [scriptures] must be returned to the repository as soon as the borrower has finished. Do not lose any [items from the collection]. A master's contribution [to his disciples] is his teaching. Do not lose or disperse [the collection].

My collection of texts at Hongakubō, however, has been scattered and lost in recent years. None [of my collection] is left [at Hongakubō]. Scriptures left [at Hongakubō] were entrusted to Sen'un,[38] the reader (*dokushi*)[39] of Yamashiro province. There is a separate catalogue [of his collection]. These scriptures should be kept at that residence [Hongakubō]. The masters of Esoteric Buddhism (*ajari*) Senga and Shōku should understand this arrangement. They must examine the collection to prevent it from becoming scattered and lost. The reason is the same as above.

As for Myōgōbō's[40] collection of scriptures, I reviewed and sealed it after the funeral service on the forty-ninth [day after the death] of the master and senior administrator of Mount Hiei [Kakue]. Because my schedule was very tight, I have not perused the collection.

I request our co-practitioner Jōan to be in charge of examining the collection. Both of our fellow practitioner Senmi and Heiyu should also be informed about the condition of the collection. They should prevent it from being scattered and lost.

Item: Ritual implements

One bell. One sword. One five-pronged *vajra* (*goko*): [These items] are stored at Master (*daibu*) Ban's [n.d.] residence.

One mirror. One scalpel.[41] Five flower vases (*kebyō*): These are kept in a lacquered box that is old and damaged. After the great master and senior administrator [Kakue] passed away, these [articles] have been in the possession of his fellow practitioners. They should be installed properly at Myōgōbō's altar for the Buddha (*Butsudan*) as soon as the construction is done. I request that our fellow practitioner Jōan be in charge of this.

Eight bells.

One three-pronged *vajra* bell (*sankorei*). One single-pronged *vajra* bell (*dokkorei*). One jeweled bell (*hōrei*). [These articles] are fairly new. [These items] were sold (to me) by Arishige [n.d.]. These three items are to be given to Myōkōbō.

One five-pronged *vajra* bell (*gokorei*) from the T'ang [dynasty]. One reliquary bell (*sotobarei*) which is old. These two items have been installed at the Buddha-shrine. They should remain at their current location.

One five-pronged *vajra* bell. I have used [this instrument] for years. The above-mentioned item [blank]

One reliquary bell. New. [This item] was sold by Arishige. A relic of the Buddha is installed inside. The above-mentioned item [blank]

One reliquary bell. Old. [This item] was sold by a disciple of the late worthy Nyoshō [n.d.]. Shōō[42] mediated the purchase; a relic of the Buddha is installed inside. The above mentioned item [blank]

Four five-pronged *vajra*.

One *vajra*, which I have used for years, is to be given to the prime minister [Fujiwara no Koremasa].

One *vajra* is to be given to Zenji no kimi.

One *vajra*, which I used for years, is currently at Myōshō's[43] residence. [This item] is to be given to Myōshō.

One *vajra* is currently at Master Ban's residence. I have received benefits from his household for years. It should not be taken back [from him].

Two single-pronged *vajra* (*dokko*).

One is at the residence of the third daughter of the emperor[44] [Hōshi naishinnō, 919–957]. [This item] is a bequest to the princess. It should not be taken back [from her].

The other is in my possession; it should be given to [blank]

Two bells (*rei*).

One is at the residence of a tonsured consort of the emperor (*nyūdō nyōgo dono*). It should not be taken back [from her].

The other is at the residence of the middle controller of the right (*uchūben*). Our co-practitioner Jōan mediated its purchase. [The administrator] should request the return [of this item] immediately and keep it in our custody. [This item] originally belonged to the late lay servant of Sei[45] [Kiyohara].

Meditation beads (*nenju*).

Two strands of [meditation beads] made from bodhi-tree seeds (*bodaishi*). One is to be given to [blank]. One is to be given to Zenji no kimi. They are kept in the incense-burner case (*kōrobako*).
One string of [meditation beads] made from *rudrākśa*-tree seeds (*kongōshi*). [This item] is given to [blank].
[A string of meditation beads] made from crystal.
One string of [meditation beads] made from green beads (*ryokuju*).
[A string of meditation beads] made from lotus seeds (*renshi*).
[A string of meditation beads] made from soapberry seeds (*mukuroji*).
[A string of meditation beads] made from white sandalwood (*byakudan*).
[A string of meditation beads] made from red sandalwood (*shitan*).

Four sets of incense-burners (*kōro*).

One set of brass (*chūseki*).
One set of silver.
One set of white copper (*hakudō*).[46]
One set of new copper (*shindō*).

One wish-fulfilling [scepter] (*nyoi*).
Two sets of surplices made of patches of cloth (*nōgesa*).
Two sets of three robes.

Item: Concerning [my] funeral service

I will select the site of my grave myself. Please choose some pleasant site to the north [of my residence] if I pass away before I select the site.

A coffin (*kan*) should be made while I am alive. If I pass away before the coffin is ready, please have it ready by the end of the day and place [my body] in it during the night. Do not wait to chose a lucky day or an hour. [The body] must be buried within three days after I pass away. Do not delay the schedule. My disciples are not to dress in white mourning clothes (*sofuku*) or wear flax rope belts (*nawaobi*). Do not disobey the teaching [of the Buddha]. At the site of my grave, a mourning chamber (*takaya*), a wooden fence (*itagaki*), and other arrangements should be prepared according to custom.

The following people are in charge of placing my body in the coffin: Jōan, Kyōu, Ikoku, Ryōun, Ryōchin, Anshin, Genzen, Myōun, Shōō.

Cremation (*yakisho*). Officiants: Jōan, Kakuzen no kimi (he is a very good friend whom I appoint because we have made promises to each other on this matter), Dōchō, Ryōun, Chinjō, Anshin, Genzen.

Miscellaneous responsibilities: Dōho, Shukukyū.[47]

Collection of bones (*shūkotsusho*): This should be done by the people who are in charge of my coffin and cremation.

I would like to prepare a stone *stūpa*[48] and install it at my grave site while I am alive. Please erect a temporary *stūpa*, if I pass away before it is installed. Then dig a hole about three or four *shaku* deep, place my bones at the bottom of the hole, and fill up the hole with soil. A stone *stūpa* should be made within forty-nine days[49] to replace [the temporary one]. [The stone *stūpa*] is a marker for my disciples who will visit the site. Mantras, such as *zuigu, daibutchō, sonshō, kōmyō, goji,* Amida,[50] are to be placed inside the *stūpa*. I plan to copy them while alive. If I pass away before I copy them, I ask Ryōshō, Dōchō, Kyōu, and other fellow practitioners to copy them.

Caretakers (*rusunin*): Ninju, Kyōu, Shōō, Kōkō, Hyōkaku.

Nenbutsu and other merit-offering services (*tsuifuku*)[51] should be performed for forty-nine days.

Lotus Hall. Twelve priests to perform repentance services[52] at the main hall three times a day.[53]

Constant-walking Meditation Hall (Jōgyōdō). Fourteen priest to perform *nenbutsu* at the main hall three times a day.

Nenjudō.[54] Ten priests for *sūtra* chanting (*dokyōsō*). During the morning and evening sessions, the *Lotus Sūtra* should be chanted; during the first and last night sessions, the mantra of *sonshō* should be recited.[55] Ten priests for *nenbutsu* practice who will perform the *nenbutsu* three times a day.

The first seventh-day [memorial service]. The fee for *sūtra* chanting is a set of robes for daily use. The service should be held at Nenjudō.

The third seventh-day [memorial service] shall consist of *sūtra* chanting. The service should be held at the Constant-walking Meditation Hall.

The fifth seventh-day [memorial service] shall consist of *sūtra* chanting. The service should be held at the Lotus Hall.

The seventh seventh-day [memorial service] shall consist of *sūtra* chanting.

The above-mentioned [instructions] have been recorded as I lay in my sickbed between the third and sixteenth day of the fifth month. I shall make amendments to these instructions later, if I find revision necessary.

[The following was written on the back of the end of the scroll.]

On the day of my death, two seals, the official seal of the prayer-offering [temple] and a private seal, are entrusted to Myōkōbō. One seal, that of the Ryōgon'in,[56] is entrusted to the manager of the temple. He must follow the directions of [the administrator of] Saki no tōin.[57]

An official letter (*gemon*) of request to appoint Myōkōbō to become the supervisor of the prayer-offering temple (*gogan'in kengyō*) should be presented as soon as [the services] for the forty-nine-day period [after my death] are completed.

[The following was written on the back of the seam of the last sheet of the scroll.]

Nineteen sheets. [Signature, (*kaō*)]

Appendix 4
Takamitsu's Retreat to Tōnomine

To understand Takamitsu's retreat to Tōnomine, a brief history of the site is useful. Tōnomine was established when the remains of the founder of the Fujiwara clan, Nakatomi no Kamatari (614–669), were exhumed and moved there by his eldest son Jōe (635–714), a monk who had returned from a ten-year stay in China. Jōe had a thirteen-story pagoda built above the grave, a lecture hall called Myōrakuji to the south of it, and an ancestral hall called the Shōryōin to the east of it. Kamatari's second son, Fuhito (d. 720), had a wooden image of his father installed. From the beginning, Tōnomine was both a mausoleum and a temple, but it was treated primarily as a mausoleum and a private institution in the *Engishiki*. Its monks were not subjected to the restrictions of the Ritsuryō regulations, but they also were not eligible to receive appointments to prestigious posts as were the monks from officially sanctioned monasteries. Although Tōnomine fell into disrepair shortly after its founding, Fujiwara interest in the site eventually revived as Fujiwara fortunes improved and members of the Fujiwara clan commissioned buildings there. For example, Morosuke's father Tadahira had the original buildings refurbished between 914 and 945; he had a large refectory built in 935 and a shrine (*sōja*) in 926. The increased building at Tōnomine reflected the growing fortunes of the Fujiwara clan. Similar activities occurred at other sites traditionally associated with the Fujiwaras such as Kōfukuji and Kasuga Shrine.

Tōnomine was transformed into a monastery and placed firmly under Tendai influence in the tenth century by a Tendai monk named Jisshō (892–956).[1] Jisshō had gone to Tōnomine at the age of thirteen to serve as one of the monks performing services at Kamatari's grave. His teacher eventually sent him to Mount Hiei to study under the *zasu* Genkan, who ordained him. In 918, he was named a court chaplain and a master of Esoteric Buddhism. In 919, he returned to Tōnomine to serve as *kengyō* and later as *zasu*. During his time there, he instituted a number of religious services including lectures on the *Lotus Sūtra,* an assembly on the *Sūtra of the Benevolent King,* an assembly to bathe the Buddha, and Tendai debates. Later he was appointed a guardian monk for Emperor Murakami, to various posts in the Office of Monastic Affairs, and as abbot of the Urin'in. His deep involvement with Emperor Murakami, the Fujiwara clan, and Tendai involved him with many of the same people as Ryōgen. Perhaps because his Tendai teacher Genkan had been one of the few *zasu* from Ennin's lineage, Jisshō seems to have been more of an ally of Ryōgen than a competitor.

In 950, Jisshō was asked by Morosuke to perform ceremonies to protect the young Prince Norihira. At the same time, Morosuke refurbished the Golden Hall (Kondō) and installed an image of Amitābha in it. The following year, Tōnomine received six ordinands to perform the Lotus meditation. The award of ordinands was symbolic of the court's recognition of Tōnomine as an officially sanctioned monastery.[2] Morosuke's activities at Tōnomine presage the vows that he would make several years later at Yokawa when he built a Lotus Meditation Hall to further his clan's fortunes. Thus Takamitsu's family had deep connections with Tōnomine.

Tōnomine seems to have declined after Jisshō's death in 956. By 960, the leaders of Tōnomine seem to have realized the importance of renewing their political and religious ties with the Fujiwara clan, leading to Kakuei's invitation to Takamitsu to come to Tōnomine.

Once Takamitsu was in Tōnomine, he lived in quarters called the Hōunbō (Jeweled cloud hall). The northern half of the hall was used for religious practices and the southern half as his living quarters. From 962 to 969, Takamitsu practiced his constant-walking meditations alone in that hall. Finally, in 970, his older half-brother Koremasa became minister of the right upon Saneyori's death and had a hall built for the practice of the constant-walking meditation, thus following the precedent of his father Morosuke, who had commissioned a Lotus Meditation Hall at Yokawa and asked that the power of the meditation enable his family to rule. Koremasa also had a *maṇḍala* hall built at Tōnomine that year. Finally, at Takamitsu's urging, Koremasa gave land for the hall that was to be used to support six practitioners and one manager (*azukari*). Practice at the hall was to consist of an annual ninety-day period of meditation beginning in the seventh month during which the practitioners would chant a text on Amitābha's thirty-two physical marks and recite the *nenbutsu* without cease.[3]

In addition to his constant-walking meditation, Takamitsu studied Esoteric Buddhism and Chih-i's treatise on meditation, the *Mo-ho chih-kuan*, under Zōga, a disciple of Ryōgen who had gone to Tōnomine at Takamitsu's urging.[4] Takamitsu and Zōga might have become close friends during the months that Takamitsu had spent at Yokawa before and after his ordination. Because Zōga was critical of some of Ryōgen's political uses of Buddhism, Takamitsu probably found Zōga sympathetic to his needs. Takamitsu seems to have been a very serious practitioner; he is described as reading only texts on Buddhism and Confucianism.[5] Moreover, he composed few, if any, poems after he left Yokawa for Tōnomine.[6] The date of Takamitsu's death is unclear, but Hori and Tamai place it between 977 and 986.[7]

Appendix 5
A Record of the Ōwa Debates

I have examined the records of the Ōwa debates (*Ōwa shūronki*), held during the reign of Emperor Murakami, the sixty-second emperor to preside at our court, on the twenty-eighth day of the fourth month of the first year of Ōwa [961] (the year of *kanoto tori*), [and found that] Ryōgen of Mount Hiei visited [the emperor] at his quarters in the palace (Seiryōden).[1] After he listened to the words of his Highness, Ryōgen presented his views to his Highness, stating that he did not understand why the Hossō school had always been given the favored position as the supervisor of the six schools. Privately Ryōgen gathered from the emperor's response that his Highness did not object [to his opinion]. Therefore, Ryōgen, on the fifteenth day of the fifth month of the same year, wrote to Genkei of the Kegon school and to Ittei of the Sanron school urging them to file a petition to the emperor. In the letter [Ryōgen] wrote,

> All schools of Buddhism have originated from the same wondrous sphere of true thusness. There is no difference [in the spiritual worth of each Buddhist school]. But the disciples of Chihō,[2] in particular, have always been given the favorable position of supervising officer of the six schools. I presented my opinion [to the emperor, explaining] that [the favored position of the Hossō School] is unreasonable. [His Highness] agreed with [my opinion]. Therefore, I urge you, too, to present your opinion swiftly to the emperor [regarding the position of the supervisor of the six schools]. Sincerely, Ryōgen.

Each school's representative presented his opinion on this issue to the emperor by letter. A petition from the Kegon school was entrusted to the minister of defense, Prince [Noriakira, 924–990],[3] on the eighth day of the eighth month of the first year of Ōwa. A petition from the Sanron school was entrusted to the minister of civil administration, Minamoto no Masanobu [920–993], on the third day of the tenth month of the same year. A petition from the Tendai school was entrusted to the middle captain of the right division of the headquarters of the inner palace guards, [Minamoto no] Nobumitsu, on the sixth day of the eleventh month of the same year.

In the third month of the second year of Ōwa [962], an official notice from the emperor was released to each school. The notice stated, "Judging from the petitions, I think the claims [filed by the various schools] are not unreasonable. [The position of the supervising officer of the six schools] should be decided by the excellence of the teaching [of each school]. I urge each [school of Buddhism] to present an official report [concerning its doctrine]."

Although the official notice from the emperor was issued, the official reports [from the Buddhist schools] were not filed. Therefore, on the fifth day of the sixth month of the third year of Ōwa [963], another official notice from the emperor was released [to each school]. The notice stated, "A service [to celebrate the completion of the copying of the *Lotus*] *Sūtra* by his Highness will be held on the coming nineteenth day of this month. [Representatives of each school] are required to attend the service." The service scheduled on the nineteenth day of the six month was postponed to the thirteenth day of the seventh month. The service scheduled on the thirteenth day of the seventh month was postponed again.

On the eleventh day of the eighth month, the middle controller of the left, Lord Fuminori, released a notice. "The great minister of the left (*sadaijin*) has received an imperial order that states, 'On the twenty-first day of this month, the day of *kanoe ne,* a special service will be held at the Seiryōden, the sovereign's private residence. [The service] will last for five days. Twenty monks will be invited to discuss the teaching of the *Lotus Sūtra.* [In every session during the service,] each leader of the service is requested to present his doctrinal interpretation of the *sūtra.*'"

During the five days, there were ten sessions in total. In each session, a monk was nominated lecturer. The following is a list of the nominated monks.

Sanron school, Kanri, Master of Discipline, Tōdaiji.
Kegon school, Genkei, Master of Discipline, Tōdaiji.
Hossō school, Anshū, Certified Lecturer (*ikō*), Kōfukuji.
Hossō school, Hōzō, Certified Lecturer, Tōdaiji.
Hossō school, Ninga, declined.
Hossō school, Tanshō, Tōdaiji.

Hossō school, Hyōshū.
Hossō school, Senri, declined.
Hossō school, Shinki, Kōfukuji.
Hossō school, Chūzan, Kōfukuji.

The above-mentioned ten monks were [nominated] from the Hossō, Sanron, and Kegon schools of the Southern Capital [Nara].

Tendai school, Zen'yu, Enryakuji.
Tendai school, Ryōgen, Enryakuji.
Chikō
Jujō
Tendai school, Shōku, Enryakuji.
Tendai school, Senkan, declined.
Tendai school, Zōga, declined.
Tendai school, Yokei.
Nōe
Gashū

These ten monks were [nominated] from the Tendai school of the Northern Capital [Kyoto].

Among these twenty nominees, four monks, Ninga, Senri, Senkan, and Zōga, declined.

Substitute for Ninga: Hossō school, Zōso, Yakushiji.
Substitute for Senri: Hossō school, Sentō, Kōfukuji.
Substitute for Senkan: Sūju, Enryakuji.
Substitute for Zōga: Kakugyō, from Enryakuji.
Zōso also declined. The substitute for him was the Sanron school
    monk Engei from Tōdaiji.

On the twenty-first, at the hour of the snake [9 A.M.], the leader of the service of the opening session, Kanri, lectured on the *Wu-liang-i ching*. The questioner was Yokei.

The leader of the service in the evening session, Genkei, lectured on the first fascicle of the *Lotus Sūtra*. The questioner was Nōe.

On the twenty-second, the leader of the service in the morning session, Anshū, lectured on the second fascicle [of the *Lotus Sūtra*]. The questioner was Gashū.

The leader of the service in the evening session (this session began at the hour of the ram [1 P.M.]) was Hōzō of the Hossō school. The questioner was Kakugyō. During the fourth session, the questioner argued against the lecturer, claiming that a sentient being of no-nature does not exist at all. The manner of the [counter]argument of the leader of the service, the great Dharma master Hōzō, was so dignified [that the questioner backed off] before Hōzō raised his verbal sword an inch. His skilled argument during the *sūtra* lecture was unrivaled. The courtiers [who heard his argument] were most impressed. At this point, Ryōgen of Tendai entered into [the debate between the two] and argued that a sentient being of no-nature does not exist at all. Heated debate between the two schools continued until the fourth quarter of the hour of the dog [8:30 P.M.]. In consideration of the exhaustion of the audience, the leader of the service [Hōzō] suspended his response [to Ryōgen] and informed [the audience] that he would answer the question on the following day.

On the twenty-third, at the hour of the snake [9 A.M.], the leader of the service in the morning session, Ryōgen, lectured on the fourth fascicle [of the *Lotus Sūtra*]. Hyōshū was the questioner [of this session] at the emperor's request. During Ryōgen's *sūtra* lecture, the audience was exceedingly impressed. From the emperor to the courtiers, [all those who attended] were moved to tears. The debate continued until the fourth quarter of the hour of the ram [2:30 P.M.]. During this session, the great [Dharma] master Hōzō presented his reply to the previous day's question.

The leader of the service in the evening session, Zen'yu, lectured on the fifth fascicle [of the *Lotus Sūtra*]. The questioner was Sentō (absent).

On the twenty-fourth day, the leader of the service in the morning session, Chikō, lectured on the sixth fascicle [of the *Lotus Sūtra*]. The questioner was Shinki (with honors).

The leader of the service in the evening session, Tanshō, lectured on the seventh fascicle [of the *Lotus Sūtra*]. The questioner was Sūju (absent).

During the evening lecture, which was the eighth session, Nijō [from the audience] asked a question. The leader of the service continued, saying, "This lecture is on the 'Chapter of Commissioning [the Dharma].'[4] During the lecture on 'Chapter of Commissioning [the Dharma],' the questioner and attending monks [customarily] do not argue with each other."

On the twenty-fifth, at the hour of the dragon [7 A.M.], the leader of the service in the morning session, Juchō of the Tendai school, lectured on the eighth fascicle [of the *Lotus Sūtra*]. The questioner was Chūzan of the Hossō school.

After the morning session, the questioner was summoned into the archery rooms.[5] The head chamberlain, Lord Nobumitsu, said, "Your argument during this morning's session was superb. Your argument met the demand of his Highness and he was extremely impressed. [The emperor has requested] that you serve [as the questioner] again during the debate in the evening session. [The emperor] also requests that you add a section on Buddhist logic. His Highness, however, would like you to leave out the profound details of the argument for the sake of the audience." (These were the requests of the emperor.)

The leader of the service in the evening session, Shōku of the Tendai school, lectured on the *P'u-hsien ching*. The questioner was Chūzan, having been reappointed at the request of his Highness.

At this point, the Master of Discipline Kanri stated, "Buddhist logic is very subtle and profound, and it is too difficult for the audience to understand. I would like to request from [your Highness] permission to exclude the section on Buddhist logic [from the debate]." Shortly afterward, [his Highness] told the assembly to exclude the section of Buddhist logic. The debate continued and the argument touched upon the issue whether a sentient being of no-nature exists or not. Chūzan immediately quoted Ryōgen's arguments of two days earlier, including his interpretation of the passage on the universal presence of Buddhanature,[6] on the three [essential] vows of the bodhisattva and the four salvific methods of the bodhisattva.[7] He made counterarguments against each of Ryōgen's statements, and scoffed at his every argument. Ryōgen sat with closed mouth and fixed eyes. All those in both the upper and lower seats of the audience were impressed [by Chūzan's argument]. At last, on the twenty-fifth at about midnight, the emperor's statement was handed down to Fuminori. Chūzan was summoned to the seat of his Highness. While all the subjects put the palms of their hands together, the son of heaven presented him with a grail. Chūzan held up the silver [grail] in his hands. The solemn luster [of the grail] shone throughout the palace. Since that time, the Hossō school has permanently maintained its position as the supervisor of the six schools, and it has never been relinquished to another school. In addition, [his Highness] granted to the Hossō school the position of supernumerary supervisor (*gonchōja*). The banner of the Tendai school, therefore, bent before the wind of Ōwa era [961–964]. Out of the dust of Tenryaku era [947–957], the Hossō school won the debates. For everyone who is able to distinguish right from wrong, it is obvious that the Tendai school clearly lost the debate. Because [the Tendai school] lost the Ōwa debates, it should not be on equal terms with the Hossō school.

Appendix 6
Ten Doubts Concerning the Hossō School

1. The Tendai position on the realization of Buddhahood by grasses and trees confuses the sentient and non-sentient.[1] It is difficult to distinguish the ways in which they are not the same.[2]

2. As for the Tendai position on the realization of Buddhahood by grasses and trees, it is not the case that [grasses and trees] realize Buddhahood by themselves.[3] Rather it is through the perfuming (*rikun*) and functioning (*kōyō*) of Suchness that the environment (*shoe*) constantly realizes Buddhahood.

3. The Tendai position on the realization of Buddhahood by grasses and trees is that all non-sentient beings] realize Buddhahood through their own efforts (*shōbō*), not through the environment's (*shoe*) [realization of Buddhahood in dependence on a sentient being realizing Buddhahood]. [Tendai] misses the significance of grasses and trees [realizing Buddhahood] while retaining the name.[4]

4. The [correct interpretation of] realization of Buddhahood by grasses and trees is that they realize Buddhahood when a Buddha does so (*etashin*). Thus, according to a *sūtra*, "When one Buddha realizes enlightenment, he discerns the Dharma-realm." This indicates that it is not the case grasses and trees have the innate capacity (*tokubun*) to realize Buddhahood.[5]

5. The doctrine of realization of Buddhahood by grasses and trees goes against the words of the Buddha (*kongon*). According to the *sūtra*, "As for those who hear the teaching, the group that lacks Buddha-nature does not realize Buddhahood."[6] It violates this teaching.

6. As for the realization of Buddhahood by grasses and trees, they have not yet manifested the physical forms of Buddhahood. Thus the sounds of the wind and waves are not the Buddha's sermons.

7. Because grasses and trees do not have minds, they do not have Buddha-natures of practice (*gyōbusshō*).[7] Because they do not have Buddha-natures of practice, how can you explain their development of the aspiration to enlightenment and religious practice?

8. As for the aspiration of enlightenment and practice by grasses and trees, [such an explanation would] depend on the three poisons and obstacles. But grasses and trees do not have the three poisons and karmic obstacles (*gosshō*). How can you then explain their aspiration to enlightenment and religious practice?[8]

9. As for the aspiration of enlightenment and practice, an explanation depends on the opposition of subject and object.[9] But grasses and trees do not have any opposition of subject and object. How could the aspiration of enlightenment and practice exist?

10. As for the aspiration of enlightenment by grasses and trees, such a teaching is not found in the wondrous teachings[10] of the Mahāyāna. On what is this teaching based?

The answers are profound (*jinpi*).[11] Jie daishi.[12]

1. [As for the Hossō argument], "If grasses and trees develop the aspiration to enlightenment, then sentient and not-sentient are confused," [they say this] because they do not know that everything innately embodies Suchness (*shōgu*).[13]

2. [As for the Hossō argument], "The aspiration to enlightenment by grasses and trees does not refer to aspiration to Buddhahood by (grasses and trees) themselves, but to the perfuming of all by Suchness," the [Hossō monks do not understand that] within the principle of Suchness, self and environment are not separate.[14]

3. [As for the Hossō argument] that the realization of Buddhahood by grasses and trees is only through sentient beings, [Hossō monks] do not know that things just as they are embody the wondrous (*tōi sokumyō*) and innate without any change in the mind.

4. [As for the Hossō teaching] that [grasses and trees] realize Buddhahood on the basis of another's [realization], from the beginning grasses and trees have attained Buddhahood. Thus when a Buddha realizes Buddhahood, he sees the grasses and trees realize Buddhahood.

5. [As for the Hossō argument] that this violates the passage that be-

gins "As for those who hear the teaching," this is because you do not know the non-differentiating intent of the wondrous tenet that all in the ten realms [realize Buddhahood].[15]

6. As for your claim that the forms and characteristics of Buddhahood are not manifested [by grasses and trees], you don't see them because your eyes are not perfected.[16]

7. You say that because grasses and trees do not have minds, they lack the Buddha-nature of practice (gyōbusshō). This is because in your position, you do not yet know about the Buddha-nature of practice by grasses and trees.

8. As for your claim that practice is based on the three poisons and karmic obstructions, [Hossō monks] do not know the aspiration to enlightenment and practice in the ten realms.[17]

9. [As for the Hossō argument that grasses and trees lack the] opposition between subject and object, [Hossō monks] do not know that although [grasses and trees] are without subject and object, subject and object are still established.[18]

10. [As for the Hossō claim that] this teaching is not found among the wondrous Mahāyāna teachings, this is based on the passage concerning how phenomena reside in the Dharma (hōi) and how the [characteristics of the] world [constantly abide].[19]

As for these ten positions, their school was finally defeated. They lack detail, but you should depend on the tenth position.

Appendix 7
Zōga as an Eccentric

Zōga is famous as one on the most eccentric monks in Japanese history. He is said to have been offered high honors and to have refused them. According to both the *Hokke genki* and the *Tōnomine ryakki*, the retired emperor Reizei ordered him to serve as court chaplain, but Zōga refused. He was asked to serve as a teacher for Empress Fujiwara no Senshi, but used coarse language to an attendant. The mention of his bizarre behavior, even though the entries are brief, suggests that he must have engaged in some eccentric behavior. In the *Hokke genki*, his unusual behavior is explained as "expedient means that were used so that he could turn away from the world," or, in other words, reject the fame and high position similar to those that Ryōgen had gained.[1]

In contrast to the view that Zōga was an eccentric, parts of the *Tōnomine ryakki*, Zōga's dream diary, and some of the earlier sources generally portray Zōga as a serious monk who helped establish institutions on Tōnomine that paralleled those on Hiei. The relationship between Zōga and Morosuke's son Takamitsu was similar to that between Ryōgen and another of Morosuke's sons, Jinzen. Just as Ryōgen was helped by a powerful patron, Fujiwara no Morosuke, so was Zōga helped by Morosuke's son, Fujiwara no Koremasa. Although the institutions established by Zōga gave Tōnomine a political role, Zōga also strove to establish a form of Tendai that was closer to Chinese T'ien-t'ai than that on Hiei.

As a result, Hori Daiji rejects almost all of the stories that Zōga was an eccentric, noting that Zōga is referred to as a court chaplain several times in the *Tōnomine ryakki*, thereby indicating, that, in fact, Zōga did serve at court. The support from Fujiwara no Koremasa while he was at Tōnomine also indicates that he was not averse to cultivating relationships with member of the nobility.[2] Miki Sumito, however, discounts the evidence in the *Tōnomine ryakki* that Zōga was a court chaplain, finding little other evidence to support it, noting that it appears only in some versions of the *Tōnomine ryakki*.[3] As a result, Miki treats the stories of Zōga's eccentricity much more seriously than does Hori. For example, he speculates that Zōga might have resorted to eccentric behavior in an effort to ameliorate the future emperor Reizei's bizarre behavior.[4]

The presence of vague statements about Zōga's eccentric behavior in a few early sources may indicate that he acted in a bizarre fashion on several occasions, though probably not to the extent that later authors suggest. Although Zōga did help build Tōnomine into a major monastic institution, he did not hold offices in the Sōgō and seems to have done little to further his own career. He might well have been critical of Ryōgen's rise to high office. For example, some of Zōga's later biographies suggest a strained relationship with Ryōgen. At a celebration in honor of Ryōgen, Zōga is said to have led the procession by using a dried salmon (*sake*) as a sword and riding an emaciated female water buffalo, asking who was more appropriate than he to ride in the vanguard of Ryōgen's entourage.[5] Zōga may have been alluding to his long relationship with Ryōgen when he announced that he should lead the parade. His choice of a water buffalo has been equated with the bull that served as Daiitoku's vehicle and may have been a parody hearkening back to one of the five-platform ceremonies that Ryōgen participated in earlier in his lifetime. The dried salmon as a sword may have been part of the parody, suggesting the weapons carried by Daiitoku. Or the salmon (*sake*) may have been part of a play on words suggesting a woman's genitals (*sake*); the choice of a cow rather than a bull as a mount might have been part of such an allusion to some event in Ryōgen's life.[6] Although such interpretations add to the richness of the tales, whether they have a historical basis cannot be known.

If the stories of Zōga's criticisms of Ryōgen are taken as having some element of historical truth, Zōga's attitude must be seen as also including affection and concern for Ryōgen. According to other sources, Zōga returned to Mount Hiei to participate in rituals without incident. For example, in 980 he led a group of monks participating in the dedication of the Central Hall (Chūdō) that Ryōgen presided over, apparently without incident.[7] At some point, he also sent one of his disciples, Sōjo (d. 993), to study in Yokawa on Mount Hiei, suggesting continuing ties between Tōnomine and Ryōgen's power base at Yokawa.[8]

As time passed, the serious side of Zōga's personality was ignored by the authors of tales, and the stories of his eccentric behavior emphasized and elaborated. In one of the most famous episodes, he was summoned to the palace to act as preceptor (*kaishi*) in the ordination of Empress Fujiwara no Sonshi. However, once he had finished cutting her hair off, he commented that they had probably invited him to preside over the ceremony simply because they had heard that he had an enormous penis as a youth. He then stated that he was suffering from severe diarrhea, went over to a porch-high rail in the southern hall, raised his robes, relieved himself with an enormous noise (and created a terrible stench), and departed.[9] These legends cannot be traced to early sources, however, and so many inconsistencies exist between various versions that almost all of them must be dismissed as the product of later authors who were indirectly criticizing the increasing secularization of the monks on Mount Hiei. Zōga was probably the subject of many of these stories because he had rejected the worldly rewards that awaited him if he had agreed to Ryōgen's schemes and instead chose to retire to a more austere life in Tōnomine.[10]

The traditions about Zōga can be thus be interpreted in two very different manners: as portraying a serious monk who rejected personal honor but strove to help develop Tōnomine into a major Tendai monastic center or as stories about an eccentric recluse whose bizarre activities exposed the pretensions and hypocrisy around him. Early sources indicate that he played a major role in building Tōnomine but did not seek high positions for himself. Although several vague references to unusual behavior exist in early sources, they are not emphasized at all. Later legends describe a sincere monk who had retired to Tōnomine because he disagreed with many aspects of the political use of Buddhism for worldly gain; Ryōgen serves as a target of criticism in several of these tales. According to these tales, Zōga resorted to bizarre behavior to protect himself from the adulation that lay believers sometimes bestowed on recluses. Through these stories, people could express their criticism of Tendai's political role and their admiration for those reclusive monks who adopted practices and stances that lay outside establishment Buddhism.

Appendix 8
Invocation of Tendai Abbot Ryōgen

Ryōgen, head [of the Tendai school], a supernumerary lesser bishop, a master of the Dharma-eye,[1] sincerely calls [all Buddhas, bodhisattvas, and guardian deities of Mount Hiei to witness this invocation]. In order that the Dharma shall forever endure, I establish the following twenty-six articles on various issues [regarding the conduct of monks at Mount Hiei].

1. The chief officer (*bettō*) supervising the ceremony for the Buddha's relic (*shari-e*) is prohibited from providing gifts of clothing (*kazukemono*) at the service and from holding a reception for the administrative officers (*shoshi*)[2] [of the temple] before and after the service. On the day when the chief administrator of the ceremony for the Buddha's relics nominates those who will hold special offices (*shikishu*)[3] at the service and after the official announcement [closing the service], he is prohibited from holding receptions for the temple administrators and other officiants who are in charge of the service (*shoshi*).[4] He also may not provide gifts of clothing and other presents to them. From now on, the prohibition will be strictly enforced by law. In order to maintain this great assembly forever, the chief administrator of the service should remember the significance of this rule every year. However, offerings for those who hold special roles (*shikishu*) at the service are exempted from this restriction because such gifts are the rewards for their participation. Be thrifty and do not waste.

2. The lecturer of the assembly of the sixth month (Minazuki-e) is prohibited from holding a reception for the audience and the administrative officers. Our wise predecessors started this assembly to commemorate the compassionate deeds of our great master [Saichō]. The temple administrators should handle the reception for the monks invited to the assembly. The invited monks should concentrate on the dis-

cussion concerning the profound meaning expounded in the *sūtra*. In the old days, only plain tea was served to quench the thirst of the guests. Simple refreshments were served to the monks in charge of the protocol for the assembly (*igisō*). Nowadays, however, the lecturer does not work on scriptural exegesis. Instead, he focuses on ways to feed the audience. Bowls of offerings arrive like banks of clouds that cover the peaks [of Mount Hiei] from east to west. For days, tasty food fills the residences of masters and guests. Venerable monks are invited to the guesthouse. A feast every morning makes them forget the taste of pine needles. Groups of sages are led to private parties. A reception with the strong scent of boiling tea every evening surprises them. People wait for the evening of the seventh day, when the lectures on the three *sūtras* [of the *Lotus*] are completed. Venerable monks gather together like flocking pigeons. They peck at all kinds of delicacies. Famous monks waddle like a parade of wild geese. Strange ornaments glow in their palms.

When we consider this state of affairs, although we are joyful at the offerings given to the Buddha and order, the valleys and peaks [of Mount Hiei] regret that this present situation is very wasteful. Officiants are assigned to their duty by turns, not by their virtues. Officiants should avoid waste while they are on duty. Therefore, [during the period of the service] the custom of preparing food bowls, cooking food, providing breakfast every morning and dinner during the six evenings are all prohibited. If someone unexpectedly receives gifts such as paper, brush, tea, or fans, he is required to surrender them at the lecture of the fifth fascicle [of the *Lotus Sūtra*]. If a monk adds these offerings of gifts to the Buddha along with the harmonious chants praising the Buddha, that monk will multiply the virtues received from the service. Do not ask for gifts if you do not receive any. The spirit of the great assembly, however, should be maintained as usual. Consequently, the temple administrators are allowed to raise a small amount of funds sufficient to meet the needs of the lecturers. They also are allowed to encourage devout families to practice the spirit of offering. I heartily urge the venerable monks selected [to participate in this service] to concentrate on lectures on the wondrous [*Lotus*] *sūtra* that expound the superior principles in order to propagate the joy of the Dharma promoted by the great master [Saichō]. Do not attend this service for trivial purposes and with the same attitudes as laypeople.

3. The candidate (*ryūgisha*) in the doctrinal debate at the assembly [of the sixth month] is prohibited from preparing food bowls, serving

tea, and making offerings to the monks in charge of the protocol for the ceremony. The candidate in the doctrinal debate at the assembly [of the sixth month] is appointed according to seniority in the monastic order, but sometimes the appointment does not follow seniority. If the appointee has many disciples and attendants (*sōmonja*), there is no problem in handling the situation. However, if the appointee is a solitary and serene monk with only a few attendants, [he might feel embarrassed accepting this appointment for fear that] he might lose face because he could not adequately serve monks in the assembly. In terms of scholarship, the academic excellence of the appointees should be equal regardless of their seniority. Whether embarrassed or confident, all appointees [to the position of respondent to the doctrinal debate] should be qualified scholars. Therefore, the customs of preparing bowls of food, serving tea, and having receptions for the monks in charge of protocol are all prohibited.

Appointees as candidates for the examination on broad learning (*kōgaku ryūgi*) are to be chosen from among the most able [Tendai scholars]. Hence, they are not necessarily restricted by this rule, but should be admonished against unseemly extravagance. Do not waste; be thrifty.

The promotion of the candidate is solely determined by his performance in the debates. Although the imperial order[5] states that "one must be a learned scholar (*kōgaku*) [of Buddhism]," students should not wait for another lifetime to attend the doctrinal debate at the assembly. Young and bright students who wish to advance their academic careers must study assiduously even if they must read by the light of fireflies [during the summer] and the reflection of the moon on the snow [during winter].

4. The lecturer of the assembly of the eleventh month (Shimotsuki-e) is forbidden to prepare food, serve tea, and make offerings to the monks in charge of the protocol of ceremony. The above-mentioned prohibitions on [the lecturer of the assembly of the eleventh month] are the same as in the former articles. But the lecturer is not prohibited from holding courtly [style] doctrinal debate (*uchi rongi dō*)[6] to encourage scholars aspiring for enlightenment. The respondent who has successfully completed his duty in this doctrinal debate is given priority as a candidate for the doctrinal debates (*ryūgi*) for the next year. This has been the custom since the first year of Anna [968]. The custom is endorsed as a permanent rule. A monk who has demonstrated his excellence in scriptural lectures and doctrinal interpretation at the assem-

bly is promoted to a higher academic position regardless of his seniority in the monastic order. Any monk who wishes to advance his academic
career swiftly should devote himself to study.

5. The lecturer at the retreat during the rainy season (*ango*) is prohibited from preparing food and sending it to the administrative
officers [of the service]. This prohibition is the same as in the previous
rules. The purpose in holding a lecture meeting during the summer is
to protect the state and to ensure a good harvest. The appointee should
concentrate on lecturing on the teachings of the *sūtra* and expound-
ing the principles of the doctrine. Lecturers, however, in recent years
are only interested in advancing their careers and do not understand
the true meaning of the teaching. They deserve to be reprimanded because of the inefficacy of their prayers. Once a monk is appointed to
the seat [of lecturer], he should single-mindedly study the triple *sūtra*
[of the *Lotus Sūtra* group]. Until the day the lecture begins, until the
morning that he ascends the lecturer's platform, the lecturer should
examine the title and text of the *sūtra* from beginning to end. The lecturer should discuss the details of the *sūtra* as well as the doctrinal principles; one should not lose the mind [that distinguishes] fruit from
flowers.[7] Externally, he must sever attachment to secular affairs, and in-
ternally he must conquer mental distractions in order to pray for the
year's good harvest and protection for the state. To expect a bountiful
harvest in the autumn, we need to conduct many *sūtra* lectures during
the summer. Once the virtue of conventional truth is settled, the merit
of absolute truth can be revealed. But if the twofold truth of reality is
not sustained [during the summer retreat], the ninety days [of the re-
treat] are simply a waste of time.

6. Monks are prohibited from wearing wooden clogs in temple
buildings. Monks must wear straw sandals in temple buildings. This is
the rule in accordance with the precepts since the ancient period.
Monks in recent years, however, often wear wooden clogs [in temple
buildings]. This violates traditional customs. People tend to forget the
traditional style. Thoughtful monks all lament [this neglect of tradition].
This [traditional] custom is now confirmed as a rule. Both in one's own
residence and when visiting temple buildings, monks must wear straw
sandals. When a monk enters a temple building from the outside, he
must change to the correct sandals for use inside the temple. Inside the
Buddha halls, however, straw sandals are not allowed. This issue is
confirmed by the *sūtras* and the texts on precepts. One should follow

the rule accordingly. A monk who does not follow this rule will not be allowed to sit in the section for monks (*sōza*), but will be seated instead as a novice (*shami*).

7. A monk who buys ritual articles (*katsumamotsu*)[8] at an auction (*keiru*) and does not meet the date of payment will be expelled from the order. Orders to punish a monk who buys ritual articles at an auction and does not meet the date of payment have been issued repeatedly— eight or nine times—in the order since the first year of Jōgan [859]. We must rethink the current condition [of the order]. The term "Buddhist order" (*sōgya*) means "harmony and mutual respect" and the term "ritual" (*katsuma*) refers to the "pure Dharma." In principle the price of articles should be determined by their actual value. Also one should have the funds before bidding on articles and buying them at auction. But some monks do not care about price because they covet the articles. (Even though the value of an article is only one or two *kan*,[9] [a buyer] tends to raise the price by two, three, four *sen* without being aware of it [at the auction], because the mind [of the buyer] is attached to the article out of his intense greed for the object.) Some monks bid a higher price [than the actual value] without concern for their loss [of money], because they wish to be ostentatious. (Some monks raise the price [at an auction] as if they were playing a game, even though they do not need the article. They compete with other monks who actually do need the articles on sale. At the auction, however, the former type of monk thinks while bidding on the price, "I am 'an [important] man.' I must beat him because he is not as good as me. How can he compete with me?" Because of his conceit, he buys cheap articles at a high price ignoring the money he will later lose.) After he wins the price competition, however, the excitement in his mind created by his greed and pride gradually fades away. He begins to regret the high price [he bid]. Some return the auctioned article. Some do not pay. In some cases, a monk simply buys the articles without preparing funds to buy them so does not have sufficient money to pay for them after he has received the articles. He delays the payment for months or, sometimes, even years. If the payment received for articles [sold at the auction] is to be added to the funds of the resident monks (*daishu*) [at the temple that held the auction], then the monks who do not receive payment on time [for an article sold] denounce him to the assistant temple administrators (*dōtatsu*). If the [defaulted] payment for the article is to be applied to the funds for repair [of the

temple], the workers for the monks have to suspend their construction work.

[Delaying, or not paying one's dues] is an act against the principle [of Dharma]. [A monk who commits this act] should be punished. In order to limit greed and conceit, I reiterate this rule to confirm the process of auction. Once an article is bought, the payment must be delivered before the due date without remorse or any alteration of conditions or price even though the price has been bid carelessly up or the item is bought mistakenly by competing for it. As for the terms of payment, see the order issued on the fifteenth day of the twelfth month of the first year of Jōgan. Here, the terms are determined according to the order [of 859]. Payment must be delivered within five days if the purchase is over five *kan,* within seven days if the purchase is over ten *kan,* within ten days if the purchase is over twenty *kan,* and within fifteen days if the purchase is over thirty *kan.* Anyone who violates this order is to be permanently expelled from the order in accordance with orders issued reiterated in Jōgan (859–877), Kanpyō (889–898), Shōtai (898–901), Enchō (923–931), and Tengyō (938–947) eras. There are no exceptions to this rule.

An administrative officer who falsely claims the unpaid due as paid on behalf of the debtor is also to be prosecuted according to the order issued on the twelfth day of the seventh month of the fifth year of Tengyō [942].

8. A monk who does not attend the fortnightly assembly will be suspended from the order for three years. The "fortnightly assembly" (*fusatsu*) means "pure abode" (*jōjū*) and "Buddhist order" means "harmonious meeting" (*wagō*). [Vairocana] on the lotus throne becomes your master, manifesting incarnations [of Śākyamuni] on the day of the fortnightly assembly. The list of rules is your guide. How could they not lead you to the ultimate? Therefore, it is transmitted among the ten myriads of Buddhas on the [lotus] blossom; it is taught in the universes on the ten thousand leaves of that lotus.[10] As a result, the light of the precepts radiates from the monk's mouth twice a month and leads him toward enlightenment moment by moment.[11] Hence, once a monk has accepted the bodhisattva precepts, he must come to the assembly hall and listen to the recitation of the precepts every fortnight. How could he neglect his duty when his turn comes to officiate at the service? But some monks, upon seeing the summons to officiate, will not sign it to indicate their acceptance. Other monks sign it, but fail to appear at the

service. This is a serious act of negligence to one's duty toward the administrative office of the temple (*jike*) and an act against the strict rules established by the World Honored [Buddha]. From now on, a monk who fails to attend the service is suspended [from the order] for three years. [Such misconduct by a monk] was never allowed. However, a monk who is physically unable to recite the precepts, chant hymns, or officiate at the service (*ina*) can request that a substitute who is skilled in these functions perform them for him while he listens. The original appointee, however, is also required to attend the service with the substitute monk.

9. A monk, after ascending the ordination platform and being ordained, must go to the hall for the fortnightly assembly, recite the precepts, chant hymns, and officiate at the service. The above-mentioned issue is discussed in the *Fan-wang ching* [Brahmā's net *sūtra*] as follows: "A monk who has received the bodhisattva precepts yet does not recite these precepts is neither a bodhisattva nor a seed which becomes a buddha."[12] The *sūtra* also states, "A disciple of the Buddha who observes the precepts while walking, standing, sitting, and lying down during the six periods in the day and night is [indestructible] like a *vajra* (*kongō*). The disciple is able to swim across the ocean like someone with a float filled with air."[13] In addition, the *sūtra* states, "A bodhisattva newly admitted to the order is required to recite the ten major precepts and the forty-eight minor precepts on the day of the fortnightly assembly. One monk leads the recitation [of the precepts] at a fortnightly assembly attended by only one monk. At a fortnightly assembly attended by two, three, or even a hundred or a thousand monks, one monk leads the recitation."[14] (The fortnightly assembly is to be held in accordance with the number of resident monks of a temple.)

Wise people of ancient times, in order to confirm their faith in the words of the Buddha, did not forget to recite [the precepts] and to attend every meeting. Some Buddhists in recent years do not observe the precepts, do not study [the precepts], and do not attend the fortnightly service. The great tradition of the fortnightly assembly will soon cease [if the current situation continues]. Since Śākyamuni's entry into *nirvāṇa*, sages and worthies have passed away one after another. For Buddhists during the end of the Period of Imitated Dharma (Zōmatsu),[15] only the precepts can serve as their teachers. If the tradition of the fortnightly assembly completely ceases, upon what will they rely? All monks in the great assembly, as well as worthies, should understand the significance [of the precepts], earnestly recite and study them, as well as encourage others to recite and study them so that the Dharma shall long endure in the world and all rapidly realize enlightenment. A monk who has just awakened the aspiration for enlightenment and accepted the precepts should resolve to recite them from the first day [he receives them] on the ordination platform.

10. A monk must practice the methods of reading *sūtras,* singing verses, chanting hymns, and properly scattering flowers at services. [This rule is formulated because] many monks do not practice the methods for chanting, singing, and performing rituals at the ceremonies. [Among these are] the monks in charge of circumambulation (*gyōdōshu*) at the new year service (*shōgatsu*) and the second month (*nigatsu*) services; the monks in charge of praises (*san*), chanting (*bonnon*), and carrying staffs with metal rings[16] (*shakujō*) at the ceremony for the Buddha's relic; the monks in charge of chanting at the service for the great masters (*daishiku*)[17] [of the Tendai school] on the sixteenth day of the seventh month [for Saichō and Ennin][18] and the twenty-fourth day of the eleventh month [for Chih-i]; the monks in charge of chanting at the Esoteric consecration ceremony (*kanjō*); and the monks who sing the praises at the ceremony on the day of the lecture of the fifth fascicle [of the *Lotus Sūtra*] at the assemblies for the *Lotus Sūtra* (*Hokke-e*) in the sixth month and the eleventh month. They keep their mouths shut during the service. A few of them occasionally open their mouths, but they have not learned these rituals adequately from their masters, and the audience ridicules [their chanting for being out of tune]. Above all, monks who participate in the group singing congratulatory hymns[19] (*kikkyōsan*) on the night of [their master's] Esoteric consecration (*kanjō*) ceremony should at least recite the first three parts, even if they are not able to memorize all nine parts. But often they can barely recite the first section and stop midway. Or they mumble the rest along with the sound of cymbals. How sad indeed that the great path has declined so far. From now on, every monk must carefully practice each ritual under the guidance of a skilled master [of ritual]. How much more so is this the case if he is to serve in one of the leadership positions (*shikishu*) for a ceremony. Once a monk receives a letter of summons to a service, he should practice reciting the [texts] while walking, standing, sitting, and lying down. On the day of the service, he should be able to recite [the text] without pause and inspire the audience with a feeling of joy. (Listed are

praising, singing, scattering flowers, chanting, verses praising the staff
with metal rings (*shakujō*), verses welcoming the teachers (*sonshi*), verses
in praise of carrying firewood,[20] and so forth.)

11. Monks must attend the services transmitting the Dharma and lectures on the [*Fan-wang*] *sūtra*. The above-stated article is based on a passage in the *Fan-wang ching* that states,

> A disciple of the Buddha should attend lectures on the rules (*bini kyō-
> ritsu*)[21] wherever they are held. Those bodhisattvas who have just begun
> to study them should visit their Dharma masters, bring the text of the
> scriptures with them, listen [to the lecture], and discuss [the Dharma].
> They should listen to lectures on the Dharma at every available oppor-
> tunity, regardless of whether it is held on a mountain, in the woods, un-
> derneath a tree, within the confines of a monastery, or at a residence of
> a monk.[22]

Various other *sūtras* and commentaries also expound the same idea.
Buddhists in ancient times all observed the words [of the *sūtra*]. They
always went and listened to all available Dharma lectures. But in recent
years, there is no audience to listen at the services observing the transmission of the Dharma, at lectures on *sūtras,* and at doctrinal debates
other than those monks who have been summoned [to officiate].
These monks not only ignore the precepts established by the Buddha,
but also lose the opportunity to attain wisdom in the future. Disciples
of Śākyamuni who appreciate the joy of the Dharma should earnestly
study the teachings, and, without fail, attend meetings where they can
observe the transmission of the Dharma, *sūtra* lectures, and listen to
doctrinal debates. Thus, the Dharma will be preserved and their wisdom will mature. Do not be lazy, and do not forget this.

12. [Administrators] must carefully select a person suitable for receiving the Dharma (*hōki*) as a candidate to be a yearly ordinand. This
rule is based on the eight-article regulations (*Hachijō-shiki*)[23] issued by
the great master [Saichō] on the twenty-seventh day of the eighth month
of the ninth year of Kōnin [818]: "A candidate [for yearly ordinand]
(*tokugō*) must complete six years of course work before he is eligible to
take the qualifying examination."[24] The regulation also states, "A candidate [for yearly ordinand] whose character is not in accordance with
the Dharma and who does not follow the rules sanctioned by the order
will be reported to governmental offices and be replaced [by another
person]."[25]

When the current state of affairs is considered, the requirement of six years of course work has not been in effect for many years, and it is not realistic to reinforce the curriculum as it was originally designed. But the administration should carefully select a candidate whose character is in accordance with [the Dharma] and who is both talented and knowledgeable. Without careful selection, a suitable person will not be found. Therefore, within the space of a year or two, an unqualified student should be terminated.

Included in the same regulation [in the eight articles issued by Saichō is the requirement that], a student must practice the four meditation practices (*shishu zanmai*) during his required twelve years of residence on Mount Hiei. In recent years, however, students practice only the constant-walking meditation. The reason for serious decline of the [three types of] meditative practices is simply that the administration does not properly select students on the day of the qualifying examination. Wise men who follow the Dharma should understand the meaning of this article and carefully select persons as candidates for yearly ordinand who are suitable for the Dharma (*tokubun*). The ideal candidate is between the ages of fourteen and twenty years. He should not have physical defects and should be strong enough physically and mentally to persevere in cultivating the meditative practices.

13. A monk who is undergoing the [twelve years of] confined practice on Mount Hiei (*rōzan*) is not allowed beyond the confines of the mountain. (The eastern limit is Hiden, the southern limit is Hannyaji, the western limit is Mizunomi, and the northern limit is the Ryōgon'in. [The sequestered practitioner] is not allowed to cross these borders.) The above-mentioned article is based on the aforementioned [eight-article] regulations [issued by Saichō] that state,

> A candidate who [has completed the requirements to be a yearly ordinand and] has received the full precepts is not permitted to leave the gates of the mountain monastery for twelve years. He is required to devote himself to study and practice [during this period]. During the first six years he should devote himself primarily to listening lectures; the practice of contemplation and meditation is secondary. Each day two-thirds of his study is devoted to Buddhism and one-third to other subjects (*gegaku*). Extensive lecturing (*jōgō*) [on scriptures] is his practice, and preaching the Dharma is his discipline. During the next six years, his first priority will be to practice contemplation and meditation; secondary emphasis will be placed on lectures. A student whose major is [Tendai] exoteric doctrine based on the *Mo-ho chih-kuan* (*Shikangō*) must practice the

four meditations. A student whose major is Esoteric Buddhism (*shanagō*) must practice contemplation and recitation according to the three divisions (*sanbu*)[26] [of Esoteric practices].[27]

In the regulations, the phrase "the gates of the mountain" refers to the boundaries (*kekkai*) [of Mount Hiei].

But in recent years, [administrators] have heard that [some yearly ordinands] have gone to Ōhara and others to Ono freely and without hesitation by crossing the borders in the four directions [before they have completed their twelve years of confined practice on Mount Hiei]. [Student misconduct] occurs because their masters neither observe the regulations issued by the great teacher [Saichō] nor discipline the unlawful conduct of their disciples. From now on, [the administration] shall strictly enforce these rules. [A yearly ordinand who has not completed his twelve years of residence practice on Mount Hiei] who habitually leaves the confines will immediately be expelled [from the monastery]. Furthermore, [a yearly ordinand] must cultivate wisdom through listening to lectures, contemplation, and meditation during both the prior and latter six-year periods in accordance with the regulations [issued by Saichō].

14. A junior monk may not dress in prohibited colors (*kinjiki*).[28] The above-mentioned article is based on the aforementioned [eight-article] regulations [issued by Saichō] that state,

> The Dharma-robes for winter and summer shall be obtained through alms-begging from various donors in order to cover the body; [this shall be carried out] in accordance with Mahāyāna teachings. Thus monks will be able to clothe themselves and will not backslide in their practice. Thatched roof huts shall be their residences and bamboo leaves their seats. The Dharma should have priority over their personal needs. Thus, we will protect the state by forever upholding the Dharma.[29]

But time has passed, and society has changed. [Monks] do not observe regulations; they have abandoned thatched huts and are reluctant to wear robes made of scraps of cloth (*funzō*). The buildings [on Mount Hiei] are gorgeously adorned and they [sit] high above the clouds. Patterned silks and the fragrance of incense waft in the [mountain] wind. The luxurious lifestyle on the mountain deserves public criticism. In the first place, there is no residence of monks, either on the peak or in the valley, that does not enshrine an image of the Buddha or dedicate [a shelf] to the scriptures. Although [the ceiling is] high and [the room is] spacious, [the resident monks] should adjust their [lifestyles to their] environment. A monk should wear just enough clothing to protect himself from the winter cold and the summer heat. He should not pay attention to the beauty and the style of his clothes. For this purpose, a regulation was issued in the fourth year of Kōhō [967] and [an announcement] has been posted at the Constant-walking Meditation Hall. [The announcement] contains the details of the regulation. All robes made of patterned silk cloth or embroidered with colorful threads are prohibited. A monk should wear a robe of [simple] color whether it is new or old, rough or fine, depending on whatever is simply available. A monk is not allowed to throw away an old robe or request a new robe or disdain a roughly [patched robe] in favor of a fine [silk robe]. Strive earnestly and do not abrogate the rules.

15. A monk who neglects his duty to attend the *sūtra* chanting services, be it either a private or public service, is permanently excluded from all official services. According to this rule, because devout lay believers in both their official and private capacities seek guidance in the Perfect teaching of Tendai and pray for the spiritual power of the deities [of Mount Hiei], they visit the halls of powerful Buddhas and hold *sūtra*-chanting services. Monks invited to rituals should abide in the Dharma and benefit others. They should attend services in the morning and evening, devote themselves to the contemplation of the words, phrases, and syllables [of the *sūtras*], and reveal the wonderful virtues of the king of the *sūtras* [the *Lotus Sūtra*] and thereby satisfy the wishes and vows of donors. However, some monks attend only the morning service and not the evening service. Other monks are only present at the opening session initiating the vow [for the service] but not present at the session concluding the vow [for the service]. [The services of these monks] exist in name only; and their practices do not reflect the true meaning [of the word "service"]. They are not only disrespectful of the sincere offerings of their donors, but also lack universal compassion.[30] The [bad reputation of some monks] has gone beyond the mountain and reached the city. Therefore, an order is issued that [monks] must attend the morning, afternoon, and evening services without fail and must be in attendance from the opening session initiating the vow [that is the occasion for the service] to the closing session that concludes the vow [for the service]. If a monk finds it difficult [to attend a service], he should immediately explain the reason at the administrative office and request a substitute. Once a monk enters the hall for a service, he

is neither allowed to be absent from a session [of the service] nor may he be excused from his duty [to attend] the middle [of the service]. A monk who neglects this order will not be invited to any of the major or minor official services. This order is established as a firm rule.

16. [Donors] are prohibited from delivering food baskets (*warigo*) as offerings to the monks on the mountain. The above-mentioned food baskets are part of the travel items of laypeople and hold smelly and greasy foods.[31] Such containers are impure. Monks (*sōke*) should have nothing to do with them. But some donors who sponsor Dharma services, and some guests who visit monks, deliver defiled food containers to our pure abode. Making a food offering to a monk is an act that produces merit and happiness. But contaminating the pure with the defiled will produce seeds of evil [karmic retribution].

Moreover, the container includes the destructive and forbidden taste [of liquor]. Although the acts of drinking and selling [liquor] are respectively minor and major offenses, both lead to hell.[32] For this reason, the great master [Saichō] in his dying remarks stated, "[Alcoholic drink] is not allowed to be used in this monastery on Mount [Hiei] even if it is for medical purposes, and certainly not for the purpose of consumption."[33] This regulation was reiterated during the Tentoku era [957–961], and again an official announcement of the regulation was posted at the eastern and western sides of the mountain during the Kōhō era [964–968]. Unruly monks, however, break this rule and prevent this regulation from taking effect [on Mount Hiei]. Now, the prohibition [of alcoholic drinks] is issued again. If a monk discovers a person who tries to smuggle [a prohibited food basket into the mountain], he must turn the person away from [the mountain] immediately. If [a monk] refuses to return [a food basket], he will be arrested and taken into the custody by the administrative office [of Enryakuji]. As a matter of course, a bottle [of liquor] must be returned without regard to its size, whether large or small.

17. Cattle and horses grazing within the confines of the monastery on Mount Hiei should be captured and entrusted to the left and right divisions of the Bureau of Horses (Meryō).[34] As mentioned above, the sage masters in the past established what lay within and without the sacred grounds (*kaiji*) [of Mount Hiei]. Moreover, emperors from generation to generation established august prayer-offering temples to the east and west, thereby making [Mount Hiei] a peaceful residence specifically for [Buddhist monks who are like] the dragons and ele-

phants [protecting] the three jewels [of Buddhism]. How can [the mountain monastery] be used as a pasture for the six kinds of livestock,[35] especially cattle and horses? It is, however, rumored that some monks who like horses and are fond of cattle put them out to pasture within the sacred confines of the mountain whenever they please during the day and secretly keep them in the back rooms of their residence hall within the confines of the monastery during the night. As a result, they contaminate the serene and pure mountain with various defilements, and they turn the cave for the divine spirits into a pit for manure. We have become known for the ugly bellowing sounds [of these animals] throughout the country, and we fear that the repercussion of public condemnation [against us] may even move the earth deities. Monks and laypeople who witness the decline [of morals among] Buddhists and the frivolous deeds of [the monks of] the Perfect teaching [of Tendai] publicly and loudly denounce [them]. From now on, [allowing animals to graze in the confines of Mount Hiei] is totally forbidden. Any livestock illegally grazing [within the confines of Mount Hiei] is to be confiscated and entrusted to the left and right divisions of the Bureau of Horses according to the court order issued on the seventeenth day of the ninth month of the first year of Jōgan [859].[36] There are no exceptions.

18. Monks who cover their heads [and faces] and disrupt the Dharma are banned [from Mount Hiei]. According to this rule, women customarily cover their face to conceal their identity, but monks who are men should not do so. However, in recent years, when the sun sets in the west and the darkness of night comes, the halls for the practice of the *nenbutsu* and the lecture halls are filled with mobs of monks who cover their heads and faces, fill the front courts, wear dirty shoes, and forcibly enter the buildings. With rough words and curses, they harass monks who try to restrain them. They chase and flail monks by brandishing swords and halberds. Those cultivating religious practices fled [from the meditation hall] upon seeing them coming, and people who came to listen to the Dharma were frightened by them and rushed away from [lecture meetings]. Such serious disturbances of the Dharma had never been observed [in years past]. For this reason, an order [to restrain disruptive monks] was issued on the first day of the eighth month of the eighth year of Kōhō [967], and was posted at the Constant-walking Meditation Hall. After the or-

der was issued, [many] judicious monks complied with the order. But some monks who have no aspiration to the Dharma have not yet complied. Therefore, this order is reissued.

During the practice of continuous (*fudan*) *nenbutsu* at the new year service, the second month service, or at the debate hall built for rituals in the courtly style (*uchi rongi dō*), as well as during the lectures on scriptures and doctrinal debates in various other places, both attendants and audience must wear proper attire in a dignified manner. Face masks (*zōmen*) and head coverings (*katō*) are all prohibited. The officers in charge of administering these rules should cite the names of violators of this rule on the spot and report them to the administrative officers [on Mount Hiei]. Violators shall be punished immediately without exception.

19. [Any monk] who arms himself and comes and goes from the residence halls or who roams the mountainside should be arrested and surrendered to the authorities. Arms are carried by warriors who live in the secular world; but scriptures are studied by practitioners who have renounced the secular world. A warrior, who lives in the secular world, may study the scriptures. But a person who has renounced the secular world must have nothing to do with arms. Above all, the monks on this mountain are to cultivate the doctrines of perfect interpenetration and the unconditioned (*ennyū musa*). With every step [they take], they are to abide in the compassionate [mind] that ferries sentient beings across [the sea of transmigration]. Novices and attendants (*dōji*) should follow the guidance of their master monk and cultivate the compassionate mind of the Buddha. How can they create karma that leads to suffering and the [three] poisons that lead to the three lower realms of existence?[37] How can they be like unrestrained people who commit the ten evil [acts]?[38]

According to the *Fan-wang ching*, "A disciple of the Buddha should not return anger with anger; nor should he return a blow for a blow. Even if one's father and mother, brothers and sisters [or other members] of one's six relatives[39] were slain, one should not retaliate. Responding to killing by killing is not in accord with filial piety."[40] Again, the *sūtra* states, "A disciple of the Buddha should not posses a sword, halberd, bow, arrows, pike, axe or any other fighting device. Even if one's father and mother were slain, one should not retaliate. How much more so is this the case for all sentient beings?"[41]

According to reports, some monks have formed cliques or gangs; they have forgotten their indebtedness [to other sentient beings] and harm others. They carry swords underneath [their robes] and go in and out of the monks' quarters just as they wish. Carrying bows and arrows, they trample the sacred ground [of Enryakuji]. They assail and wound [other monks] as they please. They are no different from butchers. They are filled with violence and evil, just like drunken elephants. They bring shame to the [Tendai] school and tarnish the three treasures. The laments [of monks] shake the mountain, and voices criticizing [the misconduct of Tendai monks] echo throughout society. The roots [of the misconduct of Tendai monks] in some cases are to be found in masters who have not strictly punished their disciples' misconduct and, in other cases, in disciples who do not faithfully obey the instructions of their masters.

From now on, the ban [on arms] is strictly enforced. Both masters and disciples must observe the precepts related to bodily and verbal acts. They must learn to follow the solemn manner of sages and saints at all times of the day and night, abandon all their swords, halberds, bows, and arrows forever, devote themselves to practicing compassion and charity at every moment, and vow to protect the state and benefit the realm of sentient beings. A monk who disregards the order issued by the administration of the temple or does not obey the instructions of his master will first receive punishments (*myōbatsu*) from the benevolent spirits who protect the Dharma. Thereafter, courageous men devoted to the Dharma will arrest him and send him to the administrative office to be turned over to the authorities.

20. Within the confines of the monastery on Mount [Hiei], a monk is prohibited from inflicting punishments arbitrarily [upon anyone]. The above-mentioned order is based on the twenty-three regulations[42] issued on the twenty-third day of the fifth month of the first year of Tenchō [824], which state, "A disciple of the Buddha should have a mind of compassion and use gentle words." As the great master [Saichō] admonished, "We, the members of the community [of monks], who equally share the Dharma, should not beat our attendants, nor should anyone be punished within the confines of the temple. A monk who fails to understand the significance of my words is not a member of our community of the Dharma, is not a disciple of the Buddha, and is not a person who studies the Dharma." Here I cite the words of the great master [Saichō] in order to convey his message to the disciples of the

later period. "In order to protect the Dharma, [a monk] should not punish [anyone in his community]. [A monk] should not beat his young [attendants] even with his fingers or palms. [A monk] who violates this rule is not a member of this mountain community. He is called a different kind [of being] than us (*irui*)."[43]

According to the *Fan-wang ching*,

> A bodhisattva should plant the roots of goodness and produce no thought of argument in any sentient being and should always maintain a compassionate mind. But, on the contrary, some monks scold with foul words in the presence of sentient and non-sentient beings (*hishujō*).[44] In addition, the offending monks punch them with fists or harm them with swords and halberds and still are not satisfied. Even though the [scolded] person wants to repent and apologize sincerely, [the monk scolding him] can hardly contain his anger. This is considered to be one of the gravest offenses (*haraizai*)[45] [within the community of] bodhisattvas.[46]

The *Fan-wang ching* also states, "A [disciple of the Buddha] should not keep male and female slaves and should not hit and curse them. He [should not add] innumerable verbal wrongdoing to the karma created from the three kinds of acts [bodily, verbal, and mental] in his everyday life."[47]

In recent years, however, it is occasionally heard that some monks on the mountain disregard the orders issued by the great master [Saichō] and violate the *tathāgata*'s admonitions (*yuikai*) by carrying out punishments within the confines of the monastery on Mount [Hiei]. Incidents of beating young attendants are often reported. From now on, [meting out of punishments within the confines of the monastery on the mountain] is completely prohibited. [A monk] who violates this rule will be expelled from the community. He is called a different kind [of being] than us (*irui*). How could he be called [a member of the community of monks who] share the Dharma (*dōhō*)?

21. Monks are prohibited from disturbing and interrupting the ordination ceremony. The ordination ceremony is the entrance that guides a person entering the family of the Buddha (*bukke*); it is the way in which beings are directly led to the place of enlightenment. [The ceremony confirming the precepts] is one of the most significant matters for the state. There is no other [ceremony] more crucial for the advancement of the [Tendai] school. But during the confirmation when the precepts are being given, some vicious people who do not observe the precepts unlawfully disturb the official ceremony because they hold

personal grudges. An ordinand is sometimes forcibly dragged out of the ceremony and humiliated by [the unlawful people at the ceremony]. And occasionally the ceremony is interrupted by [a mob of unruly people] who burst into the ceremony and start a brawl while [the ordinand] is on the [ordination] platform. No words can express the unlawfulness of these incidents.

From now on, [such unlawful conduct during ordinations is prohibited. [This ordinance is installed] to change the current situation. A monk who is concerned [about the ordination] should file a complaint describing the details of his situation to the administrative office (*mandokoro*) [of Enryakuji], and an immediate investigation should be conducted. A person who unlawfully disturbs [the ceremony], as if he were following a customary practice, will be permanently expelled from the order if he is a monk of this temple [Enryakuji]. If he is a monk of another temple, [whether] a novice or an attendant, he will be arrested and turned over to the police office (*kebiishi*). No misconduct [during the ceremony] should be overlooked.

22. [Each residence hall on Mount Hiei] is required to file a head monk's register (*bōzuchō*) [of residents to the administration office of Enryakuji] semiannually, once in the spring and once in the fall. This order is based on the above-mentioned regulation [issued on the twenty-third day of the fifth month on the first year of Tenchō (824)] which states,

> Each residence hall of [Enryakuji] temple [on Mount Hiei] must file a head monk's register [of residents] for every room to the administration office [of Enryakuji] semiannually, once in the spring and once in the fall. The register must include each resident's Dharma name (*hōgō*), province, county, family name, and given name. All [residents], regardless of age and position, should be registered without omission. This rule should always be followed. The person who does not follow this rule will be classified as a masterless wanderer (*rōnin*). Such a person is not eligible for benefits [on Mount Hiei], because he is not a member of the order on Mount [Hiei] (*sanshū*)."[48]

In recent years, however, this rule has not been observed and the registers have not been filed. The distinction between those on the mountain and those not residing on it has become difficult because of this [neglect]. From now on, [each residence hall] must keep a record [of all residents] for each term. [The register] must be filed before the deadline.

The above-mentioned regulation required that all residents, including lay servants[49] (*gonji*) and attendants (*dōji*), be included. This is because the regulation was issued when the number of the residents on Mount [Hiei] was still small and there were not so many resident halls. The regulation as it was stated [in 824] is not applicable to the current situation [on Mount Hiei]. Therefore, the register should be limited to the names of the monks currently in residence. One should neither miss the deadline nor fail to file [the register].

23. The registration of a current resident monk is to be certified by his attendance at the semiannual *sūtra* chanting services for Sannō.[50] Sannō guides us with his compassion and beneficence like our father, mother, master, and lord. We have already received his compassion and beneficence. How could we not be thankful [to Sannō]? Each monk should show his respect by transferring merit and glorifying [Sannō] through turning [the pages of] the *sūtras* (*tengyō*)[51] during the day and through memorized recitation [of a *mantra* or a *sūtra*] (*nenju*)[52] during the night in his own residence, dedicating [the merits for Sannō's] adornments. All current residents of the Eastern and Western [pagodas] should assemble at the Dharma Hall, once in the spring and once in the fall, and chant *sūtras* in unison [for the sake of Sannō].

In the old days, the number of the resident monks was calculated by those who attended the services [for Sannō]. The services [for Sannō] have been conducted during each of the four seasons since the Tengyō era. Many monks, however, have been lax in attendance, and few attend the services. [These absent monks] not only destroy the unity of the assembly of the service, but they also confuse [the administrators] as to the number of current residents [on Mount Hiei] as opposed to those on leave.

From now on, therefore, returning to the older tradition, the service [for Sannō] is to be held semiannually. A monk who does not attend the next season's service will be immediately removed from the register. The registration of a monk [who is removed from the register] will be restored at the following service [for Sannō] if he attends. But if a monk is sick, has become ritually defiled, or is invited to an official or private service [on the day of the service for Sannō], he must notify the administration office [of Enryakuji at least] three days before the service. He is allowed to fulfill his duty of *sūtra* chanting at the place where he is staying.

Also, the resident monks at Ryōgon'in [at the Yokawa area], in which almost two hundred residents are currently staying, have great difficulty in attending [the service] because their residence is over steep peaks and valleys far away [from the Dharma Hall]. [All resident monks at the Yokawa priory] should assemble at the central hall [of the Ryōgon'in] and perform the service [for Sannō] with utmost sincerity. The chief administrator (*inshi*) and other officers (*shikkō*) [of Ryōgon'in] must confirm [their attendance at the service] and forward the information [to the administrative office of Enryakuji]. This order is confirmed as a permanent rule.

24. On the day of the ceremony for the Buddha's relics, the temple officials (*kōi*) and the assistant temple administrators (*dōtatsu*) are prohibited from visiting the residence of the chief administrator (*bettō*) [supervising the assembly]. It has been customary for temple officials and assistant temple administrators to visit the residence of the chief administrator after the above-mentioned great assembly. Beginning with this year's assembly, the custom is abolished. [The custom is prohibited] for the following reasons. Although the *sūtras* state that we should take pleasure when good faculties are established, the rules and customs for the service should be more flexible. The [greeting] words [of monks visiting the chief administrator] have little sincerity. [For example,] even if the weather were not fine [on the day of the service], the monks [customarily] would say that the weather was fine. Even if [the service were] not observed according to the prescribed method, the monks would say that it was. The words [of such monks] are false and delusory in order to keep up momentary appearances. [After the service] everyone is tired and wants to be left to his own devices. But the hosts and guests [still have to] sit facing each other in accordance with unbearable rules and customs. Therefore, [the custom] is discontinued. In addition, the audience and the temple officials at the assembly of the sixth month are also prohibited from visiting the residence of the lecturer on the sixth day of the service.

25. The senior and junior officiants [of the services on Mount Hiei] are prohibited from visiting the residence of the head [of the Tendai school] to offer their congratulations [for the successful completion of the service]. The custom of the officiants visiting the residence of the head [of the Tendai school] to offer their congratulations has for many years been observed on the day of the annual services of the ceremony for the Buddha's relic, ordinations, and Esoteric consecrations. From

now on, this custom should be discontinued. The purpose of this prohibition is similar to that of the former article [24]. A newly appointed
head monk (*kanshu*)[53] [on Mount Hiei], however, is allowed to see vis-
itors when he officiates at a service for the first time.

26. The senior and junior officiants [of the official services on
Mount Hiei] should observe the rules of etiquette towards each other.
The *sūtras* and commentaries explain in detail [the principle] that one
should respect those above him and be sympathetic to those below. Even
certain birds or animals observe [this etiquette]. How much more so
should Buddhist monks observe [such etiquette]. But in recent years
monastic officials have often failed to observe the rules of etiquette. How
can [such impolite manners of monks] be tolerated in the light of the
Dharma? From now on, officials who sit in the middle or lower positions [at an assembly] must not disrupt [monks] who sit in the upper
or middle positions [respectively], even if conduct of the latter is improper. Upper- and middle-level officials must not ridicule lower- and
middle-level [monks], even if the latter make laughable statements. First,
everyone should be given an opportunity to present his opinion. A decision should be made after listening to everyone. Because the senior
official sits in the superior position, junior officials must respectfully obey
him. Because junior officials are sure to become senior officials in the
future, senior officials should not look down upon them. [All officials]
should respect and observe the rules of etiquette toward each other.

Some of the various articles stated above are based on the teaching of
the Tathāgata; others are from the admonitions of past masters. Yet, only
a few abide by these rules; those who disobey them are many. The winds
of old tradition do not sweep the moon shining over the cold valleys
any more. Traces of preceding [masters] are almost completely buried
beneath the evening clouds covering the peaks [of Mount Hiei]. If I
am alone in sincerely lamenting [the current situation] and if I grow
old idling beneath the [three] guardian stars[54] (*daisei*) [of the heavenly
palace], I fear that even after I am gone, my white bones will remain to
weep as the heavens pass above. Therefore, I exert my foolish self [and
write these articles]. Most humbly I present [this invocation to be
confirmed] before the clear mirror of the great master [Saichō]. I
present [this invocation] to all senior and junior officiants of the Eastern and Western [pagodas] and to the entire [Tendai] community on
Mount Hiei to polish the three disks (*sanrin*) [of bodily, verbal, and men-

tal acts of the monks inside] of the gate of the pine trees (*shōmon*).[55] I sincerely call [upon all buddhas, bodhisattvas, and guardian deities of Mount Hiei] to witness this invocation.

THE SIXTEENTH DAY OF THE SEVENTH MONTH
OF THE FIRST YEAR OF TENROKU [970].

The abbot [of Enryakuji], *supernumerary lesser bishop,
master of the Dharma-eye,*
Ryōgen [signature].

EXECUTIVE OFFICERS

The senior supervisor of the clerical affairs (jōza) [of Enryakuji],
a great master in the transmission of the lamp [of Dharma],
Hotchin[56] [signature].

The temple master [of Enryakuji],
a great master in the transmission of the lamp [of Dharma],
Juren [signature].

The chief director of the clerical affairs (tsuina) [of Enryakuji],
a great master in the transmission of the lamp [of Dharma],
Shōtō [signature].

Notes

Chapter 1. Ryōgen's Place in the History of the Tendai School

1. For some of the better scholarship on Chinese T'ien-t'ai teachings in English, see Leon Hurvitz, "Chih-i (538–597): An Introduction to the Life and Ideas of a Chinese Buddhist Monk"; Paul L. Swanson, *Foundations of T'ien-t'ai Philosophy;* and Neil Donner and Daniel Stevenson, *The Great Calming and Contemplation.*

2. For studies of the revival of T'ien-t'ai during the Sung, see Daniel Aaron Getz, "Siming Zhili and Tiantai Pure Land in the Song Dynasty"; and Chi-wah Chan, "Chih-li (960–1028) and the Formation of Orthodoxy in the Sung T'ien-t'ai Tradition of Buddhism."

3. Ryōgen's text on Pure Land is discussed briefly in the *Kuhon ōjōgi* (Doctrine of the nine classes of rebirth); a short description of the text in English can be found in James Dobbins, "A Brief History of Pure Land Buddhism in Early Japan," pp. 123–127. Ryōgen's text on path structure is titled *Hishōgi shiki* (Private record of opinions on when a practitioner receives a new teaching and enters the path for it); see Ōkubo Ryōshun, *Tendai mikkyō to hongaku shisō,* pp. 227–264. A short text on the debates between Hossō and Tendai scholars on the realization of Buddhahood by grasses and trees is translated in appendix 6.

4. Sasayama Haruo, "Kodai kokka no hen'yō: tenkōki to shite no jūseiki."

5. For example, Ryūkoku daigaku Bukkyōgaku kenkyūshitsu, ed., *Bukkyōgaku kankei zasshi ronbun bunrui mokuroku,* vol. 4, which covers essays published from 1970 to 1983, lists 236 articles on Saichō but only 30 on Ryōgen. The numbers are inflated for Ryōgen because of articles published in anticipation of the 1,000th anniversary of his death in 1984. The bibliography itself reflects the split in Japanese scholarship between historians and scholars in Buddhist Studies since few if any historical journals are included in the Ryūkoku bibliographies.

6. Kuroda Toshio, "The Development of the Kenmitsu System as Japan's Medieval Orthodoxy," p. 262.

7. Taira Masayuki, "Kuroda Toshio and the *Kenmitsu Taisei* Theory," pp. 442–443. For more detailed critiques of Kuroda's theories see *Japanese Journal of Religious Studies* 23.3–4 (1996), which contains a fine selection of Kuroda's writings translated into English as well as several critiques of his views.

8. Honda Kōyū, ed., *Yakuchū Jikaku daishiden,* pp. 10–11; Ono Katsutoshi, *Sanzen'in-hon Jikaku daishiden,* pp. 16, 38.

9. Ogami Kanchū, "Dengyō daishi nyūmetsugo no Tendaishū kyōdan," pp. 212–213. A set form for such certificates was included in the *Engishiki* (*KT* 26:365).

10. Kakimura Shigematsu, *Honchō monzui chūshaku*, 1:328–332. My translation is based on the annotation of Kakimura; the exact nature of the incidents that involved Tokiyoshi and Kimiyasu is not clear.

11. Nihon koten bungaku daijiten henshūiinkai, ed., *Nihon koten bungaku daijiten*, 5:648–649; Ienaga Saburō, ed., *Nihon Bukkyōshi*, 1:305.

12. A text that probably corresponds to Kakuun's biography of Ryōgen was published by Yamaguchi Kōen, "Seiraiji *Jie daishi Daisōjōden* kō." I am indebted to Nishimura Keishō for pointing out this source to me and giving me a photocopy of the Seiraiji manuscript.

13. The four sources are based on an analysis of the earliest biography of Enchin by Tokoro Isao, "*Enchin oshōden* no sozai to kōsei." It seems likely that Ryōgen's biography used the same type of sources. In fact, Tokoro notes that the process of compiling the *Jie daisōjōden* was similar to that used in *Enchin oshōden* (p. 48).

14. Enchin's biography was used in this manner (Tokoro, "*Enchin oshōden* no sozai to kōsei," p. 34); however, no statement is found in the *Jie daisōjōden* that the text was compiled for use by court historians.

15. For further analysis of the differences between the two biographies, see Kushida Ryōkō, "Jie daishiden no shinshiryō ni tsuite," and Hirabayashi Moritoku, *Hijiri to setsuwa no shiteki kenkyū*, pp. 21–40.

Chapter 2. The Early History of Factionalism within the Tendai School

1. *Denjutsu isshinkaimon*, *DZ* 1:640; Groner, *Saichō*, p. 286. The ambiguities in the seniority of the two men are examined in Shijō Masami, "Shuzen daishi Gishin no kenkyū," *Bukkyōgaku kenkyū* 38 (1982): 78.

2. *Denjutsu isshinkaimon*, *DZ* 1:593. In this passage, the Tendai monks are described as having no food. The two temples had loose ties to the Tendai school because they had been founded by Prince Shōtoku, who was said to have been an incarnation of the second Chinese T'ien-t'ai patriarch, Hui-ssu (514–577). Tendai monks such as Ennin lectured at these temples later (Groner, *Saichō*, p. 281).

3. Shibuya Jigai, ed., *Kōtei zōho Tendai zasuki*, p. 7.

4. Recent scholarly discussion has considered why a number of important events in Saichō's life are omitted from his earliest biography, the *Eizan daishiden*. Nakao Shunpaku has suggested that the debates with Tokuitsu and Saichō's Esoteric initiations from Kūkai were not mentioned either to promote harmony with the Nara schools ("Enshu to Enchin," 237:5) or because they would not give a favorable picture of the Tendai school (*Sange gakushōshiki josetsu*, pp. 143–144). Kiuchi Gyōō ("*Eizan daishiden* no yakuwari," p. 97) has criticized Nakao's conclusions and suggested that the biography was compiled with the intention of supporting Gishin as *zasu*. Events in which Gishin played little role or that cast his rival Enchō in a favorable light were omitted. Later, Enchin excerpted passages from the *Eizan daishiden* and compiled a shorter biography of Saichō, the *Gyōgōki DZ* 5 [*furoku*]: 49–56), which also described Gishin's accomplishments and qualifications as a

leader. The claims of Nakao and Kiuchi do not seem mutually exclusive. The tendency to ignore Kūkai is found in other Tendai sources; for example, Ennin does not mention the respect that his teacher, the Chinese monk I-chen, had for Kūkai in his diary, but Enchin records I-chen's high regard for Kūkai. The difference in their attitudes may have been due to Enchin's family ties to Kūkai (Saeki Arikiyo, *Chishō daishi den no kenkyū*, pp. 56–58).

5. *Ruijū kokushi*, fasc. 185, *KT* 6:291.

6. The organization of monastic ranks at this time is a difficult subject because the system was frequently amended; for a good survey, see Nakai Shinkō, s.v. "sōi," *Kokushi daijiten* 8:508c–509a.

7. Shibuya, ed., *Tendai zasuki*, p. 7.

8. For comments concerning the authenticity of the letter, see Groner, *Saichō*, pp. 82 (n. 25) and 288. Early Tendai attitudes toward Kūkai need to be investigated more thoroughly. Ennin ignores Kūkai in his travel diary, but Enchin mentions Kūkai in a number of documents and possessed a number of texts either copied or authored by Kūkai (Saeki, *Chishō daishiden no kenkyū*, p. 57).

9. Groner, *Saichō*, pp. 287–290. In recent years, Sekiguchi Shindai has forcefully argued that the *Tendaishū gishū* provides a better introduction to Tendai doctrine than Chegwan's *T'ien-t'ai ssu-chiao-i*, the text traditionally used as to present Tendai teachings to students (for the English translation, see Chegwan, *T'ien-t'ai Buddhism*. Paul Swanson has translated the *Tendaishū gishū* into English for inclusion in the Bukkyō dendō kyōkai series of translations. The text has also been the subject of a detailed study in French by Jean-Noël Robert, *Les doctrines de l'école japonaise Tendaï ai début du IXe siècle*.

10. For more on the controversy between Gishin and Enchō, see Groner, *Saichō*, pp. 286–290.

11. "Tendai Hokkeshū nenbun tokudo gakushō meichō," *DZ* 1:252. The document notes that the decision to go to Mount Takao was made privately and thus was not part of Saichō's plans to have his students study with Kūkai.

12. Nakao Shunpaku, "Enshu to Enchin"; reprinted in Nakao, *Nihon mikkyō no kōryū to tenkai*, pp. 289–335.

13. *Denjutsu isshinkaimon*, *DZ* 1:644.

14. "Enshu to Enchin," 237:2. Saichō's relations with Gomyō and Kūkai are discussed in Groner, *Saichō*, pp. 77–87, 146–148.

15. Shibuya, ed., *Tendai zasuki*, p. 8; and *Eigaku yōki*, *GR* 24:544.

16. For a study of Gomyō, see Sakuma Ryū, "Gomyō ni tsuite," pp. 71–92.

17. Enchō's interests in Esoteric Buddhism are discussed in Yūki Yoshifumi, "Enchō no kenkyū," pp. 93–112.

18. The relationship between Gishin and Shintai is based on a short letter found in "Kōya zappitsushū," in Katsumata Shunkyō ed., *Kōbō daishi chosaku zenshū*, 3:540. Also see Sonoda Kōyū, "Sōsōki Murōji wo meguru sōryo no dōkō," pp. 411–426. For a discussion of Shuen's interest in the Esoteric tradition brought back by Saichō, see Groner, *Saichō*, pp. 65–67.

19. Nakao Shunpaku, "Murō Tendai to Chishō daishi Enchin," p. 692. According to Jōjin's (1011–1081) diary, Chōnen (d. 1016) reported that Ennin did not submit the last fascicle of his travel diary because he wished to keep the court from knowing the details of the persecution in China (*San Tendai Godaisan ki*, in Suzuki

gakujutsu zaidan, ed., *Dainihon Bukkyō zensho,* 72:256a). This source is hereafter cited as *BZ;* because two editions of *BZ* exist and I have used both, the edition is cited.

20. For an analysis of some of the questions concerning the realization of Buddhahood with this very body (*sokushin jōbutsu*), see Groner, "Shortening the Path;" pp. 439–474.

21. The date of Enshu's arrival in China is established by a passage in Enchin's *Gyōryakushō* that mentions his arrival with Eun (798–869). It is not clear that Kenne accompanied Enshu to China, but because of the subsequent details of the story, it seems likely (Ono Katsutoshi, *Nittō guhō gyōreki no kenkyū,* 1:122; Oyamada Kazuo, "Kenne to Enchin," pp. 241–243).

22. *Kechimyaku zuki, BZ* (Suzuki ed.), 65:206. The text and a detailed analysis are included in an article by Ono Katsutoshi, "Nittōsō Enshu Kenne to sono *Kechimyaku zuki.*" Kuang-hsiu did not actually sign the document because he had died the previous year, shortly after conferring his teachings on Enshu but before the document had been prepared (*Sung kao-seng chuan, T* 50:895a).

23. *Shoku Nihon kōki, KT* 3:167; Nakao, "Murō Tendai to Chishō daishi Enchin," pp. 689–690. The passage in *Shoku Nihon kōki* describes Enshu as a monk of Tōdaiji with the rank of *dentō jūi* (junior rank of the transmission of the flame, the rank below *dentō man'i*), perhaps indicating that his form of Tendai adopted a much more open approach to the Nara Schools than that of Enryakuji. The name of the temple, Jion'in, suggests a connection with the Hossō tradition because Jion is the Sino-Japanese reading of the characters for Tz'u-en, the de facto founder of the Fa-hsiang (J. Hossō) school.

24. Although little information on Izumodera survives, it was probably a moderately large complex with buildings commissioned by several members of the imperial family. The temple may have been the clan temple of the Izumo family. According to later Tendai traditions, Saichō had built a grass hut on the spot. When Enchin first returned from China, he spent about a month at Izumodera, perhaps indicating his sympathy for Enshu's movement (Ono Katsutoshi, *Nittō guhō gyōreki no kenkyū,* 2:397–399). During the tenth century, it is mentioned as receiving government funds for assemblies for angry ghosts (*goryō-e*) and for services for the deceased (*urabon-e*). Thus the temple complex may have been important at the time Enshu retired there (Gotō Kuniharu, s.v. "Izumodera," in Tsunoda, ed. *Heian jidaishi jiten,* 1:131c).

25. *Genkō shakusho, BZ* (Suzuki ed.), 62:226b; *Nihon kōsōden yōmonshō, BZ* (Suzuki ed.) 62:50b. According to the *Nihon kōsōden yōmonshō,* all the participants were among the learned men of their day, suggesting that Enshu might have been a more impressive scholar than most surviving sources indicate.

26. Nakao, "Murō Tendai to Chishō daishi Enchin," p. 685. Butsuryūji was about four kilometers southwest of Murōji; it was named an official temple (*jōgakuji*) in 890 (Takei Akio, s.v. "Butsuryūji," in Tsunoda, ed., *Heian jidaishi jiten,* 2:2233c).

27. *Daitōkoku Nihonkoku fuhō kechimyaku zuki, BZ* (Suzuki ed.), 65:206b; Nakao, "Murō Tendai to Chishō daishi Enchin," p. 689; Oyamada, "Kenne to Enchin," p. 245. Kenne eventually was considered to have been a Shingon monk; according to some traditions, he accompanied Kūkai to China. However, these traditions are not supported by any authentic documents. Instead, they were probably invented by a later Shingon monk who lived at Kenne's temple, Butsuryūji (Oyamada, "Kenne to

Enchin," p. 245). Several documents concerning him are included in Nagatani Hōshū, ed., *Kōbō daishi shodeshi zenshū*, 2:469; and *Nittō shoke den kō, BZ* (Suzuki ed.), 68:174b–175c. They have been discussed in Nakao Shunpaku, "Tendaisō Kenne," pp. 181–184. One of these documents indicates that Kenne was appointed as *risshi* (master of discipline) to the Office of Monastic Affairs in 860; if the document were authentic, Kenne would have been one of the few Tendai monks so honored at that time. However, no corroborating evidence for Kenne's appointment has been found.

    28. *Sannōinzō, T, Hōbō sōmokuroku*, 3:767a.

    29. *Daitōkoku Nihonkoku fuhō kechimyaku zuki, BZ* (Suzuki ed.), 65:206c. Another version of the same text contains the notation that it was hidden in the Tōin (*Chishō daishi yohō hennen zasshū, BZ* [Suzuki ed.], 72:216b), a circumstance that might help explain why Enshu and Kenne have remained obscure figures for much of Tendai history.

    30. Oyamada Kazuo argues for a different interpretation of the notation that Enchin had received the lineage from Kenne. He notes that the document describing the lineage still survives and that it appears to be a copy of an original. Thus the original lineage itself would not have been turned over to Enchin, but rather only a copy. Kenne's intention remains obscure in Oyamada's explanation, but he might have intended the lineage to serve as a means of preserving Tendai claims on Butsuryūji (Oyamada, "Kenne to Enchin," pp. 248–249).

    31. Shinzei was one of Kūkai's most able students, receiving the dual consecration at the early age of twenty-five; he was the first Shingon monk named archbishop. Shinzen became the leader of the faction that was based at the Kongōbuji on Mount Kōya. If these two monks had successfully studied in China, they might have saved Shingon doctrine from stagnation after Kūkai's death (Tsuji Zennosuke, *Nihon Bukkyōshi*, 1:337).

    During Engyō's trip to China, he made offerings before an image of Kūkai's teacher, Hui-kuo. He returned to Japan in 839 with 69 texts in 133 fascicles, as well as a number of ritual implements and relics. Although the bibliography of texts he carried back boasts of the significance of his accomplishment, it would seem to be overstated (Ono Katsutoshi, *Nittō guhō junrei kōki no kenkyū*, 1:409–411). Moreover, he accomplished little after his return (Sonoda Kōyū, in Ienaga Saburō, ed., *Nihon Bukkyōshi*, 1:229).

    Jōgyō studied under the Risshū monk Buan and the Shingon school founder Kūkai. Although he traveled to China as a long-term Sanron student, he studied Esoteric Buddhism in China and returned by 840. His most notable achievement was his successful advocacy of Esoteric rituals for Taigensui (or Taigen) myōō (Skt. Āṭavaka), a *yakṣa* general said to protect the emperor and the state. He came to be regarded in most histories as a member of the Shingon school. Much of the biographical information about Engyō and Jōgyō is collected in the *Shingonden, BZ* (Suzuki ed.), 68:30b–31b; *Nittō goke den, BZ* (Suzuki ed.), 68:160a–c, 163c–164a; and *Nittō shokeden kō, BZ* (Suzuki ed.), 68:168b–c.

    Two monks named Kaimyō traveled to China. The first was from Daianji; he went to China late in the Nara period. In 779, he brought back the *Shih mo-ho-yen lun*, a commentary attributed to Nāgārjuna on the *Ta-sheng ch'i-hsin lun* (Awakening of faith according to the Mahāyāna). Although the text was criticized as apocryphal,

Kūkai regarded it as authentic and used it in his doctrinal scheme. Little is known about the second Kaimyō, who was from Yakushiji. His movements in China are unknown. After his return, he stayed in Tsukushi and then in Bingo, where the governor became his patron and helped him commission a copy of the canon. Eventually he went to Yakushiji, where he established the Tōin (Chinese Hall). Kaimyō is said to have brought back an image of the Fa-hsiang patriarch installed at Yakushiji. The two monks are often confused in most sources; for a clear discussion of the latter, see Ono Katsutoshi, *Nittō guhō junrei kōki no kenkyū*, 1:411–412.

32. Edwin Reischauer, trans. *Ennin's Diary*, pp. 90–91; Ono Katsutoshi, *Nittō guhō junrei kōki no kenkyū*, 1:432–433.

33. *Sung kao-seng-chuan*, *T* 50:895a; *Tendai kahyō*, *BZ* (Suzuki ed.), 41:218a. The commentary by Prince Shōtoku was an appropriate gift because Shōtoku was said to have been the rebirth of the T'ien-t'ai patriarch Hui-ssu.

34. Ennin may have alluded to the problems with the money (Reischauer, *Ennin's Diary*, p. 321, n. 1234); however, Ono Katsutoshi does not comment on the financial issues (*Nittō guhō junrei kōki no kenkyū* 3:457–458). Also see Nakao Shunpaku, "Ensai (2)," p. 222). Only Enchin mentions the sexual offenses and farming (Ono Katsutoshi, *Nittō guhō gyōreki no kenkyū*, 1:121–122).

35. Reischauer, *Ennin's Diary*, pp. 90, 339, 377; Ono Katsutoshi, *Nittō guhō junrei kōki no kenkyū*, 1:432–433; 4:203. The title *zenji* does not necessarily indicate that Ensai performed meditation; it was often applied to monks of superior virtue regardless of whether they were noted for meditation. During the latter part of the ninth century, Tendai monks were known to have overlooked sexual lapses in monks in Japan (Paul Groner, "Annen, Tankei, Henjō, and Monastic Discipline in the Japanese Tendai School," pp. 134–135).

36. Reischauer, *Ennin's Diary*, p. 377; Ono Katsutoshi, *Nittō guhō junrei kōki no kenkyū*, 4:201.

37. *Shoku Nihon kōki*, *KT* 3:199–200, 212–213; Ono Katsutoshi, *Nittō guhō gyōreki no kenkyū*, 1:49, 51. Ninkō probably had first gone to China in 838 accompanying Ensai. The rank of *dentō daihosshi* was the highest in the system of nine ranks in use at that time.

38. Ono Katsutoshi, *Nittō guhō gyōreki no kenkyū*, 1:116–117, 119. Enchin's use of the epithet "bodhisattva" to describe Ensai at this point is noteworthy. Later in their relationship, his feelings toward Ensai become increasingly negative.

39. Ibid., 1:120–123. Enchin's account of these events may be exaggerated.

40. Ensai's disciples Ninkō and Junshō had arrived in Nagato on 12-9-843 (*Shoku Nihon kōki*, *KT* 3:163; Nakao, "Ensai (2)," p. 225). Although Enshu returned before Ensai was given any more money by the court, he either was unable or did not attempt to prevent the court from dispatching more gold to Ennin and Ensai (*Shoku Nihon kōki*, *KT* 3:166, 168).

41. Saeki, *Enchin*, p. 98.

42. Ono Katsutoshi, *Nittō guhō gyōreki no kenkyū*, 1:121–124. Enki was one of the Tendai monks chosen to accompany Saichō to China.

43. Ibid., 1:227–230. The term "thief" and variations of it occur repeatedly in this passage.

44. Saeki Arikiyo, *Enchin*, pp. 94–95, 103.

45. Saeki Arikiyo, *Saichō to sono monryū*, pp. 126–135.

46. Evidence for the hall comes from a colophon on a text in the Tōdaiji library, quoted in Horiike Shunpei, "Ensai Ennin to Tendaisan Kokuseiji oyobi Chōan Shishōji ni tsuite," p. 44. For a discussion of various theories concerning who built the New Japanese Hall, see ibid., p. 50; and Saeki, *Chishō daishi no kenkyū*, pp. 96–103. The *Wu-pai men lun* is found in *Hsü-tsang ching*, 100:666–802, and the *Fa-hua hsüan-tsan* corresponds to *T* no. 1723. Approximately thirty other texts from a variety of traditions were sent back to Japan at the same time; for a list, see *Tendai kahyō, BZ* (Suzuki ed.), 41:218b.

47. *Honchō kōsōden, BZ* (Suzuki ed.), 63: 59a. The Hsi-ming temple was often used to house foreign monks.

48. *Nittō gokeden, BZ* (Suzuki ed.), 68:162c. For a thorough discussion of Shin-nyo, see Sugimoto Naojirō, *Shinnyo shinnō den kenkyū;* his relationship with Ensai is discussed on pp. 305–306.

49. *Honchō kōsōden, BZ* (Suzuki ed.), 63:59a; Ono Katsutoshi, *Nittō guhō gyōreki no kenkyū*, 2:451, 454–456; a number of Chinese acquaintances composed poems to send Ensai back to Japan. Enchin was well aware of Ensai's potential threat to Tendai unity and commented on his death to his students (*Tendaishū Enryakuji zasu Enchinden, BZ* [Suzuki ed.], 72:150; *Chishō daishi nenpu, BZ* [Suzuki ed.], 72:157c).

50. Ensai has been the subject of several studies, including Ōya Tokujō, "Chishō daishi no nittō guhō," *Onjōji no kenkyū* [Onjōji, 1931], pp. 124–135; Nakao, "Ensai (1)" and "Ensai (2)"; Horiike, "Ensai Ennin to Tendaisan Kokuseiji oyobi Chōan Shishōji ni tsuite"; Saeki, *Chishō daishiden no kenkyū*, pp. 96–118; Saeki, *Enchin*, pp. 84–145 passim. Saeki notes that Enchin's opinion of Ensai worsened as Enchin grew older (*Chishō daishiden*, p. 109).

51. Oyamada Kazuo, "Chishō daishi Enchin to bettō kashō Kōjō kan." For a use-ful survey of Kōjō's earlier career, see Kiuchi Gyōō, "Kōjō no jiseki." Kōjō's role in helping Enchin travel to China is mentioned in Ono Katsutoshi, *Nittō guhō gyōreki no kenkyū*, 1:39–41.

52. *Tendaishū Enryakuji zasu Enchinden, BZ* (Suzuki ed.), 72: 145b; *Chishō daishi nenpu, BZ* (Suzuki ed.), 72: 154c. For a discussion of the way in which the assembly came to such agreements, see Seita Yoshihide, "Eizan no gōgisei." The document appointing Enchin, the earliest extant Tendai manuscript using the term "*shugi*," was issued from the Administrative Center (*mandokoro*) on Mount Hiei (quoted and discussed ibid., pp. 231–232). The source of many of the procedures used in such decisions was potentially a problem because the Tendai school had rejected the *Ssu-fen lü (Dharmaguptaka vinaya)* as "Hīnayāna." However, Tendai monks still seem to have drawn many of the procedures they followed from the *Ssu-fen lü* and related sources ibid., pp. 226–230). Although the Tendai school eventually adopted sepa-rate assemblies based on chapels (*in*) or social classes, the assembly that voted to appoint Enchin seems to have included all the monks on the mountain (*manzan daishugi*).

53. *Daihizō yugaki, BZ* (Suzuki ed.), 38: 190b; the transmission is also mentioned in a document by Enchin from Onjōji cited in the secondary sources below. The transmission is confirmed by Annen (*Taizōkai daihō taijuki, T* 75:100a), who noted that Ennin taught the *mudrā* for Mahāvairocana to Enchin along with Tankei. These teachings would have been conferred sometime between 848 and 851. The trans-mission has been discussed by Oyamada Kazuo, "Ennin to Enchin to no kankei ni

tsuite no ichi shiron," pp. 42–43; Kiuchi Gyōō, *Tendai mikkyō no keisei,* pp. 317–320; and Saeki, *Enchin,* pp. 31–34.

54. *Chishō daishi yohō hennen zasshū, BZ* (Suzuki ed.), 72: 212c (s.v. *Chokuga denbō kiku chō*).

55. *Chishō daishi yohō hennen zasshū, BZ* (Suzuki ed.), 72:207c–208a, 210a (s.v. *Kōden shingon shikan ryōshū kanchō*). The source for this term is a petition relating Enchin's studies. Two versions of it exist, a rough draft and the final copy. The use of this term in both indicates that it reflects Enchin's view. Gishin is referred to as "father and teacher" and Saichō as "grandfather and teacher" in the same document. Also see *Daihizō yugaki, BZ* (Suzuki ed.), 38:190b.

56. Shibuya, ed., *Tendai zasuki,* p. 24; *Fusō ryakki, KT* 12:155.

57. Shibuya, ed., *Tendai zasuki,* p. 26; *Tōbō anri roku, BZ* (Suzuki ed.), 72: 185b. The *mandara-ku* was a ceremony in which offerings were made to the Womb and Diamond-realm *maṇḍalas.* The date for the ceremony coincided with the anniversary of Ennin's death.

58. Yanagida Shin'ei, "Chishō daishi no goyuikai." Fukuo Takeichirō ("Jikaku montō to Chishō montō no kōso ni tsuite," pp. 541–544) has effectively demonstrated that many of the articles must have been written two to three hundred years after Enchin's death because they reflect the situation after the schism had occurred. Typical of this type of entry is the ninth article: "After my death, my disciples should mix with those of Jikaku daishi (Ennin) like milk and water; their behavior should be like that of fathers and mothers or older and younger brothers" (*Tōbō anriroku, BZ* [Suzuki ed.], 72:185c). The will is found only in the *Tōbō anriroku,* a chronology and compilation of documents concerning Enchin compiled by Keikō (1740–1795); see the entry on the text in *Kaidai, BZ* (Suzuki ed.), 98:350c.

59. Shibuya, ed., *Tendai zasuki,* pp. 24–25. Saeki seems to regard the three-article admonitions as authentic (*Enchin,* pp. 279–280). For a detailed study and collated version of the text, see Sugawara Shinkai, *Sannō Shintō no kenkyū,* pp. 65–71. The Sannō cult seems to have had connections with the Jōshin'in, the temple dedicated to Emperor Ninmyō where Enchin performed rituals (ibid., pp. 74–75).

60. Sources differ about whether Enchin was appointed in 847 or 848, but Saeki effectively argues for 847 (*Chishō daishiden no kenkyū,* pp. 200–201). Sources also differ about the date when the Jōshin'in was dedicated, listing dates of 843, 846, and 847; Oyamada has argued for a date of 846 ("Ennin to Enchin to no kankei ni tsuite no shiron," pp. 34–35). Appointment to the post carried substantial financial rewards.

61. *Nihon kiryaku, KT* 10: 381; *Asabashō, T* (*zuzō*), 9:248a, 836b–c. The eight characters mentioned in the title of the ritual refer to eight syllables that symbolize Mānjuśrī's qualities. According to the *Nihon kiryaku* entry, another sixty monks were to recite perfection of wisdom texts in the Shishinden, the main ritual center in the palace. Because the original function of the Jōshin'in monks had been to chant perfection of wisdom texts, the sixty monks seem to have taken on that task while the Jōshin'in monks performed a new ritual. The ritual was used primarily by Tendai monks at first, but Shingon monks also eventually began performing it (Hayami Tasuku, *Heian kizoku,* p. 22).

62. No direct evidence of Enchin's displeasure is found in contemporary documents, but it seems likely that he might have been disturbed by Ennin's ascen-

dance (Oyamada, "Ennin to Enchin to no kankei ni tsuite no shiron," pp. 37–38). On the other hand, Saeki Arikiyo notes that Ennin must have taught the ritual to Enchin so that he could help perform it as a monk from the Jōshin'in. Thus the ritual also can be used as evidence for cooperation between the two men (Saeki, *Enchin*, p. 35).

63. Ono Katsutoshi, *Nittō guhō gyōreki no kenkyū*, 1:20.

64. The account of the dream is found in the beginning of a text that is extant in handwriting that resembles that of Enchin, leading Ono Katsutoshi to suggest it is probably authentic. Accounts of it are found in the *Chishō daishi nenpu* and *Tendaishū Enryakuji zasu Enchin kashō den* (Ono Katsutoshi, *Nittō guhō gyōreki no kenkyū* 1:39–41; Saeki, *Chishō daishiden no kenkyū*, pp. 205–206). The interpretation of these dreams in the light of the later Jimon-Sanmon schism has been the topic of a number of studies, including Itsuki Seishō, "Tendaishū shijō ni okeru Chishō daishi," pp. 180–181; Sonoda Kōyū, "Enchin nittō no dōki," *Shisō* 2; Hoshimiya Chikō, "Shoki Nihon no Tendai kyōdan ni okeru Chishō daishi," pp. 1327–1328. The studies have not agreed on Enchin's attitude toward Ennin, probably because the interpretation of such dreams is very difficult and because of the paucity of sources that indicate any direct contact between Ennin and Enchin.

65. For a painstaking analysis of these documents, see Oyamada, "Ennin to Enchin to kankei ni tsuite no ichi shiron," pp. 38–39.

66. Saeki, *Enchin*, pp. 19–23, 35–36.

67. Groner, *Saichō*, pp. 83–85.

68. Misaki Ryōshū, "Tendai no mikkyō," p. 221. Misaki notes that these numbers exceed Kūkai's 214 texts in 461 fascicles, including 137 Esoteric texts in 201 fascicles and twenty-three ritual implements.

69. Shibuya, *Tendai zasuki*, pp. 14–15; Saeki, *Jikaku daishiden no kenkyū*, pp. 295, 297–298; Oyamada Kazuo, "Ennin to Enchin to no kankei: Yokawa to Onjōji ron," pp. 142–145.

70. Shibuya, *Tendai zasuki*, p. 14; Satō Tetsuei, "Zentōin kenzaisho mokuroku ni tsuite," pp. 99–101.

71. *BZ* (Bussho kankōkai ed.), 26: 714a.

72. Satō Tetsuei, "Sannōin zōsho mokuroku ni tsuite," p. 19. The bibliography of works for the Sannōin was compiled in 925 by Enchin's disciple Kūe. Kūe was the teacher of Zengei, who served as *tandai* when Ryōgen revived the examination system on Mount Hiei. The Sannōin was just to the west of the Sōjiin.

73. Three documents in the *Chishō daishi yohō hennen zasshū* (*BZ* [Suzuki ed.], 72:212a–213a) concern this event; one of them was a decision of the assembly on Mount Hiei (*gijōsho*) and two of them were orders from the chancellor's office (*kanpu*). Only one is dated 5-1-869.

74. Ono Katsutoshi, *Nittō guhō gyōreki no kenkyū* 2:416–417.

75. *Chishō daishi nenpu, BZ* (Suzuki ed.), 72: 156b–c, 157b. The account of the dream reflects the events of the later Jimon-Sanmon schism. For example, according to traditional accounts, Enchin introduced the worship of Shiragi myōjin, but the deity seems to have been worshipped by the Ōtomo clan before Enchin's time (Saeki, *Enchin*, p. 216).

In fact, many of the documents concerning Enchin's rebuilding of Onjōji have been either altered or forged to support various claims in the schism between the

Jimon and Sanmon. Enchin supposedly specified that members of his lineage would be favored for appointments as abbot (*bettō*) of the Onjōji, but this tradition too has been questioned. For an analysis of the traditional narrative concerning Enchin and Onjōji, see Saeki, *Enchin*, pp. 207–214.

76. The *Sannōin zōsho mokuroku*, dated 925, has been printed in *Eizan gakuhō* 13 (1937).

77. The Esoteric and exoteric ladders to eminence remained separate to some extent. For example, Ryōgen's student Kakuchō submitted a petition to have Kyōen named *ajari*, but it was rejected because no precedent existed for an appointment of a monk who had already served as a lecturer at the three major assemblies in Nara. Eventually Kyōen did succeed in being named *ajari*. See Okano Kōji, "Denbō ajari shokui to yusoku," p. 326. However, the relation between Esoteric and exoteric Buddhism in Tendai deserves further study.

78. Okano, "Denbō ajari," p. 312. Although similar patterns eventually appeared in the Shingon school, the school seems to have been less centralized. Shingon efforts to centralize the appointment of *ajari* developed along with efforts to give the abbot of Tōji the preeminent position in the school. I have benefited from Okano's scholarship in writing this account.

79. The manner in which rituals for individuals, rather than for the state, were used is discussed in the chapter on Morosuke.

80. Nishiguchi Junko places the first usage of the term "*goganji*" in 827 ("Heian jidai shoki jiin no kōsatsu," 52). Earlier temples established at the wish of the emperor or empress were simply called "great temples" (*daiji*). The most famous list of great temples is the list of seven at Nara, but other documents contain variant lists (Mochizuki and Tsukamoto, eds., *Mochizuki Bukkyō daijiten*, 4:3227c–3228a). *Daiji* were eligible to receive court funds for their maintenance and upkeep, but private temples were not. *Daiji* were also distinguished from *goganji* through the style of architecture.

81. For a description of the establishment of a *goganji*, Gangyōji, see Groner, "Annen, Tankei, Henjō, and Monastic Discipline in the Japanese Tendai School," 142–148. The rising popularity of *goganji* was paralleled by the increasing use of Esoteric rituals for private ends; see the chapter on Ryōgen and Morosuke.

82. Nishiguchi Junko, s.v. "Goganji-ryō," in Tsunoda, ed., *Heian jidaishi jiten*, 1:858b.

83. Hori Daiji, "Ryōgen no 'Nijūrokkajō kisei,'" p. 21.

84. Nishiguchi Junko's study "Heian shoki ni okeru Yamato-kuni shoji no dōkō" compares the strategies that led to success and failure among the Nara temples in the early Heian period.

85. *Goganji* were supported lavishly with major tracts of land. For example, the *Engishiki* lists a number of *goganji* that were to receive between 10,000 and 30,000 *soku* of grain from provincial taxes. Nishiguchi ("Heian jidai shoki jiin no kōsatsu," 49) lists twenty-one tracts of land totaling 840 *chō* that were given to the Jōganji between 862 and 867.

86. Both *jōgakusō* and *ajari* had to be approved by monastic and court authorities. Officially authorized monks (*jōgakusō*) could be appointed to a variety of temples, including both official temples such as the *kokubunji* and semiofficial tem-

ples such as the officially designated temples (*jōgakuji*). Thus such monks were not limited to *jōgakuji* (Tsunoda, ed., *Heian jidaishi jiten*, 1:1303b–c).

87. The Office of Monastic Affairs during Ryōgen's time is discussed in the chapter on Ryōgen's appointment as *zasu*. The origins and adoption of the *zoku bettō* system by other temples is extensively discussed in Kikuchi Kyōko, "Zoku bettō no seiritsu."

88. Sone Masato, "Jōgakuji" and "Jōgakusō" in Tsunoda, ed., *Heian jidaishi jiten*, 1:1202d–1203b.

89. *Eigaku yōki, GR* 24:541–543; Ono Katsutoshi, *Nittō guhō gyōreki no kenkyū*, 2:411.

90. Okano, "Enryakuji zoku bettō to Tendai zasu," pp. 96–100. Okano notes that *zasu* in non-Tendai temples usually focused on propagation of teachings and did not have the administrative responsibilities that the Tendai *zasu* assumed. In addition, the lay supervisors for non-Tendai temples at this time usually had more administrative responsibilities than Tendai lay supervisors. Lay supervisors for non-Tendai temples frequently served at several temples concurrently, suggesting that they served more as bureaucrats than as lay patrons.

91. Hori Daiji, "Ryōgen no 'Nijūrokkajō kisei,'" p. 26. For a general study of the issues discussed here, see Neil McMullin, "The Sanmon-Jimon Schism in the Tendai School of Buddhism."

92. *NS* 1.2:65–69; no entry for Yuishu is found in Saeki, *Chishō daishiden no kenkyū*.

93. *NS* 1.2:163–165; Saeki, *Chishō daishiden no kenkyū*, pp. 389, 398–399. The available information on Tokuen is collected in Saeki Arikiyo, *Dengyō daishi no kenkyū*, pp. 581–585.

94. *NS* 1.2:655–658; Saeki, *Chishō daishiden no kenkyū*, pp. 389–390.

95. *NS* 1.3:730–733, 930.

96. Shibuya, ed., *Tendai zasuki*, pp. 30–31; *NS* 1.2:728–731. Yūsen's inclusion in the *Tendai zasuki* probably indicates that he functioned in a manner similar to a *zasu*.

97. Kiuchi, "Kōjō no jiseki," pp. 336–337. Apparently, he was unable to stop the increasing interest in Esoteric Buddhism; a chancellor's order issued on 6-3-864 admonishes monks against partiality to either Tendai (*shikan*) or Esoteric studies (*Sandai jitsuroku, KT* 4:187). An order issued 9-19-881 warns monks of the Tendai and Shingon schools not to engage in heated debates about appointments as lecturers and readers and establishes a rotation system so that nominations for such posts will be distributed evenly (*Ruijū sandaikyaku, KT* 25:132). Recently, Uejima Susumu has cited such events to argue that Esoteric Buddhism did not dominate early Heian Buddhism as thoroughly as many modern scholars have maintained ("Chūsei zenki no kokka to Bukkyō").

98. *NS* 1.6:1–27.

99. *NS* 1.5:442–445; Shibuya, ed., *Tendai zasuki*, p. 33.

100. Although a number of scholars have commented on the importance of the *Juketsushū*, relatively little research has been done on the text. Tajima Tokuon has raised the possibility that the text as it stands today might have additions (*BKD* 5:107b–108c), but Kiuchi Hiroshi (*BZ* [Suzuki ed.], 97:289c–290c) and Akao Eikei

("*Juketsushū* no ikkōsatsu") accept the story of its transmission to Ryōyū. The text thus helped to define the increasing factionalism on Mount Hiei.

101. Genshō studied Esoteric Buddhism with Ennin and Chōi. He played an important role on Mount Hiei for Ennin's lineage in two ways. First, he served as a teacher of Esoteric Buddhism for many of the monks who would become prominent once the Sanmon secured leadership positions on Mount Hiei. Second, he propagated the study of logic among Sanmon monks. The two roles are emphasized by the Sanron-Esoteric master Shōbō, who, after seeing Genshō defeat the Nara monk Seihan (no biography) in a debate on logic at court, said, "The world calls Genshō 'king of *goma*,' but now that we have seen this, we should call him the 'king of logic'" (*Honchō kōsōden, BZ* [Suzuki ed.], 63:64b).

102. Although little is known about Genkan, he obviously played an important role as a transitional figure in Tendai leadership. Most of the available information is found in *Honchō kōsōden, BZ* (Suzuki ed.), 63:287a–b; Shibuya, ed., *Tendai zasuki*, pp. 33–34; *NS* 1.5:795–797.

103. Tsuji, *Nihon Bukkyōshi*, 1:421–422. See the chapter on Ryōgen and Morosuke for more information on the *godanhō*.

104. Key sources for Son'i's biography are found in *NS* 1.7:680–711; Shibuya, ed., *Tendai zasuki*, pp. 34–35; and *Sō-sōjō Son'i Hosshō sonja ryakufu, ZTZ, Shiden*, 2:144–154. His dreams of Enchin are mentioned in the *Son'i sō-sōjō den, NS* 1.7:687. Uesugi Bunshū considers him to be a member of Enchin's lineage (*Nihon Tendaishi*, 1:329). While this would generally seem to be the case, initiations by Genshō and an appointment as administrator of the books that Ennin brought back from China indicate more significant ties with Ennin's disciples (*ZTZ, Shiden*, 2:144–145). In addition, the argument over the appointment of Yokei as abbot of the Hosshōji (discussed later in this book) indicates that Ryōgen argued that he was part of Ennin's faction. The tendency to classify these early Tendai monks in terms of lineages that can be traced back only to Ennin and Enchin is often overstated because of the later disputes between the two factions.

105. *NS* 1.8:457–458, 460, 523, 655 f.; Shibuya, ed., *Tendai zasuki*, pp. 36–37.

106. *NS* 1.11:340–355; Shibuya, ed., *Tendai zasuki*, pp. 38–40.

Chapter 3. Ryōgen's Early Years

1. For example, a genealogy of the Aeba clan gives the personal names of Ryōgen's mother and father; but this text is inconsistent on many points. See Hirabayashi Moritoku, *Ryōgen*, pp. 214–221.

2. *Daisōjōden, NS* 1.22:43.

3. *Genkō shakusho, BZ* (Suzuki ed.), 62:90bc.

4. Ishida Mizumaro, *Gokuraku Jōdo e no izanai*, p. 20; Hayami Tasuku, *Genshin*, p. 17.

5. Ōsumi Kazuo, "Josei to Bukkyō." The increase in stories about the mothers of monks may also be due to changes in the roles of women in society; see the discussion of Ryōgen's later treatment of his mother and her enshrinement in a Women's Hall in the chapter on finance. Matrilocal patterns of marriage among some Japanese also may have led to close ties between mothers and sons.

6. *Daisōjōden, NS* 1.22.43. Similar stories exist for other Japanese monks. For example, the Hossō monk Chūzan, later a participant in the Ōwa debates, met his teacher at the age of six or seven when his teacher noticed him playing (*Genkō shakusho, BZ* [Suzuki ed.], 62:90a).

7. *Shūiden, NS* 1.22.55–56.

8. Hirata Toshiharu, *Sōhei to bushi,* pp. 92–93.

9. Hirabayashi, *Ryōgen,* p. 8.

10. Ōsumi, "Josei to Bukkyō," pp. 5–6.

11. Tsunoda Bun'ei, ed., *Heian jidaishi jiten,* 2:2332a.

12. *Daisōjōden,* NS 1.22.43; Kakue is discussed in the next chapter.

13. See the discussion of how Ryōgen reconciled combining his religious sentiments with his aspiration for high office in the chapters on the rise to prominence and the Ōwa debates.

14. Taga Munehaya, *Jien,* pp. 18–20.

15. *NS* 1.22.19–20. Most of the lineages in which Ryōgen is included do not mention Risen, probably because he died while Ryōgen was young.

16. Population statistics from 1107 suggest that four out of every seven monks on Mount Hiei lived at Tōdō, two at Saitō, and one at Yokawa (Kageyama Haruki, *Hieizanji,* p. 61). When Ryōgen went to live at the Hōdōin, the numbers probably favored Tōdō even more. For a discussion of the establishment of Yokawa, see the chapter on the rise to prominence and appendix 1.

17. For an illustration and description of the tower from a late Heian or early Kamakura document, see Nishimura Keishō, "Hieizan Sōrintō ni tsuite," p. 1048. Kageyama Haruki (*Hieizan,* p. 66) includes a very rough sketch in which the Hōdō looks like a pole. In fact, the *hōdō* originally was a pole, but was later given a more elaborate shape, like that of a pagoda (Ono Katsutoshi, *Nittō guhō junrei kōki no kenkyū,* 3:154).

18. Kageyama, *Hieizanji,* p. 63; Ishida Mizumaro, "Tendai kyōdan hatten katei ni okeru teikō to dakyō," p. 19.

19. The Hōdōin is included as one of a list of sixteen halls in documents attributed to Saichō (*Eigaku yōki, GR* 24:506). This list is generally believed to have been a later compilation. However, the discovery of an early manuscript concerning the Hōdōin and the absence of other dates or theories concerning the construction of the tower have led some scholars to argue that it may have been built during Saichō's lifetime (Nishimura, "Sōrintō," pp. 1056–1057; Kageyama, *Hieizanji,* pp. 63–64, 67).

20. The yearly ordinands were conferred upon Eryō in 859 because of his service in praying for Crown Prince Korehito (850–880) who was crowned Emperor Seiwa in 858. Because Korehito was Emperor Montoku's fourth son, his eventual success in rising to emperor was not assured and Eryō was amply rewarded when Seiwa became emperor. The two yearly ordinands granted to Eryō were the first Tendai ordinands to serve *kami* (Kamo and Kasuga), protectors of the imperial and Fujiwara lineages. Eryō's yearly ordinands also were significant because they were to chant the *Vimalakīrti* and *Nirvāṇa sūtras.* Although both texts are highly regarded in the Tendai school, Eryō's choice of these scriptures may indicate that he was moving toward reconciliation with the Hossō school. The *Vimalakīrti-sūtra* was the primary text used at the Yuima-e at the Hossō and Fujiwara clan temple, Kōfukuji; the

Yuima-e is discussed further in the next chapter and the chapter on examinations. The *Nirvāṇa-sūtra* may have been chosen because it advocated adherence to the Hīnayāna precepts. For more on Eryō's proposals, see Ishida Mizumaro, "Tendai kyōdan hatten katei ni okeru teikō to dakyō," pp. 174–205.

21. *Sandai jitsuroku, KT* 4:372.

22. Archeological excavations of the Saitō area in 1964 and 1965 revealed that a number of smaller buildings surrounded the Hōdōin (Nishimura, "Sōrintō," p. 1046).

23. *Honchō kōsōden, BZ* (Suzuki ed.), 63:53a–b; *Genkō shakusho, BZ* (Suzuki ed.), 62:133b.

24. By the time of Ryōgen's ordination, the Tendai school had more yearly ordinands allotted to it than any other school except the Shingon. For a list of yearly ordinands awarded and their sectarian affiliations, see Ogami Kanchū, "Nenbundosha ni mirareru kashiki seido," pp. 148–150. However, only two yearly ordinands had been allotted to Saitō, the area in which Ryōgen lived. These two yearly ordinands were not simply Tendai positions. They had been used to further Tendai efforts at reconciliation with the Nara schools. Although their status at the time of Ryōgen's ordination is not known, they might very well have been subject to various restrictions. For more on them, see Ishida Mizumarō, "Tendaishū hatten katei." The rest of the Tendai yearly ordinand positions on Hiei were controlled by various halls within Tōdō. Ryōgen could have been ordained as a monk from Gangyōji, the Tendai temple near Kyoto at which he later served as abbot, but no evidence exists that he knew any of the monks of Gangyōji before his ordination.

The importance of being a yearly ordinand at this time is not clear. Most of the research on yearly ordinands concerns the Nara and early Heian periods; scholars have suggested that the system was probably declining or a mere formality by the time of Ryōgen. Recent research by Matsuo Kenji, however, has demonstrated that novices were tested and appointed as yearly ordinands well into the Kamakura period (*Kamakura shin-Bukkyō no seiritsu,* pp. 52–73). However, the many vicissitudes in the system during this period have not been traced. Consequently, the significance of it during Ryōgen's time cannot be determined with precision. At the very least, being named a yearly ordinand must have carried some prestige.

25. *San'e jōitsuki, BZ* (Bussho kankōkai ed.), 123:296; Onkun was appointed to the Sōgō in 931 and eventually rose to be provisional lesser bishop (*gon-shōsōzu*). See Hirabayashi Moritoku and Koike Kazuyuki, eds., *Sōryaku sōran,* p. 31.

26. Fukihara Shōshin (*Nihon yuishiki shisōshi,* p. 457) has noted that historical records reveal virtually no interaction between the Hossō monks of Kōfukuji and Yakushiji around the time of Ryōgen's ordination. The first two of four transmissions of Hossō from China had centered on Gangōji; as a result, these traditions were known as the Nanji transmission. The monks who had brought these teachings to Japan had studied with Hsüan-tsang and Tz'u-en. In contrast, monks who had studied under later Fa-hsiang masters and had been based at Kōfukuji had brought the third and fourth transmissions, known as the Hokuji tradition, back. As a result, the Hokuji tradition had been more sectarian than the Nanji tradition, probably reflecting Tz'u-en's views.

27. Hirakawa Akira, *Ritsuzō no kenkyū*, p. 519. A woman, however, could be ordained as a nun at the age of twelve if she was a widow.

28. *Jubosatsukaigi, DZ* 1:319.

29. Hayami, *Genshin*, pp. 25–26. Monks ordained on other ordination platforms were also less than twenty. For example, a chart of Shingon monks ordained at both Tōdaiji and Enryakuji during the thirteenth century shows that the average age at ordination was sixteen; one person was only twelve when he was ordained (Matsuo, *Kamakura shin-Bukkyō no seiritsu*, p. 159).

30. Hori Ichirō, "Waga kuni gakusō kyōiku seido," 3:594.

31. Ibid., p. 595.

Chapter 4. Ryōgen's Rise to Prominence

1. The Yuima-e is discussed further in chapter 8.

2. For detailed analyses of the varieties of lectures and debates, see Ozaki Kōjin, *Nihon Tendai rongishi no kenkyū;* and Willa Tanabe, "The Lotus Lectures."

3. Hirabayashi, *Ryōgen*, p. 16; for the account, see *Shūiden, NS* 1.22:56. Kiren was appointed supernumerary master of discipline (*gon-risshi*) in 956, two years before his death. Jōe, with Ryōgen's support, became a master of Esoteric Buddhism in 966, court chaplain in 968, and supernumerary master of discipline in 981. Jōe was ordained in 929, just two years after Ryōgen, suggesting that they were contemporaries. According to one version of the *Sōgō bunin*, he was born about 907, making him five years older than Ryōgen. He died one or two years before Ryōgen (Hirabayashi and Koike, eds., *Sōryaku sōran*, p. 159).

4. *Nihon kiryaku, KT* 11:29. The term "*kengyō*" was used instead of "*zoku bettō*" when the officeholder was a minister of the right or left (Okano Kōji, "Enryakuji zoku bettō to Tendai zasu," p. 111). Although the original function of the lay supervisor had been to oversee such administrative tasks as ordinations, these functions had been taken over by the *zasu* so that the lay supervisor was primarily a major patron of the Tendai school. However, in many of the other temples that had adopted lay supervisors, administrative tasks were still a part of their functions. The *Shou-ming ching* (*T* 1136) is a one-fascicle text translated by Amoghavajra. Chanting the *dhāraṇī* in it was said to prevent death while young.

5. Hirabayashi and Koike, eds., *Sōryaku sōran*, p. 211; nothing is known of Unnichi's career.

6. See note 24 of this chapter for more information on Kizō.

7. Senkan is mentioned in many sources from Onjōji, a major center for Enchin's lineage (*NS* 1.20:186–214). He is discussed further in the chapter on the Ōwa debates.

8. For discussions of the role of logic in East Asian Buddhism, see the section on Ryōgen's studies of logic later in this chapter and the chapter on examinations.

9. *Shūiden, NS* 1.22:56.

10. Hirabayashi, *Ryōgen*, p. 18.

11. Groner, *Saichō*, pp. 122, 128, 134.

12. *Mudōji konryū daishiden, ZTZ Shiden*, 2:121b. The term "eight fields of merit"

appears in the ninth minor precept of the *Fan-wang ching* along with the notation that nursing the sick is the most important (Ishida Mizumaro, *Bonmōkyō*, pp. 154–157). The contents of the eight fields of merit are not specified and vary among commentators.

13. *Sanne jōitsuki, BZ* (Bussho kankōkai ed.), 123:296–297; also see Ogami Kanchū, "Ōwa no shūron to shūyō gika no kakuritsu," p. 59.

14. Two of the Tendai monks appointed before Kizō as lecturers for the Yuima-e were included in the same lineage for studies of logic as Kizō and Ryōgen. See Nemu Kazuchika, "Jie daishi no inmyōgaku to sono keifu," pt. 1, p. 232.

15. The *igisō* or *igishi* was a monk who was responsible for the protocol at ceremonies such as initiations and ordinations. By Ryōgen's time, it was considered to be a step that might lead to appointment in the Office of Monastic Affairs.

16. Arihira's biological parents were archbishop Nyomu (d. 938) of Kōfukuji and the daughter of Yoshimine no Takami, but Arihira had been adopted by his father's older brother Fujiwara no Ariyoshi, governor of Tajima. He had a resplendent career at court, eventually rising to grand minister of the left shortly before his death. He was noted for his studiousness and pleasing manner, but not for brilliance. Arihira's actual father, Nyomu, was the first son of a noble other than the Tendai monk Henjō to be appointed to the Office of Monastic Affairs (Hirabayashi and Koike, eds., *Sōryaku sōran*, p. 150; *Honchō kōsōden, BZ* [Suzuki ed.], 63:66b). If Nyomu had influenced Arihira's studies, then Arihira, as the imperial emissary sent to observe the debates at the Yuima-e, might have followed them with unusual interest.

17. Ninkō was a member of the Fujiwara clan who served as lecturer at the Yuima-e in 827, ten years before Ryōgen attended the assembly; Ninkō subsequently served as lecturer at the other two major assemblies in Nara. He was appointed to various posts in the Office of Monastic Affairs, eventually attaining the rank of supernumerary greater bishop.

18. According to the *Honchō kōsōden* (*BZ* [Suzuki ed.], 63:67c), the situation is reversed from the *Daisōjōden* account, with Ryōgen being the senior monk and refusing to debate Gishō. This account also notes that Gishō was chosen to face Ryōgen because of his skill at debate. Ryōgen's major patron, Fujiwara no Morosuke, later sponsored Gishō as a lecturer on the *Lotus Sūtra* at Yakushiji.

19. *Sanne jōitsuki, BZ* (Bussho kankōkai, ed.), 123:297. The use of the term "*tsugai rongi*" to refer to debates between young boys (today they are usually elementary school boys) is said to date from the twelfth century (Yamagishi Tsuneto, *Chūsei jiin shakai to Butsudō*, p. 392; Oda Tokunō, *Bukkyō daijiten*, p. 1235). However, the term may have been used in the *Sanne jōitsuki* (completed in 1566) to indicate that the debate between Gishō and Ryōgen consisted of men younger than usual and that it was performed for the enjoyment of the emissary rather than as part of the official ceremonies. The *tsugai rongi* is still performed on Mount Hiei today; for an account, see Tsukuma Sonnō, "Hokke daie Kōgaku ryūgi," 53–55. For an account of *tsugai rongi* from the perspective of Kōfukuji that does not mention Ryōgen, see Takayama Yuki, *Chūsei Kōfukuji Yuima-e no kenkyū*, pp. 245–255.

20. *NS* 1.9:377–379; Sone Masato, s.v. "Ninkō," in Tsunoda, ed., *Heian jidaishi jiten*, 2:1874d.

21. *Daisōjōden, ZTZ Shiden*, 2:193; Hirata Toshiharu, "Akusō ni tsuite," p. 127. For more on the emergence of warrior monks, see chapter 11.

22. Little is known about Gishō; he merits only a brief mention in the notes (*uragaki*) of the *Sōgō bunin* and apparently never held a post in the Office of Monastic Affairs (Hirabayashi and Koike, eds., *Sōryaku sōran*, p. 76). He studied Sanron at Gangōji, but later moved to Tōdaiji. He was famed as a youth for his brilliance and was later known as a lecturer. Ten years after he debated Ryōgen, Tadahira asked that he be appointed lecturer at the Yuima-e, but this did not come to pass. In 948, he served as the priest who led the scattering of flowers (*sangeshi*) at the dedication of the Hall for Mahāvairocana (Dainichiin) at Saitō on Mount Hiei. In 954, he participated at lectures in honor of Emperor Murakami's copying of the *Lotus Sūtra* and in another series on Mount Hiei (Horiike Shunpei, s.v. "Gishō," Tsunoda, ed., *Heian jidaishi jiten* 1:612c–d).

23. *Inmyō keizu*, quoted in Nemu "Jie daishi no inmyōgaku," pt. 1, p. 232. The date and the authenticity of the lineage have not been clearly established. However, because the text does not contradict any reliable source and because no other source concerning Ryōgen's studies of logic is extant, the lineage is probably reliable.

24. No biography for Kizō survives. He is mentioned several times in the *Sōgō bunin* (Hirabayashi and Koike, eds., *Sōryaku sōran*, pp. 73–74, 193). He studied under Eryō and Jōbō of the Hōdōin and was appointed lecturer at the Yuima-e in 937 at the age of sixty-five. Since Ryōgen's teacher Risen is also said to have studied under Eryō, Risen and Kizō probably knew each other well (Uesugi, *Nihon Tendaishi*, "Nihon Tendai keifu"; *Tendai hokkeshū kechimyakuzu*, NS 1.22: 20).

25. See Nemu "Jie daishi no inmyōgaku," for a thorough discussion of the scanty sources on Ryōgen's studies of logic.

26. Nemu ("Jie daishi no inmyōgaku," pp. 240–241) has demonstrated that Ryōgen and Chūzan held similar positions on some issues in logic.

27. *Dengyō daishi shōrai mokuroku* (*Taishūroku*), *BZ* (Suzuki ed.), 95:230c. Four works on logic attributed to Saichō are listed in such later bibliographies as the *Dengyō daishi gosenjutsu mokuroku* (*DZ* 5 [*bekkan*]: 153, 156, 171, 184, 187, 188). However, these works are not listed in earlier sources or bibliographies, nor are any of them even discussed in such standard works as Shioiri Ryōchū's *Dengyō daishi* or Tamura Kōyū's *Saichō jiten*. These works may have been attributed to Saichō to bolster the Tendai position in debates with Hossō monks.

28. *DZ* 2:567–568.

29. Ono Katsutoshi, *Nittō guhō junrei kōki no kenkyū* 2:96–97; 4:591, 602.

30. Satō Tetsuei, "Sannōin zōsho mokuroku ni tsuite," p. 12; Ono Katsutoshi, *Nittō guhō gyōreki no kenkyū*, 2:464, 477, 489. When this bibliography is compared with the Tōdaiji monk Enchō's *Kegonshū shōsho narabini inmyōsho* of 914 (*T* 55:1134c–1135b), the Tendai school appears to have had almost twice as many texts on logic as some Nara institutions.

31. According to Takemura Shōhō ("Nihon ni okeru inmyō kenkyū" pp. 30, 52), Enchin is credited with a work titled *Shisōiki* (Record concerning the four logical errors). Takemura praised Enchin's studies of logic, but he does not even mention Ennin, a treatment that suggests that Enchin's lineage may have had the more developed tradition. However, Takemura does not maintain this attitude in his later work, *Inmyōgaku* (pp. 153–154), which simply lists the texts each brought back from China.

32. *Shūiden*, p. 83. Sakai Keijun ("Kawa no ryū no mikkyō," pp. 81–92) has col-

lected and analyzed many of the traditions concerning Ryōgen's Esoteric training. The relationship with Kakue is also mentioned in four lineages found in *NS* 1.22:24–26. Ryōgen is also said to have received other Esoteric traditions, including one that originated with Enchin and another that was an elementary initiation into the Ono-ryū of the Shingon school (*NS* 1.22:27–28). These claims are suspect because of the competition between Ryōgen's lineage and these other traditions. For Henjō's biography, see Groner, "Annen, Tankei, Henjō, and Monastic Discipline in the Japanese Tendai School."

The term "pure Esoteric Buddhism" is a later term not in use during Ryōgen's lifetime. However, I use it here provisionally to indicate the difference between Esoteric Buddhism that was directed toward spiritual goals and Esoteric Buddhism that was directed toward more this-worldly goals (*zōmitsu*).

33. The identification of the *shoson yuga goma* involves difficult problems; but it probably refers to the *Chin-kang-ting yü-ch'ieh hu-mo i-kuei* (*T* 909), often called the *Yuga goma giki* in Japan. This text was translated by Amoghavajra and brought to Japan by Ennin and others (Ono Katsutoshi, *Nitto guhō junrei kōki no kenkyū* 4:570). This ritual text is considered the authoritative work on the *goma* ritual in the Shingon school. Said to be the first text solely devoted to the *goma* ceremony, it was based on both the Taizōkai and Kongōkai traditions (Ōmura, *Mikkyō hattatsushi*, p. 621). Tendai monks are said to have used another work, the *Chien-li mant'u-lo hu-mo i-kuei* (*T* 912) compiled by Fa-ch'üan and brought to Japan by Shūei. It was based solely on the Taizōkai tradition (*T* 820). In addition, differences in the arrangement of altars and classification of ceremonies are found in the two texts. However, Amoghavajra's text was used as a secondary text by the Sanmon faction of Tendai monks. The Jimon faction of the Tendai school is said to have regarded Amoghavajra's text as equal in importance to Fa-ch'üan's work. However, Amoghavajra's text may have supplanted Fa-ch'üan's work even earlier. According to Kakuchō (960–1034), Amoghavajra's work had been the main authority for the *goma* within the Tendai school for some time. The mention of *Yuga goma* in Ryōgen's biography suggests that this process had begun by the time of Ryōgen's youth (Mikkyō jiten hensankai, ed., *Zotei shinpan Mikkyō daijiten*, p. 639c).

34. Kiuchi *Tendai mikkyō no keisei*, pp. 315–323; Ono Katsutoshi, *Nittō guhō gyōreki no kenkyū*, pp. 19–20, 40. See chapter 2 for a discussion of the relationship between Ennin and Enchin.

35. For example, Chen Jinhua makes a forceful argument that later Tendai monks, especially Annen, might have produced spurious ritual texts. These texts were produced and treated as texts that Saichō had brought from China and used by later Tendai monks to answer Shingon questions about Saichō's Esoteric initiations (Chen Jinhua, "The Formation of Tendai Esoteric Buddhism in Japan"; idem, "The Construction of Early Tendai Buddhism").

36. *Honchō kōsōden, BZ* (Suzuki ed.), 63:64b.

37. *Kanko ruijū*, in Tada Kōryū et al., eds., *Tendai hongakuron*, p. 285. The *Kankō ruijū* contains one of the earliest mentions of an Original Enlightenment (*hongaku*) tradition that Saichō received secret texts in China. These were handed down through a series of teachers to Ryōgen. When Ryōgen was on his deathbed, he transmitted the most important teachings to Genshin, but withheld them from Kakuun

and his other disciples. Although the *Kankō ruijū* is attributed to Chūjin (1065–1138), it was probably composed between 1250 and 1300 (ibid., p. 541).

Eryō was ordained by Gishin, but he later studied both Tendai Esoteric and exoteric Buddhism with Enchō and Ennin. He played an active role in the administration of the Hōdōin in Saitō. As the guardian monk of Prince Hitoyasu from his birth until his enthronement as Emperor Seiwa, he was an influential Tendai monk. All that is known of Manga is that he was a disciple of Eryō.

38. *NS* 1.22:23–24.

39. *Daisōjōden, NS* 1.22:44–45.

40. Tadahira's place in court ritual is discussed in Yamanaka Yutaka, *Heian jidai no kokiroku to kizoku*, pp. 78–79.

41. Okano, "Enryakuji zoku bettō to Tendai zasu," pp. 104–105.

42. Inoue Mitsusada, "Fujiwara jidai no jōdokyō," p. 150.

43. Okano, "Enryakuji zoku bettō to Tendai zasu," p. 104. Okano's article carefully traces the development of the offices of *zoku bettō* (another term for lay supervisor) and *zasu*.

44. *Daisōjōden, NS* 1.22:45.

45. Ibid. According to the *Shūiden* (*NS* 1.22:58), Ryōgen's decision to retreat to Yokawa was caused by an inauspicious dream.

46. *Tendai shōbu shūshaku, BZ* (Suzuki ed.), 41:89b–104a. A short description of the text in English can be found in Dobbins, "A Brief History of Pure Land Buddhism in Early Japan," pp. 123–127.

47. Kakehashi Nobuaki, "Ryōgen *Kuhon ōjōgi* no ikkōsatsu."

Chapter 5. Ryōgen and the Fujiwaras

1. Yamada Etai, "Ganzan daishi no mikkyō to minkan shinkō," p. 50.

2. *ZTZ Shiden*, 2:193b–194a. The *Tao-kan yu ching* refers to a set of texts contained in the *Ta-ching chi* (*Mahāsaṁnipata*), *T* 708–712, that explain the metaphor of comparing Buddhist teachings to the growth of rice plants; I have not identified the exact citation. The term "*shitsuji*" is translated as "perfection" or "accomplishment." Accomplishments without perceptible form (*musō no shitsuji*) would be spiritual attainments such as enlightenment, while accomplishments with form (*usō no shitsuji*) would include more worldly goals such as the ability to fly or perhaps appointment to high office.

3. *Daisōjōden, NS* 1.22:52–53. Numbers have been added to the translation for clarity.

4. Mabuchi Kazuo and Kunisaki Fumimaro, eds., *Konjaku monogatarishū*, fasc. 15, 2:133–138; the story has been exhaustively analyzed by Takahashi Mitsugu ("Genshin sōzu no haha no hanashi"). Takahashi has pointed out that the basic attitudes that Genshin and his mother exhibit in the story can be supported by statements in Genshin's writings. The story is also representative of the manner in which the mothers of monks were often idealized in biographies of this period. Zōga is discussed in the chapter on the Ōwa debates and in appendix 7.

5. Tsunoda Bun'ei, "Morosuke naru jinbutsu," pp. 15–16.

6. The *kōi* (literally, "clothes-changer") was a position given to women from families of counselors and lower ranks. It was second in rank to the junior consort (*nyōgo*). Women appointed to either position served in the emperor's sleeping quarters.

Motokata had been appointed adviser (*sangi*) in 939, middle counselor (*chū-nagon*) in 942, major counselor (*dainagon*) in 951, and major counselor and head of the Ministry of Popular Affairs in 953. Primary source materials for Motokata are collected in *NS* 1.9:920.

7. Prince Hirohira would later hold the titles of minister of war and governor-general of Dazai-fu before his death at the young age of twenty-one.

8. Motokata did not limit his patronage to Tendai monks in his efforts to ensure success. He had a Hall of Longevity (Enmeiin) built on the mountain above Daigoji that was later given to the eminent Shingon monk Ninkai (951–1046), who had it designated a *goganji* during the Chōryaku era (1037–1040). Motokata's descendants served as patrons of the temple for many years (Takei Akio, s.v. "Enmeiin [2]," in Tsunoda, ed., *Heian jidaishi jiten*, 1:316a; Nishiguchi Junko, "Heian jidai shoki jiin no kōsatsu," p. 57).

9. *Asabashō, T* (*zuzō*), 9:404b–c; 837c. The entry in the *Asabashō* notes that the incident does not appear in diaries and suggests that Ryōgen ended it before completing the ceremony, leading Hayami (*Heian kizoku*, p. 117) to consider it highly suspect. In addition, the ceremony gained popularity about a century later and thus was probably attributed to Ryōgen later (Hayami Tasuku, *Jujutsu shūkyō no sekai*, p. 143). The other entries in the *Asabashō* indicate that the ceremony was generally used to ensure safe birth as much as to ensure the birth of a male child. Ucchuṣma, who does not appear in either the Womb-realm or Diamond *maṇḍalas*, was chosen for these ceremonies because he was thought to purify places of any pollution and would be able to handle the pollution arising from childbirth. He is a good example of the major roles that previously minor figures came to play in rituals at this time.

The *Asabashō* (Compilation concerning *a*, *sa*, and *ba*) is a huge work of 233 fascicles compiled from 1242 to 1279 by the Tendai monk Shōchō (1205–1282) and several of his disciples. It is one of the most important sources for the study of the Taimitsu tradition. Hayami Tasuku has done the most extensive research on the text. Hayami argues that the entries concerning Esoteric ceremonies are generally reliable (*Heian kizoku*, p. 2). The title of the text is derived from the three categories into which images in *maṇḍalas* are classified: Buddha, Lotus, and Diamond. Those three categories are represented by the Sanskrit syllables *a*, *sa*, and *va*. Two printed versions of the text are currently available. The *Taishō* version is more accurate than that in the *Dainippon Bukkyō zensho*.

10. H. C. McCullough, trans., *The Taiheiki*, p. 12; Hayami, *Jujutsu shūkyō no sekai*, p. 143.

11. See Hayami, *Heian kizoku*, p. 103, n. 88.

12. Morosuke's actual role in having his grandson appointed crown prince is not completely clear; Tsunoda Bun'ei argues that Anshi's close relationship with Emperor Murakami was more important ("Morosuke naru jinbutsu," pp. 16–17).

13. William McCullough and Helen McCullough, trans., *A Tale of Flowering Fortunes*, 1:76; Matsumura Hiroji and Yamanaka Yutaka, eds., *Eiga monogatari*, 1: 32. According to the *Eiga monogatari*, Yūhime refused to eat. The resentment of Mo-

tokata's entire line is emphasized in the *Eiga monogatari* through the incorrect claim that both Yūhime and Hirohira died shortly after Motokata.

14. *NS* 1.12:53.

15. The first *gojisō* is said to have been Saichō, and to have dated from his appointment as court chaplain and one of the ten meditation masters in 797. Other monks associated with Esoteric Buddhism such as Kūkai also performed this role; eventually monks from the major Esoteric Buddhist monasteries at Tōji, Enryakuji, and Onjōji monopolized the position. *Gojisō* were also known as *yoinosō* (literally, "monks who spent the night" because they were expected to spend the night in the palace in a room called the Ninoma, where they would perform constant ceremonies to ensure the crown prince or emperor's well-being. By the thirteenth century, the number of monks called *gojisō* had increased from one to eight or nine.

16. *Zoku honchō ōjōden*, in Inoue Mitsusada and Ōsone Shōsuke, eds. *Ōjōden Hokke genki*, pp. 230–231; Miki Sumito, *Tōnomine hijiri dan*, p. 59.

17. *Shūiden*, *NS* 1.22. 60. See Groner, "Annen, Tankei, Henjō, and Monastic Discipline in the Japanese Tendai School;" pp. 138–139, 141, 147–148, for a description of the post of *ajari* and some of the men who held it in the late ninth century.

18. *Shūiden*, *NS* 1.22.60. The Gangyōji temporarily had been awarded four *ajari* during Henjō's lifetime, but because Henjō's position was a special one because he was the son of a high court official, he had not been replaced when he died. Ryōgen established four *ajari* as the constant number at the temple.

19. The Urin'in serves as the location for the opening of the *Ōkagami* (Helen Craig McCullough, trans., *Ōkagami the Great Mirror,* p. 65; Matsumura Hiroji, ed., *Ōkagami*, p. 35).

20. *Daisōjōden, ZTZ Shiden*, 2:194a; *Mon'yōki*, *NS* 1.10: 123–125 (this passage is not found in the *Taishō* version of *Mon'yōki*). The *Mon'ōki* account, said to be based on Morosuke's diary, is particularly detailed. Certain details of the *Mon'yōki* account seem questionable, however. For example, eighteen hundred monks are said to have met Morosuke. A note in *NS* identifies the *zasu* who met Morosuke at the Lecture Hall as Ryōgen, but Ryōgen did not attain this position until later. Elsewhere in the passage, Ryōgen is referred to as an *ajari*. A more natural reading of the text would have Morosuke meeting the *zasu* at that time, Enshō, and then proceeding to Yokawa for talks with Ryōgen. Finally, the *Daisōjōden* describes Morosuke as surveying the land at Yokawa and suddenly (*tachimachi*) deciding to build a Lotus Meditation Hall. Perhaps Ryōgen had staged events so that Morosuke would be inspired to have the appropriate building constructed.

21. *NS* 1.22:127–128; Brown and Ishida, *The Future and the Past*, p. 45; Okami Masao and Akamatsu Toshihide, eds., *Gukanshō*, pp. 157–158. Morosuke's father had dedicated the rebuilding of the Shōryōin at Tōnomine to the success of his clan. A ceremony similar to that performed by Morosuke was performed by Fujiwara Michinaga at Kohata in 1019 (McCullough and McCullough, *Flowering Fortunes*, 2:508–509; Matsumura, ed., *Eiga monogatari*, 1: 452–453). The lamp was to be kept burning at all times, much as Morosuke's lineage was to continue to flourish.

In Buddhist terms, Morosuke's actions might be interpreted as the dedication of karmic merit to his descendants; but later authors suggest that Morosuke had used both heterodox and Buddhist rituals to come back as a ghost to attack his enemies and defend his descendants. The specific rituals employed for this are not mentioned, but his vow at the dedication of the Lotus Meditation Hall was certainly viewed by later authors as contributing both to Morosuke's powers after his death and to his family's success.

22. Tsunoda, "Morosuke naru jinbutsu," pp. 13–14. Morosuke seems to have been fond of such vows; he is also described as having rolled the dice in a game of backgammon with the prediction that if they came up double six, Anshi would give birth to a son (H. C. McCullough, *Ōkagami*, p. 137; *KT* 21A:79).

23. McCullough and McCullough, *Flowering Fortunes*, 1: 80, 85; Matsumura and Yamanaka, *Eiga monogatari*, 1: 36–37, 42–43.

24. Little is known of Kansan; in fact, he is so obscure that his name is written with a variety of characters. He is mentioned several times in the *Ōkagami*, where he is called a court chaplain (H. C. McCullough, *Ōkagami*, pp. 83, 138; *KT* 21A:20–21, 81). In some texts such as the *Hyakurenshō* (*KT* [*fukyūban*], p. 15), references to a monk named Gajō (887–967) are similar to those to Kansan, leading to speculation that the two are identical (Tsunoda, ed., *Heian jidaishi jiten*, p. 569a). For example, in different sources one or the other is said to help Motokata's spirit cause Emperor Sanjō's eye ailment by covering the emperor's eyes with their wings. Gajō was appointed as *zasu* of Hōshōji in 965 and master of discipline in 966 (H. C. McCullough, *Ōkagami*, p. 257; Matsumura, *Ōkagami*, p. 444). Gajō also is mentioned as one of the participants in an early five-platform ceremony (*Asabashō, T* [*zuzō*], 9:342b), perhaps giving him an air of being acquainted with various supernatural powers. For more on Gajō, see the chapter on Ryōgen's appointment as *zasu*.

25. The early history of angry ghosts is difficult to trace. Among the issues that have not been resolved are such basic problems as to what extent the emergence of angry ghosts was due to continental influence. William McCullough argues that spirit possession was decisively influenced by the Chinese ("Spirit Possession in the Heian Period," pp. 97–98). Similarities with Korean and Chinese beliefs in ghosts and the role that Sino-Japanese readings of key terms such as "*rei*," "*onryō*," and "*goryō*" play in the cults from an early date suggest that continental conceptions must have influenced the Japanese. Shibata Minoru, however, finds the origins of angry ghosts in early Japanese fears of the dead (*Kokushi daijiten,* 6:58–59, s.v. "*goryō shinkō*"). One of the major difficulties in such investigations lies in the bias toward the upper classes present in almost all the sources, rendering views about the beliefs of farmers and other members of the lower classes highly speculative.

26. In a seminal article first published in 1939, Higo Kazuo traced the development of angry ghosts to the growing recognition of individuality among the nobility (see Higo Kazuo, "Heian jidai ni okeru onryō no shisō," pp. 13–36).

27. For a study of a *goryō* cult in English, see Neil McMullin, "On Placating the Gods and Pacifying the Populace." Many of the major Japanese articles on *goryō* beliefs have been collected in Shibata Minoru, ed., *Goryō shinkō.*

28. Both Tsuji Zennosuke (*Nihon Bukkyōshi,* 1:697) and Hayami Tasuku (*Heian kizoku,* p. 85; idem, *Jujutsu shūkyō no sekai,* p. 102) consider Motokata to be the first documented example of a ghost that attacks a specific lineage. Higo Kazuo also treats the intrigues between Morosuke and Motokata as the beginning of a new stage in the individualization of angry ghosts ("Heian jidai ni okeru onryō no shisō," pp. 26–28).

29. *Hyakurenshō, KT* (*fukyūban*), p. 8. The passage is apparently taken from the

Shōyūki. The *Shōyūki,* the diary of Fujiwara no Sanesuke, is noted for the care with which the author recorded events from 982 to 1030. The sixty-year period is based on the calendrical cycle used in East Asia. Fujiwara no Jushi is the daughter of Fujiwara no Naritoki (941–995). The passage is discussed in Hayami, *Heian kizoku,* p. 86; and idem, *Jujutsu shūkyō no sekai;* pp. 97–99. Daiitoku (Skt. Yamāntaka) is based on Śiva and exhibits many of the fierce qualities sometimes associated with that deity. He was often portrayed with six arms, six legs, and angry expressions on his six faces; the image was surrounded by flames.

30. In such cases, women were not merely passive victims of hysteria. They might actively use spirit possession to protest their treatment by men or to aid in the redefinition of their relationships. For a fascinating study of spirit possession in the Heian period that utilizes the insights of anthropologists studying contemporary cultures, see Doris Bargen, "Spirit Possession in the Context of Dramatic Expressions of Gender Conflict."

31. Hori Daiji, "Jinzen to Myōkōin" 1, p. 5.

32. See, for example, Takeuchi Rizō, ed., *Heian ibun,* 2:444.

33. Jinzen's later career as the *zasu* succeeding Ryōgen is discussed in the chapters on finance and factionalism during and after Ryōgen's tenure as *zasu.*

34. The exact date of death for Takamitsu is difficult to determine. Tamai Yukinosuke (*Tōnomine shōshō monogatari,* p. 149) has suggested that he died sometime between 977 and 985. Nihon koten bungaku daijiten henshū iinkai, *Nihon koten bungaku daijiten* (5: 289c) suggests 994, but notes the existence of other theories.

35. H. C. McCullough, *Ōkagami,* p. 135; Tamai, *Tōnomine shōshō monogatari,* p. 50. The *Tōnomine shōshō monogatari* (The tale of the lesser captain of Tōnomine) was probably written by a woman close to Takamitsu's wife, perhaps her wet nurse. The text may have been written during the summer of 962, after Takamitsu had climbed Mount Hiei but before he had left for Tōnomine (Tamai, *Tōnomine shōshō monogatari,* pp. 132–136); but some authorities have suggested that it was written several decades later (Nihon koten bungaku daijiten henshū iinkai, *Nihon koten bungaku daijiten* 4:433b). It is generally considered to be an accurate, though sometimes terse and ambiguous, account of the events around Takamitsu's ordination.

36. Tamai, *Tōnomine shōshō monogatari,* pp. 106–108.

37. Other interpretations of Ryōgen's protests are possible. They may have been a formality to some extent, used initially to refuse a request until it had been repeated several times, or Ryōgen may have been ascertaining the depth of Takamitsu's desire; similar ordinations can be cited in which the protesting teacher clearly had no political motive (Nitta Takako, "*Tōnomine shōshō monogatari*"). Miki Sumito describes Ryōgen's actions as being less political than I believe they were. For example, Ryōgen is praised for ordaining Takamitsu once he realized how serious his religious intentions were. However, Miki's explanation does not cite the *Ōkagami uragaki* (*KT* 21A:82) entry noting that Koremasa gave permission for Takamitsu's ordination, suggesting that Ryōgen ordained him only after he received permission to do so (Miki, *Tōnomine hijiri dan,* p. 73).

38. *Ōkagami uragaki, KT* 21A:82; Tamai, *Tōnomine shōshō monogatari,* pp. 50–55. The *Tōnomine shōshō monogatari* is often terse, leaving room for several interpretations. The explanation followed here is based on articles by Hori Daiji ("Takamitsu to Zōga") and Hirabayashi Moritoku ("*Tōnomine shōshō monogatari* ni miru Takamitsu

shukke no shūhen"). Other scholars such as Ashida Kōitsu, have offered an interpretation that minimizes the opposition to Takamitsu's ordination from Ryōgen and Jinzen. Moreover, they have argued that Takamitsu went to Tōnomine primarily because he wished to serve in the Fujiwara ancestral mausoleum there, not because he was not welcomed in Yokawa by his brother. For a good summary of Ashida's arguments see "Fujiwara Takamitsu ni okeru Yokawa to Tōnomine no ichi." Hirabayashi, however, has effectively answered Ashida's criticisms ("Tōnomine shōshō monogatari wo dō yomu ka").

39. *Tōnomine ryakki, BZ* (Bussho kankōkai ed.), 118:493. The *Tōnomine shōshō monogatari* states only that an accomplished teacher (*ajari*) was involved. As a result, many traditional accounts identified the teacher as Zōga because Takamitsu later studied under him at Tōnomine. The identification of that teacher as Ryōgen was first made by Hirabayashi Moritoku ("*Tōnomine shōshō monogatari* ni miru Takamitsu shukke no shūhen"). Hirabayashi argued that although Zōga later became Takamitsu's teacher, Zōga was not known well enough to have been referred to simply as "*ajari*." Moreover, Zōga had not been officially named an *ajari* (*ācārya*), the official designation of master of Esoteric Buddhism, but Ryōgen had received the title ten years previously. Takamitsu went to Ryōgen because of Ryōgen's close relations with his father, Morosuke, and because Ryōgen had ordained his brother Jinzen. Hori Daiji ("Takamitsu to Zōga," pp. 51–52), Tamai Yukinoske (*Tōnomine*, p. 54), and Miki Sumito (*Tōnomine hijiri dan*, p. 73) have agreed with Hirabayashi's thesis.

40. Hori Daiji, "Takamitsu to Zōga," p. 57.

41. Hiraoka Jōkai, *Tōdaiji jiten*, pp. 250–251; Hirabayashi and Koike, eds., *Sōryaku sōran*, pp. 169–170; Kokushi daijiten iinkai, ed., *Kokushi daijiten*, 7:782a–b.

42. *Ruijū sandaikyaku, KT* 25:74.

43. *Mudōji konryū daishiden, ZTZ Shiden,* 2:126b; Hayami, *Heian kizoku*, pp. 52–53.

44. Additional information on the privatization and factionalism that affected Esoteric ritual can be found in the chapters on finances and factionalism.

45. Ryōgen's works on Esoteric ritual are mentioned in a subcommentary on the *Ta-jih ching* titled the *Dainichikyō gishaku sōketsushō*, compiled by Ninkū from 1379 to 1381 (Yamada Etai, "Ganzan daishi no mikkyō to minkan shinkō," p. 49). The ritual texts are not mentioned in the studies of Ryōgen by Hirabayashi and Hori. Because the source for these texts is late and because I have not been able to locate any scholarly discussion of their authenticity or any mention of them in earlier works, I have not considered them in this study, but the study of Esoteric Buddhist ritual has not advanced very far, and the topic may merit further study.

46. Sources differ about whether the seven Buddhas in this ceremony are Bhaiṣajyaguru and six manifestations, seven manifestations of Śākyamuni, or seven separate Buddhas. See Mochizuki and Tsukamoto, eds., *Mochizuki Bukkyō daijiten*, 2:1919–1920.

47. H. C. McCullough, *Ōkagami*, pp. 159–160, 262; Matsumura, ed *Ōkagami*, pp. 162–163. The pregnancy described in *Ōkagami* is a poignant rendering of the fears with which many women of the nobility viewed childbirth. Morosuke's efforts to court Kōshi, including sneaking into her quarters, are also described.

48. *Asabashō, T* (*zuzō*), 8:1066c, 1067c; 9:830c. Hayami Tasuku comments that

some form of mixed Esoteric (*zōmitsu*) belief in the seven healing Buddhas was present during the Nara period (*Heian kizoku*, p. 22), but still credits Ennin with the first performance of an Esoteric ceremony based on the seven healing Buddhas (p. 92). In the *Asabashō* passages concerning the performance by Ryōgen, the date "Tenryaku 10" (956) should read "Tenryaku 11" (957).

One month before the rite of the seven healing Buddhas, Ennin also arranged for the first performance in Japan of an Esoteric ceremony called the eight-character Mañjuśrī rite (*Monju hachiji hō*) to help the ailing emperor recover.

49. Hayami, *Heian kizoku*, p. 93.

50. The *Chi-fo ching* (*T* 451) has been translated into English in Raoul Birnbaum, *The Healing Buddha*, pp. 173–220. The passage concerning the efficacy of worship of the seven manifestations of Yakushi for pregnant women is found on p. 202.

51. Hayami, *Heian kizoku*, pp. 92–94.

52. Ibid., pp. 89–92; idem, *Jujutsu shūkyō no sekai*, pp. 101–102.

53. *Nihon kiryaku*, *KT* 11:97–98. The Jijūden was the hall in the palace where the emperor generally resided. After reconstruction following a fire in 960, the Seiryōden (Hall of cool and refreshing breezes) became the emperor's residence, and the Jijūden was used for court and Buddhist rituals.

54. *Asabashō*, *T* (*zuzō*), 9:342b, 837b; *Nihon kiryaku*, *KT* 11: 143; *Daisōjōden*, *NS* 1.22:49.

55. For diagrams, see *Asabashō*, *T* (*zuzō*), 9: 340c–341a. For a brief analysis of the structures of the altars for this ritual, see Hayami, *Heian kizoku*, pp. 133–134, n. 23.

56. Both statements are found in the *Asabashō*, *T* (*zuzō*), 9:340a–b, 342b, 837b.

57. Hayami, *Heian kizoku*, pp. 88–89. The McCulloughs (*Flowering Fortunes*, 1:270, n. 61; and 421) consider the five-platform ceremony to be a Tendai ceremony.

58. *Shijūjōketsu*, *T* 75:918c. The entry is dated 1046. The *Shijūjōketsu* is said to be a collection of oral transmission from Kōgei (977–1049), systematizer of Tendai Esoteric ritual. The *Godanhō nikki* (Record of performances of the five-platform ceremony) included in the *Asabashō* is a detailed record of the many performances of the ceremony (*T* [*zuzō*], 9:342b–351c).

59. *Asabashō*, *T* [*zuzō*], 9:25c, 27a.

60. The polestar was said to rule over other celestial phenomena in Taoist literature; see Edward Schaeffer, *Pacing the Void*, pp. 44–46.

61. *Asabashō*, *T* [*zuzō*], 9:40b.

62. This account is based primarily on Ennin's biography. Honda, ed., *Yakuchū Jikaku daishiden*, pp. 122–126, 130–132; Ono Katsutoshi, *Sanzen'inhon Jikaku daishiden*, pp. 61–65; Saeki, *Jikaku daishiden no kenkyū*, pp. 61–67; *Asabashō*, *T* (*zuzō*), 9:831; *Kuin Bukkakushō*, *GR* 24:578–579. Ikeyama Issaien ("Hokke Sōjiin ni tsuite," pp. 302–303) has suggested that Fujiwara Yoshifusa (804–872) played a major role in supporting the establishment of the Sōjiin.

63. Sources vary on the years during which the hall was constructed, many giving the dates as 853–862. I follow Ikeyama ("Hokke Sōjiin ni tsuite," pp. 304–305) in using 851–860 because it reflects the court's excitement over the new ritual.

64. For more information on the significance of the Tōdōin and the thousand copies of the *Lotus Sūtra* installed in it, see appendix 1. The Sōjiin was also called the Hokke sōjiin (Lotus Dhāraṇī hall).

65. For more information on the later history of the Sōjiin, see the chapter on the rebuilding of the Tendai monastic complex.

66. Hayami, *Jujutsu shūkyō no sekai*, p. 63.

67. *Kujōdono yuikai, NS* 1.10:719; Murayama Shūichi, *Nihon Onmyōdōshi sōsetsu*, p. 127.

68. Murayama, *Nihon Onmyōdōshi sōsetsu*, pp. 172–174.

69. *Shinshin keiki, NS* 1.15:192–193; Hirabayashi, *Ryōgen*, pp. 136–137.

70. Shibuya, ed., *Tendai zasuki*, p. 44. Although the *Tendai zasuki* lists Fujiwara no Yoritada as chancellor, he did not become chancellor until 10-2-978. Thus the ritual was probably performed for Kanemichi, who was gravely ill at the time.

71. Hayami, *Heian kizoku*, p. 72. According to the *Tendai zasuki*, Gikai first performed the Shijōkōhō for nobility in 941 (Shibuya, *Tendai zasuki*, p. 39). Even if this entry is correct, Ryōgen would still have been one of the first monks to apply the ceremony in this way, though not the first.

72. For a list of such monks, see Hori Ichirō, *Waga kuni minkan shinkōshi no kenkyū* 1:85.

73. Ninkū, *Gishaku sōketsushō, TZ* 13:234. Watanabe Tsunaya, ed., *Shasekishū*, p. 66. For a list of sources of legends concerning Ryōgen, see Sakaida Shirō and Wada Katsushi, *Zōho kaitei Nihon setsuwa bungaku sakuin*, pp. 440–441. Kanchō's ancestry undoubtedly contributed to his standing in the Shingon school; he was the grandson of Emperor Uda and the son of Prince Atsumi. He eventually founded the Hirosawa lineage of the Shingon school. In 986, he succeeded Ryōgen as grand archbishop. Takamitsu's younger brother, Jinkaku, was among his disciples (*NS* 2.2:98–123). The event is also mentioned in the *Shingonden*, but without Kanchō seeming inferior to Ryōgen (ibid., p. 109).

Chapter 6. The Ōwa Debates

1. *Shūiden, NS* 1.23:59. The *Fusō ryakki* (*KT* 12:234) and "Ōkagami uragaki" (Matsumura, ed., *Ōkagami*, p. 339) have a date of 5-2-960.

2. A typical example is the remark by Genji's nurse in *The Tale of Genji:* "My vows seem to have given me a new lease on life" (Edward Seidenstecker, ed., *The Tale of Genji*, p. 59); Yamagishi Norihira, ed., *Genji monogatari*, 1:125.

When Fujiwara no Michinaga became ill and renounced the world, he expected to be rewarded for his act by receiving the protection of the deities (McCullough and McCullough, trans., *Flowering Fortunes*, 1:496–497; Matsumura and Yamanaka, *Eiga monogatari*, 1:443).

3. For studies of the ordination as sacrament, see Ishida Mizumaro, "Kitō to shite no jukai"; Nakamura Kōryū, "Jukai no minzokusei."

4. McCullough and McCullough, trans., *Flowering Fortunes*, 1:82–83; Matsumura and Yamanaka, *Eiga monogatari*, 1:39–40.

5. *Ōwa shūronki, BZ* (Bussho kankōkai ed.), 124:87. The *Ōwa shūronki* was clearly written by a monk who sympathized with the Hossō school. Although neither the name of the author nor the date of compilation is known, the text is considered to be historically reliable (Tamura Yoshirō, *BZ* [Suzuki ed.], 98 (*kaidai*): 197c). Because Ittei died in 947, the account is clearly mistaken at this point. Kanri (894–974),

the Tōdaiji Sanron monk who participated in the debates, might have been the actual recipient of the letter, but this cannot be proven (Hori Daiji, "Ryōgen to Yokawa fukkō [part 1]," pp. 54–55). Hirabayashi has suggested that "Ittei" might be a mistake for "Ichiwa" (890–967 or 970) (*Hijiri*, p. 64). Although Ichiwa was a Hossō monk from Kōfukuji who, at first consideration, probably would not have supported Ryōgen's position, he had withdrawn from Kōfukuji at least twice during his lifetime and might have been critical of the political machinations of Kōfukuji (Horiike Shunpōi, s.v. "Ichiwa," in Tsunoda, ed., *Heian jidaishi jiten*, 1:156a). At the time of the letters, Ryōgen's own political aspirations might not have been clear to Ichiwa.

6. Ueda Kōen (*Nihon jōdai ni okeru yuishiki no kenkyū*, p. 15) has interpreted Ryōgen's letter as an attack on Kōfukuji.

7. Murakami's copy of the *Lotus* has not survived, but the event is recorded in the *Shinkishū* (Tsuji, *Nihon Bukkyōshi*, 1:427).

8. Takagi Yutaka, *Heian jidai Hokke Bukkyōshi kenkyū*, pp. 213–216.

9. Inoue Mitsusada, "Fujiwara jidai no Jōdokyō," pp. 195–198. Some of the interest of nobles in doctrinal issues was a development of earlier concerns with the teaching of emptiness, particularly as presented in the *Vimalakīrtinirdeśa*, the scripture in which the layman Vimalakīrti easily defeats monks and others in debates about emptiness.

10. Michinaga and Sanesuke are chosen as examples here, even though they were active decades later than the Ōwa debates, because primary sources for their period reveal their deep interest in the *Lotus* more effectively than sources for Morosuke and his contemporaries. For Michinaga and the *Lotus*, see Takagi Yutaka, *Heian jidai Hokke Bukkyōshi kenkyū*, pp. 205–209; for Sanesuke, see Sasaki Ryōshin, "Fujiwara no Sanesuke no Bukkyō shinkō."

11. *Ōwa shūron nikki narabini ongaku sōjō*, BZ (Bussho kankōkai ed.), 124:87. Temple affiliations for some participants are not included in the *Ōwa shūron nikki;* these have been included when the information was available from other sources. Ages are based on entries in the *Sōgō bunin*. Of the monks in table 6, Hōzō, Ninga, and Chūzan are discussed later in this chapter; nothing is known of Senri.

12. *Sōgō bunin*, BZ (Bussho kankōkai ed.), 123:131; *Sanne jōitsuki* BZ (Bussho kankōkai ed.), 123:299. Shunsen was a disciple of Gengan and served as abbot of Gangyōji, the temple where Ryōgen had served as master of Esoteric Buddhism. In 950, he had performed services for the protection of crown prince Norihira, Morosuke's grandson. He had also been in the selected audience for the dedication of Emperor Murakami's copy of the *Lotus Sūtra* in 954. He had also served as abbot of Tōnomine and Urin'in.

Zengei was a well-known master of exoteric Buddhism. In 968, Zengei was only the second Tendai monk to be invited to be lecturer at the Yuima-e; he was appointed supernumerary master of discipline in 968 and rose to be lesser bishop by 977. He was appointed abbot of Onjōji in 970.

13. Enshō was the current *zasu*. Bōsan, Chinchō, and Kikyō are discussed in the next chapter.

14. Very little is known about Zen'yu's life other than the list of his appointments; he was named lecturer at the Yuima-e in 966, supernumerary master of discipline and judge (*tandai*) of the Mount Hiei examinations in 977, master of discipline in 979, and supernumerary master of discipline in 986. An episode in *Genkō shakusho*

indicates that he may have been a close friend of Senkan (*BZ* [Suzuki ed.], 62:93a), a relationship that suggests possible ties to Enchin's lineage. For his role in the Tendai examination system, see the chapter on that topic.

15. Zōso (903–979) of Yakushiji was appointed lecturer at the Yuima-e in 964, supernumerary master of discipline in 969, and supernumerary lesser bishop in 977.

16. Sentō (919?–989) of Kōfukuji was a candidate at the Yuima-e in 958, lecturer in 973, and supernumerary master of discipline in 983. By the time of his death, he had risen to supernumerary lesser bishop.

17. *Ōwa shūron nikki, BZ* (Bussho kankōkai ed.), 124:88a. Nothing is known of Suju. Engei is listed as lecturer in the Yuima-e for 970.

18. Based on the *Ōwa shūron nikki, BZ* (Bussho kankōkai ed.), 124:88. In the *Jinden ainōshō* (*BZ* [Bussho kankōkai ed.], 150:397–398) Yokei is listed as Kyōso, Genkei as Ankyō, and Shinki as Shingi. In addition, the note that Chūzan replaced Engei is also based on the *Jinden ainōshō* and is not found in the *Ōwa shūronki*. The *Jinden ainōshō* was compiled in 1532 by an unknown monk (*BZ* [Suzuki ed.], 99:245). It includes quotations from a number of earlier texts. Notes concerning the substitutions made during the lectures have been added in accordance with the accounts in the two works mentioned above.

19. *Honchō kōsōden, BZ* (Suzuki ed.), 63:69b.

20. *Miao-fa lien-hua ching* (*Saddharmapuṇḍarika*), *T* 9:9b. Earlier texts such as the *Ōwa shūron nikki* mention that the subject of *icchantikas* was discussed by Kakugyō and Hōzō, but they do not mention the argument over the reading of the *Lotus Sūtra*. According to the *Hekizan nichiroku*, a diary written in the late fifteenth century (1459–1468) by the Rinzai monk Taikyoku (b. 1421), the argument over the proper readings of this passage and one from the *Ta yüan-chüeh ching* (mentioned later in this chapter) are said to have arisen in debate between Hōzō and Kakugyō (*NS* 1.11:288), but the *Jinden ainōshō* places the argument over the reading of the *Ta-yüan-chüeh ching* in the debate between Chūzan and Ryōgen. Ōno Tatsunosuke places the debate over these readings in the discussion between Chūzan and Ryōgen (s.v. "Ōwa shūron," in Kokushi daijiten henshū iinkai, ed., *Kokushi daijiten*, 2:492c–493a), possibly basing his view on Eishin's (d. 1546?) *Hokke jikidanshō*, 1:510–511.

21. If Kakugyō had been born in 927, he would have been thirty-six at the time of the debates; however, according to the *Honchō kōsōden*, Kakugyō was "barely past twenty" (*jakkan*) at the time of the debates (*BZ* [Suzuki ed.], 63:74b). Kakugyō died in 1014.

22. *Hijiri*, p. 66.

23. *Jie daishiden, NS* 1.22:91.

24. *Ōwa shūron nikki, BZ* (Bussho kankōkai ed.), 124:88a.

25. *Jie daisōjōden; ZTZ Shiden*, 2:194b. Pūrṇa was one of Śākyamuni's sixteen preeminent disciples and was particularly renowned for his elegant preaching.

26. *Ōwa shūronki, BZ* (Bussho kankōkai ed.), 124:88a.

27. *Asabashō, T* (zuzō), 9:944c.

28. Primary sources for Hōzō's biography are collected in *NS* 1.12:326–343. Also see his biography in *Honchō kōsōden, BZ* (Suzuki ed.), 63:68b–c, and comments by Nemu, "Jie daishi no inmyōgaku," p. 232.

29. *NS* 1.10:868, 925–927; Murayama, *Nihon Onmyōdōshi sōsetsu,* pp. 221, 225, 297. Scholars vary on the victor of the debate between Yasunori and Hōzō; Murayama indicates that Hōzō lost the debate because he could not substantiate his claims (p. 221), but Yamashita Katsuaki claims that Hōzō won (*Kokushi daijiten,* 12:628c). However, the decision handed down seems to have been a compromise in which each man's calculations were used for certain aspects of the astrological computations (*Asabashō, T* [zuzō], 9:457b). At any rate, by 962, Yasunori had been appointed head of the Onmyōdō (Murayama, *Nihon Onmyōdōshi sōsetsu,* p. 128).

Another factor that would have contributed to the Fujiwaras' interest in the debate was the influence that Yasunori's father Tadayuki (n.d.) had with Morosuke. In 959, at Tadayuki's suggestion, Morosuke had commissioned a performance of a rite focusing on a white-robed Kannon to put down a revolt (*Asabashō, T* [zuzō] 9:214a–b; Murayama, *Nihon Onmyōdōshi sōsetsu,* p. 237). However, at the time, few monks knew the rite. Thus Tadayuki would have been seen as source of knowledge about astrology and the proper rites.

30. *Jie daisōjōden, ZTZ Shiden,* 2:199b; *Asabashō, T* (zuzō), 9:738b; 744c.

31. Fukaura Seibun suggests that Chūzan was not originally scheduled to participate in the debate (*Shinkō Bukkyō bungaku monogatari,* p. 275), but this interpretation does not agree with the list in the *Ōwa shūron nikki,* which shows Chūzan among those initially invited. Although Fukaura does not give the evidence for his view, it may lie in the *Genkō shakusho* entries concerning Chūzan's biography and the Ōwa debates. According to these entries, Ninga and Engei were forced to resign just before their turns so that Chūzan could replace them (*BZ* [Suzuki ed.], 62:90a, 198c; Miki, *Tōnomine hijiri dan,* p. 90). If the *Genkō shakusho* version is accepted, several aspects of the story are explained. First, Chūzan was in Nara when Fuminori met him because Chūzan had not been invited to the debates. Second, Ninga was forced to resign by his own school in favor of Chūzan; Ninga may have chosen to retire to Tōnomine rather than to a Hossō temple because he resented his treatment by the Hossō school. Third, Chūzan dramatically appeared at the last minute to save the Hossō school. Although the *Genkō shakusho* provides a more dramatic interpretation of the events, the *Ōwa shūron nikki* version has been followed here because it is the earlier source.

32. Myōchō's career is described by Sasaki Ryōshin in "Hieizan seizanroku Fumonji shikō," pp. 40–42. He rose to the rank of supernumerary lesser bishop and abbot of Onjōji.

33. The Fumonji and Fuminori's role in establishing it have been described in detail ibid. pp. 20–61.

34. *Ōwa shūron nikki, BZ* (Bussho kankōkai ed.), 124:88.

35. Hirabayashi, *Ryōgen,* p. 77.

36. Neil McMullin, "The *Lotus Sūtra* and Politics in the Mid-Heian Period," pp. 132–133.

37. Later sources exaggerate Chūzan's youth at the time of the Ōwa debates. According to the *Hekizan nichiroku* (*NS* 1.16:31), Chūzan was only eighteen at the time of the debates. In a similar manner, Ryōgen's youth or his opponent's age is exaggerated in accounts of his early debates.

38. *Genkō shakusho, BZ* (Suzuki ed.), 62:90a. Primary sources for Chūzan's biography are collected in *NS* 1.16:29–69.

39. According to Tsujimura Taizen (s.v. "Chūzan," *Kokushi daijiten*, 9:497c), Chūzan's lack of family connections may have hindered his advance in monastic circles.

40. *BZ* (Suzuki ed.), 62:90a; 63:68c–69a. Ueda Kōen has collected valuable information concerning Chūzan, some of it from unpublished sources (*Jōdai yuishiki*, pp. 14, 17–18).

41. The *Hokkekyō shakumon* (Commentary on the *Lotus Sūtra; T* 2189) was written for Fuminori shortly before Chūzan's death, demonstrating that their relationship continued for a long time and that Fuminori was seriously interested in the *Lotus Sūtra*. It is a three-fascicle work comparing the positions of different schools on the readings and meanings of various terms in the *Lotus Sūtra*. In the introduction, he compares his patron Fuminori to Vimalakīrti (*T* 56:144a). The text is also called the *Hokke ongi* and *Hokke onshaku*.

42. Nemu, "Jie daishi no inmyōgaku," p. 231. The text was composed in 953. Both Chūzan's teacher Kūshō and his disciple Shinkō (934–1007) composed texts on the same subject. Chūzan thus lived during a revival of logic at the Kitain at Kōfukuji (*BKD* 1:186d). Shinkō's text corresponds to *T* no. 2277. Ryōgen's disciple Genshin also discussed logical contradictions.

43. Fukihara Shōshin, *Kenjōgi ryakumondō no kenkyū*.

44. Fukaura Seibun, *Yuishikigaku kenkyū* 2:334.

45. *NS* 1.16:30–31. A number of temples called Jionji (named after Tz'u-en, founder of Hossō) exist, making the identification of the location difficult. Other stories with Taoist elements exist; see Nagai Yoshinori, "Matsumuro sennin to katarimono: *Genpei seisuiki* no ichi sozai no seikaku." Of these one of the most interesting from the perspective of this study is found in the *Honchō shinsenden*, which mentions that Chūzan traveled to the Ryōgon'in, a building associated with Yokawa (Inoue and Ōsone, eds., *Ōjōden Hokke genki*, p. 271). If there is any truth to the story, it may suggest that Chūzan and Ryōgen met at other times.

46. The *Ainōshō* (Compilation of bags of [worldly] dust) is an encyclopedia of Buddhist stories and terms completed in 1446 by the Shingon monk Gyōyo (Nihon koten bungaku daijiten henshū iinkai, ed., *Nihon bungaku daijiten*, 1:8c). The story of Chūzan according to the *Ainōshō* can be found in *NS* 1.11:283–285, and 1.16:39–40.

47. According to Hossō doctrine, Buddha-nature in principle (*ribusshō*) refers to Suchness, which all phenomena share. However, Hossō scholars argue that Suchness alone does not allow a person to realize Buddhahood. The realization of Buddhahood is impossible without the Buddha-nature of practice (*gyōbusshō*), untainted seeds (*muro shūji*) that exist from the beginningless past. If the practitioner does not have these untainted seeds, he cannot create them no matter how much he practices, because tainted actions can never create untainted seeds. For further comments, see Groner, *Saichō*, pp. 97–101.

48. *Ta-yüan-chüeh ching, T* 17:917b. The *Ta-yüan-chüeh ching* (*Sūtra* of great enlightenment) is an apocryphal text compiled in China that was influential from the middle of the T'ang dynasty onward. Ryōgen's reading of the passage is closer to the original intent of the text than is Chūzan's.

49. Ryōgen rejects the Hossō division of Buddha-nature into *ribusshō* and *gyōbusshō*. The realization of Buddhahood is based on the same nature, Suchness,

which everything shares. He argues that since Chūzan has admitted that the trees and grasses possess Buddha-nature, he must recognize that they can realize Buddhahood. For the Chinese background of this debate, see Penkower, "T'ien-t'ai during the T'ang Dynasty."

In Japan, discussions of the problem of the realization of Buddhahood by trees and grasses can be traced back to several brief passages in Saichō's works (for example, see *Hokke shūku*, DZ 3:167–168, 183, 215; *Shugo kokkaishō*, DZ 2:524–525). Saichō also raised the issue in his questions to Tao-sui in China (*Tendaishū miketsu*, in Hsin-wen-feng, ed., *Hsü-tsang-ching*, 100:807b–808a). Further inquiries about the realization of Buddhahood by plants appear in the *Tōketsu*, the questions sent to China by Saichō's successors (see, for example Enchō's seventeenth question, Tokuen's ninth question, and Kōjō's fifth question, *Hsü-tsang-ching*, 100:817b–818b, 857a–858a, 848a–b). Ennin discussed the theme, but did not write about it. The most extensive discussions about the problem by early Tendai thinkers is found in Annen's *Shinjō sōmoku jōbutsu shiki* (Personal compilation concerning discussions of the realization of Buddhahood by grasses and trees); for the text and analysis, see Sueki Fumihiko, *Heian shoki Bukkyō shisō no kenkyū*, pp. 363–422, 705–786. In the text, Annen criticizes the San-lun, Hua-yen, Fa-hsiang, and some Tendai positions, indicating that the topic was emerging as a debate topic both with other schools and within the Tendai school. Annen repeatedly argues that trees and grasses on their own can aspire to enlightenment, practice, and the realization of Buddhahood, but never explains how they might do so.

The realization of Buddhahood by plants had clearly become a debate topic by Ryōgen's lifetime. In fact, a short manuscript from the Eizan bunko (Shinnyōzō) with the title "Hossōshū jūgi" (Ten doubts concerning the Hossō school) has been preserved; this text purports to be ten criticisms concerning the Tendai school's position on the realization of Buddhahood by trees and grasses and Ryōgen's response to them; it is translated in appendix 6. I am indebted to Ōkubo Ryōshun of Waseda University for providing me with a copy of the manuscript. The issue of how a tree might practice is considered again in a later text called the *Sōmoku hosshin shugyō jōbutsuki* (*BZ* [Suzuki ed.], 41:141b–142a). This text is purported to be a deathbed record of teachings that Kakuun (953–1007) received from Ryōgen, but is clearly later than that, perhaps dating from the twelfth century. According to the text, plants practice and realize Buddhahood through their natural ways of existence—that is, by exhibiting the four characteristics of production, abiding, deterioration, and cessation (*BZ* [Suzuki ed.], 41:141b). Thus the *Ainōshō* account of the debate and the trees blooming in response to Ryōgen's speech may have been a poetic rendering of teachings attributed to Ryōgen in this text.

50. Courtiers used cypress fans as part of their ceremonial dress. The custom was adopted by monks, probably sometime during the late Heian; the fans were used as part of formal dress rather than for cooling oneself (Okazaki Jōji, ed., *Butsugu daijiten*, p. 230). Chūzan's usage of it in this story probably reflects customs at the time of the story's composition around the fourteenth century.

51. See *Genkō shakusho*, *BZ* (Suzuki ed.), 62:89ab; *Fusō ryakki*, *KT* 241.

52. *Ōwa shūron nikki*, *BZ* (Suzuki ed.), 124:89a.

53. *BZ* (Suzuki ed.), 63:69a, 71b.

54. For more on this subject, see the chapter on the examination system.

55. The *jūzenji,* despite the literal meaning of their title as ten meditation masters, did not actually teach meditation. Rather, they were monks who were thought to have sufficient merit and power (perhaps obtained through meditation) to give them power to protect the court.

Senkan is also discussed in the chapters on debates and examinations; primary sources for his biography are collected in *NS* 1.20:186–212. According to the *Kokon chomonjū* (Stories heard from writers old and new), Senkan responded to official invitations until he met Kōya (*NS* 1.20:198; Miki, *Tōnomine hijiri dan,* p. 90). A similar entry occurs in the *Hosshinshū* (A collection concerning aspiration to salvation), but the statement concerning Senkan's response to an official invitation refers to only one occasion (*NS* 1.20:198).

56. *Fusō ryakki, KT* 12:240. The text is extant in the Tenkaizō at Eizan bunko (*NS* 1.20:204; *BKD* 10:66). The *BKD* (10:66a) also lists another text on the *Lotus* by Senkan, the twenty-fascicle *Hokke sanshū yōroku* (Essential record of the three school's views on the *Lotus Sūtra*). Its relation to the *Hokke sanshū sōtaishō* is unclear.

57. *Genkō shakusho, BZ* (Suzuki ed.), 62:90c. For lists of Senkan's works, see *Nihonkoku Tendaishū shōso mokuroku, BZ* (Suzuki ed.), 95:191–192; *Sange sotoku senjutsuhen mokuroku, BZ* (Suzuki ed.), 95:201; Ogami Kanchū, "Ōwa no shūron to shūyō gika no kakuritsu," p. 68.

58. *Nihon ōjō gokuraku ki,* in Jōdoshūten kaishū happyakunen kinen keisan junbikyoku, ed., *Zoku Jōdoshū zensho,* 17:10.

59. *Gōjūkanshō, NS* 1.20:201. The source for the vow is the fifty-fascicle text on the *Lotus Sūtra* compiled by Senkan; however, several versions of the eight rules survive. A collated set of the rules is found in Satō Tetsuei, *Eizan jōdokyō no kenkyū,* pp. 68–69. The rules also call for a strict attitude toward the precepts and for religious austerities.

60. This type of meditation is the first of sixteen described in the *Kuan wu-liangshou ching, T* 12:341c–342a; Ryūkoku University Translation Center, ed., *The Sūtra of Contemplation on the Buddha of Immeasurable Life,* pp. 26–27.

61. Satō Tetsuei, *Eizan Jōdokyō,* p. 67.

62. *Hosshinshū, NS* 1.20:199–200; *Kojidan, NS* 1.20:199–200; *Sankoku denki, NS* 1.20:200; *Fusō in'itsuden, NS* 1.20:208.

63. For Senkan, see *Fusō ryakki, KT* 12:254–255; *Nihon ōjō gokurakuki,* in Inoue and Ōsone, eds., *Ōjōden Hokke genki,* p. 29; *Nihon kiryaku, KT* 11:104. The concubines are identified with Emperor Murakami in *NS* 1.20:188, but with Emperor Suzaku in *Kokushi daijiten,* 8:389b. Yūhime was the daughter of Motokata, the loser in the power struggle with Fujiwara no Morosuke, Ryōgen's patron. She thus chose a monk not allied with Ryōgen for her teacher. She might well have found Senkan's reclusiveness attractive.

The term "*kaishi*" (literally, "teacher of the precepts") is used to describe Senkan's status at Yūhime's ordination. In a comment concerning another document, Matsuo Kenji notes that "*kaishi*" often was used to refer to the teacher in the ordination of novices and "*kaiwajō*" (literally, "preceptor") in full ordinations ("Kansō to tonseisō," p. 298). Although this distinction is made in neither the Buddhist nor *bungo* dictionaries that I consulted, Matsuo's extensive reading of ordination certificates makes his interpretation noteworthy. In addition, the manner in which the term is used in a number of cases suggests that "*kaishi*" was used to refer to the teacher at initiations of novices in many but not all cases. The usage of the term deserves more study, particularly in regard to how it might have changed over time. Its usage in referring to the ordinations by Senkan may suggest that the women were ordained as novices. However, another interpretation of the term "*kaishi*" is possible. In Tendai ordinations, Śākyamuni Buddha served as the preceptor (*kaiwajō*) who conferred (*ju*) the precepts while an eminent monk served as the master of ceremonies (*kaishi*) who transmitted (*den*) the precepts. In this case, a *kaishi* could preside over a full bodhisattva ordination.

64. Nishiguchi Junko, s.v. "Senkan," in Kokushi daijiten henshū iinkai, ed., *Kokushi daijiten*, 8:389b. Although details of the posthumous promotion are not clear, it is said to have been reported to Senkan, perhaps indicating that he served as some sort of spiritual intermediary.

65. Biographical and legendary sources about Zōga are collected in *NS* 2.4:863–889. Although the reading "Zōga" is traditionally used for this monk, his name may have originally been pronounced "Sōga." His supposed father, Tachibana no Tsunehira, served as governor in various provinces and eventually rose to be adviser (*sangi*).

66. The earliest biography of Zōga is found in the *Dainihonkoku Hokke genki* (Miraculous Japanese stories concerning the *Lotus Sūtra;* Inoue and Ōsone eds., *Ōjōden Hokke genki*, pp. 157–159), compiled approximately forty years after Zōga's death. The biography in the *Zoku honchō ōjō den* (Continuation of biographies of Japanese born in the Pure Land; ibid., pp. 237–238) was compiled approximately a century after Zōga's death. Legends about Zōga can also be found in Mabuchi and Kunisaki, eds., *Konjaku monogatarishū* (Collection of tales of times now past) fasc. 12, no. 33; fasc. 19, no. 18 (1:306–313; 2:576–580).

67. Hirabayashi, *Hijiri*, p. 59.

68. Inoue and Ōsone, eds., *Ōjōden Hokke genki*, p. 157; *Tōnomine ryakki, BZ* (Bussho kankōkai ed.), 118:492a.

69. The diary is called the *Namubō muki* (Record of dreams by the resident of the Namu lodge) and is discussed in Abe Yasurō, "*Zōga Shōnin muki*." Abe calls the authenticity of the text into question, suggesting that the text might have been compiled shortly after Zōga's death by several disciples to bolster the status of Zōga as a holy man and Tōnomine as a spiritually charged site. However, Miki Sumito argues for its authenticity (*Tōnomine hijiri dan*, pp. 100–101). Certainly a number of monks had dreams that they later interpreted as omens or predictions of events. In such an atmosphere, Zōga might well have recorded such events near the end of his life. For a useful study of the role of dreams in early and medieval Japan, see Saigō Nobutsuna, *Kodaijin to yume*. Zōga's dreams are also alluded to in the *Tōnomine engi* and *Tōnomine ryakki* (*BZ* [Bussho kankōkai ed.], 118:483a–b, 492a) in passages probably based on the *Namubō muki*.

One of the peculiarities of the dream diary is its emphasis on Vimalakīrti, an interest of Zōga not emphasized in other biographical sources. This may arise from Tōnomine as the site of Kamatari's grave and the origins of the Yuima-e as a healing ritual for Kamatari. In 974, about a decade after Zōga went to Tōnomine, he lectured on the *Vimalakīrti;* the following year, the abbot Senman established a Yuima-e at Tōnomine (*Tōnomine ryakki, BZ* [Bussho kankōkai ed.], 118:495b).

70. *Jie daisōjōden, ZTZ Shiden*, 2:199b. Miki suggests that Ryōgen may have hoped to retreat to Mudōji (*Tōnomine hijiri dan*, p. 104).

71. Hirabayashi, *Ryōgen*, p. 79. Hori Daiji takes a similar view ("Takamitsu to Zōga"). However, Miki deemphasizes the role of the Ōwa debates in Zōga's decision to leave, noting that no source specifically indicates it as a reason; rather, Zōga might have retired to Tōnomine as part of a long-held desire to retreat from the politically motivated intrigues of Mount Hiei (*Tōnomine hijiri dan*, pp. 98–199).

72. *Tōnomine ryakki*, *BZ* (Bussho kankōkai ed.), 118:492a; Abe, "Zōga Shōnin muki," p. 18. The important role that Zōga played on Tōnomine is demonstrated in the *Tōnomine ryakki*, where his biography is much longer than that of any other monk (pp. 491a–493a). Senman was abbot of Tōnomine for twenty-one years and supervised much of the construction there.

73. *Tōnomine ryakki*, *BZ* (Bussho kankōkai ed.), 118:492b.

74. Excerpts are found in *Tendai kahyō* 4.3, *BZ* (Suzuki ed.), 41:394–397; the complete text has recently been published in *ZTZ Kengyō*, 3:1–105. Tomohira was Emperor Murakami's seventh son. He was a noted literary figure and a pious Buddhist layman, probably taught by Yoshishige no Yasutane. Tomohira and Yasutane may very well have listened to Zōga's lectures on the *Mo-ho chih-kuan*.

75. The *Yugaron mondō* consisted of four hundred questions on the *Yogācārabhūmi*, the last three hundred of which are still extant (*T* no. 2259). Both the *Hokke gengishō* (compiled in 985–986) and the *Gika shiki* are mentioned in the *Tōnomine ryakki* (*BZ* [Bussho kankōkai ed.], 118: 492b), but no information is available on them. The formats, contents, and titles of several of these works indicate that they might have been used in the debates and examinations. See the chapter on the examination system for more information.

76. *BZ* (Bussho kankōkai ed.), 118:496b. Ishida Mizumaro has suggested that the passage be emended to refer to a meditation on the thirty-two marks of Amida (quoted in Nara Hiromoto, "*Tōnomine ryakki* ni mirareru jōgyō zanmai wo megutte, 4).

77. The passages on the constant-walking meditation for both versions have been published and compared in Nara Hiromoto, "*Tōnomine ryakki* ni mirareru jōgyō zanmai wo megutte." Nara argues in favor of the Nishinomiya version but does not suggest why the Shōkōkan version would have been changed. Other scholars have accepted the published Shōkōkan account of a ninety-day meditation but have not commented on the unpublished Nishinomiya text. See, for example, Satō Tetsuei, *Eizan jōdokyō no kenkyū*, p. 48.

78. *Tōnomine ryakki*, *BZ* (Bussho kankōkai ed.), 118:486a, 496a–b. Fuminori later supported Enchin's faction; see the chapter on factionalism and Ryōgen's efforts to control the order.

79. Ueda, *Jōdai yuishiki*, pp. 262–263.

80. This information appears in a note (*uragaki*) in the *Sōgō bunin* under Shinkō's entry (Hirabayashi and Koike, *Sōryaku sōran*, p. 173).

81. *Zoku honchō ōjōden*, p. 238; *Honchō kōsōden*, *BZ* (Suzuki ed.), 63:73a; Kobayashi Yasuharu, ed., *Kojidan*, no. 285, 1:296–297. Similar stories about the preservation of Zōga's body exist (Abe, "*Zōga Shōnin muki*"), reflecting the purity and spiritual power ascribed to such recluses.

82. Kōya climbed Mount Hiei in 948, was ordained by the *zasu* Enshō, and given the monastic name Kōshō, but he continued to use the name Kōya (Hori Ichirō, *Kōya*, p. 51). He seems to have had few other connections with the Tendai establishment.

83. "Roku-haramitsu-ji sōken kō," p. 138; Miki, *Tōnomine hijiri dan*, pp. 92–95.

84. *Honchō kōsōden, BZ* (Suzuki ed.), 63:70b. Also note the purported meeting between Kōya and Senkan mentioned earlier. Finally, the Rokuharamitsuji founded by Kōya was located near the Atagoyama, the site of a temple associated with Senkan.

Chapter 7. Ryōgen's Appointments as Head of the Tendai School

1. Shibuya, ed., *Tendai zasuki*, pp. 40–42.

2. *Daisōjōden, ZTZ Shiden*, 2:194b.

3. *Engi Tenryaku gokishō, NS* 1.11.475–476.

4. *Nihon kiryaku, KT* 11:97–98.

5. *Shōyūki, NS* 1.11:724–725. According to Hirabayashi Moritoku, Bonshō, author of the *Shūiden*, suggested that Ryōgen had served as a lecturer in the three assemblies in Kyoto (*Hokkyō san'e*) to bolster claims that he was qualified to be *zasu* (*Ryōgen*, pp. 84–85). However, I have not been able to locate the citation in the *Shūiden* to which Hirabayashi refers. In addition, the three assemblies in Kyoto were not organized into a system until several decades after the *Shūiden* had been composed. These three assemblies were eventually treated as the equivalent of the three Nara assemblies and were a necessary part of the qualifications for appointment to high posts in the Tendai school. For more information on the three assemblies in Kyoto, see the chapter on examinations.

6. *Sōgō bunin, BZ* (Suzuki ed.), 65:31c, 36b. A brief biography in the *Jimon denki horoku* (*BZ* [Bussho kankōkai ed.], 127: 208) does not mention Bōsan's disappointment.

7. *Fusō ryakki, KT* 12:244–245. The *Hyakurenshō* (*KT* [*fukyūban*], p. 15) entry indicates that Gajō was posthumously named *sōjō* in 1020 in compensation for not being named *zasu*, perhaps confusing him with Bōsan. Some sources also note that Gajō may have served as the protector of Prince Hirohira, the boy displaced by Morosuke's successful efforts to install his grandson as crown prince (Hirabayashi and Koike, *Sōryaku sōran*, p. 280); in some sources, he is said to have appeared as a vengeful ghost with Motokata's spirit (see the chapter on Ryōgen and Morosuke). For the lineages of Bōsan and Gajō, see Hirabayashi, *Ryōgen*, p. 85. The rank of *hōin* (Dharma-seal) was established in 864. Although it was originally intended as the rank for archbishops, it eventually was given to monks not appointed to the Office of Monastic Affairs and as a posthumous award.

8. Two versions of the *Sōgō bunin* have been followed in compiling this list (*NS* 1.22:6–7).

9. For a thorough investigation of the origins of this type of meditation teacher, see Funagasaki Masataki, *Kokka Bukkyō hen'yō katei no kenkyū*, pp. 158–205.

10. Hongō Masatsugu, "Naigubu jūzenji no seiritsu to Tendaishū." In contrast, Oyamada Kazuo argues for origins of the *naigubu* in Japan and suggests that the combined position of *naigubu jūzenji* may have been established between 772 and 797 ("Naigubu jūzenji-shoku to Enchin").

11. Oyamada Kazuo, s.v. "Naigubu jūzenji," Tsunoda, ed., *Heian jidaishi jiten*, 2:1783b.

12. *Shoreishō, GR* 24:1, 4, 35. The *teguruma* was a cart pulled or pushed by a group of men. For a picture of such a cart, see Nihon daijiten kankōkai, ed., *Nihon kokugo daijiten*, 14:214b. The previous other two monks to receive permission to enter the palace in a *teguruma* were the Shingon monk Shinga (801–879) and the Tendai monk Henjō.

13. Groner, "Annen, Tankei, Henjō, and Monastic Discipline in the Japanese Tendai School," pp. 144–145; Groner, *Saichō*, p. 271.

14. *Tendaishū Enryakuji zasu Enchinden, BZ* (Bussho kankōkai ed.), 28:11; *Sōgō bunin* (Bussho kankōkai ed.), *BZ* 123:105.

15. For more information on Henjō, see Groner, "Annen, Tankei, Henjō, and Monastic Discipline in the Japanese Tendai School."

16. Shibuya, ed., *Tendai zasuki*, p. 36.

17. Takagi, *Heian jidai Hokke Bukkyōshi kenkyū*, pp. 23–30.

18. *Sōgō bunin, BZ* (Suzuki ed.), 65:32–34. Ryōgen had to share the position of *hōmu* with one other monk at all times: Kanchū (908–977), a Shingon monk from Tōdaiji until 977, and then Jōshō (909–983), a Hossō monk active at Kōfukuji and Tōji until 983. Ryōgen was finally replaced by Kanchō (915–998), another Shingon monk from Tōdaiji in 983. The prevalence of Shingon monks in administrative positions might have made Ryōgen's task easier. Ushiyama Yoshiyuki has compiled a useful chart of appointments as *hōmu* (*Kodai chūsei jiin soshiki no kenkyū*, pp. 203–205).

19. Natsume Yūshin, s.v. "hōmu," Kokushi daijiten henshū iinkai, ed., *Kokushi daijiten*, 12:650b; Tomita Masahiro, s.v. "hōmu," in Tsunoda, ed., *Heian jidaishi jiten*, 2:2298c–d.

20. Ushiyama Yoshiyuki ("Sōgōsei no henshitsu to sōzaichō kumonsei no seiritsu," p. 17) suggests a date of 872 for the installation of the *hōmu* and rejects documents that place it earlier as incorrect; however, he notes that the establishment of the post requires further investigation. In contrast, according to the *Kokushi daijiten* (see note 19), the post was established during the Nara period and usually held by the ranking official in the Sōgō.

21. The two chief administrators were ranked, with one of them being called supernumerary chief administrator. According to Takeuchi Rizō et al., eds., *Nihonshi jiten*, p. 780; *Kokushi daijiten* (see note 19); and the *Heian jidaishi jiten* (see note 19), when the formal post of *hōmu* was first established, one monk was to oversee Esoteric temples and one was to supervise exoteric temples. This view is rejected by Ushiyama, however ("Sōgōsei no henshitsu," p. 17).

22. For evidence concerning the location of the Sōgō, see Itō Kiyoo, "Chūsei sōgōsei no kenkyū," 27–28, n. 2. The Sōgō was moved to Tōji at an unknown date when Saiji declined. Eventually, probably by the late eleventh century, even the *hōmu* ceased to run the Sōgō and were replaced by masters of decorum (*igishi*), who had originally functioned as ritual specialists. Although ultimate control of the Sōgō still rested with the *hōmu*, they did not reside at the Sōgō headquarters. The masters of decorum who oversaw Sōgō affairs were referred to as *zaichō* or *sōzaichō*, terms that reflected their positions as filling in for absentee officials. One of the earliest occurrences of the term "*sōzaichō*" is dated 995, ten years after Ryōgen's death (Ushiyama, "Sōgōsei no henshitsu," p. 23). In addition, an assistant master of decorum (*jūigishi*) was called *kumon* (secretary) because his duty was to prepare official documents. While Ryōgen was *hōmu*, he must have actively worked for Tendai in-

terests, but he did not reside at the headquarters of the Sōgō in Kyoto. Masters of decorum probably helped him with many of the details of his post, but Ryōgen was probably much more active in overseeing it than later *hōmu*. Unfortunately, documents do not survive that would enable us to specify his role in the Sōgō. For a detailed description of the role of the *hōmu*, see Ushiyama, "Sōgōsei no henshitsu," pp. 17–22.

23. For a full set of charts for the years 923–1035, see Ogami Kanchū, "Jie daishi no Tendaishū goji," pp. 22–34. New appointees to the Sōgō as well as appointees who died are counted in the figures for the year of their appointment or death. The gradual increase in numbers within the Sōgō is indicative of the trend to make appointments to the Sōgō an honorary rather than an administrative post.

24. Itō Kiyoo, "Chūsei Sōgōsei no kenkyū," pp. 20–35; idem "Chūsei sōgōsei to Enryakuji," p. 135. In several cases, members of the Sōgō did sign Sanmon ordination certificates, but Itō is unclear about whether this reflected standard procedure or was exceptional (p. 155, n. 24). Itō's studies focus on the Sōgō during the Kamakura period, approximately two centuries after Ryōgen's time, but they provide a useful guide to the role that the Sōgō came to play for the Tendai school. Matsuo Kenji suggests that the Sōgō and other governmental institutions that Saichō had excluded from overseeing ordinations did routinely sign ordination documents by the thirteenth century (*Kamakura shin-Bukkyō no seiritsu*, pp. 145–150).

25. The background of early Tendai antipathy for the Sōgō is discussed in Groner, *Saichō*, pp. 106–164 passim, 281–285. My description of the role of the Sōgō is based on Itō Kiyoo, "Chūsei Sōgōsei to Enryakuji," pp. 137–139. However, Itō differs from other scholars who describe the Sōgō during this period as existing in name only and having little or no function. For a treatment of the Sōgō that considers Itō's research, but regards the Sōgō as less active in monastic administration after the middle of the Heian period, see Ushiyama Yoshiyuki, "Sōgōsei no henshitsu," pp. 1–33.

26. This argument is based on the absence of the *zoku-bettō*'s seal on an ordination certificate included in Matsuo, *Kamakura no shin-Bukkyō no seiritsu*, pp. 136–137, and discussed ibid., pp. 146–147.

Chapter 8. Significance of Ryōgen's Revival of the Examination System

1. For discussions of the development of the Yuima-e, see Hori Ichirō, *Jōdai Nihon Bukkyō bunkashi*, 1:192–199; Horiike Shunpō, "Yuima-e to kandō no shōshin" Itō Takatoshi, "Kōfukuji Yuima-e to shoshū"; Ueda *Jōdai yuishiki*, pp. 249–289. The last two studies are particularly valuable because they refer to an important primary source that has only recently become available, the *Yuima kōji kengaku ryūgi shidai*, edited by Kunaichō shoryōbu. Ueda has published the *Yuima-e hyōbyaku* in the above-mentioned text (pp. 601–611).

2. Ueda (*Jōdai yuishiki*, pp. 261–262) argues that the account of the lectures being founded by Hōmyō seems the more convincing of the accounts.

3. *Kōfukuji engi*, BZ (Bussho kankōkai ed.), 119:321b–322a; *Fusō ryakki*, KT 12:75. The ceremony initially had been held at Kamatari's house in Suehara in Ya-

mashina; it was later moved to a number of different temples before finally being permanently established at Kōfukuji in Nara ("Yuima hyōbyaku," in Ueda, *Jōdai yuishiki*, pp. 268–270). The account of the early Yuima-e follows that found in the "Yuima-e engi," a text by the head of the Fujiwara clan, Yoshiyo (824–900), compiled during the last year of his life, that explained the role of Kōfukuji in the clan's prominence. Variant, but generally later, accounts exist, however. The date at which the Yuima-e was finally transferred to Kōfukuji is not completely clear; however, the establishment of Kōfukuji is intrinsically tied to the Yuima-e; in fact, the very name of the temple may have come from Kumārajīva's translation of the *Vimalakīrti-nirdeśa* (Ueda, *Jōdai yuishiki*, p. 272).

    4. *Ruijū kokushi, KT* 6:216.

    5. *Ruijū sandaikyaku, KT* 25:65–66. Also see *Engishiki, KT* 26:539.

    6. The exact date when an appointment as lecturer at the Yuima-e came to entail appointments to the other two assemblies is not entirely clear. According to the *Sanne jōitsuki* (*BZ* [Bussho kankōkai ed.], 123:290a) the correct date should be 839; moreover, according to an edict dated 839 in the *Shoku Nihon kōki* (*KT* 3:95) and *Ruijū kokushi* (*KT* 6:216), lecturers at the Yuima-e were to also serve as lecturers at the Misai-e, indicating that the system may have begun about that time (*BZ* [Suzuki ed.], Kaidai 98:127–128). An edict in the *Sandai jitsuroku* (fasc. 2, *KT* 4:15) dated 859 states that the Yuima-e lecturer should be appointed to the other two assemblies the following year and then to the Sōgō. Itō Shintetsu ("*Sanbō ekotoba no kenkyū*," pp. 12–13) has searched the literature for the earliest reference to a monk following this path and suggested that it can be dated as early as 843. The *Sanne jōitsuki* cites an unnamed source that gives a date of 828 as the first occurrence of a person following this path (*BZ* [Bussho kankōkai ed.], 123:289a).

    7. Tsugunaga Yoshiteru, *Kokushi daijiten*, 5:361c, s.v. "kōshi."

    8. *Ruijū kokushi, KT* 25:126–127.

    9. The edict establishing the terms and the age limits for the lecturers is found in *Ruijū kokushi, KT* 25:125–126. The *kokubunji* were official monasteries established in each province during the Nara period. While many of them declined during the Heian period, they still continued to play a role (Oishio Chihiro, *Kokubunji no chūseiteki tenkai*).

    10. Minamoto Tamenori, *Sanbō ekotoba*, 1:128.

    11. The term "*ryūgi*" (literally, "establishing the doctrine") begins to appear in Japanese sources about the time of Saichō. In court documents from 806 and 830, the term refers both to the examinations used to qualify monks for appointments to positions as lecturers or readers (the officials who oversaw the Buddhist order in the provinces) and to one of the ranks of the monks who passed those examinations (*Ruijū sandaikyaku, KT* 25:49). The examination came to play a particularly important role in the Yuima-e. I have chosen the term "examination" rather than "debate" (which I have reserved for "*rongi*") for use here because the format of the *ryūgi* is similar to an examination. In fact, the examination system often took the form of a debate and was closely related to the debates in which Ryōgen was interested throughout his life.

    The term "*rissha*" or "*ryūgisha*" means "a person who establishes or has established the teaching." I have generally translated it as "candidate," but the term sometimes refers to a person who has successfully passed the examinations (Ogami, *Hokke daie,* pp. 2–3). Japanese texts sometimes differentiate between these two usages with the terms "*miryūgisha*" (one who has not yet established the teaching) and "*iryūgisha*" (one who has already established the teaching).

12. Horiike, "Yuima-e to kandō no shōshin," pp. 201–204; my description of the development of the format of the Yuima-e is indebted to Horiike's research.

13. *Engishiki, KT* 26:534.

14. Horiike, "Yuima-e to kandō no shōshin," p. 206.

15. *Ruijū sandaikyaku, KT* 25:58.

16. *Ruijū sandaikyaku, KT* 25:61, 63; *Ruijū kokushi, KT* 6:217.

17. *Ruijū kokushi, KT* 6:217. The date of the edict was 885.

18. *Ruijū sandaikyaku, KT* 25:55; *Ruijū kokushi, KT* 6:216.

19. See, for example, the edict of 876, which specified that one of the nine candidates (*ryūgisha*) was to be a Tendai monk (*Ruijū sandaikyaku, KT* 25:58.)

20. Itō Takatoshi, "Kōfukuji Yuima-e," p. 182.

21. Horiike, "Yuima-e to kandō no shōshin," p. 214.

22. Ibid., p. 216.

23. Ibid., p. 227.

24. Itō Takatoshi, "Kōfukuji Yuima-e," pp. 188–189. Itō notes that a number of unpublished manuscripts at Tōdaiji were prepared for the Yuima-e and other debates. Their investigation would yield much information about the topics upon which monks were tested.

25. Itō Takatoshi notes that at some later Yuima-e, *rissha* were given ten problems, five each on the *Hua-yen ching* and on logic ("Kōfukuji Yuima-e," p. 194).

26. The table is taken from Hiraoka, *Tōdaiji,* p. 116. A similar but more detailed table covering the period 859–940 is found in Horiike, "Yuima-e to kandō no shōshin," p. 212.

27. Horiike, "Yuima-e to kandō no shōshin," p. 219.

28. Ibid., pp. 218–219, 222–223.

29. Ibid., p. 221.

30. Ibid., p. 225.

31. No biographies exist for the three Nara monks who are said to have presided over the examination. The monk who administers the examination is known by various terms including professor (*hakushi*), examiner (*shōgisha*), and investigator (*tandai*). "*Hakushi*" occurs rarely in the literature on Tendai examinations. The term "*shōgisha*" is used for the monks who correct any oversights that the lecturers on the *Lotus* or other text might have made. "*Tandai,*" which refers to the most important official in the Tendai examination from Ryōgen's time onward, is the most commonly used term for the person who officiates at and judges the examinations. I have generally translated all of these terms as "judge" or "examiner" when the term occurs in the context of the examinations.

32. *Shakke kanpanki,* in Hanawa Hokinoichi, ed., *Gunsho ruijū,* 24:47; *Tandai kojitsuki,* in Tendai shūten kankōkai, ed., *Tendaishū zensho,* 20:301. The following secondary sources trace the origins of the examination system to Saichō's time: Ozaki Kōjin, *Nihon Tendai rongishi no kenkyū,* p. 72; Ogami Kanchū, *Hokke daie kōgaku ryūgi,* pp. 15–16; Mochizuki and Tsukamoto, eds., *Mochizuki Bukkyō daijiten,* 2:1031c.

The passages in the *Tandai kojitsuki* and *Shakke kanpanki* are vague on a number of points. As a result, Ogami argues that the examinations were held continuously after 801 and that Tendai monks served as judges for the most part after 809 (Ogami, *Hokke daie*, p. 16). I have followed what seems to be a more natural reading of the passage.

The *Shakke kanpanki* was compiled in 1355 (Ono Genmyō, ed., *Bussho kaisetsu daijiten*, 5:12) by Prince Son'en. The *Tandai kojitsuki* (Record of precedents concerning the *tandai*) was compiled by Shungei about 1454; a number of his disciples subsequently added to it. Although the text was compiled too late to be a completely reliable source for Ryōgen's time, it is one of the earliest sources to give an overview of the Tendai examination system.

33. Inoue Mitsusada, "Fujiwara jidai no jōdokyō," p. 156, n. 32.

34. Shibuya, ed., *Tendai zasuki*, p. 42; *NS* 1.11:767–768. Because fourteen *ajari* were originally appointed to the Sōjiin, the number in Ryōgen's proposal would seem to be incorrect or the number of *ajari* may have been decreased by one for some reason. No explanation for this apparent discrepancy has been suggested.

35. Ryōgen's advocacy of Ennin's Esoteric Buddhist tradition is discussed in chapter 5.

36. Inoue, "Fujiwara jidai no jōdokyō," p. 156, n. 32.

37. "Engi Tenryaku gokishō," *NS* 1.11:734.

38. *Seikyūki, NS* 1.11:767. The *Seikyūki* is a text on ritual and court matters probably compiled sometime before 969 by Minamoto no Takaakira (Nihon koten bungaku daijiten henshū iinkai, ed., *Nihon koten bungaku daijiten* 3:573d). Its date of compilation makes it a particularly reliable source for Ryōgen's period.

39. Shibuya, ed., *Tendai zasuki*, p. 56.

40. *Tendai zasuki* variant version cited in *NS* 1.13:219. Hirabayashi Moritoku (*Ryōgen*, p. 107) suggests that Kaikō may have been reluctant to become involved in the antagonism between Ryōgen and Bōsan or might have sympathized with Bōsan's plight, a situation described in chapter 7. Kaikō's lineage is not known. According to the *Onjōji denki* (*BZ* [Bussho kankōkai ed.], 127:66), this examination was the beginning of difficulties between the Sanmon and Jimon factions because Sanmon monks were jealous of the appointment of Jimon monks. However, Ryōgen, a member of the Sanmon faction, probably appointed Bōsan and then Zengei, both members of the Jimon faction, as *tandai* to win their support or to extend his influence as *zasu* to those in Enchin's lineage. However, Bōsan may have rejected Ryōgen's overtures in a rude manner out of frustration over his own desire to become *zasu*, and Ryōgen, in turn, might have resented Bōsan's attitude.

41. Shibuya, ed., *Tendai zasuki*, pp. 42–43. Bōsan, Zengei, and Kakuen were all members of Enchin's lineage (*Jimon denki horoku, BZ* [Bussho kankōkai ed.], 127:323; *Onjōji denki, BZ* [Bussho kankōkai ed.], 127:66). Zengei had served as lecturer at the Yuima-e in 963, making him uniquely qualified to play an important role in Ryōgen's new examination system. He entered the Sōgō as supernumerary master of discipline in 968, the same year he was appointed *tandai,* and eventually rose to lesser bishop (*shōsōzu*). In 970, he was appointed abbot of Onjōji. Very little information survives concerning Kakuen and Shun'ei.

42. *Fusō ryakki, KT* 12:245.

43. *Shūiden, NS* 22.1:68; "Enryakuji Shuryōgon'in Genshin sōzuden," in Hieizan senshuin and Eizan gakuin, ed., *Eshin sōzu zenshū*, 5:661; *Eigaku yōki, GR* 24:553–554; *Sanmon dōshaki, GR* 24:499; *Mon'yōki, T* (*zuzō*), 12:3c; *Mon'yōki, NS* 1.22:102 (this en-

try is not found in the Taishō edition of this text); *Sanmonki, NS* 1.22:101. Sources are also collected in *NS* 1.12:33–37. Variations in the lecture schedule exist. For example, Kawasaki (*Genshin,* p. 13) and Hirabayashi (*Ryōgen,* pp. 91–92) reverse the contents of the spring and summer lectures and note that the *Mahāsaṃnipāta* and large *Prajñāpāramitā* were used alternately in the winter. These differences may have arisen because the lectures changed as they were performed over a number of decades; the original schedule is not known (Ogami, "Yokawa no shugaku seido," p. 59; this article contains a good description of these examinations on pages 59–60). The *Shūiden* (*NS* 1.22:68) contains a note that no more than five candidates were to be tested at each assembly, implying that tests might have been given four times annually, but Hirabayashi states that two candidates were chosen for each of the two assemblies that included examinations (Hirabayashi, *Ryōgen,* p. 92). A note is also found in the *Shūiden* that a series of thirty lectures (one lecture on each of the twenty-eight chapters of the *Lotus* and one each on the opening and capping *sūtras*) might be given during the winter on the *Lotus Sūtra.*

44. Hirabayashi, *Ryōgen,* p. 92; the passage threatening that Ryōgen's body would be exhumed is not found in his will, but in *Sanmonki,* a later text (*NS* 1.12:33).

45. Takeuchi, ed., *Heian ibun* 2:444; Hayami, *Genshin,* pp. 39–40.

46. Ryōgen was the first person to use the term "*kōgaku*" to modify "*ryūgi.*" As the *ryūgi* system spread to other Tendai monasteries, other terms were used to describe it. For example, when Onjōji instituted a system in 1017, it was called *sekigaku ryūgi* (examination for superior learning), and the system that began at Hōjōji in memory of Michinaga (966–1027) in 1035 was called the *kangaku ryūgi* (examinations to encourage learning) (*Nichūreki,* cited in Jingū shichō, ed., *Koji ruien,* 1:416–417).

47. *Tandai kojitsuki, TZ* 20:301; *Shakke kanpanki, GR* 24:47. According to these sources, before Ryōgen's time the *tandai* at the sixth- and twelfth-month assemblies was always a monk from Nara, but the candidate (*rissha*) could be from either Nara or Hiei. After Ryōgen's reform both the *tandai* and *rissha* were from the Tendai school. However, the audience seems still to have been chosen from a variety of temples, including the Tendai school's archrival Kōfukuji (Itō Kiyoo, "Chūsei sōgōsei to Enryakuji," p. 139). The inclusion of monks from other temples probably helped legitimize the Tendai assembly.

48. *Sōgō bunin, BZ* (Suzuki ed.), 65:30c–31a. Ozaki, *Nihon Tendai rongishi no kenkyū,* p. 114. Hirabayashi (*Ryōgen,* p. 105) offers a different interpretation of Zen'yu's appointment, suggesting that Ryōgen may have arranged it. Very little is known about Zen'yu. He participated in the Ōwa debates as the questioner on the fifth day when the chapter on Devadatta from the *Lotus Sūtra* was discussed. Because this chapter contained the description on the sudden realization of Buddhahood by the Nāga girl, the locus classicus for Tendai claims that their exoteric teachings could lead to the realization of Buddhahood in this very life, and because this chapter was one of the most controversial, Zen'yu must have been highly respected as a debater. He was appointed to the Sōgō in 977, eventually rising to be supernumerary lesser bishop. He served as the second *tandai* for the Tendai examinations. Zen'yu was also the author of an early Tendai work on Pure Land, the *Amida shinjūgi (Ten new doubts about Amida)* (Satō Tetsuei, Eizan jōdokyō no kenkyū, pp. 79–83; Nara Hiromoto, "Zen'yu no ōjō shisō.")

49. Hori Daiji, "Ryōgen to Yokawa fukkō (part 2)," pp. 21–22. Ryōgen's role as judge in Kakuun's examination is described in the following section of this chapter (*Zoku honchō ōjōden,* in Inoue and Ōsone, eds., *Ōjōden Hokke genki,* pp. 231–232). Factionalism within the Tendai School is discussed further in the chapters on that subject.

50. Horiike, "Yuima-e," p. 205.

51. Uejima Susumu, "Heian shoki Bukkyō no saikentō."

52. For an example of an edict admonishing monks to maintain the balance between Esoteric and exoteric studies and warning them that no monk who is not trained in both will be appointed *zasu,* see *Sandai jitsuroku, KT* 4:187 (entry for 6-3-866). Esoteric issues are rarely mentioned in early records of examinations; one of the few times questions were asked about Esoteric teachings was when Kakuun was tested (discussed later in this chapter). Examinations based on Esoteric doctrinal issues eventually did develop, but texts concerning them date from the fourteenth century and after (Hazama Jikō, *Nihon Bukkyō no tenkai to sono kichō,* 2:7). Several examples of examination texts on Esoteric topics can be found in Tendai shūten kankōkai, ed., *Tendaishū zensho,* vol. 7.

53. The only comprehensive record of the subjects of examinations around Ryōgen's time is found in the *Mii zokutōki*'s list of examinations in the early eleventh century. Topics associated with the realization of Buddhahood by the Nāga girl in the Devadatta chapter of the *Lotus Sūtra* were among the most popular subjects. Lay believers must have been aware of the importance of this topic during Ryōgen's lifetime. The lectures on the Devadatta chapter were often the high point of lecture series on the *Lotus Sūtra.* Princess Sonshi (d. 985), the ill-fated woman for whom the *Sanbō ekotoba* was composed, recited the chapter as part of her devotions (Edward Kamens, trans., *The Three Jewels,* p. 12).

54. Ryōgen's role in the Sōgō and the significance of this institution in the tenth century are examined in chapter 7.

55. Mikael S. Adolphson, "Monks, Courtiers and Warriors in Premodern Japan," p. 80.

56. Emperor Shirakawa's vow establishing the Enshūji and the Hokke-e and Saishō-e is recorded in *Fusō ryakki, KT* 13:309–310. Although the vow contained provisions for both the Hokke-e and Saishō-e, the latter was not begun until 1082 because Emperor Go-sanjō's death in 1072 resulted in its postponement. The three assemblies are also described in *Shakke kanpanki, GR* 24:24–25, 48.

57. *Shakke kanpanki, GR* 24:24–25, 48–50.

58. Shibuya, ed., *Tendai zasuki,* pp. 155, 159–161. The increasing numbers of candidates are described below in the section on the format of the examination.

59. For an explanation of the significance of this identification, see Groner, *Saichō,* pp. 260–263.

62. Mochizuki and Tsukamoto, eds., *Mochizuki Bukkyō daijiten,* 2:1032bc.

63. For an example, see Kouda, *Wayaku Tendaishū rongi nihyakudai,* and the works included in Tendai shūten kankōkai, ed., *Tendaishū zensho,* vol. 23.

64. Sonehara Satoshi, *Tokugawa Ieyasu shinkakka e no michi,* pp. 203–231.

65. For statistics of the average number of candidates since 1599, see Take Kakuchō, *Hokke daie kōgaku ryūgi ni tsuite,* p. 21.

66. The modern format of the ceremony has been described in detail by

Ogami, *Hokke daie;* Tsukuma Sonnō, "Hokke daie Kōgaku ryūgi"; and Take, *Hokke daie.* Take's study includes lists of the ceremony since 1589. For lists of special terminology and readings used in the examinations, see *Eisen gihō, TZ* 24:282–294; and Kouda, *Tendaishū rongi nihyakudai,* pp. 673–687, 717–722. Routine examinations are based on the summaries of issues presented in *Tendaishū rongi hyakudai* (One hundred issues of Tendai debate) or *Nihyakudai* (Two hundred issues); see Kiyohara Ekō, "Tendai rongi no keisei katei," p. 83. The symbolism of the ceremony after it was interpreted through *hongaku* theory is summarized in Mochizuki and Tsukamoto, eds., *Mochizuki Bukkyō daijiten,* 2:1031c–1032a.

65. Nomoto Kakujō, editor of the Zoku *Tendaishū zensho,* noted that examination manuals and records of examinations were compiled until the twentieth century. Many of these texts demonstrate the rigor of the examinations (discussion at the Second Conference on the *Lotus Sūtra* and Japanese Culture, Tokyo, Dec. 20, 1987). However, the large numbers of monks undergoing the examination in recent centuries would have precluded rigorous testing of all of them. Moreover, the increasing numbers of sons of nobles that appeared in the examinations probably would have led to a decline in rigor, much as it did in the Yuima-e.

66. Ryōgen had banned colorful robes. See rule no. 14 of the twenty-six regulations compiled by Ryōgen (*Heian ibun,* 2:435 [document 303]); for a translation, see appendix 8.

67. *Zoku honchō ōjōden,* in Inoue and Ōsone, eds., *Ōjōden Hokke genki,* pp. 231–232. Kakuun is considered the founder of the Dannain bloc within the Tendai school. Ryōgen is reported to have made similar statements concerning the balance between exoteric and Esoteric Buddhism in Kakuchō's *Sanmitsu ryōken* (*T* 75:657c).

68. See rule no. 3 in Ryōgen's list of twenty-six rules governing the Tendai school (*Heian ibun,* 2:431–432 [document 303]); for a translation, see appendix 8. In the *Mii zokutōki,* most of the candidates were in their thirties, but Shōhan in 1021 was fifteen years old and had only seven years of seniority (*BZ* [Suzuki ed.], 67:201a).

69. *Mii zokutōki, BZ* (Suzuki ed.), 67:201–203.

70. Shibuya, ed., *Tendai zasuki,* pp. 56, 120, 122–124, 150, 157. The central role that the *zasu* came to play in the examinations is reflected by the occasional cancellation of the examinations when a *zasu* had not yet been installed; for example, see ibid., p. 124. The increase in numbers of candidates obviously affected the role that the *kōgaku ryūgi* played in the Tendai school. Although the role of the *kōgaku ryūgi* for Tendai monks during Jien's tenure as *zasu* has not been determined, Jien seems to have placed more emphasis on the *kangakukō* (lectures to encourage learning) than on the *kōgaku ryūgi* as a means to revive scholarship in the Tendai school. Like the *kōgaku ryūgi,* the *kangakukō* was designed to promote studies beyond Tendai doctrine (Taga Munehaya, *Jien,* pp. 66–69, 108–110).

71. *Mon'yōki,* cited in Ogami, *Hokke daie kōgaku ryūgi,* p. 18. I have been unable to find the original citation in the *Mon'yōki,* but this text is massive, covering the larger parts of two volumes in the Taishō canon. Similar allotments based on geography were used for other rituals on Mount Hiei.

72. *Ruijū kokushi, KT* 6:313; Ogami, *Hokke daie,* p. 97. A format of ten questions to be answered orally also was used in civil service examinations; see Robert Borgen, *Sugawara no Michizane and the Early Heian Court,* p. 74.

73. *Tandai kojitsuki, TZ* 20:316, 320. A similar sentiment is expressed in the *Tandai jitsujoki,* quoted in Ogami, *Hokke daie,* p. 93. Civil service examinations were graded even more strictly than the Tendai examinations; see Borgen, *Sugawara no Michizane,* p. 132.

74. A diagram of the box, the sticks, and a discussion of its dimensions is found in *Tandai kojitsuki, TZ* 20:305–306; a photograph of one of them is included in Tsukamoto, ed., *Mochizuki Bukkyō daijiten,* vol. 9, illustration no. 1730. Later, dimensions of the *san* varied depending on one's lineage.

75. Ogami (*Hokke daie,* pp. 99–100) gives several examples of these short versions of questions and notes that several collections of them are extant as manuscripts in the Kanazawa bunko.

76. Ten questioners are mentioned in the Onjōji examinations from 1017 to 1033 in the *Mii zokutōki* (*BZ* [Suzuki ed.], 67:201). But five questioners for each candidate were used when Onjōji allowed two candidates per year in 1034, retaining a total of ten for the examinations. They experimented briefly with six questioners for several candidates in 1038, but quickly abandoned that arrangement.

A late work, the *Taikō mondōshū kuketsu* (cited in Ozaki, *Rongishi,* p. 162) indicates that the question-and-answer format in compilations of questions was not used during Ryōgen's lifetime; if this is correct, then the use of questioners may also have been a later addition to the examination format. However, a set format for questions is mentioned in Senkan's *Jūroku gika mokuroku* (*TZ* 23:25a). To the best of my knowledge, the authenticity of Senkan's text has not been discussed, but the attribution is not seriously questioned in Mochizuki and Tsukamoto, eds., *Mochizuki Bukkyō daijiten* (9:133b) or by Ozaki (*Rongishi,* p. 169); it is not mentioned, however, in Ogami Kanchū's thorough study of the establishment of *gika,* "Tendai gika no seiritsu katei," indicating that Ogami probably doubted its authenticity. The weight of the evidence would seem to suggest that questioners might have been added to the format of the *kōgaku ryūgi* several decades after its establishment.

77. *Tandai jitsujoki,* cited in Ogami, *Hokke daie,* pp. 94–95. A slightly different format is recorded in *Tandai kojitsuki, TZ* 20:317. A five-question format is also found in the *Jūroku gika mokuroku* attributed to Senkan (*TZ* 23:25a).

78. *Tandai kojitsuki, TZ* 20:316.

79. Ibid., 316, 327.

80. *Mii zokutōki, BZ* (Suzuki ed.), 67:201b. The two candidates who were given only one topic were young, only twenty-one and twenty-two years old. Scores are not recorded for either, suggesting that they might not have passed. Later candidates always had two topics even though some of them were as young as fourteen.

81. Tsukuma Sonnō, "Hokke daie kōgaku ryūgi," p. 47.

82. *BZ* (Suzuki ed.), 67:201b–c.

83. *Tandai kojitsuki, TZ* 20:325; Ogami, *Hokke daie,* p. 95. The scores that are known from other students in Ennin's lineage during the late tenth century were generally eight or nine passes. Other sources state that Genshin's score was nine passes, one failure ("Tendai hokkeshū sōjō kechimyakuzu," *NS* 2.11:283; "Kenmitsu-shū keizu," *NS* 2.11:285).

84. *Genshin sōzuden, NS* 2.11:298–299; *Enryakuji Shuryōgon'in Genshin sōzuden,* in Kawasaki Tsuneyuki, *Genshin,* p. 406. Shioiri Ryōchū (*BKD* 1:274–275) notes that the *Genshin sōzuden* was compiled within forty-five years of Genshin's death and is

one of the most important sources for his biography. For Kawasaki's analysis of Genshin's examinations, see *Genshin,* p. 14. The Tendai examinations were not alone in being graded strictly; civil service examinations sometimes were also graded in a very rigorous fashion (Borgen, *Sugawara no Michizane,* pp. 80–84).

85. Shibuya, ed., *Tendai zasuki,* pp. 195–196.

86. *Tandai shidai,* included in *Tandai kojitsuki, T* 20:303; this source is discussed in Satō Tetsuei, *Eizan jōdokyō no kenkyū,* p. 80. The *Tandai shidai* is a list of judges for the debates from the first to the seventy-seventh (appointed in 1231). Dates and ranks at the time of appointment are from Hirabayashi and Koike, eds., *Sōryaku sōran,* a compilation based on the *Sōgō bunin.*

87. Ogami, *Hokke daie,* p. 129.

88. For typical entries concerning the appointment of secretaries, see Shibuya, ed., *Tendai zasuki,* pp. 185, 188. The listing of recorders along with candidates indicates that these positions were probably filled every year and not held for several consecutive years. According to some sources, recorders were to have ten years of seniority as a monk, while candidates were to have twenty (*Shakke kanpanki, GR* 24:51).

89. *Honchō bunshū, KT* 30:203, 224–226, 245–250, 321; *Chōya gunsai, KT* 29A:36.

90. *Mii zokutōki, BZ* (Suzuki ed.), 67:201–204. This text was compiled by Sontsū (1427–1516) in 1483 from documents at Onjōji. For discussions of these topics from a Hossō perspective, see Stanley Weinstein, "The Kanjin Kakumushō."

91. Fujimoto Fumio ("Nihon Tendai ni okeru yuishiki no kenkyū") lists the Yogācāra texts brought back by Ennin and Enchin and texts on Yogācāra written by Tendai monks.

92. Sixteen of the thirty monks who participated at a series of thirty lectures at the Tōin at Onjōji in 1345 were concerned with *Abhidharmakośa* topics (*Mii zokutōki, BZ* [Suzuki ed.], 67:213b). An example of debates between Tendai and Nara monks that included *abhidharma* topics is found in a series of eight lectures on the *Lotus Sūtra* held in 1131 at the Hosshōji (founded at the wish of Emperor Shirakawa in 1077). Monks from both the Nara schools and Mount Hiei were invited to participate at these lectures. While the primary topics of the lectures were the *Lotus Sūtra,* a text on which both Tendai and Hossō had an extensive commentarial tradition, the secondary topics were taken from such sources as the *Yogācārabhūmi* (*T* no. 1579), the *Jñānaprasthāna* (*T* no. 1544), and the *Vimuttimagga* (*T* no. 1648), texts that would have required a detailed knowledge of Hossō and *abhidharma* doctrine. Primary sources for this debate are quoted by Ogami Kanchū, "Rongijō yori mitaru Nanto Hokurei no kankei," pp. 568–569.

93. Ono Katsutoshi, *Nittō guhō gyōreki no kenkyū,* 1:91, 94; Fukuhara Ryōgon, "Nihon no *Kusha* gakusha," p. 5; Fujimoto Fumio, "Tendai ni okeru *Kusharon* kenkyū no keifu." According to the *Mii zokutōki* (*BZ* [Suzuki ed.], 67:163), an Onjōji monk named Engen (1173–1239) was the author of a work on *Abhidharmakośa* with the title *Zendanshō.* An extant manuscript of the work is mentioned in *BKD* (6:399). The texts that Enchin brought back focused on the verses of the *Abhidharmakośa* rather than the prose sections; this approach was followed by subsequent Tendai monks (Funahashi Suisai, "Kushashū no ryūden oyobi sono kyōgi," pp. 159–160). According to Shimaji Daitō, Enchin began a separate tradition of *Abhidharmakośa* scholarship based on Yüan-hui's commentary that competed with that used by the

Nara schools (Shimaji Daitō, *Nihon Bukkyō kyōgakushi,* pp. 95, 119. Tendai interest in *abhidharma* was based partly on its importance for understanding Madhyamaka thought.

94. Nemu Kazuchika ("Genshin no *Inmyōronsho shisōi ryakuchūshaku* ni tsuite") notes that Genshin studied logic both with Tendai monks such as Ryōgen and Hossō monks such as Shinkō (933–1004), a disciple of Chūzan, the Hossō monk who defeated Ryōgen at the Ōwa debates. Genshin's views on logic, however, were his own and did not one-sidedly follow any of his teachers.

95. Genshin's work on logic occupies more than two hundred pages in his collected works Hieizan senshuin and Eizan gakuin, eds., (*Eshin sōzu zenshū,* 5:51–284). For Genshin's explanation of the compilation of the text and sending it to China, see ibid., pp. 51, 284; *BZ* (Suzuki ed.), 97 (*kaidai*): 171–174. Japanese Hossō monks compiled a number of commentaries on logical issues around this time.

96. For a full discussion of the influence of Yogācāra on Genshin's thought, see Yagi Kōe, *Eshin kyōgaku no kisoteki kenkyū,* pp. 35–120, 182–302. In addition to the works listed by Yagi, Nemu Kazuchika ("Eshin sōzu to *Jōyuishikiron,*" p. 138) reports the existence of a manuscript of a commentary on the *Ch'eng wei-shih lun,* the *Yuishikiron sho,* by Genshin. The text has not been published in any collection of Buddhist works, and Nemu had not been able to see a copy of it.

97. Hieizan senshuin and Eizan gakuin, eds., *Eshin sōzu zenshū,* 4:1.

98. The *Daijō tai Kushashō* occupies the entire fourth volume of Genshin's collected works, *Eshin sōzu zenshū.* Genshin's approach differed from that of Saichō, who was intent on using discrepancies in the Yogācāra texts translated by Paramārtha and Hsüan-tsang. Also see Nemu, "Eshin sōzu to *Jōyuishikiron,*" p. 140.

99. *Zoku honchō ōjōden,* in Inoue and Ōsone ed., *Ōjōden Hokke genki,* p. 233.

100. Ibid., p. 232. The notes (p. 232) identify Henku (d. 1030) as a Hossō monk from Kōfukuji, but he was in fact a Tendai monk. Apparently he has been confused with the Hossō monk Kyōku (978–1044) because the context of the story suggests that Kakuun must have been examining a Hossō monk; however, if Kakuun was in fact examining a Tendai monk on Hossō doctrine, then the story may be interpreted as additional evidence that Tendai monks seriously studied Hossō during the eleventh century.

101. *Mii zokutōki, BZ* (Suzuki ed.), 67:201–204.

102. Fujimoto Fumio, "Chikū-sen *Inmyō ken sanshi* ni tsuite."

103. *Fusō ryakki, KT* 13:312–313; *Honchō kōsōden, BZ* (Suzuki ed.), 63:80c–81b. Raizō established the Enshūji monastery and the Saishō and Hokke assemblies held at it. He invited both Tendai and Nara monks to these meetings. Raishin was a Hossō monk who rose to be archbishop and was noted for his skill in logic. The *Fusō ryakki* was compiled sometime between 1094 and 1107 (Nihon koten bungaku daijiten henshū iinkai, ed., *Nihon koten bungaku daijiten,* 5:324), close to the time of the dispute over the place of logic in Tendai studies.

104. Takemura Shōhō, *Inmyōgaku: Kigen to hensen,* pp. 23–24.

105. Hsüan-tsang had heard lectures on Dignāga's *Pramāṇasamuccaya* in India, but he did not translate the text. According to one tradition, I-ching translated the text into Chinese, but it was soon lost (Takemura, *Inmyōgaku,* pp. 24–25).

106. Wen-kuei's work on logic has survived in part. For information on textual problems, see ibid., pp. 32–34.

107. Both contained in Hsin-wen-feng, ed., *Wan Hsü-tsang-ching,* vol. 44.

108. Nemu Kazuchika, "Tōdai Tendaisō Shōkan no inmyōgaku ni tsuite."

109. Takemura, *Inmyōgaku,* p. 67–72.

110. Ibid., p. 68.

111. Ibid., p. 77 f. Takemura notes that similar tendencies may have been occurring in China during the Sung dynasty.

112. More details about the study of logic by Tendai monks are included in chapter 4. Raizō's proposal to abandon the use of logic has been discussed previously in this chapter.

113. Nomoto Kakujō, "Tendai no rongi," p. 149.

114. For the Ōwa debates, see chapter 6. The importance of the Ōwa debates on topic selections is mentioned by both traditional and modern sources. For examples, see Ozaki, *Rongishi,* p. 160, 163. For a discussion of the influence of the Ōwa debates and other confrontations between Hossō and Tendai monks on examination topics, see Ogami, "Ōwa no shūron to shūyō gika no kakuritsu."

115. Sontsū, *Kamoku sengushō,* cited in Ozaki, *Rongishi,* p. 156. For information on the *Tendai hokkeshū gishū* (*T* no. 2366), see Groner, *Saichō,* p. 288. This is one of the few cases in which Gishin's work seems to have been influential. In recent years, it has once again become an important text because Sekiguchi Shindai (*Tendai kyōgaku no kenkyū,* 684–685) has argued convincingly that it serves as a more complete and effective introductory text to Tendai doctrine than Chegwan's more popular *T'ien-t'ai ssu-chiao-i* (*T* no. 1931; Buddhist Seminar of Hawaii, trans., *T'ien-t'ai Buddhism*), which focuses one-sidedly on classification of doctrines. Gishin's text was translated into French and carefully annotated; see Robert, *Les doctrines de l'ècole japonaise Tendaï.* Paul Swanson plans to publish an unannotated English translation in the Bukkyō dendō kyōkai series.

116. Take, *Hokke daie,* p. 2.

117. For more on Tendai discussions of *sokushin jōbutsu,* see Groner, "The Lotus Sūtra and Early Tendai Discussions of the Realization of Buddhahood with This Very Body" and "Shortening the Path." Another article touches on the role of debate in the formulation of early views of *sokushin jōbutsu;* see Groner, "Tendai Interpretations of the Realization of Buddhahood with This Very Body." Ozaki (*Rongishi,* pp. 116–117) suggests that the issue of the realization of Buddhahood was probably the central issue in the debate literature.

118. The term "*shiki*" may also have been used to describe a monk's own views on the performance of Esoteric ritual. Several such works attributed to Saichō and Ennin are listed in Tendai bibliographies. See, for example, *Enryakuji mitsujō ryakumokuroku* (*BZ* [Suzuki ed.], 96:1–3) and *Mitsujō senjutsu mokuroku* (ibid., pp. 4–6).

119. Hayami, *Genshin,* pp. 51–52.

120. Sueki Fumihiko, *Heian shoki Bukkyō shisō no kenkyū,* pp. 655–690.

121. Ōkubo Ryōshun's study of Ryōgen's text on how practitioners are drawn toward the ultimate goal is noteworthy as a contribution toward an understanding of Ryōgen's doctrinal views ("Ryōgen-sen '*Hishōgi shiki*' ni tsuite"; and "Nihon Tendai ni okeru hishō-setsu no tenkai." Also note Misaki Gisen's *Shikanteki biishiki no tenkai* with its discussion of some of the aesthetic issues in this literature.

122. Annen's *Sokushin jōbutsugi shiki* can be found in Tendaishū sōsho kankōkai,

ed., *Tendaishū sōsho: Annen senshū*, pp. 179–236; *BZ* (Suzuki ed.), 41:68–84; Sueki, *Heian shoki Bukkyō shisō*, pp. 523–654. The attribution to Annen is criticized by Nara Hiromoto in "Godaiin Annen no chosaku," pp. 41–43. Other studies of the *Sokushin jōbutsugi shiki* do not raise the issue of its authenticity. For example, Ikeyama Issaien ("Annen no *Sokushin jōbutsugi shiki* to sono kechimyaku") simply treats the text as authentic, although his discussion indirectly counters Nara by demonstrating that the text deals with issues that were important to Tendai monks during the ninth century.

123. Ōkubo Ryōshun, "Nihon Bukkyō no kyōgaku kenkyū to bunken," pp. 5–10.

124. Yūki Reimon, "Nihon no yuishiki kenkyū shijō ni okeru shiki jidai no settei ni tsuite," pp. 1–5.

125. The list of *shiki* are compiled from Tendai bibliographies, particularly the *Nihonkoku Tendaishū shōsho mokuroku* (*BZ* [Suzuki ed.], 95:191b–192b), which was compiled during the Muromachi period. In the *Nihonkoku Tendaishū shōsho mokuroku*, examination texts are listed together, giving a sense of how examination topics might have been organized at that time. The bibliography includes apocryphal works and sometimes does not mention authentic texts. Because few of the *shiki* are extant, the determination of their authenticity is difficult. They are listed here to give a sense of the popularity of each subject. Among the modern studies that discuss examination topics and *shiki* are Ozaki, *Rongishi*, pp. 121–128; and Ogami Kanchū, "Ōwa no shūron to shūyō gika no kakuritsu," p. 67.

126. The list of extant works comes from Ozaki, *Rongishi*, p. 124, supplemented with several texts by Genshin in the third volume of Hieizan senshuin and Eizan gakuin, eds., *Eshin sōzu zenshū*. Other texts may be found in the *Tendai shōbushū shaku* (*BZ* [Suzuki ed.], 41:3–187), a collection of shorter Tendai works. A number of bibliographical issues must be resolved. For example, Anne's text on *sokushin jōbutsu* may actually be the *Min'yu benwakushō* found in *DZ*. Rinshō's text on the same subject may be close to or identical to that ascribed to his teacher Ennin. Senkan's *Sokushin jōbutsugi shiki* was planned for the continuation of the *Dainihon Bukkyō zensho* but was not published (*BKD* 7:78a); however, Sueki has included it in his *Heian shoki Bukkyō shisō*, pp. 691–704. Several other texts are mentioned in prospectus for the *Tendaishū zensho* published in 1935 but were not actually included in the set. In addition, some texts called *shiki* on topics not included in the usual sets of examination subjects were compiled, such as Genshin's *Sangaigi shiki* on cosmology and several texts attributed to Ennin (Ogami, "Tendai gika no seiritsu katei," p. 276).

127. The authenticity of texts on debates attributed to early Tendai authors such as Saichō and Ennin is very difficult to determine because almost all of the bibliographies of these texts are Muromachi and Tokugawa compilations. Ogami ("Ōwa no shūron to shūyō gika no kakuritsu," p. 67) argues that several discussions of debate topics attributed to Saichō and Ennin can probably be taken as authentic because they were listed in a bibliography by the Tendai monk Gennichi (846–922). However, Gennichi's bibliography survives because it was incorporated into the first fascicle of Kenjun's (1740–1812) *Shoshū shōsho mokuroku* (*BZ* [Suzuki ed.], 95:66–68) while the texts that Ogami cites are found in the second fascicle (ibid., pp. 81–88), which was compiled by Kenjun to supplement Gennichi's bibliography.

128. *Tendai kahyō*, *BZ* (Suzuki ed.), 42:122c–127b.

129. Ozaki (*Rongishi*, p. 103) lists numbers of topics for several texts. Some of

the earliest collections of *shūyō* are also discussed in Ogami, "*Shūmanshū* to *Shūen-shū* ni tsuite.*"

130. Mochizuki and Tsukamoto, eds., *Mochizuki Bukkyō daijiten,* 10:1111c. Although the terms "*shūyō*" and "*gika*"appear in early debate literature, "*mon'yō*" seems to be a later term. Sueki Fumihiko defines "*mon'yō*" as questions concerning passages in the writings of major Tendai thinkers (*Nihon Bukkyō shisōshi ronkō,* p. 325). The definitions of the terms vary over time, as does the rigor with which the categories are applied.

131. *Tandai kojitsu shiki, TZ* 20:343b.

132. *Kōen kojitsu oboegaki,* cited in Ozaki, *Rongishi,* pp. 154–155. Some debate texts (*Tandai kojitsu shiki, TZ*20:347–348, and Ozaki, *Rongishi,* pp. 154–155) include references to *ehon* editions (texts in which the main texts and principal commentaries are printed together) of Chih-i's works that often correspond to the references in the Tada Kōryū and Tada Kōbun, eds., *Tendai daishi zenshū,* and Bukkyō taikei kankōkai, ed., *Bukkyō taikei,* editions of Chih-i's *Fa-hua hsüan-i, Fa-hua wen-chü, Mo-ho chih-kuan,* and *T'ien-t'ai ssu-chiao i.* Some of the differences in lists of *gika* are surveyed in Ono Genmyō, ed., *Mochizuki Bukkyō daijiten,* 9:133b; and Ogami Kanchū, "Tendai gika no seiritsu katei."

133. Senkan's *Jūroku gika mokuroku* (List of the sixteen examination topics), a very short text occupying half a page in the *TZ* (23:25a), has a slightly different list, as do the *Tandai kojitsuki* (*TZ*20:309) and other texts. Since Senkan was one of the most prolific authors of *shiki,* he might very well have been the author of a list of major categories of examination topics. In addition, *shiki* on most of the major topics had been compiled by Senkan's time. The text is also significant for its description of the format of the five subsequent questions asked by the monks appointed to interrogate the candidate. The establishment of *gika* is attributed to Ryōgen by some later examination manuals, such as the *Gika sōdenshō* (cited in Mochizuki and Tsukamoto, eds., *Mochizuki Bukkyō daijiten,* 9:132c) and the *Tandai igi kojitsuron* (cited in Ozaki, *Rongishi,* p. 168). According to the *Tandai igi kojitsuron, gika* were also used at Kōfukuji, indicating that Tendai examination and debate formats probably had been adopted from the Hossō tradition.

134. Fujihira Kanden, "Gika shohon no rondai henka."

135. Kiyohara, "Tendai rongi no keisei katei," p. 74.

136. This traditional account attributing the establishment of *shūyō* to Ryōgen is based on the *Tandai kojitsuki* (Record of precedents for judges; *TZ*20:307b). Kan'in was a disciple of Ryōgen and Genshin. A description of *shūyō* along with a comparative chart showing the organization of these topics in works from the Eshin and Danna lineages, as well as from Kantō Tendai, is found in Mochizuki and Tsukamoto, eds., *Mochizuki Bukkyō daijiten,* 9:377–379. The comparative lists of topics match so closely that they probably were based on an early list compiled by Ryōgen (Ogami, "*Shūmanshū,*" p. 701).

137. The example of Fa-yün is found in *Gika sōdenshō* (Excerpts from transmissions of debate topics; *TZ* 23:29). The *Tendaishū rongi nihyakudai* (Two hundred Tendai debate topics; ed. Kouda), an eighteenth-century manual, is divided into three sections consisting of 94 *shūyō,* 43 *gika,* and 70 *mon'yō;* but then many of the topics in all three sections are identified as belonging to the traditional sixteen *gika.* Also see Ozaki, *Rongishi,* p. 170, for a brief discussion of this issue.

138. *Reikō mondō kakiawase, TZ,* vol. 23.

139. The three categories are not used in Take's study of the Hokke-daie (Great Lotus assembly) over the last four centuries. Instead, he divides the topics into primary and secondary topics; the same subject material can be used in either format. For a list of the frequency of topics over the last four centuries, see Take, *Hokke daie,* pp. 28–31.

140. Kiyohara, "Tendai rongi no keisei katei," p. 77.

141. For a description of some of these examinations, see Ogami, "Yokawa no shugaku seido"; and Ogami, *Hokke daie,* pp. 11–14.

Chapter 9. Rebuilding the Tendai Establishment on Mount Hiei

1. All that is known about Zōkai is that he held an appointment as one of the ten court-appointed meditation masters (*jūzenji*) and that he was from the Jō-shin'in on Hiei (*Shūiden, NS* 1.22:59). The central role of the Tōdō area can be understood by referring to one of the earliest lists of buildings planned for Mount Hiei, the nine halls (*kuin*). Eight of the nine halls were in Tōdō. The remaining one was the Hall for the Western Pagoda. For a list of the nine halls, see Groner, *Saichō,* p. 111.

2. *Fusō ryakki, KT* 12:243; *Nihon kiryaku KT* 11:99; *Tendai zasuki,* p. 42; *Shūiden,* p. 83; *Eigaku yōki, GR* 24:513. Some sources list the date as the ninth month, but the tenth month is generally accepted as correct.

3. Shibuya, ed., *Tendai zasuki,* p. 42.

4. *Fusō ryakki, KT* 12:212. Some sources list the year as 935 (Shibuya, ed., *Tendai zasuki,* p. 35).

5. The hall was first known as Hieizanji (Mount Hiei temple) and later as the One-vehicle Meditation Hall (Ichijō shikan'in) to Saichō. Its other title, Central Hall (Chūdō or Konpon chūdō), probably came from its location between the library and Mañjuśrī's Tower (*Eigaku yōki, GR* 24:509–512; *Sanmon dōshaki, GR* 24:468–471; Kageyama, *Hieizanji,* pp. 39–43).

6. The building is described as "*shimen,*" a term I have interpreted here as four bays deep in accordance with a description in Kageyama Haruki (*Hieizan,* p. 132) and Ono Susumu (*Iwanami kogo jiten,* p. 1271d). The term "*men*" is thus contrasted with the term "*ken,*" which refers to the number of bays lengthwise. However, most other dictionaries do not include this meaning; according to the *Nihon kokugo daijiten* ([Tokyo: Shōgakkan, 1974], 10:111a), during the Heian and Kamakura periods, the term "*shimen*" referred to eaves surrounding a building on all four sides. The interpretation of the term "*men*" thus may depend on the context and dating of the passage. The term sometimes can be interpreted as meaning "square."

7. The term "*mago bisashi*" generally refers to additional eaves off the main eaves; but the *Nihon kokugo daijiten,* 18:336b includes a definition referring to rooms off the eaves and has a passage concerning Ryōgen as the *locus classicus.*

8. *Genkō shakusho, BZ* (Suzuki ed.), 62:86c–87a.

9. *Tengen sannen chūdō kuyō ganmon, GR* 24:590–591; *Ganmonshū, NS* 1.18:28–30.

10. Shibuya, ed., *Tendai zasuki*, p. 42.

11. I have benefited from the detailed chronology of Ryōgen's activities by Take Kakuchō, "Jie daishiden (Ryōgen) no shōgai to sono gyōseki."

12. The fire at Gangyōji is mentioned briefly in Morosuke's diaries, *Kyūreki* (entry for 3-8-957, *NS* 1.10:321). Since Ryōgen had been appointed *ajari* at the temple six years earlier, he probably participated in the reconstruction efforts.

13. Classical Chinese T'ien-t'ai meditation has been brilliantly described by Daniel Stevenson in "The Four Kinds of Samādhi in Early T'ien-t'ai Buddhism" and "The T'ien-t'ai Four Forms of Samadhi"; see also Donner and Stevenson, *The Great Calming and Contemplation.*

14. Groner, *Saichō*, pp. 71, 139, 156, 159, 193.

15. Ibid., p. 75.

16. *Eigaku yōki, GR* 24:526a; *Enkai jūyō, TZ* 8:38b; Shigematsu Akihisa, "Eizan ni okeru shishu zanmaiin no tenkai," pp. 207; 222, n. 4.

17. According to the *Sanmon dōshaki* (*GR* 24:471b, 476b) and the *Eigaku yōki* (*GR* 24:525a), in 818, Saichō divided his disciples into groups and had them practice all four types of meditation. However, these sources were compiled several centuries later, and earlier sources have no entries corroborating this tradition.

18. *Eizan daishiden, DZ* 5 (*bekkan*): 27.

19. Minamoto no Tamenori, *Sanbō ekotoba* 2:19–24; Kamens, *Three Jewels*, p. 254.

20. *Eigaku yōki, GR* 24:524.

21. Honda, ed., *Yakuchū Jikaku daishiden*, p. 111; Saeki, *Jikaku daishiden no kenkyū*, p. 250.

22. *Sanmon dōshaki, GR* 24:481b.

23. *Tōnomine ryakki, BZ* (Bussho kankōkai ed.), 118:496a, 501a–b; *Tōnomine engi, BZ* (Bussho kankōkai ed.), 118:483a. Also see the discussions of Tōnomine and Zōga in chapter 6 and appendix 4.

24. Takagi, *Heian jidai Hokke Bukkyōshi kenkyū*, p. 208.

25. Ibid., pp. 207–208.

26. This passage is close to the *Fa-hua san-mei hsing-fa*, translated by Daniel Stevenson in "The T'ien-t'ai Four Forms of Samadhi," p. 470. Although the *Fa-hua san-mei hsing-fa* mentions the importance of repentance, it leaves no doubt that the ritual is essentially a meditation on emptiness. The use of the ceremony against the four *pārājika* offenses is significant because traditionally such offenses would have resulted in permanent expulsion from the order for a monk or nun.

27. Minamoto no Tamenori, *Sanbō ekotoba*, 2:19–24. The translation is by the author; for a translation of the full text, see Kamens, *Three Jewels*, pp. 254–259.

28. McCullough and McCullough, *Flowering Fortunes*, 2:510; Matsumura and Yamanaka, eds., *Eiga monogatari*, 1:453.

29. Shibuya, ed., *Tendai zasuki*, p. 43; *Shūiden, NS* 1.22:59–60.

30. The entries from medieval sources concerning Ryōgen's decision to move the Constant-walking Meditation Hall are inconsistent. I have followed the analysis by Mitsumori Katsumi, "Hieizan Tōdō Saitō no Jōgyōdō no kōhai ni tsuite," pp. 269–272.

31. "Tendai zasu Ryōgen goyuigō" (document no. 305), in Takeuchi Rizō, ed., *Heian ibun*, 2:447; translated in appendix 8. For discussions of the dual practice of

chanting the *Lotus Sūtra* and the *nenbutsu,* see Kiuchi Gyōō, "Chō daimoku yū nen-butsu"; Satō Tetsuei, *Eizan jōdokyō no kenkyū,* pp. 46–47.

32. Little evidence that Saichō was interested in Pure Land practices exists. Al-though the phrase "Namu Amida Butsu" is found in his *Shugo kokkaishō* (*DZ* 2:607), it is used as an exclamation in a discussion of Tokuitsu's views, not as an expression of piety. According to the *Eigaku yōki* (*GR* 24:525) and *Sanmon dōshaki* (*GR* 24:471c), Saichō had asked Ennin to practice the meditation, but no early corroborating ev-idence for this claim exists.

33. Saeki, *Jikaku daishiden no kenkyū,* p. 269; *Eigaku yōki, GR* 24:471–472a.

34. *Sanmon dōshaki, GR* 24:473. The Jōdoin is listed as one of the nine chapels that Saichō is said to have planned, but the list is probably a later fabrication (Groner, *Saichō,* p. 111). It is still the site of Saichō's mausoleum.

35. Saeki, *Jikaku daishiden no kenkyū,* p. 269; *Eigaku yōki, GR* 24:471–472a. A sim-ilar note about Fa-chao is found in Annen's *Kongōkai taijuki* (*T* 75:179a–b); the name Fa-tao in the passage is probably an error for Fa-chao. The Chu-lin-ssu was estab-lished by Fa-chao between 785 and 805 and was one of the few temples permitted to confer ordinations by the court.

36. For Ennin's contacts with Fa-chao's practice, see Reischauer, trans., *Ennin's Diary,* pp. 216–217, 228, 300; Ono Katsutoshi, *Nittō guhō junrei kōki no kenkyū,* 2:429, 3:352; *Sanmon dōshaki, GR* 24:471b–472a. Ennin brought back several texts on Pure Land, including Tao-ch'o's *An-lo chi* and hymns by Shan-tao (Ono, *Nittō guhō junrei kōki no kenkyū,* 3:354–355). A ritual text by Fa-chao is listed in Ennin's *Nittō shin-guhō mokuroku,* in Ono, *Nittō guhō junrei kōki no kenkyū,* 4:596. Ennin did not bring back an expanded (*kō*) three-fascicle version of the ritual text. The last two fascicles of this work have been found and published in fascicle 85 of the *Taishō shinshū daizōkyō.*

37. For a thorough study of Fa-chao, see Tsukamoto Zenryū's *Tō chūki no Jōdokyō: toku ni Hōshō hosshi no kenkyū,* reprinted in Tsukamoto Zenryū, *Tsukamoto Zenryū chosakushū;* for a brief survey in English, see Stanley Weinstein, *Buddhism under the T'ang,* pp. 73–74.

38. *Wu-liang shou ching, T* 12:273c. Stanley Weinstein notes that the phrase "five sounds" is not found in the Sanskrit text (*Buddhism under the T'ang,* p. 175, n. 28). According to a story included in the early Kamakura period text, the *Kojidan* (Talks about ancient matters), Ennin taught his disciples the tunes to be used in reciting the *sūtra* by using a *shakuhachi* (Kobayashi Yasuharu, ed., *Kojidan,* 1:224). In fact, a flute used by Ennin to teach the five modes is listed in an early record (Satō Te-tsuei, "Zentōin kenzai mokuroku ni tsuite," p. 109). The translation of "*wu-hui*" is problematic; Weinstein (*Buddhism under the T'ang,* p. 175, n. 8) suggests "rhythms"; Sonoda Kōyū ("Yama no nenbutsu," p. 178) suggests that "tonality" or "mode" is close to the sense of the term. The five modes seem to have involved a steadily in-creasing pace as well as changes in melody.

39. Minamoto no Tamenori, *Sanbō ekotoba,* 2:116–118; the translation is by the author, but also see Kamens, *Three Jewels,* pp. 342–344, for the full text.

40. Mabuchi and Kunisaki, eds., *Konjaku monogatarishū,* fasc. 11.27, 1:174–176; Matsumura and Yamanaka, *Eiga monogatari,* 1:454; McCullough and McCullough, *Flowering Fortunes,* 2:511.

41. A ninety-day constant-walking meditation is performed on Mount Hiei today; however, this ceremony is the result of a revival in Chih-i's works by modern Tendai

monks, not a continuation of a traditional practice on Mount Hiei (Mitsumori, "Hieizan Tōdō Saitō jōgyōdō no kōhai ni tsuite," p. 283. Satō Tetsuei (*Eizan jōdokyō no kenkyū*, pp. 33–35) argues that Ennin's practice of the constant-walking meditation was not so far removed from T'ien-t'ai practice in Chan-jan's time, noting that Shan-tao's teaching had also begun to influence T'ien-t'ai thinkers by the mid-T'ang. Although Satō's argument is interesting, the perception of the practice by the time the *Sanbō ekotoba* was written seems to have departed in many ways from the practice advocated in the *Mo-ho chih-kuan* and Chan-jan's commentary on that text.

42. Inoue and Ōsone suggest this in a note in *Ōjōden Hokke genki*, p. 398.

43. According to a note in one version of the *Sanbō ekotoba*, Kamens, *Three Jewels*, p. 343.

44. "Tendai zasu Ryōgen kishō," in Takeuchi, ed., *Heian ibun* (document 303), 2:434b–435a; the entire text is translated in the appendix 8.

45. For a discussion of the problems of dating the first Constant-walking Meditation Hall, see Mitsumori, "Jōgyōdō," pp. 263–264.

46. Mochizuki and Tsukamoto eds., *Mochizuki Bukkyō daijiten*, 3:2570–2571; Take Kakuchō, *Hiei santō shodō junpaiki*, pp. 20–22.

47. The Monjurō should not be confused with the part of the Central Hall referred to as the Monjudō (Mañjuśrī's hall). However, the Monjurō may have been built because the Monjudō was used for other purposes (Shigematsu Akihisa, "Eizan ni okeru shishu sanmaiin no tenkai," p. 222, n. 4. Shigematsu cites a number of later works that suggest that the Monjurō was the site of the constant-sitting meditation, but these works seem sufficiently late that they may have been an attempt to rationalize the system of halls by matching them with practices in the *Mo-ho chih-kuan* (ibid., p. 211).

48. Groner, *Saichō*, pp. 30, 139, n. 111.

49. *Asabashō, T* (*zuzō*), 9:248a–b, 836b–c; Ōmura Seigai, *Mikkyō hattatsushi*, p. 337.

50. Saeki, *Ennin*, pp. 252–253; idem, *Jikaku daishiden no kenkyū*, pp. 230, 313, 317, 319; Ono Katsutoshi, *Nittō guhō junrei kōki no kenkyū*, 3:380; *Eigaku yōki, GR* 24:526–527.

51. *Daisōjōden, NS* 1.22:47. Earth and stones from Mount Wu-t'ai are listed in a record of items stored at the Zentōin (Satō Tetsuei, "Zentōin kenzaisho mokuroku ni tsuite," p. 108).

52. Take, *Hieizan santō*, p. 16.

53. *Shūiden, NS* 1.22:69.

54. Shibuya, ed., *Tendai zasuki*, p. 45.

55. Ibid., p. 42. Since fourteen *ajari* were originally appointed to the Sojiin, the number in Ryōgen's proposal would seem to be incorrect (or the number of *ajari* may have been decreased by one for some reason). No explanation for this apparent discrepancy has been suggested.

56. Ibid., p. 43. The *Nihon kiryaku* (*KT* 11:116) gives the date as the night of 4–20.

57. Translated in appendix 8.

58. Shibuya, ed., *Tendai zasuki*, p. 43; *Hyakurenshō, KT* (*fukyūban*), p. 2; *Shūiden, NS* 1.22: 60. Some of the details about a major offering at the complex on 1-3-972 attended by court officials are included in *Eigaku yōki, GR* 24:522–523. The ceremony for the Buddha's relic is discussed further in chapter 12.

59. Ono Katsutoshi, *Nittō guhō gyōreki no kenkyū*, 2:409. Sources differ about whether the Sōjiin was originally associated with the Tōdōin or whether the two were combined later (see Ikeyama, "Hokke Sōjiin ni tsuite," p. 307).

60. Honda, ed., *Yakuchū Jikaku daishiden*, p. 147.

61. *Jōgyō wajō shōrai mokuroku, BZ* (Suzuki ed.), 96:37–39; *Nittō gokeden, BZ* (Suzuki ed.), 68:160a–c; Hayami, *Jujutsu shūkyō no sekai*, pp. 57–59; idem, *Heian kizoku*, pp. 18–24.

62. This ritual is described in chapter 5.

63. Ikeyama, "Hokke sōjiin ni tsuite," pp. 301–303.

64. Ono Katsutoshi, *Sanzen'in-hon Jikaku daishiden*, pp. 32–33, 64–65. Hall boys distributed lotus leaves made of paper at ceremonies. The novices, hall boys, and errand-boys are indented in the document after the five servants, perhaps indicating that they constitute a breakdown of the servants. However, the figures for the food and supplies for the two groups do not add up, suggesting that they were separate categories. In addition, novices would probably not have been called servants (*zōshi*). For other sources, see Saeki, *Jikaku daishiden no kenkyū*, pp. 266–267.

65. *Kuin Bukkakushō, GR* 24:579; Saeki, *Jikaku daishiden no kenkyū*, p. 267. Converting these measures to modern equivalents is difficult because a number of different volumes were in use for the *masu* during the Heian period. However, the following notes may serve to give some idea of the amounts involved. During the Nara period a *masu* might have been equal to approximately 720 cc (Takeuchi, ed., *Kadokawa Nihon rekishi jiten*, p. 800). Slightly larger equivalents are listed in Nagahara, ed., *Chūseishi handobukku* (pp. 465–466), but for periods that would have been later than Ennin's time. According to Kokukushi daijiten henshū iinkai, ed., *Kokushi daijiten* (7:413c, s.v. "*gō*"), one *masu* was approximately 1.8 liters; ten *gō* were equal to one *masu*. However, according to the *Heian jidaishi jiten* edited by Tsunoda, one *masu* might be equivalent to either four or six *gō* (2:2352c). Although the court made efforts to unify the system, they seem to have been largely ineffective. The measurements of a roll of cloth varied according to the type of cloth; generally one roll was sufficient to make one set of clothes.

66. *Kuin Bukkakushō, GR* 24:578; *Eigaku yōki, GR* 24:523. The two-year gap between the awarding of the fourteen monks and the beginning of the building of the Sōjiin has led Ikeyama to suggest that the Sōjiin was built between 851 and 860. While the Sōjiin was under construction, the ceremony of the Buddha of Abundant Light was probably held at the Jōshin'in (Ikeyama, "Hokke Sōjiin ni tsuite," pp. 304–305).

67. *Kuin Bukkakushō, GR* 24:581.

68. Shibuya, ed., *Tendai zasuki*, pp. 14–15; Saeki, *Jikaku daishiden no kenkyū*, pp. 295–296; Satō Tetsuei, "*Zentōin kenzaisho mokuroku* ni tsuite," pp. 97–100. Ennin's request concerning his books is found in a petition to the court dated three days before his death. Before that they had been in Ennin's quarters.

69. Shibuya, ed., *Tendai zasuki*, pp. 14–15. Later, Enchin cautions his disciples to respect this rule (ibid., p. 25), but then makes special provisions for his own disciples.

70. Ono Katsutoshi, *Nittō guhō gyōreki no kenkyū*, 2:417; Shibuya, ed., *Tendai zasuki*, p. 18; Saeki, *Enchin*, pp. 208–209. The sectarian aspects of libraries are discussed further in chapter 2.

71. Sources differ about whether the texts were deposited there in 859 or 867. The latter date seems more likely because work was begun on refurbishing Onjōji in 858 and Enchin was named its abbot in 866. Although some sources indicate that Enchin built the temple, archeological investigations suggest that it existed in the Nara period as the Ōtomo clan temple (Ono Katsutoshi, *Nittō guhō gyōreki no kenkyū*, 2:416–418). Enchin's Tōin was in Tōdō at first but moved to Onjōji later as relations between the factions worsened.

72. *Ruijū sandaikyaku, KT* 25:71.

73. Shibuya, ed., *Tendai zasuki*, p. 37. Several performances are mentioned in the *Asabashō* (*T* [*zuzō*], 9:42b), but these seem to be special occasions and do not suggest that the ceremony was necessarily performed regularly.

74. Shibuya, ed., *Tendai zasuki*, p. 37.

75. Hori Daiji, "Ryōgen to Yokawa fukkō (part 2)," p. 11.

76. *Asabashō, T* (*zuzō*), 9:42b.

77. Shibuya, ed., *Tendai zasuki*, p. 39.

78. For records of the two centuries after Ryōgen, the *Tendai zasuki, Gyōrinshō* (*T* 76:83b–99b), and *Asabashō* (*T* [*zuzō*], 9:831b–832b) may be consulted.

79. For comparative diagrams of the various central halls, see Take, *Hieizan Santō*, p. 4.

80. *Shūiden, NS* 1.22:62–63; Shibuya, ed., *Tendai zasuki*, p. 45; *Fusō ryakki, KT* 12:250. Entries from twelve sources are cited in *NS* 1.18:26–40.

81. Hirabayashi Moritoku, "Shinshutsu *Jie daishiden* shiryō dasoku," pp. 32–37. Hirabayashi notes that Bonshō is said to have died at the age of sixty-nine in 1032. If he served as transmitter (*dōtatsu*, the person who conveyed the invocation to the chanter) at the dedication of the Lecture Hall in 980, he would have been only seventeen years old at the time, a surprisingly young age for appointment to such a major role in the ceremony.

82. *Tengen sannen chūdō kuyō ganmon, GR* 24:591.

83. Shibuya, ed., *Tendai zasuki*, p. 45. Tamemitsu was Morosuke's ninth son; his mother was Princess Gashi. At the time of the dedication he would have been a major counselor (*dainagon*). By the time of his death, he had become chancellor (*daijō daijin*).

84. *Dō kuyō, NS* 1.18:32; Hirabayashi, *Ryōgen*, pp. 156–157. Although the emperor probably did not attend, Tamemitsu might have attended as his emissary in a private mode (*Kennaiki, NS* 1.18:31).

85. The source for this account is the *Dō kuyō* (*NS* 1.18:32–39), a document of questionable authenticity (see the editor's comment, ibid., p. 39), but the story of the factionalism does agree with other events around this time. See chapter 11.

86. Shibuya, ed., *Tendai zasuki*, p. 43; *Shūiden, NS* 1.22:61–62. The *Shūiden* account is particularly detailed.

87. Shibuya, ed., *Tendai zasuki*, p. 45; *Shūiden, ZTZ, Shiden* 2:208a; *Sanmon dōshaki, GR* 24:473a.

88. Saeki, *Jikaku daishiden no kenkyū*, pp. 272–273.

89. Shibuya, ed., *Tendai zasuki*, p. 46; *Hyakurenshō, KT* (*fukyūban*), p. 4; *Daisōjōden, NS* 1.22:50.

90. *NS* 2.1:66–69; Shibuya, ed., *Tendai zasuki*, p. 47.

91. Sonoda Kōyū, s.v. "Gangyōji," Kokushi daijiten henshū iinkai, ed., *Kokushi*

daijiten 3:789. For the founding and early history of the monastery, see Groner, "Annen, Tankei, Henjō."

92. McCullough and McCullough, *Flowering Fortunes*, 1:130–134; Matsumura and Yamanaka, *Eiga monogatari*, 1:97–100; H. C. McCullough, *Ōkagami*, pp. 55–56, 80–82; *KT* 21A:17–19. The two accounts differ about whether Kazan abdicated solely out of grief for a deceased concubine or was manipulated into abdicating by the Fujiwaras.

Chapter 10. Ryōgen as *Zasu*

1. *Nihon kiryaku: zenpen, KT* 10:331; *Engishiki, KT* 26:546.
2. *Engishiki, KT* 26:646.
3. Ibid., 657–659. For more information concerning early finances on Mount Hiei, see Hirabayashi, "Ryōgen to Eizan no chūkō," p. 20; Hori Daiji, "Ryōgen to Yokawa fukkō 2," pp. 4–8. The *Kokushi daijiten* (2:428–433) includes a chronological list of early contributions to Mount Hiei and a list of temple lands arranged according to province.
4. *Sanmon dōshaki, GR* 24:491b.
5. The provisions for supporting the Sōjiin are described in chapter 9; imperially sponsored chapels are discussed in chapter 2. Provisions from tax revenues for the Shōin are found in *Kuin Bukkakushō, GR* 24:584a.
6. *Nihon kiryaku: zenpen, KT* 10:420. These lands were to be tax free. According to the *Kokushi daijiten* 2:433, these were the first lands given to the monastery for use as funding sources (*jiryō*).
7. "Tendai zasu Ryōgen yuigō," in Takeuchi, ed., *Heian ibun*, 2:444 (document no. 305).
8. These contributions are mentioned in a variety of sources including *Mon'yōki, T* (*zuzō*), 12:371c, 373a.
9. *Jinzen wajō gokishō chō, GR* 24:498b; Hori Daiji, "Ryōgen to Yokawa fukkō 2," p. 8.
10. "Tendai zasu Ryōgen yuigō," in Takeuchi, ed., *Heian ibun*, 2:444 (document no. 305).
11. *Eigaku yōki, GR* 24:552; *Sanmon dōshaki, GR* 24:492. I take the phrase "four sheaves of rice" in the *Sanmon dōshaki* to be four thousand on the basis of a passage from the *Mon'yōki*, cited in Take, "Jie daishi (Ryōgen) no shōgai to sono gyōseki," p. 228.
12. *Isshin ajari bunin shidai, BZ* (Bussho kankōkai ed.), 123:433; *Shoreishō, GR* 24:13, 34. Onjōji did not receive an *isshin ajari* until 1008, and the Shingon school until 1092 (Kushida Ryōkō, s.v. "*ajari*," *Kokushi daijiten*, 1:194–195).
13. "Tendai zasu Ryōgen yuigō," in Takeuchi ed., *Heian ibun*, 2:441–448 (document no. 305); Hori Daiji, "Jinzen to Myōkōin 2," p. 2. The will is translated in appendix 8.
14. *Shoreishō, GR* 24:13.
15. See table 20 in chapter 10. For example, Jinzen went directly from lesser bishop to archbishop (*Shoreishō, GR* 24:8).

16. These entries are based on Shibuya, ed., *Tendai zasuki*, pp. 46–47; *Hyakuren-shō, KT (fukyūban)*, pp. 4–6; *Nihon kiryaku, KT* 11:152–160; and Hori Daiji, "Jinzen to Myōkōin 2," pp. 52–53.

17. *Mon'yōki, T (zuzō)* 12:373a–c; *Sanmon dōshaki, GR* 24:498a–499a; Hori Daiji, "Jinzen to Myōkōin 1," pp. 7–8.

18. *Sanmon dōshaki, GR* 24:498b.

19. Ibid., 24:496b–497a; Hori Daiji, "Jinzen to Myōkōin 1," pp. 8–9. More information on the rivalry between the two Fujiwara lineages is found in chapter 11.

20. *Sanmon dōshaki, GR* 24:493b–494a.

21. For one of the few studies on these issues, see Sasaki Kunimaro, "Myōkōin monseki-ryō ni kansuru ikkōsatsu."

22. For a vivid account of Kazan's decision to become a monk and Yoshichika's distress, see Matsumura and Yamanaka, eds., *Eiga monogatari*, 1:98–100; McCullough and McCullough, *Flowering Fortunes*, 1:131–134. For details on the lineages of the monks of the Myōkōin, see Hori Daiji's thorough study, "Jinzen to Myōkōin 1," pp. 5–7. The parentage of the monks are also mentioned in the list of abbots of Myōkōin in *Mon'yōki, T (zuzō)*, 12:379a. Iimuro was one of the valleys in the Yokawa area. The term "*nyūdō*" (literally, "entering the path") was sometimes used as a title for high officials of the third rank and above who had taken Buddhist vows.

23. Hirabayashi and Koike, eds., *Sōryaku sōran*, p. 284.

24. Kakugyō was the grandson of Major Counselor Taira no Koremochi (881–939) and was a cousin of Tadahira. Kakuun's parentage is not known. Myōgō was the grandson of Middle Counselor Fujiwara no Kanesuke (879–933). Myōku is discussed later in this chapter. He was a disciple of Ryōgen, appointed as first master of Jitokuji at the suggestion of Jinzen, and held a number of offices in the Office of Monastic Affairs from 993 to 1002 (Hirabayashi and Koike, eds., *Sōryaku sōran*, p. 285).

25. For information on Nyogen, see ibid., pp. 149–150; Hori Daiji, "Jinzen to Myōkōin 2," pp. 57–58.

26. Dōmyō is mentioned in a variety of sources, usually for his ability to chant the *Lotus Sūtra* well and to free people from the karmic consequences of their actions (*Hokke genki*, in Inoue and Ōsone, eds., *Ōjōden Hokke genki*, pp. 164–166; *Honchō kōsōden, BZ* [Suzuki ed.], 63:375c–376a). He was also a gifted poet and the subject of several stories about monks having sexual relations with women. The title of *hōin* was the equivalent of archbishop in the revision of ranks of 864.

27. Horiike, "Yuima-e," p. 207.

28. My discussion of *betsuin* is primarily based on Takagi, *Heian jidai Hokke Bukkyōshi kenkyū*, pp. 43–51. A chart of Tendai *betsuin* is included on pp. 46–47 and in Kokushi daijiten henshū iinkai, ed., *Kokushi daijiten*, 12:490.

29. Horiike Shunpō, s.v. "Matsuji," in Tsunoda, ed., *Heian jidaishi jiten* 2:2356a.

30. Groner, *Saichō*, p. 122.

31. Oishio Chihiro (*Kokubunji no chūseiteki tenkai*) has surveyed the available information concerning the later development of the *kokubunji* system. Although Oishio believes that the appointment of lecturers was important for the early Tendai school, very little information concerning actual appointments survives (pp. 45, 90). The importance of the institution for Tendai clearly declined with the increasing popularity of privately endowed temples. However, occasionally a piece of evidence

survives indicating that the *kokubunji* continued to play at least a minor role in Tendai fortunes. For example, an extent *kokubunji* document dated 955 authorizes the ordination of a monk to replace one who had died (p. 87).

32. Kusakabe, "Anne kashō kō," pp. 51–52, 55.

33. Tamenaga was the son of Koremasa; his dates are not known, but he was active around the Kankō era (1004–1012); his poetry was included in the *Goshūishū*. He rose to the fifth rank.

34. *Shūiden, ZTZ Shiden* 2:198a; Takahashi Tomio, *Tendaiji*, pp. 114–117.

35. For more on Tōnomine, see chapter 6 and appendix 4.

36. The story is found in *Konjaku monogatarishū*, fasc. 31.24; Mabuchi and Kunisaki, eds., 4:608–613. Similar stories could be cited for Tendai's control of Tōnomine. *Konjaku monogatarishū* 31.23 includes Michinaga awarding Enryakuji control of Tōnomine on the grounds that Tendai asked first (Oishio Chihiro, *Nihon chūsei no setsuwa to Bukkyō* p. 254).

37. Katsuyama Kiyotsugi, "Shōen no keisei," p. 436. See Ryōgen's will, appendix 3.

38. Katsuyama, "Shōen no keisei," pp. 439–445.

39. Neil McMullin, "The Enryaku-ji and the Gion Shrine-Temple Complex," pp. 175–176.

40. Katsuyama, "Shōen no keisei," p. 445.

41. This aspect of the story has been explored in detail by McMullin, "Enryaku-ji and Gion"; and idem, "On Placating the Gods." As McMullin points out, determining the exact situation during Ryōgen's lifetime is difficult, and scholars must avoid reading in later elements in their interpretations. In addition, McMullin's argument discussing the ideological aspects of the ritual complex at Gion is noteworthy.

42. *Shūiden, ZTZ Shidenbu*, 2:207a–b; Hirabayashi, *Ryōgen*, p. 149.

43. *NS* 1.17:202.

44. *Eigaku yōki, GR* 24:512.

45. Ogurisu Kenji, s.v. "Chikubu shima," in Tsunoda, ed., *Heian jidaishi jiten*, 2:1613d–1614a. Ogurisu notes that a Lotus assembly (*renge-e*) began in 977, the year of Ryōgen's visit, with a rain-making ceremony.

46. *Shūiden, ZTZ Shidenbu*, 2:207a; *Chikubu shima engi, GR* 1:887; Hirabayashi, *Ryōgen*, p. 145.

47. *Shūiden, NS* 1.22:67.

48. For a lucid discussion of the role of women as patrons in Chinese Buddhism and the difficulties in tracing their contributions, see Timothy Brook, *Praying for Power*, pp. 188–191.

49. For a list of early celebrations, see Hori Ichirō, *Jōdai Nihon Bukkyō bunkashi*, 1:267–270.

50. Minamoto no Tamenori, *Sanbō ekotoba*, 1:74–75; Kamens, *Three Jewels*, pp. 302–306.

51. *Tōdaiwajō Tōseiden*, annotated version in Ishida Mizumaro, *Ganjin*, p. 313; *Shōdai senzai denki*, fasc. 3, *BZ* (Suzuki ed.), 64:281b–c.

52. Ennin mentions relics in his diary several times (Reischauer, *Ennin's Diary*, pp. 235–236, 300–302; Ono Katsutoshi, *Nittō junrei guhō no kenkyū*, 3:8–9, 17–23, 352–364). Five relics are listed in catalogues of the items brought Ennin brought from China (Saeki, *Jikaku daishiden no kenkyū*, p. 286).

53. *Kuin Bukkakushō, GR* 15:580; Honda, ed., *Yakuchū Jikaku daishiden*, p. 140; Saeki, *Jikaku daishiden no kenkyū*, p. 286; Shibuya, ed., *Tendai zasuki*, p. 12.

54. *Sandai jitsuroku, KT* 4:188.

55. *Nihon kiryaku kōhen, KT* 11:7.

56. Matsumura and Yamanaka, eds., *Eiga monogatari,* 2:152; McCullough and Mc-Cullough, *Flowering Fortunes,* 2:627; Mabuchi and Kunisaki, eds., *Konjaku monogatarishū,* fasc. 11.2, 1:229–232. Ryōgen's concern for his mother and women has also inspired modern revisionist literature, such as Gotō Hiroyuki's *Nyonin jōbutsu e no kaigen,* a treatment of Ryōgen that portrays him as being much more progressive in his attitudes toward women than the evidence warrants.

57. *Shūiden, NS* 1.22:62–63. The *Tendai zasuki* (p. 44) also states that Ryōgen moved the *shari-e* to Kyoto to benefit women in general, not for his mother.

58. The Tōshōdaiji *shari-e* is mentioned earlier in this discussion. The only mention of the Gangyōji *shari-e* that I have been able to locate is found in the *Sanbō ekotoba* (Minamoto no Tamenori, *Sanbō ekotoba,* p. 76; Kamens, *Three Jewels,* p. 303); the assembly is said to have been held sporadically during the third month. Women are said to have frequented both the Tōshōdaiji and Gangyōji *shari-e.*

59. According to the *Tendai zasuki* (Shibuya ed., p. 44), the first time was on the seventh day of the fourth month, and the second time was on the twentieth day of that same month.

60. The eight groups were beings that could not normally be seen such as deities and dragons. In this case, people presumably played the parts of these beings in dances.

61. Yoshidadera might have been chosen as the site of the ritual partly because it was said to have been founded by Kibi no Makibi, who had brought Chien-chen to Japan. It first appears in Tendai literature in the biography of the Tendai *zasu* Son'i, who is said to have seen pictures of hell there as a young child (Takei Akio, "Yoshidadera," in Tsunoda, ed., *Heian jidaishi jiten,* 2:2661a–b).

62. Shibuya, ed., *Tendai zasuki,* p. 44; *Shūiden, NS* 1.22:63.

63. McCullough and McCullough, *Flowering Fortunes,* 2:627; Matsumura and Yamanaka, eds., *Eiga monogatari,* 2:150–152; Mabuchi and Kunisaki, eds., *Konjaku monogatarishū,* fasc. 11.9, 1:229–232.

64. Hosokawa Ryōichi, "Ōken to amadera."

65. See Hurvitz, *Lotus,* p. 195; Ogami, *Hokke daie,* p. 110. See rule no. 10 in appendix 8 for a possible reference to the practice.

66. For a comprehensive examination of filial piety and Chinese Buddhism, see Kenneth Ch'en, *The Chinese Transformation of Buddhism,* pp. 14–50.

67. "Tendai Hokkeshū nenbun tokudo gakushō myōchō," *DZ* 1:250, 252.

68. Kamens, *Three Jewels,* pp. 234–239; Minamoto no Tamenori, *Sanbō ekotoba,* 1:228–237.

69. *Son'i zōsōjōden, ZGR* 8:724–725.

70. *Nihon kiryaku, KT* 10:275.

71. Katsuura Noriko, "Kodai ni okeru bosei to Bukkyō," pp. 7–8.

72. *Daisōjōden, NS* 1.22:52.

73. Sūfukuji would later be refurbished by Ryōgen's disciple Anshin, an act that brought it firmly under Tendai control.

74. *Shūiden, ZTZ Shiden,* 2:203b.

75. *Shūiden, NS* 1.22:58–59. The site is identified as the Annyōin at Nōka. It is also the site of Ryōgen's mother's grave (Nomoto, *Getsugakusan Nōkaji*).

76. Katsuura, "Kodai ni okeru josei to Bukkyō," pp. 9–10.

77. *Shūiden, NS* 1.22:59. The boats usually were made in pairs and used to transport either nobility or musicians. A boatload of musicians was approximately ten musicians and four men to pole the boat. The head of the bird was thought to offer protection from shipwrecks.

78. *Shūiden, NS* 1.22:65.

79. "Tendai zasu Ryōgen yuigō," in Takeuchi Rizō, ed., *Heian ibun* (document no. 305), 2:443–444. No biography is available for Genzen. Genzen's mother is described as an "old nun" (*rōni*) in Ryōgen's will (see appendix 3), an appellation that is further discussed in chapter 12. Myōgō was a descendant of Fujiwara no Fuyutsugu. He studied under Genshin as well as Ryōgen and served as the seventh abbot of the Shuryōgon'in at Yokawa. He had risen to the rank of grand archbishop by the time of his death in 1002 at the age of forty-eight (Hirabayashi and Koike, eds., *Sōryaku sōran*, pp. 285–286).

80. Ōsumi, "Josei to Bukkyō," pp. 2, 6. Mothers played key roles in the biographies of Tendai monks such as Son'i, Ryōgen, and Genshin. Ōsumi's article includes a number of examples of monks from other schools. For an exposition of the relationships between monks who traveled to China and their mothers, see Takagi Yutaka, *Bukkyōshi no naka no nyonin*, pp. 185–269.

81. The changes in the portrayal of women in society are discussed in such works as Katsuura, "Kodai ni okeru bosei to Bukkyō," pp. 6–7; and Wakita Haruko, "Chūsei ni okeru seibetsu yakuwari bundan to joseikan," 2:76–80.

82. George Sansom, *History of Japan to 1334*, p. 155.

83. William McCullough, "Japanese Marriage Institutions in the Heian Period."

84. Take Kakuchō, *Hieizan santō shodō enkaku shi*, pp. 99–100; Shimonaka Hiroshi, ed., *Nihonshi daijiten*, 5:623c.

85. I have not found any record concerning the date of the establishment of the women's halls around Mount Hiei; however, since they are not mentioned in the literature from Ryōgen's time, they probably were constructed later. For brief references to the hall, see Kageyama Haruki, *Hieizan to Kōyasan*, pp. 179–182; Nishiguchi Junko, s.v. "Nyonindō," and Miyazawa Satoshi, s.v. "Hie taisha," in Shimonaka, ed., *Nihonshi daijiten*, 5:623c and 949a.

86. Take, *Hieizan santō*, pp. 264–265; Hirabayashi, *Ryōgen*, 216–219.

87. Nōtomi Jōten, "Nanto Bukkyō ni okeru nyonin ōjō shisō." For a record of Eison's proselytizing among women in Kamakura, see Kumabara Masao, "Eison to Kamakura josei." Eison's establishment of an order of nuns is discussed in Paul Groner, "Tradition and Innovation."

Chapter 11. Factionalism
and Ryōgen's Efforts to Control the Order

1. See chapter 9 for more information and sources for Ryōgen's rebuilding of the Mount Hiei complex.

2. Miki, *Tōnomine hijiri dan*, p. 173.

3. *Fusō ryakki, KT* 12:250 (Tengen 5-1-10). The argument based on precedent was stronger than it may seem to the modern reader. Books concerning precedents for appointments and rituals were being compiled in both lay and monastic society during this period. According to Shibuya, ed., *Tendai zasuki* (p. 46), Ryōgen objected to the appointment of Yokei on 12-15-981.

4. *Jimon denki horoku, BZ* (Bussho kankōkai ed.), 127:424b–425a.

5. *Fusō ryakki, KT* 12:250; *Shūiden,* p. 87.

6. Hirabayashi, *Ryōgen,* pp. 165–166.

7. The Kannon'in had been established 980 in the confines of the Daiunji by Yokei as a *goganji* for Emperor En'yū; it had been awarded five *ajari*.

8. *Genkō shakusho, BZ* (Suzuki ed.), 62:199b; *Onjōji denki, BZ* (Bussho kankōkai ed.), 127:68–69; *Jimon denki horoku, BZ* (Bussho kankōkai ed.), 127:310–311; *Fusō ryakki, KT* 12:250–251. The date and compiler of the *Onjōji denki* are not known, but because its latest entry is 1343, it was probably compiled in the late Kamakura period (*Kokushi daijiten,* 2:978a–b). The *Jimon denki horoku* was compiled by Shikō during the Ōei era (1394–1428; *Kokushi daijiten* 7:173a). Fujiwara Fuminori's son Myōchō (946–1014) of Fumonji was one of the leaders whose life was threatened, but he probably already lived at the Fumonji in Iwakura; see chapter 6 for more information on him.

9. *Fusō ryakki, KT* 12:251.

10. Helen McCullough (*Ōkagami,* p. 347) remarks that Kanemichi seems to have been a neurotic and boorish man who had so offended people that he had twice been dismissed from positions. Tsuchida Naoshige (*Nihon no rekishi,* pp. 52–53) suggests that Saneyori and Koremasa might have resented Kanemichi for some reason or that Kaneie was a brash and arrogant man who liked to break precedents and probably had little regard for his older brother's feelings. These events as well as Yoritada's appointment as regent are described in both the *Ōkagami* (H. C. McCullough, *Ōkagami,* pp. 111–113, 153–156, 162–166, 347–350) and the *Eiga monogatari* (McCullough and McCullough, *Flowering Fortunes,* 1:111–135). For an English-language summary, see Sansom, *History of Japan to 1334,* pp. 156–158.

11. Because of Koremasa's early death in 972 and the demise of his two sons by his principal wife in a 974 epidemic while they were still in their twenties, Kaishi was the only one of Koremasa's children to have a distinguished career (McCullough and McCullough, *Flowering Fortunes,* 1:104–105); but she lacked the political power to push her lineage forward.

12. Arai Kōjun, "Kyōke nikō," pp. 56–61. Shinki, an eminent Hossō monk who had participated in the Ōwa debates, delivered the admonition to the retired emperor when he received the ten precepts that made him a novice at Tōdaiji. However, instead of the traditional ten precepts for novices, he seems to have received the ten good precepts for reasons that are not clear today.

13. Yokei also had other patrons including Fujiwara no Fuminori, who is discussed in chapter 6, and Empress Shōshi, referred to later in this chapter.

14. "En'yū Tennō," Kokushi daijiten henshū iinkai, ed., *Kokushi daijiten,* 2:425c–d.

15. A number of discrepancies are found in Yokei's biography. The *Sōgō bunin* (Hirabayashi and Koike, eds., *Sōryaku sōran,* p. 293) suggests that he was nine years old at ordination (the difference between his chronological age and years of seniority as a monk) and gives a date of 973 for his Esoteric ordinations. The *Jimon*

denki horoku (*BZ* [Bussho kankōkai ed.], 127:209b) indicates that he was fifty-three when he became an *ajari*.

16. The Daiunji had been founded several years earlier in 972. Among those who had played major roles in its establishment were Fujiwara no Fuminori, who had tried to help Ryōgen's opponents at the Ōwa debates, and Fujiwara no Sari (also read Sukemasa, 944–998, Fujiwara no Saneyori's grandson). Sari had become a monk named Shinkaku several years earlier. Thus, the figures associated with the founding of Daiunji all had ties to factions of the Fujiwara clan and branches of the Tendai school other than the Morosuke-Ryōgen alliance. For a detailed study of the Daiunji, see Tsunoda Bun'ei, "Daiunji to Kannon'in."

17. Okano, "Denbō ajari," pp. 316–319.

18. *Nihon kiryaku, KT* 11:165.

19. "Onjōji denbō kechimyaku," *NS* 2.1:750–751. A number of later legends about Yokei describe his powers (ibid., pp. 746–758).

20. *Shōyūki, NS* 1.19:107–108, 146.

21. *Onjōji denki, BZ* (Bussho kankōkai ed.), 127:67a. Empress Shōshi (also read Masako, 950–1000) was the wife of Emperor Reizei and the only daughter of Emperor Suzaku. Probably because she was childless and estranged from her demented husband, she devoted herself to sponsoring Buddhist services. Some documents describe the Kannon'in as being an area within the Daiunji instead of being an alternate name for the entire Daiunji.

22. Okano, "Denbō ajari," p. 322.

23. *Eigaku yōki, GR* 24:583; *Daisōjōden, NS* 1.22:50; Shibuya, ed., *Tendai zasuki,* p. 46; *Nihon kiryaku, KT* 11:149.

24. *Asabashō, T* (*zuzō*), 9:194b. The only earlier mention of Nyoirin Kannon in this passage of the *Asabashō* concerns Prince Shōtoku, perhaps indicating that Ryōgen may have played a role in popularizing Esoteric practices for Nyoirin Kannon in the Tendai tradition. According to an entry in the *San'inki,* Ryōgen also performed this ceremony from 8–10 to 8–17 in 979, so that Senshi would bear an heir to the throne. Ceremonies involving Nyoirin Kannon are mentioned in earlier sources, but not in earlier Tendai sources to my knowledge, suggesting that Ryōgen may have played an important role in promoting these ceremonies. After his death, he was said to be an incarnation of Nyoirin Kannon (Take, "Jie daishi [Ryōgen] no shōgai to sono gyōseki," pp. 219–220, 238).

25. *Asabashō, T* (*zuzō*), 9:194b; *Shūiden, ZTZ Shiden,* 2:208b–209a. Jōan was a disciple of Ryōgen who had been named master of Esoteric Buddhism at Gangyōji in 975 through Ryōgen's petition. He was eventually named administrator of Gangyōji and known as the master of discipline at Gangyōji (Kazan *risshi*).

26. *Enryakuji gokoku engi, BZ* (Bussho kankōkai ed.), 431a–432b. The location of the chapel was supposedly a very auspicious one pointed out more than a century earlier by Ennin. One yearly ordinand was supposed to focus his efforts on the *Ta-jih-ching* (*Mahāvairocana-sūtra*) and another on the *Jen-wang ching.* The specialty of the third is not mentioned, but the editors of the *Dainihon Bukkyō zensho* suggest that he was probably concerned with the *Fa-hua hsüan-i.* They do not, however, give any evidence for their position. All three were probably also required to chant the *Lotus Sūtra* and *Chin-kuang-ming ching* (*Suvarṇaprabhāsa* [Sūtra of golden light]). The main image of the chapel was Mahāvairocana.

27. Shibuya, ed., *Tendai zasuki,* p. 44.

28. Ibid.

29. *Sōgō bunin, BZ* (Bussho kankōkai ed.), 123:77b; *Nihon kiryaku, KT* 11:143; *Mon'yōki T* (*zuzō*), 11:763b. This ceremony is discussed in chapter 5.

30. *Nihon kiryaku, KT* 11:147–148. The Urin'in was part of the complex of temples developing around Kyoto to serve nobles. For its background, see Groner, "Annen, Tankei, Henjō, and Monastic Discipline in the Japanese Tendai School."

31. *Daisō jōden, ZTZ Shiden,* 2:198b. The text states that Ryōgen was moved because of an illness characterized by numbness of the limbs (*fūhi*). Hirabayashi characterizes this as measles (*fūshin*), but I have not been able to find any evidence for this (Hirabayashi, *Ryōgen,* p. 175).

32. *Fusō ryakki, KT* 12:256.

33. H. C. McCullough, *Ōkagami,* pp. 134–135; Matsumura, ed., *Ōkagami,* p. 126.

34. *Zoku honchō ōjōden,* in Inoue and Ōsone, eds., *Ōjōden Hokke genki,* p. 231.

35. Shibuya, ed., *Tendai zasuki,* p. 47.

36. Jinzen's career as *zasu* is described in chapter 10.

37. *Hyakurenshō, KT* (*fukyūban*), p. 7. The *Nihon kiryaku* gives a date of 9-29, the *Hyakurenshō,* 10-1.

38. Monks from Enchin's faction had served as *zasu* for approximately the same number of years as monks from Ennin's faction, but the four monks preceding Jinzen had all been from Ennin's lineage. The edict thus reflects the events of the preceding few decades.

39. According to passages in the *Fan-wang ching* (*T* 24:1009b), *Jen-wang ching* (*T* 8:844b), and *Lien-hua mien ching* (*T* 12:1072c), when a lion dies, other animals will not eat it. But worms emerge from within and devour it. In a similar manner, Buddhism will not be destroyed by heterodox religions but will decline when evil monks emerge from within. The edict thus warns that the monks themselves will bring about the collapse of their order, not the court or another external agency.

40. Shibuya, ed., *Tendai zasuki,* pp. 47–48; *Nihon kiryaku, KT* 11:168; *Genkō shakusho, BZ* (Suzuki ed.), 62:226c. The edict is found in part in both the *Enryakuji gokoku engi* (*BZ* [Bussho kankōkai ed.], 126:432b–433c) and *Tendai kahyō* (*BZ* [Suzuki ed.], 42:74c–75a). This translation is based on a text considered by Hirata Toshiharu to be the complete text of the edict found in Hirata, *Heian jidai no kenkyū,* pp. 193–196. Hirata includes a modern translation in *Sōhei to bushi,* pp. 160–161, from which I have benefited.

41. Tokyo daigaku shiryō hensanjo, ed., *Shōyūki,* 1:207.

42. According to Shibuya, ed., *Tendai zasuki* (p. 48), Yokei resigned on 12-20; the *Gukanshō* has the date of 12-26 (Brown and Ishida, *The Future and the Past,* p. 306). Here the *Nihon kiryaku* (*KT* 11:168) date of 12-27 has been followed; for other sources, see *NS* 2.1:501–502.

43. *NS* 2.2:60–64; Inoue and Ōsone, eds., *Ōjōden Hokke genki,* pp. 105–106.

44. *NS* 2.5:793–794.

45. *Sanmon dōshaki, GR* 24:501b–502a. The account of Ennin's dream of the deity is primarily based on Ennin's biography, the *Jikaku daishiden* (Saeki, *Jikaku daishiden no kenkyū,* pp. 211–213; Saitō Enshin, trans., *Jikaku daishiden,* pp. 42–43). Although Ennin notes a dream that he had on Mount Ch'ih, the identity of the seemingly superhuman figure in the dream is not identified (Reischauer, *Ennin's*

Diary, p. 293; Ono Katsutoshi, *Nittō guhō junrei kōki,* 3:305–308). Nor does he mention in the diary of his journey to China being protected by the deity of the mountain and vowing to build a shrine in that deity's honor. Several issues of interpretation have arisen from these discrepancies. Scholars have disagreed on whether the deity is Chinese, Korean (installed by Koreans at the hall where Ennin stayed at Mount Ch'ih for seven months), or an invention of the author of the *Jikaku daishiden* devised in response to the factional disputes on Mount Hiei in the late ninth century. For a bibliography of studies of Sekisan and a good defense of the traditional Tendai account followed here, see Saitō Enshin, "Sekisan myōjin ni kansuru ikkōsatsu."

Little is known of Jōsan other than that he was appointed one of the ten meditation masters appointed by court.

46. As might be expected in this sort of dispute, versions differ. The *Fusō ryakki* (*KT* 12:260–261) indicates that the dispute was over a trifling matter. In contrast the *Sanjūgo bunshū* (*ZGR* 12:63–64) includes a bitter complaint against Jōsan's actions dated 8-14. A complaint against the Sanmon monks' unjustified destruction of Jimon buildings is found in the *Honchō seiki* (comp. 1154–1160). My account has generally followed the *Fusō ryakki* version, but with more emphasis on the importance of the Sekisan zen'in to highlight the role of the shrine in Tendai affairs. These and other accounts are also found in *NS* 2.2:33–38.

47. *Jimon denki horoku, BZ* (Bussho kankōkai ed.), 127:425b.

48. Sources differ about whether they moved one month (*Onjōji denki, NS* 2.2:36) after arriving at Daiunji or several years ("Shiragi Myōjinki," *NS* 2.2:36).

49. *Fusō ryakki, KT* 12:260–261.

50. Fukuo Takeichirō, "Jikaku montō to Chishō montō no kōsō ni tsuite," pp. 538–539.

51. For a critical view of Onjōji's early history, see Sonoda Kōyū, s.v. "Onjōji," in Shimonaka, ed., *Nihonshi daijiten,* 1:1297–1298. For a more traditional view of the origins of Onjōji, see Hoshimiya Chikō, "Miidera no rekishi," p. 138.

52. Hiraoka Jōkai, "Onjōji no seiritsu to kaidan no mondai."

53. For a discussion of earlier and later sets of rules for the Tendai School, see Ogami Kanchū, "Tendaishū ni okeru kyōdan goji no shomondai." Color photographs of the manuscript of Ryōgen's rules are included in Eizan gakuin, ed., *Ganzan Jie daishi no kenkyū.* The actual manuscript was unpublished until it was discovered at Rozanji and published in 1860; its authenticity has not been questioned. The rules have been published in Takeuchi Rizō, ed., *Heian ibun, komonjo-hen* 2:431–440. A modern Japanese translation of them by Watanabe Eshin appears in "'Jie daishi kisei nijūrokkajō' ni tsuite," pp. 1–16. An English translation is included in the appendix 8.

54. Translated and discussed in Groner, *Saichō.*

55. Fifteen of the twenty-two rules in Ninchū's *Enryakuji kinsei shiki* are found in *Tendai kahyō, BZ* (Suzuki ed.), 42: 4b–5b; the last seven rules in this text are not extant, making it impossible to completely determine what influence they might have had on Ryōgen's set. Ennin's *Shuryōgon'in shiki* is translated in appendix 1. The 866 edict is found in *Sandai jitsuroku, KT* 4:188–189. A set of twelve rules composed by Enchin is mentioned in the *Eigaku yōki,* but its content is not clear. Ryō-

gen might well have ignored the rules given the increasing sectarianism on Mount Hiei at the time he compiled his. Analyses of the influences of these and other sources are found in Hori Daiji, "Ryōgen no 'Nijūrokkajō kisei,'" pp. 14–28; and Ogami Kanchū, "Jie daishi 'Nijūrokushiki' to Tendaishū kyōdan," pp. 339–340.

56. Hori Daiji, "Ryōgen no 'Nijūrokkajō kisei,'" pp. 13–14.

57. Ogami, "Jie daishi 'Nijūrokushiki,'" pp. 346–347.

58. The translation of the term "*dōji*" as "attendant" rather than "youth" is based on Ogami, "Jie daishi 'Nijūrokushiki,'" pp. 347–348. Ogami notes that such terms as "*dōjichō*" (head of the servants) and "*Yase dōji*" (servants from Yase) have led him to feel that the term referred to a broad spectrum of servants.

59. These issues are discussed in Groner, *Saichō*, pp. 286–303; and idem, "The *Fan-wang ching* and Monastic Discipline in Japanese Tendai."

60. *Tendaigaku gairon* 1:656–657.

61. See, for example, Hotta Tesshin, "Ganzan daishi igo ni okeru sanjō no enkai ni tsuite," pp. 55–56; and Fujishi Tetsudō, "Jie daishi no tanju gokai ni tsuite," pp. 28–31.

62. In the journal of essays issued in 1984 in honor of the thousand-year anniversary of Ryōgen's death, the issue is not even mentioned (*Eizan gakuin kenkyū kiyō* 6); these essays, as well as a collection published in 1934, were republished that same anniversary year (Eizan gakuin, ed., *Issen-nen onki kinan Ganzan Jie daishi no kenkyū*).

63. Groner, *Saichō*, pp. 140–141, no. 114. For other information about *Fan-wang* fortnightly assemblies, see Satō Tatsugen, *Chūgoku Bukkyō ni okeru kairitsu no kenkyū*, p. 462; Ishida Mizumaro, *Ganjin*, pp. 253–267; Groner, "The *Fan-wang ching* and Monastic Discipline in Japanese Tendai," p. 256.

64. Shibuya, ed., *Tendai zasuki*, p. 12. This ceremony was performed for the benefit of Grand Empress Junna, who is discussed further in chapter 12.

65. *Fugen bosatsu gyōhōgyō monku gōki*, BZ (Bussho kankōkai ed.), 26:508a–b.

66. *Daisōjōden*, ZTZ Shiden, 2:195b.

67. *T* 24:1004b.

68. *Shūiden*, ZTZ Shiden 2: 207a–b; Hirabayashi, *Ryōgen*, pp. 146–147. For Azuma-asobi, see Maegawa Akihisa, "Azuma asobi," in Tsunoda, ed., *Heian jidaishi jiten*, 1:36d–37a.

69. See rule no. 23 in appendix 8.

70. Okano, "Enryakuji zoku bettō to Tendai zasu," p. 100.

71. *Daisōjōden*, ZTZ Shiden 2:196a; *Hie sannō rishōki*, ZGR 2A:665.

72. Hirabayashi, *Ryōgen*, p. 148.

73. Okano, "Enryakuji zoku bettō to Tendai zasu," p. 100.

74. *Shūi ōjōden*, in Inoue and Ōsone, eds., *Ojōden Hokke genki*, p. 291.

75. Nagamori Ryōji ("Jiin monbatsuka no ichi kaitei," pp. 1–2) suggests that the same problems contributed to the decline of Tōdaiji and the difficulties it had with its manors.

76. Hioki Shōichi, *Nihon sōhei kenkyū*, pp. 19–21.

77. Hirata, *Sōhei to bushi*, p. 163.

78. For a thorough study that demonstrates that such factionalism was present in the Hossō and Shingon schools as well as Tendai, see Mikael S. Adolphson, *The Gates of Power*.

Chapter 12. Ryōgen and the Role of Nuns

1. For a discussion in English of the eight weighty rules, see I. B. Horner, *Women under Primitive Buddhism*, pp. 118–161.

2. I have discussed some of these issues in several places; see *Saichō;* "The *Fan-wang ching* and Monastic Discipline in Japanese Tendai," pp. 251–290; "Annen, Tankei, Henjō, and Monastic Discipline in the Japanese Tendai School"; and "The Ordination Ritual in the *Platform Sūtra.*"

3. For a discussion of ordination platforms, see Groner, *Saichō*, pp. 26, 277–281.

4. For an English-language survey of these procedures, see Kyōko Motomichi Nakamura, *Miraculous Stories from the Japanese Buddhist Tradition*, pp. 19–25. Numerous studies exist in Japanese; typical is Sakuma Ryū, "Kansō ni tsuite," pp. 1–34. The precision with which terms were used in regard to nuns is speculative since no ordination documents concerning nuns exist from this early period. However, several petitions, called *ubai kōshinmon*, that ask for initiation as novices are extant. For a study of them, see Takagi, *Bukkyōshi no naka no nyonin*, pp. 75–82.

Officially sanctioned ordinations were also performed in many other parts of the Buddhist world. Kenneth Ch'en has amply documented the Chinese case in *The Chinese Transformation of Buddhism*, pp. 81, 83–84, 86–91. Michael Aung-Thwin has described the Burmese case in "The Role of Sasana Reform in Burmese History."

5. The distinction between the terms "*kansō*" and "*shido*" appears during the Nara period; for example, see *Shoku Nihongi*, *KT* 2:451.

6. For example, in the *Nihon ryōiki*, a "highly disciplined female novice" (*rengyō shamini*) is described as the head of a devotees' organization that proselytized using pictures (Endō Yoshimoto and Kasuga Kazuo, eds., *Nihon ryōiki*, p. 154; Nakamura, *Miraculous Stories from the Japanese Buddhist Tradition*, pp. 150–151). In the *Nihon ryōiki*, Gyōki is called a novice (*shami*) by Chikō, perhaps for similar reasons (*Nihon ryōiki*, p. 193; Nakamura, *Miraculous Stories*, p. 168; Groner, *Saichō*, p. 242).

7. Futaba Kenkō, "Gyōki no shōgai to hanritsuryō Bukkyō no seiritsu," 56–59. Because Gyōki had been trained by Dōshō, a Hossō master who studied under Hsüan-tsang in China, and because the *Fan-wang ching* might not have played a significant role in Japan until Tao-hsüan (702–760) brought it from China in 736, Gyōki probably followed the precepts from the *Yogācārbhūmi*, a seminal Yogācāra text that differs in important ways from the *Fan-wang ching* and *Ssu-fen lü*. Ishida Mizumaro has argued that Gyōki followed the *Fan-wang ching* precepts, but I do not find his argument convincing ("Gyōki ron"; *Nihon Bukkyō ni okeru karitsu no kenkyū*, p. 281). More recently, Yoshida Yasuo has argued that Gyōki used a mixture of the precepts from the *Yogācārabhūmi* and the *Fan-wang ching* by comparing the precepts with the activities that Gyōki was criticized for performing, but his argument seems forced (*Gyōki to ritsuryō kokka*, pp. 291–297).

8. According to an entry in the *Shoku Nihongi* (*KT* 2:68) from 717, "These days an ordinary monk named Gyōki and his disciples fill the streets and irresponsibly preach wrongdoing and good fortune." This terse and ambiguous statement has been the object of speculation by a number of scholars. One of the more reasonable explanations has been that Gyōki taught that karmic laws applied equally to commoners, the nobility, and the emperor. For a survey of some of the interpretations of this passage, see Yoshida, *Gyōki to ritsuryō kokka*, pp. 116–122.

9. For a discussion of Gyōki's groups, see Groner, *Saichō,* pp. 236–246.

10. For a discussion of the procedures of self-ordination, see Groner, "The Ordination Ritual in the *Platform Sūtra,*" pp. 231–235. Although self-ordinations could be classified as a type of private initiation (*shido*), I distinguish between the two on the basis of whether an order of practitioners is involved and whether the precepts are received directly from the Buddha.

11. Nakai Shinkō, *Nihon kodai no Bukkyō to minshū,* pp. 186–191.

12. Ishida Mizumaro, "Bikuni kaidan."

13. The possibility that the Japanese terms "*ama*" or "*ni*" may refer to either *bikuni* (fully ordained nun) or *shamini* (female novice) is not referred to in either the classical Japanese or Buddhist dictionaries I consulted, but most do indicate the wide range of women to whom the term referred. For example, "*ama*" (the Japanese reading [*kun-yomi*] of "*ni*") is interpreted as referring to women who had received the full precepts; but at times it also was applied to women who had taken the eight precepts of abstinence (*hassaikai*) for lay believers. By the late-Heian period, the term had become so loosely defined that it could refer to women who cut their hair to shoulder length or to women who lived at home in a "religious" manner. The ambiguity of the term "*ni*" certainly contributed to the confusion surrounding the history of Japanese nuns.

14. Hanna Havnevik, *Tibetan Buddhist Nuns,* pp. 44, 64.

15. For more on this issue, see Tessa J. Bartholomeusz, *Women under the Bo Tree.*

16. Nakamura Hajime, ed., *Bukkyōgo daijiten,* p. 671b.

17. The contents of the precepts for novices are often difficult to determine, even for monks. The Tendai school used three different sets at various times: the ten good precepts (*jūzenkai*), the ten major precepts from the *Fan-wang ching,* and the ten precepts for novices specified in the *Ssu-fen lü* (Groner, *Saichō,* pp. 118–120).

18. The entries on nuns in such standard reference works as *Mochizuki Bukkyō daijiten* (ed. Mochizuki and Tsukamoto), and *Bukkyō daijii* (ed. Ryūkoku daigaku; s.v. "ama," "ni," "bikuni") jump from a description of nuns during the Nara period to nuns during the Muromachi period. Even more specialized studies such as Araki Ryōsen, *Bikuni shi,* and Sōtōshū nisōshi hensankai, ed., *Sōtōshū nisōshi,* treat nuns in much the same manner. Kasahara Kazuo's *Nyonin ōjō shisō no keifu,* an important study of the status of women in the Kamakura schools, does not adequately treat the period between Saichō (766/767–822) and Hōnen (1133–1212); for a critique of Kasahara's book, see Taira Masayuki, "Kyū-bukkyō to josei."

19. W. G. Aston, trans., *Nihongi,* 2:101, 118; Sakamoto Tarō et al., eds., *Nihon shoki,* 2:148, 168.

20. Ōsumi, "Josei to Bukkyō," p. 1.

21. Aston, *Nihongi,* 2:154; Sakamoto, *Nihon shoki,* 2:210; *Fusō ryakki, KT* 12:47. For a discussion of the status of nuns in China about this time, see Li Yü-chen, *Tang-tai te pi-ch'iu-ni.*

22. Katsuura Noriko, "Gyōki no katsudō in okeru minshū sanka no tokushitsu," p. 51.

23. For a discussion of the chapels (*in*) for women that Gyōki founded and the corresponding chapels for men, see Horiike Shunpō, "Nara jidai ni okeru niji to nisō," pp. 548–555.

24. Katsuura Noriko has suggested that like the leaders of the Sect of the Three Stages in China, Gyōki may have appealed to women, but she admits that the evidence does not exist to conclusively prove her hypothesis ("Gyōki no katsudō ni okeru minshū sanka no tokushitsu," pp. 53–54).

25. Although no historical evidence supports this interpretation, it seems likely because no specific passage in the *Lotus Sūtra* qualifies it as a text appropriate for protecting the nation. In contrast, the *Suvarṇaprabhāsa* (Sūtra of golden light), the text chosen for the monasteries, was probably composed specifically to appeal to rulers. The connection between the *kokubun* nunneries and the Nāga girl in the *Lotus Sūtra* is also pointed out by Takagi Yutaka (*Heian jidai Hokke Bukkyōshi kenkyū*, p. 196) and Ishida Mosaku (*Tōdaiji to Kokubunji*, p. 21).

26. *Shoku Nihongi, KT, (zenpen)*: 193–194; Saitō Tadashi, "Kokubunniji no seikaku," p. 51.

27. Horiike, "Nara jidai ni okeru niji nisō," p. 559; Ishida Mizumaro, "Bikuni kaidan," p. 8.

28. Saitō Tadashi, "Kokubunniji," pp. 53–61.

29. The shifts in the meaning of the term "*sō*" are reflected in Nakamura Hajime, ed., *Bukkyōgo daijiten*, 2:873a–b. The significance of dropping the term "*ni*" from many edicts has been ably demonstrated by Ushiyama Yoshiyuki, "Ritsuryōsei tenkaiki ni okeru ama to amadera," pp. 11–19.

The issue of the extent to which institutions and titles became empty formalities or took on new functions in later periods is an important topic of research among contemporary scholars interested in the history of Japanese Buddhism. Among the topics that recently have been reevaluated for Heian-period Buddhism are the Office of Monastic Affairs, the ordination system, and the provincial temple system. Ushiyama's studies of nunneries are another example of such revisions of Japanese Buddhist institutional history.

30. *Shoku Nihongi, KT* 2:109; Ushiyama, "Ritsuryōsei tenkaiki ni okeru ama to amadera," pp. 11–14.

31. *Shoku Nihongi, KT* 2:411.

32. *Fusō ryakki, KT* 12:185.

33. These figures, compiled from the six national histories from the Nara and early-Heian periods, are based on a chart in Ushiyama, "Ritsuryōsei tenkaiki ni okeru ama to amadera," p. 16. Ogami Kanchū's thorough study of ordinations and yearly ordinands includes a chart that confirms the broad trends of Ushiyama's figures but is based only on the *Ruijū kokushi* ("Nenbundosha ni mirareru kashiki seido," p. 135).

34. *Ruijū kokushi, KT* 6:313. Ushiyama was the first scholar to suggest that this edict had excluded women ("Ritsuryōsei tenkaiki ni okeru ama to amadera," pp. 16–18). I commented on the historical circumstances surrounding this regulation in *Saichō*, pp. 12–13, but like many other scholars missed its significance for the history of nuns.

35. *Ruijū sandaikyaku, KT* 25:136 (fasc. 3). Ikeda Genta notes that the sudden interest of women in the Hokkeji might have been due to secularization (*zokka*) or popularization (*taishūka*) of the nunnery ("Hokkeji no enkaku," p. 203). Although the court obviously viewed the increase of numbers with alarm, Ikeda seems to suggest that a decline in the quality of nuns may have been behind the edict, but he notes little evidence to support the claim.

36. For a thorough study of yearly ordinands, see Ogami, "Nenbundosha ni mirareru kashiki seido." For a brief discussion of the yearly ordinands and the popularity of periods of seclusion for monks in the early Heian, see Groner, "Annen, Tankei, Henjō, and Monastic Discipline in the Japanese Tendai School," pp. 144–145.

37. Ushiyama, "Ritsuryōsei tenkaiki ni okeru ama to amadera," pp. 19–29.

38. A few exceptions to this rule do exist—for example, a nun mentioned in the *Kūya rui* and the *Rokuharamitsuji engi* who is said to have had twenty-five years of seniority as a nun when she died at age seventy (cited in *NS* 1.14:53).

39. Ushiyama Yoshiyuki ("Kodai ni okeru ama to amadera no mondai," pp. 58–59) argues for the earlier dates for these changes and notes some of the sources for further investigation into the dates of these social shifts. A number of articles on the subject can also be found in Joseishi sōgō kenkyūkai, ed., *Nihon joseishi*, vols. 1 and 2.

40. Okada Seishi, "Kyūtei miko no jittai"; Takatori Masao, *Shintō no seiritsu*, pp. 266–268. Takatori sees the decline as being more extensive than Okada does.

41. Ushiyama Yoshiyuki ("Ritsuryōsei tenkaiki ni okeru ama to amadera," pp. 8–11) notes that the *Sōniryō* (Regulations for monks and nuns) treats the two orders in the same manner.

42. Iinuma Kenji, "Chūsei zenki no josei no shōgai," 2:40–41, 58–59.

43. Katsuura Noriko, "Josei to kodai shinkō," 1:74–77.

44. *Shikyō ruijū*, in Yamagishi Tokuhei et al., ed., *Kodai seiji shakai shisō*, p. 44. Kibi was from a powerful clan in the countryside. He traveled to China twice, in 717 and 751; the first time he spent seventeen years there as a student, and the second time he helped lead an official mission there. He was well versed in Confucianism, astronomy, and military matters. Under the female emperor Shōtoku, he eventually rose to minister of the right. The combination of scholarship and political acumen made him an influential figure in the late Nara period. The *Shikyō ruijū* is a compendium of his advice to his descendants modeled after Yen Chih-tui's *Yenshih chia hsün* (Family instructions for the Yen clan).

45. Obara Hitoshi, "Tennyo jōbutsu setsu no juyō ni tsuite," p. 22.

46. This argument is based on Ushiyama, "Kodai ni okeru ama to amadera no mondai," pp. 54–55.

47. Borgen, *Sugawara no Michizane*, pp. 6, 88, 288–289.

48. For a good discussion of women and Confucianism, see Theresa Kelleher, "Confucianism," pp. 135–159. Indian Buddhist sources also contained similar descriptions of women's positions (Mochizuki and Tsukamoto, eds., *Mochizuki Bukkyō daijiten*, 2:1542c–1543a).

49. Taira Masayuki, "Chūsei Bukkyō to josei," 2:79.

50. *Ruijū kokushi*, *KT* 5:267–272. For a thorough discussion of the significance of these passages, see Obara, "Tennyo jōbutsu setsu no juyō ni tsuite," pp. 17–19.

51. Obara, "Tennyo jōbutsu setsu no juyō ni tsuite," p. 20; Shimode Sekiyo, "Heian jidai ni okeru shūkyō to rinri," 14–20.

52. Shirai Yūko, "Heian jidai shotō no Bukkyō to josei," p. 106. For a brief survey of Confucianism in Japan, see Hisaki Yukio, s.v. "Jukyō." Hisaki notes that although attempts were made to spread Confucian influence to the masses during the eighth and ninth centuries by emphasizing the importance of chastity for women and filial behavior for children, these efforts were unsuccessful (p. 324d).

53. See Taira, "Kyū-Bukkyō to josei," pp. 18–21, for a lucid discussion of Buddhist traditions concerning women.

54. Groner, *Saichō*, p. 8, n. 13.

55. Chien-chen's biography, the *Tōdai wajō tōseiden* (see the annotated version in Ishida Mizumaro, *Ganjin*, p. 313), lists three nuns who accompanied Chien-chen from China. Chien-chen also brought a twenty-four-fascicle collection of biographies of nuns (p. 314). The fate of these three nuns is not mentioned in any trustworthy sources; however, a document composed several centuries later indicates that they may have been given a separate place to live (discussion with Katsuura Noriko, Dec. 17, 1989).

56. Tsutsui Eishun, ed., *Tōdaiji yōroku*, p. 323.

57. See Horiike, "Nara jidai in okeru niji nisō," pp. 565–566, for a detailed study of nuns between 740 and 760.

58. For a discussion of the few nuns that did travel over the sea to Japan, see Takagi, *Bukkyōshi no naka no nyonin*, pp. 214–223. Takagi suggests that because the sea *kami* were female, taboos that forbade women from boarding ships may have added to the difficulty nuns would have had crossing the ocean.

Another possible approach to the ordination of nuns might have been to define the ordination as one occurring in outlying areas and performing it with a smaller order. Such an approach was used for ordinations of monks in outlying areas of Japan, but no evidence exists that it was ever discussed as an option for ordinations of nuns.

Hirakawa Akira notes that only the *Wu-fen lü* (*T* 1421, *Mahīśāsaka-vinaya*) specifies that ten nuns had to be in the ordination, leaving the possibility that five nuns might have been enough (*Genshi Bukkyō no kenkyū*, pp. 514, 517). However, Tao-hsüan (596–667), the leading interpreter of *Vinaya* in East Asia, specified that ten nuns were required (*Ssu-fen-lü hsing-shih ch'ao*, *T* 40:152a–b; Ishida *Mizumaro*, "Bikuni kaidan," p. 2).

Ordinations with five nuns, even if they had been performed, might have been viewed as being inferior to ordinations with ten nuns. For example, in the fourteenth century such ordinations for monks were considered to be inferior to those with ten monks. Monks with such inferior ordinations were said to lack the qualifications to serve at important assemblies (Matsuo Kenji, "Chūsei Chikuzen Kanzeonji Shimotsuke Yakushiji ryōkaidan ni okeru jukaisei," 1:82).

59. *Shoku Nihongi*, *KT* 2:271; *Nihon kiryaku*, *KT* 10:221. My discussion of Kōmyō generally follows Hayashi Rokurō, *Kōmyō Kōgō*, pp. 86–126, 135–148; Mikoshiba Daisuke, "Kōmyōshi no Bukkyō shinkō," pp. 73–104; and Sakuma Ryū, *Nihon kodai sōden no kenkyū*, pp. 113–115.

60. Another factor in the presence of officially ordained nuns might have been how closely women were associated with the shamanistic rituals of early Japanese government. In other words, as *miko* ceased to play a central role in governmental and shrine affairs, the role of nuns in ceremonies to protect the state also might have been affected.

61. *Kanshō Tendaishū nenbun gakushōshiki*, *DZ* 1:15; *Eizan daishiden*, *DZ* 5 (*bekkan*): 39. For English translations of the relevant passages, see Groner, *Saichō*, pp. 135, 159. Other scholars have suggested later dates for the banning of women from monasteries; but their dates reflect the development of rationales and legends for

the exclusion of women rather than the actual rules banning them. For an argument that places it in the eleventh century, see Ushiyama, "Kodai ni okeru ama to amadera no shōchō," pp. 50–51.

62. See Groner, "Annen, Tankei, Henjō, and Monastic Discipline in the Japanese Tendai School," p. 145, n. 34.

63. Hōnen criticized this practice in the *Muryōjukyō shaku* (Ōhashi Shunnō, ed., *Hōnen Ippen*, p. 55); however, I have not been able to determine when women were first barred from Tōdaiji. Certainly the monastery originally did not have such a restriction since Empress Kōmyō played a major role in its establishment and dedication. However, according to a later legend, the main gate of the Buddha Hall broke when Empress Kōmyō attempted to enter it. Women were subsequently prohibited from entering it (*Nanto shichidaiji junreiki, BZ* [Bussho kankōkai ed.], 120:7a). The passage from Hōnen's work has been emphasized in Kasahara Kazuo's *Nyonin ōjō shisō no keifu* as evidence that the Kamakura schools held much more liberal attitudes than earlier forms of Buddhism. His views have been criticized by Taira Masayuki in "Kyū-Bukkyō to josei."

64. According to the *Engishiki*, female novices were to be ordained at the Tōdaiji and the other two ordination platforms associated with it (*KT* 26:544). The *Engishiki* also specifies the procedures that should be carried out in issuing ordination certificates. However, no evidence exists that such ordinations were conducted during the mid- and late-Heian periods. A recent survey of surviving ordination documents by Matsuo Kenji has revealed that no evidence exists suggesting that ordinations of nuns were performed at Tōdaiji (*Kamakura shin-Bukkyō no seiritsu*, pp. 115–116).

65. This position has been followed by Kasahara Kazuo, *Nyonin ōjō no keifu*, pp. 16–21.

66. Taira Masayuki, "Chūsei Bukkyō to josei," p. 82; Takeuchi, ed., *Heian ibun*, 1:134b (document no. 156).

67. Ushiyama Yoshiyuki, "Kodai ni okeru ama to amadera no shōchō," pp. 50–51; Nishiguchi Junko, *Onna no chikara*, pp. 116–129.

68. Most of these stories, no matter what temple they concern, involve a female practitioner of great power named Toranni or variations on that name; for a discussion, see Abe Yasurō, "Nyonin kinzei to suisan."

69. Taira, "Chūsei Bukkyō to josei," p. 90.

70. Miyata Noboru, *Kami no minzokushi*, pp. 39–72; Makita Shigeru, *Kami to onna no minzokugaku*, pp. 41–54. Many of the medieval legends about women who tried to climb prohibited mountains concern Mount Kōya, but a few concern Mount Hiei. Katsuno Ryūshin has suggested that this might have been due to Tendai teachings that stressed the universality of the Buddha-nature, but this claim needs to be justified with more evidence (*Hieizan to Kōyasan*, pp. 239–240).

71. *Jie daisōjō shūiden, ZTZ Shiden*, 2:206a. At some point, small paths for women to go on pilgrimage from the women's halls to Oku no in on Mount Kōya were demarcated even though the rest of Mount Kōya remained off limits to them (Hotta Shinkai, *Kōyasan Kongōbuji*, p. 183).

72. *Honchō seiki, KT* 9:729.

73. When Oda Nobunaga burned the temple complex on Mount Hiei in 1571, many women and children were killed (Neil McMullin, *Buddhism and the State in*

Sixteenth Century Japan, pp. 147–148). During earlier periods, some of them were mistresses of monks; such women often lived near sacred mountains; see Nishiguchi, *Onna no chikara,* pp. 186–209.

74. Matsumura and Yamanaka, eds., *Eiga monogatari,* 1:169; McCullough and Mc-Cullough, *Flowering Fortunes,* 1:192.

75. Matsumura and Yamanaka, eds., *Eiga monogatari,* 1:186, 204, 206, 213–216; McCullough and McCullough, *Flowering Fortunes,* 1:209–230.

76. Shigematsu Nobuhiro (*Genji monogatari no Bukkyō shisō,* p. 367) remarks that *Genji monogatari* records no instances of nuns being unchaste. The traditional encyclopedia—Jingū shichō, ed., *Koji ruien* (*Teiō-bu* 15 [Tokyo: Yoshikawa kō-bunkan, 1982], pp. 910–911)—records only one other case of an empress who was ordained and then reentered the court, Reisei Mon'in (1303–1333). Men and women could return to secular life after ordination only with great difficulty (Katada Osamu, "Ōchō kizoku no shukke nyūdō," pp. 382–383).

However, some evidence does exist that nuns were not always chaste. For example, Fujiwara no Korechika (973–1010) worried about the future of his daughters shortly before his death: "We can't even make nuns of them unless we want to be called mad—to say nothing of the very distinct possibility of their both winding up as companions to renegade monks (*ayashi no hōshi no gu*)" (McCullough and McCullough, *Flowering Fortunes,* 1:302–303; Matsumura and Yamanaka, eds., *Eiga monogatari,* 1:289–290). Katsuura Noriko has argued that the reduced financial circumstances of many nuns might have led them into sexual liaisons with monks or caused them to allow their dwellings to be used for assignations ("Amasogi kō," pp. 36–37).

77. Katsuura Noriko, "Amasogi kō," p. 28. Princess Sonshi, mentioned below, is another example of a woman cutting her own hair to become a nun. I have not encountered any examples of men cutting their own hair to become monks in the Heian period, but have not done a thorough search of the literature. One case of a retired emperor doing so, dated 1467, is found in *Koji ruien, Teiō-bu* 15, p. 886.

78. Mentioned in Ryōgen's will, translated in appendix 3.

79. The description of Sonshi is based on Kamens, *Three Jewels,* pp. 7–13.

80. *Honchō monzui, KT* 29:346.

81. Nagata Mizu, "Butten ni miru boseikan."

82. The suffering that arose from childbirth and women's position in society was eventually attributed to pollution and past sins. For a fascinating portrayal of the complex evaluations of motherhood and religion in the middle ages, see Wakita Haruko, "Bosei sonchō shisō to zaigōkan."

83. For Senkan, see *Fusō ryakki, KT* 254–255; *Nihon Ōjō gokurakuki,* in Inoue and Ōsone, eds.; *Ōjōden Hokke genki,* p. 29; *Nihon kiryaku, KT* 11:104. According to *Konjaku monogatari,* Atsutada's daughter had a dream that verified Senkan's rebirth into the Pure Land (Mabuchi and Kunisaki, eds., *Konjaku monogatarishū,* fasc. 15.16, 2:78).

The consorts are identified with Emperor Murakami in *NS* 1.20:188, but with Emperor Suzaku in Kokushi daijiten henshū iinkai, ed., *Kokushi daijiten* 8:389b. Yūhime was the daughter of Motokata, the loser in the power struggle with Fujiwara no Morosuke, Ryōgen's patron. She thus chose a monk not allied with Ryōgen for her teacher. She might well have found Senkan's reclusiveness attractive. Senkan does not seem to have been opposed to Morosuke, however. The award of a posthumous elevation of rank to Morosuke's wife Seishi was performed under Senkan's auspices.

The term "kaishi" (literally, "teacher of the precepts") is used to describe Senkan's status at Yūhime's ordination. In a comment concerning another document, Matsuo Kenji notes that "*kaishi*" was used to refer to the teacher in the ordination of novices and "*kaiwajō*" (literally, "preceptor") in full ordinations ("Kansō to tonseisō," p. 298). Although this distinction is made in neither the Buddhist nor *bungo* dictionaries that I consulted, Matsuo's extensive reading of ordination certificates makes his interpretation noteworthy. In addition, the manner in which the term is used in a number of cases suggests that "*kaishi*" was used to refer to the teacher at initiations of novices in many, but no all, cases. The usage of the term deserves more study, particularly in regard to how it might have changed over time. Its usage in referring to the ordinations by Senkan may suggest that the women were ordained as novices. However, another interpretation of the term "*kaishi*" is possible. In Tendai ordinations, Sākyamuni Buddha served as the preceptor (*kaiwajō*) who conferred (*ju*) the precepts while an eminent monk served as the master of ceremonies (*kaishi*) who transmitted (*den*) the precepts. In this case, a *kaishi* could preside over a full bodhisattva ordination.

84. Seidenstecker, trans., *Genji*, pp. 620, 1051; Yamagishi Norihira, ed., *Genji monogatari*, 16:385, 18:356–357). Both Tendai and Nara monks conferred the five precepts. In fact, according to the Tendai Esoteric text, the *Asabashō*, five precepts are to be conferred to lay believers when they are sick (*T* [*zuzō*], 9:568c), as is the case in *The Tale of Genji*.

85. For example, they rejected the elaborate funerary rites performed in the imperial family. Kachiko wanted a "shallow grave," perhaps the result of Mohist influence. For a thorough study on their religiosity, see Ōe Atsushi, "Junna Taikō Seishi Naishinnō to Junnain," pp. 142–173.

86. *Montoku jitsuroku, KT* 3:10–11.

87. Ikeda Genta has suggested that Zen'un might have been one of the many women who entered the Hokkeji about 797 when the court issued an edict admonishing the nunnery against allowing so many women to enter it ("Hokkeji no enkaku," pp. 203–204; *Ruijū sandaikyaku, KT* 25:136 [fasc. 3]).

88. Egaku made two or three trips to China. During his second trip he obtained an image of Kannon. When he was trying to return to Japan, he was shipwrecked on the coast of China. He interpreted this as a sign that the image was not to leave China and established a temple near the shipwreck site. His fate is not known, but Ono Katsutoshi suggests that he may have been laicized during the 845 persecution of Buddhism and have chosen to remain in China (*Nittō guhō junrei kōki*, 3:406–408, 4:206).

89. This account is primarily based on I-k'ung's biography in the *Genkō shakusho* (*BZ* [Suzuki ed.], 62:98b). However, Egaku's biography in the *Genkō shakusho* (*BZ* [Suzuki ed.], 62:149c) places these events in the Saikō era (854–856), much too late since Kachiko died in 850. Egaku may have traveled to China as many as six times (Tamura Enchō, *kaidai* [explanation] of the "Egaku wajō nenpu," *BZ* [Suzuki ed.], 98:345a). As a result, a number of problems arise in determining the chronology of these events. I have followed Ono Katsutoshi (*Nittō guhō junrei kōki*, 3:406–408) and Ōno Tatsunosuke ("Egaku," Kokushi daijiten henshu iinkai, ed., *Kokushi daijiten*, 2:243c) in this account. The primary source materials concerning Egaku and I-k'ung are compiled in Hashimoto Shinkichi's "Egaku wajō nenpu," *BZ* (Suzuki ed.), 72:136–140.

90. *Montoku jitsuroku, KT* 3:11. The term "*in*" was used to refer to a variety of buildings including country palaces and chapels at monasteries.

91. For studies of such merit-making ordinations, see Ishida Mizumaro, "Heian chūki ni okeru zaike shinja no jukai seishin no tenkai"; Katada Osamu, "Ōchō kizoku no shukke nyūdō." Charts in Katada's article (pp. 379–380) indicate that this pattern became common about middle of the tenth century.

92. Ishida Mizumarō, "Bikuni kaidan," p. 13, n. 6. Ishida has questioned the use of this term in this passage, suggesting that it was used as a term of respect and that such ordained women were probably novices when considered according to the *Vinaya*.

93. *Montoku jitsuroku, KT* 3:10–11. Also see the entries on Danrin kōgō in Mochizuki and Tsukamoto, eds., *Mochizuki Bukkyō daijiten*, 4:3528b–3529a, and Ryūkoku daigaku, ed., *Bukkyō daijii*, 5:3280b, and the entry on the Saganoin in Kokūshi daijiten henshū iinkai, ed., *Kokushi daijiten*, 6:273c.

94. *Sandai jitsuroku, KT* 4:450 (Gangyō 3-3-23).

95. *Shoku Nihon kōki, KT* 3:147 (*Jōwa* 9-12-5).

96. Ōe, "Junna Taikō Seishi Naishinnō," pp. 145–150.

97. Katsuura, "Josei to kodai shinkō," 1:96.

98. For information on Tsunesada, see his biography in *Gōshūi ōjōden*, in Inoue and Ōsone, eds., *Ōjōden Hokke genki*, p. 648; obituary in *Sandai jitsuroku, KT* 4:572; and a biography, the *Tsunesada Shinnō den*, in the *ZGR* 8A:47–49. Little is known of the relationship between Tsunesada and Shinnyo; see Sugimoto, *Shinnyo shinnō-den kenkyū*, p. 231.

Shinnyo became a monk shortly after he lost his position as crown prince in 810 as a result of the Kusuko disturbance. He studied Sanron under Dōsen and Shingon under Kūkai. In 862, he traveled to China, where he studied Esoteric teachings under Fa-ch'üan. He died, probably on the Malay Peninsula, in an attempt to reach India.

99. *Sandai jitsuroku, KT* 4:503.

100. *Sandai jitsuroku, KT* 4:450; Minamoto no Tamenori, *Sanbō ekotoba*, 2:38–43; Kamens, *Three Jewels*, pp. 272–274.

101. *Sandai jitsuroku, KT* 4:51.

102. *Sandai jitsuroku, KT* 4:341.

103. *Sandai jitsuroku, KT* 4:370. For a study of the establishment of the Daikakuji, see Hiraoka Jōkai, *Nihon jiinshi no kenkyū*, pp. 507–522.

104. *Gōshūi ōjōden*, in Inoue and Ōsone, eds., *Ōjōden Hokke genki*, p. 648; *Kanke bunsō*, cited in Horioka, *Nihon jiinshi no kenkyū*, p. 514.

105. *Sandai jitsuroku, KT* 4:481, 508. For a brief discussion of the difficulties of locating these tumuli, established even though Empress Junna did not want one, see Ōe Atsushi, "Junna Taikō Seishi Naishinnō to Junnain," p. 170, n. 40. The position of *bettō* was eventually monopolized by the Minamoto clan (Fūzanbō kokushi jiten hensanbu, ed., *Kokushi jiten*, 4:974a–c).

106. *Sandai jitsuroku, KT* 4:450; *Shoku Nihon kōki, KT* 3:147.

107. The *Ying-lo ching* (*T* no. 1485) is an apocryphal text, that is, a work purporting to have been preached by the Buddha in India but which was actually compiled in China. It was closely associated with the *Fan-wang ching* and used by many Tendai thinkers to interpret the *Fan-wang ching*.

108. For discussions of liberal aspects of the bodhisattva precepts, see the discussion of the *Fan-wang ching*'s universal order in Groner, "The *Fan-wang ching* and Monastic Discipline in Japanese Tendai," pp. 255–257; and the discussion of self-ordinations in the *Fan-wang ching* and *Ying-lo ching* in Groner, "The Ordination Ritual in the Platform Sūtra," pp. 229–233. Saichō mentions these themes and notes that "husbands and wives can ordain each other" and that "the ordained and laiety have a single essence" (*shinzoku ikkan*) (*DZ* 1:19, 133, 543). Because such liberal views would have proven to be unworkable in administering an order and in maintaining good relations with the government, Tendai monks such as Ennin began to restrict ordinations as soon as Saichō died (Groner, *Saichō*, pp. 300–302).

109. This position is maintained in the *Engishiki* (*KT* 26:544). No mention is made in the *Engishiki* of ordinations of nuns at any Tendai institution.

110. Saeki, *Jikaku daishiden no kenkyū*, pp. 286–288. The term "*bosatsu daikai*" would seem to imply a fuller set of precepts than those granted to some other believers, but the exact contents of the full precepts (*daikai*) is not clear. According to the *Tendai zasuki*, the *Fan-wang* fortnightly assembly was the very first performed (Shibuya, ed., *Tendai zasuki*, p. 12). However, the entry must refer to the first *Fan-wang* assembly performed under Tendai auspices; others had been performed during the Nara period. Gyōnen notes that Dōyū (d. 729) performed the first such ceremony at Tōdaiji (Tokuda Myōhon, *Risshū gairon*, pp. 534–535). The ceremony was probably used by Tendai monks and lay believers to make merit rather than to enforce monastic discipline. For a thorough study of *Fan-wang* fortnightly assemblies, see Ishida, *Ganjin*, pp. 253–267. The *sanmaya* precepts are discussed further in Groner, "The *Fan-wang ching* and Monastic Discipline in Japanese Tendai," pp. 262–266.

111. Saeki, *Jikaku daishiden no kenkyū*, p. 290.

112. *Jikaku daishiden, ZGR* 8:696a. Honda, *Yakuchū Jikaku daishiden*, p. 48; Saeki, *Jikaku daishiden no kenkyū*, pp. 296–298. Nothing in the *Ken'yō daikairon* (*T* no. 2380) refers to the empress' wishes. Ennin probably intended to support her wishes in a general way by replying to Nara criticisms of the Tendai ordination system. Ennin's remarks in the will were probably addressed to his disciple Henjō (817–890).

113. Ono Katsutoshi, *Nittō guhō junrei kōki no kenkyū*, 2:381; Reischauer, trans., *Ennin's Diary*, p. 207.

114. Minamoto no Tamenori, *Sanbō ekotoba*, 2:39–43; Kamens, *Three Jewels*, pp. 272–275. An English translation from Pāli of the story of the admission of the first women to the order of nuns is found in Henry Clarke Warren, trans., *Buddhism in Translations*, pp. 441–447.

115. Kamens (*Three Jewels*, pp. 272–275) describes the nunnery as existing through the eleventh century; but gives no details about it. The Kokushi daijiten henshū iinkai, ed., *Kokushi daijiten* (7:424d) entry on the Junnain includes no information about the institution's later functions as a nunnery.

116. Minamoto no Tamenori, *Sanbō ekotoba*, 2:60; Kamens, *Three Jewels*, p. 291. Tamenori comments about the Hokkeji in Yamato, "Since the founding of this convent by the Empress [Kōmyō], there has been no interruption in its habitation by nuns." However, the history of Hokkeji is filled with ambiguities. Although it is listed in the *Engishiki* as the only nunnery to be included among major monasteries, other sources indicate that it had fallen into disrepair by the eleventh century or had be-

come subject to Kōfukuji or Saidaiji; for a thorough analysis of extant sources on the Hokkeji during the Heian period, see Ikeda, "Hokkeji no enkaku," pp. 203–215.

117. *Ruijū sandaikyaku, KT* 25:98; *Ruijū kokushi, KT* 6:242–243.

118. *Sandai jitsuroku, KT* 4:295 (Jōgan 13-19-28). The term "*rakusai*," translated here as "shedding ornaments," may be a homonym for a term meaning "cut the hair" (Nihon daijiten kankōkai, ed., *Nihon kokugo daijiten*, 20:262b). The *Jikaku daishiden* (Saeki, *Jikaku daishiden no kenkyū*, pp. 290–291) mentions that Eun conferred the Hīnayāna precepts on her and bestowed the religious name Hongaku (original enlightenment) on her, but no date is given for the ordination nor is the set of precepts in question identified specifically. The passage concludes by noting that she subsequently received the bodhisattva precepts and a new religious name from Ennin, implying that she saw the error of her Hīnayāna ordination and accepted the Tendai view that only its precepts were truly Mahāyānist.

119. Katsuura, "Josei to kodai shinkō," 1:96–97.

120. *Jikaku daishiden*, in Saeki, *Jikaku daishiden no kenkyū*, pp. 290–291; *Sandai jitsuroku, KT* 4:127, 4:295; *Genkō shakusho, BZ* (Suzuki ed.), 62: 149c; Saeki, *Ennin*, pp. 241–242.

121. Shirato Waka, "Manshuin-hon *Shukke sahō* ni miru girei to Heian Bukkyō," pp. 172–174, 181, n. 32. For information about Manshuin, see Tsunoda, ed., *Heian jidaishi jiten*, 2:2367a. Chūjin was especially active in supporting the Manshuin and in reviving scholarship among Tendai monks (ibid., p. 1630c–d).

122. *Shōyūki* (Shōki mokuroku 9-28-786), cited in Katsuura, "Josei to kodai shinkō," 1:88. The Rokuharamitsuji, founded by Kōya, seems to have had a long history of appealing to women. For example, the second day of an annual four-day series of lectures on the *Lotus Sūtra* had been specifically dedicated to the salvation of women (*Honchō monzui, KT* 29:238). Several nuns are reported at the temple in the *Hokke genki* (Inoue and Ōsone, eds., *Ōjōden Hokke genki*, p. 183). If sources for a history of nuns at the temple existed, they would contribute immensely to our knowledge of nuns from the lower classes.

123. Katada "Ōchō kizoku no shukke nyūdō," p. 383.

124. See Ushiyama, "Kodai ni okeru ama to amadera no shōchō," pp. 61–65. Ushiyama has compiled a number of sources demonstrating the disappearance of nunneries during the mid- and late-Heian periods (ibid., p. 61–67).

125. Occasionally the monks and nuns of *kokubunji* are mentioned in the *Engishiki* (see, for example, *KT* 26:656), but these cases may very well be regulations carried over from earlier documents rather than an indication of an active order of nuns.

126. Saitō Tadashi, "Kokubunniji no seikaku," p. 48. Saitō's article includes citations to a number of passages concerning the nunneries through 853 (pp. 50, 61, n. 1).

127. *Sandai jitsuroku, KT* 4:558; Usami Masatoshi, "Jōgakuji no seiritsu to henshitsu," pp. 93–94.

128. *Sandai jitsuroku, KT* 4:634. Usami considers this entry to be so unusual that he suggests that the term "nun" may have been a copyist's error ("Jōgakuji no seiritsu to henshitsu," pp. 93–94).

129. Defining measures such as *soku* is difficult becuse they frequently varied according to time and place. One *soku* was generally the equivalent of ten sheaves

(*taba* or *ha*), a measure defined as the amount of grain, presumably still on the stalk, that could be grasped between the thumb and the middle finger. Eventually the measure came to be considered the measure of rice from a certain amount of land.

130. *Sandai jitsuroku, KT* 4:474 (Gangyō 4-5-19). Takagi Yutaka, *Bukkyōshi no naka no nyonin*, p. 285.

131. The connection between religious women and the washing of monks' robes was first indicated by Katsuura Noriko, "'Sentaku to onna' nōto.'" Nishiguchi Junko (*Onna no chikara*, p. 138) has indicated that some of the communities of women at the foot of Mount Hiei and Mount Kōya probably included women, some of them nuns, who washed and sewed monks' robes.

132. A nun at Rokuharamitsuji interpreted dreams (Inoue and Ōsone, eds., *Hokke genki*, in *Ōjoden Hokke genki*, p. 183); some of the nuns attending Hōjōji guided pilgrims or regularly made offerings at the Buddha hall (McCullough and McCullough, *Flowering Fortunes*, 2:575–579; Matsumura and Yamanaka, eds., *Eiga monogatari*, 76:92–96). Although the nuns usually were not portrayed as receiving anything for their efforts in these accounts, Michinaga does make a provision for one nun who had regularly made offerings of flowers (*hana no ama;* Matsumura and Yamanaka, eds., *Eiga monogatari*, 72:91; McCullough and McCullough, *Flowering Fortunes*, 2:574; others might well have provided for other nuns.

133. The nuns at Hōjōji lived nearby (McCullough and McCullough, eds., *Flowering Fortunes*, 2:571; Matsumura and Yamanaka, eds., *Eiga monogatari*, 2:89). For a number of examples of this type of arrangement, though slightly later, see Nishiguchi, *Onna no chikara*, pp. 156–162.

134. Ushiyama, "Kodai ni okeru ama to amadera no shōchō," p. 66.

135. Chinkai, *Bodaishin shū*, in Jōdoshu kaishū happyakunen kinen keisan junbikyoku, ed., *Jōdoshū zensho*, 15:525. Chinkai was a noted Sanron scholar who also practiced Esoteric Buddhism. Late in life he turned toward Pure Land traditions. Among his noted works are texts on Sanron thought, *Abhidharmakośa*, logic, and the *Lotus Sūtra*. Note that Chinkai considered the ordination platform to be necessary for a full ordination; moreover, the expression "*shamini no ama*" for novices indicates that he recognized the ambiguity of the term "*ama.*" East Asian nuns in the Vinaya school tradition actually received the 348 precepts of the *Ssu-fen lü;* the figure five hundred is simply a representative number found in many sources.

136. Ishida Mizumaro, "Bikuni kaidan."

137. *Sandai jitsuroku, KT* 4:481. Although the terms "*daini*" and "*shōni*" are not found in dictionaries, they would seem to be similar to "*daisō,*" a "greater" or fully ordained monk as opposed to a "lesser monk" or novice (*shōsō*). See Nakamura Hajime, ed., *Bukkyōgo daijiten*, p. 924a.

Similar terms—"*daini-ko*" and "*shōni-kō*" ("*kō*" is an honorific)—are found in Nara-period documents, but they probably refer to older and younger nuns of noble birth (Horiike, "Nara jidai ni okeru niji nisō," 1:556–559). However, the editors of the Jingū shichō (*Koji ruien, Shūkyō-bu* 27:677) comment that "*daini*" might have referred to a woman who had been properly ordained and "shōni" to a woman who acted as a nun but had not received a proper ordination, someone equivalent to a privately initiated *shamini* during the Nara period. Of course, the definition of a "proper ordination" is problematic. Whatever the exact meaning of the term was in the early Heian period, it clearly indicated the existence of a hierarchy of practitioners. For other examples of these terms, see Ushiyama, "Ritsuryōsei tenkaiki ni okeru ama to amadera," p. 7.

Another possibility is that the terms differentiated between women of noble birth and their servants, who were often ordained with them. This pattern is seen in Kamakura-period Risshū temples; see Hosokawa Ryōichi, "Medieval Nuns and Nunneries."

138. Katsuura Noriko, "Amasogi kō"; forthcoming English translation as "Tonsure Forms for Nuns."

139. Katsuura, "Amasogi kō," pp. 25–26.

140. Richard Bowring, *Murasaki Shikibu*, p. 55; Fujioka Tadaharu et al., eds., *Izumi shikibu nikki, Murasaki shikibu nikki, Sarashina nikki, Sanuki no suke nikki*, p. 171. Ishida Mizumaro has discussed the worldly benefits that led both men and women to take the precepts in Heian Japan. See his "Kitō to shite no jukai"; *Nihon Bukkyō ni okeru kairitsu no kenkyū*, 421–435; "Heian chūki ni okeru zaike shinja no jukai seishin no tenkai."

141. Takagi Yutaka has suggested that this hairstyle might have arisen early in the eleventh century (*Bukkyōshi no naka no nyonin*, pp. 121–122).

142. Matsumura and Yamanaka, eds., *Eiga monogatari*, 2:264–266; McCullough and McCullough, eds., *Flowering Fortunes*, 2:714, 716. The ambiguities in the status of nuns are demonstrated by the differences in interpretation of this event by the McCulloughs and Ishida Mizumaro. The McCulloughs comment that Shōshi's first ordination might have been the six precepts of a provisional nun and the ordination on the platform a full ordination. Ishida's reading of the situation suggests that the first set of precepts would have been the ten for novices and the second for a full nun. The McCulloughs attribute the other nuns' happiness to the opportunity to receive the precepts along with Shōshi; in contrast, Ishida argues that they were happy because this would enable them to become fully ordained nuns instead of novices (Ishida, "Bikuni kaidan," pp. 6–7).

143. *Shōyūki* (3-27-Manju 4), cited in Matsumura and Yamanaka, eds., *Eiga monogatari*, 2:589 (note for p. 253). Shōshi's first ordination had been performed by her cousin, a monk from Miidera (McCullough and McCullough, eds., *Flowering Fortunes*, 2:713–714), but had also been attended by monks from Mount Hiei.

144. *Ōkagami uragaki*, in Matsumura Hiroji, collator, *Ōkagami*, p. 307; *Fusō ryakki*, *KT* 12:284. The *Fusō ryakki* passage calls the 1039 event a "reordination" (*jūjukai*), a term that would suggest that the ordination was simply a repetition of her earlier ordinations, but this interpretation may reflect monastic biases that did not recognize a hierarchical system of ordinations for women. Myōson (971–1063) was an able scholar and skilled poet who led the Miidera faction of Tendai; he was appointed *zasu* of the Tendai school in 1038 and 1048, but forced to resign both times. The choice of Myōson for the ordination may indicate an alliance between Shōshi and Miidera as each lent prestige to the other. In other words, Shōshi's actions might have suggested recognition of Onjōji's efforts to establish an ordination platform, and Myōson's ordination may have indicated monastic recognition of a fully ordained Tendai lineage of nuns.

145. *Fusō ryakki*, *KT* 12:295; Ishida Mizumaro, "Bikuni kaidan," p. 6. The *Fusō ryakki* passage mentions an ordination platform among the structures destroyed, without identifying it as that built for nuns.

146. *T* 54:262a.

147. Katsuura, "Amasogikō," pp. 23–27. Katsuura notes that the evidence joining shaving the head with the transformation into men is not conclusive.

148. Ōishi Masaaki, "Ama no Hokkeji to sō no Hokkeji," pp. 186–188.

149. Katsuura, "Josei to kodai shinkō," 1:95–101. As has been noted in several of the examples cited above, some of the historians who recorded these events may have interpreted them so that they fit Confucian values.

150. *Nihon ōjō gokuraku ki*, in Inoue and Ōsone, eds., *Ōjōden Hokke genki*, p. 39. A similar story can be found in *Sange ōjōki*, ibid., pp. 681–682. Ono no Takaki's appointment as governor of Yamashiro in 887 serves to give an approximate date for these events.

151. This statement is based on conversations with Elizabeth Napper and Tessa Bartholomeusz in April and May 1990; however, Matthew Kapstein questioned this characterization of Tibetan nuns in a conversation in June 1990. The financial resources of nunneries probably plays an important role in age restrictions because poor nunneries might favor younger nuns who could work or rich older women who would contribute their wealth to the institution's financial base. Impoverished nunneries may well have been reluctant to take on the burden of caring for elderly poor women, even if such women were pious.

152. For a list of such passages, see Katada, "Ōchō kizoku no shukke nyūdō," p. 379. Numerous passages concerning ordinations can be found in Jingū shichō, ed., *Koji ruien, Shūkyō-bu*, 27:639–680; *Teiō-bu*, 15:859–913. Katada's whole article (pp. 377–401) contains a lucid discussion of the meaning of the ordination of nobles.

153. These terms seem to have become prevalent during the Kamakura period Nihon daijiten kankōkai, ed., (*Nihon kokugo daijiten*, 1:414c). The unusual term "*ie no ama*" appears in Mabuchi and Kunisaki, eds., *Konjaku monogatarishū*, fasc. 3.350, 24.27.

154. Ishida Mizumaro, "Bikuni kaidan," pp. 7–8.

155. *Honchō monzui*, *KT* 29:346; Kamens, *Three Jewels*, p. 12.

156. The significance of the *Lotus Sūtra* for women was commented on in a variety of sources by authors of several schools. See Taira, "Chūsei Bukkyō to josei," 2:85–89. Another text, the *Tennyo jōbutsukyō* (Sūtra on transformation of women and realization of Buddhahood) is also mentioned often from the mid-Heian period onward; for examples, see *Honchō monzui*, *KT* 29:346–347.

157. Kamens, *Three Jewels*, p. 13; *Honchō monzui*, *KT* 29:346. Yoshishige no Yasutane, who wrote about Sonshi, was also the author of the *Nihon Ōjō gokurakuki* (Accounts of Japanese births in the paradise), a text that included a number of biographies of women and nuns who performed Pure Land practices.

158. Nishiguchi, *Onna no chikara*, p. 115.

159. Matsumura and Yamanaka, eds. *Eiga monogatari*, 2:141–142; McCullough and McCullough, eds., *Flowering Fortunes*, 2:619–620. Queen Śrīmālā is the only woman to occupy the central place and to preach a Buddhist scripture, the *Sheng-man ching* (*T* no. 353; Skt. *Śrīmālādevī sūtra*). The text, one of three *sūtras* on which Prince Shōtoku is said to have written a commentary (*T* no. 2185), was well known in Japan.

160. *Hokke genki*, in Inoue and Ōsone, eds., *Ōjōden Hokke genki*, p. 181.

161. *Zoku honchō ōjōden*, ibid., p. 252. The editors of the Nihon koten bungaku

taikei edition of the text have convincingly argued that this biography concernsGanshō rather than Gansai as indicated in the manuscripts (ibid., p. 424). Ganshō (d. 1034) was Genshin's youngest sister. Since Genshin was one of the most eminent scholars of his day, the evaluation of his sister's learning, even if hyperbole, is significant.

162. Minamoto no Tamenori, *Sanbō ekotoba*, 2:61. The locus classicus for this passage is the *Ta-chih-tu lun*, *T* 25:161a–b; for other stories of Utpalavarṇā, see Akanuma Chizen, *Indo Bukkyō koyū meishi jiten*, pp. 715–716. The story seems to have been popular in the Japanese Tendai tradition; it is cited by Ennin in the *Ken'yō daikairon* (*T* 74:701a–b) and in the Manshuin ordination manual for nuns (Shirato Waka, "Manshuin-hon *Shukke sahō* ni miru girei to Heian Bukkyō," p. 157). The context in which the story was cited was crucial to its interpretation. In the *Ken'yō daikairon*, the story probably was an anecdote that encouraged people to be ordained even if they were not sure they could observe the precepts. However, in the *Sanbō ekotoba*, it might be interpreted as a rationale allowing lax observance of the precepts by nuns. The story might also have been cited to console aspiring nuns to be content with their lower status because the precepts could serve as a karmic cause for spiritual progress in future lifetimes.

163. For some of the doctrinal rationalizations for such behavior, see Groner, "The *Fan-wang ching* and Monastic Discipline in Japanese Tendai," pp. 273–277.

Chapter 13. Epilogue

1. *Jie daisōjōden, DS* 1.22:53. The characters for *Jie* have long been written in two different ways. Determining which was the original form is difficult, but Hirabayashi suggests that using the character *e* from *chie* (wisdom) is probably the original form rather than the form using the character read *megumu* (*Ryōgen*, pp. 179–180).

2. On the basis of a passage in the *Chikanaga kyōki* (12-18-1493, cited in Murayama Shūichi, "Jie daishi no shinkō," pp. 74–75), Murayama raises the possibility that a decree was issued sometime later awarding the title of *daishi* to Ryōgen.

3. Watanabe Shujun, *Setsuwa bungaku no Eizan Bukkyō* pp. 77–95. Also note the very few mentions of Ryōgen in Oishio Chihiro, *Nihon chūsei no setsuwa to Bukkyō*.

4. *ZTZ Shiden*, 2:198–199.

5. Ibid., 199.

6. *Myōshō ryakuden* and *Genkō shakusho*, cited in *DS* 1.22:77, 80. A portrait of Ryōgen surrounded by celestial bodies that reflects this theme is included in Murayama, *Kodai Bukkyō no chūseiteki tenkai*, frontispiece, plate 3.

7. *ZTZ Shiden*, 2:199.

8. Ibid., 210.

9. *Goshūi ōjōden*, cited in *DS* 1.22:73.

10. For example, Ryōgen is identified with Kokūzō in the *Myōshō ryakuden, DS* 1.22:77; with Nyoirin Kannon in the *Taiheiki, DS* 1.22:100; with Shōgun Jizō and *kami* in *Tōeizan Kan'eiji ganzan daishi engi* (comp. Inkai in 1673–1680), *DS* 1.22:309.

11. *Jie daishi ekotoba, DS* 1.22:85.

12. Anonymous, "Ganzan daishi shinkō ni kansuru chōsa hōkoku." This report

includes the results of questionnaires sent to 3,028 temples, of which 933 responded. Of those responding, 298 had images of Ganzan daishi installed, 26 as the main image and 166 as an attending image. In 98 temples, Ganzan daishi was installed in his own hall separate from the main hall. In 293 temples, amulets of Tsuno daishi were produced; 57 temples had amulets of Mame daishi.

13. Kageyama Haruki, "Hieizan ni okeru Mieidō to byōbō," p. 203.

14. Kageyama, "Mieidō," pp. 199–200.

15. Mochizuki, ed., *Bukkyō daijiten,* 1:791a–b.

16. Kageyama Haruki also dates the Ganzan-e from the Heian period (s.v. "Ganzan-e," Tsunoda, ed., *Heian jidaishi jiten,* 1:569a). Wakabayashi Haruko traces it back to memorial services performed the year after Ryōgen's death and then continued by the Fujiwaras ("From Conqueror of Evil to Devil King," p. 485). However, Murayama Shūichi suggests that the literature for the assemblies dates from the Kamakura ("Jīe daishi no shinkō," p. 68). The ritual clearly evolved during the Heian and Kamakura periods, and the process of changes in the Ganzan-e has not yet been adequately investigated. Murayama's research suggests that the Kamakura period marked a high point in the appearance of images of Ryōgen, a development that would have been necessary for the assemblies to focus more on remembrance of Ryōgen and the request that he protect Mount Hiei than on the education of monks.

17. *DS* 1.22:331.

18. Hieizan senshuin fuzoku Eizan gakuin, ed., *Eshin sōzu zenshū,* 5:593–95; Yamada, *Ganzan daishi,* p. 282.

19. Yagi, *Eshin kyōgaku no kisoteki kenkyū,* p. 384; Murayama, "Jie daishi no shinkō," p. 68. Murayama places virtually all of the texts for the assemblies in the Kamakura period or later.

20. Brown and Ishida, *The Future and the Past,* p. 46. Jien places Ryōgen in a group with Prince Shōtoku, Fujiwara no Kamatari, and Sugawara no Michizane, whom he considers to be manifestations of Kannon.

21. *T* 9:57b. I have followed Yagi Kōe's analysis of the lines; see Yagi Kōe, *Eshin kyōgakushi no sōgōteki kenkyū,* pp. 282–287.

22. Ōshima Ryōkō, "Jie daishi wasan no seiritsu ni kansuru ikkōsatsu"; Minamoto Kōshi, "Hōchibō Shōshin no 'Jie daishi kōshiki' ni tsuite." Both scholars accept the attribution of the *Jie daishi kōshiki* and *Jie daishi wasan* to Shōshin. Ōshima has pointed out that these works are closely based on the *Jie daishiden.* A number of hymns to Ryōgen are included in the *Tendai kahyō, BZ* (Suzuki, ed.), vols. 41–42. Also see *DS* 1.22:222–250.

23. Yamada, *Ganzan daishi,* pp. 281–283.

24. See Tōkyō kokuritsu hakubutsukan, ed., *Hieizan to Tendai bijutsu,* p. 130.

25. A number of stories concerning miracles associated with the worship of Ryōgen are included in Yamada, *Ganzan daishi,* pp. 233–305. Of particular interest is one concerning the eminent Tendai scholar Shioiri Ryōchū (1889–1971), contained on pp. 277–281. Examples of historical figures who chanted the *Fumon* are found on p. 283.

26. For examples of claims that Ryōgen could free one from illness, see *Tōeizan Kan'eiji Ganzan daishi engi, DS* 1.22:310, 315; and *Ganzan daishi rishōki, DS* 1.22:319.

27. Citations are from Watanabe Shujun, *Sōhei seisuiki,* p. 14.

28. Nomoto Kakujō, "Kike bunken ni mirareru Jie daishi Ryōgen," pp. 252–253.

29. Ishida Mizumaro, *Bonmōkyō*, pp. 134–137.

30. Nagamizu Yasuaki and Shimada Isao, eds., *Kokon chomonshū*, pp. 451–452.

31. Hirabayashi, *Ryōgen*, p. 209.

32. Toriimoto Yukiyo, "Jie Daishi to hōe: Soken ranshō-setsu wo megutte"; Mochizuki and Tsukamoto, eds., *Mochizuki Bukkyō daijiten*, 4:3147a–3148a (a picture of the robe is included in this entry).

33. Inoue and Ōsone, eds., *Ōjōden Hekke kenki*, p. 654.

34. *Sanmon dōshaki, GR* 24:486; Murayama, "Jie daishi," pp. 65–66.

35. The vows are cited in *DS* 1.22:257–259, 260–263. Four of Eijō's images survive (Murayama, *Hieizanshi*, p. 141). For an excellent reproduction of the image on Mount Hiei, see Tendaishū, Kōyasan Shingonshū, and Mainichi shinbunsha, eds., *Hieizan Kōyasan meihōten*, p. 74; also see Tōkyō kokuritsu hakubutsukan, ed., *Hieizan to Tendai bijutsu*, p. 227.

36. Murayama, *Hieizanshi*, p. 140.

37. *Mon'yōki, DS* 1.22:204–205.

38. *BZ* (Suzuki ed.), 62:89c.

39. Nishimura Keishō, "Seiraiji 'Ganzan daishi miei' sōdō ni tsuite." For a picture of Ryōgen alone, though in a *mandala*-like setting, see Tōkyō kokuritsu hakubutsukan, ed., *Hieizan to Tendai bijutsu*, p. 129.

40. Nishimura, "Seiraiji."

41. *Ganzan daishi mikuji shoshō, DZ* 1.22:241–242.

42. For amulets of Ryōgen, see Hirabayashi, *Ryōgen*, pp. 212–213; Yamada Etai, "Ganzan daishi no mikkyō to minkan shinkō," p. 54. For pictures of the talismans, see either of these sources or Michel Strickmann, *Mantras et mandarins*, p. 367.

43. Hirabayashi, *Ryōgen*, pp. 213–214.

44. Murayama, "Jie daishi no shinkō," pp. 73–74; Nakamura Kōichi, *Ichiban daikichi*, p. 230.

45. Nakamura Kōichi, *Ichiban daikichi*, p. 260.

46. For a firsthand account of a divination at Ryōgen's quarters at Yokawa, see ibid., pp. 214, 260–261.

47. *DS* 1.22:339–340, 342; Yamada, "Ganzan daishi no mikkyō to minkan shinkō," p. 54. For examples of the divinization texts, see Fujii Sahyōe, ed., *Ganzan daishi mikuji;* Noda Senbei, ed., *Ganzan daishi hyakusen, Kannon hyakusen ketsugenkai.* Nakamura Kōichi includes the poems, pictures, and explanations in *Ichiban daikichi*, pp. 268–318; a list of printed versions of the text from the Tokugawa period is found on pp. 226–227.

48. Nakamura Kōichi, *Ichiban daikichi*, pp. 123–126. The actual text was discovered by the classical scholar Cheng Chen-tuo at a bookstore in Beijing about 1930; it has been published as the *T'ien-chu ling-ch'ien* in his *Chung-kuo ku-dai pan-hua ts'ungkan* (n.d.). I thank Hiraoka Shōshu of Hanazono University for pointing out the origins of Ryōgen's divination texts and introducing me to several of the sources mentioned in this chapter.

49. Nakamura Kōichi, *Ichiban daikichi*, pp. 41, 218–221. Nakamura rejects theories that identify the text as having been transmitted by Ennin.

50. Ibid., pp. 213, 215.

51. For an insightful analysis of these developments, see Wakabayashi, "From Conqueror of Evil," pp. 491–503.

52. See Yagi, *Sōgōteki kenkyū*, pp. 284–287; H. C. McCullough, trans., *The Tale of Heike*, p. 215; Takagi Ichinosuke, ed., *Heike monogatari*, 1:416.

53. Murayama, *Hieizan shi*, pp. 140–141.

54. Itō Masatoshi, *Chūsei no jisha seiryoku to keidai toshi*, pp. 75–76.

55. Jacqueline Stone, *Original Enlightenment and the Transformation of Medieval Japanese Buddhism;* Mikael S. Adolphson, *The Gates of Power.*

Appendix 1. Ennin and Yokawa

1. Groner, *Saichō*, pp. 91, 180.

2. See Kageyama, *Hieizan*, p. 14, 18, for detailed maps showing the distances between parts of Mount Hiei and the contours of the area.

3. The *Śuraṅgama-samādhi* appears in Hui-ssu's works as a meditative state in which the practitioner masters the six perfections while engaging in everyday activities; see Stevenson, "The Four Kinds of Samādhi in Early T'ien-t'ai Buddhism," p. 96.

4. *Eigaku yōki, GR* 14:546–548.

5. For a discussion of factionalism during the decade after Saichō's death, see Groner, *Saichō*, pp. 286–292, and chapter 2.

6. *Eigaku yōki, GR* 15:542–543.

7. This interpretation of Kōchi's influence on Ennin has been presented by Hori Daiji in a number of papers. For example, see his "Yokawa Bukkyō no kenkyū," p. 208.

8. Honda, ed., *Yakuchū Jikaku daishiden*, p. 1.

9. According to one version of the *Jikaku daishiden,* Kōchi saw purple clouds when Ennin was born and went to Ennin's home and had Ennin's parents promise to entrust their newborn son to him. Ennin was then sent to study with Kōchi at the age of nine. When Ennin was fifteen, Kōchi took him to Mount Hiei to study with Saichō. Because Kōchi is not mentioned in the earliest version of the *Jikaku daishiden,* the *Sanzen'inbon,* Kōchi's role in Ennin's biography has been questioned. However, Saeki Arikiyo, in a thorough study of Kōchi, has found a letter by Enchō that states that Ennin was a disciple of Kōchi. The story that Ennin's birth was marked by the appearance of purple clouds probably is patterned after the biography of Tz'u-en, the Hossō patriarch. Although such influence may seem improbable in a Tendai influence, Ennin was very interested in Tz'u-en's teachings, and this interest might have led Ennin's disciples to allow such influence in their teacher's biography (Saeki, *Jikaku daishiden no kenkyū,* pp. 333–357; Saeki, *Ennin,* pp. 5–7).

10. Honda, ed., *Yakuchū Jikaku daishiden*, pp. 11–12. The date of the opening of Yokawa has been subject to much debate. According to the *Jikaku daishiden* (*ZTZ Shiden,* 2:46, 61), Ennin was forty and would have gone to Yokawa in 833. However, according to the biography of Ennin in some versions of the *Sandai jitsuroku* (*KT* 4:124), he was thirty; and the *Eigaku yōki* notes that he was thirty-six (*GR* 15:547). Although the bulk of the evidence suggests that Ennin was forty years old when he went to Yokawa, he is also said to have attended the dedication at Saitō the following year and been chosen to study in China the year after that. Several scholars have suggested that these activities would suggest that he must

have moved to Yokawa before he was forty. Hori Daiji suggests that he moved there in 831 at the age of thirty-eight ("Yokawa Bukkyō no kenkyū," p. 205). Kageyama Haruki has suggested that Ennin went to Yokawa when he was thirty-six and completed his training there when he was forty ("Ennin no konpon nyohōkyō to Yokawa no hattatsu," p. 76). However, Saeki Arikiyo, the author of the most detailed studies of Ennin's biography has argued for keeping the date of 833 (*Ennin*, p. 54). I have followed Saeki in my discussion. For a detailed discussion of positions and sources in the debate, see Oyamada, "Ennin to Enchin to no kankei," pp. 134–142.

11. *Mon'yōki, T* (*zuzō*), 11:626.

12. The term "*konpon*" (basic) suggests that the hall was to be the central hall in the complex, much as the Konpon chūdō (Basic central hall) had been for Saichō in the Tōdō area. The term "*nyohō*" (according to the Dharma) describes the manner in which the *Lotus Sūtra* was copied.

13. The term "*kōjiki*" or "*irogonomi*" is ambiguous and can refer either to interest in members of the opposite sex, a matter already mentioned in the first rule, or to connoisseurship, such as an interest in robes. In this passage, the emphasis is probably on coveting what one sees, whether it is beautiful items or objects of sexual desire. The term also appears in the *Fan-wang ching, T* 24:1007c, in a passage that includes using any of the senses in an improper manner. See Nakamura Hajime, *Bukkyōgo daijiten*, p. 391c; Nihon daijiten kankōkai, ed., *Nihon kokugo daijiten*, 2:412b.

14. *Tendai kahyō*, fasc. 5.1, *BZ* (Suzuki ed.), 42:5–6.

15. *Eizan daishiden, DZ*5 (*bekkan*): 39; translated in Groner, *Saichō*, pp. 158–159.

16. *Eizan daishiden, DZ*5 (*bekkan*): 40–41; translated in Groner, *Saichō*, pp. 159–160.

17. *Tendai kahyō*, fasc. 5.1, *BZ* (Suzuki ed.), 42:5.

18. Honda, ed., *Yakuchū Jikaku daishiden*, p. 146; Shibuya, ed., *Tendai zasuki*, p. 13.

19. *Hotchū bunin, ZGR* 4A:432a.

20. Ibid., 428–429.

21. *Shūiden, NS* 1.22:58. Chinchō was from the Tachibana clan. He was appointed abbot of Hosshōji in 946, to the Office of Monastic Affairs in 948, and eventually rose to be greater bishop. He was appointed *zasu* at the end of his life, but died shortly thereafter. A number of nobles and members of the imperial family were among his patrons.

Appendix 2. A Note on Morosuke's Interests

1. Tsunoda, "Morosuke naru jinbutsu," pp. 22–24.

2. For a list of Morosuke's children and brief notes on their accomplishments, see McCullough and McCullough, eds., *Flowering Fortunes*, 1:367. Morosuke's strategic marriages are analyzed by Tsunoda in "Morosuke naru jinbutsu," pp. 22–39.

3. The terms "*kyū*," "*kujōdono*," and "*kujō*" in the titles of texts by Morosuke all refer to Morosuke through the site of his home in the Kujō district of Kyoto.

4. The titles of Saneyori's diary are based on his posthumous name (*okurina*) Seishin (Pure and prudent). The term "*suishin*" comes from taking the two radicals of his posthumous name.

5. See the various entries in *Kokushi daijiten* for the texts mentioned in the above

paragraphs, all written by Yamanaka Yutaka. For a more extensive study of these issues, see Yamanaka, *Heian jidai no kokiroku to kizoku*.

Appendix 3. Dying Instructions of the Great Archbishop Jie

1. "Jie daisōjō goyuigō," in Takeuchi, ed., *Heian ibun*, 2:441–448; for photographs of the original manuscript, see Komatsu Shigemi and Hirabayashi Moritoku, *Heian: Jie daishi jihitsu yuigō*.

2. Ryōgen's residential quarters at Yokawa.

3. One *ken*, the width between posts of a house, is approximately six feet.

4. The Myōkōbō was the residence of Jinzen (943–990), a disciple of Ryōgen and the tenth son of Fujiwara no Morosuke, at Yokawa. In this document, Ryōgen refers to him by the name of his residence.

5. Kujō was the section in the capital where Morosuke's residence, Bōjōdai, was built. In this document, Ryōgen often refers to Morosuke as the lord of Kujō.

6. Here Ryōgen refers to Fujiwara no Anshi (d. 964), a consort of Emperor Murakami. Ryōgen calls her an empress because she was the mother of the emperors Reizei (r. 967–969) and En'yū (r. 969–984).

7. A unit for measuring quantity. One *koku* is approximately 180 liters, but the amount varied according to region and time period.

8. "*Zenji*" means "meditation master," an expression that did not necessarily imply that a person was engaged in or taught meditation. Rather, it indicated that a person possessed the dignity and other qualities that were thought to arise in skilled meditators and virtuous practitioners. Ryōgen adds an expression of respect *kimi* (lord) for Jinzen because of his noble birth.

9. The dual *maṇḍala*, consisting of the diamond (*kongōkai*; Skt. *vajra-dhātu*) and womb or matrix-store (*taizōkai*; Skt. *garbha-dhātu*) *maṇḍala*, are foundational for Esoteric Buddhist practices. These two *maṇḍala* represent the wisdom (*chi*) and principle (*ri*) of Vairocana Buddha.

10. The residence quarters that Ryōgen built when he first moved to Yokawa in 949.

11. Ryōgen may have inherited this residence from his master Risen.

12. Enshō (880–964), the fifteenth *zasu* of Enryakuji, was appointed *zasu* in 946. His highest rank in the Office of Monastic Affairs was as archbishop (*sōjō*) to which he was appointed in 958. Emperor En'yū granted him the posthumous name Jinen in 979.

13. One of the three main administrative positions (*sangō*) of a temple, also referred to as *jōza*.

14. Ennichi's dates are not known; *hosshi* is a title for an ordinary priest.

15. A meditation hall for the *samādhi* of freely following one's thoughts. According to the *Sanmon dōshaki*, the building was one of the four *samādhi* practice halls planned by Saichō; it was established as a prayer-offering temple for the emperor Seiwa (850–880; r. 858–876) during the Jōgan era (859–877). *GR* 19:162.

16. Senga (914–998), a disciple of Ryōgen, became an *ajari* at Gangyōji in 968, the twenty-second abbot of Enryakuji in 989; he was also known as Hongakubō *zasu* (abbot) because he inherited Hongakubō from Ryōgen.

17. Shōku (909–998) was a disciple of Ryōgen and Senga's older brother. He became an *ajari* of Enryakuji during the Tenroku era (970–973).

18. Kannon who has a thousand arms with an eye on each palm. One thousand is a symbolic figure that indicates Kanno's boundless salvific power, but icons of this type of Kannon usually have only forty arms.

19. A guardian deity of Buddhism.

20. Jōan (925–998) was originally a disciple of Kakue (872–954), but was entrusted to Ryōgen after Kakue died. He is called a co-practitioner (*dōhō*) because he was still an ordinary priest in 972. Jōan became an *ajari* of Gangyōji in 975 on the recommendation of Ryōgen. He is also called Kazan risshi.

21. The Jōshin'in, a temple built in the Tōdō area, was one the nine major temples of Enryakuji planned by Saichō.

22. Ryōyū (855–923) was the eleventh *zasu* of Enryakuji.

23. "*Daihosshi*" (great Dharma master) is a term of respect for a monk; it was the highest rank a monk held prior to being appointed to the Office of Monastic Affairs.

24. One *shaku* is approximately 0.303 m, or 0.994 ft.

25. Kazan(ji) is another name of Gangyōji in Yamashina. Myōgōbō was the residence of Kakue.

26. The use of the term "*shinden*" here is not completely clear. The term may refer to a house in the palace style. However, the size of the building does not seem large enough to fit that description. Another possibility might be quarters for sleeping (Nihon daijiten kankōkai, ed., *Nihon kokugo daijiten*, 11:224b); however, the financing described for the building suggests that it is something more.

27. Genzen (n.d.) was a disciple of Ryōgen.

28. Nōka is a village east of Yokawa at the foot of Mount Hiei. Ryōgen built a residence for his mother there in 955.

29. Anshin (?–998), a disciple of Ryōgen, became a master of discipline in 988 for his efforts in reconstructing Sufukuji in Ōmi province. He became the head administrative officer of the temple. He was appointed supernumerary lesser bishop (*gon-shōsōzu*) in 998.

30. A manor at Takashima-gun in Ōmi province, present-day Shiga prefecture. Ryōgen acquired this manor from the Tsuno family through their connection with Fujiwara no Morosuke, who represented Ryōgen as a mediator.

31. A manor at Gamō-gun in Ōmi province, present-day Shiga prefecture. Ryōgen acquired this manor from Fujiwara no Morosuke's family.

32. Taxation on farming land, usually paid with rice.

33. A unit for measuring grain. One *gō* is approximately 0.381 U.S. pint, or 180 ml.

34. Bōjō refers to Morosuke's residence, named Bōjōdai.

35. A manor at Yasu-gun in the southeastern part of Ōmi province, present-day Shiga prefecture.

36. A manor at Takashima-gun in the western part of Ōmi province, present-day Shiga prefecture.

37. Kanzaki-gun is in the western part of Ōmi province, present-day Shiga prefecture.

38. A disciple of Ryōgen; dates unknown.

39. Readers assisted lectures (*kōji*) as monks officially appointed to terms at the provincial temples (*kokubunji*).

40. The residence of the master of Esoteric Buddhism (*ajari*) Kakue at Gangyōji.

41. The scalpel was used in Esoteric ritual; just as the scalpel removed cataracts that obscured vision, so did the ritual remove the wrong views that obscured wisdom.

42. A disciple of Ryōgen; dates unknown.

43. A disciple of Ryōgen; dates unknown.

44. The third daughter of the emperor Murakami and consort of Fujiwara no Kaneie (929–990).

45. An abbreviation of Kiyohara family.

46. A kind of bronze that contains a larger portion of nickel.

47. All of the people named in connection with Ryōgen's funeral are probably his disciples; virtually none of their dates are known.

48. A stone *stūpa* (*ishi sotoba*), a marker of a burial mounds. An octagonal stone post set up on the burial mound. It is called *sotoba* (Skt. *stūpa*) because the tablet is in the shape of a *stūpa*.

49. A period of seven weeks after death during which the deceased remains in an intermediate state between death and the next life (J. *chūu;* Skt. *antarā-bhava*).

50. *Zuigu* refers to a mantra of bodhisattva Zuigu (wish-fulfilling), an incarnation of Avalokiteśvara, which appears in the *Zuigu-kyō* (*T* no. 1153). The mantra is effective for fulfilling the practitioner's wish. *Daibutchō* refers to the *Daibutchō-ju,* which appears in the *Shuryōgongyō* (*T* no. 945). The mantra is effective for driving away evil spirits and curing diseases. *Sonshō* refers to the mantra of Butchō-sonshō, the most august sage manifested from the Buddha's head; Butchō-sonshō removes hindrances. This mantra is effective for ensuring longevity and preventing natural disasters. *Kōmyō* refers to the *Fukū daikanjōkō shingon,* a spell that is effective for removing evil karma. This mantra is believed to remove all evil karma of the deceased when sand empowered with this mantra is sprinkled over the body or grave (*dosha kaji*). *Goji* refers to *goji-Monju-ju* (five-syllable Mañjuśrī spell), which consisted of five Sanskrit syllables (*a, ra, pa, ca,* and *na*). Amida refers to mantras of Amida Buddha. There are three spells: *ichijiju* (one-syllable spell), *shōju* (small spell), and *daiju* (great spell). These mantras are all effective for extinguishing evil karma and producing virtue for the deceased.

51. The performance of virtuous deeds with the dedication of merit to the deceased.

52. The *Hokke senbō* (Lotus repentance), or *Hokke zanmai senbō* (Lotus concentration and repentance), was a method of eradicating wrongdoing based on the *Lotus Sūtra.*

53. Morning, midday, and evening.

54. A hall for Esoteric *nenju* ritual in which practitioners intensely focus their attention on a Buddha (*nen*) and recite a *sūtra,* a Buddha's name, or a mantra (*ju*).

55. Approximately 8 P.M and 4 A.M.

56. Also known as Shuryōgon'in, headquarters of Yokawa, established by Ennin in 831.

57. Also known as Zentōin. Originally Ennin's resident quarters at Tōdō. The building became a memorial hall for Ennin, called Tōin (T'ang hall), in which his

disciples kept the scriptures and other articles Ennin brought back from T'ang China. Later this hall was called Saki no Tōin (or Zentōin), which means "prior Tōin," because a similar memorial hall was established for Enchin; it was called Nochi no tōin (latter Tōin) or Kōtōin.

Appendix 4. Takamitsu's Retreat to Tōnomine

1. Jisshō is mentioned repeatedly in the *Tōnomine ryakki, BZ* (Bussho kankōkai ed.), 118:491, 495–496, and is the author of the *Yōki* (Record of essentials), cited in the *Tōnomine ryakki*. One passage notes that "after [Jisshō], Tōnomine naturally became a branch temple of Mount Hiei" (p. 487b). I have benefited from an article by Shikasono Daiji (later known as Hori Daiji) on Jisshō, "Tōnomine to Jisshō," pp. 111–122.

2. *Tōnomine ryakki, BZ* (Bussho kankōkai ed.), 118:496, 501.

3. Ibid., p. 496; the ninety-day practice at Tōnomine has recently been called into question; see the discussion of Zōga in chapter 6.

4. *Tōnomine ryakki, BZ* (Bussho kankōkai, ed.), 118:492.

5. Ibid., p. 493.

6. Hori, "Takamitsu to Zōga," p. 80.

7. Ibid., pp. 79–80. Hori thus rejects the 994 date for Takamitsu's death found in most reference works, including Tsunoda, ed., *Heian jidaishi jiten,* p. 2122d.

Appendix 5. A Record of the Ōwa Debates

1. This text, which includes Ryōgen's letter forwarded to various schools, is in *BZ* (Bussho kankōkai ed.), 124:87–89. The author and the date of the text are both unknown. According to the notes attached to the text, it was one of the documents stored in Kōfukuji; the author is said to have been a Hossō monk. The currently available edition of the text is bound together with another text called *Onkaku sōjō,* a petition of a Hossō monk of Kōfukuji, Onkaku (d. 1162), that was composed in 1162. This document may indicate the date of the *Ōwa shūronki.*

2. Chihō (n.d.) was a native of Silla who lived in Japan. In 703, he was ordered by the court to go to China, where he studied Fa-hsiang under Tz'u-en's disciple Chih-chou. He then returned to Japan, where he was credited with the third transmission of Hossō doctrine. Three years after his return, he served as one of the first lecturers at the Yuima-e. Because this transmission was comparatively late, it reflected more of the sectarian qualities of Hossō than earlier ones. Ryōgen might well have been implying that Chihō represented a more degenerate and sectarian transmission than the earlier ones.

3. The son of Emperor Daigo and Fujiwara no Kinsue's daughter.

4. The twenty-second chapter of the *Lotus Sūtra.* "*Shokurui*" means "transmission, attachment, or entrustment." In this chapter, the Buddha entrusts the teaching of the *Lotus Sūtra* to the audience to propagate the *sūtra.* See Shioiri Ryōdō, "The Meaning of the Formation and Structure of the *Lotus Sūtra,*" p. 29.

5. A room at the northeastern corner of the palace archives in the inner palace (*dairi*).

6. The statement repeated numerous times in the twenty-fifth fascicle of the *Nirvāṇa Sūtra* (*Nieh-p'an ching*) which states that all sentient beings are endowed with Buddha-nature.

7. The three vows (*sangan*) consist of the three fundamental vows common to all bodhisattvas: to awaken sentient beings, to spread the Dharma, and to protect the Dharma. The four salvific methods (*shishō*) are the four methods that bodhisattvas employ to save sentient beings: giving the gift of Dharma, using kind words, performing beneficial actions, and working together with sentient beings.

Appendix 6. Ten Doubts Concerning the Hossō School

1. Although the title of the text (*Hossōshū jūgi*) would suggest that it concerns a wide variety of topics in Hossō doctrine, it focuses on the realization of Buddhahood by grasses and trees, a topic that is said to have been used in the Ōwa debates. The authenticity of this text has been discussed by Ōkubo Ryōshun, who notes that nothing in the contents of the text proves that it was a later production; however, he adds, the text also contains nothing that decisively indicates that it was a record of Ryōgen's arguments (*Tendai mikkyō to hongaku shisō*, pp. 65–66). It can be taken as representing many aspects of the debate over the realization of Buddhahood by grasses and trees.

2. In both the *Tōketsu*, a collection of letters on doctrinal issues exchanged between early Chinese and Japanese Tendai monks, and in works by Annen, the position is taken that the seeming difference between sentient and non-sentient beings ceases when a mind-only (*yuishin*) position or the sudden-perfect discernment is attained. The Hossō position would be that Tendai has misunderstood the mind-only position to allow the non-sentient to realize Buddhahood through their own efforts.

3. In the *Shinjō sōmoku jōbutsu shiki,* Annen had argued emphatically that plants and grasses realized Buddhahood by themselves. He thus went beyond the Chinese T'ien-t'ai position that an individual's realization of Buddhahood led to the transformation of his environment or world.

4. Tendai is criticized as losing the significance of the term "realization of Buddhahood" because all realize it whether they have minds or not.

5. According to a passage in Annen's *Shinjō sōmoku jōbutsu shiki,* "According to the *Chung-yin ching*, 'When one Buddha realizes the path and discerns the Dharma-realm, the grasses, trees, and land all realize Buddhahood. The light from his body illuminates everything and all can preach. These Buddhas are called Buddhas of Wondrous Enlightenment'" (Sueki, *Heian shoki Bukkyō*, p. 713). The imagery in this passage may be loosely based on a text called the *Chung-yin ching* (*T* 12:1064b), but nothing like the exact passage exists in the extant text. Miyamoto Shōson, without considering Annen's *Shinjō sōmoku jōbutsu shiki,* suggested that it is an apocryphal passage that first appeared in the *Kankō ruijū* (Miyamoto Shōson, "Sōmoku kokudo shikkai jōbutsu no Busshōronteki igi to sono sakusha"; Tada Kōryū et. al., eds., *Tendai hongakuron*, pp. 215–216). Miyamoto also suggested that the passage could be dated

no later than Ryōgen (912–985), but its inclusion in Annen's texts would require moving his estimate back approximately a century. Annen refers to the passage in several other texts (*Bodaishin ron shō*, *T* 75:436b; *Bodaishingishō*, *T* 75:484c [similar citation]). Heian scholars do not seem to have questioned the authenticity of the text; it is even accepted by Hōchibō Shōshin, a scholar famed for his close adherence to textual analysis (Nomoto Kakujō, "Tendai no rongi," p. 117).

6. The *sūtra* referred to is the *Lotus Sūtra* (*Miao-fa lien-hua ching*, *T* 9:9c). The original sense of the passage is that of all those who can hear the teaching, not a single one will fail to realize Buddhahood. Because grasses and trees do not hear, they could not realize enlightenment. However, Hossō monks punctuated the text in a different manner, so that it could be interpreted as excluding certain people from being able to realize Buddhahood. In contrast, the Tendai interpretation allows all, even plants, to realize Buddhahood. The passage played an important role in the Ōwa debates; see chapter 6.

7. Hossō monks made a distinction between two types of Buddha-nature in order to interpret many of passages in *nyoraizō* (*tathāgatagarbha*) texts that suggested that their teaching of five types of nature was incorrect. Buddha-nature in principle (*ribusshō*) referred to the non-substantiality that all phenomena shared. According to Hossō monks, Buddha-nature in principle did not suggest that phenomena could realize enlightenment. That could only occur if phenomena had Buddha-nature in practice (*gyōbusshō*) that would enable them to practice and realize their true nature. Thus Buddha-nature in principle could be thought of as being a passive aspect of the nature of phenomena, while Buddha-nature in practice was more active and applied to only some sentient beings. Tendai monks rejected the distinction between the two types of Buddha-nature. For Annen's views concerning this issue, see Sueki, *Heian shoki Bukkyō shisō no kenkyū*, pp. 747–778.

8. The classic definitions of the Buddhist path focus on overcoming various defilements such as anger, lust, and ignorance. Because such defilements are mental, Hossō monks argued that plants could not practice because they had no minds.

9. The opposition between subject and object is given considerable space in Annen's *Shinjō sōmoku jōbutsu shiki*. If the two were different, then objects would seem to be passive and subjects active. But a famous passage in the *Hua-yen ching* argues that the triple realm is mind-only, thereby suggesting that even the world is mind-only. Such positions problematized the seemingly obvious distinction between subject and object.

10. The term "wondrous teachings" (*myōsetsu*) probably refers to the *Lotus Sūtra*. In that case the Hossō monks would have been arguing that the Tendai monks were holding a position that was not found in their most important text.

11. The claim that the answers are profound (*jinpi*) also has a sense of their being secret. Such claims are found frequently in discussions of the realization of grasses and trees by thinkers after Ryōgen's time and reflect the tradition of secret oral transmissions (*kuden*). However, the answers in this text contain nothing that seems to reflect these later traditions (Ōkubo, *Tendai mikkyō to hongaku shisō*, p. 66). However, if this document did indeed reflect Tendai preparations for a debate, Tendai monks might well have wished to keep their responses secret.

12. The title Jie daishi was not used until 1030 and thus could not have originally been in the text if Ryōgen composed it. However, the title may have been added

when the text was copied later. The title Jie is reminiscent of Ennin's posthumous title Jikaku daishi (Hirabayashi, *Ryōgen,* p. 94). In fact, Ryōgen was said to have been the rebirth of Ennin.

13. One of the basic Tendai approaches to the realization of Buddhahood by grasses and trees was to argue that the difference between sentient and non-sentient vanished or was rendered unimportant in the light of the common characteristics of nonsubstantiality possessed by both.

14. Annen devoted considerable energy to criticizing the seeming difference between self and environment. In doing so, the difference between those with minds (subject or self) and those without minds (environment) would have been obviated.

15. Because each being in the ten realms has the potential to become any of the others, any can realize Buddhahood.

16. Ryōgen argues that the inability of Hossō monks to discern the realization of the non-sentient reveals their own shortcomings and does not prove that the non-sentient do not realize Buddhahood.

17. The answer here is weak because the ten realms included only sentient beings ranging from hell-dwellers to Buddhas; no grasses and trees are included in the list. It also plays virtually no role in the *Shinjō sōmoku jōbutsu shiki,* Annen's major work on the realization of grasses and trees.

18. The Tendai argument here is reminiscent of statements by Saichō concerning the manner in which distinctions can both be made and transcended (*Hokke shuku, DZ* 3:264).

19. *Miao-fa lien-hua ching, T* 9:9b. Burton Watson translates this passage from the *Lotus Sūtra* as follows: "These phenomena are part of an abiding Law. . . . The characteristics of the world are constantly abiding" (*The Lotus Sutra,* p. 41). The passage refers to the unchanging quality of non-substantiality and quiescence found in all phenomena. That unchanging quality played a key role, as did this passage, in Japanese Tendai efforts to affirm the importance of this world. Ennin in a short passage in the *Zokutai fushō fumetsu ron* (Essay on how provisional truth neither arises nor ceases; *BZ* [Suzuki ed.], 41:29c) was one of the first to realize the importance of the passage. Ennin is said to have received the teaching from Saichō (Ōkubo, *Tendai kyōgaku to hongaku shisō,* p. 81; *Jikaku daishi den, ZGR* 8b:648). Thus Ryōgen once again demonstrates the importance he places on Ennin's views.

Appendix 7. Zōga as an Eccentric

1. *Hokke genki,* in Inoue, and Ōsone, eds., *Ōjōden Hokke genki,* p. 157; *Tōnomine ryakki, BZ* (Bussho kankōkai ed.), 118:492a. Itō Kōko ("Zōga shōnin to kigyō setsuwa") uses Zōga's dislike of fame as an explanation for his bizarre behavior through the tales about him.

2. Hori, "Takamitsu to Zōga," p. 59; for an example of Zōga referred to as court chaplain (*naigubu*), see *Tōnomine ryakki, BZ* (Bussho kankōkai ed.), 118:495b.

3. Miki, *Tōnomine hijiri dan,* p. 128.

4. Ibid., p. 60.

5. This incident appears in a number of different sources. It is unclear at what

event it supposedly occurred, but Ryōgen's appointment to one of the following three positions would seem to be a likely serious possibility: head (*zasu*) of the Tendai school; archbishop (*sōjō*); grand archbishop (*daisōjō*). For a detailed analysis of the story, see Miki, *Tōnomine hijiri dan*, pp. 131–146. A typical rendition of the story is found in *Zoku honchō ōjōden*, in Inoue and Ōsone, eds., *Ōjōden Hokke genki*, p. 237.

6. Miki, *Tōnomine hijiri dan*, pp. 143–146. A later story in the *Uji shūi monogatari* about Shōbō describes him as riding through the capital naked with a dried salmon as a sword (D. E. Mills, *A Collection of Tales from Uji*, pp. 363–364).

7. *Eigaku yōki*, *GR* 24:534a; *Chūdō kuyō ganmon*, in *Tendai kahyō, BZ* (Suzuki, ed.), 41:317c.

8. *Shuryōgon'in nijūgo zanmai kechien kakōchō*, in Kawasaki, *Genshin*, pp. 384–385.

9. The full legend is found in *Konjaku monogatarishū* 19.18 (see Mabuchi and Kunisaki eds., *Konjaku monogatarishū*, 2:578–579). For a different version translated into English, see Mills, *Collection of Tales from Uji*, pp. 362–363. The *Tōnomine ryakki* contains only a brief legend noting that the empress, identified as Senshi, respected Zōga as a teacher (*BZ* [Kokusho kankōkai ed.], 118:492a); it makes no reference to his outrageous behavior.

10. The various stories about Zōga's eccentric activities have been analyzed in Hirabayashi, *Hijiri*, pp. 256–278.

Appendix 8. Invocation of Tendai Abbot Ryōgen

The manuscript is from the Rosanji archives. A photographic reproduction of the text has been published in Eizan gakuin, ed., *Ganzan Jie daishi no kenkyū*, plates following p. 335. The text has been published in *NS* 1.13:203–218 and in Takeuchi, *Heian ibun*, 2:431–440. A modern Japanese translation appears in Watanabe Eshin, "'Jie daishi kisei nijūrokkajō' ni tsuite."

1. An honorary monastic rank that the imperial court conferred on monks that was equivalent to a bishop (*sōzu*) in the Office of Monastic Affairs.

2. According to Nakamura Hajime (*Bukkyōgo daijiten*, p. 683c), "*shoshi*" is a general term for the three main administrative positions (*sangō*) of a temple: *jōza* (senior supervisor of the clerical affairs); *jishu* (temple master); and *tsuina* (chief director of the clerical affairs); it also may be used as a more inclusive term to refer to monastic administrators in general. This latter usage seems to be followed in these rules since the term "*kōi*" appears later in this rule and would correspond to the first narrower meaning. However, Ishida Mizumaro defines it as the monks in charge of secular affairs (*Reibun*, p. 601a).

3. The term "*shikishu*" refers to monks who are in charge of chanting the hymns (*bonbai*) and scattering flowers (*sange*) during the service.

4. "*Dōtatsu*" refers to the officials who assist the director of a ceremony. He is also one of seven officiants at ceremonies; he hands the petition to the invoker (*juganshi*), who reads the sponsor's petition. "*Kōi*" is used as a general term for the top officials in the monastery, similar to a narrow usage of "*shoshi*."

5. Issued on the twenty-sixth day of the twelfth month in 966.

6. A doctrinal debate in the same style as one that was held in the imperial

palace (*uchi*) at the end of the imperial assembly (*misai-e*). One monk would be chosen as lecturer, one as questioner, and a debate on doctrine would ensue.

7. The meaning of this phrase is not completely clear, but it may refer to the metaphor of the flower dropping to produce the fruit discussed in Chih-i's *Fa-hua hsüan-i.*

8. This refers to the ritual articles required to conduct ceremonies specified in the monastic rules; see Hirabayashi, *Ryōgen,* p. 110.

9. A unit of money; one *kan* is equivalent to one thousand *sen* or *mon.*

10. The imagery in this passage is based on the *Fan-wang ching* in which Vairocana sits on a lotus throne. The petals of that lotus throne have additional lotuses on them with Śākyamuni Buddhas on the various petals of each lotus.

11. This passage is based on the opening of the second fascicle of the *Fan-wang ching* in which the bodhisattva precepts are expounded (*T* 24:1003c–1004b). When Ryōgen established a fortnightly assembly using the *Fan-wang* precepts, light is said to have issued from his mouth as he recited them.

12. *T* 24:1004b.

13. *T* 24:1007b (thirty-fourth minor precept).

14. *T* 24:1008a (thirty-seventh minor precept).

15. The term "*zōmatsu*" is ambiguous and can be interpreted to mean either the periods of the semblance of the Dharma and the end of the Dharma or the end of the period of the semblance of the Dharma. Because Saichō used it in the latter sense when he discussed the precepts, Ryōgen may well have used it in a similar fashion; see Groner, *Saichō,* pp. 171–173.

16. The staff is mentioned as one of eighteen items that a person who has received the *Fan-wang* precepts should carry. It was to be used while begging. It assumed a role in Buddhist rituals with hymns praising it.

17. The services to commemorate the Tendai masters with a posthumous title of *daishi* (great master) conferred by the emperor.

18. The day in 866 on which the court awarded the posthumous titles of great master to both Saichō (Dengyō daishi) and Ennin (Jikaku daishi); this marked the first time such a title had been conferred in Japan.

19. Hymns sung on the occasion of a consecration qualifying one to receive the innermost teachings (*denbō kanjō*).

20. This is probably a reference to the procession held in the capital on the fifth day of the great Lotus assembly; see chapter 10 on finances for more information.

21. The term "*bini kyōritsu*" is interpreted in a variety of ways by commentators. Chih-i explains it as meaning Mahāyāna *sūtras* and *vinayas* in general. Fa-tsang argues that it refers to the *Fan-wang ching.* Other commentators presented variations on these explanations; see Ishida Mizumaro, *Bonmōkyō,* p. 150 for a summary of their positions.

22. *T* 24:1005b–c; this is from the seventh minor precept.

23. The full title is *Kanshō Tendaishū nenbun gakushō shiki* (Regulations to encourage Tendai's yearly ordinand students), commonly called *Hachijō-shiki.* The text is available in *DZ* 1:13–16. For an analysis and complete translation of the articles, see Groner, *Saichō,* pp. 130–137.

24. The first article of the *Hachijō-shiki;* see *DZ* 1:13–14; Groner, *Saichō,* pp. 131–132.

25. The third article of the *Hachijō-shiki;* see *DZ* 1:14; Groner, *Saichō,* p. 132.

26. Ryōgen's interpretation of the term "three divisions" (*sanbu*) is not clear. Saichō probably referred to the three divisions of the *taizōkai:* Buddha, Lotus, and Diamond. He also might have referred to the three *sūtras* of Esoteric Buddhism that Saichō mentioned in the *Hieizan Tendai Hokkein tokugō gakushōshiki,* namely the *Ta-jih ching* (*T* no. 848), *K'ung-ch'iao ching* (*T* no. 982), and *Shou-hu kuo-chien ch'u t'o-lo-ni ching* (*T* no. 997). After Ennin introduced the Soshitsuji rituals, the three divisions in Tendai Esotericism generally referred to the three great traditions of Esoteric practices (*sanbu daihō*): Kongōkai, Taizōkai, and Soshitsuji. See Groner, *Saichō,* pp. 127, 133.

27. The fourth article of the *Hachijō-shiki;* see *DZ* 1:14; Groner, *Saichō,* pp. 123–133.

28. Ishida Mizumaro comments that this refers to rules that certain colors of robes are limited to monks of certain ranks (Ishida, *Reibun,* p. 198b).

29. The fifth article of the *Hachijō-shiki;* see *DZ* 1:15.

30. The expression "*fumon no jihi*" also refers to the universal compassion of bodhisattva Kannon (Avalokiteśvara), which is expounded in the twenty-fifth chapter in the *Lotus Sūtra.*

31. The reference here is to meats and pungent vegetables such as onions, items prohibited by Mahāyāna codes popular in China.

32. Selling liquor is prohibited by the fifth major precept and drinking by the second minor precept in the *Fan-wang ching.*

33. The second article in the *Konpon daishi rinjū yuigon* (Last instructions of the founding great master [Saichō]), *DZ* 1:299; Groner, *Saichō,* p. 159.

34. An office in the court that was in charge of the administration of the stables in the court and the state horse ranches in the provinces. The office was divided into two divisions, left (*sameryō*) and right (*umeryō*).

35. The six types of livestock are horses, cows, sheep, dogs, pigs, and chickens.

36. Ryōgen cited the third article in Ennin's *Kansei shijō* (Official proclamation in four articles). The text of the *Kansei shijō* is available in the *Tendai kahyō,* fasc. 3.1, in *BZ* (Suzuki ed.), 41:307c.

37. The three lower realms of existence are hell, animals, and hungry ghosts.

38. The ten evil acts are killing, stealing, illicit sex, lying, harsh words, words creating enmity, flattery, greed, anger, and wrong views.

39. The six relations are father, mother, older and younger brothers (or sisters), spouses, and children.

40. *T* 24:1006b (twenty-first minor precept).

41. *T* 24:1005c (tenth minor precept).

42. The *Enryakuji kinseishiki* set forth the rules of conduct at Enryakuji, it was compiled by Ninchū, a disciple of Saichō, in 824. An existing edition of the text cites only fifteen articles out of the original twenty-two regulations. The text is available in *Tendai kahyō,* fasc. 5, in *BZ* (Bussho kankōkai ed.), 4b–5b. Ryōgen mistakenly claims that it had twenty-three regulations, but twenty-two is correct.

43. The fourth article in the *Enryakuji kinseishiki, Tendai kahyō,* fasc. 5, *BZ* (Suzuki ed.), 42:4o. A similar admonition is found in the fourth article in the *Konpon daishi rinjūyuigon, DZ* 1:299.

44. The term "hishujō" is difficult to interpret; Fa-tsang interprets it as "non-

sentient," an interpretation that seems odd because it would mean that a person would commit a *pārājika* offense toward the non-sentient. I-chi prefers the meaning of "sage" (one who has gone beyond a normal sentient being). Such an interpretation avoids the problem of offenses toward the non-sentient (Ishida Mizumaro, *Bonmōkyō*, p. 117).

45. In the *Fan-wang ching*, the term "*haraizai*" (Skt. *pārājika*) refers to the ten major precepts (*jūjūkai*). Committing one of these offenses results in rebirth in the three evil realms of existence (*sanmakudō*), those of hell, animals, and hungry ghosts; see *T* 24:1005a.

46. *T* 24:1005a (ninth major precept).

47. *T* 24:1006b (twenty-first minor precept). The mention of female slaves may seem odd, but many of the precepts were intended for lay believers as well as monks.

48. The tenth article in the *Enryakuji kinseishiki, Tendai kahyō*, fasc. 5, *BZ* (Suzuki ed.), 42:5a.

49. The term "*gonji*" often refers to lay believers; however, Tendai documents from this period use the term to refer to lay servants (Ishida, *Reibun*, p. 340b).

50. The Mountain King (Sannō) guardian deity of Mount Hiei.

51. The term "*tengyō*" refers to the chanting of scriptures. However, when texts had a large number of fascicles, monks might read only excerpts from the beginning, middle, and ending parts of each volume of the *sūtra* and skip the rest. Sometimes monks read the title only.

52. Recitation of a memorized *mantra*, a *sūtra*, or a name of a Buddha.

53. The term "*kanshu*" is a synonym for "*zasu*" (Ishida, *Reibun*, p. 153).

54. The three guardian stars (*daisei*) of the heavenly palace are situated around the North Star. An epithet for the three highest positions of the imperial court: prime minister, minister of the left, and minister of the right.

55. A gate made of pine trees. Ryōgen used this phrase as a metaphor of Enryakuji on Mount Hiei.

56. No dates are available for Hotchin, Juren, or Shōtō.

Glossary

Aeba　饗場

Agura-chō　上蔵町

Ainōshō　壒囊鈔

ajari　阿闍梨

ajaribō　阿闍梨房

Aki　安芸

akusō　悪僧

ama　尼

ama-nyōbō　尼女房

ama-nyūdō　尼入道

amasogi　尼削

amasogitaru chigo　尼削ぎたる児

Amida　阿弥陀

ango　安居

Anjōji　安祥寺

Ankai　安海

Ankyō　安慶

An-lo chi　安楽集

Anne　安慧

Annen　安然

Annyōshū　安養集

Anrakuin　安楽院

Anshi　安子

Anshin　安真

Anshū　安秀

Araki Ryōsen　荒木良仙

Ariaki　有明

Arishige　有茂

Asabashō　阿娑縛抄

Asake　朝明

Ashida Kōitsu　芦田耕一

Asuka　飛鳥

Atagoyama　愛宕山

Atsumi　敦実

Azai-gun　浅井郡

azukari　預

Azuma-asobi　東遊

ban, Ban　伴

bansō　番僧, 伴僧

Benzaiten　弁才天

besson　別尊

betsuin　別院

betsunōsho　別納所

bettō　別当

bettō daishi　別当大師

bikuni　比丘尼

bikuni jiritsusha　比丘尼持律者

bikuni kaidan　比丘尼戒壇

Bikuni shi　比丘尼史

Bingo　備後

bini kyōritsu　毘尼経律

Biwa　琵琶

bō　房

bodai　菩提

463

bodaiji　菩提寺

bodaishi　菩提子

Bodaishin shū　菩提心集

Bōjō　坊城

bonbai　梵唄

Bonmōkyō　梵網経

bonnō　煩悩

bonnon　梵音

Bonshakuji　梵釈寺

Bonshō　梵照

Bōsan　房算

bosatsu　菩薩

bosatsu daikai　菩薩大戒

bōshi　房司

Boshidō　母子堂

bōzuchō　房主帳

Buan　豊安

bukke　仏家

Bukkyō daijii　仏教大辭彙

Bun'ei　文永

bungo　文語

Butchō-sonshō　仏頂尊勝

Butusubu　仏部

Butsudan　仏壇

Butsuda shōnin　仏陀聖人

Butsudo　仏土

Butsuryūji　仏隆寺

butsu yōraku　仏瓔珞

byakudan　白檀

Byōdōbō　平等房

Byōdōin　平等院

Byōjuin　平聚院

Ch'ang-an　長安

Ch'an-lin-ssu　禅林寺

Chegwan　諦観

Cheng Chen-tuo　鄭振鐸

Chen-yūan　貞元

Ch'eng wei-shih lun　成唯識論

chi　智

Chi-an　斉安

Chiben　智弁

chie　智慧

Chien-chen　鑑眞

Chien-li man-t'u-lo chi hu-mo i-kuei　建立曼荼羅及護摩儀軌

Ch'i-fo ching　七仏経

Ch'ih　赤

Chih-chou　智周

Chih-i　智顗

Chihō　智鳳

chiin　知院

Chikanaga kyōki　親長卿記

Chikō (Tendai monk)　智興

Chikō (in the *Nihon ryōiki*)　智光

Chikubu　竹生

chin　鎮

Chinchō　鎮朝

Chinjō　陳常

Chin-kang-ting yü-ch'ieh hu-mo i-kuei　金剛頂瑜伽護摩儀規

Ch'ing-kan　清幹

Ching-lung-ssu　青龍寺

Ching-shuang　鏡霜

Ching-t'u wu-hui nien-fo lüeh-fa-shih i-tsan　淨土五会念仏略法事儀賛

Ching-ying-ssu Hui-yüan　浄影寺慧遠

Chinkai　珍海

Chin-kuang-ming ching　金光明経

Chisō　智聡

Chi-tsang　吉蔵

Ch'i-yin　斉隠

chō (measure of land)　丁 or 町

Chōi　長意

chokue　勅会

chokushi　勅使

chokushibō　勅使房

Chōnen　奝然

chōotsu rissha　超越竪者

Chōryaku　長暦

chōsha　長者

chōshu　聴衆

Chōya gunsai　朝野群載

Chūdō　中堂

chūgū　中宮

Chūin　中院

Chūjin　忠尋

chūjō　中将

chūki　註記

Chu-lin-ssu　竹林寺

chūnagon　中納言

Chung-guo ku-dai pan-hua ts'ung-kan　中國古代版画叢刊

chūseki　鑢石

Chūzan　仲算

Daianji　大安寺

Daibirushana jōdōkyō gishaku moku-roku　大盧遮那成道経義釈目録

daibu　大夫

daibutchō　大仏頂

Daibutchō-ju　大仏頂呪

Daibutsu　大仏

Daigo　醍醐

Daigoji　醍醐寺

daihosshi　大法師

Daiitoku　大威徳

daiji　大寺

daijin　大臣

daijō daijin　太政大臣

Daijō-e　大乗会

Daijōin　大乗院

Daijō tai Kushashō　大乗対倶舎抄

daiju　大呪

daikai　大戒

Daikakuji　大覚寺

Daikichisanji　大吉山寺

Daikōji　大興寺

daimyōjin　大明神

dainagon　大納言

daini　大尼

Dainichiin　大日院

Dainichikyō gishaku sōketsushō　大日経義釈捜決抄

Dainichi nyorai　大日如來

Dainichi nyorai taizō son hō　大日如來胎蔵尊法

Dainipponkoku Hokke genki　大日本国法華験記

dairi　内裏

daisakan　大屬

daisei　台星

Daishidō　大師堂

daishi jōkō　大師上網

daishiku　大師供

daishōni　大小尼

daishu　大衆

daishu kariya　大衆仮屋

daisō　大僧

daisōjō　大僧正

Daisōjōden　大僧正伝

daisōzu　大僧都

Daiunji　大雲寺

dajōdono　太政殿

dajō kanpu　太政官符

Dannain　檀那院

danpō　壇法

Danrinji　檀林寺

den　伝

denbō ajari　伝法阿闍梨

denbō kanjō　伝法潅頂

denbō kuryō　　伝法供料

Dengyō daishi　　伝教大師

dentō daihosshi　　伝燈大法師

dentō jūi　　伝燈住位

dentō man'i　　伝燈満位

Dewa　　出羽

dochō (initiation certificate)　　度牒

Dōchō　　道朝

Dōchū　　道忠

dōdōji　　堂童子

Dōho　　道保

dōhō (co-practitioner)　　同法

dōji　　童子

dōjichō　　童子長

dokko　　独鈷

dokkorei　　独鈷鈴

dokushi　　読師

Dō kuyō　　堂供養

Dōkyō　　道鏡

dokyō (chanting scriptures)　　読経

dokyōsō　　読経僧

dōmon　　同門

Dōmyō　　道命

Dōsen　　道詮

dosha kaji　　土砂加持

dōshi　　導師

Dōshō　　道昭

dōshu　　堂衆

dōsō　　堂僧

dōtatsu　　堂達

Dōyū　　道融

e (as in *chie*)　　慧

e (as in *megumu*)　　恵

Echigo　　越後

Edo　　江戸

edo　　穢土

Egaku　　恵萼

ehon　　会本

Eiei　　栄榮

Eiga monogatari　　栄華物語

Eigaku yōki　　叡岳要記

Eijō　　栄盛

Eika　　容荷

Eikō　　栄好

Eikyū　　永久

Eishin　　栄心

Eison　　叡尊

Eizan bunko　　叡山文庫

Eizan daishiden　　叡山大師伝

Enchin (Shingon monk)　　延敒

Enchin (Tendai monk)　　円珍

Enchō　　円澄

Engei　　円芸

Engen　　円元

Engishiki　　延喜式

Engyō　　円行

Enjaku　　円寂

enju no hi　　延寿之日

Enken　　延賢

Enki　　円基

Enkyō　　延教

Ennichi　　円日

Enmeiin　　延命院

Ennin　　円仁

En no gyōja　　役行者

ennyū musa　　円融無作

ennyū santai　　円融三諦

Enryakuji　　延暦寺

Enryakuji kinseishiki　　延暦寺禁制式

Enryakuji mitsujō ryakumokuroku
　　　　延暦寺密乗略目録

Ensai　　円哉

Enshō　　延昌

Enshu　　円修

Enshū　円秀

Enshūji　円宗寺

En'yū　円融

En'yūin　円融院

En'yūji　円融寺

Eryō　恵亮

Eshin'in　恵心院

Eshin-ryū　恵心流

etashin　依他心

Eun　恵運

Fa-chao　法照

Fa-chin　法進

Fa-ch'üan　法全

Fa-hsiang　法相

Fa-hua hsüan-i　法華玄義

Fa-hua hsüan-tsan　法華玄賛

Fa-hua wen-chü　法華文句

Fan-wang ching　梵網経

Fa-tao　法道

Fa-tsang　法蔵

Fa-yüan i-lin ch'ang　法苑義林章

Fa-yün　法雲

fudan nenbutsu　不断念仏

Fudō myōō　不動明王

fūhi　風痺

Fuhito　不比等

fūshin　風疹

Fujimotobō　藤本坊

Fujiwara no Akihira　藤原明衡

Fujiwara no Anshi　藤原安子

Fujiwara no Arihira　藤原在衡

Fujiwara no Arikuni　藤原有国

Fujiwara no Ariyoshi　藤原有頼

Fujiwara no Asamitsu　藤原朝光

Fujiwara no Atsumitsu　藤原敦光

Fujiwara no Atsumoto　藤原敦基

Fujiwara no Atsutada　藤原敦忠

Fujiwara no Chōshi　藤原超子

Fujiwara no Fuhito　藤原不比等

Fujiwara no Fuminori　藤原文範

Fujiwara no Fuyutsugu　藤原冬嗣

Fujiwara no Jushi　藤原娍子

Fujiwara no Junshi (Ninmyō's consort)　藤原順子

Fujiwara no Junshi (En'yū's consort)　藤原遵子

Fujiwara no Kaishi　藤原懐子

Fujiwara no Kamatari　藤原鎌足

Fujiwara no Kaneie　藤原兼家

Fujiwara no Kanemichi　藤原兼通

Fujiwara no Kanesuke　藤原兼輔

Fujiwara no Kanezane　藤原兼実

Fujiwara no Kanshi　藤原寛子

Fujiwara no Kinsue　藤原公季

Fujiwara no Kiyoko　藤原聖子

Fujiwara no Korechika　藤原伊周

Fujiwara no Koremasa　藤原伊尹

Fujiwara no Kōshi　藤原媓子

Fujiwara no Michinaga　藤原道長

Fujiwara no Michitaka　藤原道隆

Fujiwara no Michitsuna　藤原道網

Fujiwara no Morosuke　藤原師輔

Fujiwara no Morotada　藤原師貞

Fujiwara no Motokata　藤原元方

Fujiwara no Motona　藤原元名

Fujiwara no Nagayoshi　藤原長良

Fujiwara no Nakamaro　藤原仲麻呂

Fujiwara no Narifusa　藤原成房

Fujiwara no Naritoki　藤原斉時

Fujiwara no Nobuko　藤原述子

Fujiwara no Onshi　藤原穏子

Fujiwara no Sadakata　藤原定方

Fujiwara no Sanesuke　藤原実資

Fujiwara no Saneyori　藤原実頼

Fujiwara no Sari　藤原佐理

Fujiwara no Seishi　藤原盛子

Fujiwara no Senshi　藤原詮子

Fujiwara no Sukemasa　藤原佐理

Fujiwara no Sukeyo　藤原佐世

Fujiwara no Tadahira　藤原忠平

Fujiwara no Tadanobu　藤原斉信

Fujiwara no Tadatoshi　藤原斉敏

Fujiwara no Takamitsu　藤原高光

Fujiwara no Tamemitsu　藤原為光

Fujiwara no Tamenaga　藤原為長

Fujiwara no Teishi　藤原定子

Fujiwara no Tokihira　藤原時平

Fujiwara no Tokikata　藤原時方

Fujiwara no Tokiyoshi　藤原時善

Fujiwara no Yorimichi　藤原頼通

Fujiwara no Yoritada　藤原頼忠

Fujiwara no Yoshichika　藤原義懐

Fujiwara no Yoshifusa　藤原良房

Fujiwara no Yoshiko　藤原歡子

Fujiwara no Yoshimi　藤原良相

Fujiwara no Yūhime　藤原祐姫

fukuchi　福智

Fukuda Gyōei　福田堯穎

Fukū daikanjōkō shingon　不空大潅頂光真言

Fu-liang　福亮

Fumonji　普門寺

fumon no jihi　普門之慈悲

Funaki Yoshimi　船木良見

funzō　糞掃

fusatsu　布薩

Fushō　普照

Fusō ryakki　扶桑略記

Gaen　賀縁

gagaku　雅楽

Gajō　賀静

gakusō　学僧

gakuya　楽屋

Gangōji　元興寺

Gangyōji　元慶寺

Ganjin　鑑真

Ganmon　願門

Gansai　願西

Ganshō　願証

Ganzan　元三

Ganzan daishi　元三大師

Ganzan-e　元三会

Gashi　雅子

Gashū　賀秀

gazō　画像

Gedatsuji　解脱寺

gegaku　外学

gejin　外陣

gemon　解文

Genbō　玄昉

Genji monogatari　源氏物語

Genkan　玄鑑

Genkei　玄慶

Genkōji　現光寺

Genkō shakusho　元亨釈書

Genkyū　元久

Gennichi　玄日

Genpei jōsuiki　源平盛衰記

Genshin　源信

Genshin sōzuden　源信僧都伝

Genshō　玄昭

Genzen　源漸

gi　義

gigaku　伎楽

gijōsho　議定書

gika　義科

Gikai　義海

Gika shiki　義科私記

gikasho　義科書

Gika sōdenshō　義科相伝抄

Gion (shōja)　祇園（精舎）

Gishin　義真

Gishō　義昭

gō　合

gōbuku　降伏

Godaidō　五大堂

godai myōō　五大明王

godanhō　五壇法

Godanhō nikki　五壇法日記

gogan'in kengyō　御願院検校

goganji　御願寺

goganjo betsuin　御願所別院

gōgi　業義

Go-Ichijō　後一条

goji (five periods)　五時

goji (five syllables)　五字

gojisō　護持僧

gokai (five lay precepts)　五戒

gokai (five qualifications)　五階

goko　五鈷

gokorei　五鈷鈴

goma　護摩

gomi　五味

Gomyō　護命

gonchōja　権長者

gon-daisōzu　権大僧都

gonge　権化

gonji　近士

Gonen'in　護念院

Gonkō　厳公

Gonku　厳久

gonnokami　権守

gon-risshi　権律師

gonrō　近廊

gon-shōsōzu　権少僧都

gon-sōjō　権僧正

Gonzō　勤操

Goreizei　後冷泉

goryō-e　御霊会

Go-sanjō　後三条

goshin　五辛

goshō　五障

goshō kakubetsu　五性格別

Goshui ojōden　後拾遺往生伝

Goshūishū　後拾遺集

goshūki　御周忌

gosshō　業障

Go-uda　後宇多

Gōzanze　降三世

Guhōji　弘法寺

Gukanshō　愚管抄

Gundari　軍荼利

gusokukai　具足戒

gyakushu　逆修

gyōbusshō　行仏性

gyōdō shamini　形同沙弥尼

gyōdōshu　行道衆

gyōji　行事

Gyōki　行基

Gyōnen　凝然

Gyōyo　行誉

ha　把

Hachibudō　八部堂

hachibushu　八部衆

Hachijō-shiki　八条式

hakase　博士

hakkō　八講

hakudō　白銅

Hakuhō　白鳳

hakushi　博士

Han　伴

hana no ama　花の尼

Hokuin　北院

Hokuji　北寺

hōmu　法務

Hōmyō　法明

Honchō bunshū　本朝文集

Hōnen　法然

hongaku　本覚

Hongakubō　本覚房

Hongakusan　本覚讃

hongō　本業

Hongō Masatsugu　本郷真紹

honjō　本情

honmyōshō　本命星

hōnō　法能

honshi　本師

honzon　本尊

hōrei　寶鈴

Hori Daiji　堀大慈

Horikawa　堀川

Hōrinji　法琳寺

Hōryūji　法隆寺

Hōshi naishinnō　保子内親王

Hosoehama　細江浜

hosshi　法師

Hosshinshū　発心集

Hosshōbō　法性房

Hosshōji (Shirakawa's *goganji*)　法勝寺

Hōsshōji (Tadahira's temple)　法性寺

Hossō　法相

Hossōshū genjōgi mondō　法相宗賢聖義問答

Hossōshū jūgi　法相宗十疑

hōtaku　宝鐸

Hotchin　法傹

Hōtō　宝塔

Hōunbō　宝雲房

Hōzō (Hossō monk)　法蔵

hōzō (treasury or library)　宝蔵

Hsi-ming　西明

Hsing-ch'an　行㴲

Hsing-man　行満

Hsüan-tsang　玄奘

Hsüan-tsung　宣宗

Hua-yen ching　華厳経

Hui-ch'ang　會昌

Hui-chao　慧沼

Hui-hui　慧暉

Hui-ssu　慧思

Hyōban　平範

hyōbyaku　表白

Hyōdai　平代

Hyōgen　平源

Hyōkaku　平覚

Hyōsen　平仙

Hyōshū　平州

I-chen　義真

I-chi　義寂

Ichigyō zanmaiin　一行三昧院

ichijiju　一字呪

ichijitsu ennyū　一実円融

Ichijō　一条

Ichijōji　一乗寺

Ichijō shikan'in　一乗止観院

ichimon　一門

I-ching　義浄

Ichiwa　壱利

ie　家

ie no ama　家の尼

igishi　威儀師

igisō　威儀僧

Iimuro　飯室

Ikeda Genta　池田源太

Iken jūnikajō　意見十二箇条

Ikeyama Issaien　池山一切円

iki　位記

ikō　已講

Ikoku　伊谷

I-k'ung　義空

I-li　儀礼

in　院

ina　維那

inge　院家

inju　院主

Inkai　胤海

inmyō　因明

Inmyō nisshōriron sho　因明入正理
論疏

Inmyō nisshōriron shoki　因明入正理
論疏記

Inmyō ronsho myōtōshō　因明論疏明
灯抄

Inmyō ronsho shisōi ryakuchūshaku
因明論疏四相違略註釈

Inmyō shishu sōi ryakuchūshaku　因明
四種相違略注釈

Inmyō shishu sōi shiki　因明四種相違
私記

inshi　院司

irui　異類

iryūgisha　已堅義者

Ise　伊勢

Ishida Mizumaro　石田瑞麿

ishi sotoba　石剽都婆

Ishitsukuri　石作

Isoko　磯子

isshin　一真

isshin ajari　一身阿闍梨

isshūki　一周忌

itagaki　板垣

itaya　板屋

Itō Kiyoo　伊藤政朗

Ittei　壱定

Iwakura　岩倉

Iwate　岩手

Izu　伊豆

Izumo　出雲

Izumodera　出雲寺

jake　邪気

jakkan　弱冠

Jakuen　寂円

Jen-wang ching　仁王經

ji　慈

jido　自度

Jie　慈慧 or 慈恵

Jie daishi　慈慧大師 or 慈恵大師

Jie daisōjōden　慈恵大僧正伝

Jie daisōjō shūiden　慈恵大僧正拾
遺伝

Jiei　慈叡

Jien　慈円

Jijūden　仁寿殿

jike　寺家

Jikaku daishi　慈覚大師

Jikaku daishiden　慈覚大師伝

jikidō　食堂

Jikō　慈光

Jimon　寺門

Jimon denki horoku　寺門伝記補録

Jin den ainōshō　塵添𡏖嚢鈔

Jin'en　尋円

jinin (shrine attendant)　神人

Jinin (Jinzen's posthumous title)
慈忍

Jinkaku　深覚

Jinkō　尋光

jinpi　深秘

Jinshin　壬申

Jinzen　尋禅

Jion-e　慈恩会

Jion'in　慈恩院

Jionjisan　慈恩寺山

jiryō (temple stipend)　寺料

jiryō (monastic landholdings)　寺領

jisei jukai　自誓受戒

Jishi　慈氏

jishi nenryō　地子年料

jishu　寺主

jishu sanshō　寺主三聖

jisō　事相

Jison'in　慈尊院

Jisshō　実性

jissō　実相

Jissōin　実相院

Jitō　持統

Jitokuji　慈徳寺

jō　掾

Jōan　静安

Jōdoin　浄土院

Jōe (Kamatari's son)　定恵

Jōe (Tendai monk)　乗恵

jōgakuji　定額寺

jōgaku niji　定額尼寺

jōgakusō　定額僧

Jōgan　貞観

Jōganji　貞観寺

jōgō　長講

Jōgyō　常暁

Jōgyōdō　常行堂

Jōgyōin　常行院

Jōjakkōdo　常寂光土

Jōjin　成尋

Jōjo　定助

jōjū　浄住

Jōjuin　常寿院

jōkō　上網

Jōmyōji　浄妙寺

jōroku　丈六

Jōsan　成簒

Jōshinbō　定心房

Jōshin'in　定心院

Jōshō　定昭

jōshōsha　定聖者

jōtō　常灯

Jōtōmon'in　上東門院

jōtōryō　常燈料

Jōwa no hen　承利変

jōza　上座

Jōza zanmaiin　常坐三昧院

Jōzō　浄蔵

ju (confer)　授

ju (mantra)　呪

Juchō　寿肇

Juei　寿永

jugan　咒願

juganshi　呪願師

jugusokukai　受具足戒

jūigishi　従威儀師

jūjukai　重受戒

jūjūkai　十重戒

jukai　受戒

Juketsushū　授決集

jūmyō　十妙

jūni innen　十二因縁

junmitsu　純密

Junna　淳和

Junnain　淳利院

Junshō　順昌

jūnyoze　十如是

Juren　寿連

Jūroku gika mokuroku　十六義科目録

jūzenji　十禅師

jūzenkai　十善戒

kaebumi　替文

Kaguraoka　神楽岡

kaichō　戒牒

kaidai　解題

kaidan　戒壇

kaidan'in　戒壇院

kaiji　戒地

Kaikō　会弘

Kaimyō　戒明

kairō　回廊

kaishi　戒師

Kaishindani　戒心谷

kai ukesase　戒受けさせ

kaiwajō　戒利尚

kaji　加持

Kajōji　嘉祥寺

kake-mandara　懸曼陀羅

Kakehashi Nobuaki　梯信暁

Kakuchō　覚超

Kakue　覚恵, 覚慧

Kakukei　覚慶

Kakuen　覚円

Kakugyō　覚慶

kakuretaru maki　秘巻

Kakuun　覚運

Kakuzen no kimi　覚禅君

Kamakura　鎌倉

kami (deity)　神

kami (governor)　守

Kamo　賀茂

Kamoku sengushō　科目専愚抄

Kamo no Tadayuki　賀茂忠行

Kamo no Yasunori　賀茂保憲

kamon no suke　掃部助

kan　間

kan (coffin)　棺

kan (unit of money)　貫

Kanchō　寛朝

Kanchū　寛忠

Kan'eiji　寛永寺

kangaku-e　勘学会

Kan'in　寛印

kanji　官寺

Kanjin kakumushō　観心覚夢鈔

kanjō　灌頂

kanjōdō　灌頂堂

Kanju　勧修

kanmon　貫文

kanmotsu　官物

Kanmu　桓武

Kannōji　神呪寺

Kannon　観音

Kannon'in　観音院

Kannon-sen　観音籤

kanoe ne　庚子

kanoto tori　辛酉

kanpaku　関白

kanpu　官符

Kanpyō　寛平

Kanri　観理

Kansan　桓算, 観算, 寛算

Kansei shijō　官制四条

kanshōfushō　官省符庄

Kanshu (monk's name)　観修

kanshu (synonym for *zasu*)　貫首

kansōni　官僧尼

Kantō　関東

Kanzaki-gun　神崎郡

kaō　花押

Karasaki　唐崎

Kasahara Kazuo　笠原一男

Kasuga　春日

Kasuga myōjin　春日明神

katō　裏頭

katsuma　羯磨

katsumamotsu　羯磨物

Katsuno Ryūshin　勝野隆信

Katsuura Noriko　勝浦令子

Kawa no ryū　川流

Kawasaki Tsuneyuki　川崎庸之

Kazan　花山

Kazan chūin　花山中院

Kazanji　花山寺, 華山寺

Kazan risshi　花山律師

Kazan-ryū　花山流

Kazan zasu　花山座主

kazukemono　被物

kebiishi　検非違使

kebyō　花瓶

kechien　結縁

Kechimyakufu　血脈譜

Keikō　敬光

Kegon　華嚴

keibyaku　啓白

keiru　競留

keka　悔過

kekkai　結界

kemari　蹴鞠

ken (bay)　間

ken (sword)　劍

kengyō (abbot or supervisor)　検校

kengyō (exoteric Buddhism)　顕教

Kenjun　謙順

kenmitsu taisei　顕密体制

kenmon　券文

Kenne　堅慧

Ken'yō daikairon　顕揚大戒論

kenzoku myōgi　眷属妙義

Kibi no Makibi　吉備真備

Kii　紀伊

kijitsu　忌日

Kikyō　喜慶

kindei　金泥

kinjiki　禁色

Kioka　木岡

Kiren　喜蓮

kishu　貴種

Kitain　喜多院

Kitano　北野

Kita-shirakawa　北白川

Kiuchi Gyōō　木内尭央

kiya　木屋

Kiyohara　清原

Kiyohara Naohira　清原直平

Kiyomizudera　清水寺

Kiyoyuki　清行

Kizō　基増

kō　公

kō (expanded version of text)　広

kō (assembly)　講

Kōbun　弘文

Kōchi　広智

kōdō　講堂

Kōen (editor of *Fusō ryakki*)　皇円

Kōen (Ryōgen's disciple)　弘延

Kōen kojitsu oboegaki　講演古実覚書

Kōfukuji　興福寺

kōgaku　広学

kōgaku ryūgi　広学竪義

Kōgei　皇慶

kōgō　皇后

Kōhō　康保

kōi (junior consort)　更衣

kōi (temple administrator)　網維

kōji　講師

Koji ruien　古事類苑

kōjiki　好色

Kōjō　光定

Kōken　公顕

Kōkō　康公

Kokon chomonjū　古今著聞集

koku　斛

kokubunji　国分寺

kokubun niji　国分尼寺

kokumai　黒米

kokushi　国師

Kokūzō　虚空蔵

Kōmyō (empress' name)　光明

kōmyō (mantra)　光明

Kōmyō (monk's name)　光妙

Kondō　金堂

kongō　金剛

Kongōbuji　金剛峯寺

Kongōkai taijuki　金剛界対受記

kongon　金言

kongōshi　金剛子

Kongō yasha　金剛夜叉

Kōnin　弘仁

Konjaku monogatarishū　今昔物語集

Konoha daishi　木葉大師

konpon　根本

konpon anshitsu　根本菴室

konpon bōchi　根本房地

Konpon chūdō　根本中堂

Konpon daishi rinjū yuigon　根本大師
　臨終遺言

Konpon kyōzō　根本經蔵

Konpon nyohōdō　根本如法堂

Korehito　惟仁

kōro　香炉

kōrobako　香炉筥

Kōsai　庚濟

Kōshi　康子

kōshiki　講式

Kōshin　光審

Kōshō (Kōya as a Tendai monk)
　光勝

Kōshō (Daianji monk)　孝聖

kōtō　勾當

Kōtōin　後唐院

Kōya　空也

Koyama　小山

kōyō　功用

kōzetsu　講説

Kozu　木津

Kuan-ching shi　観経疏

Kuang-hsiu　広修

Kuan P'u-hsien ching　観普賢經

Kuan wu-liang-shou ching　観無量
　寿経

kubon ōjō　九品往生

kuden　口伝

Kūe　空恵

kugen　公験

kugyō bettō　公卿別当

Kuhon ōjōgi　九品往生義

kuin　九院

Kuin Butsukakushō　九院仏閣抄

Kujō-ryū　九条流

Kujōdono ki　九条殿記

Kujōdono yuikai　九条殿遺誡

Kujō nenchūgyōji　九条年中行時

Kujō-ryū　九条流

Kūkai　空海

Kumano　熊野

kumon　公文

kun　訓

kunsei　葷腥

Kuo-ch'ing-ssu　国清寺

kuraryō　内蔵寮

Kurodae-nishi　黒田江西

Kurodani　黒谷

Kuroda Toshio　　黒田俊雄
kuruma yado　　車宿
kuryō　　供料
kushi　　駈使
Kūshō　　空昭
Kusuko　　薬子
Kuwana Tadamura　　桑名忠村
Kūya rui　　空也誄
kyakusō　　客僧
Kyōen　　教円
Kyōen　　慶円
kyōhan　　教判
Kyōku　　経求
Kyōshun　　慶俊
Kyōso　　慶祚
kyōsō　　教相
Kyōu　　教有
kyōzō　　慶相
Kyōzō　　経蔵
kyūkyūryō　　救急料
Kyūreki　　九暦
Lien-hua mien ching　　連華面経
magobisashi　　孫廂
mago-magobisashi　　孫孫廂
Mame daishi　　豆大師, 魔滅大師
mandara　　曼陀羅
mandara-ku　　曼陀羅供
mandokoro　　政所
mandokoroya　　政所室
Manga　　満賀
Manshuin　　曼殊院
Man'yōshū　　万葉集
manzan daishugi　　満山大衆義
maō　　魔王
Mappō　　末法
Masako　　雅子
masu　　升

matsudai　　末代
matsuji　　末寺
Matsumuro　　松室
Matsuo Kenji　　松尾剛次
megumu　　恵む
men　　面
Meryō　　馬寮
metsuzai　　滅罪
Miao-fa lien-hua ching　　妙法連華経
Mie　　三重
mihan　　未判
Miidera　　三井寺
Mii zokutōki　　三井続灯記
Mikawa　　三河
Miki Sumito　　三木紀人
mikkyō　　密教
miko　　巫女
Mimyō daishi　　御廟大師
Minamidani konpon bōchi　　南谷根本房地
Minamoto no Junshi　　源順子
Minamoto no Masanobu　　源雅信
Minamoto no Nobumitsu　　源延光
Minamoto no Takaakira　　源高明
Minamoto no Takakuni　　源隆国
Minamoto no Tamenori　　源為憲
Minamoto no Yoritomo　　源頼朝
Minamoto no Yoshitō　　源能遠
Minazuki-e　　六月会
mi ni kawarite　　代身
Mino　　美濃
Minoo　　箕面, 簑尾
Min'yu benwakushō　　愍諭辧惑章
miryūgisha　　末竪義者
misai-e　　御斎会
Misaki Gisen　　三崎義泉
Mitsuhama　　三津浜

Mitsujō senjutsu mokuroku　密乗撰述目録

Mitsu no mikuri　三津厨

Miwa myōjin　三和明神

Miyoshi no Kiyoyuki　三好清行

Miyoshi no Tameyasu　三好為康

Mizunomi　水飲

Mo-ho chih-kuan　摩訶止観

Mokuzan　穆算

mon　文

Mon'en　文円

monja　問者

Monjudō　文殊堂

Monju hachiji hō　文殊八字法

Monjurō　文殊樓

monoimi　物忌

Mononobe　物部

Montoku　文徳

mon'yō　問要

Mon'yōki　門葉記

Mudōji　無動寺

mukuroji　木患子

Muneaki　致秋

Murakami　村上

Murasaki Shikibu　紫式部

Murayama Shūichi　村山集一

Murōji　室生寺

muro shūji　無漏種子

Muryōjuin　無量寿院

Muryōjukyō shaku　無量寿経釈

Musashi　武蔵

Mushiroda-gun　席田郡

musō no shitsuji　無相悉地

Mutsu　奥州

myō　妙

myōbatsu　冥罰

myōbetsu gitsū　名別義通

Myōchō　明肇

Myōfu　明普

Myōgō　明豪

Myōgōbō　妙業房

Myōkōbō　妙香房

Myōkōin　妙香院

Myōku　明救

Myōrakuji　妙楽寺

Myōsen　明詮

myōsetsu　妙説

Myōshinji　妙心寺

Myōshō　明証

Myōson　明尊

Myōtatsu　明達

Myōun　妙雲

Nachi　那智

Nagaoka　長岡

naigubu　内供奉

naigubu jūzenji　内供奉十禅師

naishinnō　内親王

Nakao Shunpaku　仲尾俊博

Nakatomi no Kamatari　中臣鎌足

Nakatsukashō　中務省

Namubō muki　南無房夢記

nanja　難者

Nanji　南寺

Nanzan　南山

Nara　奈良

narabi-dō　竝堂

Nara Hiromoto　奈良弘元

nawaobi　縄帯

Nemu Kazuchika　根無一力

nen　念

nenbundosha　年分度者

nenbutsu　念仏

nengō　年号

nenju (meditation beads)　念珠

nenju (recitation)　念誦

Nenjudō　念誦堂

ni　尼

ni-e　二会

Nieh-p'an ching　涅槃経

Nieh-p'an shu　涅槃疏

nigatsu　二月

Nihon kiryaku　日本記略

Nihonkoku Tendaishū shōsho mokuroku　日本国天台宗章疏目録

Nihon kōsōden yōmonshō　日本高僧伝要文抄

Nihon ōjō gokuraku ki　日本往生極楽記

Nihon ryōiki　日本霊異記

niin　尼院

nijōbu　二乗部

nijūgo zanmai-e　二十五三昧会

Nijūsan(ni)kajō seishiki　二十三（二）箇条制式

ninai-dō　荷堂

Ninchū　仁忠

Ninga　仁賀

Ninju　仁樹

Ninkō (Hossō monk)　仁敦

Ninkō (Tendai monk)　仁好

Ninkū　仁空

Ninmyō　仁明

Ninnaji　仁和寺

Ninoma　二間

Ninomiya no gongen　二宮權現

Nishinomiya-zōhon　西宮蔵本

nitai　二諦

Nittō shin-guhō mokuroku　入唐進求法目録

Nittō Shōnin　日灯上人

Nōe　能恵

nōgesa　衲袈裟

Nōka　苗鹿

Nōkain　苗鹿院

Nomoto Kakujō　野本覚成

Noriakira　章明

Norihira　憲平

Nyogen　如源

nyōgo　女御

nyohō　如法

nyoi　如意

Nyoirin Kannon　如意輪観音

nyoju　女孺

Nyokaku　如覚

Nyomu　如無

nyonindō　女人堂

nyōō　女王

nyoraizō　如来蔵

Nyoshō　如照

nyūdō　入道

nyūdō nyōgo dono　入道如御殿

nyūshitsu deshi　入室弟子

Nyūzen　入禅

ōbō　王法

Oda Nobunaga　小田信長

Ōe Masafusa　大江匡房

Ogami Kanchū　尾上寛仲

Ōhara　大原

Ōjōden　往生伝

Ōjō gokurakuki　往生極楽記

Okada Seishi　岡田精司

Ōkagami　大鏡

Okaya　岡屋

Ōkubo Ryōshun　大久保良俊

Oku no in　奥の院

okurina　贈り名, 諡

Ōmi　近江

omikuji no ganso　おみくじの元祖

Ōmine　大峯

O-mi-t'o ching　阿弥陀経

Ōmiya no gongen　大宮權現

omoya　母屋

on　恩

Oni daishi　鬼大師

Onjōji　園城寺

Onjōji denki　園城寺伝記

Onkaku　恩覚

Onkaku sōjō　恩覚奏状

Onkun　恩訓

onmyōdō　陰陽道

Ono　小野

Ono Katsutoshi　小野勝年

Onomiya　小野宮

Ononomiya-ryū　小野宮流

Ononomiya kojitsu kyūrei　小野宮古実旧例

Ononomiya nenchūgyōji　小野宮年中行時

Ono no Takaki　小野喬木

Ono-ryū　小野流

Ōno Tatsunosuke　大野達之助

onryō　怨霊

Onshi　穏子

Ōsumi Kazuo　大隅利雄

ōtakiya　大炊屋

Ōtomo　大友

Ōtomo no Ōji　大友皇子

Ōtomo no Yotamaro　大友与多麿

Ōtomo Sukuri　大友村主

Ōtsu　大津

Ōwa　応和

Ōwa shūronki　応和宗論記

Ōwa shūron nikki　応和宗論日記

Oyamada Kazuo　小山田利夫

Ōyamagui no mikoto　大山咋命

Ōyumi no shi　大弩師

Pan-chou san-mei ching　般舟三昧経

Raga　羅賀

raidō　礼堂

Raigō　頼豪

Raishin　頼真

Raizō　頼増

rakusai　落彩

Ranpa Keishin　蘭坂景茛

rei　霊

rei (bells)　鈴

Reifuri daishi　鈴振大師

Reisei Mon'in　礼成門院

Reizei　冷泉

Rendaibō　連台房

rendan　連壇

renge-e　連華会

Rengein　連華院

Rengeji　連華寺

Rengeshiki　連華色

rengyō shamini　練行沙弥尼

renshi　連子

ri　理

ribusshō　理仏性

rikun　理薫

rinji　臨時

rinji dosha　臨時度者

Rinsei　憐西

Rinshō　憐昭

Risen　理仙

rissha　竪者

risshi　律師

Risshū　律宗

Ritsuryō　律令

roban　露盤

Rokugatsu-e　六月会

Rokuharamitsuji　六波羅蜜寺

Rokuharamitsuji engi　六波羅蜜寺縁起

rokusoku 六即

rongi 論議

rōni 老尼

rōnin 浪人

rōya 廊屋

Rōzan (Hossō monk) 良算

rōzan (sequestration) 籠山

Rozanji 盧山寺

Ruijū kokushi 類聚国史

rusunin 留守人

ryaku 略

ryakuchū 略註

Ryakukyū 暦珍

ryō 両

ryō (head) 領

ryōbu 両部

ryōbu daihō 両部大法

ryōbu mandara 両部曼荼羅

Ryōchin 良陳

ryō-e 両会

Ryōgen 良源

Ryōgon'in 楞厳院

Ryōhen 良遍

ryōke 良家

ryokuju 緑珠

Ryōshō 良昭

Ryōso 良祚

Ryōun 霊雲

Ryōun (Ryōgen's disciple) 良運

Ryōyū (Manshuin monk, fl. 1087–1094) 良祐

Ryōyū (eleventh Tendai *zasu*) 良勇

ryū 流

ryūgi 竪義, 立儀

ryūgisha 立義者

ryūtō gekishu 龍頭鷁首

sachūben 左中弁

sadaiben 左大弁

sadaijin 左大臣

Saeki Arikiyo 佐伯有清

Saga 嵯峨

Sagami 相模

Saganoin 嵯峨院

Saichō 最澄

Saidaiji 西大寺

Saien 最円

saiin 斎院

Saiin (alternative name for Juunain) 西院

Saiji 西寺

Saikō 斉衡

Sairyūji 西隆寺

Saishō-e 最勝会

Saitō 西塔

Saitōin 西塔院

Sakamoto 坂本

sake 裂

sake (salmon) 鮭

sakiama さきあま

saki no chūgū 前の中宮

Saki no tōin 前唐院

sakon'e no chūjō 左近衛中将

sakuryōmai 作料米

sameryō 左馬寮

san (praises) 賛

Sanbō ekotoba 三宝絵詞

sanbu 三部

sanbu sanmaya 三部三昧耶

sandai 算題

Sandai jitsuroku 三代実録

san'e 三会

Sangaigi shiki 三界義私記

sangan (three views) 三観

sangan (three vows) 三願

sangan isshin　三観一心

Sange (monk's name)　山下

sange (scattering flowers)　散花

Sange gakushōshiki　山家学生式

Sange ōjōki　三外往生記

sangeshi　散花師

Sange yōki senryaku　山家要記浅略

Sange yōryakki senryaku　山家要略記
　浅略

sangi　算木

sangō　三網

San'inki　三院記

sanji　三時

Sanjō　三条

sanjū　三従

sankai　三階

sankorei　三鈷鈴

sankō tenshi　三光天子

sanmaiden　三昧田

sanmakudō　三悪道

sanmaya　三昧耶

sanmen　三面

Sanmon　山門

Sanmon dōshaki　山門堂社記

Sanmonki　山門記

sanmon shika daihō　山門四箇大法

sannaku　三惑

Sannō　山王

Sannōin　山王院

Sannōin zōsho mokuroku　山王院蔵書
　目録

Sannō myōjin　山王明神

sanrin　三輪

Sanron　三論

sanruikyō　三類境

sanshin　三身

sanshō nishi　三聖二師

sanshū　三周

santō　三塔

sanwaku　三惑

Sanzen'inbon　三千院本

Sei　清

Seihan　勢範

seihei　精兵

seikai　制誡

Seikyūki　西宮記

Seiraiji　西来寺

Seiryōden　清冷殿

Seishi (Empress Junna)　正子

Seishi (Morosuke's wife)　盛子

Seishin　清慎

Seishinkōki　清慎公記

Seiwa　清和

sekigaku　碩学

Sekiguchi Shindai　関口眞大

Sekizan Myōjin　赤山明神

sen (thousand)　千

sen (unit of money)　銭

Senga　暹賀

senju　千手

Senjuin　千手院

Senju sengen Kannon　千手千眼
　観音

Senkan　千観

Senkōin　千光院

Senman　千満

Senmi　千美

Senri　千理

Senshi　詮子

Sentō　千致

Sen'un　千雲

setsuryō　摂領

setsuwa　説話

Settsu　摂津

Shakadō　釈迦堂

Shakke kanpanki　釈家官班記

shaku　尺

shakujō　錫杖

Shakuzenji　積善寺

shami　沙弥

shamini　沙弥尼

shamini no ama　沙弥尼の尼

Shan　剡

shanagō　遮那業

Shan-kuang-ssu　善光寺

Shan-tao　善導

shari-e　舎利会

Sheng-man ching　勝鬘經

shi　私

Shibata Minoru　柴田実

Shiba Tatto　司馬達止

Shibungi gokuryaku shiki　四分義極略私記

Shibunritsu　四分律

shichi butsu yakushihō　七仏薬師法

shichishō　七聖

shido　私度

Shiga　滋賀

Shigeakira　重明

Shigematsu Nobuhiro　重松信弘

Shih mo-ho-yen lun　釈摩訶衍論

Shih-shih yao-lan　釈氏要覧

shijōkōhō　熾盛光法

Shijōshiki　四条式

Shijūjōketsu　四十帖決

shikan　止観

Shikangō　止観業

shiki　私記

Shikibu　式部

Shiki-kōdō　四季講堂

shiki-mandara　敷曼陀羅

shiki senbō　四季懺法

shikishamani　式叉摩尼

shikishu　色衆

shikkō　執行

Shikō　志晃

Shikyō ruijū　私教類聚

Shima　嶋

Shimane　島根

shimen　四面

shimobe　下部

Shimotsuke　下野

Shimotsuki-e　霜月会

Shinden　神殿

shinden (palace-style)　寝殿

shindō　新銅

Shin-enmeiin　新延命院

Shinga　真雅

Shingi　真義

Shingō　真興

Shingon　真言

Shingondō　真言堂

Shingon gakutō　真言学頭

Shingon'in　真言院

Shingonzō　真言蔵

Shinjō sōmoku jōbutsu shiki　斟定草木成仏私記

Shinkaku　真覚

Shinki　真喜

Shinkishū　宸記集

shinnan　信男

Shin Nihon-dō　新日本堂

Shinnyo　真如

Shinnyozō　真如蔵

Shinshō　真紹

shinsoku　神足

Shintai　真泰

Shinzei　真済

Shinzen　真然

shinzoku ikkan　真俗一貫

Shiōin　四王院

Shioiri Ryōchū　塩入亮忠

Shiragi myōjin　新羅明神

Shirakawa　白川

Shishinden　紫辰殿

shishō　四摂

shishūki　私集記

shishu zanmai　四種三昧

Shisōiki　四相違記

shitan　紫檀

Shitennōji　四天王寺

shitsuji　悉地

Shitsumi-no-ho　志積浦

shōbō　正報

Shōbō (Shingon monk)　聖宝

Shōchō　承澄

Shōden　聖天

shoe　所依

shōen　荘園

shōgatsu　正月

shōgisha　精義者

shōgu　性具

Shōgun Jizō　将軍地蔵

Shōhan　清範

shōji (manor administrator)　庄司

shōji (ordained servant)　承仕

shōju　小呪

shōko　庄子

Shōkōkan　彰考館

Shōkokuji　相国寺

Shōku　聖救

Shoku Nihongi　続日本紀

Shoku Nihon kōki　続日本後記

shokurui　嘱累

Shōmon　松門

Shōmu　聖武

shōmyō　声明

shōni　小尼

Shōnin　承仁

shōnin (eminent priest)　上人

Shōō　昌応

Shōrengein　勝連華院

Shōryōin　聖霊院

Shōsan (Jimon monk)　勝算

Shōsan (Sanmon monk)　正算

Shōshi (Michinaga's daughter)　彰子

Shōshi (Murakami's consort)　庄子

Shōshi (Reizei's consort, 950–999)　昌子

shoshi (temple administrators)　所司

Shōshinshi gongen　聖真子權現

Shoshū shōsho mokuroku　諸宗章疏目録

shōsō　小僧

shoson yuga goma　諸尊瑜伽護摩

shōsōzu　少僧都

Shōtai　昌泰

Shōtō　聖燈

Shōtoku (female emperor)　称徳

Shōtoku (prince)　聖徳

Shou-ming ching　守命経

Shōyūki　小右記

shōzei　正税

Shu　疏

Shūei　宗叡

Shuen　修円

shugaku　修学

Shugakuin　修学院

shugi　衆義

shūgi　宗義

Shūi ōjōden　拾遺往生伝

Shukaku 守覚
shukke 出家
shukke sahō 出家作法
shūkotsusho 拾骨所
shukubō 宿房
Shukukyū 宿久
Shun'ei 春叡
Shungei 舜芸
Shunsen 春暹
Shuryōgongyō 首楞厳経
Shuryōgon'in 首楞厳院
Shuryōgon'in kengyō shidai 首楞厳院
検校次第
Shuryōgon'in shiki 首楞厳院式
Shūshi 脩子
shūyō 宗要
sō 僧
soegi 副義
sofuku 素服
Sōgō 僧綱
Sōgō bunin 僧綱補任
sōgya 僧伽
sōhei 僧兵
sōja 総社, 惣社
Sōjiin 総持院
Sōjo 相助
sōjō (archbishop) 僧正
sōjō hōin 僧正法印
sōke 僧家
soken 素絹
soku 束
sokusai zōyaku 息災増益
sokushin jōbutsu 即身成仏
Sokushin jōbutsugi shiki 即身成仏義
私記
Sōmoku hosshin shugyō jōbutsuki 草木
発心修行成仏記

sōmoku jōbutsu 草木成仏
sōmonja 相問者
Son'en 尊円
sōni 僧尼
Son'i 尊意
Sōniryō 僧尼令
Sonshi 尊子
sonshi (teacher) 尊師
sonshō 尊勝
sonshōhō 尊勝法
Sontsū 尊通
Sōō 相応
sōrintō 相輪塔
Soshitsuji 蘇悉地
sotobarei 剽都婆鈴
sōza 僧座
sōzaichō 惣在庁
sozei 租税
sōzu 僧都
Ssu-fen lü 四分律
Suehara 陶原
Sueki Fumihiko 末木文美士
Sūfukuji 崇福寺
Sugawara no Michizane 菅原道真
Suikai 垂誡
suikotō 出挙稲
suishin 水心
Suishinki 水心記
Suju 崇寿
sukuyō 宿曜
Suzaku 朱雀
Tachibana no Kachiko 橘嘉智子
Tachibana no Kimiyasu 橘公廉
Tachibana no Toshisada 橘敏貞
Tachibana no Tsunehira 橘恒平
Tachibana no Tsunesada 橘恒貞
Ta-chih-tu lun 大智度論

Tado jingūji　多度神宮寺

taifu　大輔

Taigen(sui)　太元（帥）

Taiheiki　太平記

Taikō mondōshū kuketsu　大網問答集口決

taikōgō　太皇后

Taikyoku　太極

Taira Masayuki　平雅行

Taira no Kimimasa　平公正

Taira no Kiyomori　平清盛

Taira no Koremochi　平伊望

Taira no Muneaki　平致秋

Taira no Muneyori　平致頼

Taira no Tsunemasa　平恒昌

taishōkoku　大相国

taishūka　大衆化

taizōkai　胎蔵界

Ta-jih ching　大日経

Tajima Tokuon　田島徳音

Takahashi Mitsugu　高橋貢

Takagi Yutaka　高木豊

Takaiko　高子

Takano　高野

Takao　高雄

Takashima-gun　高島郡

Takatori Masao　高取正男

takaya　高屋

Takemura Shōhō　武邑尚邦

Taketsure　武連

Tamai Yukinosuke　玉井幸助

tandai　探題

Tandai igi kojitsuron　探題異義故実論

Tandai jitsujoki　探題実助記

Tandai kojitsuki　探題故実記

Tandai shidai　探題次第

tani no zasu　谷座主

Tankei　湛契

Tanshō　湛照

Tao-ch'eng　道誠

Tao-ch'o　道綽

Tao-hsing　道興

Tao-hsüan (596–667)　道宣

Tao-hsüan (702–760)　道璿

Tao-kan yü ching　稲幹喩経

Ta pan-jo ching　大般若経

Ta-sheng ch'i-hsin lun　大乗起信論

Tateiri　立入

tatsumi no sumi　巽角

Ta yüan-chüeh ching　大円覚經

teguruma　輦車

teihatsu　剃髪

Teimyō　程妙

Teishinkōki　貞信公記

Ten'anji　天安寺

Tenchi　天智

Tenchō　天長

Tendai　天台

Tendai Hokkeshū gishū　天台法華宗義集

Tendai Hokkeshū sōjō kechimyakuzu　天台法華宗相承血脈図

Tendai shikyōgi　天台四教儀

Tendai zasuki　天台座主記

tengu　天狗

Tengu zōshi　天狗草紙

tengyō　転経

Tengyō (era name)　天慶

Tenji　天智

Tenkai　天海

Tenkaizō　天海蔵

Tenmu tennō　天武天皇

tennyo jōbutsu　転女成仏

Tennyo jōbutsukyō　転女成仏経

Tenroku　天禄

Tentoku　天徳

T'ien-chu ling-ch'ien　天竺霊籤

T'ien-chu-ssu　天竺寺

T'ien-t'ai ssu-chiao-i　天台四教儀

Tobatsu Bishamon　兜跋毘沙門

Tōbō　唐房

Tōbō anriroku　唐房行履録

tochi　橡

Tōdaiji　東大寺

tōdan jukai　登壇受戒

Tōdō　東塔

Tōdōin　東塔院

Tōeizan Kan'eiji ganzan daishi engi
東叡山寛永寺元三大師縁起

Tōen　東縁

toga wo kotowaru　科を義わる

Tōgoku　東国

Tōin　唐院

tōi sokumyō　当位即妙

Tōji　東寺

tōkanshiki　沓冠式

Tōkata　遠名

Tōketsu　唐決

Tōkōji　東光寺

toku　得

tokubun　得分

Tokuen　徳円

Tokugawa Ieyasu　徳川家康

tokugō　得業

Tokuitsu　徳一

Tomohira　具平

Tomoyui　鞆結

Tōnan'in　東南院

Tōnomine　多武峰

Tōnomine engi　多武峰縁起

Tōnomine ryakki　多武峰略記

Toranni　都藍尼

Tōshōdaiji　唐招提寺

Totsu-hama　富津浜

Tsu　津

tsugai rongi　番論義

tsuifuku　追福

tsuina　都維那

Tsui-sheng-wang ching　最勝王經

Tsujimura Taizen　辻村泰善

Tsukushi　筑紫

Tsuneyasu　常康

tsuno daishi　角大師

Tsuno Shigekata　角重名

Tsuno Takeyasu　角武廉

Tsuno Yoshiko　角好子

Ts'un-shih　存式

Tsurakuni　貫邦

T'un-lin　遁麟

Tz'u-en　慈恩

Tzu-sheng-ssu　資聖寺

Ubai kōshinmon　優婆夷貢進文

ubuyu　産湯

uchi　内

uchi rongi　内論議

uchi rongi dō　内論議堂

uchūben　右中弁

Uda　宇多

udaiben　右大弁

Ueda Kōen　上田晃円

Uharake　優鉢羅花

Uji　宇治

ujidera　氏寺

ujigami　氏神

umeryō　右馬寮

Unnichi　運日

Unshō　運昭

urabon-e　盂蘭盆会

uragaki　裏書

Urin'in　雲林院

Usa hachiman　宇佐八幡

usō no shitsuji　有相悉地

Ususama　禹擦

Wakasa　若狭

wagō　和合

warigo　破子

wasan　和讃

Wei-mo ching　維摩経

Wen-chi p'in　問疾品

Wen-kuei　文軌

Wen-shu-shih-li p'u-sa pa-tzu san-mei fa
文殊師利菩薩八字三昧法

Wen-ts'an　文漸

Wu-fen lü　五分律

wu-hui nien-fo　五会念仏

Wu-kou-ch'eng ching　無垢称経

Wu-liang-i ching　無量義經

Wu-pai men-lun　五白問論

Wu-t'ai　五台

Yagi Kōe　八木昊恵

yakisho　焼所

Yakushi　薬師

Yakushidō　薬師堂

Yakushiji　薬師寺

Yakushi nyorai　薬師如來

Yamada Etai　山田恵諦

yama no ajari　山の阿闍梨

Yamashina　山階

Yamashita Katsuaki　山下克明

Yamashiro　山城

Yamato　大利

Yang Jen-lu　揚仁侶

Yase dōji　八瀬童子

Yasu-gun　野洲郡

Yasuhito　懐仁

Yen Chih-tui　顔之推

Yen-shih chia hsün　顔氏家訓

Ying-lo ching　瓔珞經

Yin-ming cheng-li-men lun　因明正理
門論

Yin-ming ju-cheng-li lun　因明入正
理論

Yin-ming ju-cheng-li lun i-tuan　因明
入正理論義斷

Yin-ming ju-cheng-li lun-shu　因明入
正理論疏

Yin-ming ju-cheng-li lun tsuan-yao
因明入正理論纂要

yin-yang　陰陽

yoinosō　夜居僧

Yokawa　横川

Yokei　余慶

Yōki　要記

Yoshidadera　吉田寺

Yoshida Yasuo　吉田靖雄

Yoshimine no Yasuyo　良岑安世

Yoshishige no Yasutane　慶滋保胤

Yōshō　陽生

Yü-chieh lun　瑜伽論

Yü-chüan-ssu　玉泉寺

Yüan-hui　円暉

Yuga goma　瑜伽護摩

Yuga goma giki　瑜伽護摩儀規

Yugaron　瑜伽論

Yugaron mondō　瑜伽論問答

yuikai　遺誡

Yuima-e　維摩会

Yuimae hyōbyaku　維摩会表白

Yuima kōji kengaku ryūgi shidai　維摩
講師研学竪義次第

Yuisei　遺制

Yuishikishō　唯識章

Yuishikiron sho　唯識論疏

yuishin　唯心

Yuishu　惟首

Yūken　猷憲

Yūki Reimon　結城令聞

Yün-huang　雲黄

Yūsen　幽仙

yuya　湯屋

zaichō　在庁

zasu　座主

Zendanshō　禅談鈔

Zengei　禅芸

zenji　禅師

Zenji no kimi　禅師の君

Zenju　善珠

Zenrinji　禅林寺

Zenshinni　善信尼

Zentōin　前唐院

zentoku　全得

Zen'un　禅雲

Zen'yu　禅瑜

zōbu　雑部

Zōga　増賀

Zōho　像法

Zōkai　増快

zokka　俗化

zoku-bettō　俗別当

Zoku honchō ōjō den　続本朝往生伝

Zokuruihon　嘱累品

Zoku Tendaishū zensho　続天台宗全書

zōmatsu　像末

zōmen　蔵面

zōmitsu　雑密

Zōmyō　増命

Zōrindō　雑林堂

zōsha　雑舎

zōshi　雑使

Zōso　蔵祚

zōyaku　雑役

Zōzen　増全

zuigu　隨求

Zuigu-kyō　隨求経

Zuijiidō　隨自意堂

Zuijii-in　隨自意院

zuiki　隨喜

Bibliography

Abe Yasurō. 1989. "Nyonin kinzei to suisan." In *Miko to joshin*, ed. Ōsumi Kazuo and Nishiguchi Junko, 154–240. Tokyo: Heibonsha.

———. 1983. "*Zōga Shōnin muki:* Zōga-den no shinshiryō ni tsuite." *Bukkyō bungaku* 7: 17–26.

Adolphson, Mikael S. 2000. *The Gates of Power: Monks, Courtiers, and Warriors in Premodern Japan*. Honolulu: University of Hawai'i Press.

———. 1996. "Monks, Courtiers, and Warriors in Premodern Japan: The Secular Power of Enryakuji in the Heian and Kamakura Eras." Ph.D. diss., Stanford University.

Akamatsu Toshihide. 1966. "Fujiwara jidai Jōdokyō to Kakuchō." In *Zoku Kamakura Bukkyō no kenkyū*, ed. Akamatsu Toshihide, 305–332. Kyoto: Heirakuji shoten.

Akanuma Chizen. 1967. *Indo Bukkyō koyū meishi jiten*. Kyoto: Hōzōkan.

Akao Eikei. 1989. "*Juketsushū* no ikkōsatsu." In *Chishō daishi kenkyū*, ed. Chishō daishi kenkyū henshū iinkai, 775–786. Kyoto: Dōhōsha.

Anonymous. 1984. "Ganzan daishi shinkō ni kansuru chōsa hōkoku." *Eizan gakuin kenkyū kiyō* 6: 299–316.

Arai Kōjun. 1994. "Kyōke nikō: shamikai dōshi kyōke, fujuku." In *Chūsei jiin to hōe*, ed. Satō Michiko, 56–78. Kyoto: Hōzokan.

Araki Ryōsen. 1929. *Bikuni shi*. Tokyo: Nisōdō shoten.

Ashida Kōitsu. 1980. "Fujiwara Takamitsu ni okeru Yokawa to Tōnomine no ichi." *Kokugo to kokubungaku* 57, no. 6: 12–27.

Aston, W. G., trans. 1972. *Nihongi: Chronicles of Japan from the earliest times to A.D. 697*. Rutland, VT.: C. E. Tuttle.

Aung-Thwin, Michael. 1979. "The Role of Sasana Reform in Burmese History: Economic Dimensions of a Religious Purification." *Journal of Asian Studies* 38, no. 4: 671–688.

Bargen, Doris. 1988. "Spirit Possession in the Context of Dramatic Expressions of Gender Conflict." *Harvard Journal of Asiatic Studies* 48, no. 1: 95–130.

Bartholomeusz, Tessa. 1990. "Women under the Bo Tree." Ph.D. diss., University of Virginia.

———. 1994. *Women under the Bo Tree: Buddhist Nuns in Sri Lanka*. New York: Cambridge University Press.

Birnbaum, Raoul. 1979. *The Healing Buddha*. Denver, Colo.: Shambala.

Borgen, Robert. 1986. *Sugawara no Michizane and the Early Heian Court*. Cambridge: Harvard University Press.

Bowring, Richard. 1982. *Murasaki Shikibu: Her Diary and Poetic Memoirs*. Princeton, N.J.: Princeton University Press.

Brook, Timothy. 1993. *Praying for Power: Buddhism and the Formation of Gentry Society in Late-Ming China*. Cambridge: Harvard University Press.

Brown, Delmer M., and Ichiro Ishida, trans. 1979. *The Future and the Past: A Translation and Study of the "Gukanshō."* Berkeley: University of California Press.

Buddhist Seminar of Hawaii, trans. 1983. *T'ien-t'ai Buddhism: An Outline of the Fourfold Buddhism*. Tokyo: Daiichi shobō.

Bukkyō taikei kankōkai, ed. 1917–1921. *Bukkyō taikei*. Tokyo: Bukkyō taikei kankōkai.

Bussho kankōkai, ed. 1912–1922. *Dainihon Bukkyō zensho*. Tokyo: Dainihon Bukkyō zensho kankōkai.

Chan, Chi-wah. 1993. "Chih-li (960–1028) and the Formation of Orthodoxy in the Sung Tien-t'ai Tradition of Buddhism." Ph.D. diss., University of California at Los Angeles.

Chegwan. 1983. *T'ien-t'ai Buddhism: An Outline of the Four Teachings*. Trans. David Chappell. Honolulu: University of Hawai'i Press.

Chen Jinhua. 1998. "The Construction of Early Tendai Buddhism: The Japanese Provenance of Saichō's Transmission Documents and Three Buddhist Apocrypha Attributed to Śubhākarasiṁha." *Journal of the International Association of Buddhist Studies* 21, no. 1: 21–76.

———. 1997. "The Formation of Tendai Esoteric Buddhism in Japan: A Study of Three Japanese Esoteric Apocrypha." Ph.D. diss., McMaster University.

Ch'en, Kenneth. 1973. *The Chinese Transformation of Buddhism*. New York: Columbia University Press.

Cheng Chen-tuo. N.d. *Chung-guo ku-dai pan-hua ts'ung-kan*.

Dobbins, James C. 1998. "A Brief History of Pure Land Buddhism in Early Japan." In *Engaged Pure Land Buddhism: Challenges Facing Jōdo Shinshū in the Contemporary World, Essays in Honor of Alfred Bloom*, ed. Kenneth Tanaka and Eisho Nasu, 113–165. Berkeley: Wisdom Ocean Publications.

Donner, Neil, and Daniel Stevenson. 1993. *The Great Calming and Contemplation: A Study and Annotated Translation of the First Chapter of Chih-i's Mo-ho-chih-kuan*. Honolulu: University of Hawai'i Press.

Eishin (introduction by Ikeyama Issaien). 1979. *Hokke jikidanshō*. 3 vols. Kyoto: Rinsen shoten.

Eizan gakuin, ed. 1984. *Issen-nen onki kinen Ganzan jie daishi no kenkyū*. Kyoto: Dōhōsha.

Endō Yoshimoto and Kasuga Kazuo, eds. 1967. *Nihon ryōiki*. Tokyo: Iwanami shoten.

Ennin. 1955. *Ennin's Diary: The Record of a Pilgrimage to China*. Trans. Edwin O. Reischauer. New York: Ronald Press.

Fujihira Kanden. 1988. "Gika shohon no rondai henka." *Tendai gakuhō* 30: 130–133.

Fujii Sahyōe, ed. 1983. *Ganzan daishi Omikuji*. Kyoto: Konshōdō.

Fujimoto Fumio. 1988. "Chikū-sen *Inmyō ken sanshi* ni tsuite." *Tendai gakuhō* 30: 57–61.

———. 1986. "Nihon Tendai ni okeru yuishiki no kenkyū." *Tendai gakuhō* 29: 84–89.

———. 1984. "Tendai ni okeru *Kusharon* kenkyū no keifu." *Tendai gakuhō* 26: 129–134.

Fujioka Tadaharu et al., eds. 1971. *Izumi shikibu nikki, Murasaki shikibu nikki, Sarashina nikki, Sanuki no suke nikki.* Shinpen Nihon koten bungaku zenshū, vol. 26. Tokyo: Shōgakkan.

Fujishi Tetsudō. 1984. "Jie daishi no tanju gokai ni tsuite." In *Issen-nensonki kinen Ganzan jie daishi no kenkyū*, 28–32. Kyoto: Dōhōsha.

Fukaura Seibun. 1978. *Shinkō Bukkyō bungaku monogatari.* Kyoto: Nagata bunshōdō.

———. 1954. *Yuishikigaku kenkyū.* 2 vols. Kyoto: Nagata bunshōdō.

Fukihara Shōshin. 1970. *Kenjōgi ryakumondō no kenkyū: Chūzan jutsu.* Nakamura insei kabushiki kaisha.

———. 1944. *Nihon yuishikishi.* Kyoto: Daigadō.

Fukuda Gyōei. 1968. *Tendaigaku gairon.* 2 vols. Tokyo: Bun'ichi shuppan.

Fukuhara Ryōgon. 1970. "Nihon no Kusha gakusha." *Ryūkoku daigaku ronshū* 392: 1–20.

Fukui Kōjun, ed. 1973. *Dengyō daishi kenkyū.* Tokyo: Waseda Daigaku shuppanbu.

———, ed. 1964. *Jikaku daishi kenkyū.* Tokyo: Waseda Daigaku shuppanbu.

Fukuo Takeichiirō. 1931. "Jikaku montō to Chishō montō no kōsō ni tsuite." In *Onjōji no kenkyū*, ed. Tendaishū jimonha goonki jimukyoku, 527–578. Ōtsu: Onjōji.

Funagasaki Masataki. 1985. *Kokka Bukkyō hen'yō katei no kenkyū: Kansō taisei shijō kara no kōsatsu.* Tokyo: Yūzankaku shuppan.

Funahashi Suisai. 1985. "Kushashū no ryūden oyobi sono kyōgi." *Nanto rokushū*, ed. Hiraoka Jōkai and Yamasaki Keiki, 156–162. Tokyo: Yoshikawa kōbunkan.

Futaba Kenkō. 1961. "Gyōki no shōgai to hanritsuryō Bukkyō no seiritsu." *Nanto Bukkyō* 5: 1–75.

Fūzanbō kokushi jiten hensanbu. 1940–1943. *Kokushi jiten.* 4 vols. Tokyo: Fūjzanbō.

Getz, Daniel Aaron. 1994. "Siming Zhili and Tiantai Pure Land in the Song Dynasty." Ph.D. diss., Yale University.

Gotō Hiroyuki. 1984. *Nyonin jōbutsu e no kaigen: Omikuji daishi Ryōgen no monogatari.* Tokyo: Mainichi shinbunsha.

Groner, Paul. 1987. "Annen, Tankei, Henjō, and Monastic Discipline in the Japanese Tendai School: The Background of the *Futsū jubosatsukai kōshaku*." *Japanese Journal of Religious Studies* 14, nos. 2–3: 129–159.

———. 1990. "The *Fan-wang ching* and Monastic Discipline in Japanese Tendai: A Study of Annen's *Futsū jubosatsukai kōshaku*." In *Chinese Buddhist Apocrypha*, ed. Robert Buswell, 251–290. Honolulu: University of Hawai'i Press.

———. 1989. "The *Lotus Sūtra* and Saichō's Interpretation of the Realization of Buddhahood with This Very Body (*sokushin jōbutsu*)." In *The Lotus Sūtra in Japanese Culture*, ed. George Tanabe, Jr., and Willa Tanabe, pp. 53–74. Honolulu: University of Hawai'i Press,

———. 1990. "The Ordination Ritual in the *Platform Sūtra* within the Context of the East Asian Vinaya Tradition." In *Fo Kuang Shan Report of International Conference on Ch'an Buddhism*, 220–250. Kaohsiung, Taiwan: Fo-kuang shan.

———. 1984. *Saichō: The Establishment of the Japanese Tendai School.* Berkeley Buddhist Studies Series, 7. Berkeley: Center for South and Southeast Asian Studies/Institute for Buddhist Studies, University of California.

————. 1992. "Shortening the Path: The Interpretation of the Realization of Buddhahood in This Very Existence in the Early Tendai School." In *Paths to Liberation: The Mārga and Its Transformations in Buddhist Thought*, ed. Robert
Buswell and Robert Gimello, 439–474. Honolulu: University of Hawai'i
Press.

————. 1997. "Tendai Interpretations of the Realization of Buddhahood with This
Very Body (*sokushin jōbutsu*) after the Death of Saichō: Sources and Preliminary Considerations." In *Taeyŏn Yi Yŏngja paksa hwagap kinyŏm nonch'ong
ch'ŏnt'ae sasang kwa tongyang munhwa*, ed. Taeyŏn Yi Yŏngja paksa hwagap
kinyŏm nonch'ong kanhaeng wiwŏnhoe, 131–155. Seoul: Pulchisa.

————. Forthcoming. "Tradition and Innovation: Eison, Kakujō, and the Re-
establishment of Orders of Monks and Nuns during the Kamakura Period."
In *Buddhist Precepts and Ordinations in East Asia*, ed. William Bodiford.

Hanawa Hokinoichi, ed. 1893–1902. *Gunsho ruijū*. Tokyo: Keizai zasshisha.

————. 1923–1930. *Zoku gunsho ruijū*. Tokyo: Zoku gunsho ruijū kankōkai.

Havnevik, Hanna. 1989. *Tibetan Buddhist Nuns*. Oslo: Norwegian University Press.

Hayami Tasuku. 1988. *Genshin*. Tokyo: Yoshikawa kōbunkan.

————. 1975. *Heian kizoku shakai to Bukkyō*. Tokyo: Yoshikawa kōbunkan.

————. 1987. *Jujutsu shūkyō no sekai: Mikkyō no shuhō no rekishi*. Tokyo: Hanawa shobō.

Hayashi Rokurō. 1961. *Kōmyō Kōgō*. Tokyo: Yoshikawa kōbunkan.

Hazama Jikō. 1972. *Nihon Bukkyō no kaiten to sono kichō*. 2 vols. Tokyo: Sanseidō.

Hieizan senshuin fuzoku Eizan gakuin, ed. 1975. *Dengyō daishi zenshū*. 5 vols. Tokyo:
Sekai seiten kankō kyōkai.

Hieizan senshuin and Eizan gakuin, eds. 1984. *Eshin sōzu zenshū*. Kyoto: Shibunkaku.

Higo Kazuo. 1984. "Heian jidai ni okeru onryō no shisō." In *Goryō shinkō*, ed. Shibata Minoru, 13–36. Tokyo: Yūzankaku.

Hioki Shōichi. 1972. *Nihon sōhei kenkyū*. Tokyo: Kokusho kankōkai.

Hirabayashi Moritoku. 1981. *Hijiri to setsuwa no shiteki kenkyū*. Tokyo: Yoshikawa
kōbunkan.

————. 1981. "Roku-haramitsu-ji sōken kō." In *Hijiri to setsuwa no shiteki kenkyū*, ed.
Hirabayashi Moritoku, 126–144. Tokyo: Yoshikawa kōbunkan.

————. 1976. *Ryōgen* Jinbun sōsho, vol. 173. Tokyo: Yoshikawa kōbunkan.

————. 1981. "Ryōgen to Eizan chūkō." *Rekishi to kyōiku* 12, no. 6 (1964). Reprinted
in *Hijiri to setsuwa no shiteki kenkyū*, ed. Hirabayashi Moritoku, 7–20. Tokyo:
Yoshikawa kōbunkan.

————. 1981. "Shinshutsu *Jie daishiden* shiryō dasoku." In *Hijiri to setsuwa no shiteki
kenkyū*, ed. Hirabayashi Moritoku, 21–40. Tokyo: Yoshikawa kōbunkan.

————. 1963. "*Tōnomine shōshō monogatari* ni miru Takamitsu shukke no shūhen."
Gengo to bungei 5, no. 5. Reprinted in *Hijiri to setsuwa no shiteki kenkyū*, ed.
Hirabayashi Moritoku, 41–56.

————. 1981. "Tōnomine shōshō monogatari wo dō yomu ka: Ashida Kōitsu-shi no
hihan ni kotaete." *Kokugo to kokubungaku* 58, no. 3: 22–34.

Hirabayashi Moritoku and Koike Kazuyuki, eds. 1976. *Sōryaku sōran*. Tokyo: Kasama
sakuin sōkan.

Hirakawa Akira. 1964. *Genshi Bukkyō no kenkyū*. Tokyo: Shunjūsha.

————. 1970. *Ritsuzō no kenkyū*. Tokyo: Sankibō Busshorin.

Hiraoka Jōkai. 1981. *Nihon jiinshi no kenkyū.* Tokyo: Yoshikawa kōbunkan.

———. 1989. "Onjōji no seiritsu to kaidan no mondai." In *Chishō daishi kenkyū,* ed. Chishō daishi kenkyū henshū iinkai, 423–488. Tokyo: Dōhōsha.

———. 1977. *Tōdaiji.* Tokyo: Kyōikusha.

———. 1980. *Tōdaiji jiten.* Tokyo: Tōkyōdō shuppan.

Hirata Toshiharu. 1977. "Akusō ni tsuite." In *Shūkyō shakaishi kenkyū,* ed. Risshō daigaku shigakkai, 125–143. Tokyo: Yūzankaku shuppansha.

———. 1943. *Heian jidai no kenkyū.* Tokyo: San'ichi shobō.

———. 1965. *Sōhei to bushi.* Nihonjin to tame no kokushi sōsho, vol. 12. Tokyo: Nihon kyōbunsha.

Hisaki Yukio. 1979–1994. "Jukyō." In *Kokushi daijiten,* ed. Kokushi daijiten iinkai, 7:324a–325c. Tokyo: Yoshikawa kōbunkan.

Honda Kōyū, ed. 1963. *Yakuchū Jikaku daishiden.* Otsu: Tendaishū kyōgakubu.

Hongō Masatsugu. 1985. "Naigubu jūzenji no seiritsu to Tendaishū." *Bukkyō shigaku kenkyū* 28, no. 1: 1–19.

Hori Daiji. 1966. "Jinzen to Myōkōin 1: Yokawa Bukkyō kizokuka no ichimen." *Nihon Bukkyō* 23: 1–11.

———. 1966. "Jinzen to Myōkōin 2." *Nihon Bukkyō* 23:52–64.

———. 1967. "Ryōgen no 'Nijūrokkajō kisei' no seitei no igi." *Shisō* 25:12–39.

———. 1964. "Ryōgen to Yokawa fukkō (part 1): toku ni Ennin montō to no kanren wo megutte." *Kyoto joshi daigaku jinbun ronshō* 10:24–55.

———. 1966. "Ryōgen to Yokawa fukkō" (part 2): toku ni Hieizan chūkō to kanren shite." *Kyoto joshi daigaku jinbun ronshō* 12: 1–34.

———. 1971. "Takamitsu to Zōga." *Bukkyō bungaku kenkyū* 10:43–83.

———. 1962. "Tōnomine to Jisshō." *Ryūkoku shiden* 50:111–112.

———. 1983. "Yokawa Bukkyō no kenkyū." In *Genshin,* ed. Ōsumi Kazuo, 205–232. Tokyo: Yoshikawa kōbunkan.

Hori Ichirō. 1975. *Jōdai Nihon Bukkyō bunkashi.* 2 vols. Tokyo: Daitō shuppansha, 1941; reprinted Kyoto: Rinsen shoten.

———. 1971. *Kōya.* 3d ed. Tokyo: Yoshikawa Kōbunkan.

———. 1978. "Waga kuni gakusō kyōiku seido." In *Hori Ichirō chosakushū 3 (Gakusō to gakusō kyōiku),* ed. Kusunoki Masahiro, 547–692. Tokyo: Miraisha.

———. 1953. *Waga kuni minkan shinkōshi no kenkyū.* 2 vols. Tokyo: Sōgensha.

Horiike Shunpō. 1957. "Ensai Ennin to Tendaisan Kokuseiji oyobi Chōan Shishōji ni tsuite." *Nihon Bukkyōshi* 3: 43–57.

———. 1982. "Nara jidai ni okeru niji nisō." In *Nanto Bukkyōshi no kenkyū* 1 (Tōdaiji-hen), 546–567. Kyoto: Hōzōkan.

———. 1988. "Yuima-e to kandō no shōshin." In *Chūsei jiinshi no kenkyū,* ed. Chūsei jiinshi kenkyūkai, 193–230. Kyoto: Hōzōkan.

Horner, I. B. 1975. *Women under Primitive Buddhism.* Delhi Motilal Banarsidass.

Hoshimiya Chikō. 1990. "Miidera no rekishi." In *Chishō daishi sen-hyaku nen goonki kinen: Miidera hihōten,* ed. Tōkyō kokuritsu hakubutsukan et al., 138–143. Tokyo: Nihon keizai shinbunsha.

———. 1973. "Shoki Nihon no Tendai kyōdan ni okeru Chishō daishi." In *Dengyō daishi kenkyū,* ed. Fukui Kōjun, 1319–1342. Tokyo: Waseda Daigaku shuppanbu.

Hosokawa Ryōichi. 1999. "Medieval Nuns and Nunneries: The Case of Hokkeji." In *Women and Class in Japanese History,* ed. Hitomi Tonomura, Anne Walthall, and Wakita Haruko, 67–79. Ann Arbor: Center for Japanese Studies, University of Michigan.

———. 1989. "Ōken to amadera: Chūsei josei to shari shinkō." In *Onna no chūsei,* ed. Hosokawa Ryōichi, 124–160. Tokyo: Editā skūru shuppanbu.

Hotta Shinkai. 1972. *Kōyasan Kongōbuji.* Tokyo: Gakuseisha.

Hotta Tesshin. 1984. "Ganzan daishi igo ni okeru sanjō no enkai ni tsuite." In *Issennen onki kinen Ganzan jie daishi no kenkyū,* ed. Eizan gakuin, Fukkoku ronbun, 53–65. Kyoto: Dōhōsha.

Hsin-wen-feng, ed. 1977. *Wan Hsü-tsang-ching.* Taipei: Hsin-wen-feng.

Hurvitz, Leon. 1980. "Chih-i (538–597): An Introduction to the Life and Ideas of a Chinese Buddhist Monk." *Mélanges chinois et bouddhiques* 12.

———, 1976. trans. *Scripture of the Lotus Blossom of the Five Dharma, Translated from the Chinese of Kumārajīva.* New York: Columbia University Press.

Ienaga Saburō, ed. 1967. *Nihon Bukkyōshi.* Vol. 1. Kyoto: Hōzōkan.

Iinuma Kenji. 1990. "Chūsei zenki no josei no shōgai." In *Nihon josei seikatsushi,* ed. Joseishi sōgō kenkyūkai, 2:31–74. Tokyo: Tōkyō Daigaku shuppankai.

Ikeda Genta. 1986. "Hokkeji no enkaku." In *Shinshū Kokubunji no kenkyū.* Vol. 1: *Tōdaiji to Hokkeji,* ed. Tsunoda Bun'ei, 178–250. Tokyo: Yoshikawa kōbunkan.

Ikeyama Issaien. 1974. "Annen no *Sokushin jōbutsugi shiki* to sono kechimyaku." In *Annen oshō no kenkyū,* ed. Eizan gakkai, 8–23. Kyoto: Dōhōsha.

———. 1964. "Hokke Sōjiin ni tsuite." In *Jikaku daishi no kenkyū,* ed. Fukui Kōjun, 299–316. Tokyo: Waseda Daigaku shuppanbu.

Inoue Mitsusada. 1983. "Fujiwara jidai no Jōdokyō." In *Genshin,* ed. Ōsumi Kazuo and Hayamai Tasuku, 142–204. Tokyo: Yoshikawa kōbunkan.

Inoue Mitsusada and Ōsone Shōsuke, eds. 1974. *Ōjōden Hokke genki.* Tokyo: Iwanami shoten.

Ishida Mizumaro. 1978. "Bikuni kaidan: Ama no tokui na seikaku." *Musashino joshi daigaku kenkyū kiyō* 13:1–15.

———. 1971. *Bonmōkyō.* Butten kōza, vol. 14. Tokyo: Daizō shuppan kabushiki kaisha.

———. 1974. *Ganjin: Sono kairitsu shisō.* Tokyo: Daizō shuppansha.

———. 1976. *Gokuraku Jōdo e no izanai: Ōjō yōshū no baai.* Nihonjin no kōdō to shisō, vol. 35. Tokyo: Hyōronsha.

———. 1956. "Gyōki ron." *Shūkyō kenkyū* 150:5–6.

———. 1986. "Heian chūki ni okeru zaike shinja no jukai seishin no tenkai." In *Nihon Bukkyō shisō kenkyū: Kairitsu no kenkyū,* ed. Ishida Mizumaro, 2:239–263. Kyoto: Hōzōkan.

———. 1970. "Kitō to shite no jukai." In *Nihon shūkyō no genze riyaku,* ed. Nihon shūkyō kenkyūkai, 67–81. Tokyo: Daizō shuppansha.

———. 1963. *Nihon Bukkyō ni okeru karitsu no kenkyū.* Tokyo: Zaike Bukkyō kyōkai.

———. 1997. *Reibun Bukkyōgo daijiten.* Tokyo: Shōgakkan.

———. 1985. "Tendai kyōdan hatten katei ni okeru teikō to dakyō." In *Dengyō daishi to Tendaishū,* ed. Shioiri Ryōdō and Kiuchi Gyōō, 174–205. Tokyo: Yoshikawa kōbunkan.

Ishida Mosaku. 1966. *Tōdaiji to Kokubunji.* Tokyo: Shibundō.

Itō Kiyoo. 1979. "Chūsei sōgōsei no kenkyū: Kamakuraki wo chūshin ni." *Rekishi* 53: 20–35.

———. 1980. "Chūsei sōgōsei to Enryakuji." In *Toyoda Takeshi hakushi koki kinen: Nihon chūsei no seiji to bunka,* ed. Toyoda Takeshi sensei koki kinenkai, 131–157. Tokyo: Yoshikawa kōbunkan.

Itō Kōko. 1979. "Zōga shōnin to kigyō setsuwa." *Taishō daigaku sōgō Bukkyō kenkyūjo nenpō* 3: 55–66.

Itō Masatoshi. 1999. *Chūsei no jisha seiryoku to keidai toshi.* Tokyo: Yoshikawa kōbunkan.

Itō Shintetsu. 1971. "*Sanbō ekotoba* no kenkyū: toku ni Tendaishū Bukkyō girei wo chūshin to shite." *Bukkyō daigaku bungakubu jinbungaku ronshū* 5: 29–101.

Itō Takatoshi. 1979. "Kōfukuji yuima-e to shoshū." *Komazawa daigaku Bukkyō gakubu ronshū* 10: 180–196.

Itsuki Seishō. 1976. "Tendaishū shijō ni okeru Chishō daishi: toku ni Jikaku daishi to no kankei ni tsuite." In *Hieizan to Tendai Bukkyō no kenkyū,* ed. Murayama Shūichi, 170–185. Tokyo: Meicho shuppan.

Jingū shichō, ed. 1982. *Koji ruien: Shūkyō-bu.* Tokyo: Yoshikawa kōbunkan.

———. 1982. *Koji ruien: Teio-bu.* Tokyo: Yoshikawa kōbunkan.

Jōdoshū kaishū happyakunen kinen keisan junbikyoku, ed. 1971. *Jōdoshū zensho.* 23 vols. Tokyo: Sankibō Busshorin.

———. 1972–1974. *Zoku Jōdoshū zensho.* 19 vols. Tokyo: Sankibō Busshorin.

Joseishi sōgō kenkyūkai, ed. 1982. *Nihon joseishi.* Tokyo: Yoshikawa kōbunkan.

Kageyama Haruki. 1964. "Ennin no konpon nyohōkyō to Yokawa no hattatsu." In *Jikaku daishi kenkyū,* ed. Fukui Kōjun, 73–90. Tokyo: Waseda Daigaku shuppanbu.

———. 1966. *Hieizan.* Tokyo: Kadokawa shoten.

———. 1978. *Hieizanji.* Kyoto: Dōhōsha.

———. 1976. "Hieizan ni okeru Mieidō to byōbō," In *Hieizan to Tendai Bukkyō no kenkyū,* ed. Murayama Shūichi, 186–207. Tokyo: Meicho shuppan.

———. 1980. *Hieizan to Kōyasan.* Tokyo: Kyōikusha.

Kakehashi Nobuaki. 1994. "Ryōgen *Kubon ōjōgi* no ikkōsatsu." In *Shinran no Bukkyō: Nakanishi Chikai Sensei kanreki kinen ronbunshū,* ed. Nakanishi Chikai sensei kanreki kinen ronbunshū kankōkai, 713–729. Kyoto: Nagata bunshōdō.

Kakimura Shigematsu. 1922. *Honchō monzui chūshaku.* 2 vols. Tokyo: Naigai shuppan kabushiki kaisha.

Kamens, Edward, trans. 1988. *The Three Jewels: A Study and Translation of Minamoto Tamenori's "Sanbōe."* Ann Arbor: Center for Japanese Studies, University of Michigan.

Kasahara Kazuo. 1975. *Nyonin ōjō shisō no keifu.* Tokyo: Yoshikawa kōbunkan.

Katada Osamu. 1985. "Ōchō kizoku no shukke nyūdō." In *Chūsei Bukkyō to Shinshū,* ed. Kitanishi Hiroshi sensei kanreki kinenkai, 377–401. Tokyo: Yoshikawa kōbunkan.

Katsumata Shunkyō, ed. 1970. *Kōbō Daishi chosaku zenshū.* Tokyo: Sankibō Busshorin.

Katsuno Ryūshin. 1966. *Hieizan to Kōyasan.* Tokyo: Shibundō.

Katsuura Noriko. 1989. "Amasogi kō: Kamigata kara mita ama no sonzai keitai." In *Ama to amadera,* ed. Ōsumi Kazuo and Nishiguchi Junko, 11–42. Tokyo: Heibonsha.

———. 1982. "Gyōki no katsudō ni okeru minshū sanka no tokushitsu." *Shigaku zasshi* 91, no. 3: 37–59.

———. 1990. "Josei to kodai shinkō." In *Nihon josei seikatsushi*, ed. Joseishi sōgō kenkyūkai, 1:69–104. Tokyo: Tōkyō Daigaku shuppankai.

———. 1983. "Kodai ni okeru bosei to Bukkyō." *Nihon shisōshi* 22: 3–17.

———. 1995. *Onna no shinjin: tsuma ga shukke shita jidai*. Tokyo: Heibonsha.

———. 1995. "'Sentaku to onna' nōto." *Gekkan hyakka* 261 (1984); reprinted Katsuura Noriko, *Onna no shinjin: tsuma ga shukke shita jidai*, 185–206. Tokyo: Heibonsha.

———. Forthcoming. "Tonsure Forms for Nuns: The Classification of Nuns by Hairstyle." In *Engendering Faith: Women and Buddhism in Premodern Japan*, ed. Barbara Ruch. Ann Arbor: Center for Japanese Studies, University of Michigan.

Katsuyama Kiyotsugi. 1978. "Shōen no keisei." In *Shinshū Ōtsushi-shi*, ed. Hayashiya Shinsaburō et al., 1 (Kodai): 426–448. Ōtsu: Ōtsu-shi yakusho.

Kawasaki Tsuneyuki. 1983. *Genshin*. Nihon no meicho, vol. 4. Tokyo: Chūō kōronsha.

Kelleher, Theresa. 1987. "Confucianism." In *Women in World Religions*, ed. Arvind Sharma, 135–159. Albany: State University of New York Press.

Kikuchi Kyōko. 1982. "Zoku bettō no seiritsu." In *Saichō*, ed. Shioiri Ryōdō and Kiuchi Gyōō, 390–433. Tokyo: Yoshikawa kōbunkan.

Kiuchi Gyōō. 1978. "Asa daimoku yū nenbutsu." In *Bukkyō girei: Sono rinen to jissen*, ed. Nihon Bukkyōgakkai, 233–244. Kyoto: Heirakuji shoten.

———. 1982. "*Eizan daishiden* no yakuwari." *Tendai gakuhō* 24: 90–98.

———. 1990. "Kōjō no jiseki." In *Nakao Shunpaku sensei koki kinen Bukkyō to shakai*, ed. Nakao Shunpaku sensei koki kinenkai, 323–338. Kyoto: Nagata bunshōdō.

———. 1984. *Tendai mikkyō no keisei*. Tokyo: Keisuisha.

Kiyohara Ekō. 2000. "Tendai rongi no keisei katei." In *Rongi no kenkyū*, ed. Chisan kangakkai, 65–109. Tokyo: Seishi shuppan.

Kobayashi Yasuharu, ed. 1981. *Kojidan*. Tokyo: Gendai shichōsha.

Kokushi daijiten henshū iinkai, ed. 1979–1997. *Kokushi daijiten*. Tokyo: Yoshikawa kōbunkan.

Komatsu Shigemi and Hirabayashi Moritoku. 1977. *Heian: Jie daishi jihitsu yuigō*. Nihon meiseki sōkan, vol. 13. Tokyo: Nigensha.

Kouda Ryōsen. 1972. *Wayaku Tendaishū rongi hyakudai jizaibō*. Tokyo: Rinkōin.

———. 1966. *Wayaku Tendaishū rongi nihyakudai*. Tokyo: Ryūbunkan.

Kumabara Masao. 1961. "Eison to Kamakura josei." *Kanazawa bunko kenkyū kiyō* 1: 113–118.

Kunaichō shoryōbu, ed. 1973. *Yuima kōji kengaku ryūgi shidai*. Tokyo: Yoshikawa kōbunkan.

Kuroda Toshio. 1996. "The Development of the Kenmitsu System as Japan's Medieval Orthodoxy." *Japanese Journal of Religious Studies* 23, nos. 3–4: 233–270.

———. 1980. *Jisha seiryoku: Mō hitotsu no chūsei shakai*. Tokyo: Iwanami shoten.

———. 1994–1995. *Kuroda Toshi chosakushū*. 8 vols. Kyoto: Hōzōkan.

Kuroita Katsumi, ed. 1929–1966. *Shintei zōho Kokushi taikei*. Tokyo: Yoshikawa kōbunkan.

Kusakabe Kōbō. 1997. "Anne kashō kō." *Tendai gakuhō* 39: 49–56.

Kushida Ryōko. 1979–1997. "Ajari." In *Kokushi daijiten*, ed. Kokushi daijiten henshū iinkai, 1:194–195.

————. 1966. "Jie daishiden no shinshiryō ni tsuite." *Indogaku Bukkyōgaku kenkyū* 14, no. 2: 507–513.

Li Yü-chen. 1989. *T'ang-tai te pi-ch'iu-ni.* Taipei: Tai-wan hsüeh-sheng shu-chü.

Mabuchi Kazuo and Kunisaki Fumimaro, eds. 1972. *Konjaku monogatarishū.* Nihon koten bungaku taikei. Tokyo: Shōgakkan.

Makita Shigeru. 1981. *Kami to onna no minzokugaku.* Tokyo: Kōdansha.

Matsumura Hiroji, ed. 1960. *Ōkagami.* Nihon koten bungaku taikei, vol. 21. Tokyo: Iwanami shoten.

Matsumura Hiroji and Yamanaka Yutaka, eds. 1964–1965. *Eiga monogatari.* Nihon koten bungaku taikei. Tokyo: Iwanami shoten.

Matsuo Kenji. 1988. "Chūsei Chikuzen Kanzeonji Shimotsuke Yakushiji ryōkaidan ni okeru jukaisei." In *Chūsei jiinshi no kenkyū,* ed. Chūsei jiinshi kenkyūkai, 1:75–115. Kyoto: Hōzōkan.

————. 1988. *Kamakura shin-Bukkyō no seiritsu.* Tokyo: Yoshikawa kōbunkan.

————. 1985. "Kansō to tonseisō: Kamakura shin-Bukkyō no seiritsu to Nihon jukaisei." *Shigaku zasshi* 94, no. 3: 1–45.

McCullough, Helen Craig. trans. 1980. *Ōkagami the Great Mirror: Fujiwara Michinaga and His Times.* Princeton, N.J.: Princeton University Press.

————. 1959. *The Taiheiki: A Chronicle of Medieval Japan.* New York: Columbia University Press.

————. 1988. *The Tale of Heike.* Stanford, Calif. Stanford University Press.

McCullough, William. 1967. "Japanese Marriage Institutions in the Heian Period." *Harvard Journal of Asiatic Studies* 27: 103–167.

————. 1973. "Spirit Possession in the Heian Period." In *Studies on Japanese Culture,* ed. Ōta Saburō and Fukuda Rikutarō, 91–98. Tokyo: Japan P. E. N. Club.

McCullough, William H., and Helen Craig McCullough. 1980. *A Tale of Flowering Fortunes: Annals of Japanese Aristocratic Life in the Heian Period.* 2 vols. Stanford, Calif.: Stanford University Press.

McMullin, Neil. 1984. *Buddhism and the State in Sixteenth-Century Japan.* Princeton, N.J.: Princeton University Press.

————. 1988. "The Enryaku-ji and the Gion Shrine-Temple Complex in the Mid-Heian Period." *Japanese Journal of Religious Studies* 14, nos. 2–3: 161–184.

————. 1989. "The *Lotus Sūtra* and Politics in the Mid-Heian Period." In *The Lotus Sūtra in Japanese Culture,* ed. George Tanabe, Jr., and Willa Tanabe, 119–142. Honolulu: University of Hawai'i Press.

————. 1987. "On Placating the Gods and Pacifying the Populace." *History of Religions* 27, no. 3: 270–293.

————. 1984. "The Sanmon-Jimon Schism in the Tendai School of Buddhism: A Preliminary Analysis." *Journal of the International Association of Buddhism* 7: 83–105.

Miki Sumito. 1988. *Tōnomine hijiri dan.* Kyoto: Hōzōkan.

Mikkyō jiten hensankai, ed. 1979. *Zotei shinpan Mikkyō daijiten.* Taipei: Hsin wen feng ch'u p'an.

Mikoshiba Daisuke. 1989. "Kōmyōshi no Bukkyō shinkō: Sono Bukkyōteki kankyō to Kokubunji Kokubunniji sōken e no ka'yō ni tsuite." In *Ama to amadera,* ed. Ōsumi Kazuo and Nishiguchi Junko, 73–104. Tokyo: Heibonsha.

Mills, D. E. 1970. *A Collection of Tales from Uji: A Study and Translation of Uji Shūi Mono-gatari.* Cambridge: Cambridge University Press.

Minamoto Kōshi. 1970. "Hōchibō Shōshin no 'Jie daishi kōshiki' ni tsuite." *Indo-gaku Bukkyōgaku kenkyū* 18, no. 2: 749–769.

Minamoto no Tamenori. 1982. *Sanbō ekotoba,* ed. Eguchi Takao. Tokyo: Gendai shichōsha.

Misaki Gisen. 1999. *Shikanteki biishiki no tenkai.* Tokyo: Perikansha.

Misaki Ryōshū. 1977. "Tendai no mikkyō." In *Kōza Mikkyō.* Vol. 2: *Mikkyō no rekishi,* ed. Miyasaka Yūshō, 218–234. Tokyo: Shunjūsha.

Mitsumori Katsumi. 1977. "Hieizan Tōdō Saitō no Jōgyōdō no kōhai ni tsuite." In *Bukkyō shigaku ronshū,* ed. Futaba Hakushi kanreki kinenkai, 263–284. Kyoto: Nagata bunshōdō.

Miyamoto Shōson. 1961. "Sōmoku kokudo shikkai jōbutsu no Busshōronteki igi to sono sakusha" *Indogaku Bukkyōgaku kenkyū* 18: 264–268.

Miyata Noboru. 1979. *Kami no minzokushi.* Tokyo: Iwanami shoten.

Mochizuki Shinkō and Tsukamoto Zenryū, eds. 1931–1967. *Mochizuki Bukkyō dai-jiten.* Tokyo: Sekai seiten kankō kyōkai.

Murasaki Shikibu. 1976. *The Tale of Genji.* Trans. Edward Seidenstecker. New York: Alfred A. Knopf.

Murayama Shūichi. 1994. *Hieizanshi: Tatakai to inori no seiiki.* Tokyo: Tōkyō bijutsu.

———. 1976. "Jie daishi no shinkō." In *Kodai Bukkyō no chūseiteki kenkyū,* ed. Mu-rayama Shūichi, 61–75. Kyoto: Hōzōkan.

———. 1981. *Nihon Onmyōdōshi sōsetsu.* Tokyo: Hanawa shobō.

———, ed. 1976. *Kodai Bukkyō no chūseiteki kunkyū.* Kyoto: Hōzōkan.

Nagahira Keiji, ed. 1973. *Chūseishi handobukku.* Tokyo: Kondō shuppansha.

Nagai Yoshinori. 1966. "Matsumuro sennin to katarimono: *Genpei seisuiki* no ichi sozai no seikaku." In *Nihon Bukkyō bungaku kenkyū,* ed. Nagai Yoshinori, 1:251–264. Tokyo: Toshima shobō.

Nagamizu Yasuaki and Shimada Isao, eds. 1966. *Kokon chomonshū.* Nihon koten bun-gaku taikei, vol. 84. Tokyo: Iwanami shoten.

Nagamori Ryōji. 1955. "Jiin monbatsuka no ichi kaitei: Heian kōki jiin sōzoku no ichi keikō." *Kanazawa daigaku kyōiku gakubu kiyō* 3: 1–10.

Nagata Mizu. 1985. "Butten ni miru boseikan." In *Bosei wo tou,* ed. Wakita Haruko, 1:259–286. Kyoto: Jinbun shoin.

Nagatani Hōshū, ed. 1942. *Kōbō Daishi shodeshi zenshū.* Kyoto: Rokudai Shinpōsha.

Nakai Shinkō. 1973. *Nihon kodai no Bukkyō to minshū.* Tokyo: Hyōronsha.

Nakamura Hajime, ed. 1975. *Bukkyōgo daijiten.* Tokyo: Tōkyō shoseki kabushiki kaisha.

Nakamura Kōichi. 1999. *Ichiban daikichi: Omikuji no fōkuroa.* Tokyo: Taishūkan shoten.

Nakamura Kōryū. 1972. "Jukai no minzokusei." In *Satō Hakushi koki kinen: Bukkyō shisō ronsho,* ed. Satō Mitsuo hakushi koki ronbunshu kankokai, 889–906. Tokyo: Sankibō Busshorin.

Nakamura, Motomichi Kyōko. 1973. *Miraculous Stories from the Japanese Buddhist Tra-dition.* Cambridge: Harvard University Press.

Nakao Shunpaku. 1976. "Enshu to Enchin Kanazawa bukohon 'Murōsan nenbun-dosha sōjō' ni yosete" *Kanazawa bunko kenkyū* 22, no. 2: 1–16; 22, no. 3 (1976): 1–6.

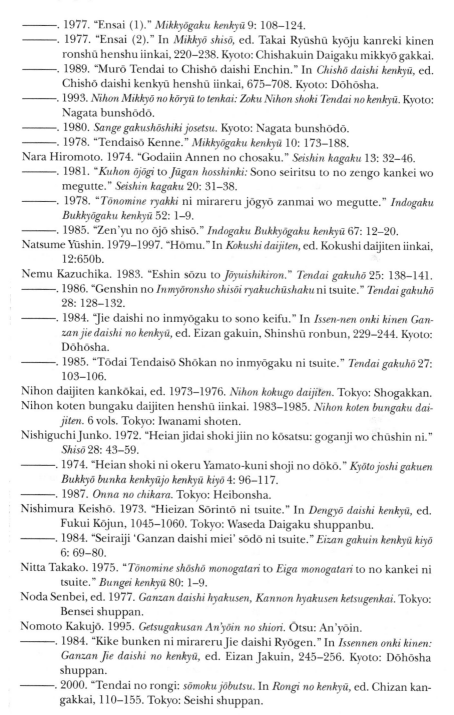

———. 1977. "Ensai (1)." *Mikkyōgaku kenkyū* 9: 108–124.

———. 1977. "Ensai (2)." In *Mikkyō shisō*, ed. Takai Ryūshū kyōju kanreki kinen ronshū henshu iinkai, 220–238. Kyoto: Chishakuin Daigaku mikkyō gakkai.

———. 1989. "Murō Tendai to Chishō daishi Enchin." In *Chishō daishi kenkyū*, ed. Chishō daishi kenkyū henshū iinkai, 675–708. Kyoto: Dōhōsha.

———. 1993. *Nihon Mikkyō no kōryū to tenkai: Zoku Nihon shoki Tendai no kenkyū*. Kyoto: Nagata bunshōdō.

———. 1980. *Sange gakushōshiki josetsu*. Kyoto: Nagata bunshōdō.

———. 1978. "Tendaisō Kenne." *Mikkyōgaku kenkyū* 10: 173–188.

Nara Hiromoto. 1974. "Godaiin Annen no chosaku." *Seishin kagaku* 13: 32–46.

———. 1981. "*Kuhon ōjōgi* to *Jūgan hosshinki*: Sono seiritsu to no zengo kankei wo megutte." *Seishin kagaku* 20: 31–38.

———. 1978. "*Tōnomine ryakki* ni mirareru jōgyō zanmai wo megutte." *Indogaku Bukkyōgaku kenkyū* 52: 1–9.

———. 1985. "Zen'yu no ōjō shisō." *Indogaku Bukkyōgaku kenkyū* 67: 12–20.

Natsume Yūshin. 1979–1997. "Hōmu." In *Kokushi daijiten*, ed. Kokushi daijiten iinkai, 12:650b.

Nemu Kazuchika. 1983. "Eshin sōzu to *Jōyuishikiron*." *Tendai gakuhō* 25: 138–141.

———. 1986. "Genshin no *Inmyōronsho shisōi ryakuchūshaku* ni tsuite." *Tendai gakuhō* 28: 128–132.

———. 1984. "Jie daishi no inmyōgaku to sono keifu." In *Issen-nen onki kinen Ganzan jie daishi no kenkyū*, ed. Eizan gakuin, Shinshū ronbun, 229–244. Kyoto: Dōhōsha.

———. 1985. "Tōdai Tendaisō Shōkan no inmyōgaku ni tsuite." *Tendai gakuhō* 27: 103–106.

Nihon daijiten kankōkai, ed. 1973–1976. *Nihon kokugo daijiten*. Tokyo: Shogakkan.

Nihon koten bungaku daijiten henshū iinkai. 1983–1985. *Nihon koten bungaku daijiten*. 6 vols. Tokyo: Iwanami shoten.

Nishiguchi Junko. 1972. "Heian jidai shoki jiin no kōsatsu: goganji wo chūshin ni." *Shisō* 28: 43–59.

———. 1974. "Heian shoki ni okeru Yamato-kuni shoji no dōkō." *Kyōto joshi gakuen Bukkyō bunka kenkyūjo kenkyū kiyō* 4: 96–117.

———. 1987. *Onna no chikara*. Tokyo: Heibonsha.

Nishimura Keishō. 1973. "Hieizan Sōrintō ni tsuite." In *Dengyō daishi kenkyū*, ed. Fukui Kōjun, 1045–1060. Tokyo: Waseda Daigaku shuppanbu.

———. 1984. "Seiraiji 'Ganzan daishi miei' sōdō ni tsuite." *Eizan gakuin kenkyū kiyō* 6: 69–80.

Nitta Takako. 1975. "*Tōnomine shōshō monogatari* to *Eiga monogatari* to no kankei ni tsuite." *Bungei kenkyū* 80: 1–9.

Noda Senbei, ed. 1977. *Ganzan daishi hyakusen, Kannon hyakusen ketsugenkai*. Tokyo: Bensei shuppan.

Nomoto Kakujō. 1995. *Getsugakusan An'yōin no shiori*. Ōtsu: An'yōin.

———. 1984. "Kike bunken ni mirareru Jie daishi Ryōgen." In *Issennen onki kinen: Ganzan Jie daishi no kenkyū*, ed. Eizan Jakuin, 245–256. Kyoto: Dōhōsha shuppan.

———. 2000. "Tendai no rongi: *sōmoku jōbutsu*. In *Rongi no kenkyū*, ed. Chizan kangakkai, 110–155. Tokyo: Seishi shuppan.

Nōtomi Jōten. 1977. "Nanto Bukkyō ni okeru nyonin ōjō shisō." *Indogaku Bukkyō-gaku kenkyū* 25, no. 2: 32–37.

Obara Hitoshi. 1990. "Tennyo jōbutsu setsu no juyō ni tsuite." *Nihon Bukkyō shigaku* 24: 13–28.

Oda Tokunō. 1969. *Bukkyō daijiten.* Tokyo: Daizō shuppan kabushiki kaisha.

Ōe Atsushi. 1989. "Junna Taikō Seishi Naishinnō to Junnain." In *Ama to amadera,* ed. Ōsumi Kazuo and Nishiguchi Junko, 141–174. Tokyo: Heibonsha.

Ogami Kanchū. 1973. "Dengyō daishi nyūmetsugo no Tendaishū kyōdan." In *Dengyō daishi kenkyū,* ed. Fukui Kōjun, 211–236. Tokyo: Waseda Daigaku shuppanbu.

———. 1979. *Hokke daie kōgaku ryūgi.* Hieizan: Hokke daie jimukyoku.

———. 1976. "Jie daishi 'Nijūrokushiki' to Tendaishū kyōdan." In *Okuda Jiō sensei kinen: Bukkyō shisō ronshū,* ed. Okuda Jiō sensei kinen: Bukkyō shisō ronshū ronbun kankōkai, 339–354. Kyoto: Heirakuji shoten.

———. 1984. "Jie daishi no Tendaishū goji." In *Ganzan jie daishi no kenkyū,* ed. Eizan gakuin, 17–34. Kyoto: Dōhōsha shuppan.

———. 1982. "Nenbundosha ni mirareru kashiki seido." In *Saichō,* ed. Shioiri Ryō-dō and Kiuchi Gyōō, 123–172. Tokyo: Yoshikawa kōbunkan.

———. 1970. "Ōwa no shūron to shūyō gika no kakuritsu." *Tendai gakuhō* 12: 58–68.

———. 1984. "Rongijō yori mitaru Nanto Hokurei no kankei." *Indogaku Bukkyōgaku kenkyū* 32, no. 2: 566–574.

———. 1970. "*Shūmanshū* to *Shūenshū* ni tsuite." *Indogaku Bukkyōgaku kenkyū* 18, no. 2: 701–706.

———. 1970. "Tendai gika no seiritsu katei." *Indogaku Bukkyōgaku kenkyū* 19, no. 1: 274–279.

———. 1973. "Tendaishū ni okeru kyōdan goji no shomondai." *Nihon Bukkyōgakkai nenpō* 39: 151–171.

———. 1968. "Yokawa no shugaku seido." *Tendai gakuhō* 11: 53–63.

Ōhashi Shunnō. 1971. *Hōnen Ippen.* Tokyo: Iwanami shoten.

Ōishi Masaaki. 1997. "Ama no Hokkeji to sō no Hokkeji." In *Hotoke to onna,* ed. Nishiguchi Junko, 181–217. Tokyo: Yoshikawa kōbunkan.

Oishio Chihiro. 1996. *Kokubunji no chūseiteki tenkai.* Tokyo: Yoshikawa kōbunkan.

———. 1999. *Nihon chūsei no setsuwa to Bukkyō.* Tokyo: Yoshikawa kobūnkan.

Okada Seishi. 1982. "Kyūtei miko no jittai." In *Nihon joseishi,* ed. Joseishi sōgō kenkyūkai, 1:43–73. Tokyo: Tōkyō daigaku shuppankai.

Okami Masao and Akamatsu Toshihide, eds. 1967. *Gukanshō.* Nihon koten bungaku taikei, vol. 86. Tokyo: Iwanami shoten.

Okano Kōji. 1995. "Denbō ajari shokui to yūsoku." In *Ritsuryō kokka no seimu to girei,* ed. Torao Toshiya, 30–343. Tokyo: Yoshikawa kōbunkan.

———. 1985. "Enryakuji zoku bettō to Tendai zasu." *Komazawa shigaku* 33: 93–114.

Okazaki Jōji, ed. 1982. *Butsugu daijiten.* Tokyo: Kamakura shinsho.

Ōkubo Ryōshun. 1996. "Nihon Bukkyō no kyōgaku kenkyū to bunken." *Nihon no Bukkyō* 5: 1–17.

———. 1998. "Nihon Tendai ni okeru hishō-setsu no tenkai: kihonteki jikō wo chūshin ni." In *Tendai kyōgaku to hongaku shisō,* ed. Ōkubo Ryōshun, 236–264. Tokyo: Sankibō Busshorin.

————. 1994. "Ryōgen-sen 'Hishōgi shiki' ni tsuite." *Tendai gakuhō* 36: 89–95.

————. 1998. *Tendai mikkyō to hongaku shisō.* Tokyo: Hōzōkan.

Ōmura, Seigai. 1918. *Mikkyō hattatsushi.* Tokyo: Bussho kankōkai zuzōbu.

Ono Genmyō, ed. 1964–1988. *Bussho kaisetsu daijiten.* 14 vols. Tokyo: Daitō shuppansha.

Ono Katsutoshi. 1982–1983. *Nittō guhō gyōreki no kenkyū: Chishō daishi Enchin hen.* 2 vols. Kyoto: Hōzōkan.

————. 1969. *Nittō guhō junrei kōki no kenkyū.* 4 vols. Tokyo: Suzuki gakujutsu zaidan.

————. 1958. "Nittōsō Enshu Kenne to sono *Kechimyaku zuki.*" In *Ishihama Sensei koki kinen: Tōyō ronshū.* Osaka: Ishihama Sensei koki kinenkai.

————. 1967. *Sanzen'in-hon Jikaku daishiden.* Kobe: Goten shoin.

Ōno Susumu, Satake Akihiro, and Maeda Kingorō, eds. 1974. *Iwanami kogo jiten.* Tokyo: Iwanami shoten.

Ōno Tatsunosuke, "Egaku." 1979–1997. In *Kokushi daijiten,* ed. Kokushi daijiten hen-shū iinkai, 2:243c. Tokyo: Yoshikawa kōbunkan.

————. 1979–1997. "Ōwa shūron." In *Kokushi daijiten,* ed. Kokushi daijiten henshū iinkai, 2:492c–493a. Tokyo: Yoshikawa kōbunkan.

Ōshima Ryōkō. 1984. "Jie daishi wasan no seiritsu ni kansuru ikkōsatsu." *Eizan gakuin kenkyū kiyō* 6: 257–272.

Ōsumi Kazuo. 1983. "Josei to Bukkyō: Kōsō to sono haha." *Shiron* 36: 1–10.

Ōya Tokujō. 1931. "Chishō daishi no nittō guhō." In *Onjōji no kenkyū,* 124–135. Ōtsu: Onjōji.

Oyamada Kazuo. 1989. "Chishō daishi Enchin to bettō kashō Kōjō kan." In *Chishō daishi no kenkyū,* ed. Chishō daishi kenkyū henshū iinkai, 755–774. Kyoto: Dōhōsha.

————. 1978. "Ennin to Enchin to no kankei ni tsuite no ichi shiron." *Nihon Bukkyō,* no. 47: 33–48.

————. 1986. "Ennin to Enchin to no kankei: Yokawa to Onjōji ron." In *Ronshū Nihon Bukkyōshi,* ed. Hiraoka Jōkai, 3 (Heian jidai), 133–162. Tokyo: Yūzankaku shuppan.

————. 1990. "Kenne to Enchin." In *Chishō daishi Enchin no kenkyū,* ed. Oyamada Kazuo, 236–254. Tokyo: Yoshikawa kōbunkan.

————. 1994. "Naigubu jūzenji." In *Heian jidaishi jiten,* ed. Tsunoda Bun'ei, 2:1783b.

————. 1990. "Naigubu jūzenji-shoku to Enchin." In *Chishō daishi Enchin no kenkyū,* ed. Oyamada Kazuo, 196–216. Tokyo: Yoshikawa kōbunkan.

Ozaki Kōjin. 1971. *Nihon Tendai rongishi no kenkyū.* Ōtsu: Hokke daie jimusho.

Penkower, Linda. 1993. "T'ien-t'ai during the T'ang Dynasty: Chan-jan and the Sinification of Buddhism." Ph.D. diss., Columbia University.

Reischauer, Edwin, trans. 1955. *Ennin's Diary: The Record of a Pilgrimage to China in Search of the Law.* New York: Ronald Press.

Robert, Jean-Noël. 1990. *Les doctrines de l'école japonaise Tendaï ai début du IXe siècle: Gishin et le Hokke-shū gi shū.* Paris: Maisonneuve and Larose.

Ryūkoku daigaku, ed. 1935–1936. *Bukkyō daijii.* 7 vols. Tokyo: Fuzanbō.

Ryūkoku daigaku Bukkyōgaku kenkyūshitsu, ed. 1986. *Bukkyōgaku kankei zasshi ronbun bunrui mokuroku.* Vol. 4. Kyoto: Nagata bunshōdō.

Ryūkoku University Translation Center. 1984. *The Sūtra of Contemplation on the Bud-*

dha of Immeasurable Life as Expounded by Śākayamuni Buddha. Kyoto: Ryūkoku
    University.

Saeki Arikiyo. 1989. *Chishō daishiden no kenkyū.* Tokyo: Yoshikawa kōbunkan.

———. 1992. *Dengyō daishi no kenkyū.* Tokyo: Yoshikawa kōbunkan.

———. 1990. *Enchin.* Tokyo: Yoshikawa kōbunkan.

———. 1989. *Ennin.* Tokyo: Yoshikawa kōbunkan.

———. 1999. *Hiun no kentōsō: Ensai no sūki na shōgai.* Tokyo: Yoshikawa kōbunkan.

———. 1986. *Jikaku daishiden no kenkyū.* Tokyo: Yoshikawa kōbunkan.

———. 1993. *Saichō to sono monryū.* Tokyo: Yoshikawa kōbunkan.

Saigō Nobutsuna. 1972. *Kodaijin to yume.* Tokyo: Heibonsha.

Saitō Enshin. 1984. "Sekisan myōjin ni kansuru ikkōsatsu." *Tendai gakuhō* 26:
    162–165.

———, trans. 1992. *Jikaku Daishi Den: The Biography of Jikaku Daishi Ennin.* Tokyo:
    Sankibō Busshōrin.

Saitō Tadashi. 1969. "Kokubunniji no seikaku: Toku ni Kokubunsōji no hikaku wo
    chūshin to shite." *Bukkyōshi kenkyū (Taishō daigaku)* 4:47–62.

Sakai Keijun. 1984. "Kawa no ryū no mikkyō." In *Issen-nen onki kinen Ganzan jie daishi
    no kenkyū,* ed. Eizan gakuin, Shinshū ronbun, 81–92. Kyoto: Dōhōsha.

Sakaida Shirō and Wada Katsushi. 1976. *Zōho kaitei Nihon setsuwa bungaku sakuin.*
    Tokyo: Seibundō.

Sakamoto Tarō et al., eds. 1965–1967. *Nihon shoki.* Nihon koten bungaku taikei, vols.
    68–69. Tokyo: Iwanami shoten.

Sakuma Ryū. 1987. "Gomyō ni tsuite." In *Higashi Ajia to Nihon: Shūkyō bungaku
    hen,* ed. Tamura Enchō Sensei koki kinen kai, 71–92. Tokyo: Yoshikawa
    kōbunkan.

———. 1983. "Kansō ni tsuite." In *Nihon kodai sōden no kenkyū,* 1–34. Tokyo:
    Yoshikawa kōbunkan.

———. 1983. *Nihon kodai sōden no kenkyū.* Tokyo: Yoshikawa kōbunkan.

Sansom, George. 1958. *History of Japan to 1334.* Stanford, Calif. Stanford University
    Press.

Sasaki Kunimaro. 1974. "Myōkōin monseki-ryō ni kansuru ikkōsatsu." *Indogaku
    Bukkyōgaku kenkyū* 22, no. 2: 781–785.

Sasaki Ryōshin. 1981. "Fujiwara no Sanesuke no Bukkyō shinkō." In *Ronshū Nihon
    Bukkyōshi,* ed. Hiraoka Jōkai, 3 (Heian jidai): 223–238. Tokyo: Yūzankaku
    shuppan.

———. 1981. "Hieizan seizanroku Fumonji shikō." *Bukkyō shigaku kenkyū* 23, no. 2:
    20–61.

Sasayama Haruo. 1993. "Kodai kokka no hen'yō: tenōki to shite no jūseiki." In
    Shinpan kodai no Nihon, ed. Tsuboi Kiyotari and Hirano Kunio, 1 (Kodaishi
    sōron): 363–382. Tokyo: Kadokawa shoten.

Satō Tatsugen. 1986. *Chūgoku Bukkyō ni okeru kairitsu no kenkyū.* Tokyo: Mokujisha.

Satō Tetsuei. 1979. *Eizan jōdokyō no kenkyū.* Kyoto: Hyakkaen.

———. 1937. "Sannōin zōsho mokuroku ni tsuite." *Eizan gakuhō* 13: 236–254.

———. 1964. "Zentōin kenzai mokuroku ni tsuite." In *Jikaku daishi kenkyū,* ed. Fukui
    Kōjun, 97–140. Tokyo: Waseda Daigaku shuppanbu.

Schaeffer, Edward. 1977. *Pacing the Void.* Berkeley: University of California Press.

Seita Yoshihide. 1980. "Eizan no gōgisei." In *Dengyō daishi kenkyū: bekkan,* ed. Fukui Kōjun, 225–247. Tokyo: Waseda Daigaku shuppanbu.

Sekiguchi Shindai. 1978. *Tendai kyōgaku no kenkyū.* Tokyo: Daitō shuppansha.

Shibata Minoru. 1979–1992. "*Goryō shinkō.*" In *Kokushi daijiten,* 6:58–59.

———, ed. 1979. *Goryō shinkō.* Tokyo: Yuzankaku shuppan,

Shibuya Jigai, ed. 1973. *Kōtei zōho Tendai zasuki.* Tokyo: Daiichi shobō.

———, ed. 1973. *Teisei Nihon Tendaishū nenpyō.* Tokyo: Daiichi Shobō.

Shigematsu Akihisa. 1980. "Eizan ni okeru shishu zanmaiin no tenkai." In *Dengyō daishi kenkyū: bekkan,* ed. Fukui Kōjun, 204–223. Tokyo: Waseda Daigaku shuppanbu.

Shigematsu Nobuhiro. 1967. *Genji monogatari no Bukkyō shisō.* Kyoto: Heirakuji shoten.

Shijō Masami. 1982. "Shuzen daishi Gishin no kenkyū." Bukkyōgaku kenkyu 38:78–98.

Shimaji Daitō. 1933. *Nihon Bukkyō kyōgakushi.* Tokyo: Meiji shoin.

Shimode Sekiyo. 1980. "Heian jidai ni okeru shūkyō to rinri: *Zoku honchō ōjōden* wo chūshin to shite." In *Nihon ni okeru rinri to shūkyō,* ed. Shimode Sekiyo, 1–33. Tokyo: Yoshikawa kōbunkan.

Shimonaka Hiroshi, ed. 1992–1994. *Nihonshi daijiten.* Tokyo: Heibonsha.

Shioiri Ryōchū. 1937. *Dengyō daishi.* Tokyo: Nihon hyōronsha.

Shioiri Ryōdō. 1989. "The Meaning of the Formation and Structure of the *Lotus Sūtra.*" In *The Lotus Sūtra in Japanese Culture,* ed. George J. Tanabe, Jr., and Willa Tanabe, 15–36. Honolulu: University of Hawai'i Press.

Shioiri Ryōdō and Kiuchi Gyōō, eds. 1982. *Saichō.* Tokyo: Yoshikawa kōbunkan.

Shirai Yūko. 1989. "Heian jidai shotō no Bukkyō to josei." In *Ama to amadera,* ed. Ōsumi Kazuo and Nishiguchi Junko, 105–140. Tokyo: Heibonsha.

Shirato Waka. 1978. "Manshuin-hon *Shukke sahō* ni miru girei to Heian Bukkyō." In *Bukkyō girei,* ed. Nihon Bukkyō gakkai, 151–181. Kyoto: Heirakuji shoten.

———. 1997. "Nihon Tendai no sōmoku jōbutsu setsu to sono keii." In *Le Vase de béryl: Études sur le Japon et la Chine en hommage à Bernard Frank,* ed. Jacqueline Pigeot and Hartmut O. Rotermund, 557–567. Arles, France: P. Picquier.

Sonehara Satoshi. 1996. *Tokugawa Ieyasu shinkakka e no michi: Chūsei Tendai shisō no tenkai.* Tokyo: Yoshikawa kōbunkan.

Sonoda Kōyū. 1953. "Enchin nittō no dōki." *Shisō* 2.

———. 1979–1997. "Gangyōji." In *Kokushi daijiten,* ed. Kokushi daijiten henshū iinkai, 3:789. Tokyo: Yoshikawa kōbunkan.

———. 1981. *Heian Bukkyō no kenkyū.* Kyoto: Hōzōkan.

———. 1992. "Onjōji." In *Nihonshi daijiten,* ed. Shimonaka Hiroshi, 1:1297a–1298a. Tokyo: Heibonsha.

———. 1959. "Sōsōki Murōji wo meguru sōryo no dōkō." In *Kokushi ronshū,* ed. Kokushikai. Kyoto: Kyōto daigaku bungakubu.

———. 1981. "Yama no nenbutsu." In *Heian Bukkyō no kenkyū,* ed. Sonoda Kōyū, 163–191. Kyoto: Hōzōkan.

Sōtōshū nisōshi hensankai, ed. 1955. *Sōtōshū nisōshi.* Tokyo: Sōtōshū nisōdan honbu.

Stevenson, Daniel. 1987. "The Four Kinds of Samādhi in Early T'ien-t'ai Buddhism." In *Traditions of Meditation in Chinese Buddhism,* ed. Peter Gregory, 45–97. Honolulu: University of Hawai'i Press.

———. 1987. "The T'ien-t'ai Four Forms of Samādhi and Late North-South Dynasties, Sui, and Early T'ang Buddhist Devotionalism." Ph.D. diss., Columbia University.

Stone, Jacqueline. 1999. *Original Enlightenment and the Transformation of Medieval Japanese Buddhism.* Kuroda Institute Studies in East Asian Buddhism, vol. 12. Honolulu: University of Hawai'i Press.

Strickmann, Michel. 1996. *Mantras et mandarins: Le bouddhisme tantrique en Chine.* Paris: Gallimard.

Sueki Fumihiko. 1995. *Heian shoki Bukkyō shisō no kenkyū.* Tokyo: Shunjūsha.

———. 1993. *Nihon Bukkyō shisōshi ronkō.* Tokyo: Daizō shuppan kabushiki kaisha.

Sugawara Shinkai. 1992. *Sannō Shintō no kenkyū.* Tokyo: Shunjūsha.

Sugimoto Naojirō. 1965. *Shinnyo shinnō-den kenkyū.* Tokyo: Yoshikawa kōbunkan.

Suzuki gakujutsu zaidan, ed. 1972–1975. *Dainihon Bukkyō zensho.* Tokyo: Suzuki gakujutsu zaidan.

Swanson, Paul L. 1989. *Foundations of T'ien-t'ai Philosophy: The Flowering of the Two Truths Theory in Chinese Buddhism.* Berkeley: Asian Humanities Press.

Tada Kōryū and Iada Kōbun, eds. 1985. *Chūkai gōhen Tendai daishi zenshū.* Tokyo: Nakayama shobō busshorin.

Tada Kōryū, Ōkubo Ryōjun, Tamura Yoshirō, and Asai Endō, eds. 1973. *Tendai hongakuron.* Nihon shisō taikei, vol. 9. Tokyo: Iwanami shoten.

Taga Munehaya. 1959. *Jien.* Tokyo: Yoshikawa kōbunkan.

———. 1971. "Kizoku to sōryō." *Bukkyōshi kenkyū* 5: 13–26.

Taira Masayuki. 1990. "Chūsei Bukkyō to josei." In *Nihon josei seikatsushi,* ed. Joseishi sōgō kenkyūkai, 2:75–108. Tokyo: Tōkyō Daigaku shuppankai.

———. 1996. "Kuroda Toshio and the *Kenmitsu Taisei* Theory." *Japanese Journal of Religious Studies* 23, no. 3–4: 427–448.

———. 1989. "Kyū-Bukkyō to josei." In *Hōken shakai to kindai,* ed. Tsuda Hideo Sensei koki kinenkai, 3–29. Kyoto: Dōhōsha.

———. 1997. "Sesshō kindan no rekishiteki tenkai." In *Nihon shakai no shiteki kōzō: kodai chūsei,* ed. Ōyama Kyōhei kyōju taikan kinen kai, 149–172. Kyoto: Shibunkaku shuppan.

Takagi Ichinosuke, ed. 1959–1960. *Heike monogatari.* Nihon koten bungaku taikei, vols. 32–33. Tokyo: Iwanami shoten.

Takagi Yutaka. 1988. *Bukkyōshi no naka no nyonin.* Tokyo: Heibonsha.

———. 1973. *Heian jidai Hokke Bukkyōshi kenkyū.* Kyoto: Heirakuji shoten.

Takahashi Mitsugu. 1967. "Genshin sōzu no haha no hanashi." *Bukkyō bungaku kenkyū* 5: 129–171.

Takahashi Tomio. 1977. *Tendaiji: Michinoku shugo no tera.* Tokyo: Tōkyō shoseki kabushiki kaisha.

Takakusu Junjirō and Watanabe Kaigyoku, eds. 1922–1933. *Taishō shinshū daizōkyō.* Tokyo: Taishō issaikyō.

Takatori Masao. 1979. *Shintō no seiritsu.* Tokyo: Heibonsha.

Takayama Yuki. 1997. *Chūsei Kōfukuji Yuima-e no kenkyū.* Tokyo: Benseisha.

Take Kakuchō. 1987. *Hiei santō shodō junpaiki.* Ōtsu-shi: Eizan gakuin.

———. 1993. *Hieizan santō shodō enkaku shi.* Ōtsu: Dōhōsha.

———. 1995. *Hokke daie kōgaku ryūgi ni tsuite.* Hieizan: Enryakuji Hokke daie jimukyoku.

————. 1984. "Jie daishiden (Ryōgen) no shōgai to sono gyōseki." *Eizan gakuin kenkyū kiyō* 7: 209–244.

Takei Akio. 1994. "Butsuryūji." In *Heian jidaishi jiten*, ed. Tsunoda Bun'ei, 2:2233c. Tokyo: Kadokawa shoten.

Takemura Shōhō. 1981. *Inmyōgaku: Kigen to hensen.* Kyoto: Hōzōkan.

————. 1970. "Nihon ni okeru inmyō kenkyū." *Ryūkoku daigaku ronshū* 394: 30–52.

Takeuchi Rizō. 1957–1958. *Ritsuryōsei to kizoku seiken.* 2 vols. Tokyo: Ochanomizu shobō.

————, ed. 1974. *Heian ibun.* Tokyo: Tōkyōdō shuppan.

———— et al., eds. 1969. *Nihonshi jiten.* Tokyo: Kadokawa shoten.

Tamai Yukinosuke. 1981. *Tōnomine shōshō monogatari.* Tokyo: Hanawa shobō.

Tamura Kōyū. 1979. *Saichō jiten.* Tokyo: Tōkyōdō shuppan.

————. 1992. *Saichō kyōgaku no kenkyū.* Tokyo: Shunjūsha.

Tanabe, Willa. Winter 1984. "The Lotus Lectures: *Hokke Hakkō* in the Heian Period." *Monumenta Nipponica* 39, no. 4: 393–407.

Tendai shūten hensanjo, ed. 1987–1999. *Zoku Tendaishū zensho.* 15 vols. Tokyo: Shunjūsha.

Tendai shūten kankōki, ed. 1974. *Tendaishū zensho.* Tokyo: Daiichi shobō.

Tendaishū, Kōyasan Shingonshū, and Mainichi shinbunsha, eds. 1997. *Hieizan Kōyasan meihōten.* Tokyo: Sankei shinbunsha.

Tendaishū sōsho kankōkai, ed. 1922. *Tendaishū sōsho: Annen senshū.* Tokyo: Tendaishū Daigaku shuppanbu.

Tokoro Isao. 1968. "*Enchin kashōden* no sozai to kōsei." *Bukkyō shigaku* 14, no. 3: 41–42.

Tokuda Myōhon. 1969. *Risshū gairon.* Kyoto: Hyakkaen.

Tōkyō daigaku shiryō hensanjo, ed. 1959–present. *Shōyūki.* Dainihon kokiroku. Tokyo: Iwanami shoten.

————. 1901–present. *Dainihon shiryō.* Tokyo: Tokyo Daigaku shuppankai.

Tōkyō kokuritsu hakubutsukan, ed. 1986. *Hieizan to Tendai bijutsu: Hieizan kaisō nihyakunen kinen.* Tokyo: Asahi shinbunsha.

Tomita Masahiro. 1994. "Homū." In *Heian jidaishi jiten*, ed. Tsunoda Bun'ei, 12:650b. Tokyo: Kadokawa, shoten.

Toriimoto Yukiyo. 1984. "Jie daishi to hōe: Soken ranshō-setsu wo megutte." In *Issennen onki kinen: Ganzan jie daishi no kenkyū*, ed. Eizan gakuin, shinshū ronbun, 287–297. Kyoto: Dōhōsha shuppan.

Tsuchida Naoshige. 1971. *Nihon no rekishi: Ōchō no kizoku.* Vol. 5. Tokyo: Chūō kōronsha.

Tsuji Zennosuke. 1947. *Nihon Bukkyōshi.* 10 vols. Tokyo: Iwanami shoten.

Tsukamoto Zenryū. 1976. *Tō chūki no Jōdokyō: toku ni Hōshō Hosshi no kenkyū.* In *Tsukamoto Zenryū chosakushū*, 4:209–510. Tokyo: Daitō shuppansha.

Tsukuma Sonnō. 1980. "Hokke daie kōgaku ryūgi." *Tendai* 1: 47–61.

Tsunoda Bun'ei. 1984. "Daiunji to Kannon'in." In *Tsunoda Bun'ei chosakushū 4: Ōchō bunka no shosō*, 260–297. Kyoto: Hōzōkan.

————. 1983. "Morosuke naru jinbutsu." In *Heian no haru*, ed. Tsunoda Bun'ei. Tokyo: Asahi shinbunsha. Reprinted Tokyo: Kōdansha, 1999 (13–44).

————, ed. 1994. *Heian jidaishi jiten.* Tokyo: Kadokawa shoten.

Tsutsui Eishun, ed. 1944. *Tōdaiji yōroku.* Osaka: Zenkoku shobō.

Uchida Keiichi. 1988. "Saidaiji Eison oyobi Saidaiji-ryū no Monju shinkō to sono zōzō." *Bijutsushi kenkyū* 26: 42–61.

Ueda Kōen. 1985. *Nihon jodai ni okeru yuishiki no kenkyū.* Kyoto: Nagata Bunshōdō.

Uejima Susumu. 1996. "Chūsei zenki no kokka to Bukkyō." *Nihonshi kenkyū* 403: 31–64.

———. 1997. "Heian shoki Bukkyō no saikentō." *Bukkyō shigaku kenkyū* 40, no. 2: 38–68.

Uesugi Bunshū. 1935. *Nihon Tendaishi.* 2 vols. Tokyo: Kokusho kankōkai, 1972; originally published Nagoya: Hajinkaku shobō.

Usami Masatoshi. 1976. "Jōgakuji no seiritsu to henshitsu." In *Nihonshi ni okeru minshū to shūkyō,* ed. Shimode Sekiyo, 85–109. Tokyo: Yamagawa shuppansha.

Ushiyama Yoshiyuki. 1990. *Kodai chūsei jiin soshiki no kenkyū.* Tokyo: Yoshikawa kōbunkan.

———. 1990. "Kodai ni okeru ama to amadera no shōchō." In *Kodai chūsen jiin soshiki no kenkyū,* ed. Ushiyama Yoshiyuki, 44–82. Tokyo: Yoshikawa kōbunkan.

———. 1990. "Ritsuryōsei tenkaiki ni okeru ama to amadera." In *Kodai chūsei jiin soshiki no kenkyū,"* ed. Ushiyama Yoshiyuki, 1–43. Tokyo: Yoshikawa kōbunkan.

———. 1982. "Sōgōsei no henshitsu to sōzaichō kumonsei no seiritsu." *Shigaku zasshi* 91, no. 1: 1–42.

Wakabayashi, Haruko. 1999. "From Conqueror of Evil to Devil King: Ryōgen and Notions of *Ma* in Medieval Japan Buddhism." *Monumenta Nipponica* 54, no. 4: 481–507.

Wakita Haruko. 1982. "Chūsei ni okeru seibetsu yakuwari bundan to joseikan." In *Nihon joseishi,* ed. Joseishi sōgō kenkyūkai, 2:65–102. Tokyo: Tōkyō Daigaku shuppankai.

———. 1985. "Bosei sonchō shisō to zaigōkan: Chūsei no bungei wo chūshin ni." In *Bosei wo tou,* ed. Wakita Haruko, 1:172–193. Kyoto: Jinbun shoin.

———, ed. 1985. *Bosei wo tou.* Kyoto: Jinbun shoin.

Warren, Henry Clarke. 1963. *Buddhism in Translations.* New York: Atheneum.

Watanabe Eshin. 1984. "'Jie daishi kisei nijūrokkajō' ni tsuite." In *Issen-nen onki kinen Ganzan jie daishi no kenkyū,* ed. Eizan gakuin, shinshū ronbun, pp. 1–16. Kyoto: Dōhōsha shuppan.

Watanabe Shujun. 1984. *Setsuwa bungaku no Eizan Bukkyō.* Osaka: Izumi shoin, 1996.

———. *Sōhei seisuiki.* Tokyo: Sanseidō.

Watanabe Tsunaya, ed. 1966. *Shasekishū.* Nihon koten bungaku taikei, vol. 85. Tokyo: Iwanami shoten.

Watson, Burton. 1993. *The Lotus Sutra.* New York: Columbia University Press.

Weinstein, Stanley. 1987. *Buddhism under the Tang.* Cambridge: Cambridge University Press.

———, trans. and ed. 1965. "The Kanjin Kakumushō." Ph.D. diss., Harvard University.

Yagi Kōe. 1977. *Eshin kyōgaku no kisoteki kenkyū.* Kyoto: Nagata bunshōdō.

———. 1996. *Eshin kyōgakushi no sōgōteki kenkyū.* Kyoto: Nagata bunshōdō.

Yamata Etai. 1959. *Ganzan daishi.* Tokyo: Daiichi shobō.

———. 1982. "Ganzan daishi no mikkyō to minkan shinkō." *Tendai* 6: 48–54.

Yamagishi Norihira, ed. 1958–1963. *Genji monogatari.* Nihon koten bungaku taikei, vols. 14–18. Tokyo: Iwanami shoten.

———, et al., eds. 1979. *Kodai seiji shakai shisō.* Nihon koten bungaku taikei, vol. 8. Tokyo: Iwanami shoten.

Yamagishi Tsuneto. 1990. *Chūsei jiin shakai to Butsudō.* Tokyo: Hanawa shobō.

Yamaguchi Kōen. 1935. "Seiraiji *Jie daishi daisōjōden* kō." *Eizan gakuhō* 9: 1–23.

Yamanaka Yutaka. 1988. *Heian jidai no kokiroku to kizoku.* Tokyo: Shibunkaku shuppan.

Yamashita Katsuaki. 1979–1997. "Hōzō." In *Kokushi daijiten,* ed. Kokushi daijiten henshū iinkai, 12:628c–d. Tokyo: Yoshikawa kōbunkan.

Yanagida Shin'ei. 1973. "Chishō daishi no goyuikai." *Tendai gakuhō* 15: 37–42.

Yoshida Yasuo. 1987. *Gyōki to ritsuryō kokka.* Tokyo: Yoshikawa kōbunkan.

Yūki Reimon. 1975. "Nihon no yuishiki kenkyūshijō ni okeru shiki jidai no settei ni tsuite." *Indogaku Bukkyōgaku kenkyū* 23, no. 2: 498–502.

Yūki Yoshifumi. 1987. "Enchō no kenkyū." In *Higashi Ajia to Nihon: Shūkyō bungaku hen,* ed. Tamura Enchō Sensei koki kinen kai, 93–112. Tokyo: Yoshikawa kōbunkan.

Index

Abe Yasurō, 399n.69
Abhidharmakośa: Tendai study of, 147, 151–152, 156, 411n.92–93
Abundant Light: Ritual for Buddha of, 43, 90–92, 119, 137, 183, 185, 195, 229, 420n.66
Adolphson, Michael, 303
alcohol, 293–294, 307–308, 357
Amida Hall, 227
Amitābha (Amida), 176–177, 271
Ānanda: confession rites dedicated to, 274–275
Anjōji, 275–276
Ankai, 161
Anne, 34, 38–40, 160–161, 202, 233, 274, 308–309, 414n.126
Annen, 159–161, 239, 455nn.3, 5, 456n.9, 457nn.14, 17
Annyōin, 216, 426n.75
Annyōshū, 68–69
Anrakuin, 36
Anshin, 207, 317, 425n.73, 452n.29
Anshū, 98n.3, 101, 332–333
apocryphal texts, 384n.35
Asabashō, 386n.9
Ashida Kōitsu, 390n.38
assembly of the sixth month (Rokugatsu-e or Minazuki-e), 121, 126, 345–347, 364
astrology, 90–91, 103, 395n.29

Benzaiten, 207
betsuin (affiliated temples), 201
Bishamon (Vaiśravaṇa), 168

Bonshakuji, 49
Bonshō, 11, 421n.81
Bōsan, 99, 119, 138, 233, 401n.7, 406n.40
branch temple (*matsuji*), 201
Buddha-nature, 338–339, 396nn.47, 49, 456n.7
Butsuryūji, 22, 370nn.26, 27, 371n.30
Byōdōin, 69

candidate in debates (*ryūgi*), 131, 404n.11
Central Hall (Chūdō), 21, 31, 168–169, 171–172, 181, 184–188, 219, 342
Ch'an, 34, 269
Chan-jan, 26
Ch'an-lin-ssu, 21
Chen Jinhua, 384n.35
Ch'eng wei-shih lun, 152
Chi-an, 269
chief administrator (of the Office of Monastic Affairs), 124–125
Chien-chen (Ganjin), 10, 19–20, 208, 260–262, 306, 436n.55
Chi-fo ching, 88
Chih-chou, 155–156
Chih-i, 18, 54, 113–114, 158, 160–161, 174, 178, 329
Chihō, 130, 331, 454n.2
Chikō, 100–101, 334
Chikubu Island, 171, 206–207
Chinchō, 99, 118, 309
Ch'ing-kan, 155

511

About the Author

Paul Groner, who received his doctorate from Yale University, is a professor of religious studies at the University of Virginia. He is the author of numerous articles on the Tendai school and a book-length study, *Saichō: The Establishment of the Japanese Tendai School*. His translation of Hirakawa Akira's *History of Indian Buddhism: From Śākyamuni to Early Mahāyāna* was published in 1990; he is at work on the translation of the second volume.

Printed in the United States
By Bookmasters